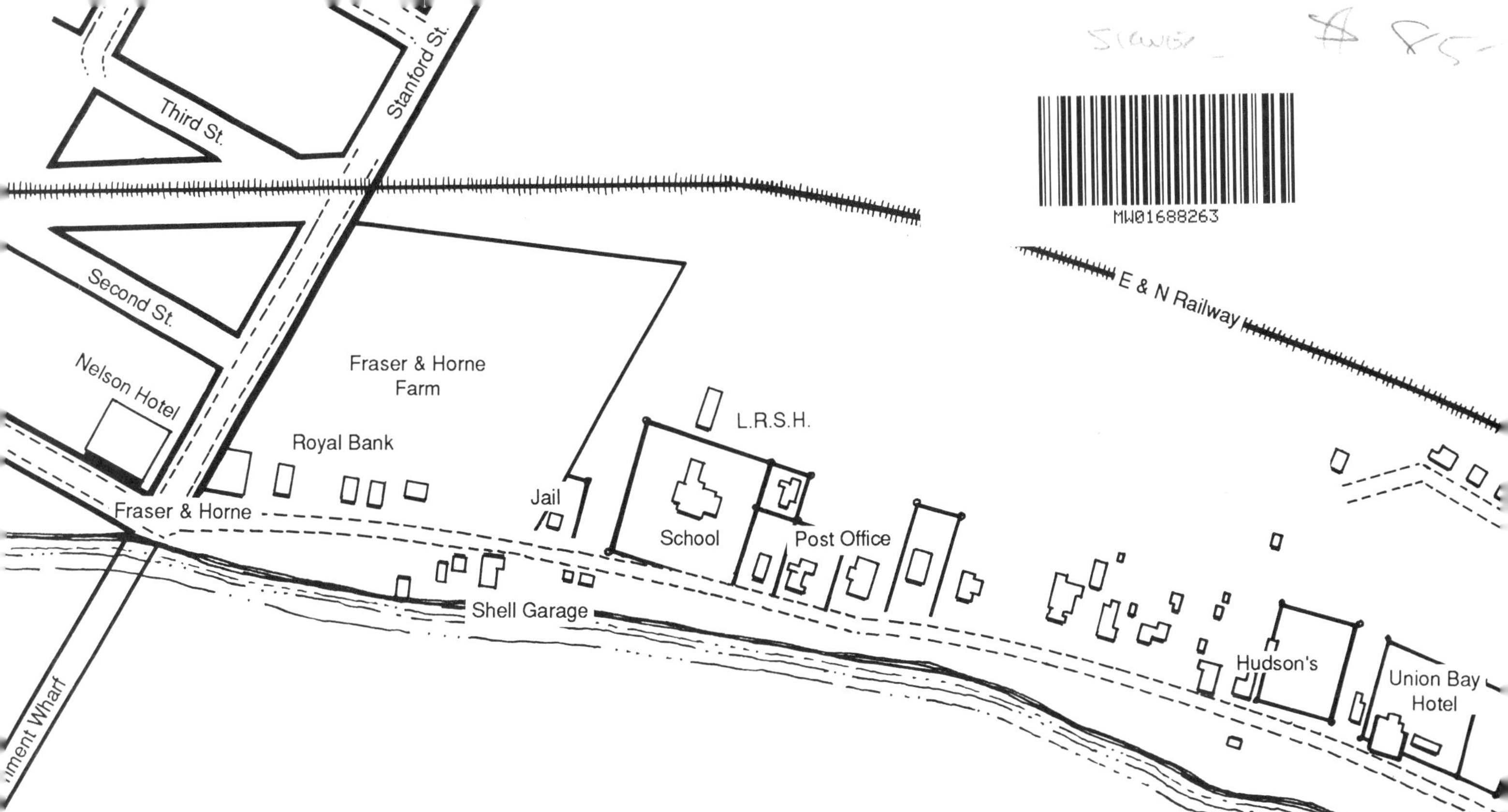

Third St.
Stanford St.
Second St.
Nelson Hotel
Fraser & Horne
Farm
Royal Bank
Fraser & Horne
E & N Railway
L.R.S.H.
Jail
School
Post Office
Shell Garage
Hudson's
Union Bay
Hotel
ment Wharf

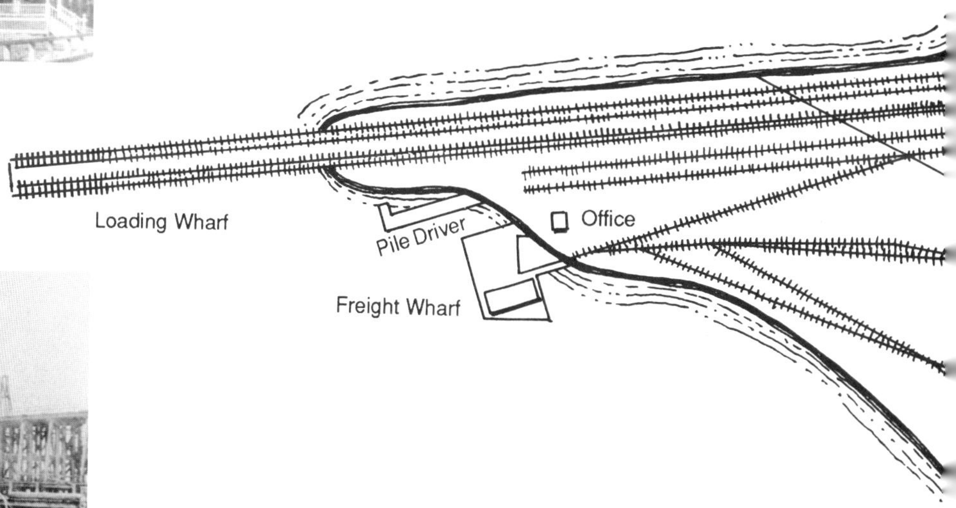

Loading Wharf
Pile Driver
Office
Freight Wharf

THE FRIENDLY PORT

A History of Union Bay 1880·1960

by
Janette Glover-Geidt

To Michael.
Enjoy,
Janette

Janette Glover-Geidt
Published by
Douglas R. Geidt

Printed by Kask Graphics Ltd.
1372 Island Highway, Campbell River, B.C.
V9W 2E1

Page and cover design by C.V. Words & Images, Ltd.
Courtenay, B.C.

Canadian Cataloguing in Publication Data

Geidt, Janette Glover, 1934-
The friendly port

ISBN 0-9694760-0-0

1. Union Bay (B.C.) --History. I. Title.
FC3849.U5G44 1990 971'.12 C90-091529-3
F1089.5.U5G44 1990

Printed and bound in Canada

This book is dedicated to

My parents, Winnie and Harry Glover,
my grandparents, Clara and William Bowden,
Ann and Herbert Glover
&
All the pioneers of Union Bay.

For the enjoyment of

My children: Lloyd, Jennifer, Jocelyn, Juliette,
their children,
&
all the children
of Union Bay: past, present, future.

Acknowledgements

Book Design - C.V. Words & Images, Ltd.
Henriette Beaudoin
Sandy Reber
Carol Neufeld

Research and Preparation Assistants
Jocelyn Geidt
Juliette Geidt
Jennifer Geidt-Keenan
Harry Glover
Jacqueline Gordon

Cover Design and Artwork
Henriette Beaudoin
Margaret Hansen

Photography
Douglas Geidt
Backdoor Gallery & Studio
Spectro 80
Studio One

Proof Readers
Margaret and Wilf Bowden
Mildred Coe
Douglas Geidt
Winnie and Harry Glover
Daphne and Bill Hamilton
Myrtle and Bill McKay
Emily and Fred Peters
Muriel and Ken Peters
Edna and Leroy Richardson
Audrey Sawchuck
Gladys and Buster Sherburn

Contributors

Myrtle Adamson
Annie & John Aitken
Dennis Aitken
Jan Aitken
Marjorie Aitken
Jack & Dot Anderson
Fanny Auchinvole
Alice Bannerman
Ron Bannerman
Alice Batty
Dorothy Bell
Jean Bennett
Don & Lois Bennie
Rachel Bennie
Charles Benson
Lillian Bohn
Grace Boudreau
Margaret & Wilf Bowden
Jack Bradley
Beverly Brown
Doug Brown
Delores Bullen
Alice Bundy
Annie Campbell
Bruce Campbell
Katherine Carter
Art Chafer
Mildred Coe
George & Audrey Cooper
Marge Cooper
Hilda Cullen
Ingles Dalziel
Donella Davis
Henry Davis
Pauline Dougherty
Thelma & George Dutfield
Nola Eastman
Margaret Egger
May Ellingsen
Charles Ennals
John Ennals
Daniel Gallacher
Fanny Bay Inn
Gilbert & Cheryl Francklyn
Irene Fudge
Alma Geary
Ethel & Wilf Glover
Jack Glover
Winnie & Harry Glover
Jacqueline & Robert Gordon
Ann Graham
Bus & Margaret Griffiths
Mildred Haas
Victor & Marjorie Haggart
Ethel Hallstrom
Bill & Daphne Hamilton
Alma Hardiman
Beryl Hargood-Ash
Henry Hatch
Jessie Hastings
Irene Hawkins
Showney Higashi
Ticki Higashi
Joy Hilton
Vera Hong
Isabel Hood
Hector & Aina Hooper
Vi Hudson
Julie Isbister
Dick Isenor
George James
William Johnstone
Nettie Jones
Kenneth Keenan
Harold Kennedy
Lorelei Kilvert
Mary Kine
Nellie King
Sarah Kirkwood
Helen Konetzha
Terry Kovar
Eva Leighton
Shirley Lenner
Bob & Gladys Lennox
John Lockner
Irene & Donald McDonald
Nelson and Joan McInnis
Bill & Myrtle McKay
Bob McKay
Donna McKay
Florence McKay
Jim & Bessie McKay
Tom & Milla McKay
Warren McMurtrie
Hazel Macartney
Bessie & Louis Magnone
Kim Mah
Alex & Ester Mar
Bill Marshall
Duncan & Marge Marshall
Ruth Masters
Margaret Matthews
Edith Munro
Gordon & Lil Murdock
Dover Muschamp
Kyoshi & Suzie Nakamura
Scutta & MitzieNakamura
Winanne Naylor
Annie Nelson
Emily & Fred Peters
Harold & Edna Peters
Muriel & Ken Peters
Bob Pollock
Ann Pratt
Debbie Prouse
Geoff Rainey
Jim Reid
Thelma Rennison
Elizabeth Renwick
Edna & Leroy Richardson
Wilma Richardson
Clara Ridgway
Gertrude Robertson
Violet Rutherford
Rubina Ryan
Steve Sampson
Audrey Sawchuck
Art & Etta Searle
Buster Sherburn
Margaret Shillito
Mildred Simpson
Frances Stasek
Cassie Stephens
Gerry & Catherine Stewart
Lyle & Barb Stewart
Kathleen Strachan
Delores Street
Robert Swanson
Rita Treloar
Mrs. A. Vanyo
Bob Veale
Mame Vowels
Doris Walker
Joe Walker
Althea Watson
Nora Watson
Bob & Donna White
Mary Winterburn
UnionBay Community Club
Union Bay Fire Department

Staff and Resources of
Campbell River Museum - Jeanette Taylor, Irene Ross
Courtenay Museum - Catherine Siba
Cumberland Museum - Barb Lemky
Courtenay Public Library
Union Bay Public Library - Bryanna Clark
Vancouver Public Library
Public Archives of British Columbia, Victoria
Royal Bank Archives, Ottawa
B.C. Provincial Museum - Dr. D. Gallacher

Table Of Contents

Please Note...

Good Canadian history books should include discussions of the geological history of the area, aboriginal peoples, and explorations by the first Europeans. As this book does not, the reader is referred to the first three chapters of the publication *Land of Plenty - A History of the Comox District* by Isenor, McInnis, Stevens and Watson. The authors have covered these topics which pertain to Union Bay as well as the whole of the Comox District in a very thorough manner.

The very birth of Union Bay was a result of the need for a shipping port for coal. The source of the coal, the Cumberland mines is not dealt with herein. The reader is referred to *One Hundred Spirited Years: A History of Cumberland* by Isenor, Stevens and Watson for a discussion of the topic.

Newspapers

Many articles have been used, starting with the Nanaimo Free Press in 1880 then switching to the first paper printed in the Comox Valley in 1892. They are indicated in the book with ⊸ and indexed with the following numbers.

1.	Victoria Colonist	Random
2.	Nanaimo Free Press	May 1880 - December 1896
3a.	Weekly News, Courtenay	November 1892 - September 1894
3b.	Weekly News, Cumberland	October 1894 - December 1896
4.	Cumberland News	January 1897 - December 1915
5.	Cumberland Islander	June 1910 - July 1931
6.	Comox Argus	May 1917 - December 1960
7.	Comox District Free Press	August 1927 - December 1960

Preface

Growing up in a company house in a company town, I woke to the quarter to seven whistle, and dashed off to meet Daddy when the four o'clock whistle blew. In bed I was lulled by the chug-chugging of the locomotives shunting coal cars on the wharf and snuggled down a little further when the big giants let off a gush of steam. Approaching the port, a freighter gave its haunting call. All was right with my little world and so to sleep.

Both sets of my grandparents lived in town as well as numerous aunts, uncles and cousins. Those that didn't live in town came "home" for summer holidays. Cousin Carolyn proclaimed Union Bay to be "the best place in the whole wide world". Mom always planned fun things after we first picked berries, stacked wood or helped can salmon. Together the extended family and friends spent the warm afternoons (I don't remember rain) swimming at Coal Beach, diving off the wharf, hiking up Washer Creek to play in the flume, boating to Tree Island, picnicking at Holmes' Field. No kid could ask for more.

Now when I walk over the "Coal Hills" I remember the coke ovens, the Washer, the trestle and all the shop buildings. Dad often took my sisters and I down on week-ends when there were extra jobs in. There was something magical when he threw the switch which started the conveyor belts. All the machines came alive with power. I can still hear the clack-clack of the belts, see the dazzling white and blue sparks of the welder's torch on metal and smell the flux. Dad knew every locomotive personally by the size and number of its wheels, shape of the tender, or a weld on its boiler. We were allowed to climb all over these monstrous machines, or pump a speeder up and down the track.

I never want to lose these things, so I have recorded my memories and those of the many oldtimers I interviewed. I hope the stories will serve to trigger recognition in older readers and provide the young people with a picture of Union Bay in her glory days.

The Friendly Port could not have been written without the support and help of my parents, Harry and Winnie Glover, and the encouragement and assistance of my husband Douglas. Of course the most important contributors are the pioneers. Their stories have grown into a rather large book about a small town that we love and call home.

Janette Glover-Geidt

COLLIERIES

FIRST MINES

Nanaimo coal fields started producing in 1852, the same year that Joseph McKay wrote to James Douglas about coal discoveries near Comox. A year later the Hudson Bay factor visited the district. He poled up the Puntledge River and was impressed by pieces of coal lying on the river bank.

In 1864 Dr. R. Brown led an expedition that explored the Puntledge and its tributaries, discovering coal seams on the river that bears his name. Prospectors began exploring all over the district.

Two years later, a six month lease was taken out for $55 on 11 acres of land along the Tsable River. Two seams of coal, 6' to 7' feet thick, had been discovered. The Baynes Sound Coal Co. was established, but at the end of the lease it had shown little practical interest in developing the mine. The Surveyor-General was convinced that the lease was obtained for speculation, with the company planning to sell to capitalists from California. He refused to renew the lease and in turn sold it to the Black Diamond Coal Co. of San Francisco. The American company was no better than the Canadian, so in July 1867 the Baynes Sound Coal Mining Co. regained the lease with two stipulations: that six properly equipped men must start immediately, and that $25,000 be spent within the first year.

The company, headed by David Lenevu, was financed by the B.C. Investment and Loan Co. Their mine site was about 2 1/2 miles inland, situated 200' above sea level. David Pickle did the surveying for the company and laid out the tramway route from the mine, along the north side of the Tsable River. To reach the wharf on Baynes Sound, the rails came out of the ravine and across the north flats at the mouth of the river. A steam sawmill was built which cut the timbers for the mine, wharf and railroad. The 3' narrow gauge tramway was constructed from the mine to the wharf, a distance of 3 1/2 miles. The wharf was a wooden structure 410' in length, standing 25' above high water mark. At the mine site, a tunnel 6' wide and 6' 8" high accommodated an underground railway to bring the coal to the surface. Coal bunkers were also built at the mine. Active mining was started at the Gaston seam in 1875.

Near the mill and wharf the little town named Quadra was growing. Cottages were built for the miners. For several years it was the main center for people living on Baynes Sound, Denman Island and Hornby Island. A post office was established there in October 1876, with W. M. Dingwall as postmaster.

The Inspector of Mines gave a glowing report of the mine in 1876. The output for that year was 600 tons, with 98 tons being sold locally. The rolling stock was reported to be an 8 1/2 ton Baldwin locomotive and twenty-one 4 ton coal cars. There were fifty-five men employed at the Gaston seam. The forty-two white miners received $2.00 a day, while the thirteen Chinese made $1.00. The output in 1877, until it was closed, was 1,500 tons.

The high grade steaming coal was sold mainly in California, and when that market slumped the mine ceased operation. In less than a year after the little locomotive pulled its first load down to the wharf, the buildings and equipment were dismantled and sold. It was returned to the mortgage holder.

1882 AUGUST ⊷ The steamer *Alexander* left for Comox to tow down the barque *Malay* loaded with railway irons from Quadra. [2]

Some of the miners stayed in the district, with many pre-empting land on Hornby and Denman. Before the mine opened, David Pickle had left the mining company and had a well-established farm to supply the miners with meat and produce.

Phillip Buckley also worked for the mining

Provincial Archives of B.C. HP81807

Discovery of coal gave Union Bay its beginning as shipping port for the "black gold"

company, and when the mine folded he stayed on as a squatter on the property. The big man in well-patched overalls became a rancher. The flat land at the mouth of Tsable River was a perfect place to let his rangy cattle run. Over the years the little settlement which was once Quadra became known as Buckley Bay.

Later, the Dunsmuir Co. acquired the mine. In the 1890's Thomas Keenan traded the mineral rights to his property on Denman to the Dunsmuir Co., for 160 acres at the mouth of Tsable River. He also inherited Mr. Buckley and his cattle. Every autumn Keenan's sons, William and Charles, took the horses up the old railway grade and brought coal down from the decaying bunkers to heat their home. They enjoyed fruit from the old orchard beside the mill. Today when grandson Ken ploughs the north field he often turns up a small railway spike.

The Perseverance Coal Company was the second mining interest in the district. It was located in the Jap Mountain region, with claims along Bradley Creek behind Union Bay. A trail was built from the beach (where the post office is today) to their camp beside the tunnel, into the mine seam known as the Beaufort Coal Mine. The company, which filed a request for permission to build wharves out into Baynes Sound in 1885, developed little further than the exploration stage. The Perseverance Trail with its several branches was used for years by hunters.

The third mining company organized was registered by eight partners, including the names of Samuel Cliffe, John Dick and Frank Little. After George Drabble surveyed the coal reserve, the Union Coal Company selected and purchased 1,016 acres along Coal Creek. They explored some of the seams along the creek, and by the fall of 1871 had cleared part of the right-of-way for the railway bed to Royston.

Much capital was needed to bring a prospective mine into production. Often the original owners had to sell to larger, better-financed companies. This was the case when the Dunsmuir Company bought out the Union Coal Co. in the 1880's.

Robert Dunsmuir came to British Columbia under a coal miner's indenture to the Hudson's Bay Co. He and his uncle first prospected around Fort Rupert Mines on the north end of Vancouver Island. After two years he transferred to Nanaimo where, because he did not join a miners' strike, he was rewarded with a Free Miner's licence from Governor Douglas. This meant he could prospect for himself in his spare time. In 1869 he discovered the Wellington coal seam. Because he did not have enough capital to develop the mine, he sold shares to a group of naval officers led by Lieutenant W.N. Diggle. During the next twelve years the mine developed so well that Dunsmuir was able to buy out Diggle's interest.

To build the Esquimalt to Nanaimo railway in 1883, the Dunsmuir syndicate was granted about a quarter of Vancouver Island, $750,000, and coal rights on the east side of the island. The railroad was finished in 1886, completing the agreement between the Dominion and Provincial governments when B.C. was brought into Confederation. The Dunsmuir Company operated the railway until 1905, when they sold it to the CPR.

By the late 1880's the Hon. Robert Dunsmuir was well-settled in Victoria and active in government. He attended to running his railroad and was not eager to develop his newly-acquired holdings. His two sons, James and Alexander, with brother-in-law John Bryden, were managing the family enterprises and anxious to bring the Union Mine into production. In August 1888 these men formed the Union Colliery Co. They kept the word "Union" as they also planned to sell coal to the Union Pacific Railroad in the United States.

The original Union Coal Co. had planned to ship coal from Royston, so had built a primitive road from the beach to the mine site. The Dunsmuirs deemed that the bay at Royston was too shallow, so plans were made to route the railroad to Port Augusta. They attempted to buy 300 acres from James Robb who owned the desired land on Comox Bay. The price proved too high, but early in 1888 Dunsmuir and Sons acquired the Perseverance Coal Co. claim. They also acquired the adjacent 160 acres that Emerson Muschamp had preempted less than a year before. This property included Langley Point (Hart's Point) which provided Dunsmuir with a deep sea port.

1888 FEBRUARY ➾ The people of Comox were greatly excited on Thursday afternoon on receiving the Free Press with news of the opening up of two coal mines on Messrs. Dunsmuir and Sons property. The settlers felt quite jubilant and it is said that the price of farms went up 100% at one bound. Some showed their joy by having a jolly time all night. [2]

New Coal Mines!

The Union and Perseverance Seams of Coal at Comox!

To Be Opened Up At Once!!

Messrs. R. Dunsmuir & Sons Arranging for Exploration and Surveying Parties!

MR. JOHN DICK WILL LEAVE AT ONCE TO PROSPECT AND OPEN OUT THE SEAMS.

Coal to be Shipped at Jack Hart's Point.

James Dunsmuir

James Dunsmuir had for several years been supervising the Wellington mines. With John Bryden's assistance he spent many months supervising the sinking of shafts, installing pumps and machines, and constructing the railway and wharves. In May 1888 the aging Robert Dunsmuir inspected the mine, when the first coal seam had only been developed to a depth of 30'. He died before the first coal was shipped from Union Wharf and left his wife, Joan, over ten million dollars.

Fred Little was appointed superintendent, and John Dick underground manager, to get the new mine into production. These men were two of the original eight owners of Union Mines. Joseph Hunter, superintendent of the E&N, supervised the building of the railroad, and Mr. Pinder was in charge of the survey crew. W.E. Blackett had the contract to build the bridges, trestle and wharf.

1888 MARCH ➡ T. Whyte and S. Davis, with several other miners, left for Comox on the steamer *Robt. Dunsmuir* to assist Mr. John Dick, manager, in opening up the the Union and Perseverance seams of coal. The steamer *Pilot* returned Wednesday, after landing Joseph Hunter, Superintendent of the E&N, at Jack Hart's Point. Mr. Hunter is having a railway line surveyed from the Point to the seam of coal. Operations are much retarded due to 4' of snow which lay on the ground. [2]

All of the men and equipment had to be loaded off the steamers onto barges, row boats and rafts, then beached and unloaded. Mr. Blackett was drowned bringing in a load of machinery and was replaced by R. Gibson. Some of the equipment, such as the steam plant and Grant's saw mill, was unloaded on Royston beach. It was taken up the old trail by a team of oxen which had walked from Nanaimo, most of the way along the beach.

George Clinton supervised two hundred Chinese labourers who were put to work clearing and building the 13 mile railroad bed. It followed the ridge beside the beach to Royston, then parallelled the wagon trail. Six miles were completed in two months.

1888 APRIL ➡ The arrangement was that the Chinamen thrown out of work by the exclusion of the Chinese from the Wellington Collieries, were to go to Comox to assist in the construction of the railway there. [2]

By summer, work started on the trestle and loading wharf. The trestle approach was 2,060' long, with 560' stretching out into the bay. Built of 12" square timbers, the superstructure was braced with a capacity for supporting a 100 ton locomotive and train of coal cars. The wharf stood on 360 copper-sheathed bearing piles driven into the ocean floor. The top deck was 60' above high tide, and the surface was 48' wide, with three tracks running the full length of it. On each side, eight travelling sets of triple chutes opened, one above each other at the side of the wharf, in order to accommodate different stages of the tide. The travelling chutes eliminated the need to move the ship as each hatch was filled. Two of the largest colliers afloat could load at once, with room left for small craft and barges at the beach end. The bottom deck was level with the ground, with sets of stairs leading to the top deck. The wharf was enlarged still further in 1910.

With a wharf to land supplies and equipment, construction moved faster, especially after the first locomotive arrived.

1888 NOVEMBER ➡ The steamship *Wellington*, with Captain Jordan, sailed from San Francisco for the Union Colliery with the first of three large locomotives. It will be landed on the wharf at Jack Hart's Point and start working. [2]

The next week, wooden ties from Chemainus arrived aboard the *Isobel*, and steel rails aboard the *Antrim*. The locomotive, driven by engineer Alf Walker, pushed a flatcar loaded with rails and ties to be laid ahead of it. Trent River bridge was built using 700,000 board

V. Hudson

The dock of the shipping wharf was 60' above high tide; the surface was 48' wide. c. 1900

L. Magnone

Dunsmuir's ship *Wellington* which transported the first locomotive to Union Bay

Cumberland Museum

Train on coal shipping wharf, before the gantries for the coal conveyors were built, loading a sailing vessel probably bound for California. On the left can be seen the transfer slip and freight shed under construction. c. 1895

feet of lumber, and had steel on it by Christmas. Early in January the rails reached the mine's mouth, but work ballasting the road continued for several months.

V.Hudson

Two ships loading simultaneously. c.1914

1889 JULY ➻ The standard gauge railway is 11 miles in length as originally surveyed, to the station which was the first log cabin at Union City, known as John Dick's cabin.

The line is extended a third of a mile beyond this to No.1 slope, and a branch to what is known as the "22" seam. It is also being continued on to Coal Creek, where the original discovery of coal was made. A quarter mile distance from Union Wharf are two long sidings on either side of the main line, where bunkers will eventually be erected. [1]

Arriving aboard the *San Mateo* in March were the fittings for the first fifty cars. They were made at the wharf from a pattern car imported from Pennsylvania.

1889 JULY ➻ The cars are 31' 6" in length, with a breadth of 8' and a depth of 4' 6". Built of Douglas fir and lined with sheet iron, they have a carrying capacity of 25 tons. The box is built with sloping ends, with a hopper bottom that opens by a lever to start the coal running out. [1]

At the end of June 1889 the *San Mateo* was back, to transport the first shipment of coal to market. Built in England earlier in the year, the all-steel freight ship was built for the East Indian trade. It made just one trip to Bombay before being bought by the Southern Pacific Improvement Co. for hauling coal. She was 340' long with a 40' beam, and 25' deep holds which could carry 4,500 tons. Her average speed was 9 1/2 knots, and she could make the trip from Union Wharf to San Francisco in about ninety-five hours.

After just sixteen months and an expenditure of over half a million dollars, the first coal was ready to be hauled over the new line and loaded from the new dock.

1889 JULY ➻ The officers of the ship speak in highest praise of the appliances for rapid loading provided by this new company. They have visited all the coal loading bunkers on the coast, and unhesitatingly award the "broom" to Union Wharves. The cars hold 25 tons each, and on strict time seven of those 25 ton cars were unloaded in the almost unprecedented time of 17 minutes, beating the Tacoma Tournament all hollow. That was less than 2 1/2 minutes per car or, at the rate of 10 tons a minute, 6,000 tons in a ten hour day. [2]

Comox Coal was a high grade bituminous coal with fine coking properties. It had a reputation as the best steam coal on the west side of North America. In 1893 a huge sample of it was sent to the World Fair in Chicago.

Cumberland Museum

Construction of the Washer. It required 400,000 board feet of lumber and towered four stories high. c. 1895

Cumberland Museum

Looking south to the Washer, which processed 600 tons of coal a day. In the background is the long flume which carried waste to the "coal hills"

WASHER

Coal was washed, not to get it clean but to separate the coal from the rock. The first coal sold was called "mine run". This was coal in any shape or size as it came out of the mine. Later, at the tipple, a screen separated the lumps over 5" from the small pieces which were sold "as mined". This was weighed, and the miner was penalized if it contained too much rock. The lumps moved along a plate conveyor, with men standing on either side knocking off the rock with picks.

Early in the 1890's, a Sheperd Improved Washing Machine was installed at the mine in Union. This could clean 850 tons of coal a day, but there was a loss of "the fines" (fine coal). A Washer was constructed at Union Wharf in conjunction with the first coke ovens. W.C. Cunningham came from Scotland to superintend the erection of his company's Luhrig Cone Washer.

1895 OCTOBER ➺ With 400,000 board feet of lumber from Grant and Mounce's mill, the Washer building is assuming shape. It towers four stories above us mortals, and will have a metal roof. The way the workmen handle themselves and the heavy timbers away up in the air would make the fat boys of Union green with envy. The *Joan* made an extra trip with 60 tons of machinery for the new plant. [3b]

The Washer was situated next to the trestle, near the head of the first row of coke ovens. This complex was called the Alexandra Colliery. It started into production with a capacity to wash 600 tons of coal in a ten hour day.

1896 OCTOBER ➺ The Washer is an immense affair provided with elevators, sifters, washers, etc. and run by steam created by the gas conducted from the coke ovens, a most economical and ingenious arrangement. The coal deposited in the Washer is the residue left after the lump or commercial coal has been shipped. This, without these works, would be worthless. Here it is washed, passed through a separator, then the fines are elevated into a large bunker erected over the car road of the ovens. The separated nut coal is in demand for commercial purposes. In case there is not enough fine coal for the ovens, the nut coal is passed through a crusher and converted into fine coal. Lately a large crusher has been placed in position for crushing the lump coal if needed. [3b]

A siding for ten cars was built on the trestle beside the Washer. A mile up Washer Creek a reservoir was built, and water flowed in a 6" pipe to the Washer and coke ovens. About 1900, Canyon Creek was bridged and a 10" pipe laid to the Washer from Langley Lake. This provided lots of pressure to power the Pelton wheel at the Washer. When the lake was low in the summer an auxiliary coal boiler was fired up.

When power was brought to Union Bay in 1914 the pipe was no longer needed so a diversion dam was built about 3/4 of a mile up the creek. A flume with a trail beside it was built from there to the Washer. The ditch, about 3' wide with a 1% grade, was dug into the

D. Bennie

David Haggart building the flume to carry the waste from the Washer to the "coal hills"

Cumberland Museum

A new coal washing machine, the "Visac Jig", waiting to be installed. c. 1941

ground. Depending on the terrain, the flume was about 3' deep, with wooden portions built up over little creeks or gullies. It went under the E&N, then was raised and travelled through a wooden box across the Company Hill before being piped under the road to the Washer.

As well as powering the Washer, the water was used to wash the coal and continued down a long metal-lined flume carrying all the rock to the end of the point. For years it was David Haggart's job to keep this clear, and extend or shorten the flume as the piles grew, forming the coal hills we know today.

The fresh water flume was used to wash the coal until the late 1930's. Then a flume was built along the edge of the wharf. An electric motor pumped the salt water up to this flume and it flowed along to the Washer. In the '50s a pipeline replaced this flume.

Over the years the Washer was improved and enlarged. In the 1940's a new washing machine was installed. The "Visac Jig" was built in Vancouver by the "inventor" Mr. Visac, who also sold the briquet plant to the company. It was later discovered that the jig was not an original invention. The plans had been copied from a firm in Belgium.

After many design and mechanical changes at the machine shops, the new Washer worked well. It could handle all coal 6" and smaller, with the large lumps still cleaned at the pit head. First the coal passed over a 3/8" vibrating screen to sift out the fines. These were then mixed with water which flowed over slightly tilted 6' x 10' slatted vibrating tables. This separated the coal from the rock. Then the fine coal and water flowed into a settling tank at 3,000 gallons a minute. The fines settled to the bottom and were scraped up by a conveyor. This carried them into a bucket elevator which deposited them into a bin. For years the fines were shipped by barge to the Bamberton Cement Works. They were also used to make briquets.

The larger coal was fed into the Visac Jig which had a 3/8" sloping screen at the base with a water chamber below. The coal ran into the end of the jig, with the water pulsating through a revolving butterfly valve which lifted the coal and rock up and down. Every time a surge of water was jetted into the chamber, it carried coal onto screens. When the rock at the bottom became heavy enough, an electric circuit was completed. This caused a star valve to revolve, allowing the rock to discharge to waste.

The coal was sized by passing over various size screens, which produced "pea" sold for domestic stoker coal and "nut" used mainly by steam tugs. The remainder went over the end and was sold as "cobble".

The company chemist was the supervisor of the Washer. Dr. Thurm first held the position, until 1918 when he was replaced by Alf Matheson. In the early '30s Paul Grundy took on the job with George Slaughter as foreman. In the late '30s, until he joined the army, Archie Dick also worked as a chemist in the lab.

In the lab beside the Washer, coal was tested for the amount of BTU's produced when it burned, as well as the amount of ash left. Every day Mr. Grundy's helper, Kwong Joe, took coal samples from selected coal cars. In the lab the chemist ground up the samples, mixed them, then ground a small portion to dust. This dust was tested in a cylindrical container called a "bomb". It was about 4" in diameter and 5" high, and had a gold lining. The bomb was filled with pure oxygen, then set in a given amount of water. A spark plug ignited the coal and it exploded, burning the

D. Walker

Building the embankment for construction of the coke ovens. Almost all the leveling was done by Japanese workers. c. 1895

coal and heating the water. From this experiment the exact number of BTU's could be calculated for a ton of coal. The amount of ash created was also weighed. Similarly, the chemist checked the amount of ash in the coal coming off the vibrating tables, and adjusted the angle to improve the wash.

COKE

The coke produced at Union Bay was neither drunk nor snorted. This grey, light, knobby product was a solid carbonaceous fuel obtained by heating coal in ovens to remove the gases. When further burned, the coke produced the high heat necessary in the smelting of copper.

After the mine had been producing for a few years, trials began to determine if a quality coke could be produced from Comox coal. The "fines", which up until then had no commercial value, were used. The product was said to be superior, with 66% coke produced from the coal burned. So work began on a double battery of fifty ovens in the fall of 1895.

Messrs. Piercy and Hunter won the contract to do the embankment work. Using three teams of horses and twenty men, mainly Japanese, the ground was graded. Limestone was brought over from the quarry on Denman and used for the foundation. Dozens of bricklayers were employed to build the walls. They were constructed of brick from a Victoria brickyard. Large pieces of oblong sandstone, also from Denman, were used to face the first ovens. A year later a brickyard which used clay from No.4 mine was built at Union Wharf, under brickmaker A.F. Barnam. Situated next to the coke ovens, it made use of the heat from them. These local bricks were used in part of the construction of subsequent ovens.

By February the foundation and the front and back walls were completed. Then work shut down awaiting the arrival of the fire bricks. Shipped around the Horn from Bonnybridge, Scotland, 350,000 fire bricks arrived in April. On board were a crew of skilled stonemasons: G. Hay, J. Nelson, C. McDonald and others. Ed Drew, a German bricklayer, also worked on the early construction and stayed to do maintenance and build later ovens. One hundred giant beehive ovens were constructed in six months. At a total cost of $260,000, the coke ovens went full blast into production.

D. Walker

One hundred beehive coke ovens being constructed by skilled stonemasons brought from Scotland to do the job of installing 350,000 fire bricks

A. Searle

The completed coke ovens, with chimney at each end, were capable of producing 50,000 T. of coke annually. The sheds beside the ovens were for cooling the hot coke before loading

1896 OCTOBER ➻ The double row of ovens is 681' long, fifty ovens facing each way. At both ends is a massive smoke stack 100' high. On either side is a row of substantially built sheds, with brick floors extending out to the ovens, forming a platform between. Upon the roof of the ovens, two cars, constructed of steel and provided with chutes, are run back and forth by an endless chain, operated by a steam engine. These cars are filled with fine coal which is deposited into the ovens. [3b]

A man drove the little chain-driven cars which were loaded with coal from the bunker under the Washer. Six and a half tons of coal were dumped through the charging hole in the roof of an empty oven. Both Andrew McKay and Joe Walker had the hot job of driving the little train, at $3.30 for a nine hour day. The production of coke from coal took seventy-two hours.

The first supervisor of the Washer and coke works was Matthew Marshall, who brought nineteen years experience with him from Glasgow. J. Todhunter, M. Laird, John Cook and William Riley were coke burners. By the turn of the century Charles Hooper was in charge of the coke ovens. Mr. Hooper came with his family from Victoria to Comox, where his stepfather farmed on land where the hospital is today. Charles married Minnie Stewart and they lived in Courtenay while he worked at No.1 mine, driving back and forth in a horse and buggy. In Union Bay they first lived in a company house, then when Rays were forced out of their house (five houses north of the post office) during the strike, the Hoopers moved in. The couple had five boys and two girls.

All the other jobs were done by Chinese and Japanese. Mr. Hooper supervised these poor men working in the nearly unbearable heat and poisonous gases. The ovens were never allowed to cool and stayed at about 600° F., so that as soon as the coal was spread out on the 12' diameter floor, it began burning. When the coal was burning fiercely, a cast iron cover was put over the top hole. The large arch-shaped door was then bricked in, using mortar that contained no cement so that it could be easily dismantled.

By choking off the air supply the coal burned slower, burning off the volatile materials to leave fixed carbon. After seventy-two hours an oven was opened. The bricks were taken down from the doorway, which had a cast iron frame with notches at different heights protruding from it. A 20' long iron rake was set in a notch and pulled back and forth across the 12' floor to rake out the coke. The worker had to quickly clean off the bricks in readiness to reseal the door to repeat the process. To cool it, the coke was piled in the sheds facing each oven, then with a coke fork, was put into coal cars which were pushed onto barges via the transfer wharf.This eliminated any breakage in dumping.

Some of the gas was used as fuel for the boiler that generated steam for the stationary engine. Some was used to heat the kilns in the brick plant, but there was no means of more by-product recovery. It just went up the chimneys. It was a twenty-four hour operation, so there were always ovens being "charged" and "pulled". When the ovens were sealed, the smoke and gases were carried off through the two tall chimneys. Before the lid was put on, flaming gases shot up through the charging hole, producing a beautiful glow in the night sky.

"When visiting at Mr.& Mrs.Searle's home in April 1918, I admired the rosy glow reflected against the background of evening."

Margaret Egger

The air was full of pollutants, with a strong smell of sulphur. The many acids tarnished silverware the day after the housewife had cleaned it. No one knew what it did to the lungs.

The coke industry was far from stable. Over the twenty-five years of production, tonnage varied from 5,000 to 50,000 per year. Initially, the smelters on the Pacific coast obtained their coke from Belgium and England. The Union Bay product made inroads into that market, and also sold to smelters in California and Mexico. Sales were good for several years, and 100 more ovens were built in 1898, with 35,000 tons produced that year. Copper smelters in B.C. were going into production. Coke was sold to Trail and Nelson in the Kootenays, until the Crows Nest Pass Coal Company built ovens and undersold Dunsmuir. From about 1900 to 1908, demands by smelters at Ladysmith and Crofton kept production up. Then ovens were built at Ladysmith, and Crofton imported coke from Australia. Due to the miners' strike, no coke was produced from 1911 to 1914. When work resumed, the Granby Co. had built a smelter

Cumberland Museum

On the floor is a 20' iron coke rake used to pull coke out of ovens. The author is holding a small coke fork which was used to pile coke into cars, and a long scraper for cleaning ovens prior to recharging

Union Bay School Collection

The coke ovens were never allowed to cool and held a temperature of 600°F. This bank of 100 are in full production

D. Aitken

The briquet plant was built in 1941 in an attempt to market the coal "fines"

up the coast at Anyox. Some coke ovens were replaced, while others were repaired, and the company was back into high production to supply Anyox. Two of the best years followed; 49,500 tons sold in 1916, and 54,300 tons in 1917. In less than two years the Granby Co. bought coking coal properties at Nanaimo and built ovens next to their smelter in Anyox. This was the first by-product plant to make metallurgical coke as a unit of a copper smelter. It rang the death knell for the coke industry at Union Bay. The last coke was produced in 1922 and was sold to the Trail smelter.

BRIQUET PLANT

For years after the coke ovens shut down, all the "fines" (coal under 1/4") were sold to the Bamberton Cement Company, but in the early 1940's this plant converted to oil. Looking for a use or market for the "fines", the CC(D)L officials were talked into buying a secondhand plant from Washington state. It made a "wonderful" product, the briquet, for the domestic market. Faulty from the start, the machine was accompanied by the salesman who was a smooth-talking Belgian consulting engineer named Visac. For six months he made himself unpopular, overseeing the installation of both the briquet plant and the new "Visac Jig" in the Washer.

The impressive frame building was situated beside the Washer. It was 125' long, 28' wide, and towered 74' above the trestle. Painted "carshop red" outside, the inside was sparkling white (to begin with), and floodlit throughout for night operations.

Paul Grundy, the chemist, oversaw the procedure. He experimented for months to determine the proper binding material and best combination. Hundreds of small briquets were manufactured with a hand press. Hoping to make the plant more efficient, Bill Auchinvole and Harry Glover made many design changes.

The briquets were made of 90% coal and 10% asphalt (which acted as a binder). The oil came from Ioco via the E&N in specially insulated cars, at a temperature of 430° F. It was immediately pumped from the cars into a 8,500 gallon insulated tank containing steam coils, which kept it in a liquid state.

A coal-fired boiler supplied the superheated steam which was under 100 lb. pressure. A conveyor carried the washed coal to a main elevator which lifted it to the top of the building. Here it entered a horizontal paddle conveyor which was heated to 600°. The hot dry coal was then mixed with the asphalt and went into the huge 32 T. press, which consisted of two rollers surfaced with shallow cups. The coal mixture was scooped into the cups on each roller which came together to form one briquet. They dropped from the press hot onto an endless belt and were cooled as it carried them outside to a waiting coal car. Syd Waterfield ran the presses and Buster Sherburn fired the boiler. The plant also employed three others.

"Production was poor! We made hundreds of adjustments to the plant. The oil was difficult to keep at the right temperature, the coal was hard to regulate, and the rollers had to be kept very tight. One day the briquets would be good, the next day the halves wouldn't stick together. On top of all that, sales were poor because they were very smoky and burned like creosote."

Harry Glover

Barge loads were sold to the B.C. Electric Co. of Vancouver, but the domestic market never caught on. Housewives hated the smoky things. The plant closed in less than a year and was the butt of many jokes.

"Lizzie Renwick made some cookies out of them for one of the crib wind-ups. She took half a dozen briquets and iced them and put the "cookies" on a cake plate. Bert Geary was the first to take one. He bit into it and realized what it was so set it down, then sat back and watched the others!"

John Aitken

Cumberland Museum

Briquets dropping from the conveyor into a waiting coal car

RAILROAD

The Wellington Colliery Railway, owned and operated by the Dunsmuir family, was incorporated in 1883 to transport coal from the Dunsmuir mines at Wellington to Departure Bay. Following the coal seam eight miles south of Wellington, Dunsmuir found the main seam, and development got under way in 1898. The town was called Extension, and another Wellington Colliery Railway was built to the beach at Oyster Bay (renamed Ladysmith in 1900). The railroad between Union Mine and Union Wharf, built in 1888, was also part of this railway. It became part of the Canadian Colliery (Dunsmuir) Limited holdings in 1910 but the old name stuck.

Robert Dunsmuir also built the E&N in 1883, and the family operated it until it was sold to the CPR in 1905.

H. Macartney

Mr. and Mrs. George Davis with ten of their twelve children beside the family home at the Crossing: Albert, Henry, Beattie, George, Clifford, Mr. and Mrs. Davis, Hazel, Lucy, Emma, Ada, Violet

The Minister of Mines Report for the Union Colliery in 1895 states there was a standard (4' 8 1/2") gauge railway line 12 miles long. The rolling stock included four locomotives, 150 coal cars of 25 tons each, and one passenger coach. By the Minister's report in 1911 the railroad was 18 miles long, with two large and four switching locomotives travelling on it. The coal cars had increased to 185 and were supplemented with 100 larger steel hopper cars. There were coaches, box cars and flat cars which totalled thirty-four. In the '20s about 400 coal cars served all the mines. The box cars were used to haul great quantities of freight from the dock to Cumberland and the mines, as well as all supplies to Comox Logging. The coal and logging tracks tied into each other near Royston.

Gradually, additions and improvements were made to the railway and wharves, until there were 22 miles of track joining the four mines to the main line which went to the beach. There were twenty sidings totalling 3 miles of track, as well as an interchange with the E&N at Bayton, 2 miles north of the wharf. Eighty pound rail was used on the main line, and 56 lb. rail used for the sidings and around the yard at the wharf. The roadmaster and his two Chinese crews, one from Union Bay and the other from Cumberland, maintained the tracks, travelling back and forth on velocipedes.

1894 SEPTEMBER ➻ A train of sixteen cars made the thirteen mile run from Union to the Wharf in nineteen minutes. This shows that the track is in good repair under an old C.P.R. man, John Harwood. [3a]

Mr. Harwood, the first roadmaster, lived on a farm at Trent River, and was followed by Alf Shields. In 1910 most of the railway was rebuilt to higher standards. Ralph Gibson became roadmaster, managing the rails and road crew for many years. Later, Allan Nunns was trainmaster.

The heat in the summer, the heavy braking coming from the mines with loaded cars, and power-pulling back to Cumberland, all caused the rails to slowly creep toward the end of the wharf. About twice a year the railway crew drove the rails back the 5' to 10' they had moved. A 40' length of rail was hung on a tripod at the end of the wharf. The crew lined up on either side of the suspended rail and swung it to hit the last rail on the track. With a rhythmic thud which could be heard all over town, the rail was pushed back up the line, inch by inch.

To supply water for the locomotives, water tanks were situated on the wharf, at the bunkers, and at the mines in Bevan, Cumberland, and No.8. The tank on the wharf stood on 15' legs so that the water chute was higher than the locomotive. Made of wooden staves, the barrel was about 14' tall with a 16' diameter. Hinged from the bottom, the steel pipe could drop to the desired height to fill the saddle tanks or the tank on the tender.

A turntable was situated a quarter of a mile north of the Washer. It was about 60' long so could accommodate all the locomotives,

Cumberland Museum

Loaded coal cars ready for dumping

B. Sherburn

Trestle under repair. c. 1922

although the yard trains rarely turned, but shunted cars back and forth in reverse or forward. An engine was run onto the turntable which was fitted with rollers for easy turning. Then the train crew pushed on the large handles to turn the turntable 180°, reversing the direction of the locomotive. The "Y", situated at the company farm near the entrance to Cumberland, was also used to turn locomotives on their way back to the mine. The locies backed the empty cars into the mines, so were then in position to haul the loaded cars back to the beach.

Boys would often gather at the turntable for some fun. They would push the turntable and jump on for a ride as it gained speed. Once the 30 ton table got moving there was no stopping it. In 1927 little Griffin McColgan was killed when he fell into the pit. From that day on, the turntable was locked with a chain and padlock.

F. Peters

The Foo Foo Gang who repaired the wharves and bunkers

Across the tracks, the weigh station was built in 1914, consisting of railway scales and an office. The train slowly passed over the giant scales, one car at a time, and the gross weight was recorded by the weigh man. This job was held in the early years by G. Parks, W. Whyte and W. Harrison. In the '20s, R. Fogg held the position, then Jim Kerr and later Harry Tappin.

Next to the office was a house for drying sand. Sand was barged from Denman, shovelled onto a flat car and taken up to the sand house. Here Har, George Davis' Chinese assistant, lit a big oil drum stove to dry the sand. As the sand dried it ran through two screens. This fine sand was put in the sand dome on top of each locomotive boiler. The engineer could release the sand in front of the driver wheels to cause friction on slippery tracks and when braking.

Situated near the bunkers, between the upper and lower tracks, was a building which housed supplies for lubricating the cars. It contained bales of waste wool and barrels of heavy black oil. The first car inspector was J. Skinner, until George Davis was given the job.

"My Dad lost a leg in the mines, and had a peg leg. Everyone said he should sue Dunsmuir and get some money. But Dad wanted to work, so he went to Mr. Dunsmuir and asked him if there was some kind of job that he could do. That's how he became car inspector."

Henry Davis

Mr. Davis bought several acres at the crossing north of Union Bay from Marshall Laird. There he and his wife raised a large family of seven boys and five girls.

With Har's help, George checked the empty cars for lubrication, worn brake shoes, or "hot boxes". On the end of each pair of wheels was the journal box. This cast iron box was packed with wool waste which was saturated with heavy oil and acted as a wick to lubricate the axle journal. If the box was allowed to dry out, the bearing would run hot, melting the babbit and possibly starting a fire in the journal box. This could result in cutting off the end of the axle, causing a derailment. So Mr. Davis and Har were careful to top up the box with oil and wool, as well as send cars with worn axles, wheels or bearings to the shops to be repaired.

When the mines were in full production they occasionally shut down because all the coal cars were full, so provision was made to stockpile coal.

1897 MARCH ➻ GOOD NEWS! The rumour that the company will build a bunker at Union Wharf is well-founded. This will do away with the necessity for the mines to lay off now and then because the cars are full and expected ships have not arrived. It is a very important undertaking and means much to Union employees and the town. [4]

About 3/4 of a mile from the wharf, the bunkers were constructed beside the main track. Built of wood, about 30' wide, the bottom was higher than a coal car so that the cars could be brought along side and reloaded from chutes at the side of the long continuous bunker. On top, a track ran the whole length so that the hopper-bottomed cars could be unloaded into any section. In 1903 the bunkers were lengthened to 400', with a capacity to store about 5,000 tons of coal.

Union Bay Community Hall

The Tsable River Mine which operated from 1945 - 1960

D. Wilkie

Locie No. 14 is switching the last carloads of coal prior to the shutdown of Tsable River Mine. c. 1960

The road crew maintained the railroad, and the "Foo Foo Gang" made all repairs and improvements to the wharves, trestles, bridges and bunkers. Norman Searle was foreman for several years of the all-white crew of carpenters and helpers. In 1924 Albert Jones, fondly called "Putt-Putt", led this genial group of workers. Jack Campbell, who had worked with the gang for many years, took over when Mr. Jones retired.

"One day about six of us had to push a car. Fred Peters had just started working with us. All except Fred slacked off, but we kept saying it was too hard and that we needed some elbow grease. Finally we sent Fred over to get a requisition from Mr. Jones for some elbow grease. "Putt Putt" wouldn't go along with it and said, 'They're just trying to pull your leg, my boy.' The Foo Foo Gang was always playing a joke on someone."

Bill Hamilton

The upper structure of the wharf was rebuilt many times. When the Weldwood Company dismantled the wharf seventy-eight years after it was installed, some of the original pilings were still sound. The copper casing was gone but the copper had penetrated the wood, turning it green. Many of the pilings were barged to Squamish where they were used to build a wharf for the company's pulp mill.

When all the mines were closed at Cumberland in 1950, the main line was taken up and the rails stored at Union Bay. In 1960 they were sold to Comox Logging at Ladysmith.

After the First World War the CC(D)L sent a team of prospectors into their Tsable River claim. A road was built from Buckley Bay, and several log cabins and a barn were constructed for the diamond drillers who worked the area for a number of years. Rumours flew that the mine would be opened and a soldier's settlement started, much the same as the one at Merville. But it was not until 1945, when the mines in the Cumberland area were almost finished, that the Tsable River Mine was put into production.

The miners were bussed from Cumberland, and the coal was trucked to the Washer at the Bay by Roy Davis Trucking. A new conveyor was built at the north end of the Washer where the trucks dumped the coal. The coal was screened before it was loaded into the train cars. The switching locomotives were retained to load the ships and store coal.

The cement works at Bamberton changed over to oil, and with its biggest customer gone, the company closed Tsable River mine in 1960. Including the mine and shipping facilities, 250 men were out of work.

A syndicate of three Colliery employees formed the Comox Mining Company Ltd.: Stan Lawrence, president and former mine manager; George Dutfield, vice-president and former electrical engineer; Paul Grundy, secretary-treasurer and former chemical engineer. The new company applied for and received a federal loan especially set up for coal companies. An agreement was worked out with the old company to use much of their equipment.

1960 MAY ➾ It is felt by the syndicate that the mine, which now employs about 250 men, could have its operations streamlined and employ about seventy men to produce 70,000 tons per annum.The present production is about 177,000 tons. [7]

The new company won a contract from the provincial government to supply Essondale

J. Stewart

Coal from Tsable River Mine was transported to the shipping wharf at Union Bay by Roy Davis Trucking. c. 1956

L. Magnone

The first locomotive to work at Union Bay was a Baldwin Saddleback 2-4-2. Loco No. 1 known as "Betsy Jane" switched cars around the yard for over 50 years

E. Hallstrom

Engineer John Lockner and his wife Mary on Locie No. 10

hospital with 8,000 tons in six months. As well, the airport contract was kept, and coal was sold locally. Mining started May 9, 1960. The new company screened and sized the coal at the mine, and it was shipped from Buckley Bay, the first and last coal shipping port in the district.

LOCOMOTIVES

Over the years about twelve locomotives numbered between one and twenty served the coal company. There were usually three large locomotives transporting coal over the main line. Three smaller engines shunted the coal cars back and forth at the port, loading ships and filling bunkers. To the train crews each engine possessed a personality of its own. Many of them were given nicknames, such as *McGinty*, *Victoria*, and *Duchess*. Some were saddle tank engines, meaning that extra water for the boiler was carried in tanks which fit over the boiler. The others carried water in a tank on the tender. Nut coal was used for fuel and was carried on the tender or behind the cab on the saddle tank engines.

Cumberland Museum

Loco No. 14 pulling a train load of coal cars from the mine at Cumberland to the wharf at Union Bay

Loco No.1, a light switching locomotive of 25 tons, was a Baldwin bought from the Central Pacific Railway in the States. It was a saddle back 2-4-2 engine, and may have been the first one brought to the port after the wharf was built. It pushed the flat cars loaded with rails as the men laid the tracks ahead of it. *Betsy Jane*, as it was fondly called, spent its life working on the wharf and around the yard at Union Bay until the early 1950's, when it was scrapped. Its 40 lb. bell was saved and designated for use in perpetuity at the Union Bay United Church.

1900 APRIL ➾ Loco No.1, in charge of J. Sargeant, ran off the track on the approach to the coal wharf and fell 30' to the ground, completely demolishing the cab, water tank and pipe fittings. The boiler and frame work was not damaged. Alex Shaw, the brakeman, went over the trestle with the engine but had no broken bones. Engineer Sargeant jumped to safety. [4]

Little is remembered of Loco No.2 or No.3 except that they were similar to No.1 and served for a time at Union Bay.

When Dunsmuir sold the E&N in 1905, he kept several of the engines and transferred them to the Wellington Railway Company. No.10 was one such engine. With a wheel configuration of 4-6-0, the 85 ton locomotive with tender worked the main line.

About the turn of the century, No.11, No.12 and No.13 arrived to take their place at Union Bay. They were all similar, 35 ton saddle back Baldwins bought from Park & Ocean Railway Co. Used on a scenic railway in California, they were decorated with bright colours which were, in the early days, touched up when the locies were in for an overhaul. The two old work horses, No.11 and No.12, carried on working into the 1950's. No.12 is well remembered as *McGinty*, the engine on the wharf. It was driven for many years by Bill Marshall and Dick Ray. Bad luck seemed to plague No. 13. In his excitement to get to Cumberland and bring medical help for a sailor who had fallen overboard, engineer R. Cameron crashed the engine into coal cars parked on the same track. Both he and brakeman Duncan were suspended. No.13 was retired in 1914.

Cumberland Museum

Loco No. 5, later numbered 15, was an 85 ton 4-6-0 engine built at the Baldwin works in Philadelphia

W.R. Swanson

Loco No. 17, a 75 ton Baldwin saddle tank engine, was known as the *Galloping Goose* because modification made her nose heavy

No.14 had a varied and long career which spanned 62 years with the coal company. The 85 ton 4-6-0 engine was equipped with a four wheel pony truck in front. Built in the Baldwin works in Philadelphia, it was delivered new to Union Wharf in April 1898 and numbered 4. That same summer it went down with the Trent River bridge, taking with it the crew and six passengers.

1898 AUGUST •➜ The body of engineer Alf Walker was in the underside of the engine, but at 12 noon he was taken out. He had died at his post. It was not until Mr. Mellado arrived and gave direction where to excavate, that his son, Alex Mellado, brakeman, was taken out terribly crushed - dead. [2]

Fireman Hugh Grant was badly injured but survived, while a second brakeman, Matt Piercy, jumped to safety (see accidents). No.4 was retrieved from the bottom of the ravine and was painstakingly repaired, then renumbered 14. Its engineers claimed that the frame was never completely straightened out, making it a "rough-riding loco". Some of the gully was filled in and a shorter bridge was built. In 1926 the Canadian Bridge Company replaced the old wooden bridge with a steel span.

In 1901, No.14 was called upon to rush medical supplies to assist in the rescue operations after the disaster at No.6 mine. It was also in an accident that year, and again nine years later.

1910 JUNE •➜ Shortly after 3:00 p.m. on Saturday, an accident occurred on the railway just south of the Trent River Bridge. Eleven coal cars left the track due to the spreading of the rails, and over 50 yds. of track was completely torn up, the ties splintered into matchwood. The train, which was in charge of J. Lockner driving engine No.14, was very fortunately travelling at a slow speed... Strange to say the engine and two loaded cars passed over the break with safety but the following cars left the rails. [5]

In 1926 No.14 had the honour of transporting Governor-General Baron Byng to Cumberland. It was the last locomotive to work at Union Bay, stripping the site of all equipment and rails, then transporting them to the E&N railway. On a very foggy day No.14 gave a sad, last wail as it left Union Bay on the E&N, bound for Puget Sound. There it was to be an attraction on the railroad buffs' Snoqualmie Valley Railroad.

"I saw No.14 in 1984 in Snoqualmie on a siding, trees and bush all around it, cab all rusted away. It had never been fixed. I couldn't even get a picture; it was so overgrown."

Buster Sherburn

E. Renwick

Loco No. 16 and crew Dobie Somerville, Louis Magnone and Frank Davidson with Dave Renwick, wharfinger

Cumberland Museum

Loco No. 20, the biggest at 110 T and last to be purchased, was a 2-8-2 Mikado built by Baldwin. It was the heaviest engine ever to operate on the mining railways of Vancouver Island. Here the powerful locomotive is seen about to leave Cumberland with a long train of 30 loaded hopper cars. Left to right: D.R. McDonald, Fraser Watson, Bill Wood, Dobie Somerville, Geordie Richardson

It is probable that No.5, later numbered 15, also came from E&N. A mainliner, it was the same size and type as No.14. In 1905 the "big mogul" was towing a train of fifty-two empties from the wharf, when it collided with engine No.17 pulling a loaded train from No.4 mine. The collision took place at the siding near Cumberland's Chinatown, and both engines, travelling at 25 m.p.h., were badly damaged. The new shops at the Bay were still under construction, so the locomotive with the most damage was sent to Ladysmith for repairs. The mines had to be closed until another locomotive was sent up from Ladysmith.

No.16, a small saddle tank engine, worked at Ladysmith and occasionally relieved at the Bay. Built before 1898, No.17 worked alongside No.14 until the end. The 75 ton Baldwin arrived as a 0-6-0 saddle tank engine. Later, as it was needed on the main line and because it could not carry enough fuel to make the long haul from Cumberland, a 3,000 gallon water and fuel tender was added. As the coal was to be stored in the tender, the fuel hopper from behind the cab was removed, causing the engine to be nose heavy. After that, No.17 was known as the *Galloping Goose*. Still later, a two wheel pony truck was added. This was placed under the front end to balance the load.

The locomotive that went through the most changes was No.19, known as the *Wellington*. Bought by Dunsmuir in 1889, it was a 15 ton 0-6-2 locie, and started its career on the narrow gauge (3') railway at the Wellington Mines. When those mines closed it was sent to Extension. This new route travelled mainly over the E&N rails, so the engine had to be converted to standard gauge. In 1932 an engine was needed at No.4 Mine to pull cars from Scott's Slope across the trestle over the end of Comox Lake. This railway had the unusual gauge of 2' 11", so the *Wellington* was brought up and its gauge changed at the shops. After No.4 Mine closed, the gauge had to be changed back to 3'. To gain the necessary 1", instead of moving the wheels, the tires were "shrunk on" 1/2" farther out. No.19 was sent south again and ended its working days in 1953 at No.10 Mine at South Wellington. Eventually the old *Wellington* was put on display at Piper Park in Nanaimo.

The last locomotive to be acquired was No.20, the biggest of all the engines at 110 tons. It was a 2-8-2 Mikado locie with tender.

1913 APRIL ➾ A powerful new locomotive arrived at Union Bay for the CC(D)L company. The modern engine is built according to B.C. government specifications, the tank will hold 4,500 gal. of water. It is expected to haul 600 tons of coal over a 1% grade. That is about thirty cars of coal. [5]

After forty-five years on the mainline, No.20 was scrapped in 1958 because no one wanted it.

D. Geidt

Bill Woods was the last engineer and his fireman was Jimmy Brown. Lloyd Geidt and Mark Naylor had the thrill of their young lives when they went for a ride on No. 14

All new locomotives or engines coming in for repairs from Ladysmith came by boat or barge, and were unloaded on the transfer slip which was built in 1895. After the E&N was finished, the locomotives came via the railroad. A few came up under their own steam but most of them were towed. The E&N would not accept any responsibility, so shop men were assigned to prepare and look after the engines.

"I was on old No.19 when she came up to have the gauge changed in 1932. Three of us went down to Nanaimo and it took us a day to get her ready. Because she didn't have air brakes, we had to put an air line through and we also did some work on the couplings and so on. I rode on her and kept her lubricated on the way up."

Harry Glover

The engineer was responsible for his locomotive on the road. He had to have enough knowledge to know what was dangerous and what was not. He took great pride in the giant he controlled and reported any problems to the shop foreman. Every month the locomotives were brought into the shops to have their boilers cleaned and routine repairs made.

In the 1920's new standards for engineers were introduced. The men had to take courses on steam pressure, gauge work, water tables and valve settings. Strict exams had to be passed before they were given a certificate and the right to drive an engine. The old timers like Johnny Lockner, Dick Ray, Bill Marshall and Bob Abrams were automatically given tickets.

"Bill Woods was the last engineer down here. He took the exams when he got his ticket. He was probably the best engineer for looking after his engine. His fireman, Sam Davis, spent all his time polishing the engine. When Sam got in the cab in the morning he ate his lunch. It was the first thing he did. He got that out of the way and could spend his lunch hour polishing the brass."

Harry Glover

Firemen, such as Harry Sherburn and Jimmy Brown, were crucial to the well-being of the locomotive. They and the engineers worked as a team. It was the fireman's job to keep the fire at an even temperature for the engineer who checked gauges and controlled the water level to keep the steam up. Any rapid change in temperature could cause cracks in the fire box, broken stays, and leaky tubes. So the fireman always closed the firebox door quickly between shovelfuls of coal when he was stoking up.

Usually the locomotives worked round the clock, so they always had steam up. However, if there was no night crew working, the fireman would fill the firebox with green coal and leave the grates partly open. In the morning he would arrive early, break up the coals, spread them out, add fresh coal, and away the fire would go.

The brakemen, such as Geordie Richardson and Plunky Bradley, had the responsible job of being in charge of the whole train at all times. The train crews on the main line lived in Cumberland, and the crews on the yard and wharf trains lived in Union Bay. There were two shifts on the main line. Although they did not bring any loads down at night, the crews were kept busy shifting cars to and from the tipple. On the siding, a train of loaded cars was ready to leave first thing in morning.

At busy times there were two trains with two shifts of train crew working at the Bay -

T. Dutfield

District Superintendent Alexander Auchinvole and Mrs. Auchinvole with their three boys: Bill, Harry and Alex

loading ships, filling bunkers, or shifting empties. During a lay-off the citizens of the town had trouble sleeping, without the chugging and blowing of the engines throughout the night.

"My Dad worked all the time. 6:00 a.m. to 6:00 p.m. for a week, then one day off and on to night shift 6:00 p.m. to 6:00 a.m. Just work and sleep. He always drove the train on the wharf and Bert Brown was his fireman."

Bill Marshall

Following is a partial list of the train crews over the years.

ENGINEERS	FIREMEN	BRAKEMEN
A. Walker	M. Piercy	A. Melado
D. Young		
C. Whyte		F. Davidson
J. & H. Miller		T. Hudson
J. Putz		S. Grieves
T.L. Ray		R. Cameron
J. Humphrey		
R. Cameron		J. Hudson
F. Day		H. Whyte
W. Marshall	B. Brown	J. Sargeant
R. Abrams		G. Richardson
W. Clark		A. Bradley
J. English	S. Davis	
J. Lockner	H. Sherburn	J. Murdock
R. Ray	J. Brown	
H. & J. Walker		J. Buchanan
L. Magnone	R. Sherburn	
T. Miller		F. Peters
F. Watson		
W. Wood		

COLLIERY COMPANY MINE OWNERS

1888 Union Colliery Co. of B.C.
Dunsmuir family
1900 Wellington Colliery Co. Ltd.
Dunsmuir family
1910 Canadian Collieries (Dunsmuir) Ltd.
1914 Vancouver Island Coals Ltd.
Same company with name changes
1957 Canadian Collieries Resources Ltd.
Same company with name changes
1960 Weldwood Canada Ltd.

MANAGEMENT

Working out of Cumberland, F.D. Little was the first superintendent of the Union Coal Company. During his term Mr. Little saw mines No.1, No.2 and No.3 begun and abandoned, and the next three mines opened. He was followed by J. Lockard. In 1910 Dunsmuir sold his coal enterprise to Mackenzie and Mann of the Canadian Northern Railway for $7,000,000. The new company kept the founder's name in the title, Canadian Colliery (Dunsmuir) Ltd. They greatly expanded the wharves and practically rebuilt the railway. With four mines working, coal production at 518,426 tons was at an all-time high, with W.L. Coulson as General Manager. He guided the company through most of the bitter years of the strike.

In 1915 the head office at Victoria was moved to Cumberland and the old office there remodelled. It featured a plate glass window in the superintendent's office. From here, besides enjoying the view, Mr. Lockard managed the mines, shipping and shops. In 1917 Thomas Graham, a consulting engineer, was brought in as General Superintendent. Alexander Auchinvole, a Scotchman, who had connections with the CC(D)L company in Victoria, moved to Union Bay and was appointed District Superintendent.

A beautiful home was built for the Auchinvoles, three houses north of the post office. With the help of Chinese gardeners the grounds became a showpiece, and were loaned to many worthy causes for garden parties and teas. The family, with three teenaged sons, became very involved in the community and helped form many music, social and sport clubs. The chatelaine of the big house was famous for her fancy dress balls.

In 1928 the CC(D)L gained controlling interest in the Western Fuel Corp. Ltd. in Nanaimo. Mr. Graham left to run for Parliament and Lt. Col. Villiers became General Manager. The company now owned all the large producing coal mines on the Island. At this time

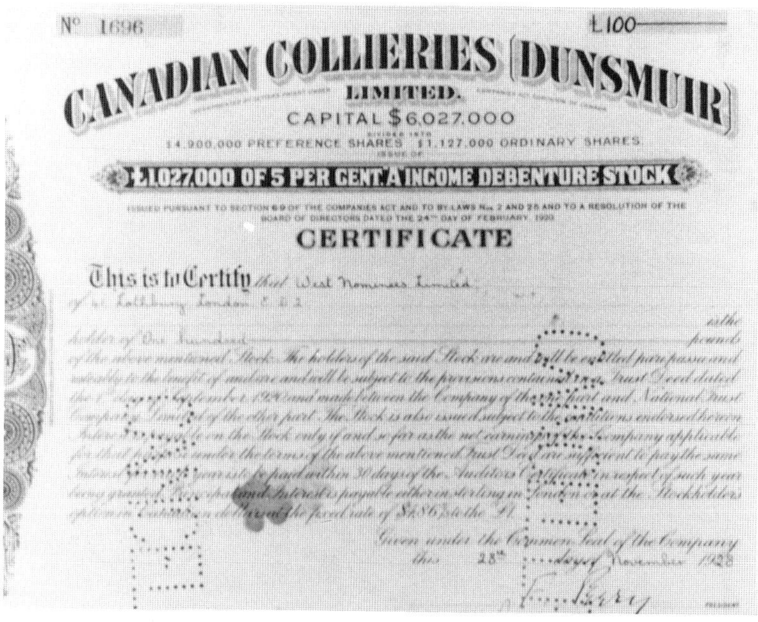
No 1696 £100
CANADIAN COLLIERIES (DUNSMUIR) LIMITED.
CAPITAL $6,027,000
£4,900,000 PREFERENCE SHARES £1,127,000 ORDINARY SHARES
£1,027,000 OF 5 PER CENT A INCOME DEBENTURE STOCK
CERTIFICATE
This is to Certify that West Nominees Limited

Union Bay School collection

A 100 pound debenture used to raise capital for the CC(D)L in 1928

D. Bennie

Office Staff, about 1920 - E.T. Searle, Rachel Haggart, Gertie Hudson, Andy Kay, Edith Bickle

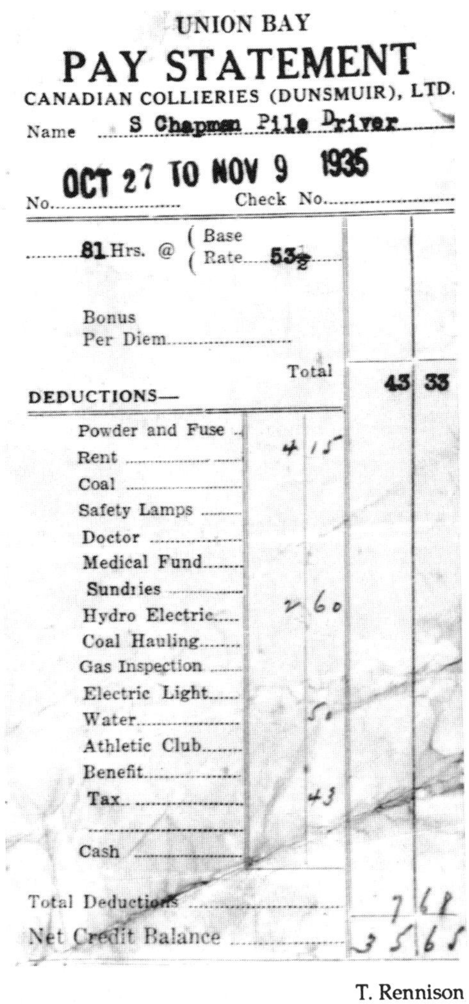

UNION BAY

PAY STATEMENT

CANADIAN COLLIERIES (DUNSMUIR), LTD.

Name S Chapman Pile Driver

OCT 27 TO NOV 9 1935

No. Check No.

81 Hrs. @ (Base Rate 53½

Bonus

Per Diem

Total 43 35

DEDUCTIONS—	
Powder and Fuse	
Rent	4 15
Coal	
Safety Lamps	
Doctor	
Medical Fund	
Sundries	
Hydro Electric	2 60
Coal Hauling	
Gas Inspection	
Electric Light	
Water	50
Athletic Club	
Benefit	
Tax	43
Cash	
Total Deductions	7 68
Net Credit Balance	35 65

T. Rennison

Pay statement of Sandy Chapman for a two week period

Mr. Auchinvole's responsibilities increased to include all railways, wharves, stores, shops, washeries and powerplants in the Ladysmith, Nanaimo and Comox Districts. The coal output in 1930 was half what it was twenty years earlier.

Col. Villiers died in 1938 and was succeeded by H.R. Plommer from the Vancouver office. Shortly after, Mr. Auchinvole retired, and some of his work load was taken over by Mr. Plommer, as the mines through the '40s became less productive. George Dickson came from Nanaimo to become superintendent at Union Bay, and moved into the big house.

In 1941 the company bought the McLeod River Hard Coal Company in Alberta. Some coal was actually brought from Alberta via the CPR and E&N to be shipped from Union Bay. CC(D)L headquarters in Vancouver were moved to Nanaimo in 1945. About this time Bob Dunn moved from the company office in Mercoal, Alberta to become purchasing agent. The buying had formerly been done through Nanaimo.

The Tsable River mine was opened in 1945, and by the '50s all the mines in Cumberland were closed. In 1957 the CC(D)L became Canadian Colliery Resources Ltd. The Nanaimo office closed and some of the staff moved to Union Bay. Herb Glover, who had started as an office boy in Nanaimo after the First World War, came home to Union Bay as comptroller of the company.

Through the years at Union Bay, the master mechanic was in charge of the works. W.G. Pillsbury was the first, followed by A. McKnight (who testified at the Trent River inquest in 1898). About the turn of the century George McLaughlin took over, followed for a few years by E. Fox. A beautiful house was built beside the post office in 1913, and J. Tompkins was the first master mechanic to occupy it. F. Sawford, A. Hamilton and A. Pollock each served short terms. Bill Auchinvole became the general superintendent in 1929 and held the post until he died, one year before the company folded.

In 1916 E.T. Searle left his job working on the weigh scales in Cumberland to become paymaster at Union Bay. Mr. Searle had a good deal of office experience, first working

D. Bennie

Switch board operator Rachel Haggart and stenographer Jean Potter in the CC(D)L office

R. Treloar

Office staff in the 1950's - Wilf Glover, Rita Treloar, Bob Dunn, John Morre, absent is Bill Auchinvole

Courtenay Museum

Piles of lumber in front of Grant & Mounce Sawmill, Cumberland

LUMBER
All Kinds of Rough and Dressed lumber always on hand and delivered at short notice.

MOULDINGS
Also all kinds of sawn and split shingles and dressed pine and cedar.

STUMPING
Stumping done at reasonable rates by our Giant Stumper.

WOOD
Coal, brick and lime on hand and delivered at short notice.

R. Grant & L. Mounce, Proprs.

in a bank in London, then ten years in a railroad office in Washington. Ted and Caroline, with three boys and a girl, initially lived in a company house near Russell Hill, before buying land from Mr. Harwood and building the big house on the beach. Mr. Searle was very community-minded, and belonged to and was secretary for many groups, from the school board to the crib club.

Bookkeepers, such as A.G. Butters and J. McFarlane, and the paymaster had an office in the administration building, which held the drafting room, lecture room, accounting department and telephone exchange. The only female company employees worked here as stenographers and telephone operators. One of the first girls to fill the position was Hazel Whyte. She was followed by Edith Bickle, Rachel Haggart, Gertrude Hudson, Bernice Shirley, Dorothy Renwick and Jean Potter. Greta Kay attended the business school in Courtenay. In 1931 she joined the office staff and became an institution, with her naive manner and little girl voice. Later, several Cumberland girls worked in the office with Rita Treloar who was with the company to the end.

The large store with warehouse was presided over by the Company storekeeper, who bought all supplies needed and kept a large stock of often requested items. Herbert Glover was storekeeper for the E&N in Wellington, until Dunsmuirs sold the company. Mr. Glover moved to Union Bay to manage the store there for a few years. W. Richard filled in until the 1920's, when Andy Kay took over until he died, then Ted Greig managed the store.

SAWMILL

When the company started developing the mine, a sawmill was needed to supply the works with lumber for the pit-head, railroad, wharves and houses. Robert Grant was brought up by the Dunsmuirs from their Wellington operations where he had run a successful mill. Grant imported a steam plant and sawmill machinery from San Francisco. They were hauled by three yoke of oxen from the beach at Royston, up the original trail to a site just outside of Union. Lewis Mounce became a partner and the mill was known as the Grant & Mounce Sawmill.

This mill cut the Douglas fir to construct the first coal cars in 1889. The company installed a machine to saw and split shingles in 1893, which sped up the construction of homes for the miners. They further improved their production by purchasing a portable mill which could be taken into the timber. A fire destroyed the main mill in 1911 and the coal company ceased to have a mill associated with it until the 1940's.

All of the mines required great quantities of mine props for shoring up the roofs. Cut by contractors on company land, these 6" to 12" diameter poles were originally taken from small old-growth, then from second growth. As time passed larger timber was used, so a small mill was built in the yard at the end of the coke ovens. Mainly supplied by logger Paul Leynard, the mill was run by Jim McKay and a small crew. It cut rough lumber for mine roofs, railway ties, and timbers used on the trestle and around the shops.

J. Anderson

The Machine Shop, Car Shop, Foundry and Blacksmith Shop built in 1905

MACHINE SHOPS

1889 MARCH ➾ The axle of the big locie at Union Mines is broken, so a man was sent by canoe to Englishman's River and from there walked by road to Wellington. A new axle will soon be sent up. [2]

From the beginning the coal company needed facilities and mechanics to make repairs. So a shop was set up at the Wharf to service and install equipment as it arrived. A small shop was also maintained at Cumberland until 1935.

The big new shops were built in 1905. J. Fowler, who had succeeded Andrew McKnight as master mechanic, was in charge of construction of the works. Before this, large repair jobs had to be shipped to Ladysmith. After the new shops were built, all large repairs to CC(D)L locomotives and mine machines from Cumberland, Ladysmith and Extension were done at Union Bay. When some of the mules at the mine were replaced by mechanical haulage in 1910, it meant a great deal of work for the shops in the initial installation, and later in maintenance. New machinery was also designed and built for all aspects of the operation.

1908 JUNE ➾ The company's steamer *Wellington* is at sea again after extensive repairs to engine, boiler and hold at Union Bay machine shops. Everything is working like a charm. People would like to see another big steamer in for repairs. [4]

The biggest building contained the machine shop, with the locomotive bay situated at the west end. Two rail lines ran the length of the locie bay. A crane travelled the length of the building and extended out about 200' beyond the shop. This crane went over the two rail lines to the car shop. Steam produced by a coal-fired boiler drove the engine which supplied power to the overhead drive shafts. The main drive shaft ran the length of the shop and extended outside. From here a right-angled drive shaft supplied power to the blacksmith and car shops. These shafts drove all the machines by belt drive.

The steam from the boiler blew the whistle which governed the whole town. Families lived by the whistle.

"In the morning it blew at quarter to 7:00 and we all started for work, then again at 7:00 when work started. Two whistles for quarter to and one for seven. Then for lunch one whistle at 12:00, two at quarter to 1:00, and one toot at 1:00. One whistle at 4:00 signalled quitting time."

Harry Glover

When electricity arrived in 1914, motors replaced the boiler and ran the central driveshaft. At this time an air compressor was installed to run some of the tools, and it also blew the whistle.

The machine shop had a large variety of power tools. At least three of the six lathes were always running. Coal car axles were turned and the wheels bored for a press fit of about 40 tons. When locomotive tires were worn they were turned on the lathe to the

Cumberland Museum

Two sets of tracks ran the full length of the locomotive bay of the Machine Shop

Cumberland Museum

The interior of the Machine Shop where all repairs to CC(D)L locomotives and mine machines from Cumberland, Ladysmith and Extension were done

proper size and contour. Steam engine cylinders were bored and pistons fitted. Shafts up to 16" in diameter were turned on the 24' variable gap lathe. Pieces up to 7' diameter were machined on this lathe. To cut keyways and flat surfaces, the shaper was used with an 8' planer to machine large surfaces up to 4' x 7'. Usually two of the three small drill presses were running, as well as the drill press with a 6' radial arm which easily handled the larger jobs. There were also threading machines, gear cutters and many small tools.

Electric driven equipment could only be used underground in designated areas free from fire or explosive hazards, so air driven pumps, winches and tools were used. Both electric and air-driven pumps used at the mines were overhauled and made at Union Bay. These pumps varied from 4 to 400 gal. per minute with the pressure ranging from a few pounds to 500 p.s.i. Air-driven winches were also designed and made. Repairs and installations were made to the Washer. Vibrating screens, shaker tables and reciprocating plate feeders were designed and built in the shop. On the wharf new conveyor systems were installed, and a fine coal unloader designed and built by the shop crew.

The locomotive end of the shop was always busy. There was always at least one locomotive in for a complete overhaul and this employed five men full time. As well, each engine had its boiler washed out every month to clear it of impurities. In some areas boilers had to be cleaned every week, but water in the Comox Valley was quite pure and even after a month little scale was found. After five years of work, each locomotive was brought in, stripped down, thoroughly cleaned, repaired and reassembled to pass government inspection. The men at the shops took pride in their work, with the result that the locomotives were always in top condition.

1960 JUNE ➻ The engines were in absolutely marvelous mechanical condition despite their age. No.14 and 17 were both in A-1 shape, although 17 had not been used recently as she was due for an internal inspection. No.14 holds her steam well and hasn't a leak anywhere. Her staybolts are all in good shape with none cracked.

Doug Cummings, editor of The Steam Chest

The complete overhaul of a locomotive and tender was a long involved process. All

Cumberland Museum

Two locomotives in for overhaul stand in front of the machine shop

the driving wheels were removed and the old steel tires machined or replaced. New tires were bored undersize and heated by a ring of fire jets. When the tire was expanded enough it was pushed into position on the wheel, and when cool was very tight due to the "shrink fit". The bearings, pins and shaftings were replaced where necessary. Cylinders often had to be rebored and new pistons made, as well as piston rods. Most of the locomotives were supplied with Westinghouse airbrakes. These systems had to be overhauled. Springs and spring gears had to be checked and renewed if necessary.

The interior of the fire box was one of the first things to go. The hot fire over a long period of time, and sudden temperature changes, would crack the high grade steel.

Over the years, locies No.14, 15, 17 and 20 all had new boilers installed. More often they were repaired and parts replaced. Several hundred 2" tubes went through the boiler, taking the hot gasses from the fire box to heat the water, then up the smoke stack. Leaky tubes were repaired and all flat walls were stayed, as otherwise they would bulge and burst with the pressure. The inside walls were also attached to the outside walls of the firebox with stay bolts.

"A stay bolt had a hole through the center, and if it broke water would spurt out and the engineer knew that it was broken, so watched for more. You could have three or four broken if they were well spaced, but if too many were broken the boiler would explode. All broken stays were replaced at the monthly wash out."

Harry Glover

All of the valve gears were overhauled, and the valves reset for the proper timing of the inlet and exhaust of the steam.

The stripped down locomotive was ready to be rebuilt. The wheels were put in and the dome cover and safety valves were added. When all the tubes were put in, the boiler was filled with water and government inspected with a hydrostatic pressure 1 1/2 times the working pressure. If the boiler passed the test, the insulation was put in place and the covering jacket put over it. The valve gear was installed and all main rods and side rods were fastened in

Sillence

Men from the Union Bay shops pose in front of the largest locomotive No. 20, driven by little "engineer" Herbert Lund. c. 1932
Back Row, left to right: Chinese - ?, Chinese - Dick, Bert Geary, Yorkie Dunn, ?, Charile Shillito, Alex Auchinvole, Chic Graham, Ross Ray, George Cooper, Jack Medrich, Jim Kerr, John Fulcher, Harry Glover Jr., Bill Auchinvole, Ted Searle. Front row, left to right: George Walker, Bill Treloar, Jim Walters, Tweet Bradley, George Strachan, Wilf Glover, Dunc Marshall, Henry Davis, Bob Campbell, Tom Campbell, Albert Glover, Eddie Hughes, Harry Glover Sr., Bunt Bradley

place. The completed engine, tender and pony truck were given a fresh coat of black paint. Then the engine number and company logo were painted on in white. The boiler was fired up and the shop crew took it for a test run.

In the machine shops there were usually about sixteen men, made up of machinists, helpers and apprentices. Probably the first foreman of the small shop was J. Fowler. He was followed by W. Haggart, a cousin to David Haggart. Next came J.F. Street and then A. Kyle held the job for a few years, until Harry Glover succeeded him in the early '30s and continued as foreman until the company closed.

BOILER SHOP

All the plate work and welding was done in the boiler shop which was attached to the machine shop. Numerous plates were rolled or pressed into different shapes to suit the application. Power shears cut and punched 1/2" plate. Several gas welders and cutting torches were used. Later, two electric welders were used, and oxyacetylene welding was introduced. Chute and bin shapes were made with heat and press applications. Short tubes taken out of one boiler could be welded into a boiler requiring shorter tubes. To lengthen the tubes so that they could be reused in the same boiler, tube welding rolls were used to add short pieces.

The boilermakers were all welders. James Grady was probably the first foreman, with P. Harris next. He left and was replaced by Jack Medrich in 1925. In the 1930's, Mr. Medrich brought his three step-sons, Fred, Art, and Bill Treloar, to Union Bay. They had all served their time in Victoria and were superior welders. The B.C. Boiler Inspector proclaimed Art to be the best welder in the province.

BLACKSMITH SHOP

Shapes of all kinds, from simple tools to crankshafts, were forged in the blacksmith shop. Steel was heated in one of the three forges, and the blacksmith used a hand hammer to shape the forging into chisels, punches or hammer heads on the anvil. The hammerman wielded the sledge hammer for larger jobs, as when mine car irons were made.

Running the full length of the blacksmith shop, the overhead driveshaft powered machines for drilling and sharpening. It also powered the pressing and shaping cylinders. Later, a heating furnace for large forgings

Cumberland Museum

Building coal cars in the Car Shop. A new car was ready for the road every month

was installed. Steel billets could be heated and forged under the air hammer which had an 800 lb. head. Forgings for locomotives and mine machinery were made in dies, then one or two blows of the air hammer would shape them.

When No.4 mine closed, Locie No.19 and over a hundred coal cars were changed from 2' 11" to 3' (narrow gauge) at the blacksmith shop. Each axle, two to a car, was heated red hot and pounded to stretch it 1". This project took about three months.

Marsilla Magnone and Lindsay Ray were two of the first blacksmiths working for the Union Coal Company. Marsilla's son, Louis, married Bess McKay, and his daughter, Jennie, married E. Mugford. Both brought up their families in Union Bay. Mr. Ray was married to Sadie Grant and some of their eight children were born in Boston before the couple moved to Union Wharf. They built a house on company land south of the Wilson Hotel. Their oldest son, Dick, married Emma Baird and they brought up a family of four at the Bay. Both Louis and Dick worked on the locomotives.

Before the turn of the century, William and Alf Horne came from Nanaimo where they worked in the Renwick and Horne blacksmith shop. Waddy Wilson was for many years hammerman. R. Turnbull was foreman of the foundry until George Davis Jr. took over in the late 1920's.

"George Davis' hands were very tough, just like a dog's paw. He would pick up a piece of hot metal from the forge and hand it to you... you'd drop it fast."

Harry Glover

FOUNDRY

When the patterns were finished, moulds were made in two part boxes. The bottom was called the drag, and the top the cope. Natural sand or river silt which was dug from sand pits was arranged in parallel piles on the foundry floor. The drag, mounted on a bottom board, was set up between the sand piles. The pattern was placed on the bottom board and rammed with sand. This was topped by another board and the whole assembly turned over. The sand in the drag was coated with parting sand, then the cope was placed on the top and rammed with sand. The cope was taken off and the pattern extracted, then the cope replaced. Pouring holes were made in the mould.

A center-mount revolving crane serviced the whole foundry. A cupola, lined with fire brick, was used to melt up to three tons of cast iron. Under this, a steel plate was lined with clay. A wood fire was started on the clay bed, topped with a layer of coke, then a layer of cast iron chunks weighing about 500 pounds. Alternate layers of coke and iron were piled on, then a fan forced air into the fire, making it very hot. The heat melted the iron and it collected on the clay bed. When required, the molten metal flowed out of the cupola into the main ladle of 1000 lb. capacity. The ladles were carried by the crane or by hand, and the metal poured into the mould box. Metals other than iron were melted in crucibles over an oil fire. The machine shops repaired and constructed pumps for the mines, with the bronze castings made in the foundry. Cores for the patterns were made of sand and water mixed with a binder of molasses, sugar, flour or oil. These were baked in the core oven.

Working in the foundry were four molders, a core maker and several labourers. E. Navey was followed by Bert Geary as foreman. A.C. Dunn worked for over thiry years as a moulder and Jimmy Walters was a long-time core maker. Other molders were Charlie Bradley, Archie Miller and Bob Geary.

"One day for a joke, Yorkie Dunn cast a set of false teeth for Johnny Aitken who rarely wore any."

Buster Sherburn

CAR SHOP

A few coal cars originally came from Nanaimo, but the remainder were built at the car shop. Constructed of wood, they were of 25 ton capacity, which was later raised to 30 tons with the addition of a plank around the top. Axles and wheels manufactured in the eastern states were assembled in the machine shop and shunted across to the car shop on the railway that connected the two buildings. There the boxes were built. The overhead driveshaft ran the length of the car shop to power the band and circular saw, planer, boring machine and many small tools. One rail line ran inside the shop and the other outside, where the cars were spray painted "car shop red" with red oxide. Each new car had a white number painted on both sides, as well as the initials CC(D)Ltd. A new car was ready for the road every month. Repairs were also made on all the cars which were sent in by the car inspector.

One hundred 60 ton steel cars with double hoppers were purchased from eastern Canada about 1915 but the salt water used in the Washer soon corroded them. They were rebuilt with wooden sides and some were still in use in 1960. Numerous box cars, and coaches for miners and passengers were built in the car-shop.

"Built of wood and painted a dull barnyard red, they looked more like freight cars with windows than a vehicle to carry passengers... Always looking as if they needed a coat of paint, there was no mistaking the industry they served. But one feature that made these coaches something out of the ordinary was the huge potbellied stove with its cast-iron chimney sticking through the roof."

William Johnstone

1915 April ➺ A first class railway passenger coach was completely made for the new passenger service on the CC(D)L railway at the machine and car shops at Union Bay. [5]

John Work built the first car shop, and later he became an E&N car inspector. For many years George Campbell managed the car shop, and was succeeded by Peter Reid in the 1920's.

Patterns for the foundry were also made in the car shop. The many intricate patterns for pumps, hoists and mining machines were designed in the drafting room, and the plan given to the pattern maker who then cut and carved the pattern out of white pine. One of the first pattern makers was J. Haggerty. A. Ellis was the draftsman when apprentices from each shop spent six months learning drafting. Wilf Glover designed and built many patterns during thirty years as pattern maker and draftsman.

APPRENTICESHIP

All of the departments had an apprenticeship program. Many of the young boys finished school at grade eight and went straight into one of the shops to learn a trade. All apprentices served five years before becoming journeymen.

SHOP:	**TRADE:**
Machine	Machinist
Boiler	Boilermaker or Platemaker
Blacksmith	Blacksmith
Foundry	Moulder
Car	Carpenter or Pattern maker

"To be a pattern maker it took four years as an apprentice and one year as an improver. This was the same for all trades. After four years you could call yourself a patternmaker. You got paid 50¢ a day for the first year, $1.00 a day for the second year, $1.50 a day for the third year, and $2.00 a day the fourth year. As an improver you got a little better but not full wages. As a journeyman the pay was $5.00 a day."

Wilf Glover

Each apprentice spent six months in the drafting room to make him familiar with drawing and reading blueprints. Night classes were held by the foreman of each department, and government exams were written.

1918 JANUARY ➺ The Union Bay Technical Class held in the lecture rooms of the CC(D)L started its second term. Twelve pupils are studying shop mechanics and drafting under Mr. Ellis. [6]

Many of the men stayed on after their apprenticeship was finished. In later years Bill Auchinvole became the Master Mechanic, and Harry Glover the General Foreman. George Davis was made foreman of the blacksmith shop, and Bert Geary the foreman of the foundry, where in time he trained his own son, Bob. Below is a partial list of apprentices who trained in the various shops:

Machine Shop - T. Campbell, D. Renwick, H. Brown, H. Baldwin, W.Whitehouse, W. Auchinvole, H. Glover, E. Mazzolini, F. Street, R. Pollock, R. Ray, H. Davis, D.Marshall, A. Dunn, A. Searle, G.Strachan, H. Jones, P. Graham, T. Ferryman, A. Geary, H. Sherburn, D. Haggart, J. Haggart

Boiler Shop - G. Walker, S. Nakamura, B. Davis

Blacksmith Shop - G. Davis, D. Johnson

Foundry - S. Hooper, W. Hooper. H. Geary, A. Miller, C. Bradley, R. Geary

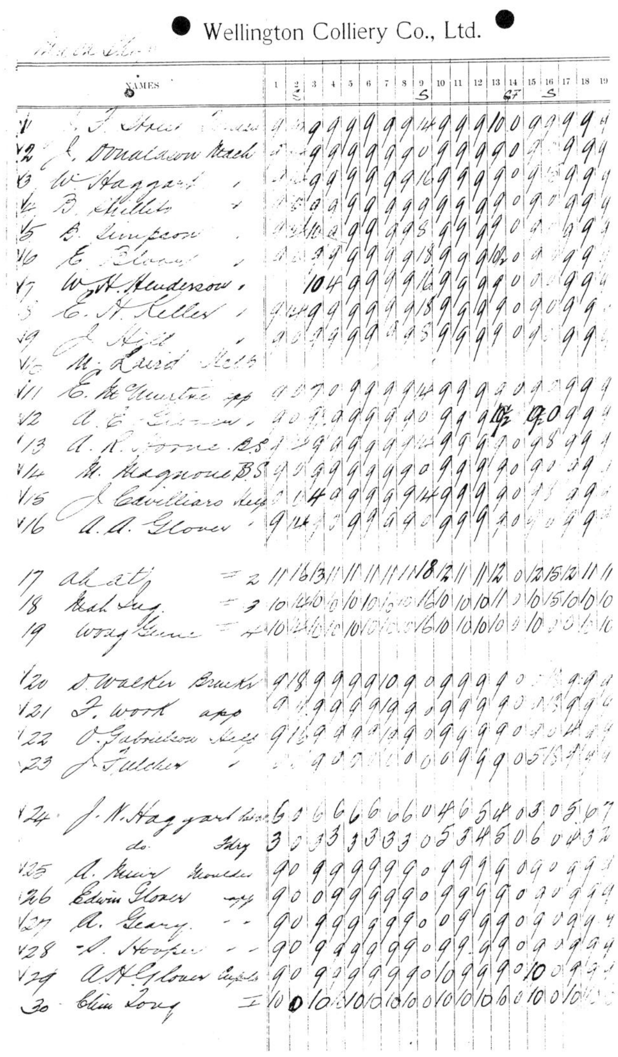

Car Shop - Carpenters: D. Haggart, W. Marshall, B. Bradley
Pattern Maker and Draftsman: W. Glover

Every year a new candidate was taken into the machine shops to start an apprenticeship. The first year was spent helping mechanics and cleaning machines. The job also included firing up the stationary boiler and keeping it clean. All mechanics wore bib overalls, and the apprentices got theirs slick with grease. One day Ross Ray, Henry Davis and Bob Pollock decided to make themselves a washing machine. They sawed a grease barrel in half, cleaned it out, bored a hole in the bottom, and put a jet of steam through it from the boiler. When the whistle blew for quitting time on Saturday, the barrel was filled with water. The first man changed and threw in his overalls and half a can of lye. The second and third added theirs, as well as more lye. The cauldron bubbled away until Monday morning. When they went to retrieve their overalls, all that was left were the buckles, buttons, and the double cloth for the bib, waist, fly and cuffs.

Cumberland Museum

The colliery yard beside the beach looking north to the briquet plant, washer, office and shops. Clam shell in foreground used for loading coal from stockpiles in yard

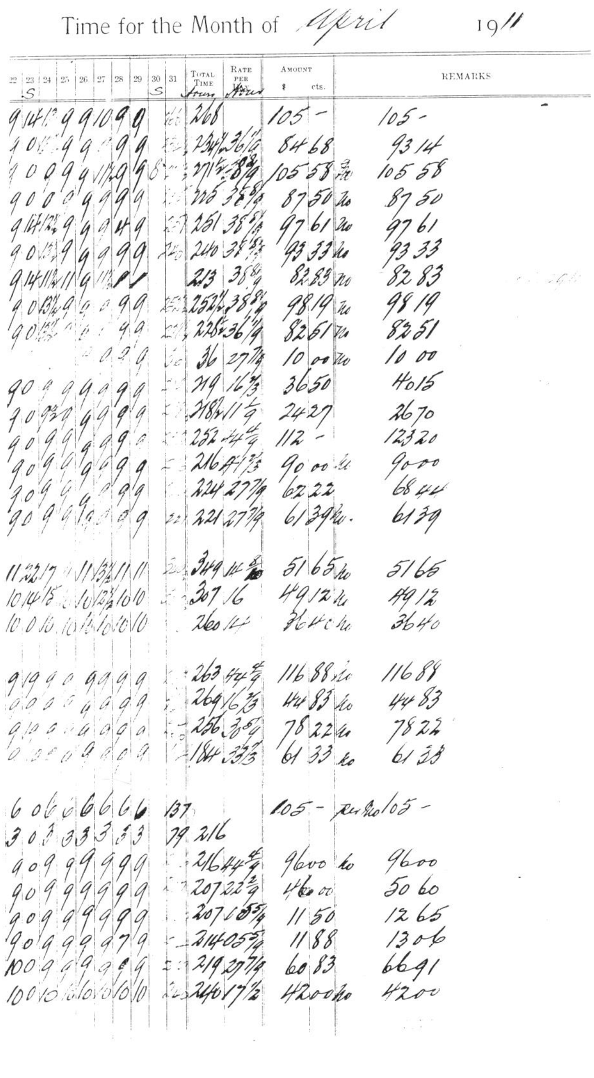

Time for the Month of April 1911

22 23 24 25 26 27 28 29 30 31 | Total Time Hours | Rate per Hour | Amount $ cts. | Remarks

"None of us was very old. There was a waterpipe in the shop, and one day Alex Auchinvole and I started a water fight. Alex was on the locomotive waiting to get me with the hose as I ran around. But who should walk in the door just then and get it? Old Man Auchinvole! There was trouble from then on."

Bob Pollock

Between the shops and the beach sat a row of four toilets over a little ditch of running water that took everything out to sea. If the stalls were all full and some of the older men sitting there too long, the young fellows would take a piece of oily waste, light it with a match, and float it down the ditch. One by one the occupants could be heard to jump up, shouting and swearing.

SHIPPING

Comox coal was shipped all over the world, even to Newcastle when a miners' strike there in 1939 caused a coal shortage in Britain. Coal production was tied to sales, which in turn were tied to world conditions. A shortage in one part of the globe meant that more demand was put on another. Before the First World War, ships engaged in the North Pacific trade transported coal to Australia and the Orient. During both wars coal was in high demand, with both naval and merchant marines loading up. During construction of the Panama canal, steamers coaled at Union Bay before departing with loads of B.C. lumber. When the canal opened it took less than a month to go from Union Bay to New York, but steamships bunkering on Vancouver Island decreased alarmingly.

G. Murdock

Mr. and Mrs. D. Renwick with Dorothy, Percy, Grace and Dave in their yard across the road from the Washer

L. Kilvert

Mrs. Fred Brown holding daughter Laura (named after Mrs. J. Dunsmuir) and a Dunsmuir grandchild while holidaying on the *Dolaura*

1914 February In the past, ships cargoing lumber from Vancouver and grain on the Columbia River for the U.K., as well as those loading on Puget Sound, all came to Vancouver Island ports for coal. They had to have enough fuel to go around the Strait of Magellan. Now, coal can be obtained very cheaply at Colon at the eastern entrance to the Panama Canal. So ships, by coaling after passing through the canal, save quite a tidy sum in tolls through the draft of water being many inches less. Many of the big Blue Funnel liners fill up in Hong Kong, and can make the trip to Victoria and return without refilling. [4]

Later, as it was cheaper to ship goods by water via the Panama Canal than by rail across Canada, more ships called for bunker. But oil was to seal the doom of the coal trade. Gradually, steamers and large manufacturing plants converted to oil all over the world.

The wharfinger was in charge of all loading. He decided where the ships were berthed, which coal chutes were used, and gave orders to the train crew regarding the emptying of coal cars. John Brent and George Reid served as wharfinger before the turn of the century, then Fred Beveridge had the job. Mike Manson took over until 1907. Fred Brown was next, and when he left about 1910, his assistant Dave Renwick managed a shift for over twenty years. Dave was born in Nanaimo where his father was a partner in Renwick & Horne blacksmith shop. He married Mary Ann Morgan and they had four children, Percy, Dave, Grace and Dorothy. The family followed Dave's sister, Jenny, and her husband, Mike Manson, to Union Bay about 1905 and lived for years in the second colliery house south of Chinatown.

A large house was built at the foot of Russell Hill for the wharfinger and his family. Michael Manson was the first to live there, followed by Fred Brown. James Dunsmuir and company officials often stayed there when they were in town on business. Both the Mansons and Browns were good friends of the Dunsmuirs, from early days in Nanaimo. Mrs. Brown (Sarah Horne) grew up with the Robert Dunsmuir family, and named her youngest daughter after James' wife Laura. James' family of twelve children often travelled up the coast on their yacht. Mr.

Output of District Mines in Tons. All shipped through the Port of Union Bay

1888	2,000	1910	518,426
1889	31,204	1911	437,335
1890	69,537	1912	475,803
1891	114,792	1913	508,095
1892	68,928	1914	394,731
1893	143,927	1915	260,841
1894	241,372	1919	552,196
1895	264,550	1920	455,914
1896	233,610	1930	243,929
1897	265,642	1940	357,244
1901	253,468	1950	216,385
1906	408,258	1960	88,764
1907	390,545		

The Dunsmuir family often came to Union Bay on their steam yacht *Dolaura*

R. Treloar

A frequent visitor was the *SS Makura*, a passenger liner from New Zealand. Her crew often challenged locals to soccer games

Dunsmuir bought the *Thistle* from Michael Manson. Then after it was destroyed by fire in 1907, the large steam yacht *Dolaura* was built. It was a beautiful sight pulling into dock, and the family was always welcome at Union Bay, where people could only imagine a life of such splendor.

The wharfinger relied on the Boss Chinaman to supply him with trimmers. It was their job to load the ship so that the cargo of coal was spread evenly and the boat balanced. (See Chinese chapter). Boats could be loaded at the rate of 200 tons per hour.

"I remember the worst job I ever did was trimming a tug boat on Chinese New Years. The Chinese, of course, wouldn't work because it was their holiday. So George Walker, Herb Muschamp and I trimmed this tug for 75¢ an hour, which was twice what I got normally as an apprentice. The hold was about 10' high with a little hole about 3'x 3' at the top where the elephant trunk poured the coal through. Trimming was taking the coal and pushing it in all the corners until you got them full. That was a piece of cake until it started to get higher and higher. You'd gone through standing, bending over, and kneeling, now you're lying down and that dirty wet nut coal keeps coming. You take the big shovel over and fill it up under the chute and pull it past you and push it over to a corner. You're about a foot from the roof and the coal is still coming in. Whoo! You know you got to go out where the coal's coming in. That's the worst job I ever had."

Dunc Marshall

Very often, if a boat was in for cargo coal, it would have ballast in the hold in the form of rocks, loaded where the last cargo was deposited. This ballast had to be unloaded in Baynes Sound before loading could take place. A few exotic animals or snakes, loaded with the ballast, washed up on shore and became a curio for a few days. Rats on board and on shore were often a problem. Most families had cats which kept the rat population down.

"They put rat guards up on the ships so the rats couldn't get on and couldn't get off. They were a round tin with a slot in it and they hung it over the rope, just off the side of the ship. Then the rats couldn't walk up the rope."

Wilf Bowden

Many large and small ships came to Union Bay for bunker coal. This was coal burned by the boat for fuel. These vessels included ships of the British and Canadian navies, as well as government coastal patrol boats. In 1918 a big contract to sell coal to the U.S. Navy was obtained. Large colliers delivered coal from Union Bay to Pearl Harbour. The Russian, American and Canadian sealing and whaling fleets stopped in for coal on their way north to the hunt.

A. Searle

Dunsmuir's tug *Lorne* towing a sailing ship into port. The windjammers did not travel the inside passage under sail

E. Renwick

An Irish captain, a friend of Ellen McKay's, entertains locals while in port. Standing: Captain, Mary McKay, Bess Muschamp, Eva Small, Elizabeth Walker, Jackson Arthur. Seated: Ellen McKay, Captain Cain

1934 MAY ➾ The *SS Gray*, mother ship of the Consolidated Whaling Corporation of Victoria, has just left for the Queen Charlotte Islands. There she is making 5,000 ton dumps of coal at two locations for her four sister ships cruising for whales in the Bering Sea. They are all fitted with the most modern appliances for taking the big fellows of the Pacific. When she has completed coaling she will return to Victoria to be fitted with tanks for carrying whale oil. [6]

Local ferries and mail boats took bunker. Large ships got bunker before transporting B.C. lumber, canned salmon and wheat.

1926 MAY ➾ During the month of April, Union Bay has taken on a semblance of its old time glory, with sailors from deep-water ships from ports all over the seven seas walking its street. The *SS Burma* was loaded with lumber for Japan; the *SS Balboa* was loaded with coal for Mexico. The *SS Triever* steamed through the stormy Straits of Magellan to Union Bay in ballast to load with Comox coal, which says something for the quality of coal. She left to load grain at Portland. The *SS Wairuna* was bound for Australia with a general cargo; the *SS Arabia* left Union to load with lumber at Vancouver for Japan; the *SS Delamoor* left for Seattle to load grain for the United Kingdom; the *SS Carpsey* left for Vancouver to load with ties for Egypt; the *Waiotapu* had a cargo of paper from Powell River for Australia; the *SS Kenilworth* left Vancouver to load grain for the United Kingdom; the government boat *Canadian Seigneur* left for Vancouver to load with lumber for the United Kingdom; the *SS Wolhandel* left for Portland to load with wheat for Europe; the *SS Woron* and the *Queenmoor* both left for New Westminster to load with lumber for New York. [6]

A few passenger ships also called for bunker coal. Usually the passengers were left at Vancouver or Victoria while the ship came for coal. It was exciting when the big *Empress of Japan* arrived. While loading, any passengers and family of the crew were required by law to leave the ship. They took rooms along with the pilots in the Nelson Hotel, or stayed with the wharfinger and his family. Keeping food fresh during the long journeys was a problem, so animals were taken aboard "on the hoof". Cows, pigs and sheep were brought ashore to graze on the land which eventually became the ball field.

Cargo coal was loaded onto big colliers. When the Union mines went into production, the last of the big sailing barques were still hauling coal. After a few mishaps travelling up the inside passage under sail, they stopped at Esquimalt and were towed up, usually by

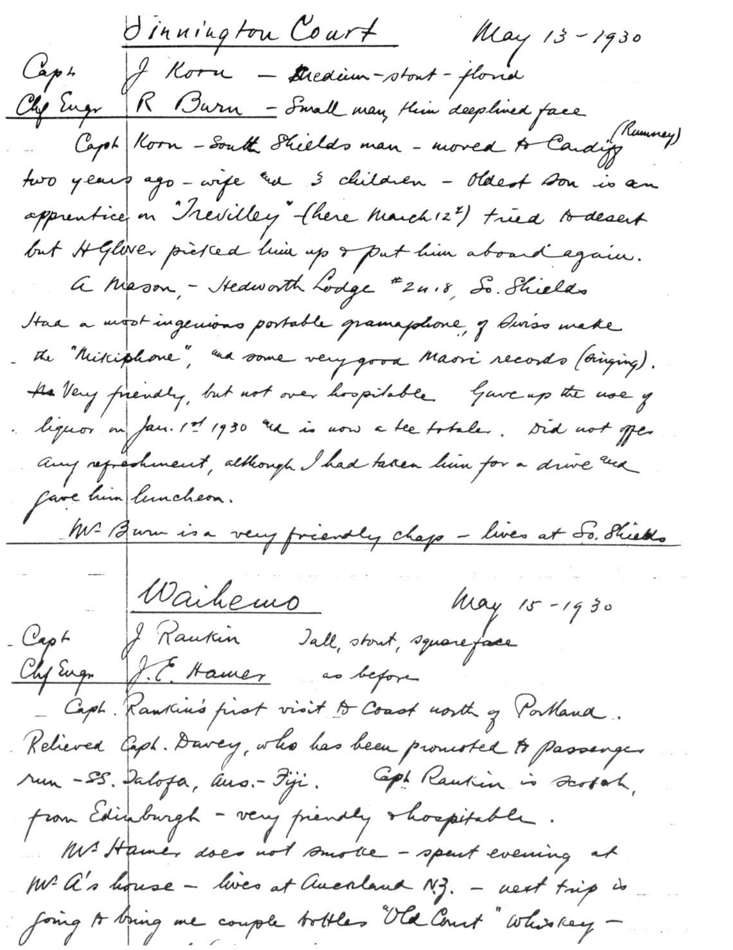
Dinnington Court May 13 – 1930
Capt J Korn – Medium – stout – florid
Chf Engr R Burn – Small man thin deeplined face
Capt Korn – South Shields man – moved to Cardiff (Rumney) two years ago – wife and 3 children – Oldest son is an apprentice on "Trevilley" – (here March 12th) tried to desert but H Glover picked him up & put him aboard again.
A Mason, – Hedworth Lodge #2418, So. Shields
Had a most ingenious portable gramaphone, of Swiss make the "Mikiphone", and some very good Maori records (singing). Very friendly, but not over hospitable. Gave up the use of liquor on Jan. 1st 1930 and is now a tee totaler. Did not offer any refreshment, although I had taken him for a drive and gave him luncheon.
Mr Burn is a very friendly chap – lives at So. Shields

Waihemo May 15 – 1930
Capt J Rankin Tall, stout, square face
Chf Engr J.E. Hamer as before
Capt. Rankin's first visit to Coast north of Portland. Relieved Capt. Davey, who has been promoted to passenger run – SS. Talofa, Aus. – Fiji. Capt Rankin is Scotch, from Edinburgh – very friendly & hospitable.
Mr Hamer does not smoke – spent evening at Mr A's house – lives at Auckland NZ. – next trip is going to bring me couple bottles "Old Court" Whiskey –

A page from the diary of shipping agent E.T. Searle

Dunsmuir's tug, the *Lorne*. The large ocean-going steamships also stopped and took a pilot on board to guide them through Juan de Fuca and Georgia Staits. This did little to help the *San Pedro* in 1891, which left Union Wharf with an experienced pilot aboard. The ship ran aground at the entrance to Victoria Harbour on a clear calm night with both captain and pilot on the bridge.

1893 OCTOBER ➻ Foreign Coal Shipping from Union for September.

SS Mineola for Los Angeles	3,500 tons
SS Barracouta for Panama	1,500 tons
Bk. Palmyra for Port Angeles	2,000 tons
SS City of Puebla for Seattle	1,100 tons
Bk. McNear for Honolulu	1,368 tons [2]

The shipping agent took orders and arranged schedules of boats coming for coal. He had personal contact with the officers and was in charge of paying them a "commission" (payola) for choosing to coal at Union Bay. The shipping agent often entertained the captain and engineer, or drove them to town for business and lunch. His office was situated near the freight shed. James McLean was the first shipping agent, followed by George Booth after the turn of the century. Herbert Glover held the position for about ten years, followed by Percy Fogg, then E.T. Searle and John Moore. Much of the early coal was shipped to American firms in Pacific coast cities. Tugs with scows delivered coal to many local industries up and down the B.C. coast. The coast guard ships *Quadra*, *Estevan* and *Stewart* called for coal to deliver to the lighthouses up and down the coast.

E. Renwick

Captain Desmond Champion entertains customs officer Percy Renwick and shipping agent John Moore while *Pamir* is loading 4000 tons of coal for New Zealand

DEEP WATER VESSELS THRONGED UNION BAY

Demand for Comox Coal Gave Old-Time Importance To Bunkering Port

The very welcome activity in coal orders at Cumberland during April is reflected in the bunkering at Union Bay. Fourteen deep-sea ships bunkered at Union Bay during April and quite a number of coastwise vessels. The list is given below.

April 8th	Siam City from Vancouver for New York
April 8th	Mt. Balboa from 'Frisco for Mexico
April 11th	S.S. Burma, from Japan to Vancouver
April 11th	S.S. Triever from Buenos Aires to Portland
April 14th	S.S. Wairuns, from Ocean Falls for Australia
April 20th	S.S. Arabia from Yokohama to Vancouver
April 22nd	S.S. Dalemoor from Seattle to Portland
April 24th	S.S. Carspey from Vancouver to Egypt
April 25th	S.S. Waiotapu from Powell River to Australia
April 27th	S.S. Kenilworth from Japan to Vancouver
April 27th	S.S. Canadian Seigneur from Vancouver to Davenport, Eng.
April 28th	S.S. Wolhandel from Vancouver to Portland
April 29th	S.S. Woron from Vancouver to New York via New Westminster
April 30th	S.S. Queensmoor from Seattle to New York

Many of the ships were like old friends, returning again and again. Their captains and crews often formed part of the social life at the little port. Several of Ellen McKay's brothers and cousins were sailors and captained ships that came in for coal. Family and friends were always welcomed aboard. Besides the *Joan*, every week there was at least one of Dunsmiur's boats, the *Robt. Dunsmuir*, *Barnard Castle*, or *Wellington*, in for coal. The *Marmion*, an old north sea trawler, called regularly to take coal to Bamberton for the B.C. Cement Co.

"The "Pilot" came in often. Everyone knew the whistle. When we were in school and the whistle blew, there would be a yell, 'There's the "Pilot"'. We all knew Captain Scarf."

Violet Rutherford

Many ships with an interesting history, crew, design or cargo, called for coal. Sailing ships like the *J.D. Peters*, *Detroit*, *Matilda*, *Martha Davis*, *Enoch Talbot*, and *Richard III* always drew people's curiosity, especially after their number decreased.

1916 JUNE ➻ The full rigged sailing ship *Golden Gate* sailed from Union Bay Saturday with 3,500 tons of coal for San Francisco. It was the first sailing ship to enter the port in ten years, and will make two more trips under tow of the tug *Dauntless*. [5]

E. Renwick

The *Cyclops*, like all ships of the Blue Funnel Line, had double masts which were nicknamed the "goalposts"

In 1946, long after the others had gone to Davy Jones' locker or the scrap heap, the *Pamir*, flying the New Zealand flag, came for coal.

"She was a wonderful sea boat. Despite her vast bulk, she could "wear ship" in seven minutes. She handled like a dream."

Captain Desmond Champion

Originally built in Hamburg in 1905 for the Chilean nitrate trade, she became one of the Flying P Line. All eighteen ships had names starting with the initial "P". Rigged as a four masted barque, she was 331' long with registered tonnage of 2,385. The citizens of the Bay never saw her sail, as she was towed to and from port.

R. Ryan

Best remembered ship to coal at Union Bay was the four masted barque *Pamir*. She was 331' long and her masts stretched 168' skyward. Local artist Chas. Pickles painted her several times, the largest of which is in the possession of the author

"Under all canvas the Pamir set thirty-one sails, her full sail area being 5/6 of an acre. The Pamir followed the fashion of her time in having a full bridge deck amidship, in which officers and men were housed in greater comfort than in the poop and forecastle of the older sailing ships. After she was loaded with 4,000 tons of coal at the Bay, she was towed out to the open sea by the tug Snohomish.

Charles Pickles

From a photo, Mr. Pickle, an old salt as well as an artist, captured her on canvas. In the 1950's the *Pamir* was sold to the German navy and used as a training ship. On September 21, 1957 she foundered in a hurricane and sank in the South Atlantic, with only six survivors out of a crew of eighty-six.

Probably the best remembered and loved of the many ships were the beautiful vessels of the British Blue Funnel line. The large 7,000 to 10,000 ton boats were easily distinguished, not only by the blue funnel but also by the double mast, which was nick-named the "goal post". These were used for derricks and winches during loading. With names like the *Ixion, Progressist, Onfra, Cyclops* and *Ning Chow,* they were always a welcome sight pulling into port.

The wharf became a billboard, advertising all the ships that came for coal.

1939 SEPTEMBER ⊷ It is the habit of the artist bloke that is on nearly every ship that tramps the seven seas, to use his ample time while coaling in affixing a board at the wharf head. There are dozens of them, some pretty crude on the sides of packing cases, some real works of art. Some months ago a Teuton ship came to coal at the Bay. Her artist proceeded to adorn his placard with a board bearing the legend "South, East, North, West, Good old Germany is Best," with the swastika appended.

Soon after, along came a British ship. The Nazi emblem greeted his irate eye. He took a board, wrote on it "NURTS" and nailed it over the offending sign. After the Britisher left, a Slav ship hove in sight. This was before the Russo-German pact was even dreamt of, and Stalin was calling Hitler all the fancy names he could think of. So the Russian artist wrote a word that means something far too obscene and offensive for print in a family journal, and pasted it on the German sign. Next came an Italian boat. Now at that time Il Duce was very much enamoured of the German alliance. Egg-headed Nazis had not

Union Bay Community Hall

This painting of the Blue Funnel ship *Xion* hung for years in the Union Bay post office. It is now in the Community Hall

K. Carter

The Russian ice-breaker *SS Krassin* loading up before heading to Leningrad through the frozen Arctic Sea

planted themselves arrogantly on the Italian plazas. So Tony the dauber thought it his loyal duty to an ally to tear off the defacing strips and leave the Teuton notice in its former glory.

Once more came a Britisher. By this time the crisis with Poland was approaching, and the British tar saw with loathing the Nazi billboard. He tore it down and cast it into the sea. After that there was nothing for it but to declare war. [6]

Ships with foreign crews, interesting histories and tales of events in other countries, brought the world to the doorstep.

1893 MAY ➾ The U.S. coast survey ship, the *Albatross*, left for the Bering Sea. Many citizens visited the ship and saw many curiosities and specimens of the deep sea, fish caught four miles down, some with no eyes. [3a]

1919 DECEMBER ➾ The *SS Wairuna*, a captured "Hun" ship, coaled here. The British Admiralty used her for a troopship, and upon returning from Greece she was torpedoed off the coast and remained submerged for three months. She was raised and put into commission. Then at Dunkirk a huge hole was blown through her side by a German shell, but she managed to make England safely. [6]

1921 MAY ➾ A big Japanese liner is at Union Bay and the port is crowded with Nippon sailors. This is the most modern of Japanese boats to coal here. [6]

1922 JULY ➾ The *Equator* is the converted yacht in which Robert Louis Stevenson cruised the south seas. She was bought at the great writer's death for the Alaska fishing trade and converted to steam. She often comes into Union Bay, and to all intents and appearances is as stout a craft as when she sailed the southern seas with the great novelist aboard. [6]

1922 NOVEMBER ➾ Captain Boler of a Blue Funnel ship tells of being at Yokohama when the earthquake hit. He reported that the disaster reports were not overdrawn. Of the 400,000 population 100,000 were dead. Mr. Boler has a wonderful collection of photos. [6]

1923 FEBRUARY ➾ To pass a general order among the crew of the *SS Pawnee*, which has been coaling at Union Bay this week, would require half a dozen interpreters. For her officers are Germans, her stokehold is full of Chinese, and her crew is composed of Englishmen, Irishmen, Scotchmen, Americans, Scandinavians, natives of South American republics and a few other assorted nationalities. [6]

1923 SEPTEMBER ➾ Two freak ships have been featured this week at the Bay. A relic of the past was the whaleback *Kobe Maru*, a great old boat, with plates like armor-plate and as dry as a bone. A ship of the future is the corrugated type, *Rio Azul*. She is built in three waves or corrugations, and it is claimed that this form of construction strengthens her and that she presents less resistance to the water. [6]

1927 DECEMBER ➾ The notorious rum-runner, the *SS Federalship*, put into Union Bay for bunker. The vessel was first launched in Germany forty years ago as the *Aarnold Dwing*, and she was interned in Belgium during the war and adopted the name of *Gertrude*. Then she came to Vancouver under Panama registry and was known as the *Federalship*. After her seizure and subsequent release off 'Frisco, she was changed to the *Glendrina* under the flag of Guatemala. This was not sufficient protection for her against the influence of the "dry squad" of the United States, so she was changed to Italian registry and will probably remain unmolested under the protection of Mussolini. [6]

1931 DECEMBER ➾ The Captain of an Austalian steamer was on the first Scott Antarctic expedition and has many stories to tell. [6]

1934 MAY ➾ The *SS Krassin*, English built ice-breaker of the U.S.S.R., put her rusty nose opposite the coal bunkers at Union Bay at ten o'clock on Saturday morning. That this is no sight-seeing mission was evident since, although she had steamed all this way from the Baltic, a cruise of 13,000 miles, she did not stop at either Victoria or Vancouver but came straight to Union Bay to coal. She is going to crash her way through the ice of the Arctic Sea to Leningrad.

Hundreds of people flocked to the Bay to see the famous vessel flying the hammer and sickle. No one was allowed aboard; even a Communist delegation from Vancouver was turned away. The large crew of 157 made good use of their shore leave, and Courtenay merchants were invaded by the Soviet sailors. The crew had a pleasant time fraternizing with local people. Constable Lennox at Union Bay complimented the men on their good behavior. [6]

1939 AUGUST ➾ Two and a half months out of Leningrad on their way to Vladivostok, seven Russian vessels dropped anchor at Union Bay. It was probably the oddest flotilla ever seen in these waters. Three freighters, three sea-going tugs, and a dredge with ninety-four men and twelve women aboard, are making their leisurely way from one port of the USSR to another port in the same country by the longest way round. [6]

In the late 1930's many of the deep sea ships bunkering at the Bay were loaded with scrap iron for Japan. Often old clunkers on their last legs were loaded, and when they reached Japan were scrapped along with their cargo. This was the fate of most of the Greek ships that came to Union Bay during the war. (See WWII). During the First World War, ships were camouflaged with many coloured stripes, but during the second war all ships were painted grey. Many of the ships captured were renamed and used in the war effort.

By the end of the Second World War almost all ships had converted to oil. This meant the end of the bunker trade. There was still some cargo coal sold which was shipped out on a few ocean freighters and on barges pulled by tugs. The Japanese ships returned again as Japan was industrialized. John Moore was the shipping agent through the war years and until the last ship coaled at the old wharf. He and his wife Mary entertained the ships' officers.

"There was Captain Churchill on the "Ft. George", who celebrated his birthday standing with his men on the bridge of his ship, in the middle of a convoy under attack in the North Atlantic, while the men sang "Happy Birthday".

Captain Robson was a British captain who was held prisoner aboard the German "Graf Spee" when she was shelled by three British cruisers.

There was Thomson of the "Fort Confidence" who sailed his ship to the edge of the Polar ice cap to escape the German raiders, and Captain Vasilios Sarantidis of the Greek ship "Despena" which left for the Pacific and was sunk.

When the first Japanese ship came in after the war, they were very nervous about how they would be treated, but they could hardly be blamed, and the war was over. The "Tatsuhi Maru" came back often and the officers were almost part of our family. At Christmas the radio officer practically danced into the house carrying a parcel. When opened it was full of Japanese ornaments for our Christmas tree. The young officers spent the evening decorating the tree, while old Captain Yamamoto sat in the easy chair holding our baby in his lap, quietly smiling."

Mary Moore

M. Vowels

In 1951 the *Hikawa Maru* took on 10,000 tons of coal and was the last ship to coal at Union Bay

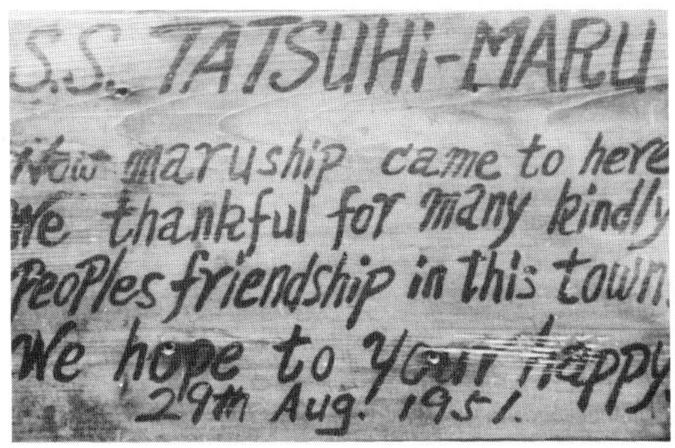

M. Aitken

This plaque was put up by the crew of *Tatsuhi Maru*, the first Japanese ship to visit after WW II

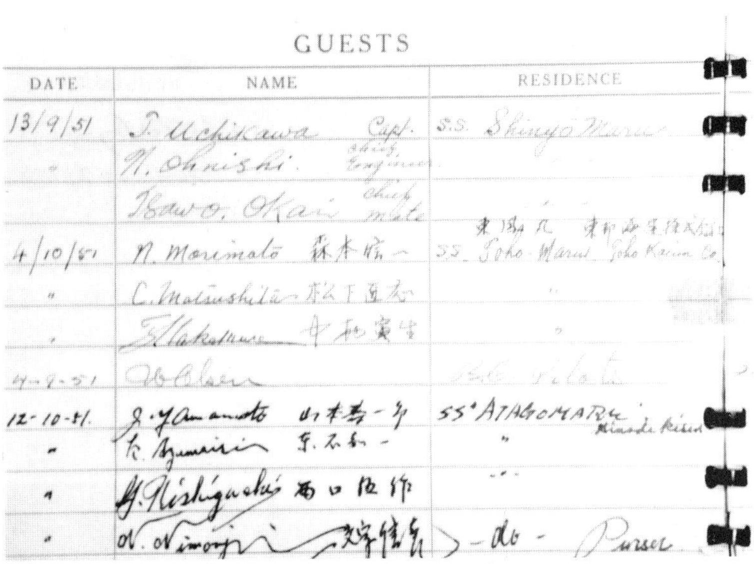

GUESTS

DATE	NAME	RESIDENCE
13/9/51	T. Uchikawa Capt.	S.S. Shinyo Maru
"	N. Ohnishi Chief Engineer	
	Isawo. Okai Chief mate	
4/10/51	N. Morimoto 森本	S.S. Soho Maru Soho Kaiun Co.
"	C. Matsushita 松下	"
"	Takenaka 中	"
4-?-51		
12-10-51	Yamamoto 山本	SS ATAGOMARU
"		"
"	Nishiguchi 西口	"
"	N. Ninomiya	- do - Purser

M. Aitken

A page from John and Mary Moore's guest book indicates the number of Japanese ships that coaled at Union Bay after the war

The last ship to take cargo coal was the *SS Hikawa Maru*, formerly a Japanese liner. She

Cumberland Museum

From 1952 to 1960 the only coal loaded from the port was shipped by barge

had been stripped down during the war and used as a hospital ship. She took 10,000 tons of coal to Japan to further their industrial development after the war. From then until the end of mining in 1960, only scows were loaded from the big wharves. Tugboats such as the *Swell* and *Master* were like old friends, returning again and again for scow loads of coal.

Originally, the pilots which took charge of the ships while in the inside passage brought the freighters right into the dock. After an American ship rammed the wharf, a small boat was used to meet the ship and take the hawser into the dock. Dave Campbell in his fourteen foot boat had the job for many years.

Cumberland Museum

Tugboats like the *Master* called regularly for scowloads of coal

SHIPPING DISASTERS

One of the first ship wrecks connected with Union Bay was the sinking of Michael Manson's *Rustler* off Nelson Island in 1889. The steamer's captain and crew managed to get into a dingy. As it happened, Mike was on the *Dunsmuir* going from Union Wharf to Nanaimo when he sighted a rowboat. The *Dunsmuir* went alongside and Mike recognized his captain. He jumped aboard the rowboat and helped the men row to Vancouver in the cold December weather. The *Rustler* had brought many supplies to the new port as it was being built. Mr. Manson's next ship, *Thistle*, was sold to the Dunsmuir Co. and in 1907 it was destroyed by fire.

Although much dangerous cargo passed through Union Bay there was never an accident. Up until about 1893 most of the mining was done by blasting. Blasting powder was used and was manufactured by a private firm, the Hamilton Powder Works at Northfield. The powder for the Union mines was shipped weekly on special trips of the *Joan*. The powder company began the manufacture of dynamite which contained nitroglycerin, a very volatile yellow liquid. This had to be transported from boats at Departure Bay by wagon to Northfield.

1896 APRIL ➾ People eating dinner at Union Mines, at ten past two on Thursday afternoon, distinctly and undeniably felt the shock of the nitroglycerin explosion by which the wagon driver Stevenson lost his life at Northfield Powder Works. Union is about fifty miles as the crow flies, so it was quite a force. [2]

A powder works was then built at Departure Bay by the coal company to eliminate the danger during transportation. But several explosions occurred at that plant with many lives lost. In 1913 a boat carrying powder blew up in Nanaimo harbour. The powder works were moved to James Island near Victoria in 1915.

In the early days of shipping, by the time many of the boats were put on the coal runs, they were old and in need of repair. Several times, crews fearing for their lives refused to ship out on unseaworthy vessels, only to be replaced by a fresh crew. The story of the *Alpha* (see Lighthouse chapter) illustrates this. As well, foolhardy captains, ever anxious to make a profit, overloaded their vessels.

1894 DECEMBER ➾ Captain Blackburn, commander of the *Montserrat*, by his numerous adventures had earned for his vessel a notoriety unequalled by any other craft on the coast. He always declared that as long as the funnel was above water he could steer his vessel into port. [2]

The English steamer *Barracouta* was six hours out of port when it was wracked by a terrible explosion in its hold. Parts of the deck boards flew as high as the masthead, and three crew members were injured.

1893 SEPTEMBER ➾ The saloon house is in a deplorable state. It was lifted bodily from the deck a couple of feet and the doors were blown from their hinges. The walls bulge outwards and the staterooms are simply an extent of loose and broken boards. In the diminutive social hall are the remains of a glossy black piano, but the instrument looks as if a couple of rusty blacksmiths had been operating on it with sledges. The floor gapes in many places, and what is left is littered with fragments of porcelain and pulverized glass. [2]

Many years later a Greek ship arrived for bunker with a fire in her hold.

1936 OCTOBER ➾ The Bay workers took off as much coal as the engineer thought necessary and then loaded the *Nereus* with Comox coal. Apparently not enough was removed, as the fire was discovered again off the Queen Charlottes. She then steamed to Victoria with 700 tons ablaze, where she was met by a tug equipped to fight the fire. [6]

December 1894 was one long storm, with a succession of gales lashing the Pacific Ocean. Any ship unlucky enough to be caught out in it was in trouble. The barque *Dominion* took thirty-one days to make the voyage from San Francisco to Puget Sound.

1894 DECEMBER ➾ During the worst of the gale she was hove to under bare sails, as she had been caught unaware and a full set of sails were blown away. Tremendous seas and winds from all points of the compass kept the barque jumping around like a cockle shell. [6]

Also out in the storm were the *Montserrat*, which had overloaded at Departure Bay, and the *Keeweenaw*, an old weak boat which loaded 3,500 tons at Union Wharf on December 8. Both were headed for 'Frisco, and when they did not arrive, tugs and coast guard cutters were sent out to search but to no avail.

1894 DECEMBER ➾ It is twenty-three days since the steamers went missing. Indians on the west coast saw rockets and believe a large boat was in difficulty. If this is so, one of the steamers must have foundered off Cape Flattery, then got into the stream up the west coast of the Island. [2]

By spring, whalers brought back reports of the Queen Charlotte Indians using wreckage from both boats to repair their homes. The nameboard of the *Keeweenaw* was used to decorate a chief's house.

Ships regularly went aground in foggy weather at Ship's Point and Deep Bay. The *H.M.S. Comux* in 1896 stayed too close to Vancouver Island and ran aground, but as there were no large rocks she was easily pulled off. Fog was again the culprit when the H.M.S. *Flora* was wrecked on Village Reef, Denman Island.

1903 ➾ While proceeding from Union Bay to Esquimalt in a dense fog, the navigation lieutenant mistook a spar buoy for a pile beacon on the other side of the channel. The vessel crashed on the rocks, the bow slid up the shelving reef and held fast, leaving her stranded with stern submerged. The sea poured in through open scuppers, nearly trapping the sleeping officers. Officers and crew took refuge on Denman Island, where tents were erected. The officers who escaped in night attire upheld the dignity of the service under trying circumstances. Two royal navy ships, the *Grafton* and *Egeria*, spent seven foggy days pumping out the boat and floating her off. When the vessel was pulled clear, the band played "A Life on the Ocean Wave" and "Rule Brittania" as the crew cheered lustily. [5]

W. Isbister

HMS *Flora* was stranded on Village Point reef in 1903. It took seven days to pump her out and refloat her

UNIONS

Although the men at Union Bay worked for the same corporation, feelings against the company never ran as high as they did in Cumberland. The terrible conditions in the mines of flooding, gas, dust and explosions did not exist at the Bay. Most of the workers, except the Chinese, worked in relatively comfortable surroundings. The smaller working force had a greater diversity of jobs.

However, Union Bay employees were not immune to the miner's situation and were eager to support their fellow workers. All of the union organizers arrived via the port, and the workers were well aware of what was happening. Each new development was reported by the train crews, who came down at least twice a day.

Before any coal had been shipped from the Wharf, the white miners objected to the Chinese miners who had come up from Nanaimo because a law there forbade them to work underground.

1889 FEBRUARY ➾ The miners strike at Union because they object to working with Chinese underground. The Chinese had a slope entirely to themselves, but when some were put on another slope with white men, the latter objected. [2]

Probably the first attempt to organize the miners was in 1890, although union workers in Nanaimo had been active long before that. That year Tully Boyce, a union president, arrived at Union Wharf and was refused transportation on the train to Union. Undaunted, he walked the ten miles.

"I got there O.K. although somewhat foot-sore and tired, and organized what promises to be a flourishing branch of the M.& M.L.P.A. From the reports I got from the miners, these mines seem to be in a very deplorable condition. The wages paid are down to the starvation point. The prices the company store charges are astonishing, and the miners are compelled to sign a cutthroat note empowering the Company to stop wages for store bills. These mines are known as the Union Mines.

D. Muschamp

Dave Walker, forced off CC(D)L property during the strike of 1913, took his house apart board by board and re-built it up McLeod Road

I would suggest that unless a more liberal policy is pursued, they hereafter be known as the Siberian Mines of British Columbia."

Tully Boyce

A few years later, in 1893 an explosion occurred aboard the *Barracouta* when it was six hours out of Union Wharf. Immediately, the officers accused the union of planting dynamite in the hold. In fact, it proved to be caused by coal dust and gases. The Nanaimo press seemed to be sympathetic with the miners, while the newspaper at Union was for years on management's side.

1893 AUGUST ➾ Shipmasters and others employing non-union men are ever ready to place the blame on union men. It is almost fair to presume that if they snore in their sleep it is the work of some union sympathizer and not the effect of nature. [2]

D. Muschamp

Mr. and Mrs. D. Walker with son David, years later, in front of their house and well established garden

1913 MARCH ➾ The curtain has dropped on the last act of the U. M.W., and to say the least there have been several, and each and every one of them injurious to the town of Cumberland... It is gratifying to know that the Canadian Colleries are making such rapid strides towards redeeming the trade lost by the "holiday." [5]

Much has been written about mining conditions and tragedies suffered by the miners. Following is a list of important milestones over the years that finally ensured the acknowledgement of the union by the company.

1888 After explosions at Nanaimo, Chinese were not allowed to work down the mine, so they were sent to Union to work.
1895 Company discharged 100 men and fourteen organizers of the Miner's Protective Society.
1896 Chinese and Japanese formed a union and asked for $1.50 per day.
1898 Trent River disaster, some suspected sabotage.
1901 Feb - Fire at No.6 Mine, sixty-four men were suffocated.
1902 J. Dunsmuir forbade any member of Western Federation of Miners to work in mines, resulting in a 3 1/2 month strike.
1903 July - Explosion at No.6 Mine, sixteen Chinese were killed.
1905 A four month long strike.
1906 Chinese pushers went on strike for higher wages.
1910 J. Dunsmuir sold his coal enterprise to Mackenzie & Mann and the company became CC(D)Ltd.
1910 Mule drivers struck and were given the increase they asked for.
1911 United Mine Workers of America formed and took over the Western Federation of Miners.
1912 Sept 16 - All miners, white and Oriental, struck in support of the miner's gas safety committee members who were dismissed.

Sept 17 - Company locked miners out and required that each man sign a separate contract under the same old conditions. Daily wage scale railroad men wanted:

Loco Engineer	$4.00	Yard Engineer	$4.00
Fireman	$3.25	Yard Fireman	$3.00
Brakeman	$3.30	Yard Brakeman	$3.00

Sept 24 - One dozen special police arrived and refuse to give white men access to Chinatown and Japtown.

Sept 25 - Orientals signed two year contract. The mines re-opened. One hundred special police arrived. Six were stationed at Union Bay.

Sept 28 - All strikers were ordered to leave rented company homes, and homes built on company property.

"We lived next to Renwick's house. Then when the strike came the people were not welcome in the company houses and we were put out. Then we went down to the other end of town and lived in a tent. I was just two and a half and Dunc was a baby. Everyone was on the beach so I guess the houses stood empty. My Dad didn't work for the Colleries for two years and we were two years in a tent. It had a floor and side of logs. I guess it was just put up in a hurry. It was a regular tent town, down past the Nelson Hotel. As kids we loved it, living on the beach. Our neighbours were the Haggarts and Donaldsons. Around that time a lot of people straggled away and went to Vancouver or Victoria.

Some men went on strike, others didn't. Mr. Renwick was a boss so he worked. Dad got a job as bartender at Humphrey's Hotel. I was young and don't remember any hardship, or incidences, or ill-feeling. Everyone remained very friendly, but in Cumberland there certainly was trouble. The workers in Union Bay went out in sympathy, or couldn't work if there was no coal."

Nettie (Marshall) Jones

"My dad came out here two years before us. He came to Vancouver to avoid strikes in the old country, and when he got there the boiler makers were on strike, so he came to Union Bay. He bought a house off Humphreys, already furnished for us to come to, but it was on company property. My dad had to take the house off the property in 1913 because the shops over here came out in sympathy with the miners in Cumberland. That was a terrible time for Mother and she had seven kids. Dad took the house apart piece by piece, and took it up the hill and rebuilt it. He was going to be a farmer."

Sarah (Walker) Kirkwood

1912 NOVEMBER ➻ Attempt was made to blow up Trent River Bridge with dynamite. Striking miners blamed. J. Hawthornewaite, MPP for Nanaimo, said the job was too bungling to be the work of miners.

1913 - A hot summer with riots on Dunsmuir Avenue. Attorney General Bowser ordered the militia into the strike areas. The Seaforth Islanders arrived, 450 at Cumberland and 50 at Union Bay. All saloons were closed. There were enough strike breakers to keep the mines going.

Oct - W.L. Coulson, general manager, resigned.

1914 July - Strike pay ended as the Union could not afford it.

Aug 4 - War declared.

Aug 20 - Miners accepted company proposal and went back to work. Miners were allowed to belong to the union but the company would not recognize it.

1916 - Shortage of miners so black-listed men (organizers) could work.

1917 June - Carbon monoxide poisoning in No.6 Mine and four men died.

1918 - Ginger Goodwin, a union man, became a martyr to the workers' cause when he was shot in the back by a policeman. A general one day strike was held all across B.C. to protest the shooting of brother Goodwin.

1919 - The last local of the Mine Workers of America faded.

1922 Aug - Explosion in No.4 Mine, eighteen miners were killed.

1923 Feb - Explosion in No.4 Mine, thirty-three miners were killed.

1925 - An eight hour day passed in B.C.

1930 - A local of Mine Worker's Union of Canada was formed.

1930 - Wage agreement

Occupation	Per Day
Machinist/ Mechanic	$4.95
Mechanic, second class	$4.63
Blacksmith	$5.11
Hammerman	$4.01
Carpenter	$4.51
Carpenter's helper	$3.80
Locomotive engineer	$5.12
Fireman	$4.16
Head Brakeman	$4.40
Second Brakeman	$4.16

1936 - Because M.W.U. of C. had communist leanings, the men chose the U.M.W. of A. to represent them.

1936 - The company recognized the union by signing an agreement providing uniform wages of $5.50 per day.

1938 - Wage agreements were drawn up through friendly open meetings of the company and union. It passed with a large majority by the Cumberland local of the U.M.W. of A. Jocky Pollock represents the Union Bay men at the negotiations.

1939 Apr - No. 8 Mine reopened. Miners struck for a week and won transportation to the mine.

1942 - J. Cameron was elected president of Cumberland local.

Oct - Miners struck in protest of the National War Labour Boards delay of approving their demands. The request was refused.

1943 Nov - Miners struck for two weeks then accepted a compromise of $1.00 a day increase, plus holiday with pay.

LOGGING

Probably the first white men to live in the Baynes Sound area were loggers. The McFarlane Bros. were located on Denman Island, and by 1880 had built a saw mill there. By this time there were several groups logging in the vicinity. Carpenter, who owned a mill at Nanaimo, worked around Mud Bay. Harry and Walter Piercy *"horse logged"* north of Buckley Bay and sold to the Sayward Mill in Victoria. Archie Pritchard set up a camp at Trent River.

1883 SEPTEMBER ➾ The *Beaver* is bringing booms of logs from Baynes Sound to mills at Cowichan and Nanaimo. [2]

G. Francklyn

Huge trees like these were commonplace in the area surrounding Union Bay. The sight of them inspired men to seek their fortune as loggers, and the felling of these giants and moving them to market is the story of logging

M. Coe

Standing on spring boards, fallers George McQueen and Jack Coe have made the undercut to determine where the tree will fall

M. Coe

With a crosscut saw the fallers saw from the opposite side to meet the undercut and timberrr!...down it falls

The very early loggers were hand loggers, working alone or with a partner. With their pole axes they cut down the big trees along the beach. If possible, they felled them into the salt chuck. When the log landed a few feet from the beach they skinned one side, and with the help of a jack slid them into the water. These were huge trees, 5' to 6' at the butt end, and some had to be left where they fell. The men travelled in small boats and slept in tents or makeshift cabins. Called "Bacon Loggers" because they often sold their logs for food, they ate pancakes, dried beans and cured meats, augmented with fish they caught or game they shot.

Next came the small companies of about six men, who logged on skid roads with oxen. This was a means of moving a little farther from the mill, beach or river. To make the road the roadmaster used an axe, pick and shovel to clear and flatten the bed. Then, every eight feet

Campbell River Museum

This giant red cedar was felled by hand in the bush behind Union Bay. It is over 12' in diameter, close to record size. Several notches for the fallers spring boards can be seen extending around the tree

A. Batty

Handbucker Carl Juvas bucking a log into lengths

a ditch was dug across it. A log up to 20" in diameter and 9' long was made into a skid. The top side was skinned and a shallow wedge-shaped notch cut into the center to direct the log. The skid was then buried two thirds into the ditch.

Fallers used their double-bitted axes for the whole process, from putting in the undercut, to chopping the tree down and bucking it into logs. The early saws, with all cutter teeth, were next to useless on the huge trees, as they became bound with sawdust. About the turn of the century the crosscut saw was invented with raker teeth. Every fourth tooth was short and allowed the sawdust to be raked out.

The pitch at the bottom of the tree was difficult to pull a saw through, so tall stumps were left. The faller made a notch to insert his springboard, and stood on it to cut a second notch, sometimes going *"three boards"* high. The undercut was made with his axe so that the tree would fall as close to the road as possible. With a man pulling on either end of the cross-cut saw, the giant was brought crashing down to the forest floor.

The buckers took over to delimb and top the tree. Then they bucked (chopped or sawed) it into lengths from 24' to 40', to span three to five skids.

Logs could be dragged from 100 yards on either side of the main skid road with hand skids. Poles about 8" in diameter were laid on top of the ground. The log was rolled onto them and more easily pulled to the road.

The hook tender prepared the logs for the road by chopping off the butt end to make a blunt point, which stopped the log from hanging up. He also barked the side it would ride on and generally smoothed out any bumps or twists, and finally drove in a hook on which to attach the chain. The chain went from the log to the yoke around the oxen's neck. These 1600 pound beasts were chosen, not for brains or speed, but for strength.

"I started in the woods in 1910 with an American company named George Doane. I was getting $2.00 a day. The oxen used to bring the logs down to the beach near our farm. We used to go down there and watch the blacksmith. I have told people about that, and they said they never shod oxen, but they did, with a split shoe. Take the oxen off the skid road and into the bush, they would fall over themselves. They are very clumsy, so they used horses in the woods to bring the logs out to the skid road, then the oxen took over."

Bob McKay

The bull puncher was in charge of the team - talking, cursing, shoving, and goading them in the right direction. Depending on the size and kind of log, two yoke of oxen could pull a turn of three logs attached one behind the other. Cedar was lighter than fir and fir lighter than hemlock, although in the early days hemlock was rarely logged because lumber companies did not buy it. Attached to the last log was the pig, a boat-like conveyance for carrying tools and fish oil.

Many a young boy started his logging career as a skid greaser. His job was two-fold. On the way down to the beach he carried a five gallon can of dog fish oil, which he swabbed onto each notch on the skid. He was able to refill the can from drums of oil along the road. On the way back he swept out the notches with a broom, since much mud and debris would collect in them, causing friction on the next advancing logs.

All along the waterfront of Baynes Sound, skid roads came down to the beach. George Doane, who managed the Fraser River Logging Co., had his team working right in town. James Miller logged with oxen at Garvin's Point at the turn of the century. Until 1911 Abraham McLaughlin logged with oxen for the Taylor Mills Co. at Coal Creek. The cumbersome oxen were eventually taken off the skid roads and replaced by horses, which were used for many years in the small camps. By filling the space between the skids with lumber, the mud was eliminated and further sped up the horses.

1925 AUGUST ➺ A party of seven Nova Scotians headed by Ira Growe will operate four miles south of Union Bay. Everyone is an experienced lumberman and logging will be carried on with the aid of horses. Nine Percherons have been brought from the prairies. [5]

"Howard Singer started down there and had the tie mill at Buckley Bay. It was 1928. I remember because that was my first job and I never got paid. I had that NSF cheque for a long time."

Bill McKay

1926 JUNE ➺ K. Kawasaki and Co., who have been logging north of Bloedel camp, have finished and will move to Sechelt. Mr. Kawasaki has been cutting this tract for the past five years. He used a skidway across the highway, at Prossor's corner, down which his horses hauled logs to the waterfront where they were boomed. [5]

L. Kilvert

A team of horses pulling logs to the beach

Courtenay Museum

A team of double yoked oxen pulling logs over a skid road

"Kawasaki dumped north of where Van West dumps now. They had one right-of-way that went under the highway bridge just south of Davis' corner. We used to go up there as kids and ride the "boat" behind the horses, back and forth."

Wilf Bowden

The next advancement was the steam winch. These single drum winches were used in the woods to pull the logs out to the skid road. They sat on the beach and pulled logs as far as one mile, down the skid road to the beach. The single line was pulled out to the logs by a horse. A choker line coupled to this main line was put around the log and the winch pulled the log in. Later, a haulback drum was added to pull the main line back, thus eliminating the horse.

"There was another logging company with a donkey where Ethel and Wilf lived. A line went up to the woods. Often we'd have to wait until the turn went past when we were going to school. They hauled the logs right down over the road. The donkey engine sat out on the rocks and it pulled them down to the water. Horses took the line back to the woods. Maybe that was Doane's too."

Bob McKay

After 1884 the B.C. government granted timber licences with a 15¢ per tree stumpage cost. Then, in 1903 the McBride government opened the Crown Lands. This meant anyone, Canadian or foreign, could buy as many timber licenses as they wished. There was massive speculation and people from all walks of life dreamed of making big money.

1909 APRIL ➺ Mr. Blaney of Union Bay has retired from the piano business and ventured into the logging business at Trent River. He is ably assisted by his partner J. Blanchford. [4]

Many of the early operators who took advantage of the timber licenses had started their logging careers in the east. When the forests around the Great Lakes were exhausted, they moved west to Oregon, Washington, and eventually B.C. These men with lots of capital established large companies. They introduced steam donkeys and locomotives to the Island. Some smaller companies had steam locomotives too, but they were very primitive affairs.

"I worked for Dave Taylor over at Henry Bay. First he had a Holtz and Bess gas tractor that pulled the trailer of logs along thin boomsticks. Later he had a locomotive that ran on the wooden tracks. We had problems keeping it on the tracks."

Bob McKay

Campbell River Museum

Single drum winches were soon replaced by donkeys with two sets of drums for yarding and loading

"Charlie Sing Chong, a big Chinaman, had the same thing at Fanny Bay. He had a gasoline locomotive and they just put cedar poles fore and aft for the flanged wheels to run on. The wheel was like a tire turned inside out. Bob Curran had the same thing down at Coal Creek."

Bill McKay

After WW I many Scandinavian loggers emigrated to the B.C. woods. These strong, hard working men were very proficient with axe and saw. Louis Schulson first worked as a faller for Jeremiahson. He felled the giant trees on the property where he later built his home, on McLeod Road, where he and his wife raised two girls and a boy. To keep the crosscut saws cutting efficiently they had to be kept sharp, so the filer became a very valued member of the team. Louis became an expert filer, working for the big companies. His son, Schulle, followed in his father's footsteps. Also living at Union Bay, Dave Rundquist became section foreman for Bloedel, Stewart & Welch. David Lindstrom was a tie maker and built donkey sleighs. Carl Juvas, a hand bucker, came to Union Bay in the 1940's and worked with fallers George McQueen, and Jack and Les Coe.

"Those were the days of the big strapping Scandinavian loggers - fellows like Alex Beckman and John Bloomingren who were fallers. They were bachelors, and would come and stay with us at the hotel when the camps shut down. They were as honest as the day was long. They'd run up a big bill, but with their first pay cheque they'd start paying it back."

Alice (Willis) Bundy

The earliest steam-driven donkeys employed a ground yarding system, and had the capacity to log a setting of about ten acres. The lines went from the donkey directly out to the logs, which were dragged in along the ground, often becoming hung-up. Later, a block was hung a short distance up a standing tree. The main line went through this and gave some lift to the logs as they were pulled in. This was the birth of high lead yarding.

High lead yarding increased the size of the setting serviced by one donkey engine to about forty acres. A tall straight tree at the landing site was chosen for the spar tree. The high rigger, who was in charge of rigging the spar tree, climbed the tree, delimbing it as he went. About 200' from the ground, he topped the tree and secured a small pass line block. With a 3/8" straw line through the block, all the blocks and guy lines were pulled up the tree and assembled there. Guy lines for stability were attached to the top of the spar and to stumps several hundred feet away. The main line block,

G. Francklyn

An early single drum steam winch on Denman Island, spewing forth steam as the logs are pulled in. Horses often took the line back into the woods

D. Aitken

High rigger Bill Burgess just completed topping the spar tree. Now it is ready for hanging the rigging (lines and blocks) so that logging can begin

Campbell River Museum

An early steam-driven donkey at Bloedel, Stewart & Welch. The front drum holds the thick main line for yarding logs while the rear drum is wrapped with the lighter haulback line used to pull the main line out to the rigging crew in the bush, a job formerly done by horses

weighing about 2,000 lb. was attached to the top of the spar and threaded with the main line. With this line leading up to the top of the spar tree and then out to the logging area, it gave the logs a good deal of lift as they were pulled in. The haulback blocks were hung around the perimeter of the setting, and moved as the logs were removed from each area. The haulback line attached to these blocks pulled the main line out to the rigging crew in the bush. The *"hook tender"* was the man in charge of the crews doing the yarding and loading. He decided where to hang blocks and lines for the best production and safety of his crew.

With a skidder skyline, up to 400 acres could be logged in one setting. This method used a main spar, with back spars located around the perimeter. The skyline, a 2" diameter wire cable, was tightly fastened from the main spar to the back spars. A carriage rode back and forth on the skyline. Attached to the carriage on the skyline was the rigging, lines with chokers. The *"rigging slinger"* chose the logs that the *"chokermen"* fastened the chokers around. With a signal from the *"whistle punk"*, the *"donkey puncher"* pulled in the mainline which tightened the choker loops around the logs and lifted them up to the skyline so they were airborne into the landing. When they arrived, the *"chaser"* unhooked the chokers and the *"turn"* was complete. The skyline, which was about 2,000' long, was moved from backspar to backspar as the area was logged. This method was very efficient in logging large areas next to a railroad, or areas inaccessible by other

D. Aitken

Left: Some high riggers did a death defying dance after topping a tree. Needless to say, companies and the W.C.B. took a very dim view of this practice
Right: A spar tree fully rigged for high lead yarding

Campbell River Museum

A "turn of logs" is ready to be pulled into the landing. Chokers attach two logs to the main line and the haulback can be seen passing the men. To avoid being "in the bight" these men would move well away from the logs before the "whistle punk" sent a go-ahead signal to the "donkey puncher"

W. Bowden

A "hayrack" (boom) used to swing the logs from the landing pile onto the railway car. The big chunk hanging is a counter weight which returned the hayrack after the donkey swung it. The "second loader" has just unhooked the tongs from a loaded log

methods. It largely went out of use with the advent of trucklogging, as roads could be built right into the timber.

As the yarder engineer could not see what the yarding crew was doing, he had to rely on signals. Originally, a light steel line was attached to the donkey's whistle and went out to a location near the rigging crew. The *"rigging slinger"* gave a signal by voice or hand to the *"whistle punk"*, who jerked the whistle wire the required number of times. This was transmitted to the engine and the whistle blew. One beep - stop, three quick beep, beep, beeps - go ahead easy, etc. The engineer could also signal to let the rigging crew know when the line was coming back to the woods. Electrically operated horns were used later.

While the yarder pulled the logs into the landing, another donkey engine, the loader, was used to load the logs. Both were operated by a *"donkey puncher"* who, in the days of steam, had to have an operating certificate. In large camps a man was employed to run each machine, but in small camps one man did both jobs. Logs were first loaded onto railway cars by parbuckling the log with lines from the steam winch. Next came tong loading. The *"first loader"* chose the log to be loaded, then he and the *"second loader"* hooked the tongs onto the log and unhooked them after the loader placed it on the car. Boom loading followed. A boom made of logs was attached to the spar tree and swung in an arc around the spar. Hooked by tongs, a log was lifted up by the boom, swung around and deposited on the railway car or truck.

The train crew consisted of an engineer, a fireman and two brakemen. The head brakeman was responsible for the operation of the whole train. A track crew was also employed to keep the railroad and bridges in repair. When the logs were dumped at the booming ground, the boom men assembled the logs into booms according to species. Each boom was about 70' wide and of varying lengths. The logs were corralled with boomsticks, fastened together with boom chains.

A few companies experimented with truck hauling in the 1920's. The very first travelled on rails, like a locomotive. With a single axle and solid rubber tires, these primitive trucks

L. Richardson

A Robert Dollar train crew which consisted of engineer, fireman, and brakeman

H. Davis

A train in the process of dumping logs at the Bloedel, Stewart & Welch booming ground which was located in front of Laird's property

needed smooth roads, so much of the road was planked.

"To make the road smoother, on soft spots and hills the road was covered with planks, "fore & aft". On steep hills an endless cable was used. The loaded truck coming down would pull up the empty one."

Bill McKay

"I built "fore & aft". We had a little machine, and we had to go and fall these trees and yard them in. Then you put down mudsills 4' to 6' apart. Then, on top, you put down "fore & aft". Two or three wide, depending on the size, and you had to flatten them with a broad axe. You spiked them down to the mudsills with drifts. If there was a corner, you put a bolt rail on so the truck wouldn't go over the edge. On the hills, of course, you put the "rip rap" on. That was a cable zigzagged over the top of the planks and stapled on. The same idea as putting chains on a tire."

Bus Griffith

Caterpillars were first used in the area in the early 1930's. They were small *"60 gas cats"*, pulling the logs to the railroad or road. Smaller companies used them to haul the logs out of the bush and down to the beach, often pulling the logs right over the highway.

1935 MARCH ➻ This new monster, the caterpillar tractor - the *"cat"* as the loggers call it - has invaded the woods with the roar of a huge engine and the uncanny skill of a living creature. It is only in its experimental stage here yet, and no one can say what effect it is going to have on British Coumbia's largest industry. [7]

The living quarters for the loggers were built so that they could be moved from one location to another. These camps were situated

F. Street

D. Aitken

Left: Early logging truck with solid rubber tires. Right: This 1920's vintage logging truck is heading to the dump at Buckley Bay. The peak log is a Western Red Cedar, the largest of which grew in this area

D. Muschamp

George Welburn (left) and Herb Muschamp are standing beside an early RD-4 "cat" which they used to haul logs

near the booming ground, or if this was too near to a beer parlour, the camp was built back in the woods.

A fresh water source was always close at hand to supply the camp and locomotives. The ram was a familiar sound around a camp. Its steady woomp, woomp, woomp was like an ever-present metronome. A pipe from a small river or creek carried the water into the ram which hydraulically lifted the water to fill a reservoir. When a camp moved, the ram was often left intact and went chugging on in solitude for many years.

The bunk houses where the men lived were usually long and narrow, built on skids. They could be floated on the ocean or lakes, pulled by donkey engines, or loaded onto flat cars and transported over the railroad. Built of rough-sawn lumber, with cedar shake roofs, the inside consisted of double bunks around the wall, with a small window for each bunk. The first mattresses were straw and each man brought his own *"turkey"* (bed roll). A large woodstove stood in the middle and was used to heat water in large, old, coal oil cans. Wet clothes were hung from nails on the walls and rafters. The central building was the cookhouse. Although sometimes the board was meager, it was recognized that to keep a crew an abundance of well-prepared food was necessary. There were always lots of complaints about the room and board. In 1911 some of the gripes were stated in a letter from a Union Bay logger to the Superintendent of the Provincial Police.

...There is at present a pool of water close to the back of the bunkhouses which I think ought to be drained, and piles of filth which have been swept out of the bunkhouses, which would put a Chinese sweatshop in the shade. There is a stench around the front doors of the bunk houses from frequent urinations, that would drive a sanitary inspector to seek fresh air. There are a number of foreigners who seem to think it smart to spit phlegm on the floor. The company charges $5.25 for board and 25¢ for the use of a vermin infested mattess.

B. Kelleher

N. King

Jack Cathew (left) and Jim McKay worked for Robert Dollar Co.

R. Dollar

A mile north of Buckley Bay, right in front of the Palmer Hotel, was the Robert Dollar Co. booming ground

"Dollar, Bloedel, Tomsen & Clarke... I stayed in them all. You shared the bed with bedbugs. One time I was de-bedbugging my bed. I got out a pill bottle and I had it full of bed bugs. Do they bite? They take a chunk out. They're great big louts!"

Tom McKay

Anderson Logging: By the 1920's the woods around Union Bay were criss-crossed with railroads. Probably the first track was a mile south of town. David Jeremiahson and Olaf Strand "ran the show" for Anderson Logging. They started their operations before the turn of the century, and put down steel in 1909. The 8 mile railroad served three "sides", and employed over one hundred men. They had a big camp about a mile up Washer Creek. Their booming ground was about one mile north of Buckley Bay, right in front of the Palmer Hotel which had been built to quench the logger's thirst when they came out of camp on Saturday night.

"When the railway was first started, ties and steel were put in. Then they put planks between the rails. The locomotives would drive down on the rails and pull the logs which slid on the planks. It was later that they got flat cars for the logs. The railway went through our property. They used to haul the coal for the locomotives by horse team from Union Bay, and they had a little bunker there. Mr. McLeod was the coal delivery man."

Annie (Muschamp) Nelson

Canadian Robert Dollar Company: In 1916 Anderson sold out to the Warren Lumber Co., which was shortly bought by the Canadian Robert Dollar Co. Four hundred feet were added to the wharf, and the railroad was pushed deeper into the bush. A Shay locomotive hauled logs on the main line and a Climax worked up in the woods. The famous American shipping magnate, with ships in the China trade, left the running of the camp to his son, James. The Dollar family lived first in the camp, and then for seven years at Union Bay in the CC(D)L house next to the post office. Their daughters, Phyllis and Dorothy, attended school and the family played an active part in the town's social life.

"It was a good company to work for; they treated you right. We came in one rainy day at supper time and Jim Dollar said to me 'How about making another trip tonight, Tom. We're going to be out of cars tomorrow.' I said, 'My gawd, it's just pouring, and look at the water just running out of my boots.' Well, he took me over to the office and gave me a brand new pair of Paris boots."

Tom McKay

With the Union Bay claim nearly logged off, the company bought out Burrard Lumber Co. at Deep Bay for half a million dollars. The next year Robert Dollar, who started working in the bush in Ontario, visited the old camp and then toured the new claim. The main camp was high on Dollar Mountain, with a view of the mainland. The booming ground was on the north end of Deep Bay. Their locomotives ran on oil, and in 1928 the big oil tank at the wharf collapsed, just after being filled. All the surrounding water and beaches were coated with oil which killed many ducks and gulls. By the early 1930's that claim was logged off, and the Dollar Co. left to log across the border.

H. Macartney

Bloedel, Stewart & Welch logged by rail behind Union Bay beginning as early as 1920. Left to right: on locomotive: Sandy Chapman - brakeman, Fred Smith - head brakeman, Henry Carter - fireman, Cliff Davis - engineer

1931 JUNE •◆ Mr. and Mrs. Dollar entertained their friends at a farewell dinner at Dollar Camp on Sunday. Flat cars met the guests at the junction of the railway and the highway, and transported them 5 1/2 miles into the mountains. Following a chicken dinner, the guests were taken to view Rosewall Canyon. The camp will be permanently closed and the steel withdrawn. [7]

Bloedel Stewart & Welch: The other large holding at Union Bay was on land south of Trent River, which was logged by Bloedel, Stewart & Welch. In February 1920 a camp and dumping ground 2 miles north of town was established.

L. Magnone

A log taken from a huge Douglas Fir. Sometimes the logs were so heavy they could not be moved and were left in the bush where they fell

Cumberland Museum

The Royston Lumber Co. was operated by Japanese owners. They supplied the lumber with which the Union Bay Hall was built

"Bloedel's logged with steam locies and had branch lines all through here. The camp was right where the railway crossed the road, but they couldn't keep the men out of the pub, so they built a camp way up Bradley Creek. The booming ground was down in front of what is Dorothy Road now."
Jim McKay

The railroad was built using the first steam shovel with caterpillar treads in B.C. The idea had been adapted from the tanks used during the war. A 1200' bridge was built to take the track above the CC(D)L and E&N roads. A 50 ton Climax worked back in the woods, and a 70 ton Shay pulled the logs to the beach.

"The whole railroad was like the Toonerville Trolley. Syd Muir and I used to go up and take clean clothes to his uncle, Hector Hooper. We'd ride on top of the tender. Wow, it would just about throw you off!"
Wilf Bowden

By 1922 there were 150 men employed in the operation at Union Bay. When the easily available timber was exhausted in the late '20s the firm moved north to Menzies Bay.

Royston Lumber Co.: The Royston sawmill was originally started by Grant and Mounce. In 1913 they built a sawmill in the woods behind Royston after their Cumberland mill burned down. Markets were poor, and the mill ran into operational difficulties. The Japanese log supplier, Mr. Fugie, could not be paid so he took over the mill. He sold out to a group of Japanese who hired Mr. Uchiyama as manager, and renamed the enterprise the Royston Lumber Company. For twenty-five years the company logged the land west of Trent River, from a railroad which tied into the Colliery tracks. They exported finished lumber via the CC(D)L and E&N railroads, as well as from their wharf which was located between the Royston government wharf and the Comox Logging wharf. This company supplied the lumber with which the community hall was built.

Baikie Bros. Logging: In 1934 Baikie Bros. took over the shingle bolt claim of a Japanese group, and first operated for two years on 8 miles of railroad track left by Bloedel, Stewart & Welch, north of Union Bay. Nicknamed the "humdergon" railroad, they pulled the logs out with an old Fordson. With a name change to Bradley Creek Logging Co., the Baikies were back at Union Bay in 1946. A large operation, they contracted out the yarding and loading to Piercy, Hurl and McKenzie. They did their own hauling to the dump, one mile north of the town. The company moved north in the '50s, and logged land around Upper Campbell Lake before it was flooded.

Van West Logging: This company logged land south of Cumberland during the 1950's. Tommy Carter was superintendent.

McKenzie Logging: Formed in 1959 by Tommy McKenzie, the company logged south of Comox Lake. They hauled the timber 16 miles by truck, using part of Van West's road to the log dump. The company later moved to the Cowichan Valley.

Fanny Bay/Deep Bay Logging: A Japanese company funded by a syndicate in Tokyo, it was managed by Mr. Kagetsu. It logged behind Fanny Bay and Deep Bay from the time of the First World War until the Japanese were deported from the coast in 1941. The large operation had several miles of poorly built tracks. The grades were steep, with one switchback that would only take three cars at a time. This company and Victoria Lumber used the same main line that went under the E&N railroad.

Campbell River Museum

Baikie Bros. first hauled logs on the abandoned Bloedel, Stewart & Welch rails using a Fordson and trailer. Wallace Baikie at the controls and Tom Feeley move a load over the "humdergon" railroad

Then they branched out onto their own wharves, one on either side of Cougar Creek, near the Fanny Bay Inn.

Most of the loggers were Japanese, but initially the donkey operators and train crews were white. Orientals were prohibited from holding a steam locomotive ticket. In the 1930's whole logs were exported to Japan on large freighters. There were many families, and the children attended Fanny Bay School and became part of the community. They also had a Japanese school in the camp, which the children attended. The company donated $250 to the Fanny Bay Hall in 1931. After the Japanese were removed from the coast, their timber land reverted back to the government, and MacMillan & Bloedel acquired it.

Grant Bros. Logging: Bob and Ab were sons of Robert Grant, owner of the first mill at Cumberland. They contracted for the Dollar Logging Co. at Mud Bay. In the early 1920's they were pioneers in truck logging. Their first vehicle was a single-axle Leyland truck with solid rubber tires.

Al Stasek: Mr. Stasek was a logger from Oregon who moved to B.C. and married Frances McKay. He logged in the Fanny Bay area from 1933 until he died in 1937. The logs were dumped at Grant's wharf in Mud Bay. Ted Glover hook tended for his friend Al and later took over the booming ground.

Beban Logging Co.: When Jack Beban first worked in the area, he was logging and hauling mine prop timber to the little mill in the CC(D)L yards at Union Bay. In 1946 he bought a block of timber up the Tsable River road. The company dumped into Buckley Bay and built a large machine shop near the highway which was destroyed by a truck accident and fire. The company moved north in 1958.

Frazer Mills Logging: Just after the turn of the century the company logged south of Anderson's. George Doane managed this and the several camps at Deep Bay and Denman Island, so it was often called Doane's Logging.

Fanny Bay Shingle Mill: A large shingle mill at Fanny Bay was built in 1914 by McDonnel & Burke Cedar Co., a Washington firm. Beside the mill there was a dry kiln that was full of shingles when it was destroyed by fire in 1918. In the '20s three logging camps supplied the mill, which shipped one car of shingles each day via the E&N. The company sold out in 1923 to a group of engineers and manufacturers.

G. James and Fanny Bay Inn

The Fanny Bay Shingle Mill. The Island Highway can be seen passing under the conveyor which carried shingles from the mill to the kiln

1924 JANUARY Because cedar is growing short in Washington and Oregon, the mills will move to B.C., predicted O.H. McGill who is secretary of Fanny Bay Mutual Mills Ltd. At present there are twenty-three white men working at the mill and a great many of them are shareholders. [6]

The mill changed hands again in 1925 when Mackie, Barnes & Horton bought the plant. They ran a night shift and employed thirty-five men. Much of the product was exported to the Orient. As well, the company sold clear-cut cedar logs in 13' and 16' lengths for the interiors of Japanese homes. Japanese freighters were loaded with as many as 2,000 logs each. In the early '30s sales were poor, and the mill closed for a year. It reopened, and six months later a $10,000 blaze destroyed the kiln, dry shed, green shed, two loaded freight cars and two million shingles. It was covered by insurance and was rebuilt, then sold to J. Forter, H. Hurndale and H. Stuart. Renamed the Totem Shingle Mill, it employed about 100 men. The large mill was built between the beach and road. A conveyor carried the shingles from the mill over the highway to the dry kiln. In 1944 the mill was sold to the International Lumber Association of America. Later, Alaska Pine & Celonese owned the mill. After they were bought out by Rainier & Co. in the early '60s, the mill was closed.

H. R. MacMillan Co.: H.R. MacMillan started his business in this area not as a logger, but as a log buyer and exporter.

"One day Jim Dollar said, 'I want to go down to the beach with you. There's some guy down there, I don't know if he's crazy or nuts or what. I've got eight booms of Pee Wee logs and he's offered me $2.00 a thousand more than I can get anywhere.' Well, it was H.R. MacMillan, and he bought the whole works. In about a week a raft came in there with a saw on it. Brother Jim worked on it. They cut the logs into 10', 12' and 14' lengths and loaded them on a big ship at Deep Bay and sent them to Japan. That was 1929 when MacMillan got his start around here."

Tom McKay

Gradually, MacMillan bought timber and equipment from some of the larger companies as they were finished logging. After the Japanese were forced to leave the coast, MacMillan acquired the Deep Bay Logging Co. claim, which was logged by Fletcher.

Fletcher Logging: This company contracted to log timber owned by H.R. MacMillan in 1944. The railroad was abandoned, and Bus Griffith with a cat and driver, Pete Biggs, was hired to build the new road for Fletcher's trucks.

G. Murdock

Tomsen & Clark logged in this area from 1924 to 1940's. This photo shows their log dump at Deep Bay

Victoria Lumber & Manufacturing Co.: In the late 1930's the Victoria Lumber & Manufacturing Co. built a railway into Block 34, and logged with high lead and skidder. The company shared the main line with the Deep Bay Logging Co., where the railway went under the E&N. The camp was first built near the highway next to Coal Creek. It proved to be too close to the Fanny Bay pub so was moved into the woods. At this time several of the houses were brought up to Union Bay, put onto foundations and redecorated. All the logs were towed to a Chemainus Mill, also owned by V.L. & M. The company worked in the Fanny Bay area until the late '40s.

Tomsen & Clark Timber Co.: In 1924 Tomsen and Clark began logging in the Deep Bay area, and built a 13 mile railway into Horne Lake, the Big Horne, and Rosewall Valley. Their first camp was at Bowser, then they moved it to the head of Horne Lake. Later, when logging around Hunt Creek, their final camp was near Rosewall Creek. By the '40s logging was finished and all the equipment was sold to H.R. MacMillan.

Howard Singer: Singer was the first company to log the area behind Buckley Bay. He built a dirt and plank road, and logged by truck.

"I remember when the "old man" was hauling for Singer. He had to go and retrieve the old Federal. It was a hard-tired truck. He never got paid so he had to go down and bring her home."

Fred Peters

H. Glover

Ted Glover, high rigger and partner-owner of Rosewall Logging Co., was killed on the job in 1960

Tansky: This company was owned and operated by Louis Tansky. He logged in the woods behind Buckley Bay in the 1930's and '40s, using the Tsable River road originally built by the CC(D)L and added to by Singer. By 1939 he was employing sixty men.

Bob Curran: Mr. Curran logged in several areas. He first logged near the Dollar railroad, and had his logs transported on it to the beach. He logged south of Langley Lake in the late 1930's, and hauled by truck down the Tsable River road. He was one of the early "cat" loggers, hauling logs across the highway in several places. He finally went broke, logging near Great Central Lake. Behind Fanny Bay a mountain was named Curran Mountain.

Green & Cochrane: Herb Green started as the foreman for Dollar Logging. Then he and Mr. Cochrane became partners of a small company, and logged near Deep Bay until they sold the claim to Glover Logging. From there, the company went to Texada where they went broke.

Rosewall Logging: Owned by the Glover brothers, the company started out as Glover Logging. Ted started his logging career working for Bloedel, Stewart & Welch, and soon became a high rigger. He managed the Rosewall operations while Harry, who continued to work for the CC(D)L, did the timber cruising and road surveying. With a Fordson donkey and White truck, the small company started logging timber in 1934 at Deep Bay. Then they moved up and logged a claim behind Union Bay, which Hamilton Logging had started before going broke. They logged for years in the Rosewall Creek area, cutting timber on land which the larger companies thought inaccessible. Their boom ground was at Mud Bay.

As they left school, many boys got their first job as whistle punk at Rosewall. Learning good logging and safety practices, they moved up the ranks, then often moved on to the larger

K. Peters

This big fir log from Rosewall Creek area was so heavy that it took the trailer with it when dumped at Glover Bros. boom ground

companies. The company had an enviable safety record. Three times they won the safety award for small companies in British Columbia. It was particularly tragic that one of their few accidents killed owner Ted, when he was run over by the company truck in the landing in 1960. That year Harry finished work with the CC(D)L and took a more active roll in the operation. Long time employee Wilf Bowden managed the camp.

End of the Large Companies: Deep Bay became a depot for old and used machinery from Horne Lake to Campbell River.

1941 MARCH ➻ "The Last Setting." At Deep Bay, a scant 20 miles south of Courtenay, one can see what happens when the larger logging companies reach the end of their timber resources, when the last setting is finished, and the last load has thundered over the dump. For here there is assembled an assortment of logging equipment which even the most veteran logger never saw at one camp in his palmiest days. All are for sale to the highest bidder. On the foreshore and on the railway sidings which wind into the bush, everything can be found in quantity which is used in the operation of a modern logging camp. Skidders, locomotives, skeleton cars, rigging-up goats, speeders, steel cable, rigging crummies, gasoline pumps, power shovels, bunk houses, warehouses full of supplies lie forlorn and all but forgotten in the wind and the weather. On the beach itself, some pulled up only a few feet above high water mark, are twenty or thirty donkeys of every description and vintage, from ancient steampots whose names have made history in the B.C. woods, to the latest Williamette skidders with extension boilers and oil-fired furnaces. Their towering stacks are covered with rusty pieces of sheet iron, their empty drums gape to the sky, and over every moving part is a thick coating of grease. The caulk-scarred skids and shiny levers testify to years of service. On each can be found reminders of their days in the woods: a grimy coffee pot with a wire handle, an old tin hat, a tattered pad of scale sheet flapping dismally in the wind. It is safe to say that many of these machines will never pull another turn of logs, for with the present trend to truck logging and gas donkeys, their day of usefulness is ending. They are too old, too heavy, or too expensive for present operations, and their ultimate destination will probably be the scrap heap. [7]

L. Stewart

Rosewall Logging Co. provided employment for Union Bay loggers for over forty years. The crew grew beards for the B.C. Centennial. Back to front, left to right: Wilf Bowden - donkey puncher, Harold Kennedy - faller, Bob Kovar - faller, Don Kennedy - rigging slinger, Lyle Stewart - first loader, Jack Glover - chokerman

LOGGING ACCIDENTS

Most editions of the local paper reported at least one accident, many of which were fatal. In the camps surrounding Union Bay there were at least two men killed every year. This was particularly true during the heyday of the big companies that logged by railroad. The focus was on production, with little regard for the safety of the men. Equipment was often poorly maintained, resulting in sudden failures.

Toward the end of the 1920's, pressure from the public, government, courts and union organizers forced companies to pay more attention to safety. They launched a safety campaign with slogans and posters of "Old Man Safety First" displayed at the camps and printed in the newspapers, but it took another decade before any appreciable reduction in the accident rate occurred.

The fallers, the majority of whom were big, strong Scandinavians, probably had the most dangerous job. Through the years many fallers were killed by *"widow makers"*, *"bent logs"*, and *"barber-chairing trees"*.

1935 NOVEMBER ➾ A widow maker killed a Japanese logger at Deep Bay Logging. Nakaji Emi suffered a fractured skull and died. [6]

1945 MAY ➾ John Bloomingren, employed by the Beban Logging Co., is believed to have been struck by a falling snag and to have died almost instantly of a broken neck and a fracture of the base of the skull. [6]

D. Aitken

With so many facets to the logging industry, accidents have been commonplace. Here a load of logs has left a seemingly safe, straight stretch of track

The loggers were strong, tough men who worked hard and played hard. At the local pub on Saturday night many of the men, isolated from a normal family life, drank and gambled their pay cheques away.

"Poker Pete Johnson was the faller who put his head in the undercut up at Bloedel's. He had been on a big bender and lost a lot of money gambling. The tree started to go, and he ran and stuck his head in there to commit suicide."

Harry Glover

Every logger always had to be on his guard to avoid positions of potential danger. This was referred to as "being in the bight", whether in the path of a falling tree, moving rigging, or approaching truck.

"In '24 Cairns was killed. A loaded car came off the track and was laying on its side, and he was below it, splicing a line. A log came off the top and flattened him. That's what I call "being in the bight"."

Tom McKay

All the large companies logged with steam donkeys, and hauled logs by steam locomotives to their dumping grounds. Many accidents happened during the loading and transporting of logs. Herb Green, a donkey puncher, was reading the height of water in the boiler when the glass tube burst and he lost an eye.

1911 ➾ At Anderson's Logging a Japanese fireman was scalded to death when the donkey engine capsized. [4]

1921 SEPTEMBER ➾ A man was run over by the logging train at the Robert Dollar camp near Union Bay. The Jury recommends that switches be blocked to prevent similar accidents. [5]

1925 MARCH ➾ For the purpose of hauling, the Deep Bay Logging Co. uses a Ford tractor mounted on wheels with a trailer. The truck was coming down the 2% grade to the booming ground at high speed. It was the custom of Wm. Stark, a young American, after he got over the rise to put the car in reverse and allow it to drift. The car and its load evidently got out of control and jumped the track. The load of logs came down on the truck, killing the driver instantly. Prior to this, Stark had been in accidents with the machine. Once, it got out of control and went half over the wharf. He had been having a number of minor accidents due to the fact that the engine got away from him, and twice it crossed the Island Highway out of control. [6]

1934 NOVEMBER ➾ Andrew Anderson of Union Bay was instantly killed on Monday. The locomotive he was driving at the Tomsen and Clark Timber Company's operations at Horne Lake, turned over. With him in the cab were Dave Renwick, fireman; Tom McKay, head brakeman; Rex South, camp foreman; and Henry Nevotny, second brakeman. [6]

"Something hit my chest and the steps hit my legs. I landed out to the side on the center truck. Dave Renwick had the bones sticking out of his arm and he was cut above the eye. Both ankles were broke. So I got him up to the track and ran half a mile down to the telephone to get help. While I was phoning I thought, 'Oh my gawd, those cars are sitting on a 7% grade and no brakes on them. They might get away and meet the speeder.' So I ran all the way back and got three brakes on and I was beat! I was black and blue all over my chest and just about pooped."

Tom McKay

Loggers, company officials and track crews

travelled to and fro on speeders. Several victims fell off and were injured or killed. Also, without modern communications the speeders often unexpectedly met trains on the same track.

1927 NOVEMBER ➾ Four lives were snuffed out in a flash when a runaway skeleton logging car gathered speed as it followed the tracks to the beach. It struck a motor speeder on the Robert Dollar track at Deep Bay, just after dark on Monday night. The speeder that the four doomed men were riding in was a Chevrolet car with flanged wheels. The hood and the roar of the engine effectively drowned the sound of the runaway car, and it must have struck the speeder without the slightest warning. The wreck was complete, part of the skeleton car being scattered for some distance in the woods, and the speeder setting fire and burning. It was, indeed, the light from the flames of the wrecked speeder that guided the first men to the scene of the accident, where they found all four men dead. [6]

1932 JULY ➾ One Japanese logger was killed, and three were injured at Deep Bay Logging Co. All four were in a runaway speeder which was hurtling down an 8% grade when it crashed into a slow moving logging train. [6]

1934 DECEMBER ➾ K. Katushita, witness, said that he noticed Fuimoto move, probably with the idea of making himself more comfortable. As he did so, the speeder passed over a joint in the rails with a jolt. At that moment he saw the deceased fall forward off the speeder, and it passed over him. The underwork rolled him further, breaking his back and several ribs. [7]

Apparently some of the railway tracks used in logging were jerry-built affairs. If the road bed was not properly prepared and the ties and rails carefully laid and maintained, the constant motion of the trains travelling the road dislodged the ties and spread or tipped the rails.

"The Jap grades were really something. They had powder boxes shaved down and used to shim the tracks. Over a dip were little stringers sitting on a rock or stump, and through the swamps they just layed logs fore and aft with ties on top. Old Bill Surgenor used to run locomotive there, and he said it was nothing to go off the track three or four times on a trip to the beach."

Bus Griffith

For many years, until the camps provided crummies, the only way for the loggers to get to the job site was by riding in or on the logging trucks. A freak accident happened in 1939 at Tansky's Camp. Bill Wortendyke was riding on the running board when he was struck dead by a plank that was thrown up by the wheels of the truck.

By the 1940's most of the larger companies had left the area, and the smaller ventures that were left were all hauling by truck and trailer. Safe logging was practiced by most companies. Accidents were greatly reduced in the landing, out in the rigging, and on the road, but they still happened.

"I was running the levers at Victoria Lumber about 1945. The heel block let loose, and as soon as I saw it rattling and banging towards me I started running. But young Howard Shupe had his back to it, watching the sky line. It just caught him in the back, all that heavy rigging. Threw him right off the load into the pile, upside down. It was so close, it could have easily been a miss. He was only eighteen."

Wilf Bowden

"Andy Rogers was running the machine, I was pulling rigging and Donald Renwick was setting chokers. A log had come off the rigging, so I went up behind to pick that up and sent the turn back. As soon as Don picked up the log with the choker, he just walked off to the side and started to roll a smoke, with his back to the turn and in front of it. When the rigging started up, the log hung up on a stump and it took a big swing. He got hit right in the back and it smashed everything in him. If he had been a yard over it would have gone right by him. Ron Pratt, Ken Keenan, Fred Peters, Andy and I took turns packing him out. He died a few days later in the hospital."

Ken Peters

In July 1947 at Buckley Bay, a runaway logging truck driven by Oscar Olson crossed the highway and crashed into a panel truck, carrying it into Beban Logging's machine shop. The gas in the truck exploded and the whole building was an inferno. Happening as it did at quitting time, several crews arrived just after the accident but were of little help.

"We were coming down in the crummy. When we got down there the shed was on fire. Some carpenters had been working in the truck shed, and they were just climbing into a panel truck when he piled into it and drove it into the shed, and the whole thing blew up. Jack Beban came out of his office and ran into the shed, and came out with a man under each arm. There were three fellows still in there and he wanted to go back in, but someone held him, as he'd never have made it. Pop Ward was first aid man, so was first to help the injured."

Bus Griffith

"I was driving truck up there and Oscar came down just behind me. His son Irvin was riding with him and he tried to get the "old man" to ditch it but he wouldn't. His eyeballs were straight ahead. He was frozen to the wheel. Oscar didn't get killed but three of the men in the panel truck were killed and one was thrown clear. Abe Orr was the carpenter who had built the shop. He was just outside and the truck hit a pole which fell over and hit him on the head, killing him. So four died."

Wilf Bowden

"We were coming down behind him and he lost the air pipe way up in the dip between the first and second pond. He should have put it in the woods

THE LOGGERS' STRIKE

3000 Loggers

are at Work Today

1800 Who Want to Work Are Turning Down---

1 ***The offer of their jobs back without discrimination—***

2 ***LOGGING WAGES RANGING FROM $6.50 to $3.20 A DAY***

As set forth in the following statement issued by the employers:—

THESE ARE THE WAGES FOR AN 8-HOUR DAY

YARDING CREW . . . . $6.50 to $3.20
ENGINEERS, SHOVEL AND FIREMEN . . . . $6.00 to $3.20
LOADING CREW . . . . $5.50 to $3.20
TRAIN CREW . . . . . 60 to 40 cents an hour
NON-LOGGING OCCUPATIONS:
Section men, $3 a day
Bedmakers and dishwashers rate, $82.50 a month.

THIS IS THE BOARD

BREAKFAST

Cereals - several kinds		Butter; Tea and Coffee
Hot Cakes, Syrup, Honey and Jam	Fruit - Canned, Dried, Stewed	Bacon and Eggs, Not Limit
	Toast, Bread, Rye Crisp	Cookies, Doughnuts, Cakes

LUNCH (at camp)

Soup	Salad and Vegetables	Hot Rolls, Bread, Rye Crisp,
Pudding, Pie	Butter	
Meat - Roast, Boiled, Cold	Sauces, Pickles, etcetera	Tea and Coffee

LUNCH (in woods)

Sandwiches - two kinds	Apples, Pie	Tea and Coffee
	Cakes, two kinds	(in Thermos flasks)

DINNER

Soup	Salad and Vegetables	Hot Rolls, Bread, Rye Crisp,
Beefsteak, Chops	Fruit - Fresh and Canned	Butter
Stewed Meat; Cold Meats	Cakes - three kinds	Honey Jams, Pickles, Sauces
		Tea and Coffee

1 The management of each company will at all times decide which and how many employees are needed in its work and when and for how long they are needed:

2 In hiring or laying off men each company will make no distinction, except upon the basis of a man's ability or competence for the work:

3 While the exact number of men immediately required at resumption of operations must naturally depend upon the existing conditions of the company's business, each company will offer jobs to their old employees as the opportunity presents:

4 From anyone in its employ each company will welcome constructive suggestions for the welfare of the employees, or the advancement of the company's business.

AS TO CAMP COMMITTEES

No Logging Business Could Operate Successfully Under Camp Committee Dictation

WE THE UNDERSIGNED, DEFINITELY REFUSE TO SUBMIT TO IT

ALBERNI PACIFIC LUMBER Co., Ltd.
B. & K. LOGGING Co., Ltd.
BLOEDEL, STEWART & WELCH, Ltd.
CAMPBELL RIVER TIMBER Co., Ltd.
COMMERCIAL LUMBER Co., Ltd.
DISCOVERY PASSAGE LOGGING Co., Ltd.
ELK RIVER TIMBER Co., Ltd.
GREAT CENTRAL SAWMILLS Ltd.
GREEN POINT LOGGING Co., Ltd.
LAMB LUMBER Co., Ltd.
MERRILL & RING LUMBER Co., Ltd.
MERRILL, RING, WILSON Ltd.
THOMSEN & CLARK TIMBER Co., Ltd.
VEDDER LOGGING Co., Ltd.

way up there. Young Olson bailed out by the railway tracks. They were still alive in there. They were screaming and hollering, but there was no way to help because it was so hot you couldn't get near it."

Fred Peters

Many of the loggers were quite superstitious. It seemed many accidents could be linked to dreams, previous happenings, or rituals done differently. Friday the 13th was particularly feared as many accidents seemed to happen that day. On Friday, June 13, 1941 three district loggers were killed in separate accidents. After forty-five years in the bush, Ted Glover, owner of Rosewall Logging Co., had a respect for Friday the 13th. In May 1960 on Friday the 13th, he was suffering from a slight hearing loss due to a bad head cold. He was standing in the landing and did not hear the logging truck driven by Wes Peters, which backed up and killed him.

From the turn of the century a few loggers, like the miners, started to agitate for better and safer logging conditions. Neither companies nor governments listened. During the First World War these International Workers of the World members were lumped together with men who would not join the fighting forces. Most of them were rounded up and jailed for anti-conscription or subversive activities. The B.C. Loggers Union was formed at the end of the war with 1500 members, but the operators would not recognize the group. In 1920 the camps of the district were on strike, demanding an eight hour day and minimum wage of $6.00 per day.

It was not until 1934 that the Lumber Workers Industrial Union mustered enough support to conduct a general strike. The industry would not recognize the union and continued working with those men willing to work. However, the government issued orders that a mimimum wage of $3.20 per day be paid all loggers. The Courtenay Local of the I.W.A. was formed in 1942, and the logging operators recognized this union the next year. It was not until the '50s that the loggers received medical coverage, cost of living bonus, base rates and more statutory holidays.

Many of the smaller camps around Union Bay were not unionized until the 1960's. In some the men were well treated and received union wages or above, so felt no need to join the union until it became mandatory.

FOREST FIRES

During the dry months from June until September, fire was a constant threat and worry to the company owners, loggers and settlers. Everyone was affected when the forest burned. The year 1922 was particularly bad as fires raged out of control around Merville, Bevan and Cumberland. Merville was again threatened in 1938 when the big fire swept down from Bloedel, Stewart and Welch, north of Lower Campbell Lake, to the Comox Logging. It burned everything in its path until the wind changed.

In the early days fire safety was not considered important. Donkeys and locomotives, particularly those with wood burning engines, spewed out great showers of sparks with every chug. Cable wires caused friction as they travelled quickly over logs and stumps. Little or no fire fighting equipment was kept near the operation to put out small fires before they took hold. By the 1920's the Forestry Service required precautions on the part of the operators, and began closing the woods during hot dry spells. However, at about this time the same department introduced the practice of slash burning to aid in reforestation. Slash fires frequently got out of control when fanned by strong winds in early spring, or during prolonged dry weather in late fall. There were some noteworthy forest fires around Union Bay.

1910 ➾ A bush fire at Anderson's Co. was started by sparks from the locomotive pulling logs to the salt water. It alarmed the whole neighbourhood and did great damage to timber, burning a distance of 3 miles. Anderson's camp was completely destroyed, including

D. Geldt

The aftermath of a forest fire. Much merchantable timber was lost annually to fire. Jennifer Geidt suveys the sad situation

all buildings, donkey engines and logging material. Loss is estimated between $15,000 and $20,000. Doane's Camp, situated 2 miles below, was only saved by the great effort of the men. [5]

"When the logging camp burned down in 1910 they thought our house would go. We had just finished harvesting so they brought gas down and burned the field to save us. Us kids got up on the barn and house roof with wet sacks and buckets of water. As the roofs took fire we put it out. I was only eleven years old.

Nellie (McKay) King

1925 In this charge it was claimed that "on the 14th day of July 1925, near Deep Bay, in the county of Nanaimo, the Canadian Robert Dollar Co. unlawfully, and did not diligently attend to the controlling and extinguishing of a fire which had originated on land upon which an operation was being carried on by the said company, for the cutting of forest material contrary to the forest closure act." The company was fined $100. It is possible that Tomsen & Clarke will sue the Dollar Co., for damages caused by the same fire which spread to their operations. [6]

"I was working up there at that time and it burned up fifteen million board feet of cold-decked timber. Forty gallon drums of gasoline would explode and fly four to five hundred feet in the air. A huge tongue of flame... that was real fire works. Some of the crew escaped by walking through to Cameron Lake."

Harry Glover

1926 Kagetsu & Co. at Fanny Bay was wiped out by fire. In the intense heat of Monday, the fire appeared to have originated in the yarder of the Japanese company. Fanned by the wind, it spread like a ribbon of molten fire down the logging track which leads over the E&N tracks to the beach. Along this track and in the path of the marching tongues of flame were many dwellings belonging to the Japanese employees, and some houses of the shingle mill employees. On swept the fire, taking in its stride the garage on the Island Highway belonging to Mr. Alec Tweedie, and his home on the bluff. With as much of their furniture as they could salvage, the Japanese women and children, evicted by the flames, made for the wharf where they huddled together with their belongings until refuge was found for them in Tweedies Hall. Some of the refugees would undoubtedly have lost their lives but for the gallant action of the locomotive engineer and crew. Louis Magnone repeatedly drove his engine through the flames, with the smoke so thick he could hardly see, until everyone was out of the danger zone and all their personal effects were brought out. One must admire such pluck. Miss Swan picked up a two week old Japanese baby lying on a pile of bedding among the flying cinders and nearly suffocated with the smoke. Its mother was frantically trying to save her belongings.

Motorists along the Island Highway gave reports of adventures when the flames were on the road. At Horne Lake the blaze covers an area of two thousand acres and is running through the dry underbrush, burning the green timber. It is not yet fully under control. One man had to take to the lake to get out ot the way of the fire. [6]

1928 Coming out of the Rosewall Canyon from the west coast like a tornado, the wind blew on the smouldering slash fire near the Robert Dollar Camp. It acted on the brush like a blow-torch, and within minutes it was a solid wall of flame 200' long, bearing down on the camp. The wind blew the flames over the old slash with a roar, and very soon a shower of sparks as thick as snow-flakes was pouring down on the buildings of the camp. In spite of all efforts to wet them down, one by one the buildings ignited and had to be abandoned. The logs on nine flat cars caught fire and were burning like torches, then the oil house exploded and it was time to get away and escape down the tracks. In less than two hours the loss included all twenty-two camp buildings and a good deal of equipment, but no merchantable timber. The cabs were burned out of three locomotives and two small donkey engines were lost. Grant Bros. Logging also suffered several hundred dollars in damage. [6]

"Fred O' Neil was sent out to burn the slash so he phoned down to Dollar and said, 'It's blowing up here, a wind off the hill'. Dollar said, 'Light her up'. Well, the fire beat Fred to camp and he had to get out another way."

Bill McKay

1935 Fire which broke out in the workings of the Deep Bay Logging Co. caused damage estimated at $70,000. Four million feet of felled and bucked timber, several flat cars, four donkeys, some steel and all bridges were destroyed. During the week-end, rumours persisted that some twelve Nipponese loggers had been trapped by the flames and burned to death. This was proven untrue when the missing men later came out of the woods. The smoke and heat had prevented their earlier appearance. [7]

"Brother Bill was firing locomotive up there at that time and the Japanese loggers had to rebuild all the bridges and repair the tracks after the fire. They had to do it all for free before they could go back to work."

Harry Glover

1938 MAY Two hundred men fight four mile slash fire in old Dollar slashing. It is the worst fire in ten years. There is no property damaged yet, but high winds are driving the fire south.

1938 JUNE The blaze at Dollar Logging now covers 12,000 acres. The Forestry look-out station on Rosewall Creek burned, and Grant Bros. have lost 20,000 board feet. [6]

1943 The fire near Fanny Bay in the Victoria

Lumber Co.'s timber is now under control. For four days 130 men fought the blaze. [6]

"That was down by the Million Dollar bridge. The skidder was just across the creek and it burned the bridge too. Four of us were picking berries there and we heard the speeder leave, then three separate fires started. Tom McKay told us kids to run down to camp and tell them. They were just about finished logging there and they wanted to burn up the machine. The next day the police came to Tom McKay's and tried to blame us berry pickers, but he told him what really happened. Tom wanted to go to court and testify but nothing ever came of it."

Fred Peters

"Beban had a fire up there in the '50s. Bob Payne was foreman and he wanted to get a good burn around the landing when he burned the slash. So he had Mac McBride haul in tar paper and spread it all over the landing to keep it dry. He lit it and did it take off! After that he was called "Tar Paper Bob"."

Bus Griffith

"Then we had a fire up by the mine about 1956. It started in the rigging and luckily we saved our pile of logs.

Wilf Bowden

When a fire threatened a large area of forest, all the loggers in the vicinity immediately became fire fighters. As well, unemployed men and even men walking down the street were conscripted to fight the fire. The pay was 25¢ an hour and the men worked twelve hour shifts, often with few breaks. If needed, they volunteered for the next shift, so put in twenty-four hour and even thirty-six hour days. Before the advent of bulldozers the men cut fire trails by hand, using saws, axes and shovels. It was hoped that the fire would come to these fire breaks and be unable to cross the cleared space. But with a wind the fire could jump as far as half a mile. The flames would sweep down a hill with a deafening roar as it devoured everything in its path.

"At one time we didn't fall the snags. Well, lots of times, if there was a fire the snags would spread the fire quite a bit, because they were so tall and burning parts would fall off them. Being a faller, I generally went snag falling during a fire. You'd be falling the burning snag by hand. Burning chunks and embers would be falling on your back and head as you were sawing away. For this I got 40¢ an hour, then had to go out and buy all new clothes."

"One time the fire was down below, so the boss sent me up to fall a couple of snags in case the fire got up that far. I had the undercut in one and I heard this noise. It sounded like a train. So I shut off the saw to listen, and it was the fire coming right up through the salal. My gas and oil can were in there so I took off fast and ran out of there."

Bus Griffith

FISHING

WHALING

The only whaling station to operate in the area was at Whaling Station Bay on Hornby Island. Moved from Cortez Island in 1871, the processing plant closed the next year because most of the big whales were depleted in Georgia Strait. This left only the killer whales.

The Indians have many stories and legends about the killer whale, but the white man also became enamoured and in awe of this large mammal, which he usually called "black fish". Often seen in Baynes Sound, the pods of whales with their big dorsal fins gleaming in the sun loved to swim and play around boats. They were always fair game and many were shot at, even with small pistols from the decks of boats. Stories were recounted of black fish coming up under boats and lifting them out of the water, or chasing rowboats onto the beach.

1895 AUGUST ⊷ Off Qualicum the *SS Joan* ran into a school of whales travelling in the direction of the mainland. Two of the biggest were swimming alongside one another and leading the school. As the *Joan* approached, the leader came right across her bow. There was a collision which made every timber in the steamer creak and the passengers rush on deck. The *Joan* struck the nearest whale and sunk it, then passed right over the other. It is probable that the first whale was killed by the impact as he was not seen to rise again. [2]

SHARKS

Sharks, along with dog fish, were caught in the 1920's for oil and fertilizer. In the '30s large sharks became a menace to fishermen in Baynes Sound. It seems they were attracted to the big flashers being used for salmon. Several fishermen were nearly pulled overboard when a big monster was hooked. Letting it have rod and tackle was the only safe response.

1939 AUGUST ⊷ Mr. E. Lloyd, fish warden, whilst on patrol off Deep Bay, has been hearing complaints from the fishermen of a great number of sharks, so he went shark fishing. He baited his hook with a three pound salmon on an inch rope and soon had sport. He believed from the wrench he got that a bigger one got away, but soon afterwards he had a 500 lb. shark on the line. He had to tow it five miles before he could get to a wharf where he and other fishermen hauled the big fellow out and killed him with a hammer. [6]

SHELLFISH

The large middens of broken shells found everywhere on the Island give evidence that the Indians enjoyed clams and oysters for thousands of years.

OYSTERS

Beaches on Baynes Sound were some of the best for growing native oysters. The succulent bivalves were free for the taking. They provided food and ready cash if no job was available.

1884 ⊷ Mr. Wm. Keddy brought down a 50 lb. sack of the large and luscious bivalves from the oyster beds discovered by him in Baynes Sound. These oysters are pronounced by connoisseurs to be superior to any found on the coast. [2]

In the 1920's the owners of the Japanese Logging Company at Fanny Bay are credited with introducing the first "pacific oysters" into the area.

"About 1926 or '27 Louis Magnone was running the locie and my Dad was firing at the Jap Camp in Fanny Bay. The owners brought in nine crates of oyster seed from Japan, and the train crew took them down to the beach. In with them was Jap seaweed seed and that sure took over. It was terrible if it got caught in your propeller."

Jack Anderson

The Pacific oyster could not readily reproduce in our colder waters, so for many years seed was imported from Japan. Along with this seed came the Manila clam. The first oyster leases were taken out in the 1940's, and it was discovered that Pendrell Sound was warm enough for the oyster to breed. Oyster men threaded old shells on strings and barged them up to Pendrell Sound, where eggs attached themselves and young oysters started to grow. They were then moved back to sheltered beaches of firm mud, sand or gravel and spread at half tide mark. Feeding on plankton as the tide rose and fell, it took from two to four years before they could be harvested.

CLAMS

G. Francklyn

Gilbert Francklyn of Henry Bay with a catch of over 40 cod fish for the market

Although not as exotic, clams were a more readily accepted food than the oyster. Chowders were the mainstay of many meals, and today people are still loyal to the chowder their mother made. Either Boston clam chowder with a milk base was favoured, or Manhattan clam chowder with a tomato base.

The native butterclam and littleneck clam grew in the sand and gravel, and were very plentiful on the sandspit from Denman to Seal Island. During the winter, families rowed over and the men dug with a fork in the sand to find the clams, while the women and older children filled sacks to take home. The kiddies followed the squirt of the geoducks down into the sand. To clean out the sand the clams were treated with one last meal of fresh water and rolled oats, before being put into the pot and steamed open. The small ones were eaten with butter, while the large ones were used in chowders or minced for clam burgers.

The Indians had long spent part of the year harvesting clams on the spit. After the turn of the century, American canneries sent ships into B.C. waters, and by employing the Indians almost robbed us of all our clams, until the government stepped in.

1907 FEBRUARY ➾ Clam Poachers Here Again. For some days the American Steamer *Electric* has been lying in Bayne Sound engaged in loading up clams for Puget Sound canneries. The method pursued is to contract with Indians for delivery on the steamer at a set price per pail. Every night last week the Denman spit was illuminated by strings of pitch torches carried by the Indian diggers of the bivalves. Is it right that a foreign country is allowed to rob us of everything of value in the way of fish? The clam beds to the south have been completely depleted and the same will happen in B.C. [4]

Clams remained plentiful, as proven by a clam digging contest in 1911. First prize of $5.00 was won by Mr. S. Yanto who dug 210 clams in two hours. Soon the B.C. canneries had the clams to themselves, but the over-harvesting continued. With the introduction of teams of horses, they ploughed the sand on the islands, exposing the clams for the Indian harvesters. This decimated the clam beds as well as killing the young clams.

Clams were in abundance again in the 1930's and '40s, when Union Bayites made some extra money by digging clams at 3¢ a pound. Scows called at the dock in the late afternoon to pick up warmly clothed men, women and teen agers with their forks, sacks and flashlights. They were barged to the spit to take advantage of the low winter tides. The imported manila clam had spread, and was dug along with the butter and littleneck clams. Several years later the spit was over-harvested again, and the fisheries department closed the area.

1942 FEBRUARY ➾ After a four year rest, clam digging again took place on Seal Island with seventy diggers under supervision of the Research Board of Canada. Observers found that a most satisfactory recovery had been made. The Island was lit up like a Christmas tree with fires of the clam diggers. [6]

FISHING

Sports fishermen caught salmon, cod and halibut for their families, and often sold the extras at 20¢ a fish to stores or fish packers, before the days of government regulations. Up and down the coast many canneries had been established by the 1890's. Cans, handmade by Chinese labourers, were filled with salmon by Indian and Japanese women. The lids were soldered on and then individually dipped into varnish to make sure of the seal. Ships loaded with canned salmon regularly called at Union Wharf for bunker coal.

Arthur Groll built and operated the Deep Bay Packing Co. in 1917. For about twenty-five years this processing plant played an important role in fishing, from Qualicum north to Johnstone Strait. The plant canned coho and pinks, using mainly the native and Japanese wives of the fishermen. Cans made and sealed by machines were introduced. A fish reduction plant was added to the cannery in 1922, which converted dogfish and shark into oil and fertilizer. The plant was sold to B.C. Packers in 1935 and two years later burned down.

1937 APRIL ➾ Deep Bay Cannery burned with a $50,000 loss which was covered by insurance. The fire broke out in the net house at 6:00 p.m. The heavily tarred nets went up fast as did two scow loads of fish oil. Twenty-five buildings on the spit were saved by the Union Bay and Courtenay fire brigades. [6]

The plant was rebuilt exclusively as an oil refining and fertilizer plant. It was eventually closed because the fishermen could get more money for the fish's liver than the refining company paid for the whole fish. Fertilizer was less valuable without the liver. Dogfish oil had long been used as a lubricant on the coast. Qualicum Tom was one of the early processors. He extracted the oil in a crude little refinery at his home on the Big Qualicum River, where spawning fish were plentiful. With his horse and buggy, he travelled up Island and sold the oil at 50¢ per gallon to the logging camps around Union Bay. It was mainly used as a lubricant on the skids, to make the logs slip easily when the oxen or horses pulled them to the booming grounds.

It was easy to tell a Deep Bayite, as the smell of rotten fish got in hair, clothes, bedding, books, funiture and car. The smell lingered for years, even after residents had moved away.

1941 SEPTEMBER ➾ "Dogfish Plant Stinks". Residents of the east coast from Bowser to Union Bay and Denman Island, file a protest with the government over the stench from B.C. Packer's plant at Deep Bay. When southeasters blow everyone must keep windows and doors closed. Some people have moved because of it, and tourists have turned back when they got a nostril full. The plant is processing dogfish which the fishermen go for when nothing else bites. The company lets the fish accumulate until it is worthwhile to start up the plant. [6]

Herring teemed in the Sound, and fishermen from B.C. and Washington reaped the harvest which varied from year to year.

1892 MARCH ➾ The Gulf of Georgia is reported to be choked with large schools of herring. Fishermen have no trouble in catching fish by the tons for shipment to the east. A remarkable and beautiful sight can be seen at night from the deck of the steamboat. The boat seems to be floating on herring, and the fish dart away from the bow in the thousands, leaving phosphorescent wakes like the flashing of countless meteorites. [2]

The fisheries department amended the fishing act in 1924, to allow pilchard and herring to be caught and used for fertilizer. A.W. Neill, MP, protested vigorously against using human food for manure, but to no avail.

1931 MARCH ➾ Herring boats have a very good catch this year. One purse seine caught 125 tons. This is the largest catch in ten years but the fish are lower in oil. [5]

All of the creeks emptying into Baynes Sound were home to spawning coho *(blueback)*, pink *(humpback)* and chum*(dog)* salmon. The entrances into the sound around Yellow Light to the south, and the bar between Cape Lazo and Seal Island to the north, were always abundant fishing areas. On the beach south of Union Bay at about half tide the Indians built fish traps. They cleared two large circles and ringed them with boulders. At certain times of the year the water was so full of fish that they were trapped there when the tide went out. The Indians were easily able to harvest them. These two circles are still evident on the beach today.

Salmon were still plentiful after the white man came, and in the fall months the river entrances were crowded with fish and boats.

"I saw a seine boat once at the mouth of Washer Creek make a set, and it got 13,000 coho in the one set. The fish were waiting for enough water to go up the creek."

Tom McKay

In the 1920's the American boats were still coming up to catch fish in Canadian waters and take them back to the canneries in Puget Sound. Several times, because of poor refrigeration, the fish would start to rot and had to be dumped by the scow load.

1920 AUGUST ➾ A good run of salmon around but the American boats are so thick that Canadian's can't catch them and Canadian canneries are short. One American boat took too many and had to dump the 13,000 salmon. They lay rotting in Deep Bay and Discovery Passage. [6]

Year after year, when the Sound was open for seine boats, the

D. Muschamp

Two trollers belonging to local fishermen who mainly fished the waters around Denman and Hornby Islands. Nights and stormy days were spent tied up at the float at Government Wharf

same few boats docked at the wharf and became friends with the townspeople. Also using Union Bay as their base were the bottom trawlers such as the *Sea Angel*, which was jokingly said to be "out uplifting soles".

Union Bay was home to a group of Japanese trollers and gillnetters during the fishing season. Whole families lived on board, helping with the chores. Some of the women lived in a house that stood on stilts, south of the "glass house". They worked on the barge salting fish. Chum *(dog salmon)* were cleaned, salted and packed in barrels for shipment to Japan.

1925 OCTOBER ➾ Once again Union Bay reminds us of a typical fishing village, with fishing boats dotting the Bay and making this their headquarters. Docked at the Government wharf is a large covered scow where fish are cleaned and salted. [5]

The troller was a purist when it came to fishing. No nets to trap or scoop up the fish. The salmon had a fighting chance, to bite the bait or not. Most of the fishermen who lived in Union Bay were trollers, men who had started their vocation as little boys who loved to fish. There was a running battle with the seiners. The trollers accused them of depleting the fish. In 1927 a fishing inquiry was held at Union Bay, with over fifty fishermen from the surrounding district presenting petitions. In district No.3, 4002 licenses had been issued in 1926, a 92% increase in three years. The fish were quickly becoming depleted, and restrictions were called for to keep the seiners out of Baynes Sound during spawning season. Eventually, restrictions were put in place that allowed for a certain number of fish to enter the creeks before the fishermen were allowed to fish. This became the foundation of today's fishing regulations, that have become more and more stringent as the fishermen become more and more proficient.

Most of the fishermen who lived in Union Bay were trollers. The Anderson family dominated the scene, starting with Pete when he returned from WW 1. Then Pete's son, Ed, in the *Veda* was followed by grandsons Jack on the *Atoimah* and Tom on the *Avonlea*. Fred McKinnel fished on the *Connie* and his brother-in- law, Bill Glover, fished on the *Nymph* 2. Later, Frank Street and Art Pickles made Union Bay their fishing base.

There was just one man to a boat, which was carefully maintained and repaired over the winter. Each year they were brought up on the ways beside the government wharf, where the hull was scraped down and copper bottomed. Ed Anderson partitioned off the tearoom of the confectionery, and used it for repairing and building small boats. In 1944 Harry and Ted Glover began building the boat of their dreams, behind the house on the company hill. The 36' long, 10' beam troller began to take shape under the careful supervision of many onlookers. The yard looked like a shipyard, complete with a long steam box used to shape the solid oak ribs which fitted onto the keelson. She was finished with beautiful teak trim and readied for the trip to the sea. Huge cedar skids were placed under her, and the town turned out on June 29, 1946 to see the monster pulled by a grader down Russell Hill to the coal spit, where she was christened *JanJacAnn* and launched in a brisk north wind. Brother Bill Glover fished her locally as well as on the north and west coasts.

H. Glover

Union Bay fleet heads out for a day's fishing

H. Glover

December 28, 1943. Harry Glover puts the finishing touches to the keel of the 36' troller *JanJacAnn* which he and brother Ted built

H. Glover

June 29, 1946 was launch day. *JanJacAnn* still fishes the waters of the west and north coasts, now skippered by the builder's nephew Bruce Glover

Land

The Baynes Sound area is composed of many bays, points, rivers and lakes. The names we use for them today came from many sources - Indian words, explorers, navy men, settlers. Here are the origins of the names as discovered in the author's research.

Baynes Sound - Named after Rear Admiral Robert Lambert Baynes, Commander-in-Chief of the Pacific Station Esquimalt, 1857-1864.

Bowser - Named after William John Bowser, Premier of B.C. 1915-1916.

Buckley Bay - Named after the squatter, Phillip Buckley, who stayed on after the Baynes Sound Mine Co. closed.

Chichlatixw - (pronounced Cheech-a-tel-wh) Early Indian name for the fertile land around the mouth of Washer Creek. (later became Watts' Flats, then the Coalhills)

Chrome Island or Yellow Rock - Probably evolved from the fact that in early spring the two acre island is covered with a mass of yellow flowers.

Coal Creek - An outcropping of coal was found there.

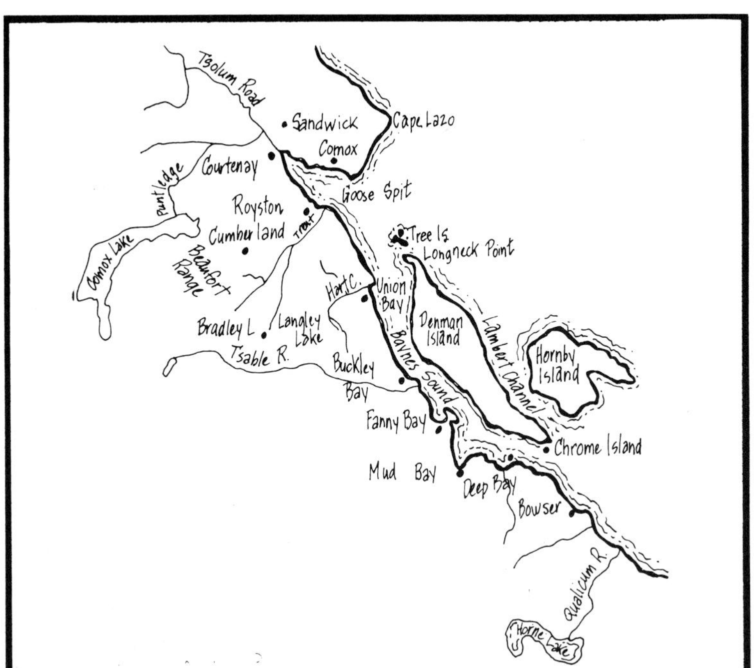

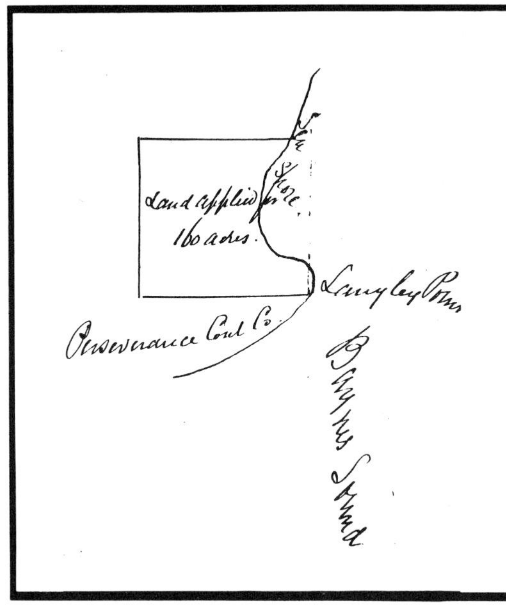

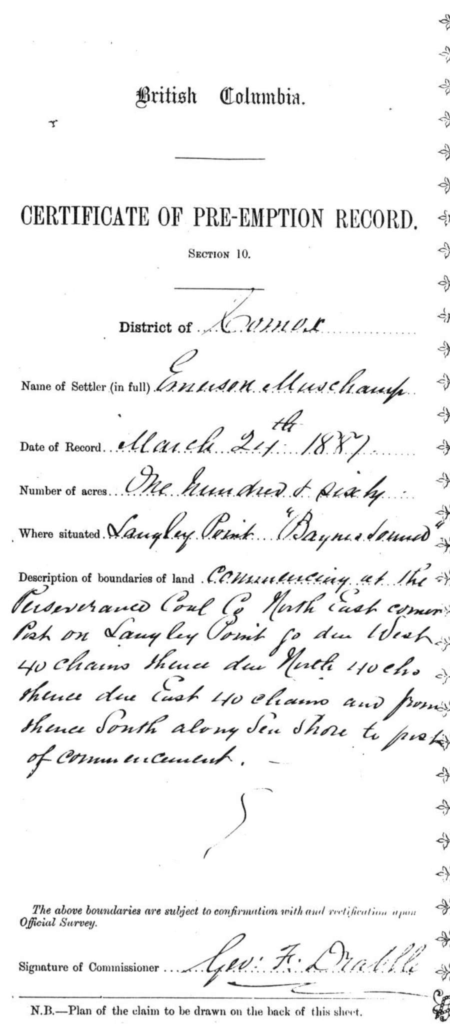

British Columbia.

CERTIFICATE OF PRE-EMPTION RECORD.

SECTION 10.

District of Comox

Name of Settler (in full) Emerson Muschamp

Date of Record March 21st 1887

Number of acres One hundred & sixty

Where situated Langley Point Baynes Sound

Description of boundaries of land Commencing at the Perseverance Coal Co North East corner Post on Langley Point go due West 40 chains thence due North 40 chs thence due East 40 chains and from thence South along Sea Shore to post of commencement.

The above boundaries are subject to confirmation with and rectification upon Official Survey.

Signature of Commissioner Geo: F. Drabble

N.B.—Plan of the claim to be drawn on the back of this sheet.

Emerson Muschamp's preemption certificate of property at Langley Point. A year later he sold this property to Dunsmuir

Cook Creek - Named for brothers Ezra and Ephram Cook who pre-empted land there in 1885.

Comox - Indian word meaning land of plenty.

Cougar Creek - Possibly one of the big cats was sighted there.

Courtenay - The river was named first, for Captain George W.C. Courtenay of *HMS Constance.*

Cumberland - Named for the county in England famous for its coal mines.

Deep Bay - Named because of the geographical structure of the bay.

Denman Island - Named after Rear Admiral Joseph Denman, Commander-in-Chief of the Pacific Station Esquimalt, 1864-1867.

Fanny Bay - Possibly named after Admiral Hornby's wife.

Hart Creek - Named for Jack Hart, Indian trader.

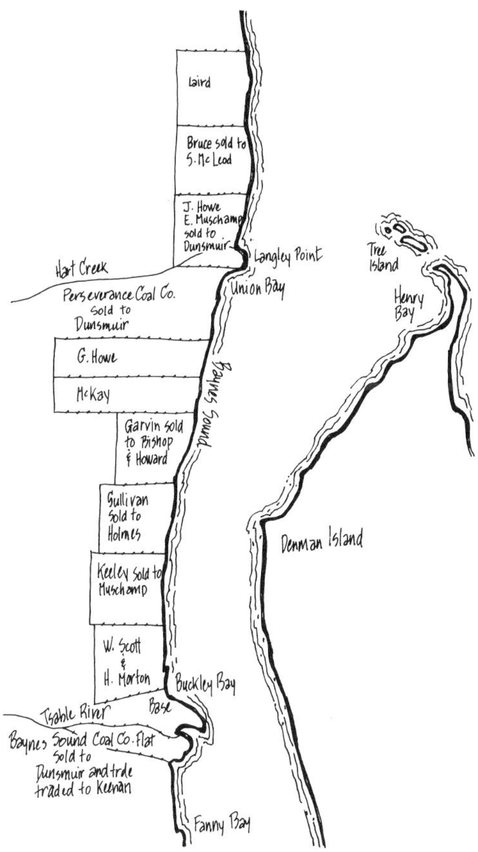

Preemptions taken out in the 1880's. The two mining company claims were established in the 1860's. The Laird, G. Howe and McKay properties were acquired in the 1890's

Henry Bay - Possibly named after Captain Henry Richards, captain of *HMS Plumper*, who in his surveys of 1857-1861 gave names to many places on the coast.

Hindu Creek - Possibly there was a Sikh camp there during the building of the E&N.

Hornby Island - Named after Rear Admiral Phipps Hornby, Commander-in-Chief of Pacific Station Esquimalt, 1847-1851.

Horne Lake - Named for the Hudson Bay Factor, Adam Grant Horne, the first white man to cross Vancouver Island from Qualicum to Barclay Sound for the purpose of opening a fur trade with the Indians. (father of Mrs. Fred Brown)

Jack Hart Point - Named for the trader who came to the point at the mouth of Hart Creek and set up a small store to trade with the Indians.

Lambert Channel - Named after Rear Admiral Robert Lambert Baynes.

Langley Point - Official name of Jack Hart Point.

Mud Bay - Named because of the low flat muddy bottom of the bay.

Nile Creek - Named after Phillip Nile who homesteaded there.

Qualicum - Derived from a Nanaimo Indian term for "place of the dog salmon" Quall-e-hum or Quallchum.

Rosewall Creek - Named for brothers H. and J. Rosewall who homesteaded at the mouth of the river and who prospected and found gold in many of the creeks in the Alberni area.

Royston - Named after one of its first settlers, William Roy.

Stray Creek - Flowed into Washer Creek from the north, near the ravine.

Trent River - Named after the river Trent in England.

Tsable River - An Indian word.

Union - Taken from the Union Coal Co. that started the mines.

Union Wharf, later Union Bay - The port from which Union coal was shipped.

Washer Creek - Hart Creek became known as Washer Creek after the Union Coal Co. built a coal washer there.

Watts' Flats - Area around mouth of Washer Creek, squatted on by Mike Watts before the Colliery started. (Coalhills)

Land in the Nelson District on Baynes Sound was put up for preemption in the 1880's. A composite map of the preemptions of this period follows.

In the next ten to fifteen years some of these properties changed hands. As John Howe did not develop his section in the required time, it reverted back to the crown, and in 1887 Emerson Muschamp preempted the same 160 acres, which contained Langley Point. The Union Coal Co. was bought by Dunsmuir, who sought a deeper port site than Royston. It is reported that Mr. Muschamp sold his property to the coal baron for $500. The Union Coal Co.

also acquired the Perseverance claim in 1888.

A few years later Daniel Sullivan sold to Joseph Holmes, and C. Keeley sold to Emerson Muschamp. Both Alex Garvin and Joseph Holmes developed their land and ran cattle there, but as the port grew they sought to sell part of it. Garvin had discovered the "famous springs" and had plans for a spa and resort. By 1893 both men had subdivided and were listing lots from $75 to $100. Later, George Harwood and Charlie Bishop bought Garvin's land, but it was not until the middle of the twentieth century that it was built on.

M. Peters

George Howe with his niece and nephew, Lil and George Harwood, leaving Union Bay for Hornby Island

George Howe left England in the 1870's, and with his cousin Jack worked his way across the states to San Francisco, then up to B.C. He worked in the Baynes Sound coal mine in '76 and stayed in the district when the mine closed. He had a farm on Hornby and a meat market in Comox. In 1893 Mr. Howe bought the land situated between the present Union Bay market and the McKay property. Here he developed the farm and built his store, hotel, and rental houses. About the turn of the century Mr. Howe sold some lots south of the hotel. The Kinnards built a two-storey house which they later sold to Mugfords. Then Alf Horne bought it and renovated it into a beautiful one-storey house. Alex McLeod built a home next door with a barn back of the house. About 1906 two prefabricated "Aladdin" houses were erected by Howe, north of the store. The walls were assembled and floated in by barge, then screwed together. They were "modern houses", featuring stained glass in all the windows. When Mr. Howe retired in 1907, he sold to Fraser and Bishop a strip of property including the buildings from the hotel to the school. The rest of the property was subdivided and offered for sale.

Union Bay Community Hall

Looking south from the Nelson Hotel up Station Road

About the turn of the century, Marshall Laird bought the section of land north of Adam Bruce. George Davis bought some acreage from Mr. Laird about 1910. Later, Sam McLeod bought the Bruce section, and in the 1940's some of it was subdivided and homes built along Spence Road.

Also about the turn of the century, Andrew McKay bought a section of land between Garvin and Howe. In 1907 he subdivided some of the farm, creating lots along the road which were soon bought up. His sister, Biddy, and her husband, Jackson Arthur, had the most northern lot. They built a home and had one son, Bill, but soon after traded the house to George Howe for some property on Hornby. Howe later sold the house to Mrs. Humphrey after her husband died. The oldest McKay girl, Elizabeth, married Louis Magnone, and got some of the property above the railroad track. Mr. Magnone bought lumber from Graham's mill on Denman and floated it across Baynes Sound on a barge. He then hauled it up McKay's road and down the railway right of way before the steel was laid. In this house the couple raised their four girls and one boy.

1908 ➡ Jackson Arthur is having a new home built at Fairview. It will greatly add to Union Bay's splendid new homes. [4]

Union Bay Townsite For Sale

700 Lots at Rock-bottom Prices

This Townsite Has Just Been Released and Title Is Assured to All Purchasers.

Unique opportunity to acquire a home or business site in one of Canada's most promising seaports.

Union Bay promises to be the future coal and shipping centre of a great and developing area.

Ideal Residential and Waterfront Lots at $50 to $200

Buy where employment at high high wages is an assured thing.

The prices now fixed hold good for a limited time only better come and see us now.

For plans and details of Lots and Prices apply

Hicks-Beach & Field
Courtenay, B. C.

Geo. John Hardy
Courtenay, B. C.

This 1919 advertisement offered lots for sale by the Harwood family. A steel mill at Union Bay was expected to be announced any day. In fact, some waterfront lots were sold in the '30s for $25.00 each

Henderson's British Columbia Gazetteer and Directory 1910

Union Bay

A post village at Union Wharf Baynes Sound, Comox-Atlin district, 7 miles from Cumberland (Union Mines) Union Bay. Is the first and last port at which the Northern steamers call and is an important coaling station. Has telegraph, Union Coal Co. have a large wharf 1,600 feet long, 40 feet wide and 60 feet above high water mark, there is accommodation for four ships along each side; a track 13 miles long connects with the mines.

Postmaster - J A Fraser
Abrams Robert engineer
Abrams S laborer
Allara Luis miner
Allen Charles I engineer
Anderson Adolf laborer
Armitage Frederick laborer
Arthur Jackson laborer
Bakewell James laborer
Balo N laborer
Beatty A S carpenter
Bennett Thomas carpenter
Bishop Charles R gen store
Bishop Charles R of Fraser & Bishop
Bland Henry laborer
Blaney Arthur clerk
Blatchford John carpenter
Booth G H frt agent
Borgaes Charles logger
Brown Frederick wharfinger
Browne Thomas L gen store
Buckley Philip farmer
Buick Miss M teacher
Cameron Alexander engineer
Campbell G C foreman
Campbell Wm mule driver
Canadian Pacific Ry. Telegraph Fred M Humber manager
Carmichael J H machinist
Carter Wm boilermaker
Cavilliaro, J blacksmith
Chapman Sandford farmer
Clark Edward storekeeper's asst
Clark Walter M engineer
Cook Nelson carpenter
Cowie Alexander farmer
Cowie David farmer
Curran Frederick laborer
Davies James W engineer
Davis George car insp
Doane George mgr Fraser River Logging camp
Dominion Govt Telegraphs, James McNeil agent
Donaldson John mechanic
Donaldson Robert mechanic
Drew Edward bricklayer
Ead John carpenter
Ellis Wm blacksmith
English James E engineer
Fox C M mechanic
Fraser & Bishop hotel, general store, meat market
Fraser John A of Fraser & Bishop
Fraser River Mills Co logging camp
Fulcher John engineer
Garvan Alex laborer
Graham E A engineer
Glover A A foundry
Glover A H laborer
Glover Edwin moulder
Glover Harry moulder
Glover Herbert storekeeper Wellington Collieries
Graham E A engineer
Haggart David N laborer
Haggart James N laborer
Haggart Wm mechanic
Hardie George laborer
Harrison Wm H weighman
Harwood W George clerk
Haywood Ernest woodsman
Hill John mechanic
Hill Wm carpenter
Hogberg Andrew farmer
Hooper Charles laborer
Horne A R blacksmith
Horne Thomas telegrap op.
Hudson Thomas line repairer
Humphreys John hotel
Humphreys John Jr engineer
Hunt Edward G machinist
Keenan C farmer
Kelly William captain
Kerton Frederick carpenter
Kesley John overman
Kidd Rev C E (Presbyterian)
Krick Charles logger
Krick H F logger
Latham D P laborer
Law R K moulder
Le Clair Joseph laborer
Lockner John loco engineer
Luck Henry moulder
McCallum Archibald carpenter
McDonald Daniel fireman
McKay A farmer
McLaughlin Abraham logger
McLeod Alexander laborer
McLeod N A carpenter
McMurtie E mechanic
McNeill James telegraph agent
McQuarrie Angus E carpenter
McRae Alexander farmer
McStephen Alexander fisherman
Magnoni Seconde blacksmith
Marshall Wm engineer
Matheson A carpenter
Nelson Hotel, Fraser & Bishop props
Olsen Ole carpenter
Patterson N laborer
Ramsay D T laborer
Ray Lindsay blacksmith
Ray Richard R engineer
Ray T L engineer
Renwick David F wharfinger
Riley Wm coke
Robertson George H blacksmith
Robertson Robert H blacksmith
Roe George deputy customs collector
Rogers John carpenter
Russell George carpenter
Stratford A C carpenter
Street J F mechanic
Struther John P carpenter
Taylor Mill Logging Co
Thrum Richard laborer
Union Bay Co-Operative Society
Waggett C M mgr Union Bay Co-Operative Society
Walker A G farmer
Walker Harley engineer
Walker James engineer
Wellington Collieries Co
Whyte Harry brakesman
Wilson Hotel John Humphrey prop
Young R J laborer

Union Bay School Collection

A picture taken from the Government Wharf showing the post office and Wilson Hotel

Union Bay Community Hall

Two prefabricated Aladdin houses arrived by barge and were screwed together to make charming homes. Mr. and Mrs. C. Bishop lived in one

1910 JULY ➾ Mr. and Mrs. Harry Glover expect to move in a week to their beautiful new residence at McKayville. Mr. Street has also moved his family there, where he hopes to build a house. [4]

T. Dutfield

The Auchinvole family enjoy the beautiful grounds of their gracious house

After George Howe died, the remaining property was willed to his nephews, the three Harwood brothers. George was the only one living in Union Bay and it became his responsibility to pay the taxes. He sold lots whenever the opportunity arose. One of the first dwellings built on the waterfront next to the first store was the house owned by Mammy King. She rented it out, and for many families it was their first house after arriving at the port. Later, the porch was glassed in and it was dubbed the "glass house", and still later, George Cooper moved it south about a quarter of a mile when the road was widened. Another early house was built by Nelson Cook and later sold to Mrs. Little. Ernie King built his home on the beach, and about the same time J. McFarlane built across the road. E.T. Searle's large home was built on waterfront in the 30's and dubbed "the Big House". Mr. Searle's parents joined the family, and built a home across the road from Kings. Other builders along the beach were Carter, McKenzie, Sherburn and McQueen. Strapped for money in the late 30's, George Harwood sold three waterfront lots at $25.00 each to Harry Chapman, who built three homes at the south entrance to Union Bay.

Some of the first families, when they arrived about 1894, lived in the large boarding house where the single men lived. Soon they leased land from the company and built homes. The McCartneys, McKays, Rays, Drews and Cooks all had houses along the front street, and in 1901 Tom Hudson built a cottage for his family next to the Wilson Hotel.

In 1897 the company constructed a row of houses facing the trestle. The Donaldson and Gibson families were some of the first occupants. These houses were small, with just four rooms and a pantry. Studs were not used in their construction. Instead, the 1" x 12" shiplap was vertically nailed onto a 2" x 4" along the ceiling and floor. Battens were put on top of the cracks in the shiplap. There were no inside walls; felt paper was put over the shiplap and calcimined. The chimney did not go to the floor but was supported by a bracket on the wall, and had holes on two sides for the kitchen stove and living room heater. Another row of these bungalows was built about the turn of the century. Two large homes were also built for company officials, on either side of Russell Hill. The big red house on the south side was occupied by the wharfinger. James Dunsmuir stayed there when he was in town, as well as captains and their wives while their ships were being loaded. By 1910 there were over 300 people living in Union Bay. During the next decade the company built more houses, and many homes were built privately. A house was built for the master mechanic in 1911, next to where the post office was later located.

In 1917 new management was brought in to run the CC(D)L. A beautiful big home was built for Alexander Auchinvole, District Superintendent. At this time the back row of the Company houses was also constructed. Six were large houses with three bedrooms down one side which were separated from the kitchen, dining room and living room by a hall. The outside walls were finished in rustic siding. They rented to company workers for $12.50 per month.

1917 MAY ➾ The CC(D)L has a gang of workers clearing land preparatory to the erection of a number of houses for its employees. Ten neat frame buildings will be put up at once and the plans seen show that they will be modern and comfortable in every respect. This is only a start on an extensive program of development work the company intends to carry out at Union Bay. [6]

The original road to the lake was part of the Perseverance trail and left the highway between

F. Peters

Originally owned by Mammy King, this house was rented to numerous families when they first arrived. The porch was later glassed in and the house dubbed 'the glass house.' Years later it was moved south and across the road by G. Cooper

D. Bennie

About 1916 carpenter and cabinet maker David Haggart built this home for his family above the E&N tracks

J. Geidt

Herbert Glover proudly shows off his newly constructed house on McLeod Road

the post office and church. Stanford Road was put in to join with this road about 1910. Because David Walker rebuilt his house there in 1913 during the strike, it was called Walker's Hill. Later it was called McLeod Road because Alex McLeod had a farm at the top of the hill. The E&N went through in 1914 and Mr. Howe offered lots in a subdivision above the track facing McLeod Road. The Haggarts, Glovers, Goods and Baldwins built homes on Shaughnessy Heights as it was called.

1917 SEPTEMBER → Mr. Herbert Glover's residence is near completion. The neat trim bungalow will be one of the most picturesque places here. [6]

Station Road was put in to provide access to the E&N. In the early 1920's Hughie Reid, Fred Dale, George Broder and Mrs. P. Anderson all built houses along it. By the mid '20s the town was developing to the north, with Tomojiro Nakamura, George Campbell, William Bowden, and Vincent Francioli all leasing land from the CC(D)L and building homes on Washer Creek Hill.

Most of the homes of the early twentieth century were small. The walls and ceiling were

Campbell River Museum, Rob Yeatman

A view down the main street of Union Bay in the 1920's. A boardwalk paralleled the street which is part of the Island Highway. Hudson's house is on the right with the post office in the distance

Union Bay Community Hall

These six large company houses were built in 1917 and featured kitchen with pantry, dining and living rooms (both with fireplaces), three bedrooms and space for a bathroom

often covered with beaver board which was painted with calcimine. Gyproc did not come onto the market until the 1930's. The earliest company houses had felt paper covering the walls, but the later ones were built with studs and had slats covering the inside walls. These slats were covered with cheese cloth, then wall papered. Stores and the company paperhangers offered a good selection of wallpaper.

1894 → Simon Leiser's has just received 1,000 rolls of wall paper to sell for 15¢ and up. How can they get out such pretty patterns so cheaply? The lumber used here is usually "green" and shrinks, hence the custom of putting on "cheap cloth" (cheesing it) and then papering is quite common. [3b]

The kitchen floor was usually covered with a printed linoleum, which soon showed signs of wear as the pattern wore off in heavy traffic areas. Battleship linoleum was preferred if one could afford it. The fir flooring in the other rooms was most often painted brown. The talented housewife decorated her floors by stippling them. A sponge was dipped into the paint and pressed onto the floor, leaving an open design. If several colours were used a pretty effect could be achieved.

Every home had a pantry, usually built onto the kitchen with a lean-to roof. Bins or shelves were in a dry sink or built onto the walls. There was not much counter space so the baking was done on the kitchen table. Food was kept in a cooler in the pantry, on the porch or in the cellar. Food was also suspended in a bucket down the well, or stored in a crock that was buried into the ground.

"We stored our milk and butter in an evaporator. There was water in the bottom of a big square tin, and a frame covered with cheesecloth to keep out the bugs. The evaporation kept the food cool."

Muriel (Harwood) Peters

The sink was set into a small drainboard, often in the pantry. If the housewife was lucky, she had a pump next to the sink. If not, water had to be carried from the family well, or a communal well down the street, until running water was installed. All the water for cooking, laundry and bathing was heated on the kitchen stove. The Gem, McClary, or Majestic held centre stage in the kitchen. A rocking chair often sat beside it and a wooden clothes line hung above, in the 12' high ceiling. As hot air rises, the floors were always cold and the top half of the room hot.

On cold days everyone gathered around the big kitchen stove. Some sat with their feet on the oven door, while many children dressed for school in front of the kitchen stove.

Mrs. McKenzie's kitchen was a favourite gathering spot for the young girls. With her husband Jim away in the logging camp, Jessie ran the house in a relaxed manner. Her three girls- Lydia, Florence and Margaret - enjoyed little discipline as did their friends when visiting.

"Mrs. Mac's was a haven for young girls. We'd sit around and talk and hear the latest gossip. She was a good cook and there was always a pan of peanuts roasting in the oven for us to nibble on whenever we liked."

Margaret (Harwood) Bowden

A. Graham

Bessie Magnone cooked for years on this beautiful Majestic cook stove

In most households on laundry day the whole family pitched in. The boys carried water and poured it into the big coal oil tins on the stove to heat. Mother and the girls manned the scrubbing boards, rubbing their knuckles raw in an attempt to get the clothes clean with Feltes naptha soap. Later, as families prospered, manually operated washing machines were set in motion by the young boys or girls. Mangles for removing the water from clothes were a great improvement over hand wringing but still required someone to turn the handle. By the late 1930's a few lucky women had electric washers with the wringers on the side that fed the clothes into the rinse tubs. There is scarcely a family that does not have a story to tell of how one of the youngsters helping out got an arm caught in the wringer.

N. King

Washday at the McKay household. Mary and Nellie help their mother scrub the clothes on metal scrub boards, then put them through the mangle

Cumberland Museum

Dora Cook and Bessie Magnone air the canary and prepare for a day of house cleaning

"Remember the Rundquists, a Swedish family. She used to take her washing down to the beach and build a fire in the rocks. She put her tubs on top of the rocks and heated the salt water. She'd wash in one tub with homemade soap and rinse in the other."

Clara (Cave) Farmer

"A couple of tubs on the back porch and there would be two or three of us girls scrubbing away on the iron scrub boards. We always let Mother do the heavy underwear and overalls, and we did the lighter stuff. We did have a mangle so we didn't have to wring the clothes by hand. Then, when it rained, the clothes were hung on the lines in the kitchen's high ceiling."

Frances (McKay) Stasek

"Auchinvole's washing machine wore out and they gave it to the Hoopers. It was one of those kinds that

D. Geidt

Laura Little's beautiful bedroom suite with high carved head board and marble topped dresser. Pillow shams are tiny cotton rosettes made by Clara Bowden

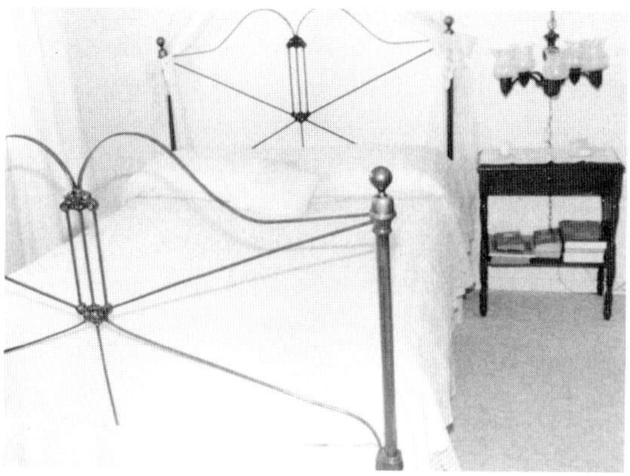

D. Geidt

This iron bedstead was once slept in by guests of the Nelson Hotel

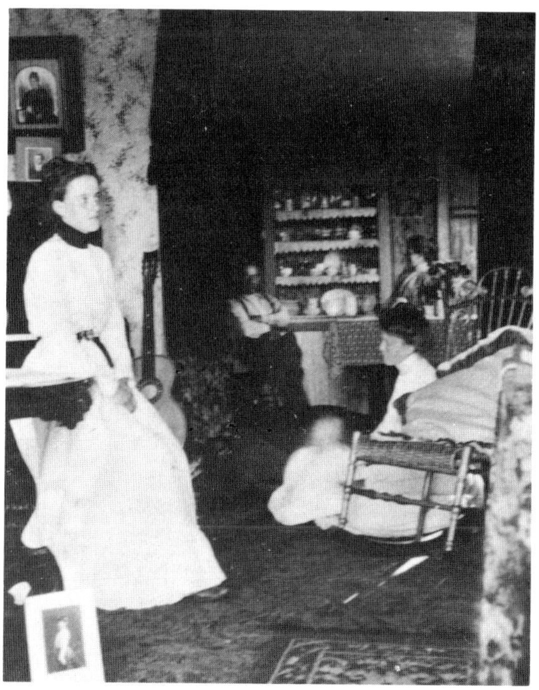

M. Vowels

you turned back and forth. As kids we took turns, a hundred times for one load of clothes. Still, it was an improvement over the scrubbing board. But it wasn't too good for really dirty things."

Hector Hooper

The next day the ironing had to be done. Most of the women's and children's clothes were starched, making it necessary to dampen the clothes with a sprinkling bottle first. The flat irons weighed one or two pounds and had to be heated on the stove, but they cooled quickly. Some women progressed to gas irons, which were often temperamental and hard to adjust, sending blue flames up over the handle.

"We would stand in the heat and iron for hours with the old sad irons. Real old heavy ones. Everything had to be starched and ironed: frilly dresses, petty coats, even pillow slips."

Annie (McKay) Aitken

In many living rooms there was a fireplace with raised coal grate, set into brick or tile, with a modest mantle above. Some homes had coal heaters with mica windows through which one could watch the flames. In the larger houses some of the bedrooms also had chimneys, and an oil drum heater was used to warm the room. A few master bedrooms boasted a tall wooden bedroom suite, but iron bedsteads were standard, with slat springs and feather or batten-filled mattesses.

"The night we moved into the new house we asked to have a fire in our bedroom heater. We'd never slept in a warm bedroom in our lives. It was so wonderful! Just the two of us sitting there reading. You know, you can't get away from a big family very often so we really enjoyed it, until it was time to get to bed. Oh, it was so hot and the room was so light from the fire that we couldn't get to sleep."

Margaret (Glover) Matthews

To start with, all of the homes had outhouses in the back yard. Some of the houses beside the ocean had the outhouse on stilts beyond high tide, with a wooden path connecting it to the house. No one worried about pollution and this had the advantage of never getting full.

Many women were house-proud and kept their castles, no matter how small, shining. Their few prized pieces of furniture bought from Grant & McGregor, Tarbell, Hitchen, or the catalogue were lovingly polished and covered with doilies or a deeply fringed silk scarf. Knickknacks and family pictures were carefully arranged on top.

FARMS

Many families had gardens and orchards. Some kept one or two milch cows for their own use, and sold a few quarts of milk to neighbours. Pigs were fattened for the dinner table with scraps from the kitchen and garden.

Left: In this interior view John and Elizabeth Cook look on from the kitchen table at daughters Myrtle Peters (seated at the black walnut organ) and Belle (playing with nephew Harold Peters)

D. Aitken

The Muschamp farm house and out buildings, with a view of Denman Island

D. Aitken

A view from the water of the McKay farm with ranch house and barn up on the bluff. The road ran along the beach behind the little cabin

"We lived next door to the Marshalls. They had two pigs. My Dad was great for making home brew, and he thought he wouldn't waste the mash so he took it over and dumped it into the pigpen. The pigs got drunk, and was Mrs. Marshall mad! But she got over it."

Hector Hooper

Some men farmed small plots while also holding a full or part-time job. Alex McLeod planted several acres up the lake road in grain to feed his livery horses.

In the very early days, on the north side of Union Bay, Adam Bruce had a farm which went right down to the beach. Beyond that, Marshall Laird owned ten acres. He sold a couple of acres to George Davis who cleared and farmed the land to feed his family.

About a mile from Buckley Bay, Alexander Garvin cleared his land and ran cattle there for about twenty-five years. North of Garvin's claim, C. Keeley had a farm which Emerson Muschamp took over at about the turn of the century. North of this property J. B. Holmes, who operated a store in Comox, had a ranch. He hired men to row him over to the ranch where he ran cattle for his butcher shop. After the turn of the century Andrew McKay bought the quarter section between Holmes' and Howe's.

Over the years there were only three large farms at the Bay. The McKays and Muschamps each operated dairy farms. George Howe, who owned the big store and hotel, maintained a produce farm. He employed Hungo, a Chinese farmer, to operate it.

The gardens Hungo tended were beautiful and they produced a bountiful harvest of vegetables. To transport them to the store, he loaded them into two large baskets hanging from a pole balanced across his shoulders. The boys of the town watched as the vegetables ripened, and they often raided the pea patch or corn field. Raw corn-on-the-cob was a delicious treat. Near the tall water tank there was a large root house where potatoes, turnips and carrots were stored for winter use.

In the early days Hungo cared for the delivery horses in the big barn. A few dairy cows were kept for the milk, cream and butter required for the hotel. About fifty chickens supplied the store with eggs. There were always five or six porkers being fattened up for the butcher's block. Beef cattle were allowed to run wild back of Union Bay or over at Henry Bay. They were brought by boat or walked down to the slaughter house beside the road and track.

The two dairy farms were operated by women. Even before Andrew McKay died in 1915, his wife Ellen took on most of the responsibility for running the farm. Her husband first worked for the Union Coal Co. and later had a livery business.

Campbell River Museum, Yeatman Collection

Hungo, the Chinese gardener, taking in some produce. The Fraser & Bishop gardens stretched from the school yard to McLeod Road

D. Bennie

Below the E&N track stood the long root house where produce was stored. The water tower supplied water to Fraser & Bishop's store and hotel

"When I think how hard Mother worked! She used to say, 'Work never killed anybody.' I guess it didn't because she just thrived on it, and lived to be ninety-nine."

Mary (McKay) Winterburn

Emerson Muschamp did not see himself as a farmer, as he held the job of road foreman for the district. Management of the dairy was left to his wife Alice.

"My mother worked like a man. My father never milked a cow in his life. He used to come up to the barn and carry the milk down to the house. He wouldn't sit down to milk a cow! Mind you, he used to garden and plow and work in the field. But when it came to cows, he had nothing to do with them."

Annie (Muschamp) Nelson

Ellen McCartney came from a seafaring family in which all but one of her brothers were captains. She left Ireland for San Francisco in 1889. There she met Andrew McKay, a fellow Irishman, who was a mate on the sailing ship *Two Brothers*. This collier transported coal between Tacoma and 'Frisco. The couple were married and their first child, Elizabeth, was born in 1890. They moved to Victoria, then to Nanaimo, where Mary was born. In 1894, along with Ellen's brother, Captain Andrew McCartney, and his wife, they moved to Union Bay. They were the first families to live in the village and Greta McCartney was the first white child born there.

When they arrived they lived in the big boarding house. Then they built a small house and barn on company property three lots north of where the post office is now.

"Our house on the main street was small, with lots of little rooms. The walls were papered with newspaper. We had horses and cows. After we moved, the Cook's moved the barn down and made it into a house. It's still there. The McCartney's lived just south of where the school is. They had an old-type Irish house with the animals living in one end. I think they left before the turn of the century."

Mary (McKay) Winterburn

The McKays bought land at the south end of town and in 1907 built a big home and barn. They set to work clearing the land.

"It was 160 acres. Most quarter sections were half a mile by half a mile but ours was a quarter mile of waterfront and one mile back. We had eight acres cleared and grew hay. We had eight horses and lots of Jersey cows."

Jim McKay

"I was the first McKay to be born on the farm. Eight kids before me and two after. It was a beautiful ranch house with a lovely view. The verandah went right around the house, from the back door to the front. In the big front room there was a grate with a huge stove under it. There was a big wood stove in the kitchen and pantry off it. All the rooms had high ceilings, good for drying clothes. Upstairs were five bedrooms and two downstairs."

Annie (McKay) Aitken

Andrew McKay died in 1915, just after his son Bill was born. Mrs. McKay had the children well-organized. Everyone worked. The oldest son, Bob, took over the livery business, transporting and ploughing all over the district. The boys cleared land, picked rocks, baled hay, and cleaned the barn. The girls tended the chickens, gathered the cows, milked, raked hay and helped with the housework.

"Mother wouldn't let the boys milk because she thought they'd make the milk dirty with their hands. The girls did the most work. We had to work in the barn and in the house too."

Nellie (McKay) King

D. Aitken

Ellen McKay at the dairy door. She often said "Work never killed anybody" and lived for 99 years

E. Richardson

The McKay family in front of their big ranch house overlooking Baynes Sound. c.1913. Left to right: Louis Magnone, Bob McKay, Frances McKay, Agnes McKay holding Alma Magnone, Bess Magnone, Beth Magnone, Mrs. Higgins with daughter Kate, Ellen Magnone, Mrs. McKay, Cassie McKay, Jim McKay

"We milked the cows morning and night in the barn, and cooled the milk in the milk house. We delivered milk twice a day to keep it fresh. Rain or shine, as far as the Company Hill before school. We carried a two gallon can in each hand. It had a lid and handle. They were heavy! We also carried a pint dipper in a flour sack to keep it clean. If you wanted a pint we filled our dipper from the can and dumped it into your jug. Ten cents a quart. Straight from the Jersey cow, cream and all. Then, when we got modern, we used bottles with cardboard lids.

Mary (McKay) Winterburn

It was a difficult life but the family shared the hardships and the joys. They even managed to help family and neighbours. Some years were more difficult than others.

"When my dad died we were living in Vancouver, so Mother brought us over to Union Bay and Grandma McKay (my dad's sister, but he spelled his name Macartney) took all five of us in. Then we moved to a house at the very top of McLeod Road."

Margaret (Macartney) Shillito

"In 1915 the snow was 8' deep. We shovelled a path to the barn and from the barn to the watering trough for the cows. We had a big sleigh and delivered the milk with it. We helped out hauling coal and took groceries to people. The store had a horse and wagon but no sleigh so couldn't get around. It was hard, people never shovelled their paths out. I've waded through snow up to my waist."

Nellie (McKay) King

"Our barn burned a year or two after we built it. It was in the fall. We had all the hay in, and about two tons of spuds. I was cutting hay on the old Garvin place but the machine broke down and I couldn't finish the job. So the guy burned our barn. He was drunk, and it was about eleven o'clock when I saw one of the fires start. I got all the horses and cows out. But one calf and all the chickens burned. We lost the buggies and all the harnesses. We had to buy hay. A

terrible hardship for us, but we built it again. The guy pulled out the next day. If I'd caught him that night I'd have put him in the fire."

Bob McKay

In 1938 Ellen McKay leased the farm to Fred Vowels who had farmed in the North Thompson area. Together with his wife, Mame (Peters), they continued selling pure fresh Jersey milk to the little settlement. Mrs. McKay moved into the front of the house and the Vowels had the rest of the big home.

"Fred modernized the dairy with an electric milking machine and cream separator. The cows roamed all over the town and kept the edges trimmed. The two Dickson boys (Foggy and Dopey) rounded up the cows for us after school and brought them home along the highway."

Mame Vowels

In 1943 Art Chafer bought the farm from Mrs. McKay, and the stock and equipment from Mr. Vowels who left the farm to work in the colliery mill. Mr. Chafer milked between thirty-five and forty cows and was the milkman for fifteen years. In the summer of 1958 he engaged an auctioneer, Mr. Ennals (Charles Ennals' father), from Saanich and the herd was auctioned off. The Chafers lived on the farm for eleven more years.

Bob Rawlins, who had taken over the Walker farm at Fanny Bay, increased his herd and included Union Bay on his route, thus saving the people at the Bay from drinking pasteurized milk for a few more years.

Emerson Muschamp, trained as a draper in England, applied for a job in Canada and was accepted by the David Spencer store in Vancouver. However, when he landed in Montreal

D. Aitken

Ellen McKay poses with her large family. Back left to right: W. Cairnes holding Roy, Mary Cairnes, Nellie, Jim, Frances, Agnes, Bess and Louis Magnone holding Alma. Front left to right: Tom, Annie, Mrs. McKay holding Bill, Cassie, Ellen and Beth Magnone. (Bob was absent)

M. Shillito

All dressed for haying, the McKay girls and friend model their overalls. Left to right: Agnes, Frances, Mary, Nellie Haggart, Annie, Nellie

D. Bennie

Jim and Bill McKay set to rake the hay

D. McKay

Jim McKay supervises his sisters haying. The girls worked in the fields as well as the dairy and house

in the 1880's he befriended some CPR surveyors and took a job with them, working his way across Canada. Eventually he got to Comox and worked there for J.B. Holmes. In 1887 he preempted 160 acres at Langley Point but did not develop it.

Alice Currans had come from her home on Thetis Island to work in the hotel at Comox and there met Emerson. They were married and soon had a little girl, Elizabeth. Mr. Muschamp clerked for several years in Courtenay at McPhee and Moore's store. Then he acquired a position with George Howe, and the family moved to Baynes Sound where they bought a 160 acre homestead from C. Keeley. Soon after, George, Herbert and Annie were born. Mrs. Muschamp came from a farming background so she was happy to return to the land.

"Our land was half a mile along the water and half a mile back. Our old house stood near the north boundry. I was born in it. I was the "boy" in the family after George died and Herb married. We delivered milk right up to Japtown. Now they talk about bears. I used to get up about five o'clock and go way up a mile or so into the bush and fetch the cows and never thought of bears and never saw one. We'd milk about eighteen to twenty cows, all by hand, morning and night. We'd keep the milk overnight in the milk house. My uncle, Mr. Ede, built it especially for storing things like apples and cooling the milk. It was a big log house built with big cedar slabs and cemented. We used to have a well down across the road. We had big tubs and we'd carry water up and sit the milk cans in them to cool it off right after we milked."

Annie (Muschamp) Nelson

Mr. Muschamp cleared a large area and planted grain for the cows. His wife took charge of the dairy. When war broke out, Emerson joined the fighting men. Alice, with the help of son Herb and little Annie, was able to carry on with the business. The beautiful farm on sloping land overlooking the water was a perfect destination for a Sunday walk. Many young ladies walked down and enjoyed tea with Mrs. Muschamp.

At war's end Emerson procured the job as road foreman for the district and Mrs. Muschamp continued running the farm. Herbert, who worked for his father on the road crew, married Matilda Walker. They built a house on the south end of the property where they raised a family of five children. Lizzie married Bob McKay, and they built a house next to Herb and had five children.

The dairy supplied milk to Dollar Logging Camp whose railway went through their farm. Later, when the company moved to Deep Bay, Annie drove the car and delivered milk to the cook house. There she met her husband, Nordale Nelson, who worked on the boom. The couple lived for several years with Annie's family, and she continued to help her mother with the dairy chores. When milk sales were down they acquired a separator, and sold thick Jersey cream to the Creamery at Courtenay.

Eventually Mrs. Muschamp turned her herd over to Mrs. McKay. When Alice Muschamp died, Elizabeth and Bob McKay moved to the Muschamp homestead, and Lizzie carried on her mother's

J. Ennals

The dairy cows roamed free all over town keeping the grass mowed and the edges trimmed. Const. Ennals trains his dog, oblivious to the cows walking by on the highway

M. Kine

Mr. and Mrs. E. Muschamp beside their newly built home

I. Hood

Right: Emerson in his army uniform and Alice Muschamp with daughters Annie (standing) and Liz (holding son George) and son-in-law Bob McKay

M. Kine

At the Muschamp farm Ellen McKay gets a ride from Emerson Muschamp on the tractor

Art Chafer

Mr. and Mrs. A. Chafer in front of their new 1946 Fargo truck which was used for milk deliveries

M. Coe

Herb Muschamp cutting firewood with a Wee McGregor

traditions of entertaining all passers-by. Mr. Muschamp died many years after his wife and the property was divided into three. Herb retained the southern third, Elizabeth the northern end, and Annie got the middle piece of land.

GARDENS

As soon as the early settlers had built a house, they cleared land for a garden. Most of the private homes had at least a quarter of an acre so there was lots of room for a big garden, and usually an orchard. Often an area to be used for a garden was fenced off, and pigs put in the enclosure. They stripped off all the weeds and rooted out most of the stumps. Chickens served much the same purpose. Most families had enough boys to dig the ground each spring. If not, a Chinese worker was hired to turn the soil, or Bob McKay and his team were hired to plough large fields.

The vegetables grown were much the same as today. In the 1920's, Cos lettuce, a butter lettuce said to have originated on the Greek Island of Kos, was introduced into Union Bay. The seed was given to Alexander Auchinvole by an Australian captain. Mr. Auchinvole's Chinese gardener planted the seeds and the crunchy lettuce became popular. A few gardeners have faithfully saved the seed from year to year, and it is much prized today.

Seeds could be ordered from mail-order houses or bought from the Creamery and Buckerfields in Courtenay. Potatoes were an easily grown staple. In lean years the housewife simply peeled the potatoes a little thicker around the "eye" and the peelings were planted for next year's crop.

Commercial fertilizers did not exist, but the soil was built up in many ways. Wood ash containing nitrogen and potash was sprinkled over the garden. Kitchen peelings and bones were dug in. Leaf mold from the forest and seaweed from the beach were collected and used. Manure from the chicken house also made excellent fertilizer. Cow, horse, and chicken manure could be bought from the farmers, but as the cows roamed freely all over town, cow plops were free for the gathering. This job was usually delegated to the children.

"We used to be in competition collecting cow plops with Bruce Auchinvole. He hated picking up the fresh plops, so to beat us to the biggest one he stuck notes on the top, 'Property of Bruce Auchinvole'."

Jacqueline (Glover) Gordon

Peas, beans, corn and tomatoes were eaten fresh and the excess canned for winter. Potatoes, turnips, carrots, beets and onions were grown in abundance because they could be stored with little

D. McKay

Tom McKay helps his mother in the vegetable garden behind the ranch house

D. Bennie

Dressed in their overalls the girls are ready for gardening, picking rocks or stacking wood. Back left to right: Nellie Haggart, Tilda Walker, Rachel Haggart, Sarah Walker. Front left to right: Ina Walker, Kathleen and Elsie Haggart

effort and used until spring. A pit was dug and lined with leaves. The vegetables were piled in and covered with more leaves and soil. Proper root houses were built into the ground with heavy logs cemented together. This made the food more accessible. Homes did not have basements, but the foundations formed a cellar which was always cold. Bins for the vegetables and plank shelves for the fruit were enclosed in wire mesh cages to keep out animals but allow for air circulation.

Orchards with thirty or more trees were planted. Many varieties of apples were popular: Gravenstein, Yellow Transparent, Golden Russet, King, Baldwin, Rhode Island Greening. Several pear and plum trees were usually planted.

Although vegetables took up the most space in gardens, a few

D. Walker

Mr. and Mrs. Drew's garden and home was titled "Rose Cottage". Three lots south of the Wilson Hotel, it was a show place for many years

gardeners cultivated flowers. Some made show places of their property, with laurel and box hedges outlining their gardens. After the turn of the century, Drew's garden, about four lots south of the Wilson Hotel, was the showplace of the community.

1912 AUGUST ➾ Cleda Iola Drew was married to John Droskie. The wedding took place at "Rose Cottage" in the beautiful garden of the bride's parents. [4]

The official residence for the head man at the Colleries was surrounded with beautiful grounds. Running through the property was a creek which was bridged in several places. A tennis court was set at the back. The Chinese gardeners saw that each season brought forth a profusion of flowers. It was the setting for many garden parties and flower shows.

1934 AUGUST ➾ The Dalhia Show for the district was again held at the home of Mr. A. Auchinvole of Union Bay. It was hosted by Mrs. Auchinvole and Mrs. Horne of the Horticultural Society. [6]

Union Bay School Collection

The residence of Alexander Auchinvole, Supt. of CC(D)L, featured a creek, bridges, fountains and a tennis court. It was the setting for many garden parties

W. Naylor

Herbert and Anne Glover pose in their lovely garden with grandchildren Herbert Glover III, Herbert and Peggy Lund

W. McMurtie

On a dry hillside overlooking Baynes Sound Harry Glover cultivated a beautiful garden which three times won the annual prize for best garden in the district

D. Geidt

At the Nelson Hotel, Miss Fraser, with the help of gardener Jackie Whitfield, kept the grounds beautiful. Across the road near the beach was a fenced area with a lawn and flowers for the enjoyment of all. Both Mr. Glovers were avid gardeners with beautiful showings of flowers and vegetables.

1934 JUNE ⊷ Mr. Frank Pigott has taken a picture of a Lillium Regale blooming in Mr. Herbert Glover's garden. There are no less than 100 blooms on it. In the same garden there is a lily with two heads. [6]

"Dad always wore a flower in his lapel to church. A rose or a flower from a potato plant, it didn't matter. He just loved flowers. One day he had a bouquet in his lapel and a lady asked him, 'What kind of a flower is that, Mr. Glover?' 'Oh, that's a "growbesidem". They're found beside the road.'"

Violet (Glover) Rutherford.

Every summer the company sponsored a big picnic with many sporting competitions. In the 1920's it introduced a garden contest, to encourage beauty and utility. A perfect balance of ornamental flowers and shrubs, as well as a bountiful vegetable garden, were what the judges looked for. Union Bay always gave a good showing, with gardeners like George Davis, Andy Kay, Ed Navey, Harry and Herbert Glover entering the contests. For three years Harry Glover won for the best garden in the district, one year with ninety-seven points.

1922 JULY ⊷ Mr. Glover, who I understand is over sixty, well deserves to win. His garden is on a very dry hillside without watering facilities. This garden shows what constant hoeing and cultivation will do. It proves that the "hoe" is mightier than the "watering can". His rose garden is beautiful and he has tree fruits, small fruits, and the proper amount of everything. Indeed, this is a well-balanced garden made under difficulties. [6]

Much later, in the 1950's Harry Glover Jr. followed in his father and uncle's footsteps and cultivated a big garden beside the beach. His spring garden is particularly beautiful with a lovely show of rhododendrons, many of which he purchased from his friend, Ted Greig, of Royston.

Since the houses on the Company Hill were rented, few had vegetable gardens. The only flowers might be a climbing rose or honeysuckle planted by an earlier renter. George Cooper's lovely garden was an exception during the 1930's and '40s. As he lived in the end house, he was able to extend the yard for his ever expanding hobby. Mr. Cooper even made a green house and was able to start seedlings to get a jump on the season.

Most women helped in the garden, and some, like Lil Shillito, found time from raising eight children to cultivate beautiful gardens. Charles and Lil moved to Union Bay in the 1930's and bought the bungalow that Mr. Nakamura had built on Washer Creek Hill. The couple screened all the soil in which Mrs. Shillito not only had vegetables but a beautiful display of flowers. A honeysuckle

The beautiful spring garden of Harry and Winnie Glover surrounds their granddaughter Jocelyn Geidt

covered the porch, and rock gardens were planted around the stumps. Some years Lil planted as many as 400 gladiolus bulbs. She was very generous with her flowers and gave them freely for weddings, teas and funerals. Another lady ever ready to share her garden was Phemie Wynne. She and her husband, who were successful market gardeners in Chemainus, moved to Union Bay in the '40s. At their home on Station Road Phemie managed a lovely garden even after husband Jim died. She kept flowers on the altar at church, from the first snowdrops of spring to Christmas roses in December.

M. Cooper

George Cooper with a prize Christmas cactus. Mr. Cooper always had a beautiful garden which he kept supplied from his green house

HONEY

The settlers at the Bay truly lived in paradise with many food items there for the taking. The ocean provided cod, salmon and herring - the beach provided oysters, clams and crabs - the forest provided salmonberries, thimbleberries, blackberries, blackcaps and strawberries. Honey could also be obtained with some patience, equipment and know-how.

Wild honey bees made their hives in hollow logs or standing snags. They were often located in the woods by loggers, hunters or berry pickers. The location was kept secret until a honey collecting party was arranged in the fall when the bees had a good store of honey to provide them with nutrition for the winter. Sometimes the honey collector would arrive only to find that "bruin" had beat him to the honey and left the tree or log torn apart and the honey all eaten.

E. Hallstrom

Always dressed in overalls Lil Shillito created a beautiful garden on Washer Creek Hill. Some years as many as 400 gladiolus were planted. Seated in the garden are her children Esther holding Helen, Eddie, and Rubina holding Bobby

Often a bee tree had to be purposely found. This was done on a quiet sunny day by careful observation and patience. A honey bee was taken off a fireweed flower and put into a little glass-topped wooden box into which were mixed a few drops of anise oil and sweet syrup. It could be observed feeding, and in a minute or two would be released. The bee would make a couple of wide circles around the box and fly off in the direction of its hive. The open box was set on a stump and soon the bee was back with one or two

Union Bay Public Library

Cutting down a bee tree. Curious bystanders outnumber the honey-seekers who have not yet donned protective clothing

other worker bees. They would collect some of the sweet syrup and repeat the process, bringing back more workers. Then the box would be closed with a few bees inside and the honey-seeker would walk a few hundred feet in the direction the bees were flying, open the box and repeat the process, getting closer and closer until the bee tree was located.

He would return a few days later with family or friends to help harvest the honey. Everyone coming within a radius of 25' had to wear protective clothing. Pant legs were tightly tied around heavy boots, and gloves pulled up and tied around shirt sleeves. To protect the head and face, netting was sewn around fedora hats and tucked tightly under the collar.

If the hive was in a standing snag it had to be felled, or the log chopped or sawed open. But first the bees were tranquillized with smoke. A wad of sacking was put into the smoker and the smoke forced into the hive with bellows on the smoker. This done, the bees were much subdued and the honey could be collected easier. When the honey comb was exposed it was cut into large pieces and put into buckets and wash tubs to be taken home. The honey was eaten in the comb or was strained out and bottled. As much as 100 lbs. could be gathered from one hive.

Some of the settlers kept their own hives, sometimes obtaining their queen and colony from bee trees they had raided. Alex McLeod had an apiary and often took the hives into the slash where fireweed was plentiful. His nephew, Wes Peters, took over the business and for years supplied the town with honey. It was used in baking and eaten on bread, toast, muffins, crackers and pilot bread.

"Mother liked pilot bread. It was a round thick biscuit with holes in it and was quite snappy when you bit into it, crunch, crunch. We used to butter it, put honey or sugar on it and pour hot tea and thick cream on it. It would be soft and we'd eat it with a spoon.

Nellie (McKay) King

WOMEN

1897 NOVEMBER ➾ There are a dearth of young ladies here at Union Bay, but those we have are very nice. [4]

Although few at first, the women of Union Bay played a very big role in the growing community. They made the houses into homes, fed and clothed the family, worked in the garden, and volunteered in the community. In addition to this, two ladies, Alice Muschamp and Ellen McKay, also operated the only dairies in town.

H. Glover

Some Glover cousins on a visit to Grandmother Russell in Ladysmith. Back: Jane Russell, Jack Glover, Eugene Glover. Middle: Lina, Bill, Anne and Ray Glover, Grandmother Russell. Front: Harry, Wilf and Margaret Glover

Most of the original settlers had large families - 15 Laird children, 13 Manson children, 12 Davis children, 11 McKay children, 10 Brown children, 9 Herb Glover children, 8 Cook children, 7 Walker and 7 Hooper children.

"Mother and Aunt Annie took ten of us cousins down to Ladysmith to visit Grandma Russell. We were walking along the street and Lina said to the little ones, 'Some of you kids walk on the other side of the street, we don't want people to think you all belong to us'.

Violet (Glover) Rutherford

Seated beneath a parasol is Annie Laird dressed in a chic Gibson girl blouse. Soon after this photograph was taken she died of T.B.

M. Ellingsen

In the early days most of the young girls, as they left school, spent a few years as a mother's help, worked as chambermaid in one of the hotels, or clerked in a store or post office before settling down into married life. There were exceptions as some of the girls left home and took further training. Following are some of the young ladies who pioneered in post secondary education. Phyllis Partridge went off to UBC in 1918 and became a teacher, as did Mary Little in the '30s. Pauline Horne graduated from UBC in 1942 and Eileen Watt passed the pharmaceutical exams in 1945 to become a druggist.

In 1919 Lina Glover became the first nurse when she graduated from Ladysmith and Vancouver General Hospitals. Margaret followed her sister into the same profession and graduated from Victoria Jubilee Hospital. Elsie Haggart took her training at Nanaimo General Hospital and graduated in '26. Also graduating from the Jubilee were Nettie Marshall in 1929, Margaret Dunn and Mary Reid in the '30s and Betty Watt and Muriel Jones in the '40s. Muriel went on to become a pharmacist.

Over the years a number of girls attended Victoria Normal School to become teachers. Nellie Ede was the first teacher, followed by the two Jones girls - Florence in the late '20s and Irene in the '30s. In the '40s Verna Campbell, Gertrude Harwood, Winanne Glover and Lorraine Watt became teachers, and in the '50s Jacqueline and Janette Glover went to Normal School.

A few of the girls took secretary training at Sprott Shaw Business school in Nanaimo or Victoria. Dorothy Renwick was probably first, followed by Greta Kay, Jessie Marshall and Rita Treloar. Winnie Glover spent two years in Vancouver apprenticing to be a dressmaker.

Women in little towns all over Canada read about the struggle for the franchise and women's rights in general. The suffragette movement became stronger after the turn of the century.

1912 ➾ On Women's Franchise. A woman had a labourious life and had lost her romantic notion. When asked if she wanted to vote said, "No, certainly not, I say if there is one thing the men folks can do alone for goodness sakes let them do it." [4]

When the vote came in 1916 the women in Union Bay had convinced enough men that they deserved the right to vote, and the referendum passed there and in the whole country. In 1921 a few women even travelled to Cumberland to hear Mrs. Pankhurst talk on social diseases (venereal). The audience was surprised at the lady's mild manner and soft voice.

CLOTHES

Early settlers had little money and no time to worry about fashions of the day. The closest they came to getting ideas from a Vogue magazine was by reading the catalogue.

Houses were not very warm and usually draughty, so during winter, inside or out, one had to be dressed warmly. This started with wool knitted underwear (faced with satin if you were lucky). Men and children wore longjohns. Women wore high knit stockings

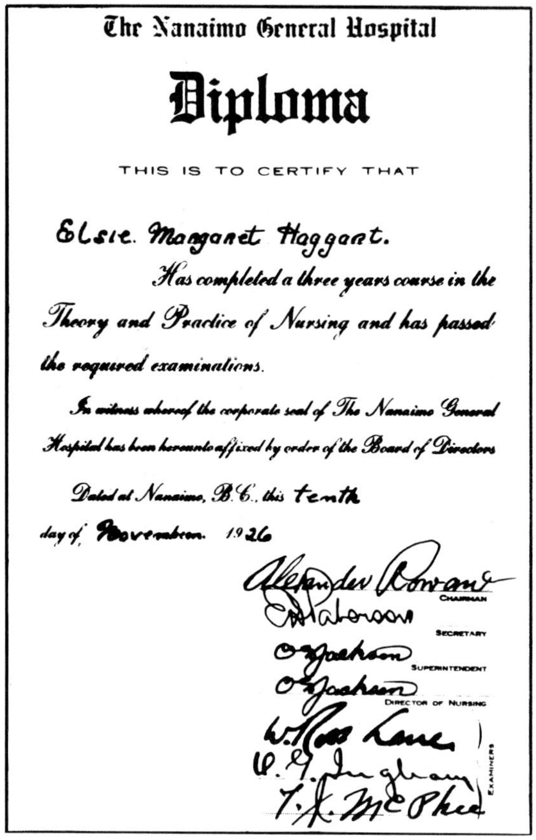

The Nanaimo General Hospital

Diploma

THIS IS TO CERTIFY THAT

Elsie Margaret Haggart.

Has completed a three years course in the Theory and Practice of Nursing and has passed the required examinations.

In witness whereof the corporate seal of The Nanaimo General Hospital has been hereunto affixed by order of the Board of Directors

Dated at Nanaimo, B.C. this tenth day of November. 1926

Chairman

Secretary

Superintendent

Director of Nursing

Examiners

W. & H. Glover

Margaret Glover

H. Glover

Lina Glover

W. Glover

Nettie Marshall

B. Veale

Elsie Haggart

C. Benson

Always setting the fashion trend at Union Bay was Bebe Muir, the town telephone operator, shown here with her mother Mrs. Hooper

W. Glover

Emily Bowden and Muriel Jones model fashions from the '30s

held up by garters attached to their corsets. Little girls held their stockings up with suspenders that hung from their shoulders.

Ladies were laced into corsets which were worn by the older women until the 1950's. They held everything in from below the bust to the hip. Later, girdles were used as tummy flatteners, and garter belts were used by thinner girls who just needed to hold up the long hose. Hosiery for everyday use was knit of cotton or wool. Silk stockings at $1.00 a pair were considered very chic and became popular as the skirts got shorter. They were very delicate, and caught and ran easily.

1927 JANUARY ⊷ According to Dorothy Gish the modern girl doesn't wear silk stockings for herself alone. The predominence of silk hosiery in feminine limbs is due entirely to the gentle sex's desire to make life easier for their male admirers. Silk seems much easier on the eyes - else why would the "sheiks" devote so many optical hours on them. [5]

All yardgoods were made of natural fibres - cotton, wool, flax. The first man-made thread was rayon, made from the cellulose in wood. It became popular in the 1930's. Silk from the Orient became scarce in the late '30s due to the war. Then the process for making the fabulous new material, nylon, was introduced.

1941 APRIL ⊷ New nylon yarn has a variety of uses. Knit goods, woven dress materials, lace and silk will all benefit from the hard-wearing, quick-drying qualities of nylon. A highly specialized possibility for nylon is making of parachutes which up till now have been made of silk from the Orient. From the filaments will be made a good bristle for brushes, fishing leader, tennis racquet strings, surgical surtures and musical instrument strings. [7]

Now crepe, satin, net and chiffon were made of nylon, as well as the nylon stocking for women. Made with a seam up the back, they fitted the leg well but it was still difficult to keep the seams straight.

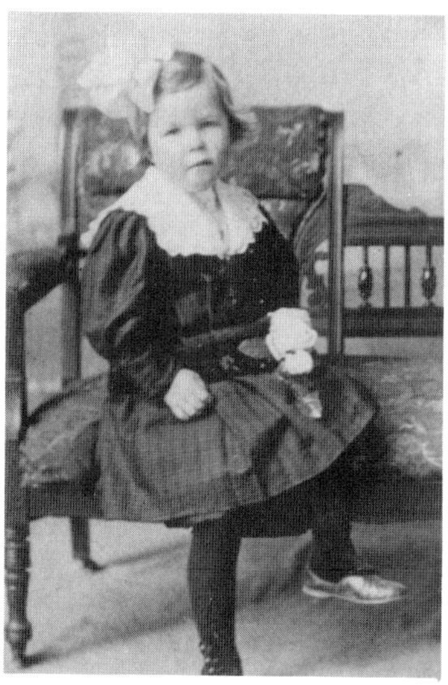

N. Jones

Little Nettie Marshall in her very best dress, puffy bow in her hair and borrowed gold locket is ready for the photographer

J. Anderson

Little boys like Jack Anderson, Les and Jack Coe wore shirts with knickerbockers, jeans or short pants

Cumberland Museum

Little sisters Nellie and Frances McKay with pinnies over their dresses and wearing lace boots. Brother Jim has on a warm woolen sweater and jeans

M. Vowels

A flapper, Mame Peters, ready to go for a spin with George and Bill Walker

Women wore long dresses, or skirts and blouses, usually of dark colours. For everyday wear the fabric was cotton or woolen. For special occasions most ladies had a dress of silk or linen, with lace trim and puffy sleeves.

"Mother wore dresses right down to her ankles. Not easy to get around in or keep clean on the muddy streets. I remember a very light linen suit she had. Can you imagine having to wash and iron it?"

Margaret (Glover) Matthews

Either for working on the farm or in the machine shop, men wore flannel shirts and denim overalls. They had one woolen tweed "Sunday go-to-meeting suit" for church, weddings, funerals, and picnics. The younger fellows had ice cream pants and shirts for dress-up in the summer.

Boys wore flannel shirts and sweaters with overalls or jeans for play and work, but to school they wore serge knickerbockers with wool knee stockings, held up by rubber bands. Mother was kept busy knitting and mending knee socks.

"We wore knickers. They were quite full, and tight below the knee. The kids called them "shit stoppers".

Jack Anderson

Little girls wore plain, dark coloured dresses to school, with sometimes a pinny to brighten them up and keep them clean. For dress-up they got frills, ruffles and bows.

"My Mom made our clothes. People would give us clothes and Mother would make them down. No dressmakers then, you made your own or sent to the catalogue. The first catalogue dress you got, you thought you were in heaven. It might have been $1.75 and you could pick it out."

Nellie King

Women and girls were never "really dressed" unless they wore hats, which had large brims and were trimmed with ribbons and flowers. They were made of felt and velvet in dark colours for winter, and straw for summer. Later, during the 1920's, smaller hats featuring veils were in vogue. Men too wore hats - felt bowlers and fedoras - all year, with straw panamas and boaters in summer. Boys wore rather floppy caps.

Everyone carried two handkerchiefs: one for show and one for blow. When the family had a cold, mother had a stack of white rags that were used. Afterwards they were boiled, washed and ironed. Men used red bandanna-type for work, and white linen for good. Women had hankies beautifully trimmed with embroidery and lace.

Men's fashions changed little over the years, but women, if they could afford it, tried to keep up with the the times.

1922 JULY "Fashion Hint": There will be little "change" in men's pockets this year. [5]

In the 1920's the flapper's dresses became plainer, chests flatter and hems shorter. The young girls dressed accordingly, but the older women kept their hems below the calf.

Mary Up To Date.
Mary had a little lamb,
That day has passed away.
No lamb could follow at the pace
That Mary sets today.

Now Mary sits at motor wheel
With skirts too short by half,
No lambkin stays her airy flight
But you can see her calf. [5]

Skirt hems again dipped to cover the knee in the 1930's and '40s. During the Second World War the War-Times Prices and Trade Board forbade the manufacture or sale of long dresses, except for brides and religious orders.

TOYS & GAMES

Children of yesteryear used their imaginations to amuse themselves. Big, burned-out stumps, or sacks tacked up around trees made wonderful playhouses. In them little girls made mud pies decorated with flowers and berries. Soapflakes were whipped up and coloured with berries to ice a pretend cake. Perfume was made from rose petals. Driftwood on the beach was transformed into trains, boats and playhouses. Many of the early toys were homemade by mother or father - sock dolls, knit balls, wooden wagons and sleighs.

"My sister, Lina, used to make dolls out of kelp for

W. Glover

Emily Bowden showing off her precious Kewpie doll

A. Watson

Gordon Horne and friend allowing a girl to ride in their beautiful wagon with spoke wheels

W. Glover

Wicker perambulators like the one Winanne Glover has were popular for both babies and dolls

me. She'd snip the trailing part for hair. Then cut eyes and a mouth in the ball part. I loved to play with them."

Margaret Glover

A great many of the bought toys, particularly china dolls and wind-up toys, came from Germany. During and after the First World War this supply ceased, and what were available became more expensive, until American and Canadian manufacturers started producing them. Every year a new "Eaton's Beauty" was featured in the catalogue, and much prized by the lucky girl that received one. Japanese imports became popular, especially the Kewpie doll.

B. Sherburn

Bob Sherburn riding on the covered wagon he and brother Buster built

1929 Toy Price List

5¢	10¢	15¢	20¢	25¢
Pencil box	Sparklers	Telesope	Blocks	Bells
Kewpies	TinHorns	Music Grinder	Kewpie	Music box
Hanky	Kewpie	Concertina	Pencil box	
	Balls	Machine toys	Monkeys	
		Kewpies	Cars	

Young people made their own fun. Games requiring no equipment such as "kick-the-can", "British bulldog", and "may I" were played by groups of neighbourhood kids. Two or three children together played "one potato, two potato", "mumblety-peg", marbles and hop-scotch.

"We used to play out on the main road. We didn't have to worry about cars because there were none. We'd play "run sheep run" every night until dark, when mother would call us in."

Mary (McKay) Winterburn

"The only cement in town was in front of the post office. It was great for bouncing balls and the only place to roller skate. We just about drove Edythe Hicks crazy with the noise."

Muriel (Harwood) Peters

Most families had pets: cats, dogs, horses, rabbits, and even parrots. Mrs. Campbell, who lived up Washer Creek Hill, had a parrot, Polly, which had quite a collection of phrases and swear words: "Bad boy", "Scratch a wee heady", "Polly want a cracker".

M. Aitken

Marjorie and Jack Moore enjoying the dog's bath more than the dog

W. Glover

Penny Adamson learning to ride a horse

She constantly called "Mildred, Mildred", in imitation of Mrs. Bowden who lived next door. When she saw Mr. Campbell coming home Polly started to chant, "Here comes Bob, Here comes Bob". During the war Mrs. Campbell left the parrot with Ruby Treloar and went back to England. The boat she was on was torpedoed, so Ruby inherited the parrot which continued to amuse everyone.

Often pets were given the surname of their master. So there was May McKay (Jim's horse), Duke Horne (Gordon's dog), and Rex Hastings (Art's dog). Rex loved people and turned up at all functions; in fact, the Ladies Aids' teas were not official unless Rex Hastings was present. The most famous cat was Joe Renwick. The Renwicks inherited Joe from Joe Damonte. He was originally named Percy but Elizabeth decided one Percy in the family was enough so named him Joe.

"Joe was quite a tomcat. Every night he was on the prowl and he kept our female cat in kittens. In fact, most of the cats in Union Bay looked like Joe. Kathleen and Cecil Stubbs were coming home late one night and saw Joe walking along the roof of the Nelson Hotel. Next day she told Elizabeth about it, who said 'Joe was just visiting some call girl cats up from Vancouver'."

Mamie Vowels

W. Richardson

Three sisters and their dollies. Wilma, Diane and Marilyn Richardson

D. Aitken

"Cowboy" Jimmy Aitken riding John Rosengren's horse "Star"

A. Graham

All sorts of treasures can be found on the beach to make and furnish a playhouse

ETHNIC

CHINESE AND CHINATOWN

Almost all of the Chinese that came to Canada were from the districts around Canton in the province of Kwangtung. These migrants were from large peasant family units that lived communally, and made up the small rice farming villages on the delta of the Pearl River. There was a large supply of labour but small supply of land, as this area was very heavily populated. The family farms needed capital to increase productivity of the land through irrigation and fertilization, so the young males emigrated and sent their savings home. When a married man went far afield to earn money for the whole village, he knew that his wife and children would be taken care of by the extended family. These hard working men, bound to the support of the family back home, became loyal, reliable employees.

Many of the original Chinese workers in the coal mines on Vancouver Island started life in Canada building the B.C. section of the CPR. To break a strike at his Nanaimo mines in 1884, Robert Dunsmuir brought in Chinese. Again, in 1885 he hired, directly from China, hundreds of Chinese to lay the bed for the E&N railroad from Victoria to Nanaimo. This year also saw the passing of the Dominion Chinese Restriction Act or "head tax". It began as a $50 levy to be paid by each Chinese immigrant as he entered the country. Soon it was raised to $100, and in 1903 to $500. As the average Chinese immigrant was poor, the hiring company paid the tax and deducted money from the worker's wages.

Chinese miners were blamed for the mine explosions in Nanaimo, where many men were killed. The other coal companies, except Dunsmuir, voluntarily excluded the Chinese miners in response to the white miners' wishes. When thirty-one whites and thirty-seven Chinese were killed in his mine in January 1888, he was forced to exclude them. Many of them still owed the "boss" for their head tax and transportation from China. Exactly one month later the Dunsmuir Company announced the opening of the Union Mines. By April, 200 Chinese were clearing the right-of-way for the railway from Union Wharf to the mine. So there were Chinese living at Union Bay from the very beginning of the shipping port's history.

Very different from the British Columbians of European background, the Chinese immigrants encountered many problems. People feared the unknown, and a racial prejudice grew against these men who were different in appearance, dress, language, customs, manners and eating habits. (Many of the men still wore their hair in a queue in the 1920's)

1891 ➾ "For Luck." At Nanaimo a lot of boys were amusing themselves by throwing rocks at a wretched Chinaman. When asked why they did it they replied: "It's always lucky to hit a Chinaman." This is hard on the "heathen," but proves that in the eyes of the small boy they are of some use to the world. [2]

1892- A "Mongolian" walked from Union Wharf and was found lying near the Bastion, played out. Doctor says he is suffering from summer fever and was sick during the long tramp. He was sent in an express cart to Chinatown. The Chinese at Chinatown were scared by the look of the man and refused to do anything for him. He was left alone and died. Had he been looked after by his own patriots he may have recovered. [2]

1904 ➾ Cumberland reports maltreatment of Chinese by young boys. When the Chinese are returning from work they are waylayed and molested, a daily occurrence in a civilized town. This is a sign of barbarism in our youth and wanton cruelty of taking a delight in the suffering of others, whether man or beast. [4]

The politicians echoed the general public's call for tighter immigration laws. At every sitting of parliament, members from British Columbia were demanding stricter laws to check the tide of Oriental immigrants. This resulted in the "head tax" gradually being raised to $500 in 1903. First it was the responsibility of the Customs Department to enforce, but later became the duty of the Immigration Department.

Each year, to avoid paying the "head tax," several Chinese would try to desert ship as it coaled at the dock. A few were killed as they tried to crawl along the hawser in the dead of night and fell onto the pilings below or drowned in the icy water. If the body was not recovered or if "John Chinaman made good his escape", the captain of the ship had to pay the $500 before leaving British Columbian waters. It was believed that many of the deserters found refuge in the large Chinatown at Cumberland and were never detected.

The "head tax" had only partial success as a political tool to limit the number of Chinese immigrants. The mine owners, like Mr. Dunsmuir, were willing to pay the tax and collect the payments with interest over a long period. This bound the Chinese to their employer and they were used as strike breakers.

In the beginning the Chinese outnumbered the white men and everyone was employed. They worked in jobs which Europeans were loathe to do, so the workers at the Bay did not feel threatened as the Cumberland miners did. By and large, the Chinese were very law-abiding humble people who lived within their tight-knit community. The white settlers adopted a "live-and-let-live" attitude. Some friendships developed between fellow workmen, but the Chinese "knew their place" and few were ever invited into the white man's home or socialized away from the job. The only exception to this was after the flood in 1912, when Chinatown was virtually wiped out. The white settlers welcomed the Chinese into their homes, and clothed and fed them. Although the adults treated the Chinese as inferiors, the children were taught to be courteous to the hard-working men. Some of the older boys played pranks on the Chinese but there was never anything malicious reported. The Chinese seemed to enjoy the young people and turned out to all the ball games to cheer on the local team.

The first trimmers were native Indians who lived at the mouth of Hart Creek, on what was known as Watt's Flats. Unaccustomed to the regular work hours and the availability of alcohol, the Indians were not a reliable work force. Ships often had to lay over after a payday and wait for the trimmers. The wages were very low; the work was hard and dirty. Finally, the Indians refused to work and asked for more money. The company responded by bringing in Chinese workers, by now a familiar way of breaking a strike. They became trimmers, and a little later, rakers, pulling the coke out of the coke ovens with long heavy rakes. Both were hard, dirty, tedious jobs which the white men were happy to leave to the Chinese.

At first the Chinese lived in tiny houses at the mouth of Hart Creek on Watt's Flats, on land which had been vacated by the Indians. It was a beautiful spot with fertile soil, and they cultivated bountiful vegetable gardens.

As the coke ovens and shops were built and the tailings from the Washer were dumped on Watt's Flats, all the Chinese relocated across the highway. On the south end a road entered and wound its way through Chinatown. To the left was the big two storey boarding house. Next to this was the store, and opposite the store was another boarding house. Set further back was a large house originally occupied by the Boss Chinaman. The cookhouse faced the highway. Most of the inhabitants of Chinatown lived in the boarding houses, while twelve to fifteen men lived privately in tiny one room shacks scattered here and there. Chinatown was inhabited by about 100 Chinese men during the early 1890's, decreasing to about 25 by the 1950's. Over the years several Chinese merchants served the community: Mar Tong, Sing Kee Jan Co., Mah Tein, Mah Fat, and the Kim Bros.

For the sixty years they lived in Union Bay, the Chinese did very little except work. When there were ships to be loaded they worked around the clock. There were two twelve-hour shifts, each made up of about sixty men. The morning shift was up before the night shift returned. They breakfasted on white rice and green tea in the cook house. When the quarter to seven whistle blew, they slipped their bare feet into oversized rubbers (the kind Englishmen wear over their dress shoes), put their large steel sheets on their backs, picked up their shovels, and shuffled single file across the road and through the field down to the wharf. At 7:00 a.m. the second whistle blew, and the men climbed into the pitch black bowels of the ship to begin their twelve hour shift.

A coal car was positioned by the locie over the chute. The coal poured down the chute into a pile on the ship's floor. It was the trimmer's job to spread the coal evenly. First, it was piled close to the ship's boilers for fuel on the journey, then the cargo coal was spread around. To make the job more efficient, large steel plates were made in the machine shops and supplied to each trimmer. They were about 30" x 18", made of plate steel, and looked much like a medieval shield. A loop of rope at one end made it easier to carry the plate to and from work, as it hung from the shovel carried over one shoulder. The coal fell or was pushed onto the plate, then was shovelled into place. The plate was used as a base so that the shovel could be easily pushed into the coal. It was a very slow, backbreaking job, as some of the lumps could be 18" thick and weigh nearly 80 lb. The coal kept pouring in, making the pile deeper and the air space less. The trimmer's lamp shed very little light into the dustfilled darkness. The lamp, built in the shops, resembled a metal coffee pot and was filled with fish oil which burned from a wick in the spout. It gave off a putrid smell and was very dangerous in the combustible atmosphere. Luckily, there was never an explosion while loading the ships. The trimmers later acquired battery-powered, underground safety lamps.

After five hours of work the trimmers climbed out of the dark depths and made their way, single file, home to the cook house. There Cook, a short rotund man, announced that dinner was ready by ringing the huge metal triangle outside the door. For lunch there was more rice, possibly accompanied by wokked garden vegetables and bits of fish, pork, chicken, or venison if available. Meals were always washed down with green tea. Occasionally soup was the fare, made from free beef bones or turkey feet collected from the butcher shop at Christmas. Cook would boil the turkey feet, scrape off the scales, then meticulously pick off the tiny bits of meat.

Cook often fished to supplement the pot, as did the other men if they had time off. He would set out with a long pole across his shoulders, buckets swinging at each end. In one

Union Bay School Collection

A Chinese aviary on the wall of the boarding house in Chinatown

bucket was a fishing line wound around a board. In the other was his bait, sea worms and shrimp collected at low tide. Cook sat patiently at the end of the wharf and took anything that chanced to bite his hook: bullheads, bass, perch, and the favourite, rock cod. The Chinese were also successful at catching crabs in homemade traps. These were constructed by bending a supple branch into a circle, tying the ends, then filling the space with a crisscross of ropes. The trap was baited with fish meat, weighted with rocks and lowered onto the ocean floor. After several hours the trap had usually attracted three or four crabs.

In the black fertile land behind Chinatown, the men cultivated beautiful gardens. There was never a weed to be seen. The finely-dug soil was built up in beds where they grew enormous cabbages, pumpkins and turnips. They cultivated a thin pea (all pod) which the white man thought useless. This was the very same snow pea much prized by gourmets today. To return a favour, some white families were the lucky recipients of a huge squash or bunch of crunchy carrots. A few men with large gardens peddled their produce around town, where they found ready buyers. During the winter their diet must have been deficient, but in the summer and fall it was well supplemented with vitamins and minerals from their bountiful gardens.

Each garden had a wooden barrel sunk into the ground. This caught the rain or was filled from Washer Creek. Their watering was done with a tin can with holes punched into it, nailed to a stick. It was very efficient unless the rows were too long; then they had to dip and run quickly to the end of the row before the water ran out. When fertilizer was required, cow plops were added to the water, producing a very potent manure tea.

Everything was utilized. Seeds were saved from year to year. Fish skins, bones of all kinds and seaweed were buried in the ground to enrich the soil. Not many of the gardens were fenced, and so provided easy picking for the wild deer, wandering cattle and wayward boys. The gardens stretched from the back of Chinatown to the E&N, and included a large area on the other side of the tracks.

Honey bees were kept in hives that were hung on the outside walls of their houses. The honey was used as a sweetener in many of their dishes.

The men also raised chickens, ducks and pigs in pens beside their homes.

"The Chinamen used to bring a load of pigs over from Denman on an open scow. They'd land at Coal Beach and drive them across the ball field to Chinatown. One day we kids were playing ball and decided to help them. Well, there were pigs and Chinamen everywhere."

Art Searle

The two boarding houses were about 20'x30', with the 2"x4"s exposed within. The two storey buildings were never painted so became grey with age. The main floor was one large room, used for gambling in one house and cooking in the other. In the cookhouse a small area of the floor was bricked and lined with sheet metal. Here they built their coal fires with free coal they carried home in sacks on their backs. The cooking was done in large cast iron pots that stood on three little legs, right in the fire. There was no chimney - just a hole in the roof - which was refined later with a 12" square wooden box projecting four feet down into the room. If there was a good draft the smoke found its way to the hole. The interiors were all black; even the two windows were coated with black greasy smoke. A coal oil lamp which cast a dim flickering light hung from the ceiling. This was later replaced by a bald lightbulb to pierce the gloom. The furniture was sparse, with just a long table and benches for eating. Upstairs were many tiny cubicles with bunks one above the other. The men slept on bare boards and covered themselves with a lone blanket.

Some of the more affluent or enterprising preferred to live in their own little homes. These tiny houses were tucked in at odd angles at the back of Chinatown. They were jerrybuilt shacks about 8'x10'. Each featured a potbellied stove placed close to the wall, with a 6" chimney pipe rigged up with wires and strings. As the Chinese grew older, this became the firemen's nightmare.

Each boarding house had a full length verandah at the front. On it the men had constructed benches of wooden planks, stretched between two blocks of wood. When there was a lay off they would sit and smoke their long pipes, chatting or reading the latest Chinese newspaper. They enjoyed a little town gossip with passersby and seemed to know all the news of the village. The men were especially interested in newly married couples, and anxiously awaited the announcement of the first pregnancy.

Coming from a culture of very strong family ties, they loved the children of Union Bay. All new babies, and especially twins, were very much admired and their names noted and remembered, usually getting a Chinese pronunciation. Thus Janette and Jacqueline became Jessie and Jin. Children were often given treats of sugar, candy and peanuts.

Although the "head tax" did not have the desired effect of limiting the number of Chinese immigrants, it greatly affected the way in which they lived. It kept them separate from the rest of the community, and forever foreigners in their adopted land. Except for the wealthy merchants, few could afford to bring their wives out, so they remained bachelors and did not establish homes or adopt western ways. Their social life was very sparse, as twelve hour working days left little leisure time. In the early days they earned a wage of 10¢ to 15¢ an hour, about $45 per month. After paying room and board to the Boss Chinaman, then possibly paying on the ticket to Canada and the $500 "head tax," there was very little left to send home, much less spend on themselves.

Some diversions were provided by opium, alcohol, gambling, or a train trip to Cumberland Chinatown. A homesick man could wander down the crooked streets enjoying the sights and smells. He could shop in a variety of grocery stores well stocked with items from home, get some advice and a cure from a herbalist, and view the latest fashions in the tailor shop. Or he could enjoy an authentic meal in the Peking Chop Suey House, then attend the colourful Chinese Theatre with acts from Vancouver, Victoria or San Francisco. He could play Fan-Tan or Mah-Jong in a Joss house, or spend an hour of pleasure with a beautiful Chinese girl in a brothel.

At Union Bay the options were not so varied. The men spent many hours in the dark interior of the gambling house. With the smell of opium in the air and Chinese music playing on a phonograph in the corner, the men bent over the tables intent on their games. Occasionally, on a warm summer day when the doors were open, a young rascal would creep up to the doorway with his slingshot, and shoot out the coal oil lamp hanging from the ceiling. The poor Chinese never caught or even saw the culprit as they stumbled out of the gambling house, and were blinded by the bright sunlight.

Alcohol was another pleasure which they enjoyed, although only a few frequented the pub. They had liquor in their homes from their own supply in Chinatown. Mah Fat had a store from which he ran a profitable bootlegging business. They drank beer and White or Dark Horse rum, but preferred the Chinese drinks.

The men were given Chinese New Year's day off to celebrate in their traditional way. Stores were decorated with paper lanterns and red streamers. "Gung Hay Fat Choy," words of welcome and good cheer echoed down the alleys. The pungent smell of burning sandalwood mingled with the smell of firecrackers exploding on all sides.

"Chinese New Year was always celebrated with lots of food, chicken, Chinese pastries, lichee nuts, ginger and sugar cane. For kids it was lots of firecrackers, fruit and nuts all day. We dressed in our best clothes and didn't do any work that day. Grown-ups generally visited each other and had a drink together to celebrate the New Year. Good luck money was wrapped in red paper, and if you were offered candy or pastry you left a packet of lucky money on the plate. That just goes for grown-ups. Of course us kids were on the receiving end of all the money. So we ended up pretty rich by the end of the day."

Vera (Mah) Lun

Although forbidden by their parents, the local children, attracted by the firecrackers, scrambled from door to door shouting "Happy New Year". They received treats of barley sugar, peanuts, huge oranges and lichee nuts.

All the notables from the town were invited - the Colliery bosses, postman, storekeepers and teachers. Grace Davis had two of the June children in her class, and responded to the invitation to help them celebrate their New Year. When she arrived she was presented with a beautiful string of cultured pearls.

It was a happy holiday, a time to celebrate, forget tomorrow and hope that the new year would be better than the last. It seldom was. Several of the Chinese met untimely deaths through accidents. Others became ill, despondent, depressed and lonely. A few commited suicide by hanging or drowning themselves.

Under the wharfinger, the Chinese contractor, or Boss Chinaman as he was known, was in charge of the Chinese crews. The boss had contacts in Canton through which new men were recruited when needed. His job was to have crews ready to trim the coal in the ships whenever needed. He employed a bookkeeper who kept a statement of the men's hours, then submitted the total to the Collieries' pay master and received the cash. From this the Boss Chinaman deducted payment for debts to the Company, as well as money for room and board if the worker lived in his boarding house. The labourer received the remainder and sent some of it home. The Boss Chinaman also owned and operated one of the two stores where the men bought their supplies, everything from rubbers to rice. Items were quickly tallied up on an abacus.

One of the first labour contractors was Mah Sue Que, who arrived in 1899 from Guangzhou near Canton. At Union Wharf he was a partner in a store and had a contract to supply the company with Chinese coal trimmers. Que learned English, probably taught by Nellie Ede, a Union Bay girl. Miss Ede had taken teacher training, and conducted her classes for the Chinese in the little company house that had been used for the first school. The knowledge of English gave Mr. Mah an advantage in his position as foreman.

While Mr. Mah was on a trip to Vancouver he met a young girl named Mah Chin Shee. At the age of eleven she had been brought to Vancouver by a well-to-do family to work as a domestic. Que proposed, and in 1917 there was great excitement as preparations were made for a Chinese wedding in Union Bay. The Mahs settled into married life and lived above the store. The large three storey house was painted rose, and decorated with filigree work above the verandah. Chin Shee was always beautifully dressed in the traditional silk costumes and tiny silk slippers. Her first son was born at Union Bay. Labour contracts declined, so Mr. Mah moved to Cumberland.

The long time contractor to supply trimmers was the family of Mah Foo Ching (Charlie Mah June). Mr. June's father came to Cumberland first and then to Union Bay where he established the contract with the Collieries to supply trimmers.

In the year 1909 Charlie Mah June followed his father to Canada. With his wife, Wong Shee, he left the farming village of Pak Sha in the Kwangtung province and set sail from Canton for Union Bay. In a few years Mr. June took over as boss of the trimmers, and also acquired the large boarding houses and store.

When Mr. and Mrs. June arrived in Union Bay they took up residence above a big general store. It was a strange land for Wong Shee. She must have been very lonely until her first child, Mae, was born in 1915. Wong Shee's son, Bill, was born two years later, then Alex, Tommy and Vera over the next eight years. The children were all given Chinese names. They also received an English name which was used at school. Mah Bow Gee became Mae Mah, Mah Kam Ming became Bill Mah and so on.

Mrs. Mah June's life was very busy tending to her large family. She cooked on a coal and wood stove as the western women did, turning out mouth-watering buns and bread to delight her family. She rarely went out, except to tend her beautiful vegetable garden. Although she lived on the premises, she never worked in the store. She seldom visited Cumberland. Wong Shee was petite in her traditional Chinese costume of pants and tunic, with silk slippers on her minute feet that had been bound as a child. She lived in Canada for sixty-seven years but never learned to speak English. Mrs. Mah June lived on at the store with Vera for many years after her husband's death. They eventually moved to Courtenay.

All five of the June children attended Union Bay school and wore western clothes. They were pitied by their Canadian classmates because they had a Chinese teacher at home. He taught them the Chinese curriculum when their Canadian school day was over. The rumour was that he wielded a cane! The children were sent to Victoria for high school.

In 1934 the Provincal government approached the older Chinese living in communities on the Island. Many of these fellows would have been a burden on the government for the rest of their lives. They were asked if they would return to their homeland if transportation was provided. Fourteen men from Union Bay and Cumberland accepted the proposal, and in January 1935 sailed from Victoria for the Orient. Originally, a graveyard was established on the bank across Washer Creek. It was the custom that after seven years the remains were exhumed, and the bones polished and sent back to China. After the turn of the century most of the Chinese were buried in the cemetery at Cumberland. There were still a number of old trimmers living at Chinatown in the fifties. The last one moved to Cumberland just before the site was cleared for the Community Hall in 1961.

CHINESE CHARACTERS

Many of the Chinese became known, loved and remembered because they were different in some way to the hundred or more other men who made up the Chinese community. Not all of them were trimmers and some did not work for the Collieries. Several worked for Fraser and Bishop, and a few worked for private families.

The locals often gave them nick-names because of some physical characteristic or peculiar habit. Thus "Goo Goo" was named because he had large poppy eyes. At the time, the song "Barney Goo Goo with the Great Big Googly Eyes" was the rage. "Pontiac" looked like the Indian chief in the Canadian School History Book. Another was dubbed "Two Cup" because he always ordered two cups of beer. "Greasy Bob" worked in the machine shops and never washed his clothes. "Cod Fisher" loved nothing better than to sit at the end of the wharf and fish.

Mah Hung arrived as a big, strong young man with a good deal of farming knowledge. Hungo, as he was known, went to work for George Howe and eventually managed the farm. All the meat, milk, cream, eggs, vegetables and fruit for the store and hotel were produced by Hungo.

In the early days the beef cattle were brought to the farm by scow, from Howe's farm on Denman where they ran wild. Once when Hungo and Mr. Howe were walking a cow from the beach to the slaughter house, the cow went a little wild. In an attempt to tie it to a tree, Hungo got his hand caught and it was permanently damaged.

He owned a tiny neat house at the back of Chinatown. Every day he rode his old black bicycle to the farm. The children would call out as he passed, "Honk your horn, Hungo". He always obliged with a smile and toot-toot of the little rubber bulb horn mounted on his handlebars.

Hungo had a soft spot for children, probably because he had left his young wife and family in China. Many little girls and boys would stop in at the big red barn for a visit. They watched as he sat on a block of wood, sorting eggs or collecting seeds, with a basket of kittens playing nearby. He would reach into his pocket and pull out gold barley sugar.

His home in Chinatown was a favourite place to visit on Chinese New Year. Dorothy Hamilton would take him a cake, and he always returned the favour three-fold. Hungo would sit beside his little gramophone playing Chinese songs, with large bowls of nuts, fruit and candies ready for all visitors.

Because he associated closely with the white community, he had fairly good English. He had a habit of stammering before he spoke, and started each sentence with "him him".

Every month the faithful husband sent money to his wife and family in China. From hard work he became a stooped, crippled old gentleman. He was quite a different sight from the handsome young man that had arrived fifty years earlier. Hungo, who had won a place in the hearts of all the townspeople, returned to China in 1947. From his home in China, he wrote letters to friends at the Union Bay store.

Slew worked in the CC(D)L store with Andy Kay. One of his jobs was to supply all the buildings with drinking water. Carrying two buckets on a pole across his shoulders, he would walk up the trail to the well on the Spring Hill. He would bring back the full

A. Watson

Mah Hung (Hungo), gardener for Fraser & Horne, had a soft spot for children. Here he stops hoeing the garden for a picture with Lyle Horne

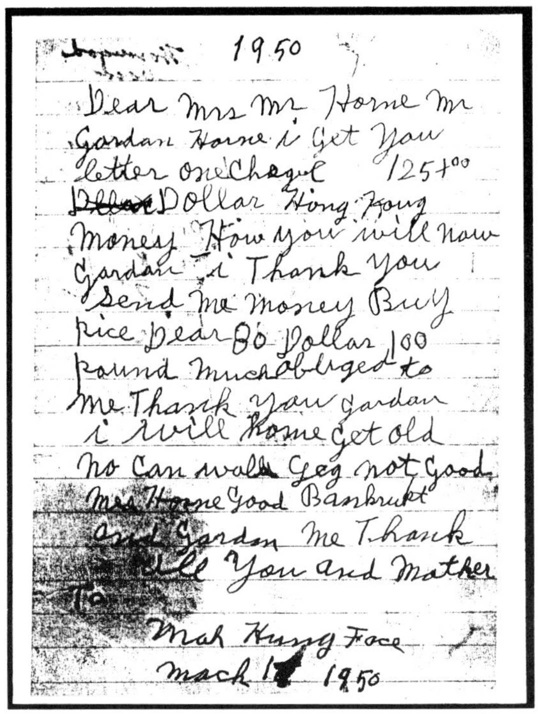

1950

Dear Mrs Mr Horne Mr
Gardan Horne i Get You
letter one Chaqul 125+00
~~Dllar~~ Dollar Hong Kong
Money How you will now
Gardan i Thank you
Send me money Buy
rice Dear 80 Dollar 100
pound much obliged to
me Thank you gardan
i will Home get old
no can walk Leg not Good
Mrs Horne Good Bankrukt
and Gardon me Thank
All You and mather
To
Mah Hung Face
mach 1? 1950

A. Watson

A letter written to Mrs. Horne and son Gordon after Hungo had been home in China three years

A. Watson

At 77 years of age Hungo went home to China in 1947 and is pictured here with his family

T. Dutfield

Posing beside Auchinvole's car is Sam, the Chinese who cooked for the family

buckets to the foundry, car shop, machine shop, boiler shop and office. Beside each bucket hung a little tin dipper used by the men to drink the clear cold spring water. During the winter the buckets were filled in the morning only, but in summer they were refilled after lunch.

Slew later became the gardener for Alex Auchinvole, and Dick took his place as water boy. Dick also worked in the shops, and later became the gardener for Bill and Thelma Auchinvole. One day while weeding, Dick proudly showed Thelma the large pile of big roots he had dug up. Much to her dismay he had dug out her entire rhubarb patch, a plant he had not seen before.

As Alex Auchinvole was District Superintendent of the CC(D)L, the company provided him with a gardener and cook. Sam cooked for the Auchinvole family and their many guests. He wore western clothes and cooked western meals. He became so much a part of the family that he was known as Sam Auchinvole.

Ling Sally started as a gardener for the Brown family when they lived in the big red house on Russell Hill. When Mr. Brown returned as postmaster, Ling Sally came and did housework once a week. Mrs. Brown paid him every Saturday with a freshly baked layer cake and fifty cents.

Har assisted George Davis in his job as railway car inspector. He checked the journal boxes for oil and filled the sand boxes on the locies.

Mah Hong (Fat Boy) and Mah Him were head loaders for each of the two shifts of trimmers. Both lived at the Bay until they died in accidents in their seventies. Mah Him was a sociable fellow and got quite animated, blinking and stuttering when he talked. Sometimes he would go into the beer parlour and buy beer for a young fellow, then offer to pay his way to Vancouver. He was an unattractive, round shouldered man who apparently had trouble getting a prostitute in the big city. His idea was to have the young fellow get a girl which they could then both enjoy.

Shortie was a little fellow with big eyes. He was a trimmer, but also had a garden and peddled his fresh produce around town. When a housewife answered the door she was greeted with "You likee lettuce, turnip and pea?" The children were quick to see the humour in the order of vegetables and it became a good joke. He called on Elizabeth Renwick one day when she was cleaning out closets. She offered him one of Percy's old rain coats and a beautiful fedora hat. Shortie gratefully accepted and went happily off in the oversize coat and hat, his trademark ever after.

"Grandpa Renwick was in charge of all the trimmers so knew them well. When he met Shortie he asked, 'Ah, you hip high tone today, where you catch him?' Shortie answered 'Percy's wife will give'."

Elizabeth Renwick

Two Cup probably associated the most with the local townspeople. He frequented the beer parlour, and his name came from the fact that he always called for two cups. He was a small man but could hold lots of beer. One night he tried to "drink Bert Geary under the table," but as the evening drew on he slowly slid under the table himself. He loved a party, and at closing time a group would often take him along to a house party. He enjoyed a sing-song around the piano and would offer a solo.

Mah Fat, a well educated man, was the bookkeeper for Charlie Mah June. He was a tall, proud gentleman, dressed impeccably in a suit and bowler hat. Carrying a cane or umbrella, he walked along to the mail and bank every day. He also ran a little well-stocked store north of the boarding house. It was a favourite stop for children with a penny to spend on candy or freshly roasted peanuts. Often two boys would enter, and one engage Mah Fat in conversation while the other stole some peanuts. One day Wilfie Bowden and Henry Davis, with mischief on their minds, entered the store. Wilfie averted Mah Fat's attention, and when Henry saw his chance he grabbed the string hanging on a spool in a holder over the counter and darted outside. Round and round it spun. Down the steps onto the highway and across the Washer Creek Bridge ran Henry, with Mah Fat in hot pursuit. Meanwhile, Wilfie howled with laughter, wondering why Mah Fat did not just cut the string.

It was a store where young boys could buy cigarettes to smoke behind the woodshed, and men could buy bootleg whiskey. In a raid, the B.C. Police found nearly 1,000 bottles of liquor in Mah Fat's store. He was fined $300 for bootlegging. He sold mainly to the Chinese but had some very regular customers among the townspeople. Just before the Collieries closed down, Mah Fat moved to Port Alberni, where he opened a store and lived to be a very old man.

The most colourful of the Chinese were Goo Goo and Gopher Gus. Due to their appearance, habits, and lack of hygiene, they struck fear in the hearts of many little girls. Lee Yeun Loya, known as Goo Goo, came to Union Bay as a coal trimmer. In 1895 his right leg was crushed under a wheel while attempting to jump onto loco No.4. The leg was amputated at the knee by Dr. Lawrence and he was fitted with a wooden leg. The crippled man never worked again and seemed to be shunned by the rest of the Chinese community. It was strongly rumoured that Goo Goo was the pick-up for drugs dropped overboard by the smugglers on the freighters.

After the accident Goo Goo became a bit strange and very slovenly. His little house was crammed full of everything, even ladies lace underwear! In each dirty ear he kept a coin, which must have impaired his hearing. His money was kept in a little wooden box filled with dirt. At the store or post office he would take out the box, slide the lid off and dig around for the right change. Because of his strange ways he became the butt of many jokes. With a wooden leg he could do little about the taunts of young boys shouting "Barney Goo Goo with the Goo Goo Googly Eyes". Several young girls arriving in Union Bay for the first time were promised a handsome young man, only to find out it was Goo Goo!

He spent each day pushing his old cart around, collecting firewood and junk on the beach. For a quicker trip around town he took his scooter. Goo Goo had rigged up a child's scooter for his wooden leg. On the platform he had nailed a metal bottle lid which kept the peg leg from slipping off. By pushing with the good leg he could move around quickly. He even took a few trips to Cumberland on his scooter.

None of the Chinese went out in a boat except Goo Goo. He had an old flat-bottomed skiff he used for picking up stray logs, and perhaps drugs. It was on just such an excursion that he apparently fell overboard and drowned. A week later, on August 30, 1929 his body was sighted close to shore, floating wooden leg up. His nephew came from Vancouver to attend to the burial. When he screwed off the wooden leg it was full of money.

Another scary Chinese was Chang Tim, known to everyone as Gopher Gus. He hated the nick-name and always corrected the speaker by emphatically saying, "My name not Gus! My name Tim, T- I-M." Tim was another unhygienic man. He had a nasty habit of getting very close, and talking with spittle flying into his listener's face. He was very nosy, always wanting to know everyone's business.

Tim was anxious to improve his English, and with his pencil and cigarette box would corner people to have words spelled for him. Sometimes he would have a list of words, perhaps a seed catalogue of vegetables, and want the names read for him. If someone tried to hurry the process by skipping a word, he would point to it and say, "What's a matter him?"

His worst habit was to offer a little girl a nickel, then grab her for a well-placed kiss on the mouth. Several girls had their mouths washed out with soap by their mothers. They quickly learned to keep out of his way.

As the Collieries operation became smaller there was less work for the Chinese. However, all the men were old, with the exception of Jim Gong (Chicken). Chicken arrived in the late 1930's and lived in the new boarding house. He was a pleasant, handsome fellow who spoke good English. Chicken married and brought his wife to Union Bay. He moved the boarding house up to the Company Hill where the Crib Club had been, and lived there for several more years. Joe, a young boy, came to live with the couple and went to school at the Bay.

OPIUM

"Opium-a drug obtained from the unripe seed pods of the Oriental poppy. After the white petals drop, raw opium is collected from cut surfaces of the seed pod. A milky resin exudes, which turns into a gummy dark brown mass when exposed to air. Opium is one of the basic folk medicines used to allay pain, induce sleep, reduce hunger, thirst and other drives, and alleviate anxiety and depression."

Encyclopedia Americana.

During the Industrial Revolution in Europe, opium was used extensively by the working class to help them tolerate their overcrowded unsanitary housing and long working hours under terrible conditions. These circumstances were not unlike those found in the Chinatown at Union Bay.

"They worked twelve hour shifts. At lunch they'd go home and have a smoke of opium, and it gave them more energy to work the rest of the day."

Bob McKay

An act of the Canadian Parliament in 1884 had prohibited the sale and use of opium. But the act had been disallowed. At one time Victoria had fourteen opium factories which advertised on the front page of the Victoria Colonist. In the 1880's there was a very lucrative opium ring operating out of Victoria, smuggling opium to the American cities of Port Townsend, Seattle, Tacoma and Portland. It was reported that every night at least one sailing ship left Victoria with opium. The *SS Wellington*, owned by Mr. Dunsmuir, had long been suspected of bringing opium into San

Francisco while delivering coal from Union Bay and Nanaimo. In 1893 one hundred eight tins of opium were found aboard. As a result Mr. Dunsmuir discharged all hands, except the officers, in an attempt to stop the smuggling.

In 1908 William Lyon McKenzie King, Minister of Labour, discovered that opium was being legally manufactured and openly sold and smoked in Victoria. On July 13, 1908 the House of Commons passed a law prohibiting the import, manufacture and sale of opium for other than medical purposes. However, through steamers coaling at Union Bay or docking at lumber ports on the Island, a supply was maintained. The authorities attempted to prevent this smuggling, but in 1911 it was reported that Union Bay was almost a free port for the smuggling of opium. The Provincial Police often raided the opium dens. Usually the men captured were only in possession of opium outfits and enough opium for their personal use. They were fined anywhere from $10 to $75 and released.

1919 NOVEMBER ➾ Four dope fiends of Union Bay were apprehended this week with opium in their possession. They were each fined $10 after pleading guilty. [5]

The Chinese had little trouble satisfying their addiction to Yen See, as they called opium. Stories abound of how the opium was smuggled into the busy port. The majority of it was sold to the large Chinese population in Cumberland. Most opium arrived via the Blue Funnel freighters that came regularly from the Orient for bunker coal.

1937 MARCH ➾ A big Blue Funnel ship is welcome after a long absence. The *SS Talthybius* came in for 900 tons of bunker, and playing around her was a swift motor launch of the RCMP. The police have been paying particular notice to all Oriental boats since a big parcel of narcotics came up on an anchor chain at New Westminster. [6]

Cumberland Museum

Implements for smoking opium - a lamp for heating the opium which was skewered on a long needle before putting it in the long stemmed pipe

Twenty-four hours a day, a customs man was posted on the gangway to check people coming and going, but the Chinese working on the boats had many opportunities. As soon as a coal car was emptied, a man could quickly scramble unnoticed up the dust-filled chute and put a bag of opium in the empty car. The locie would take the empty coal car to a siding up near the bunkers. By noting the number on the side of the car, the trimmer could later go to this virtually deserted spot and retrieve the opium.

From about 1916 the RCMP Narcotic Squad had an almost constant watch on the Chinese at Union Bay. In 1921 they managed their first big haul. Twenty-nine tins of opium worth $1500 were brought off the Blue Funnel boat *Talthybius.*

1921 JULY ➾ While members of the squad were searching a number of Chinese coal-trimmers who were coming ashore, Const. Hicks noticed a man coming from the boat along the top of the wharf. As he came down the steps to the ground, the Chinaman came face to face with the constable, who was the only one of the party in uniform. Evidently taking fright at the sight of the constable, the Celestial threw the sack down and beat it like a scared rabbit, darting through the doors of a shed nearby. The constable pursued the Chinaman but he escaped in the darkness. A little later Sgt. Bryan saw a man running at top speed towards the boat, who he pursued and arrested. This man, who was very much agitated and gave the impression of being badly frightened, was taken to the Chief Inspector of Customs, Seymour Abrams, for examination. He was later brought to Cumberland and released on $1000 bail. [5]

When the man appeared in court, Const. Hicks could not positively swear that the accused and the man who threw the sack at his feet were the same. It was late at night and the man's face was covered with coal dust. The case was dismissed.

The smugglers became more cunning. In China the opium was packed into a large slatted box filled with rock salt. When the ship docked, the box was thrown into the water where it sank. On these days there were always several Chinese fishing off the low pilings at the wharf. The salt in the crate slowly melted, and the box floated up. The fisherman's pole for carrying his bucket became very useful in landing the "fish". It took just a minute to transfer the opium from the box to buckets, and cover it with a bit of seaweed. He put the buckets on either end of the pole and shuffled back to Chinatown with his "catch." Goo Goo was named by many as a pick-up, as he was always around the waterfront with his little cart.

"A three pronged grappling hook was actually made in the blacksmith shop for the Boss Chinaman. No questions were asked about its use, but we had a pretty good idea."

Harry Glover

Opium was also brought from China packed into yard-long pieces of bamboo, plugged at each end with rock salt, and tied into bundles. At an appointed spot the smuggler aboard the ship would toss the bundles into the sea. The water melted the salt and up popped the bamboo. When the "heat" became too great in the port, the bamboo was tossed overboard near Hornby Island, where Yick Ching lived and farmed on the old Ford ranch. When the Blue Funnel ship passed Yellow Rock he was on the lookout for the bamboo. When it floated to the top, Yick went out in his thirty-five foot gasoline launch and picked it up. Soon, on a dark rainy night, the wharf crew at Union Bay would catch a whiff of opium in the air, and they knew that the boat from Hornby was coming in. He often had eight to ten bags which were passed to a man at the Bay. Yick Ching was never caught smuggling opium, but he was caught with a large amount of "moonshine" whiskey on his launch.

Opium was also smuggled from Vancouver. In 1927 it was cleverly concealed in the hearts of cabbages. Each cabbage looked perfect from the outside.

In the 1930's another big bust was made when the police found a great quantity of opium down the only septic tank in Chinatown. The opium was packed into empty shot gun shells, then waxed together in cartons.

There were several opium dens in Cumberland, but only one, so called, in Union Bay. The building was actually a two storey boarding house, with bunks rented upstairs. A small set of scales was used to weigh the opium. Several flickering lamps stood on the bunks. Skewered on a long needle, the deck of opium was held over the flame before putting it into the bowls of the long stemmed pipes. Scrapers were provided to carefully clean out the "dross" (ash) which was put into containers for a cheap smoke later. After lighting his pipe the smoker settled down into the bunk, and a dreamlike state enveloped him.

In April 1939, the Boss Chinaman was caught alone in the bunk house asleep, with four packets of opium, three pills of cocaine, and keys to the premises in his pocket. During the two day trial, he pleaded not guilty and said he had no knowledge of smoking opium. He then told a story of coming to the bunk house to get extra men for the night shift. Being exhausted after a twenty-four hour shift, he lay down beside fellow worker Lem Que to rest. He believed that the opium had been planted on his body by Que before he left the bunk house for work. The story was corroborated by a third Chinese present, who said he witnessed Que smoking but not the boss. Mr. Justice A.I. Fisher at the Nanaimo assizes found him guilty on two counts. He was sentenced to eighteen months imprisonment plus a $400 fine.

During the trial Mr. Herbert Glover, Immigration Officer, gave a good character testimony for the accused whom he said he had known for thirty years. In pronouncing sentence, the judge said that the previous good character of the accused was the only thing that saved him from a long prison term.

JAPANESE

Japanese isolation ended in 1867 when Emperor Mutsuhito gained power. He soon eliminated the feudal system and established a modern army and navy. The emperor urged his people to seek knowledge in all parts of the world, to help make Japan strong. Soon after this the first immigrants from Japan crossed the Pacific to British Columbia, leaving the overcrowded conditions of home in search of economic improvement. Fishing was their major occupation, and by 1900, four thousand Japanese were working in the fishing industry on the B.C. coast.

In January 1892 about a hundred Japanese arrived at Union Wharf aboard the *Zambesi*. They climbed onto the coal train and headed for Union Mines. The men were employed above and below ground, and were blamed for throwing whites and Chinese out of work. People warned that B.C. was facing a coming evil equal to the Chinese invasion. So from the

S. Nakamura

Japtown beside Washer Creek before the flood of 1912

beginning, these newcomers faced a hostile host country. Although the European workers did not like the Chinese, they were becoming more accustomed to them. When the Japanese arrived they became scapegoats for hatred and prejudice.

1892 FEBRUARY ➾ The 100 imported Japanese are still at Union, and proving to be not good workers - only fifteen working underground, pushing boxes and making poor pushers. They can't keep going as long as white boys and are not as smart. They are impossible at picking coal and quite incapable of doing the work. In their habits they are very little above the Chinese at Union. The one hundred live in three small shacks and sleep in bunks, one above the other as the Chinese. They are unpopular among the whites as much as the Chinese are, whom the whites are starting to regard as a necessary evil. But the importation of ignorant dirty Japanese is most distasteful to the white population. [2]

It seems that Dunsmuir was having some trouble with the Japanese workers. They were under contract to the Union Colliery and had struck work in January 1893. Some had run away and were jailed as vagrants in Nanaimo. Others were suffering from "dropsy", supposedly from the change of climate and food. Most of them could not speak English. More than once, Mr. P. Kito, the Japanese Consul in Vancouver, accompanied Mr. Dunsmuir on the *Isobel* to Union Wharf and Union, to smooth over difficulties.

At home in the Orient, the Japanese were busy trying to expand their empire, and were rivals with China for Korea. This resulted in the Chinese-Japanese war of 1894-95. Japan won the war, and China was forced to give up Korea and Taiwan to them. This animosity between the two nations was brought with the immigrants to Canada, as they vied for jobs.

1896 FEBRUARY ➾ Union Wharf Notes: Grading of the coke oven grounds has been resumed. Subjects of the "Mickydoo" are mostly employed. The Chinese complain about this class of cheap labour cutting them out in certain lines of industry, and when referring to them say "Allee same Siwashee". [2]

Both nationalities suffered and were exploited, because they were under contract and in debt to the Union Coal Co. In spite of their dislike for each other their problems were similar, and as early as 1896 they joined together and tried to form a union, demanding $1.50 per day but continuing to be hired at 75¢ to 90¢.

With the arrival of about fifty more men in Union, the Japanese community grew, and signs of a social life began. Japanese lecturers and entertainers came from Vancouver and found an eager audience.

The Russo-Japanese war in 1904 again saw the Japanese trying to expand their boundaries. England supported Japan in this rivalry and made an alliance with her in 1902.

1904 MARCH ➾ Last Wednesday Union Wharf was the scene of an animated leave-taking of a Japanese leaving for home to join the army. Japanese and British flags were borne aloft and many speeches were made to the departing soldier in Japanese. The whole concluded with three cheers for Great Britain led by Mr. Nakano of the Wharf. [4]

A big change took place in the Japanese community after the 1907 riots in Vancouver. This led to the signing of the "Gentlemen's Agreement" in 1908 which restricted immigration to 400 men a year from Japan. However, it did allow wives and families left in Japan to join their husbands. This resulted in the "Picture Brides". Marriages were arranged by families in Japan, and pictures of the prospective brides sent to the men in Canada. In 1924 restrictions were further tightened and Japanese immigration almost ceased.

In Cumberland there was a large community of Japanese living at No.1 and No.5 Japtown. At Union Wharf there was a large workforce of Japanese in the 1890's. Some were employed around the shipping wharf, building the Washer, but most worked grading the ground in preparation for the British masons who built the coke ovens. The Washer was completed in 1896, and half a dozen Japanese men were hired to run it. Two of these men met untimely deaths there. In December 1910, a worker fell into the hopper and was suffocated. Charles Nakamura, who was in charge of the Japanese at the Washer, was killed in 1922 when his shirt was caught in a revolving pulley. He left his wife and four children. Mrs. Nakamura is believed to be the first Japanese widow to receive compensation.

A little community was situated near the Japanese-owned Royston Lumber Co. There were settlements in Fanny Bay and Deep Bay, where Japanese logging companies operated. Some men worked for Anderson Logging Co. at Union Bay.

By the turn of the century, in comparison to Chinatown, Japtown at Union Bay was small. It consisted of about eight families and thirty single men. The homes were situated around Washer Creek. Like the Chinese, the Japanese suffered during the flood of 1912. The only person killed was a Japanese man. They rebuilt their homes on the north side of the creek. Because of the family units, with about a dozen children who attended school and became friends of the white children, the Japanese integrated into the community more easily than the Chinese.

Some of the family names remembered are Higashi, Hygano, Kuroda, Miyahara, Nakamura, Tateishi and Uchida. Mr. S. Nakano operated a brick and tile yard, built in 1899. The fire clay came from No.4 Mine and was made into bricks at the Union Bay yard. They were fired in two kilns housed in a two storey building.

Little is known of most of the families. Mrs. Uchida took in laundry from the townspeople. There were two girls born around the turn of the century. Ebe and Matsui attended Union Bay School. Their brother Jumbo worked in the foundry.

The story goes that Jumbo, a husky fellow, had done some Sumo wrestling. A strong man came to town, full of boasts about his strength. One day he walked into the foundry and eyed a 500 pound car wheel. He announced that he could lift it, which after much struggling he did. Jumbo had been watching the proceedings quietly from a corner. When the strong man and his admirers left, he calmly walked over to the wheel, bent down and picked it up in one motion. With a broad smile he dropped the wheel and walked away. Jumbo had lived up to his name. He was married with two children, Yungo, born about 1924 and Tsutomu, born about 1929. Yungo was known to his school chums as Georgie Jumbo, a little roly-poly boy with a big grin. He was later killed in the woods.

Tomojiro Nakamura came to Union Bay about the turn of the century. Shizu, his wife, came later as a picture bride. After the flood, Mr. Nakamura built a big house at the top of Washer Creek Hill. Mrs. Nakamura took in laundry and cooked for the single Japanese workers. They had four children: Scutta, Saburo, Himako, and Kiyoshi. All attended school and were very popular with their classmates. After school was out, they mixed and played with the other children of Union Bay. Playing house and tea parties with the Nakamura children were especially fun, as they were allowed to bring their mother's real china. Himako was very clever and won many spelling bees. The boys were members of different sports teams, and favourites at picnics and dances. They were natty dressers, often wearing ice cream pants and shirts.

"I have many fond memories of the kids I grew up with - especially Art Searle and "Butchie" (Wilfred Bowden) and I can't say enough for their parents - they were most kind, gracious and understanding."

Kiyoshi Nakamura

After he finished school Scutta became an apprentice in the boiler shop.

1927 AUGUST ➾ Misses Winnie and Louise Bowden held a very enjoyable "Court Whist" party in honour of Mr. Nakamura who is leaving for Vancouver where he has accepted a position. The happy evening was brought to a close with the singing of "For He's a Jolly Good Fellow." [7]

Saburo married Mary Carter from Cumberland, but was killed in 1934 at the Royston Sawmill where he worked. Himako married Fred Kayto of Royston. Kiyoshi, who worked in the lumber industry, married Susie Yaguchi from No.5 Japtown. After the war Scutta married Susie's sister, Mitzie.

1939 NOVEMBER ➾ A beautiful Japanese wedding was performed at Royston Mill before the brilliant, impressive altar of the Royston Buddhist church. Rev. S. Asaka united Tsuyoko (Susie), daughter of Mr. & Mrs. Yaguchi of Cumberland, and Kiyoshi, youngest son of Mrs. T. Nakamura and the late T. Nakamura of Union Bay. The couple will reside at the Bay. [6]

S. Nakamura

A wedding photo of Tomojiro Nakamura and his "picture bride", Shizu, reproduced on a painted tin picture frame

About 1910 Shizuichi Higashi came to Union Bay to work in the Washer. Tazu, his wife, arrived two years later, and they were married in Victoria. They lived in Japtown, in the house closest to the road. Because Washer Creek often used to back up along the road, their home was built on stilts with a porch and walkway along the front of the house. There were four

S. Nakamura

On the verandah of her home Shizu Nakamura enjoys a visit from Shizuichi Hagashi

M. Coe

Friends Kenneth Renwick and Tickie Higashi drink a milkshake from Hudson's store in front of Kelly's shack

children in the family, and like the Nakamura's, were integrated into the community. Many of the neighbourhood children learned to ride on the Higashi kids' bikes.

Hutchiko was the oldest in the family. After she finished school she worked for Mrs. Christie at Royston, where she learned to drive a car. She in turn taught her brothers to drive when they became old enough. Later, she became mother's help to Mrs. B. Auchinvole. Massa and Tickie were very popular with their set of friends. After the boys quit school they went to work in the Washer. Massa bought himself a 1938 Dodge, and Tickie bought a new green Chev, which he "fancied up with mud guards".

Tickie was the main means of transportation for the young fellows. If he was going to town, he would circle down to Hudson's store where the boys hung out, to see if anyone wanted to go up to the latest movie. Tickie and Fooner June were great pals. Fooner had a big "La Salle".

"We grew up with them. There was no prejudice... we never thought anything about it. We were all friends. There'd be a white guy, a Chinaman and a Jap. We all travelled together. They'd come to our house and have a sandwich or cookies, and when we went to their house it was fried perch, or sometimes dried horse clam snouts. They used to pull them up and cut the end off, and scrub them and put them out to dry. It was like chewing rawhide but it was tasty."

Bill Hamilton

Mr. Higashi attended English classes taught by Nellie Ede, but Mrs. Higashi could not speak English so the children translated for her. The neighbourhood children were always welcome. The two younger children were still in school when the Japanese were sent away from the coast in 1942. Showney and Fusako were popular with their school chums. It was a tearful day when they bade them good-bye.

"I can remember sitting at the end of the wharf and crying when the Japanese were being loaded onto the boat. Showney was my good friend."

Gertrude (Harwood) Robertson

The Japanese at Union Bay lived much as the other people did. The children and men wore western clothes. Their houses were plain and clean. The only difference was their bath houses, which were attached to their homes by a walkway. The brass tubs were set into the floor and heated with a boiler. After work the men were scrubbed by their wives, then left to soak in the tub. Their diet included rice, dried and salted fish, and soybean products like tofu and miso.

During the summer months of the 1920's and '30s, Union Bay was home to a group of Japanese fishermen. There was a house built on stilts jutting out over the beach, just past the old warehouse. The men lived on and fished from their gillnetters, and left the women on shore to salt and dry the chums that they caught. When fishing season was over, they packed up their meager belongings and sailed off, possibly to homes in Steveston.

The hard-working frugal Japanese were seen as a threat to the fishing and logging industries where they excelled. Zealots for the exclusion of the Japanese talked of a Japanese Imperialist plan to take over Canada by peaceful penetration. There were suspicions of spies on Japanese fishboats, mapping the coast and photographing the important ports and military installations. The plan supposedly included economic undertakings. The acquisition of timber leases by Japanese investors was seen as an example.

During WWI a Canadian Battalion was formed, and the young Japanese from the Comox District were well represented. They were all eager to fight for their country, Canada. In spite of this, after the war, Veterans organizations, the Native Sons of Canada, and Boards of Trade were demanding the end of Japanese immigration, and deportation of the settled immigrants back to Japan.

A.W. Neill, MP for Comox District, was a constant advocate for Japanese expatriation. In the 1930's he presented a bill to the House of Commons "to exclude all Japanese Labour Immigrants from Canada." It did not pass, because the politicians in the east had little interest in the "imagined problems" of the west coast. However, at home Neill had a great deal of support. Both local newspapers supported his stand.

A new type of seaweed, called Japanese seaweed, was growing

and flourishing on the Pacific coast. It was brown, with long thin branches covered with thousands of little seeds. It wound itself into the nets and often around the propellor shaft on small boats, stopping the motor. Some of the white fishermen were convinced that the Japanese had introduced this seaweed to sabotage the fishing industry. It probably came with the oyster seeds.

On the Pacific coast, even before Pearl Harbour, the supposed fear of the "Japanese menace" prevailed. People were very suspicious of their every move. The Japanese felt a need to display their loyal support to Canada, especially in the war with Germany.

1941 MARCH ➾ Royston's Young Men's Buddhist Association staged a splendid bazaar. The result was that Canada's defense fund gained $34.46. The hall was decorated in patriotic motifs of red, white and blue, with two huge Union Jacks draped at each end. The hall was filled with Japanese residents from all over the district. [6]

In July 1937 Japan declared war on China. This was reflected at the Bay when Chinese trimmers refused to load Japanese ships.

1939 SEPTEMBER ➾ Chinese trimmers at Union Bay refused to work when the Japanese ship *Maru Yamahgi* came in for 400 tons of bunker. She was in ballast at Union Bay, going on to Vancouver to load. The Japanese did their own trimming, and a scratch crew was organized around the Bay to help with the loading. The Chinese did not attempt to interfere with anyone else loading, but refused themselves. The ship had taken on her cargo in nine hours and was gone. [6]

Then, on December 7, 1941 Japan attacked Pearl Harbour. Very quickly, the Japanese of the district issued a statement.

1941 DECEMBER ➾ We, the Japanese residents of the district, wish to reaffirm our loyalty to Canada and state that we will continue to support to the utmost this country's war effort. [6]

However, by January of 1942 there was a great deal of correspondence sent to the government and the press, asking that restrictions be put on the Japanese. Many demands were made for their removal from the coast. Prime Minister McKenzie King claimed that the disloyal Japanese had been taken care of, and that the rest were loyal to Canada. This did not satisfy the people of British Columbia.

1942 JANUARY ➾ The Cumberland council sends a request to A.W. Neill for removal of Japanese. Mayor Maxwell declared it a grave situation. [7]

Finally, the Dominion Government announced the decision to remove enemy aliens of all origins, including the Japanese, from the defense areas of British Columbia. It mattered little that nearly all of them were Canadian born, or parents of children born in Canada.

1942 JANUARY 14 ➾ The announcement in brief stated:

1. Transfer of all alien enemies from coastal defense areas. This covers all adult Japanese.
2. Formation of a committee to look after the transfer of 1,100 Japanese fishing boats to white fishermen.
3. Organization of a Japanese "civilian corp" to work on national projects.

The decision of the government to take the action outlined above has been greeted with acclaim, as the most logical way to handle an admittedly delicate situation. [7]

A.W. Neill heartily favoured expatriation. He complained that Ottawa was far too slow making preparations, and that very few restrictions had been placed on the Japanese.

1942 FEBRUARY ➾ Neill declares, "Perhaps it is too early to talk of it, but it is well to get started. We should make arrangements to expatriate all the Japanese left in Canada after the war. Do it on fair terms. Buy them out, pay them liberally. Let us settle this once and for all, this canker that prevents us from being a united white Canada. That is what B.C. wants. [6]

By the end of January the RCMP, who were handling the removal of Japanese people from the area west of the Cascades to the interior of the province, were in the district registering the Japanese. One of the first actions taken was the removal of telephone services to all Japanese homes and places of business. Also, they were not allowed to be in possession of cars, radios, cameras or explosives. Finally, in March the order came and headlines screamed "ALL NIPPONS MUST GO."

1942 MARCH ➾ Exodus of Japs from district has begun. Those owning cars and trucks, about twenty, mostly from Cumberland, left under convoy of Provincial Police. The vehicles driven by owners to Victoria will be stored there at the owners' expense until war is over. All have obeyed curfew between dusk and dawn and have also surrendered all radios, fire arms and other forbidden equipment. [6]

It was not until about a month after the final order that the Japanese actually left the district. By now there were only the Higashi and Nakamura families living at Union Bay. It was a very anxious time, with many decisions to be made as to what to take, leave, or sell. Each adult was allowed two suitcases and a clothes bag, while the children were allowed one suitcase and a small clothes bag. Those who sold - the smartest ones as it later turned out - had to accept ridiculously low prices for their possessions.

"Their properties were seized by the Custodian of Enemy Alien Property and held "in trust" - a trust

that was later broken when the properties were sold without the owners' consent."

Price Waterhouse Study

At 5:30 a.m. on April 16, 1942, eight special Vancouver Island Coach Line buses began to shuttle back and forth between the local Japanese communities and Union Bay. Baggage went first. Next, the buses were loaded with the men, women and children, who were transferred to the Canadian National steamship *Prince George*, which was docked at the government wharf. The families at the Bay found their own way to the wharf accompanied by a few friends. Several of the older students represented the school, and presented Showney and Fusako Higashi with momentos and cards. It was a tearful scene as the school chums parted. By 10:00 a.m. the ship was loaded and steaming down the gulf, carrying away 585 confused souls to unknown destinations. This was the sad fate of a people who had contributed much to the life of the Comox District for the previous fifty years.

"I have most pleasant memories of Union Bay as a desirable and first choice place to live."

Showney Higashi

"The kindness from the school children at Union Bay was not common to other Japanese in other places. Showney still has the belt his classmates gave him when he left."

Tickie Higashi

The next evening, the few remaining spokesmen for the Japanese hosted a dinner in Cumberland, to bid their friends farewell. Several men, including Shizuichi Higashi, had been granted permits to stay to help the official custodian transfer the property to the state. Reverend Ono said that the idea of the gathering that evening was simply to say "Thank You" to all the people of the district. The speaker stated that the Japanese people were deeply grateful for all the kindnesses shown during the evacuation by the Provincial Police, and by Matt Brown, the agent for the custodian. He expressed the hope that before long this conflict would come to an end, and all could resume their natural way of living, amongst the friends they had made over a long period.

In reply, Mr. J.C. Brown stated that it was unfortunate that circumstances forced the removal of the Japanese from the district. He complimented the local Japanese residents for the way they had received the evacuation order. "They have in every instance co-operated to the fullest extent, making the work of the authorities so much easier."

The Japanese were taken first to Vancouver. Uprooted from their homes in coastal towns and on Vancouver Island, thousands of Japanese Canadians were confined in the livestock pens at Hastings Park (P.N.E. grounds).

From there, Mr. Higashi, in order to keep the family together, chose a Catholic relocation centre at Greenwood where he, Masa and Tickie became plumbing tradesmen. The Nakamura family relocated to an internment camp at Tashme, B.C. In both locations the Japanese had to obey a curfew. Living conditions were poor, and shared with other families. They suffered extreme hardships in the cold winters. After the war the Higashi family stayed in Greenwood. The Nakamuras moved to Ontario where the men found work.

HINDUS (Sikhs)

It is believed that East Indians passing through British Columbia on their way home from Queen Victoria's Diamond Jubilee, took home stories of a bountiful land with towering forests. Between 1904 and 1907 about 5,000 male Sikhs arrived in B.C., and found jobs as labourers in lumber mills, logging camps, and a few in the coal industry. These men and the ones that followed were called Hindus, often spelled "Hindoos". However, it is doubtful if there was a Hindu amongst them. These handsome proud people were Sikhs, members of a reformist religion in the northwest region of India known as the Punjab.

A group of Sikhs arrived in 1906 to work for the Union Coal Company as construction workers in Cumberland and Union Bay, where they helped build the coke ovens and Washer.

S. Nakamura

The internment camp at Tashme, B.C. where the Nakamura family spent the war years

The Sikhs were housed in a large boarding house at the head of the bay. It was built for the workmen who came to the youthful port to construct the railway. They were not allowed to bring their families to British Columbia, so the single men worked and lived together in a tight little group. Because of their language, appearance and customs, the European settlers viewed them with suspicion.

It was odd the way they squatted to cook, eat and chat. They made chipatis from whole wheat flour and water, then deftly threw the dough from one hand to the other, making it thinner and thinner. The flatbread was cooked on hot rocks or a steel plate. This chewy bread was used as a spoon to scoop up hot vegetable curry, dal, or subje that simmered over the fire, sending exotic aromas through the air.

The strangest custom of all was that of cremating their dead. Few who witnessed a cremation would ever forget the sight and smell of the huge funeral pyres, burning long into the night.

1906 NOVEMBER ➾ The first cremation in the district was performed last Saturday on the body of a Hindoo who died at Union Wharf. A huge pile of wood and coal was built up in the bush near the coal bunkers. On top of which the remains of the departed, dressed in his best clothes, were placed and scattered with sandalwood. With customary Oriental rites the pile was ignited. In a few hours nothing but a pile of white ash remained. In the olden times the widow of the dead man threw herself on the burning pile, but this custom has been abolished through the efforts of the British government. [4]

Later that month a second Sikh died, and was cremated on a funeral pyre behind the hospital at Cumberland. For the next seven or eight years, this became a common occurrence which never failed to rouse the curiosity of the community.

At home in India the Sikhs settled disputes by the sword. This tradition was continued in Canada and gained a poor reputation for the group.

JULY 1913 ➾ Some Hindoos tried to carve each other up with knives at Union Bay. [4]

The first group of Sikhs worked at Union Wharf for about eight years, until the coke ovens and Washer were complete. They returned again about 1912, when the E&N Railroad Company employed great numbers of them to build the railway from Nanaimo to Courtenay. As the railway was laid progressively up the island, the crews of Sikhs moved from river to river. As well as laying ties and rails, they cared for and drove the donkeys that moved the earth for the foundations of the bridges.

"I remember the valley at Tsable River, there must have been 200 Hindus. The cook used to go this way and that way with the dough, till it got about 8" wide in diameter, a big pancake. Then they'd get the meat and curry and sauce. They were all good workers. My mother used to say, 'Now don't you get too funny with those Hindus. But I liked them. There was one big Hindu working on the dump car, making a fill using carts and horses. I used to do little errands for him and he'd give me candy."

Joe Walker

About 200 Sikhs lived in a tent town behind Union Bay. Their cooks were supplied with food that arrived in large orders on the steamships. Living as they did in camps with everything provided, the men had little cause to go into the village. They enjoyed the children, and the brave ones who visited their camp were welcomed with gifts of fruit and sweetmeat.

The Harry Glover family lived at the south end of Union Bay next to the E&N right of way, so were able to watch the construction progress.

"One day Gertie was playing the piano and she happened to look up and there were about half a dozen Hindus standing by the gate watching her. She stopped playing and they came up the path and knocked on the door. Gertie was terrified and called Mother, and Mother told her to let them in. Well, in they tramped, such big men with their tall turbans, and pointed to the piano. Mother said 'Go ahead and play, Gertie, for heaven's sake'. Gertie played, although she was just trembling. Then they all clapped and bowed, and one gave her a nickel."

Violet (Glover, McMurtrie) Rutherford

When the railway was completed in 1914 the Sikhs moved on, with the exception of one fellow who had made friends with Andrew McKay. He was deathly afraid of war, and felt he may be conscripted because he was a British subject. This man stayed on the McKay property, clearing about four acres of land and doing odd jobs. He enjoyed carving and was a very good craftsman. For the last baby, Bill, the old Sikh carved a beautiful crib. Then, when Andrew died he made the coffin.

"He made a dozen brant decoys. He had a little bit of an axe and cut them out as smooth as can be. I still have them."

Jim McKay

After a few years he left to work on a farm in the Fraser Valley, and sent Mrs. McKay a case of luscious strawberries each summer.

NEGRO

The Union Coal Co. chartered the *Princess Louise* to take 100 black miners to Union Wharf in 1889. The miners had come through on the Pacific Express from Pennsylvania. People at Union were upset over so many coloured men, but preferred them to the Orientals or other foreigners who could not speak English.

1889 AUGUST ➾ The Coloured miners have proved themselves a very peaceful lot so far, but there is no chance of a white man getting a job. [2]

Soon there were reports of the *new coons* not being happy with their quarters, and also the charge by the company that the *coloured miners* were not earning their daily wage. Due to the wet weather in November, most of the negros were discharged and headed back to the United States, saying that British Columbia did not suit them. The following summer, thirty-one black miners were brought in from Roslyn, Washington to work in the Wellington mines. Due to a strike there, they came to Union and found work. A *coon town* was established near No.1 Mine. The settlers of Union Wharf watched these *coloured gentleman* arrive and depart, but had little to do with them.

Union Bay only had one black resident to call its own. Mammy King came and settled in Union Bay at the beginning of the century, via San Francisco, Victoria and Union. She came originally from Louisianna, and eventually returned there. It has been suggested that she ran a brothel in Cumberland, but it is as a sweet, lovable old lady that she is remembered by all in Union Bay.

She was the typical picture of a southern mammy, as wide as she was tall. She owned the "glass house", so-called because of the glassed-in verandah. She was employed as the laundress for George Howe's hotel. To make more revenue, she moved to a small log cabin on Garvin's ranch and rented out the glass house. The Harry Glover family rented the house when they arrived from England in 1905.

Every day Mammy collected the laundry, tied all the linen in one big sheet, and balanced the bundle on her head as she walked the mile and a half to her home at Garvin's field. The work had just begun. The kitchen stove was set to blazing, then well water had to be pulled hand over hand in a bucket, and poured into the big boilers on the stove. Out came the scrubbing board, and she rubbed her hands raw getting the towels and sheets clean. Wringing the water out was hard but essential work, because the more water she squeezed out, the quicker the linen would dry. Everything was hung on lines strung from tree to tree, and on warm breezy days things dried quickly. During rainy weather they often had be ironed dry with heavy flatirons. Even on sweltering summer days the stove had to be roaring hot to heat the water and irons.

She was a familiar sight on the road. Bringing the clean linen back in the early hours of the morning, she sometimes frightened people who thought they were seeing a ghost when the wide figure with a huge white ball on her head appeared.

Mammy also hired herself out as mother's help and was working at the McKay household when Annie was born. She lived in, and shared a bed with Nellie. With her ample girth Mammy made quite an indentation in the bed. Little Nellie, who was only eight years old kept sliding over, but tried hard to keep to her own side of the bed. Mammy finally said to her, "Honey, don't be afraid to touch me. I might be black but it won't rub off."

Mammy King showed loving concern for all, and was liked and respected in return. She was especially loved by the children, as she always had a bag of peppermints tucked into her apron pocket.

GYPSIES

Gypsies were paying visits to Vancouver Island in the nineteenth century. In Nanaimo in 1889 a group of Scottish Gypsies lived in tents and sold lace and spoons, but they would not buy a business licence so were run out of town.

When the road improved to the upper Island, Gypsies toured the Comox Valley in their colourful caravans, pulled by stout horses. They lived a few weeks in each settlement. The men were skilled metalworkers and made eating utensils, jewelry and small tools which they sold to the villagers. They went from door to door sharpening knives and scissors. At Union Bay the band would set up camp at the end of the baseball field, across from Chinatown.

"I guess they toured the Island. They came in wagons. At night they would have their bonfires and play music with violins and tambourines. They were dressed in their old fashioned get-ups, bright colours, embroidery, jewelry and headdresses. It was the sort you looked at but never ventured near, and we had been warned by our parents."

Wilf Bowden

In the spring of 1921, after stopping at Union Bay for a week, they pitched their tents and wagons at Headquarters. When the Japanese store keeper was missing some silk, the police searched the Gypsy camp and found a woman in a wagon, slitting a pillow with a stiletto in order to hide the silk inside. Also found were gloves belonging to the storekeeper. The Gypsies departed, less $30.00.

Again their reputation had been lived up to, and another story was added to the lore of the Gypsies. Little did it matter that many years they came and went, selling their wares without any trouble with the law.

COMMUNICATIONS
NEWSPAPERS

A child is born, the Doctor in attendance gets a $10.00 fee, the Editor notes it and gets 0. It is christened and the Minister gets $5.00, the Editor writes it up and gets 00. It marries and the Minister gets another $10.00, the Editor gets a piece of cake or 000. In the course of time it dies, the Doctor gets from $5.00 to $100.00, and the Minister perhaps gets another $5.00, the Undertaker $25.00 or $50.00, the Editor prints a notice of death and an obituary two columns long, and a set of resolutions of some lodge or organization to which the deceased belonged, and gets 0000. Then he has the privilege of running a free card of thanks, and a lot of poetry besides. [2]

For the very early settlers and miners at the Bayne Sound Mining Company, a newspaper was a rare treat. For those who were literate, the occasional steamer that stopped may have had a Victoria Colonist or San Francisco Examiner aboard, enabling them to catch up on the "outside" world news. Then, in the 1870's, the Nanaimo Free Press started publishing a weekly newspaper which soon grew into a bi-weekly published every Tuesday and Friday in time to catch the Comox Steamer.

Besides carrying world news and local news, there was a column with a passenger list of everyone travelling to and from the Comox District. In 1888 came the announcement that Dunsmuir would open up a mine at Union.

THE WEEKLY NEWS

Published Every Tuesday
At Union, B.C.
M. Whitney Editor

TERMS OF SUBSCRIPTION
IN ADVANCE

One Year	$2.00
Six Months	$1.25
Single Copy	$0.05

RATES OF ADVERTISING

One inch per year	$12.00
One inch per month	$1.50
eight col per year	$25.00
four col per year	$50.00
week per line	$0.10
Local notices, per line	$0.20

Notices of Birth, Marriages and Deaths, 50 cents each insertion.

No Advertisement inserted for less than 50 cents.

The Weekly News.

UNION, COMOX DISTRICT, B. C., TUESDAY, FEB. 25, 1896. $2.00 PER YEAR

Anyone that could afford the $3.00 yearly subscription fee for the bi-weekly had no trouble keeping pace with the developments in the mine and at the wharf. Everything was duly reported in the Nanaimo Free Press from the day the initial surveyor arrived. News items of special interest included when the Orientals first arrived to construct the railroad from the port to the mine, all the specifications of the locomotives when the track was finished, a birth announcement of the first baby to be born at Union Wharf, how the boarding houses for the miners were constructed, the unbelievable price of $25.00 a ton that the farmers were paid for potatoes.

After the mines opened, a column appeared every month listing all the foreign shipping that coaled at Union Wharf. The year-end reports of the Minister of Mines were also printed. Soon a reporter was sending "Weekly Jottings" from the new towns to the paper in Nanaimo.

In June 1889 W. H. Ellis, Proprietor of the Victoria Colonist, travelled, first on the E&N Railway to Nanaimo then on the *Cariboo Fly* to Union Wharf, to report on the first shipment of coal leaving the little harbour. Back home in Victoria, he devoted four complete columns to the Union Coal Company's mines and shipping facilities.

The district's first newspaper, the Weekly News, had a very inauspicious beginning. Mr. M. Whitney, formerly of the Steveston Enterprise, decided in September 1892 that he would start a newspaper in Courtenay. He arrived in October with his press and complete printing outfit, and announced that the first issue would hit the streets on October 23. The people of the district anxiously awaited the first edition of the Courtenay News, but it was another month in coming.

1892 NOVEMBER On the last trip, the *SS Comox* took a large shipment of paper which was omitted when the proprietor went up with machinery. On the newsprint's arrival the good people were in a great state of expectation. But when the salutary issue was about ready for the press the entire absence of ink raised yet another barrier. So, they await the next trip of the *Joan* or *Comox*. [2]

At last the Editor was off and running. He kept the district informed not only with world news but also with all the happenings at home. He regularly travelled by horse, boat or train to all the areas and reported on what he saw there - a trip to Denman one week, a report on the naval boats training in Comox Harbour the next, then a full description of the newly-opened hotel at Union Wharf.

After publishing the paper for two years in Courtenay, the Weekly News moved to Cumberland where Mr. Whitney built an up-to-date printing house at the corner of Dunsmuir and Third.

1894 OCTOBER ➾ While Courtenay has continued to grow and at no time has given evidence of a brighter future than now, and as the gateway between Union and the farming district, and from its central and charming position offers much inducement as a residence place, yet such strides has Union and Cumberland (really one place) taken within the last year, that it is now recognized as the business centre of the district. From this point the news of the district can be best gathered, as well as the cream of the more important news of the World. [3b]

Mr. Whitney, like most of the editors for the next forty years, was very conservative by today's standards. The paper generally stood firmly on the side of mine management and frowned on any union activity. During the strike of 1912-13 many union men withdrew their subscriptions because of the extreme bias (pro company) of the paper. The Weekly News followed a format similar to all weeklies of that era.

The columns of local news were entitled District Intelligence. Later, down through the years, separate communities had their own reporters. Their columns were mostly gossip under colourful headings; Courtenay Chaffs, Union Flashes, Comox Drips, Union Bay Jottings, Cumberland Lightning, etc.

About the turn of the century, in opposition to the News, Mr. Bates, a Cumberland school principal, started printing a little paper named the Enterprise. E.W. Bickle, who was a miner and fire boss, changed careers and went to work for the Enterprise. In 1910 Mr. Bickle bought the press and started publishing the Cumberland Islander. E.T. Searle, who had written for the Nanaimo Free Press, spent a short time writing for the Islander before getting a job with the coal company. The News closed in 1915, leaving one paper in Cumberland.

After the Weekly News moved to Cumberland, Courtenay did not have a newspaper until 1912 when the "Review" was published for six years. Then, during the First World War, the Argus, founded and edited by Mr. A. Hope Herd, published its first paper May 3, 1917. A few years later it was taken over by Ben Hughes who was publisher and editor until the paper folded in 1959. It was very much an agriculture paper to start with, involving itself with the farmers at Courtenay, Merville and Sandwick. Each paper published the egg production of poultry farmers of the area, as well as milk and cream production from dairies. It listed the shipping at Union Bay and often gave colourful reports of interesting ships that called at the port.

In 1927 Mr. Bickle started the Courtenay Free Press which he printed on his Cumberland press. Then, in four years, he amalgamated the Islander and Free Press under the name of the Comox District Free Press. This provided the area with two good newspapers.

Both papers had a local reporter in Union Bay. The Argus position was filled by a variety of people, but the Free Press had Mrs. Laura Little. Working at Fraser and Horne's, she had easy access to the town's news, and faithfully wrote a column every week. It was the first column to be read, to see who had made the news that week. After Mrs. Little retired, the position was filled for many years by Mrs. Mary Moore. Occasionally, Mary branched out and wrote articles about Union Bay's past.

More Free Press papers were sold in Union Bay because of the obvious ties between it and Cumberland, but people developed a fierce loyalty to either one publication or the other.

The newspaper office also did all the printing for the community - letterheads, calling cards, business cards, invitations, marriage and death announcements.

1908 JANUARY ➾ Mr. J. Humphrey of Union Bay is busy distributing a very unique business card which was printed by this office. It is a money fetcher for sure. [4]

THE ISLANDER
VOL. III., No. 36 — THE ISLANDER, CUMBERLAND, B.C., SATURDAY, NOVEMBER 30, 1912 — Subscription price, $1.50 per

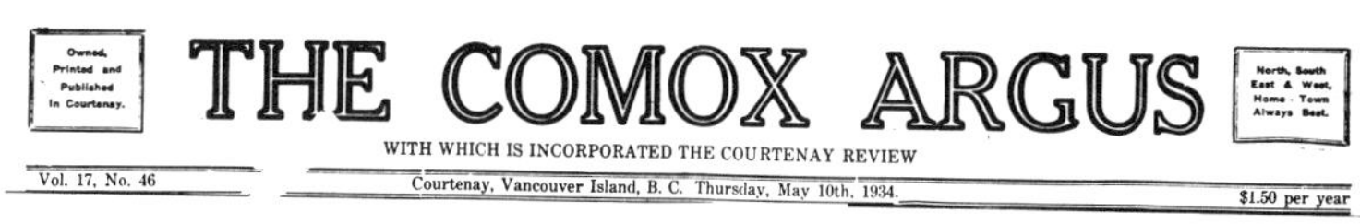
Owned, Printed and Published in Courtenay.
THE COMOX ARGUS
North, South East & West, Home - Town Always Best.
WITH WHICH IS INCORPORATED THE COURTENAY REVIEW
Vol. 17, No. 46 — Courtenay, Vancouver Island, B. C. Thursday, May 10th, 1934. — $1.50 per year

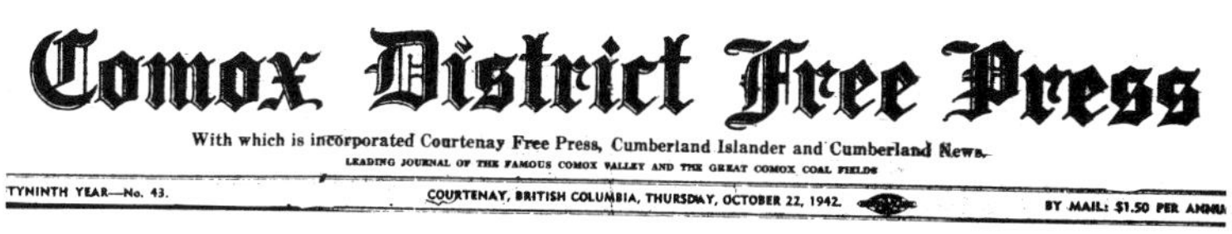
Comox District Free Press
With which is incorporated Courtenay Free Press, Cumberland Islander and Cumberland News.
LEADING JOURNAL OF THE FAMOUS COMOX VALLEY AND THE GREAT COMOX COAL FIELDS
TYNINTH YEAR—No. 43. — COURTENAY, BRITISH COLUMBIA, THURSDAY, OCTOBER 22, 1942. — BY MAIL: $1.50 PER ANNUM

As well as the local papers, a few of the avid readers received daily papers from the larger cities. Before the turn of the century, representatives went door to door selling subscriptions to the Victoria Colonist, Seattle Post Intelligencer, and San Francisco Examiner. Later, the Vancouver papers became popular. Luckily, the papers were much thinner than today, as five or six papers may have all arrived at once.

"We had lots of paper to burn. My dad got every paper that was published, even some from the old country. He loved to read."

Annie (Muschamp) Nelson

In the 1920's the Vancouver papers were becoming popular, so paper boys were hired. Some of the first to make a few extra dollars were Donald Marshall, Albert Cooper, Buster and Bob Sherburn.

By the late 1930's Bob Sherburn was delivering the Sun and Bill Hamilton the Province. The route was from one end of Union Bay to the other, with the Sun having about seventy-five homes and the Province about fifty. The paper was delivered six days a week, rain or shine. The monthly cost to the customer was 50¢ and the boys got 20¢ of that. Later it went up to 75¢ and the boys received 25¢.

Both papers came in on the 11:00 p.m. bus and were dropped off at the Nelson Hotel. Usually the proprietor brought the bundles in, but if he forgot and it was raining, the paper boy had the extra job of drying them out.

"The papers would be soaking so I'd have to take them all home and dry them. I'd hang them on the high wooden pulley line in the kitchen and anywhere else they could be draped. As they dried, I'd go out and deliver a few, then wait till a few more dried."

Bill Hamilton

The boys were down at the hotel by 5:30 a.m., even Christmas morning. Sometimes they would stay up Christmas Eve to deliver the papers after the bus came in. If the two boys were compatible they would work out a deal, one delivering both papers to the south end of town as far as Magnone's, the other doing the north end to Davis'. Some people got both papers, the Sun at the front door and the Province at the back. However, most readers were very loyal to one paper or the other. In the 1940's, the printers at the Province went on a prolonged strike, but very few of the loyal subscribers switched over to the Sun.

By the late 1920's, newspapers were encouraging the boys to increase subscriptions. On one competition Donald Marshall won a camera. Later Bob Sherburn, with a boy from Duncan, won a three day trip to Vancouver for getting the most new subscribers on the Island.

1939 MAY ➾ The two boys were met at the boat, taken to hotel rooms reserved by the Sun and then were taken on tours of Vancouver and New Westminster. Of course they had special tickets to view the Royal Procession. In fact they had a simply marvelous time. [6]

The area was growing, and by the 1940's the paperboys went as far south as Boskills and north to Creedles. Don Campbell delivered the Sun and Jack Renwick the Province. They were followed by Gerry Stewart and Jack Glover.

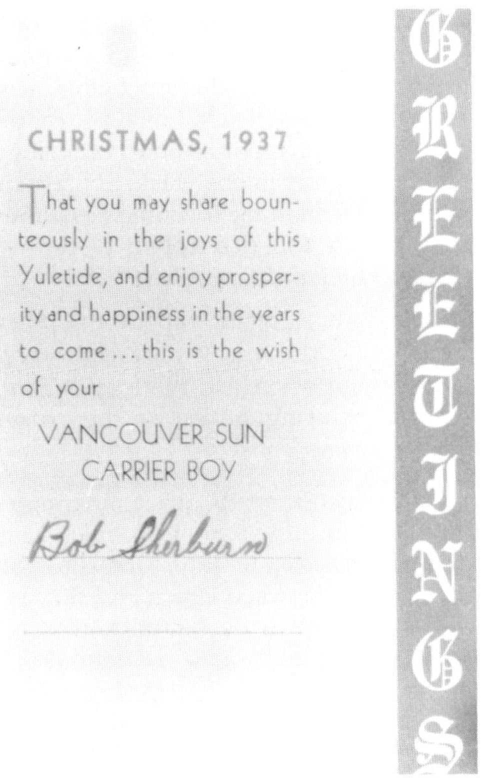

B. Sherburn

Paper boy's Christmas card

SUBSCRIPTION RECEIPT
VANCOUVER SUN
Month ending April 30, 1949
Carrier G. Stewart
Phone
Amount $1.00

"I used to have to go all the way to Mrs. Boskills with one paper. In a sou'easter you were bucking it all the way down but you just flew home. Saturday nights we'd deliver the papers after they came in at midnight, then we'd collect beer bottles at the hall after the dance. We'd be up all night, but have Sunday off."

Jack Glover

Some subscribers bought the paper for different reasons. Long Joe could not read English but he had the Sunday Sun delivered to start his fire. It provided more pages than the Province so it lasted all week. Bill Kelly claimed that the Province was printed on better quality paper. He said the Sun's paper was too thin and his fingers went through it when using it for toilet paper.

POST OFFICE

The early settlers complained about the poor mail service they received. However, with just a few people scattered along the east coast of Vancouver Island, often unable to communicate with each other, it was very hard to present a unified group to petition the Government in Ottawa.

The modern post office in Canada originated from the colonial postal service established in Massachusetts in 1639. As settlement began on the northwest coast, the colonies of British Columbia and Vancouver Island both had separate postal systems and issued their own postage stamps. They united and passed a Postal Ordinance in 1867 "to assimilate the law regulating the Postal Service". The government mail boat, the *Sir James Douglas*, was in charge of delivering the mail. In July 1868, the only Colonial Post Office on northern Vancouver Island was established in Comox, with W. Alexander sworn in as postmaster.

This was a boon to the settlers, who could paddle their canoes up to Comox to mail a letter and have an address to receive mail. Also, the mailboat, on its regular route up the Sound, could be met midstream and letters mailed on board. The early mail boats had "postal stamps" and the purser was authorized to give out mail.

When British Columbia entered Confederation in 1871 the new province came under the Dominion Postal system, which established the rates in the Postal Act of 1867. Mailing a letter became cheaper:

- 3¢ to anywhere in the province
- 10¢ to other provinces
- 6¢ to the United States
- 12 1/2¢ to Great Britain

About the same time, Joseph Spratt was awarded the contract for the East Coast Mail Service. He initiated his service using the steamer *Maude*, which, after numerous complaints, was replaced by a faster vessel with the colourful name, *Cariboo Fly*. This ship served the district well, bringing mail from Nanaimo to Comox fortnightly.

In 1875 the first mine of the district was established on Tsable River by the Baynes Sound Mining Co. Around their wharf a little town named Quadra grew up. A post office was established there in October 1876, with W.M. Dingwall as postmaster. He was followed by C.M. Cuteon in 1878 and R.S. Swan in '79. The mine only operated for about two years before it closed, and soon after the post office was moved to Denman, retaining the name Quadra until 1892 when it became known as Denman Island Post Office.

M. Peters

The first post office was housed in George Howe's store on the beach in 1894

As people complained and governments changed, the mail contract went to different shipping firms on the coast. Unreliability of the steamers was only one of the problems of getting the mail through. With ocean travel, weather was always a big factor. Southeasters could rage for days, "Qualicums" could suddenly blow up, and fog, snow, or even ice could hold up the steamer.

1880 DECEMBER ➾ The steamer *Maude* did not return from Comox till 6:00 p.m. on Thursday owing to Baynes Sound being frozen over. The *Maude* was compelled to go outside while Purser Waite and the first officer had to tramp across Denman Island and back with Baynes Sound mail. [2]

In 1883 the people of Nanaimo agitated for twice weekly mail to Victoria and weekly mail to Comox. Mr. Robert Dunsmuir, MP for Victoria, presented a resolution to that effect. It passed, and none other than the Dunsmuir company won the contract. The new weekly service started October 1, 1884 with Her Majesty's Mail being carried by Captain Rogers of the *SS Robert Dunsmuir*.

After the CPR was completed, the speed of the National Mail Service increased greatly. Instead of being transported by numerous conveyances, a letter was put on the CPR in the east and had an uninterrupted journey across Canada to Port Moody in the West. Two years later, in 1887, when the first train chugged from Montreal to Vancouver, one more step was eliminated in getting the mail from the east or Britain to the Comox District. Now postal bags could go directly from the train onto a steamer bound for Vancouver Island. However, sometimes the train would be weeks late due to blizzards on the prairie, snow slides in the Rockies, or floods in the Fraser Valley.

Discovery of coal at Union had already taken place and there was a constant flow of men and equipment being sent on the *Dunsmuir* for exploration of the mine. The announcement was made in February 1888 that Dunsmuir and Co. was opening up a mine. Men arrived at Union Wharf to construct the railway and work in the mine.

1889 FEBRUARY ⊸ Mr. D.W. Gordon, M.P. for Vancouver Island District, is using his best endeavours in Ottawa to secure the establishment of a mail service to Union Collieries at Comox. [2]

That same year a post office was established at Union, with the mail bags being unloaded off the mail boat at Union Wharf and put onto the Collieries train. For the next few years the people living at Union Wharf had to wait until the mail was sorted at Union, then their letters were delivered the next day.

The district was growing. Grantham and Sandwick Post Offices opened the same year as Union's, with the mail coming by horseback from the mail boat at Comox. Courtenay's Post Office opened in 1893, and finally one at Union Wharf in December 1894. It was to be known as the Union Bay Post Office. Soon there was a good postal business locally between the communities, albeit only once a week. The Weekly News was mailed to readers all over the district.

George Howe had established his hotel and store in the fall of 1893, so it was the natural place to put the new post office. He was sworn in as the first postmaster of Union Bay on December 1, 1894 and his salary was based on the number of stamps that were sold. The post office became a meeting place on "mail day" as townspeople gathered and anxiously awaited the arrival of the mail boat, by then the *Isobel*. As there was no public wharf, the steamer stopped out in the water in front of Howe's store, where the mail bags, freight and passengers were put onto a scow which was rowed to shore and landed on a rock platform built out into the water. On stormy days everything was unloaded at the Collieries dock. A team and wagon was sent around to the wharf to collect the load, but if just the mail was expected, a boy or Chinese was sent with a wheel-barrow. Excitement mounted as the mailbag was dumped out and the names of the fortunate recipients read out.

Post cards were a novelty. Their messages were read out for the enjoyment of all, whether the addressee was there or not. The cards were often made from photographs taken of scenes and buildings around B.C. Photographers travelled the Island taking pictures in each town, returning later to sell them as post cards to the stores.

From the early 1880's there was a road, or rather a trail, to Alberni from Nanaimo. It followed the ocean to Englishman's River where it turned inland. The mail was transported over it by horse and buggy. In the '90s the people of the Comox District felt they deserved mail more than once a week, so they took up a petition to have the thirty miles of road completed from Englishman's River to Union Wharf. The public felt that the E&N Company, with their railway and steam boats, had a monopoly on the east coast mail routes. The company had demanded an exorbitant subsidy for a tri-weekly service, which the Dominion Government had turned down.

Finally, in 1899 the new road over a distance of fifty miles was completed and the overland mail route launched.

1899 JULY ⊸ The mail will leave Nanaimo on Friday evening. The carrier will exchange mail at French Creek and at Union Bay, and by their returning will leave Cumberland on Sunday, connecting with the Alberni mail stage on its southbound trip. This new regulation will give a semi-weekly mail service between Nanaimo and Cumberland. One mail delivery going up by steamer on Wednesday. [4]

In truth, the road was not much more than a trail. Most of the rivers had to be forded as bridges had not been built. When the Big Qualicum was high, the driver hired Qualicum Tom to row him across with the mail, while the mule swam the river. The wagon sported a large umbrella which was supposed to keep the mail dry. When the stage arrived at Union Bay the driver traded his tired mule for a fresh horse from McKay's livery stable to finish the journey to Cumberland and Courtenay.

The overland route carried only letters to the 5,000 people living in the Comox District. Newspapers were too heavy and had to go by steamer, so the outside news still arrived just once a week.

The mail managed to get through during most of the year, but during the winter it was a battle all the way, with mud, swollen creeks and rivers, as well as trees blown across the trail. It was discontinued after only one and a half years of service, until the road was upgraded.

1901 JANUARY ⊸ The Overland Mail is a thing of the past. Why would the good, kind government of the Dominion of Canada attempt to force mail by land over a road that will take years to put into good condition, when a good and grand waterway exists? WE WANT MORE MAIL! [4]

G. Francklyn

The first real post office, with boxes, was attached to the new Fraser & Bishop store

awfully fine fellow, but Ern stepped in."
Violet (Glover, McMurtrie) Rutherford

The population of the Comox Valley was growing and Union Bay soon outgrew its second post office. The Government made the decision to build two identical new buildings, one in Comox and one in Union Bay, using the same design and contractor. A full time postmaster was now needed.

Fred Brown was the first train dispatcher in Victoria when Mr. Dunsmuir built the railway to Nanaimo. In 1907 he came to Union Bay and worked for the Dunsmuir Company, in charge of shipping. After six years in Union Bay the Browns moved back to Victoria.

The family had grown very fond of the little town, so a year later, when Mr. Brown was offered the post office job, he jumped at the chance. Mr. Brown had family connections in the post office, his brother-in-law Adam Horne being postmaster in Nanaimo. Also, the job entailed operating the telegraph and Fred had much experience as a telegrapher.

W. Richardson

Mr. Brown with children and grandchildren in front of the post office

One very cold, stormy day in January 1913, Fred Brown, his wife Sarah and eight of the ten children still living at home, travelled up from Victoria on the *Charmer*. When they arrived at Union Bay, the new post office was not finished. The main floor was one big room - no partitions, no equipment, and no furniture. So Mr. Brown's first task was to oversee the installation of the equipment, while the family settled in upstairs and renewed acquaintances with the villagers.

A partition made of oak was built the whole width of the building, dividing the public area from the office. A Dutch door was at one end, with a top which could be opened to pass parcels

Gradually the service improved, and by 1910 mail came four times a week, carried by different routes and vessels - Tuesday by the *Queen City*, Wednesday and Friday by the *City of Nanaimo*, and Saturday it arrived via the land route.

The population of the little town outgrew the original store, so Fraser and Bishop constructed a new one. A separate room with its own entrance was built onto the south end of the store. This housed a real post office, with boxes for each family's mail. Jack Fraser was postmaster.

It became a gathering place as people waited for the mail to be sorted. All the news of Vancouver Island, British Columbia and the world arrived by post. Most people in the community had connections in the "old country". Letters were sent home to tell of the beauties and opportunities of Canada in hopes that longed-for relatives would immigrate. This was the only means of communication, so everything came by mail, even the occasional proposal of marriage.

"We were waiting for our mail in the old post office, and Margaret Ray was standing by me. I got a letter from Hornby Island and said, "Oh Hornby Island! I wonder who?" I opened it and Margaret read over my shoulder. Here it was a proposal for marriage. She read the whole thing while I did. George Harwood was one of my admirers. He was an

L. Kilvert

Behind the wicket at the Union Bay post office. Fred Brown, first postmaster to serve in this building, is at the back. His daughter, Carrie, who assisted him is standing with Greta's daughter, Jean Abrams

through. Next to it was a narrow counter in front of the wicket where all the business was done. Another wicket served as pass-through for General Delivery. A good half of the partition was taken up by the 178 mail boxes. Most were 2"x3" with a few larger ones for businesses. Each box had a tiny door with a key hole and bevelled glass window. A foot wide step ran beneath the boxes to enable short people to reach the top. A tall, solid oak desk stood against one wall for the public's use.

Sharing the large office were the telegraph receiving equipment, the telephone switchboard, and the customshouse office. Mr. Brown wore two hats. As postmaster and telegrapher he was paid separate salaries by two different departments of the federal government.

"The telegraph department gave holidays but the Post Office didn't, so every year a telegrapher came for a week to replace Grandpa, but he still had to work in the post office."

Mildred (Hicks) Simpson

A great improvement took place in the postal systems in the towns north of Nanaimo in 1914, when the E&N railway was completed to Courtenay. The first train arrived August 6, and a month later a mail car was added. Now the community had mail by train and steamer.

1914 NOVEMBER ➾ Commencing Thursday the mail will arrive and be dispatched as follows.

Arrives via E&N	*Tue. Thurs.Sat. at 4:30 p.m.*
Dispatched via E&N	*Mon. Wed. Fri. at 10:30 p.m.*
Arrives via SS Charmer	*Wed. Fri. Evening*
Dispatched via SS Charmer	*Thurs. Sat. at 6:00 a.m.*

Mail by SS Cowichan to be discontinued. [4]

Now, letters mailed in Victoria or Nanaimo arrived in Union Bay the very next day. It was not until June 1920, a short time after the E&N started daily runs, that the mail was transported exclusively by train. Three times a week the train connected in Nanaimo with the CPR boat, and the mail bags were put aboard.

M. Simpson

Some of the large Brown family. Left to right: Mildred and Edythe Hicks, Babs?, Mr. Brown, John Doney, Mrs. Brown, Alva and Jim Kerr, Laura

E. Leighton

Mr. and Mrs. Edward Baldwin with their twin grandchildren, Harold and Evelyn Leighton

One of the cars on the E&N was a mail coach. Aboard was a postal clerk who worked as the train sped from station to station. Alf Kerr held the job for many years. He opened the bags from each post office along the way, and quickly sorted them into receiving bags which lined the wall of the coach - one for each town, which was traded at the station for the outgoing sack.

Half an hour before the train was due, Mr. Brown closed up the mail bags and entrusted the King's mail to Hungo who, with his horse and buggy, drove the 1/4 mile up Station Road to await the train's arrival. At Union Bay the train always stopped at the station, giving time to exchange the mail bags. Some of the smaller villages, such as Fanny Bay, just had a fly stop if there was no passenger wanting to get off or on.

"They hung the mail sack up on a wooden pole and the fellow in the baggage car, going at 60 miles an hour, would stick his arm out and grab the bag. At the same time he would kick the other sack out the door onto the ground. If he had some fragile mail the train would stop at Fanny Bay".

Joe Walker

In the early 1920's Charles Cave bought a little Ford car, and for a few years he had the contract to transport the mail between the station and the post office. Then in 1923 Edward Baldwin took over, and twice a day, with the bags carefully stowed in the back of his little Chevy truck, he took off for the station.

"Mr. Baldwin picked it up and made that "whip corner", ZIP, like that. I don't know how he did it, nobody else could. All in an effort to get the mail to the post office in record-breaking time."

Joe Walker

M. Vowels

Fred and Mame Vowels used this Ford Coupe to transport the mail from the post office to the train station. Seen here is son Eddie who later enjoyed the car

"Mr. Baldwin never had brakes on his car; he'd wheel into the side of the post office and bang into the gate to stop. The government had to replace the gate nearly every year. Once I left the gate open and he went sailing right through and banged up against the garage. Boy, did he bawl me out."

Mildred (Hicks) Simpson

The Baldwin family came to the Bay in 1916 from Cumberland where Harold and Eva had already started school. Mr. Baldwin, a carpenter for the company, built and lived in the fourth house above the track on McLeod Road.

Following Mr. Baldwin, in 1945, Fred and Mame Vowels combined that job with their dairy farm. The mailbags rode in the rumble seat of their Ford Coupe until 1951 when a truck brought the mail up the Island instead of the train.

"MAME'S FORD" by Frank in the mail car

Henry Ford's black chariot
Driven by Hot Rod Hariette
Has a radio and wire wheels
With lots of rattles and squawks and squeals.

The tires are nearly new
The brakes were good once too
Carburetor's not worth a hoot
And wonder if the horn will toot?

The motors still fairly good
And there's a fancy do-dad on the hood
The paint is still quite black
And there's a rumble seat in back.

The upholstery is all tattered and brown
When you get in the springs let you down
But who cares about riding in state?
If you start soon enough you'll never be late.

Twice a day it carries the mail
All through snow, wind, rain and hail
No matter what the weather is -
You can always depend on the old tin Liz.

It was two days before the E&N came through, in August 1914, that Canada declared war on Germany. Life in the community during the war years centered on the post office, with news arriving hourly via the telegraph. Letters from sons serving in Europe, and from loved ones in the British Isles, were anxiously awaited. To encourage citizens to write to the soldiers, the Government introduced a rate decrease. As of February 1915, postage for letters addressed to British and Canadian troops in Europe was 2¢.

In April 1915 the Government imposed a one cent "War Tax". This was prepaid by the sender by means of a "War Stamp" used on all letters and post cards mailed in Canada, in addition to the regular postage of 3¢.

A Parcel Post Service for Canada was initiated in 1914. Up until then all parcels came by freight on the steamers. Ottawa imposed a weight limit of 11 lb. on all parcels. Now the office needed large scales and room to store the parcels. Any parcels arriving from outside of Canada had to be claimed from Mr. Abrams, the customs man. The Government issued guidelines for wrapping parcels.

1916 NOVEMBER ➾ Note from the Post Office
As many parcels sent overseas are damaged they must be well packed and covered with canvas or linen.
Don't use light cardboard boxes like shoe boxes.
Use - Strong boxes, corrugated cardboard.
- Tin boxes such as cookie boxes.
- Strong wooden boxes. [5]

The good people of the Bay took this advice to heart, wrapping the heavy boxes with cloth (another use for the flour sack), sealing it shut with glue, and tying it up with stout cord. The packing approached half the weight of the parcel. Then the Government asked the citizens to limit the weight and number of parcels sent, stating that ammunition, food and stores for the army took first priority on the transport system.

Even the postal building was put into war use. In the basement a cookhouse was set up to supply the officer's mess which was situated in the church next door.

"The reading room in the church was the headquarters for the army and the officers' mess. The cookhouse was under the post office. We used to get free loaves of bread and everything. Oh boy, that bread was good!"

Doug Brown

Catalogue buying became very popular, and as payment had to accompany the order, a good deal of the postmaster's job was making out money orders. The cost of a money order became proportionately cheaper the larger the sum. A $10.00 money order cost 10¢ while one for $100.00 cost 40¢. It was not until 1922 that C.O.D.

service was introduced. Although a more costly way to receive items, it was easier for the customer, as exact prices and freight charges were sometimes hard to estimate accurately. Often the post master was obliged to hold the parcel a week or two until the receiver got paid and had money to pay for the C.O.D. order.

Mr. Brown conducted the King's Post in a very serious, businesslike manner. Gone were the days when everyone knew the message on your post card. One by one, as his daughters Alva, Carrie, Edythe and Laura came of age, they were sworn in as postal clerks. Mrs. Brown never ventured into the office below her living quarters, and the boys were absolutely forbidden. Fred had a loud intimidating voice.

"Brown ran the post office. As a kid, when you went into the post office Mr. Brown would ask, 'What the hell are you doing in here?'"

Hector Hooper

"Mr.Brown would give us heck. He'd say, 'Don't swear, boys, it sounds like hell. Not that I give a damn but the customers don't like it'."

Bill McKay

Fred Brown had very strict habits, starting every morning at 6:00 a.m. with a cold bath which he had poured the night before. After dressing, he tucked a white silk handkerchief into his pocket, ate breakfast, then walked down the stairs, opened the wicket, and was ready for business at 7:00 a.m. The mail bags were closed at 11:00 a.m. sharp and sent off to the station. Then the incoming mail from the district had to be sorted. Right after lunch, with one of the girls in charge of the office, Mr. Brown personally delivered the mail to Fraser and Bishop's store. There he was offered a cigar which he enjoyed while chatting with Jack Fraser.

It was a long day. The northbound train, bringing everything from the outside world, arrived at 4:30 p.m. To speed things up, the wicket was closed during sorting. Most of the year, with help, the sorting could be done in half an hour. It took much longer at Christmas with as many as five or six sacks of mail arriving, and it was not unusual to finish at 7:00 p.m. The group of eager people, with their keys clutched in their hands, waited in the outer office getting progressively noisier. Fred would silence the crowd with a loudly bellowed oath.

After the mail was sorted and parcels given out, it was upstairs to a family dinner.

"The only time my Dad ever took a drink was Sunday night at the dinner table. He took a little drink of scotch, no water, just scotch. No one else at the table was ever offered any. Dad went to bed every night at 9:00 p.m. He wouldn't give a darn who was there - the mayor, the king of England. He just said 'good night', poured his bath for the morning and went to bed."

Doug Brown

Edythe, the fifth Brown daughter, worked with her father from 1920 until her marriage to a Northwest Mounted Policeman named Russell Hicks, who was stationed in Union Bay. They moved to Alberni, and little more than a year later, in 1926, Russell died, so Edythe returned a widow with her infant daughter Mildred. She worked with her father until his death in 1935 and was then appointed postmistress.

During Mrs. Hick's tenure of over forty years, she saw several changes of great significance which improved the speed of mail delivery. In 1939 an airmail service across Canada, from Vancouver to Montreal, was initiated by the Trans-Canadian Airlines. Service to the maritimes was added in 1940, and sending letters via air across the Atlantic became a reality in 1943. It was amazing to receive a letter from your "fighting man" in only four or five days. Replacing the train in 1951, a special mail truck run by the Vancouver Island Coach Lines carried and collected the mail up and down the Island. The incoming mail arrived an hour earlier and left early in the morning.

The mail must get through! At Union Bay it usually did. Mrs. Hicks knew everyone well, so if a letter arrived with an unusual or mixed up address she usually tucked it into the right box.

Miss Mary Hart, (I don't remember
her married name.)
Union Bay, B.C.

Dear Garden Hone and Family
Union Bay, Canada

To Liz,(by the big barn on the farm that
looks across to Denman)
Union Bay. B.C.

From an article by Mary Moore

M. Simpson

Postmistress Edythe Hicks and Greta Kay ready for a spin on a borrowed motor bike

TELEGRAPH

Even before the E&N was built from Victoria to Nanaimo there was a telegraph system between the two cities. In the early 1880's Fred Brown, who much later came to Union Bay, was the telegrapher in Nanaimo. Dunsmuir had built a line to Wellington to serve his mines. The citizens of the Comox Valley had long been asking for a service to their end of the Island, with members of parliament petitioning the government in Ottawa.

1892 JANUARY ➾ D.W. Gordon, MP, finally wins a government telegraph line from Nanaimo to Comox. The line is to follow the wagon trail to Englishman's River, then along the Government trail past the Qualicums, then strike straight ahead for Union Bay. There it will follow the railroad to Cumberland and the road to Comox. Mr. D.L. McLaughlin, contractor for the line, has started to inspect a portion of the route and says contracts for getting out poles are to be let. The line will be first class all the way and is to be finished by June 30th. It will be a great convenience to shipping and commercial enterprises. [2]

Large gangs of men were hired to log and erect the poles. By May, ten miles of poles were up but the line had not arrived from England, so they could not string it as they went. This meant going back over the route again, which added to the cost. In August, when the line was within seven miles of Comox, the contractor ran out of the advanced money allowed by the Government and could not pay the workers. Many of them quit, as some had not been paid for two months.

It was decided to abandon the line from Union to Comox. Messages for Comox came to Union and were then relayed to Comox via the telephone. Finally, fifteen months after it had been started, the line was complete, but the service was not without problems.

1893 APRIL ➾ The new telegraph line from Nanaimo to Union is at last finished and yesterday was in thorough working order, but a storm last night caused a breakage which cannot be located yet. There is no competent operator at Union. The man doing the duty does not know the first thing about telegraphy. When the damage is repaired and a capable man is placed at the keys in Union, Nanaimo will finally be in telegraphic communication with that city. [2]

Mr. Fryer had the first job as operator, and apparently could send messages but could not read the messages by sound. He complained that he had been trained in England where he said the system was different. Very soon he was replaced by Mr. A. Fraser who struggled along at the job for about seven months, then left and became a customs man. David Jones had the job next, and finally, in 1894, Thomas Horne (brother-in-law to F. Brown) was hired. At last there was "an experienced hand at the bellows".

About 1895, telegraph offices were established at Comox and Union Bay. The MacDonald sisters were the first operators. Maggie was stationed in Comox, and Emma at Union Wharf. Emma lived at the Nelson Hotel. If she got a little homesick, the sisters switched jobs. Emma went home to Comox for a rest, and Maggie came to Union Wharf for a little more excitement. Father George owned the Elk Hotel.

The small telegraph building which sat beside the trestle near the beach became a very busy place. There was a constant tap, tap of the telegraphy machine as the messages kept coming. Emma carefully copied them down and passed them on. A ten word message could be sent for 25¢, with 2¢ for each additional word.

Ships were able to wire from any port on the coast and state their arrival time and the amount of coal to be purchased. Friends and families could get in touch in an emergency. Scores of football games played in Nanaimo could be obtained before the players arrived home. The Provincial Police used the telegraph to catch thieves, and the Immigration Department to find deserters.

1895 DECEMBER ➾ A constable at Johnson's Wharf in Nanaimo captured a man on the *SS Joan*. He was arrested for fraud after a telegram from Union Wharf. [3b]

The sixty-five mile line was strung through the forest with just a narrow trail beside it. With every storm the line was brought down by falling branches and trees. The first linesman was Mr. Conway, followed by young Tom Hudson at the turn of the century.

In 1886 Tommy's father was killed by gas when rescuing fellow miners after the disastrous explosion at No.1 Mine in Nanaimo. A year later, at only eleven years of age Tommy went down the mines, to help support his mother. When he was seventeen he moved to Union, and soon after married Nellie Piket. In 1901, possibly to better service the telegraph line, Tommy built a little bungalow next to the Wilson Hotel and the family moved to Union Bay. The couple had a daughter, Gertie, and three boys.

Tommy was a rough-and-ready sort of fellow with a quick temper. He loved sports, a party, and a good laugh.

1922 DECEMBER ➾ Mr. T. Hudson, working for the Dominion Telegraph Company, had just placed new poles in position on Tuesday, and climbed an old pole and diconnected the wire. The old pole immediately collapsed, and as Tom was attached to it, he came down heavily with the pole. He struck a spike on another pole and received a nasty 8" gash. But, as the genial Tommy cannot see the cut, he says, "I'll have to eat my meals standing up". [5]

Mr. Hudson was in charge of maintaining the telegraph line from Bowser through Cumberland to Cape Lazo. This was a very big and difficult area to service. Apart from the almost daily south easters during the winter, three or four times a year a westerly whistled through the forest between Union Bay and Qualicum, snapping off branches and trees as if they were match sticks. Often he had to call out extra help, and it would take days to restore the service.

Over the years the line was improved and in 1910 Mr. Hudson installed a telegraph line from Comox to Cape Lazo. This land station was a life saver for ships, which very soon were required by law to be equipped with wireless instruments and operators.

When the weather cooperated and there were no repairs needed, Tommy had other ventures to occupy him. At different times he ran a livery stable, served as a police officer, sold cars and also life insurance. If their father was away pursuing one of his other careers when a line went down, Mr. Brown, the telegrapher, would call one of the Hudson boys, Tom, Leonard, or Reg, out of school to make repairs.

At 50 years, Tom died in bed of a heart attack, after being the "life and soul" at a social held by the Native Sons of which he was a member.

1924 DECEMBER ➻ Tommy was a great athlete twenty years ago and athletics often weakens the heart. He used to sweep the board at local athletic contests in high jumping, putting the shot and short distance races, and the only man he could not beat at wrestling was "Cuddy" Johnson. [6]

Mr. Louis Cole came from Estevan to take up the duties of government linesman after Mr. Hudson's death.

About 1906 Miss MacDonald resigned her position as telegrapher to marry Richard Ray, a locomotive engineer, and a one-armed man named Jimmy McNeil got the job. He was a jovial fellow, active in the community, always ready to emcee a concert or referee a football match. He, in turn, married Emma's sister-in-law Bessie Ray.

Len Lucas took over and was the operator when the dam broke and the flood swept the little telegraph house out to sea. It was one of the most noteworthy pieces of news ever generated in Union Bay but alas, the telegrapher could not tell the world. He had heard the roar and dashed to higher ground. The building was found washed ashore on Denman.

New equipment and new accommodation were needed, so Mr. Lucas shared the customs office with George Roe in the small building next to the Wilson Hotel. Two men in such close quarters proved impossible. Mr. Roe and Mr. Lucas had one disagreement after another, until one huge row that had the whole town talking. Shortly after this Lucas left, the new post office was built, and Mr. Fred Brown was the town telegrapher.

Fred Brown was well trained. He had left his home in Prince Edward Island to join his brother in Chicago, where he learned telegraphy. From there he travelled to Nanaimo and got a job as one of the town's telegraphers, where he fell in love with Sarah, daughter of Hudson Bay factor, Adam Horne. In 1883 they travelled on their honeymoon to Yale, where CPR's Mr. Onderdonk had hired Fred as the town telegrapher and postmaster. A few years after the last spike was driven, the family moved to Victoria where Fred began his association with the Dunsmuir Company as dispatcher for the E&N.

Mr. Brown had full responsibility of setting up the new post office building in Union Bay. The telegraph equipment was situated on one wall in the main post office, along with the telephone exchange for Denman and Hornby. The tap, tap, tap of the telegraph machine could be heard by the customers in the post office. The First World War had started and the telegraph was a means of keeping abreast of troop movements and battles. Mr. Brown was also the bearer of sad tidings when one of the local sons was killed.

Also in the post office was a telephone switch board which had a direct line to the Canadian Collieries Company office. When a message came via the telegraph it could immediately be rung through to the company.

"The day the war ended my Dad got the telegram and phoned over to Mr. Auchinvole. Then all the whistles started tooting."

Doug Brown

In the early 1930's the telegraph office closed and messages then came through Courtenay.

M. Simpson

Postmaster and telegrapher Fred Brown and wife Sarah

TELEPHONE

Mr. Fred Brown was definitely a pioneer in communication on Vancouver Island.

1883 FEBRUARY ➾ Music by telephone was heard on the line between Nanaimo and Departure Bay, about three miles in length. Mr. W.C. Halleck stood in the Nanaimo office and played "The Blue Bells of Scotland" and other airs on the flute. The sweet strains were distinctly and plainly heard by Mr. C. Loat and Mr. Young at Departure Bay. Mr. F. Brown, who held the hearing tube for Mr. Halleck, said he could distinctly hear the gentlemen in Departure Bay beating in time to the music. [2]

By the 1890's there was a system of sorts connecting the district towns. In reality, it was a message center, as the public were not able to speak directly to one another.

1893 JUNE ➾ Telephone messages can be sent from Courtenay to Union and Comox for 25¢. They are written down as a telegraphic message and delivered to the recipient. It must be remembered that to hunt up and deliver the message is worth 10¢ so really the cost is not so high. Secrecy is maintained as to all dispatches. [3a]

The British Columbia Phone Company had a system from Victoria to Nanaimo, and in 1909 completed seventy more miles to connect Parksville, Little Qualicum and Union Bay, with branch exchanges at Cumberland and Courtenay. This was of great advantage for calls out of the district, but by no means meant a telephone service as we know it. Union Bay had only two pay stations that the public could use. One was situated at Fraser and Bishop's store, the other at the Exchange in Hooper's house, fifth house north of the post office. Mrs. Bebe Muir, a grass widow, was the operator. She and her three children lived with her parents, the Hoopers. Evelyn Campbell cross-shifted with Bebe, so the system was always open, to accommodate captains of tugs so that they could be in touch with Vancouver. In 1907 Mr. T. Hudson, the maintenance man, started installing poles on Denman and Hornby Islands. In the summer some of the young boys went over to help cut the brush down and were paid in candy and pop. With one central station on each Island, the settlers were connected to the exchange at Union Bay. From Union Bay, calls could be made to Fanny Bay or Cumberland for 10¢, but to call Courtenay the cost was 20¢.

C. Benson

Union Bay's two telephone operators, Evelyn Campbell and Bebe Muir, dressed in Bebe's brothers' kilts and army uniforms

Finally, in 1921 the B.C. Telephone company added additional telephone circuits at Union Bay, so that all the business firms, logging companies, stores and hotels had their own phones. The big wooden box phones were mounted on the wall with a large metal mouthpiece on the front. Calls within the community were made by cranking the side handle and ringing the right number of rings - one long and two shorts, etc.

In 1924 the long distance service within the district was improved by the addition of more copper circuits. Now, instead of ringing central, giving the name of the party you wished to speak to, then hanging up and waiting for connections to be made, the "two-number rapid fire system" came into use. This eliminated the wait, was more efficient, and with it came a rate reduction. It cost 10¢ for five minutes.

Long distance service to other parts of B.C. was also improved over the years. In 1913 the *Princess Louise* laid a cable from Vancouver to Nanaimo, making a direct phone route from the Island to the rest of the province. The wireless station at Cape Lazo was greatly improved in 1925 when a radiotelephone system was installed. Then, in 1931, the B.C. Telephone ship, the *Brico*, dropped a cable on the ocean floor linking Powell River and Cape Lazo.

At first there were so few phones in the district that it was not necessary to know the number of the party you were calling. If you gave the operator the name, she knew by heart the corresponding number. However, as phones increased this became impossible, and by the 1930's, operators refused to connect calls if only the name was given.

At Union Bay there were very few phones until after the war. On the Company Hill there were only two - Nurse Reid at the north end had a phone for emergency health calls, and Harry Glover had one for company emergency break-down calls. These two numbers managed to serve the twenty families living on the hill with a very good message service. Neighbours were constantly dropping in to use the phone, and Jim Reid and the Glover children were often called upon to deliver messages.

If Kay Carter wanted to get a message to her mother, three houses from Glover's, she would call up Winnie, have a chat and give her the message. Winnie would send one of the girls off with a note to Mrs. Formby. The Cooper girls, four doors the other way, had many admirers, and calls would often come long distance from an infatuated serviceman. Then a twin or Winanne was dispatched at top speed to bring Gladys or Phyllis to the phone. But during the war not all the calls were happy affairs. The day Ian Pollock was killed, it was Winnie Glover who had to deliver the message, "Killed in Action".

A big change came to the phone system in 1941, when the old magneto system was replaced by a "common battery" service. A new switchboard was installed at Courtenay and new telephones in the homes. This meant no more cranking. All that was necessary to signal the operator for "Number Please" was to lift the receiver.

Union Bay numbers were changed in March 1959 to ADams 5-1234. Phone numbers and party line rings were changed as well as the telephones. Automation was introduced in 1962.

New Telephone System Comes Into Service

10 P.M., Saturday, May 3

NOTE THESE IMPORTANT CHANGES:

1. **No More "Cranking."**
   You will no longer have to run a crank on your telephone. All you will have to do to signal the operator will be to lift the receiver.
2. **All Numbers To Be Changed.**
   The change of system made it necessary to re-assign all telephone numbers and party-line rings. The new numbers will be in the new telephone directory, but be sure not to use it until after 10 p.m. Saturday, May 3.
3. **New Telephone Office**
   Commencing Monday, May 5, all telephone business will be transacted at the new telephone office on the Island Highway, and the old office will be closed.
4. **Give Number To Operator**
   In making a call, please give the operator the number you want, not the name. In order to handle calls when names and not numbers are given, it would be necessary for operators to memorize every name and corresponding number. Courtenay has grown to a size that makes this impossible.

BRITISH COLUMBIA TELEPHONE COMPANY

RADIO

After the First World War, people in Union Bay started experimenting with radio. It was not just a matter of buying a crystal set; one had to have some electrical knowledge. The sets were bought in parts or kits for about $25 and put together in many ingenious ways. By all accounts, Jimmy Murdock was the first to make one in Union Bay. He lived in a little house next door to the Hornes when he bought himself a "Radiola Super-Hetrodyne". Outside he built a large diamond frame which he wrapped with wires for his aerial. Jimmy would put his head set on, and when he was lucky enough to receive something, sit and rock to the beat of the music. Like all new radio owners, he boasted of hearing stations as far away as California. But, whenever anyone was invited to share the experience, the reception, likely as not, was very poor.

For those not fortunate enough to have their own set, "radio concerts" were held by the Northern Radio Co. at the Great War Veterans Association's hall in Courtenay. People sat and listened to the sounds of singers and bands drifting over the airways from American cities. These concerts progressed to larger halls where the audience danced to the music.

By the 1930's, radio was becoming very popular and everyone was saving to buy a set. As wages were low, the new radios were expensive items, many of them between one and two hundred dollars. There were the Majestic, Spartan, Westinghouse and RCA from which to choose.

In the beginning all the stations received at Union Bay were American and music was about all that was broadcast. The lucky listeners tuned in to Seattle or Bellingham and sometimes as far away as Denver or Los Angeles. The position and size of the antenna dictated the stations received. There were some British Columbia stations but at first their signals were very weak. The commercial station in Victoria that claimed to serve the Island could not be heard past the Malahat. Soon Vancouver stations could be heard. Every Wednesday night people tuned into CKWX to hear the Roscoe Entertainers and Sammy Davis, a local boy who played with them.

Then, in November 1936 the CBC started broadcasting coast to coast, and soon acquired

a large following. The next year everyone in town with a radio was up early (London time) on May 12 listening to King George VI's coronation.

"Today, in a manner hitherto unknown in history, the King will come to his Consecration and his Crowning accompanied by his people. For, by a marvel of science, millions of them throughout the world will be able to listen to the noble words which lay this great charge upon him, as if they themselves were present in the Abbey Church of Westminster."

Rev. F.C. Chapman, Courtenay

Every morning, housewives kept happy and healthy with the "Happy Gang". People became slaves to the "little box" as they hurried home to follow the adventures of "Ma Perkins" or ate lunch to the "Farm Show". Everything stopped for "Hockey Night in Canada" with most of the Bay cheering for the Maple Leafs. The teenagers got their thrills from the "Lone Ranger" and the "Shadow". Sunday night the family gathered around the radio for "Lux Radio Theatre".

"My brother was visiting us and he needed a haircut, so he went along to Jim Guiness just before six o'clock. Jim said, 'Well, I'm sorry but you'll have to come back at seven. I have to listen to Major Bowes.'"

Elizabeth (Walker) Renwick

A $2.50 license was required yearly to operate a radio. An inspector visited the district every few months and checked homes for licenses, fining the many offenders $2.00 and costs. The inspector also investigated noise problems because the radios were susceptible to interference.

1938 MARCH •➜ A.W. Neill, M.P., brings up again the need to increase the power of the Radio Inspector, who locates interference (in way of motors or engines) for radios. "Radio Pests" are noted at all times of the day in many parts of the district. It is also noted that when the inspector is in the district it is silent, and when he goes it resumes. Give the inspector the power to fine people who will not correct their equipment. [6]

Politics

Politics was always a hot issue. In the small town everyone knew each other's political leanings. It is said that on election night families would list house by house throughout the village and guess who the occupants would vote for. When tallied up, it came very close to the figures listed in the next newspaper.

After Confederation, the Baynes Sound area was part of the Vancouver Island constituency. This federal seat included most of the Island, except Victoria, as well as settlements around Vancouver. The first polling station in the district was at Comox, with booths opening at Denman in 1874 and Hornby in 1876. Even after 1890, when Union had a polling station, people at Union Wharf had to travel to Comox. They cast their vote at the Central School House in polling station No.9.

By the election in 1900, Union Bay had a polling booth at which twenty-six people cast a vote. This had increased to forty-seven voters by 1911. For both federal and provincial elections, eligible voters had to be British subjects, which covered most of the residents, except the Chinese, at the Bay. The settlers always turned out in large numbers to hear the candidates when they came to town.

1917 OCTOBER ➾ Mr. H.S. Clements, Conservative "win the war" candidate and supporter of the Union Government in the coming election, arrived in Union Bay from the North Island to campaign in the area. [5]

Clements received 81 votes and the Liberal McInnis 41, a proportion reflected in the rest of the riding. Then, in 1921, the tide turned when A.W. Neill, an Independent Liberal, captured the district. The 217 voters at the Bay gave him 107 votes, and Clements just 91, while the first time Labour candidate, Armishaw, got 19.

The popular Mr. Neill, who worked hard to gain the Old Age Pension for Canadians, represented Comox-Alberni until 1944, and Union Bay voters were loyal to him. In 1945 the CCF had its first candidate, T. Barnett, but Union Bay stuck to the winner, another Independent Liberal, John Gibson. He was a logger from the west coast. It was not until 1953 that the voters at the Bay began their long love affair with the socialist party, even through the Progressive Conservative swing in 1958. John Moore became president of the Comox Valley Conservative Association when everyone was following John Diefenbaker.

There seemed to be more interest in provincial politics than federal. In 1861 twenty-four electors of Comox district gave Dr. John Ash sixteen votes. Because it was a smaller riding, most of the candidates came from the district and were personally known to the settlers. After B.C. joined Confederation, the second member elected to the Legislative Assembly was William Dingwall in 1882, a local who had been timekeeper for the Baynes Sound Coal Company. He strongly opposed the E&N land grant at the time when Robert Dunsmuir represented Nanaimo. Dingwall was defeated in 1887 and was followed by three "out of district" men. J. Hunter, Supt. of the E&N from Victoria, ran against the popular J. McPhee of Courtenay and won.

1890 JUNE ➾ Constable W.B. Anderson, returning officer, made a quick trip from Comox to Nanaimo in fourteen hours. He travelled from Comox to Englishman River by canoe, then walked to Wellington where he took the train to Nanaimo. The poll results for the district were:

Comox Settlement -	Hunter	67	McPhee	63
Union Settlement-	"	23	"	2
Denman Island-	"	25	"	8

Hunter was elected by a majority of 42. [2]

In 1898 Conservative James Dunsmuir who was well-known at the Bay, represented the district for two years. He then served Nanaimo for three years, at which time he was Premier. From T. B. Humphrey's victory over Dingwall in an 1888 by-election, until 1916, the district including Union Bay voted Conservative. Two Cumberland merchants, Lewis Mounce and Robert Grant (Mrs. L. Ray's brother) followed each other as MLA.

In 1909 Union Bay's own Michael Manson represented the Conservatives. His fellow Conservatives, J. Fraser, H. & H. Glover, P. Reid, D. Renwick, and E.T. Searle rallied to his aid and held political meetings. He easily won in 1909 and again in 1912.

1915 MARCH ➾ The Conservatives of Comox Electorate District met at Union Bay to nominate a candidate. The 150 delegates present unanimously endorsed Mike Manson. [5]

With the Conservatives on the decline, Premier McBride resigned in 1915. Manson faced a tough opposition and lost to Liberal Hugh Stewart.

1916 SEPTEMBER ➾ Liberals sweep the province. Prohibition and Women's Suffrage referendum carried by a large majority throughout the province. [5]

Following Stewart in 1920 was the Courtenay preacher T. Menzie, then came P. Harrison in 1924.

Jack Fraser was a good friend of Simon Tolmie and no doubt played a large part in organizing Conservative meetings.

1925 SEPTEMBER ➺ Dr. S.F. Tolmie draws a big crowd of Conservatives from all over the district to a meeting at Union Bay. Delegates came from Alberni and Parksville in the south, to Merville in the north. [6]

Dr. McNaughton, a Cumberland physician, represented the district in 1928. The doctor, very popular at Union Bay, received 111 of the 127 votes cast. With the Depression, Tolmie's government met many problems. By 1931 men were on relief and the mines were only working part-time.

1932 FEBRUARY ➺ District men on a hunger march climbed into Creech's open truck in a snow storm and motored first to Nanaimo for a rally, then on to the capital. They are camping out on the steps of the parliament buildings. [6]

The government was blamed, and in 1933 with five candidates to choose from (two Conservatives, two Liberals, and one CCF), L. Hanna was elected, receiving 75 out of the 146 votes at Union Bay. He joined T.D. Pattulo's Liberal government.

Compared with the canoe trip of Constable Anderson in 1890, the mode of travel for returning officer Len Piket reflected the changing times.

1936 OCTOBER ➺ The ballot boxes in isolated areas were collected by plane by returning officer Len Piket. The Canadian Airlines plane hired from Vancouver took off in bright weather for Kyuquot, the most western part of the Comox Electorate District. On the return trip, the clouds came in and they were forced back to Kyuquot. From there Mr. Piket got to Alert Bay where he stayed until next day. Quite a thrill in the course of his duties, as the pilot was unfamiliar with the area. [6]

Politics were also changing, and in 1937 the CCF candidate, Colin Cameron, represented the district in the Liberal government. At Union Bay he collected 92 votes against 48 for the Conservatives, and 41 for the Liberals. Almost identical numbers were cast again for Mr. Cameron in 1941.

For the next two legislative sessions the district elected a local logging operator, H. Welch, to the Coalition legislature. Union Bay remained CCF. They again supported the winner in 1952 when W. Moore, CCF, of Courtenay went to Victoria. In 1956 the Social Credit Party became a force in B.C. Dan Campbell represented Comox riding for thirteen years, but Union Bay remained loyal to the CCF.

MIKE MANSON

Michael Manson was born in 1858 at Sandwick on the Shetland Islands. At the age of sixteen he set out for Sandwick, B.C. to work on his Aunt Rubina and Uncle Oliver Duncan's farm. After a few years he moved to Nanaimo and worked as a brakeman on a coal train, then clerked in and subsequently owned, a dry goods and grocery store.

He left Nanaimo at intervals to trade with the Indians, and established a trading post at Manson's Landing on Cortez Island in 1882. During this time he became a master of the Chinook language.

In Nanaimo he courted and gave an engagement ring to Jane Renwick, whose strict religious father did not approve of Mike. Not wanting to lose such a good worker as Jenny, Mr. Renwick beat her over the hands and broke the ring. This only made the couple more determined. One evening in August of 1878, as her father was coming home from work, he passed Jenny who he supposed was going to a prayer meeting. But she was on her way to meet Mike, who had hired a canoe and six Indians for an elopement. The husky canoers paddled all night, and when they arrived at Sidney Mr. Manson hired a team and wagon to Victoria where they were married.

Back in Nanaimo, he first showed his flair for "public life" by becoming the city clerk, then secretary of the School Board. In 1887 Mike preempted land at Flint Lake on Cortez, where he built a home as well as keeping the store at Manson's Landing.

The sea beckoned and Michael bought the $6,000 steamer *Rustler*. With it he had his first contact with Union Wharf when he delivered rails for the new railroad. The *Rustler* was wrecked in 1889 off Nelson Island, with no insurance. Eight months later, in 1890, his new 123' ship, *Thistle*, was launched in Victoria. With a crew of ten, it could sleep thirty-two. Mr. Manson used his boats for coastal trade: copper ore from Texada, fish from the Queen Charlotte Islands, seals from the Bering Sea, furs from the Columbia River.

1895 SEPTEMBER ➺ The *Thistle* from Queen Charlotte's fishing banks called at the "Wharf" for coal. She had 30 tons of halibut on board. [2]

At Nanaimo Mike and Jenny started their family, and although the first daughter died in infancy, within the next ten years they had five more children. Tragedy struck again in the fall of 1890 when all the little ones caught diptheria. Mr. and Mrs. Manson nursed the children until, one after another, the four youngest children died. Jenny got the disease too, and was so sick that twice preparations were made to take her out of the house, dead. Then one evening she told Mike she was sure she would be dead before midnight. Mercifully, she fell asleep and Mike turned the clock

M. Ellingsen

Including two sets of twins, the Manson family on the verandah of the wharfinger's house. Back: Robina (twin), Michael, Wilf, Ethel (twin). Middle: Margaret, Hazel, Jennie. Front: Flossie (twin), Gwendolyn, Florence (twin)

ahead, so when she awoke the clock said 12:30. She was still alive and slowly began to recover.

1890 OCTOBER The second child afflicted. Mr. & Mrs. M. Manson mourn their son William, age three, who died in hospital from diptheria. Nine year old Robina died yesterday. Two more of the children and the mother are also sick. [2]

In 1896 James Dunsmuir persuaded Michael to leave the sea and become the wharfinger at Union Bay. He leased out the *Thistle,* and finally sold it in 1904 to Mr. Dunsmuir who used it as his private yacht.

The family followed Mike in 1898 and lived in the big house at the bottom of Russell Hill for nine years. While at Union Bay, Jenny was busy with a new family. Twin girls and two other children were born before she left Nanaimo, and another set of twin girls and a daughter arrived at Union Bay. Mike was a great community worker wherever he lived, and he was soon on the school board, teaching Sunday school, and leading a drive for a church.

The family spent most summers on Cortez Island, and in 1907 moved there. Like all of the citizens of Union Bay, the Chinese, with whom he worked closely, were sorry to see Mr. Manson leave. They presented him with 50 lbs. of tea, and boxes of Chinese candies and lichee nuts for the children.

Long interested in politics, Michael ran as a Conservative and became the Comox member of the Legislative Assembly in 1909. The Conservatives were defeated in 1916, but Mike was back in the "house" again in 1924, representing the new district of MacKenzie. He took an active interest in logging practices on the coast, and "decried the waste of small timber and second growth, destroyed in the pursuit of the big giants".

GOVERNMENT SERVICES

CUSTOMS

By the late 1880's Walter Harvey was the Sub-Collector of Customs at Comox. However, the ships that came and went from Union Wharf to ports in the United States or the Orient had to stop at Nanaimo to get customs clearance.

1893 JANUARY The *San Mateo,* loaded with coal from Union Wharf for San Pedro in California, must stop at Nanaimo to get clearance from customs. Mr. B.H. Smith is a most affable man and will get out of bed to clear the ship so it can go speedily on its way. [2]

Besides the coal operations needing customs clearance, the amount of food and equipment imported through the new port by the citizens, especially the Chinese, was on the increase. In June 1893, J.B. Holmes was sworn in as Sub-Collector of Customs at Union Wharf. Soon, Mr. Harvey resigned the position in Comox, and Mr. Holmes left to take over that office which was soon closed.

In November Alex Fraser left the job as telegrapher and was made Deputy of Customs at Union Bay. The poor man was only at the job a couple of months when things went wrong.

1894 FEBRUARY A.W. Fraser took two doses of carbolic acid, whether by accident or intentionally, and is gravely ill. Mr. Fraser was up and about until 10:30 p.m. when he went home and was found at 1:30 a.m. in a dying state. Dr. Lawrence was sent for and emetics and other restoratives were applied. Fraser was unconscious for six hours, but is conscious now and speaks rationally. [2]

Mr. George Roe immediately came up from Nanaimo and filled the position. Mr. Fraser recovered and took a job in the Indian Department. George Roe, his wife and three boys, Jack, Desmond and Gerald, lived in Union Bay for the next seventeen years, in a house just south of the Nelson Hotel. The boys were great trappers and caught enough mink to have a coat made for their mother. It was the only mink coat in Union Bay. Mr. Roe swam every morning at 7:00 a.m., rain or shine, summer or winter. One early morning a Chinese man mistook him for a seal and shot at him, narrowly missing his wet head. All foreign ships arriving or departing had to be cleared by customs. The family often entertained officers from the ships.

"When we lived on the beach, Mr. and Mrs. Roe lived across the street. All the captains had to come to Mr. Roe to enter and leave port. So in that way we met a lot of interesting people. If they were musically inclined, the Roes would have them for an evening, and then they would come over to our house for an evening and then over to Uncle Herbert's. I just loved it."

Violet (Glover) Rutherford

During the first ten months of Mr. Roe's tenure, he collected $4750.17 in duty, proving the necessity of a customs man at the port. His pay was $800 a year. He was just a Sub-Collector out of the port of Nanaimo, and this led to many problems. In its heyday, the imports at Union Bay almost equalled those of Nanaimo, but many items still had to be cleared there. For example, the Union Bay office was not supplied with the necessary liquor testing equipment, so the spirits were sent to Nanaimo for testing. The Chinese at Cumberland imported large orders from China, and if an order contained any alcohol, none of it could be cleared until samples were sent to Nanaimo. There they were tested and the results returned, usually taking two to three weeks. Many perishable goods in these held-up orders rotted at the Union Bay dock.

1910 DECEMBER •➜ The Chinese are Mad!!! A large shipment of delicacies of all kinds consigned to the Chinese merchants for Chinese New Year were frozen solid on the wharf at Union Bay, and much is practically useless. [5]

At this time Mr. Roe operated from a little office next to the Wilson Hotel, so large orders were just left on the Government dock. Later, a proper customs warehouse was built in 1914 on the company freight wharf.

In 1911 Mr. Roe left to join the police force, and a different Mr. Fraser took his place. William J. Fraser, whose wife was to become the E&N station master, was succeeded in 1913 by Seymour Abrams. Seymour, the son of Judge Abrams of Cumberland, was married to postmaster Brown's daughter, Greta. They lived three houses north of the post office. The couple had two children, Ben and Georgina. Ben became harbour master in Nanaimo, and Georgina, an artist.

The new post office was to have a customs office adjoining it, but the First World War interrupted the plans. Mrs. Brown gave up her living and dining rooms on the second floor of the post office to the customs men. The dining room was Seymour's office and the living room stored the parcels. Finally, in 1935 a customs office was built onto the north end of the post office. This lovely new addition had an adjoining door through to the post office, and when the customs man was not busy during the Christmas rush he would slip through and help sort the mail.

During the first war, imports and shipping increased so another man was needed. Percy Renwick, who grew up in Union Bay and was just 18 years old, became the assistant. There was much to keep the two men busy. Foreign parcels were passed to the customs men from the post office, the contents examined, valued, and notices sent to the recipients. Some parcels were never claimed as people could not afford to pay the duty, or refused to pay if they felt it was too high.

As well, when foreign ships arrived, the captain came any time of the day or night to have his ship cleared. The customs man had to go down to the dock or out to the ship riding at anchor, sometimes in a howling southeaster. Anything containing goods like alcohol, which might be sold, had to be sealed for the duration of their stay. Ships coming from the Orient required a twenty-four hour watch. A customs officer stood at the gang plank, checking each crew member as he came or went.

"As the Chinese crew on the Blue Funnel boats came off, they were searched for opium. Once or twice they caught them with pretty big hauls. Percy told me once that one of them had a lot of pockets in his vest, full of opium."

Elizabeth (Walker) Renwick

Elizabeth Walker's parents died when she was just a teenager in Nanaimo, so she moved to Courtenay and lived with her stepsister, Mrs. Emdy. Soon after, she got a job in the Nelson Hotel. One day, as she was sweeping the hotel verandah, she looked up and saw a handsome man in a uniform. As

Percy Renwick was just 18 years old when he became assistant customs man

G. Murdoch

there was no boat in, she asked where he had come from and found out that he was the young customs man. It was love at first sight and she married Percy Renwick. The couple had three boys.

Anything heading to the Comox District or Campbell River had to pass through the Union Bay Customs Office. This was an inconvenience for the miners in Cumberland and the farmers at Courtenay, so they constantly lobbied for an office in their towns. About 1907, when a new post office was built in Cumberland, a room was provided with a sign over the door "Customs House". This remained vacant for about four years. Then the Government posted a man there for the next twenty years. It was not until 1924 that Courtenay finally received a customs service. One of the customs men from Union Bay was instructed to spend one half-day, twice a week, in Courtenay, clearing bonded goods from an office in the newly completed post office. This became an excellent bus service as people hitched a ride to town with Mr. Renwick.

Seymour Abrams was promoted to Collector of Customs at Nanaimo in 1933. A few years later Gordon (Champ) Chilton, son of the United Church minister at Union Bay, became Mr. Renwick's assistant. Champ transferred to Nanaimo in 1947 after a stint in the armed services. He went on to open the Kitimat customs house in 1953, the first full port office to be opened in B.C. for many years.

The customs office was closed at Union Bay in 1953 due to the decrease in shipping. Percy Renwick then worked in Courtenay, where he continued to serve the district until retirement. The office later became the library.

IMMIGRATION

The problem of sailors deserting their ships came with the many foreign vessels coaling at Union Bay. Most of the sailing barques were old, unseaworthy and in need of repairs. There were several cases of men refusing to ship out on them and deserting at Union Bay. Disputes sometimes arose between officers and crew, with the result that a group of sailors would refuse duty and try to desert.

1895 MAY ➾ Six of the crew on the *J.D. Peters*, a barque coaling at Union Wharf, deserted. Special constable McCartney found the men in a cabin on Denman and soon had them arrested and in jail in Comox. Later, the six seamen broke jail by climbing through a hole in the roof, and have not been captured. The *J.D. Peters* sailed without a full crew. [2]

At first the district was served by the Immigration Officer in Nanaimo. Soon it became necessary to station an officer closer to the port. Mr. Herbert Glover left England in 1894 and followed his sweetheart, Ann Russell, across the Atlantic to Ladysmith where they were married. He worked at several jobs before becoming the storekeeper in Wellington for the E&N Railway. Mr. Dunsmuir, owner of the railway, offered Herbert a job as Storekeeper at Union Bay, so the couple moved there in 1905 with their children, five boys and two girls. (Raymond was born in Union Bay).

About 1910 Mr. Glover became the Immigration Officer from Nanaimo north to the end of the Island, including Alberni. He travelled by stage or train to check up on new immigrants. After the $500 head tax was imposed on all Chinese immigrating to Canada, there was the problem of Chinese deserting to avoid the tax. To make their escape they swam ashore or shimmied along the ropes to the wharf, then were assisted by the Chinese at the Bay to get to Cumberland. There, in the large China-town, they were easily lost to the authorities. If the man was not found, the captain of the ship had to pay the $500 head tax, so the shipping companies were as eager to catch the deserters as the Immigration man, who could hold up a ship's departure. The law also required a close watch on Japanese entering the country, so Mr. Glover made regular visits to Japanese logging camps and lumber mills.

Foreign sailors coming ashore for the few days the ship was loading would be bonded. The shipping company signed a bond for the Immigration man which could be cashed if the sailor did not leave with his ship.

"Dad would often have large amounts of money in the house. These men were supposed to stay on the ships, but they were allowed off and bonded, and then the money returned when the ship sailed with all the crew aboard. Sometimes there would be six or more ships in at once. I remember once in the middle of the night we could hear some men talking and could hear them coming up the steps. Dad got his shot gun and went to the door. There were two or three men who thought they'd skip ship, but they got scared and came up to Dad to report."

Margaret (Glover) Matthews

At the beginning of the First World War, the predominantly British population of the Comox Valley was constantly calling for the expulsion or internment of all Germans.

1914 AUGUST ➾ No German, Austrian, or Hungarian should be trusted as they are most likely spies. At present they are permitted to go freely and gather information about which boats are in the harbour and where they are destined. [4]

Soon all the "aliens" had to be registered. Then they were ordered out of the mines and sent to internment camps. In the summer of 1915, thirty-one Germans and Austrians from Cumberland, Courtenay and Bevan were sent to the army camp at Union Bay to be interned. There, the 72nd Highlanders had a camp where the men were put to work. These men, all miners, loggers or merchants, were quite unlikely to be involved in espionage. Union Bay had one German, Dr. Thrum, who was an analytical scientist for the coal company. He was strongly suspected of being a spy by some officials in the district. (see World War I)

LAW ENFORCEMENT

Probably the first law enforcement officers to uphold justice at Union Wharf were Justice of the Peace M. Piercy, Constable Joseph Rodello, and Government Agent F. Creech, all of Comox. In 1884 J. McKelvey was also sworn in as Justice of the Peace. After Rodello, W.B. Anderson became police constable as well as tax assessor and collector, all for $60 a month.

When the colliery started, local law enforcement was needed at Union and Union Wharf. Robert Grant, Andrew McKnight and William Walker were Justices of the Peace.

In 1889 Judge E. Harrison of Nanaimo made monthly journeys to hold "County Court" at Comox, taking over from Judge Crease of Vancouver. Judge J. Abrams, a Justice of the Peace and Notary Public, was appointed Stipendiary Magistrate and Coroner for the electoral district of Comox in 1895. He lived in Cumberland and travelled around the district to view the scene of a crime, or hold inquests.

Comox had a small jail where offenders were held before being tried. On a Sunday in 1896 McKnight, Grant and Walker arrested, tried and fined a Chinese man in a prostitution case in Union, because they did not have a jail to keep him in until Monday. A smart lawyer brought this to the attention of the Attorney-General, and a long court case followed.

Soon after, a new $1,000 jail was built at Cumberland which provided four cells, a court-

G. Robertson

Verna Campbell, Marjorie Peters holding David Peters and Mary Militich on Union Bay jailhouse steps during the renovations of 1946

house and a police office. After sentencing, all prisoners were sent to Nanaimo on the mail boat. In 1912 Constable Stevens drove to Cumberland where he picked up a prisoner and, for the first time by auto, transported him to the jail in Nanaimo.

If a thief, deserter or murderer was caught at Union Wharf, he had to be taken to Comox or Union to be held. In 1901 this changed when a small jail house was built.

1901 AUGUST ➼ The Provincial Jail which is near the school house promises to be a comfortable residence for those who are inclined to patronize His Majesty's Boarding House. [4]

It was built with an office in front and jail cells at back. The floor to the cell had a steel plate underneath, and the windows were all barred, so that the prisoners could not easily escape. The little building was used as an office for the police. Inquests were held by magistrates in cases where individuals met death by drowning, accidental shooting, or logging and mining related accidents. Also, the liquor licensing board met there as they travelled up Island hearing hotel applications. Actually, few "bad men" were ever behind bars, but it was used quite often as a drunk tank to sober up tipsy loggers or celebrating sailors.

The jailhouse was completely renovated in 1946, at a cost of $878.30.

"I arrived in July 1945 with a wife and two boys, and there were no houses to rent in either Union Bay or Cumberland. The house previously used as a detachment office in Cumberland and owned by the Canadian Collieries, was required by the company. So we decided to build our own home, and bought property between Vowels and Hoopers. I applied to have the detachment changed to Union Bay, and was able to persuade the government to renovate the old jail building."

Cst. Charles Ennals

In the late 1950's the last court case to be held in the little jail house was presided over by Judge Ryland. Douglas Campbell, Wayne Hayton, Terry Smith and Larry Sharp were charged with disturbing the peace in a Fanny Bay eatery and were apprehended by Constable Lowe. Three of the boys pleaded guilty, but Larry defended himself and got off.

Before the turn of the century the crime rate in the port town was not high. Clothes and food were sometimes stolen, mainly for survival. Occasionally, pirates in sailing sloops visited homesteads and stores along the coast, stealing what they could find. The illegal sale of liquor to the Indians brought with it many problems. A special constable at the port worked in conjunction with the Union police - Stevenson, Smithurst and Hutchinson - who served the community well in the early days. Union Wharf's first "special policeman" was Andrew McCartney. He was followed by Tom Hudson about 1901.

1896 MARCH ➼ Officer McCartney of Union Wharf is quite active in preserving order in that popular and fashionable resort town. [3b]

After the "head tax" was imposed on the Chinese in 1903, deserters became a problem. With the labour unrest at Union mines, the company was worried about saboteurs blowing up the wharf. The stores and hotels, like others along the coast, had been robbed. A great deal of opium was coming through the port and finding its way into the Chinatowns of the district. All this added up to the need for a resident police constable at Union Bay. James McKenzie was sent to do the job. In his big, friendly way he soon gained the trust of the small community.

At the time of the 1912-13 strike, other provincial police officers - Henry Holland, Robert Mills, James Walls - were also stationed at Union Bay. Then two men, Donald Ross and Harry Westaway, were sent in February 1913 to crack the Flying Dutchman case, which resulted in Westaway's death. (See Crime) Constable Murray, who followed McKenzie, stayed only a short time. Then came Charlie McTaggart in 1915, to be followed by a number of officers over the years. Constables Regan and Norris in the '20s, and G. Lennox and B. Tannock in the '30s.

M. Simpson

R. Lennox

Left: R.C.M.P. constable Russell Hicks with his horse was stationed at Union Bay to control opium smuggling. He married Edythe Brown from the post office.
Right: B.C. Police constable Gordon Lennox policed Union Bay in the early '30s

With little or no access to lawyers, a notary public was used for all legal matters. G. Geary, who also worked as a carpenter at the colliery, filled the post in the early days. He and his wife raised two children, Edna and Bert, at the Bay. In later years Charles Pickles filled the post of notary public.

Through the years the RCMP usually had men stationed at or near Union Bay, on the lookout for opium. Sergeant Bryan, assisted by Russell Hicks (who married Edythe Brown from the post office), discovered a big haul in 1921. The RCMP kept a constant vigil on the ships and Chinatown, ready to sweep down in a raid looking for opium.

After the war the law was enforced by Charles Ennals, probably the most respected and loved of the policemen. It was his lot to control the revellers at the Community Club's Saturday night dances. He took an interest in the youth, and with his wife, ran the Sunday School.

"Remember the time the Gee boys stole Dr. Gordon's car. They were too short to reach the pedals, so one steered and the other got down on the floor and pressed the pedal. Mr. Ennals took chase and in his attempt to shoot a tire out, shot the spot light off the police car. It took him a long time to live that one down."

Ann (Vowels) Graham

When the Provicial Police Force was taken over by the RCMP in 1950, Constable Ennals was there to make the transition, and looked sharp in the red serge. The detachment area extended from Deep Bay to Courtenay city limits, and included the area around Cumberland city and the Forbidden Plateau. Ken Atree followed Ennals. Wilf Emdy (who was killed in a plane crash in 1955) and M.G. Lowe next filled the position. In 1956 the Union Bay detachment increased to two men.

WATER

Before there was any sort of piped water supply, wells supplied the only fresh water. Individual property owners dug their own well and were lucky if they hit a spring, otherwise it might be dry in the summer. Behind the store, Mr. Fraser built a huge water tank supported on high timbers. This supplied the store and hotel with running water, so that the water jugs in each room could be kept full. The Wilson Hotel had a water tank fed by one of the many springs along the ridge from Chinatown to McLeod Road.

The Spring Hill trail wound from the Wilson Hotel through swampy ground up to the Company Hill. Half way up was a well, always full of clear cold water. For over fifty years, a Chinese with two buckets hanging from a pole over his shoulders walked there several times a day from the Colliery yards. He brought back fresh, sweet drinking water to fill the pails in the shops and offices.

This well, like the others on the hill, was cribbed and maintained by the Collieries. There was another well at the north end of the company houses between the middle and front row. This well had a boom to help draw the water up. There was also a shallow well on Russell Hill, really just a spring under a big maple tree. A pipe was laid from it to the big company house where Dunsmuir stayed when he was in town.

H. Glover

Langley Lake, at 500' elevation was first dammed to supply the Washer with water

"It was the only house with running water. I remember going up the hill once with some perch we'd caught down at the wharf, and we dropped them in the well. Browns lived there then."

Wilf Glover

Everyone went to the community wells for water. It was a great place to catch up on the local news.

"On Saturday all the women did their washing so that the kids could fetch the water. Two pails at a time and maybe three trips each. It helped to have lots of brothers and sisters. The first trip wasn't too bad, then the next trip everyone complained. Some of us had to go almost a block."

Harry Glover

Water was precious so none was wasted. After heating the water and using it for washing clothes, the water would then be used to wash the floors, and what was leftover was put on the garden.

Around the turn of the century, Langley Lake, at 500' elevation, was dammed to supply the Washer with water at 200 lb. pressure. An earth-fill dam was built with large timbers facing the toe side. Then a 10" pipe line was laid to the Washer, crossing the 200' span at Canyon Creek. It was supported by a 100' high bridge that was only 5' wide. It was a thrill for young boys who dared each other to walk along the top of the pipe. In 1912 the dam burst, flooding Chinatown and the colliery yards. The dam was rebuilt stronger and is still used today.

Just after this, a group of local men under manager W. Harrison and foreman Johnny Fulcher put in a water system. A 2" galvanized pipe was run off the 10" main at Chinatown to the company houses. From the hill it continued down behind the homes on the main street as far as the post office. When the system was complete, every house had one cold water tap into a kitchen sink, which was a luxury for $1.00 a month.

"I remember the first tap water when we lived on the hill. With the cold weather they used to say, 'Let your taps run at night, even just a drip, so the pipes won't freeze.' We had a skating rink in the kitchen in the morning because the drain froze. The houses were as cold inside as out. Mother banked the stoves, but there wasn't much heat by morning."

Nettie (Marshall) Jones

Gradually, hot water jackets were installed in the coal burning stoves to heat water tanks. Wash day was no longer quite such a burden. Then came flush toilets. The Company bosses got them first.

By the 1930's the main supply line was in need of repair, so a pump house was installed behind Chinatown with the water taken directly from the creek.

In the early 1940's the main town line was replaced and extended north as far as the weigh station, and up McLeod Road to four or five houses above the tracks. Bob and Jim McKay led a large crew of Chinese workers installing 4" wooden stave pipes. Each 16' long pipe was made of wooden staves bound together with galvanized wire. The pipes were joined with wooden sleeves. Galvanized pipes were attached from the main line to each home. After the new road was put through in 1947, the line was similarly extended south to the town limits.

By 1953 there were about seven families, each with a poor well, living at the north railway crossing. They formed the Union Bay Water Association, got permission from the Canadian Colliery to connect to their water system at the weigh scales, and went to work. Paul Bohn used his equipment to dig the ditch in lieu of paying his share of the total $3,516.24. The men laid the pipe and the women helped fill in the ditch, so everyone greatly appreciated the water when it was turned on in July.

K. Carter

The pipeline crosses Canyon Creek, a span of 200'. Tommy Formby and dog nonchalantly pose on the narrow 100' high bridge

A. Hooper

A Chinese crew in 1947 laying the pipe to homes south of McLeod Road

"I remember filling in the ditch for the water pipe along the highway. We were all women. The twins and Pauline were teenagers and had to help. They hated it and were embarrassed to be seen working like coolies, so kept their heads down when a car went by."

Betty Lund

When the company closed in 1960, it sold the water system to the newly formed Union Bay Water Board for $1.00. The board also bought Langley Lake for $1000, one of the few lakes in B.C. which is privately owned.

1960 APRIL ➾ Distribution of CC(D)L water utility at Union Bay will be handed over to the newly formed board of trustees. A water district has been formed to administer the water supply. The trustees are Tom Campbell, Harold Dane, Harry Glover, Herbert Glover, and Bill Woods. [7]

Union Wharf became "famous" for water in the early 1890's. However, this was no ordinary water, but the Comox Medicinal Water which was found at Garvin's Mineral Springs. Alex Garvin homesteaded on land at Baynes Sound, about a mile from town. Alex probably took little interest in the springs until a promoter, with an eye to making a fortune, approached him. Mr. D. R. Young was always on the lookout for a fast and easy buck (he later promoted a scheme for an electric tramway from Union to the Wharf). Young was able to interest some local businessmen, among them Judge Abrams, to bottle and sell the water. He proclaimed it to be a great healer and tonic for all diseases of the liver and stomach.

Young even invented an Indian legend to help promote his product. The story was told of a beautiful Indian maiden named Umadilla. She lay sick until a brave warrior went to the spring every day and beat off bears to bring the princess some of the life-healing water.

The output of the spring in its primitive state was about 500 gallons every twenty-four hours, but the Company hoped to develop it further. As an introductory offer, the water was sold in Nanaimo at "the unbelievably low price of 25¢ per bottle".

1895 ➾ The Comox Mineral Springs has an enviable reputation. Sunday being an off day, maimed, halt, and blind, and those who imagine they may become that way, make the pilgrimage to the waters with demijohns, lunch tins, bottles, buckets, and teakettles for a supply. White men, Indians, Chinamen, greasers, and black men wend their way. Maids of the forest too, go to pay homage to the shade of Umadilla. I hope they don't bathe in the spring, I was a very sick man for two days after my visit to it! A local rancher has a record of seven bears killed at the spring so that even the beasts of the forest seem to know a good thing when they find it. [2]

L. Bohn

A crew of housewives anxious to have water in their homes north of the Bay fill in the ditch after the water pipe was laid. Left to right: Louise Glover, Lil Bohn, Eileen Hill, Betty Lund

Durham Townsite Lots.

This Magnificent Townsite Overlooking Baynes Sound

has been surveyed into lots which are now for the first time put on the market. The most important development may be expected here. Here is located the

Famous Spring.

which has been analyzed and pronounced of the highest value.

Parties wishing to purchase can do so now at reasonable figures and on easy terms.

Applications should be made to

A. Garvin,
Union Mines.

H. Glover

This large power shovel was bought from the Panama Canal after it was finished, to do the excavating for the new power dam in 1912

V. Hudson

The 300' long impounding dam was built at the outlet of Comox Lake

POWER

The first electric power at Union Mines and Union Wharf was generated by coal. At the Wharf, the power was used by the company in its shops, where all the machines and equipment for the mine and loading wharves were made and repaired. There was a large steam boiler fired by coal which ran the main shaft. This main drive shaft supplied power to all the machines and tools in the machine shop, car shop, boiler shop and blacksmith shop.

The coal washer was built in 1895. It was originally powered by water under high pressure which was brought by pipe from the lake, and by direct drive, powered a Pelton wheel. During the summer, when the water volume was low, an auxiliary coal-powered steam engine was used.

In 1911 the Company made plans for a large electrical plant powered by water from the Puntledge River. To bring in machines and equipment, a railway was extended from the main line to the dam and plant. A large powershovel, purchased from the Panama Canal after it was completed, travelled on the tracks and did most of the digging. The impounding dam, which was 300' long, was built at the outlet of Comox Lake, and a diversion dam was constructed further down the river at Bevan. From there a huge wooden flume took the water to the plant.

1912 NOVEMBER ➾ Sidetracked at Union Bay is a huge dynamo which takes the whole of a CPR flatcar. It is consigned for #7 Power Plant. The steamship *Marmion* of the Portland Cement Co. at Todd Inlet is unloading 6,000 sacks of cement for construction of the plant. [5]

The Puntledge Power Plant was finished in August 1913. It had two 6,000 horsepower turbines that were directly connected to two generators which operated at 500 r.p.m. Electricity was generated at 13,200 volts with a frequency of 25 cycles per second.

Cumberland mines had power in 1913, but it was not until the spring of 1914 that the wooden poles and line were put through to

V. Hudson

The wooden flume under construction which carried water to the power house

a substation at Union Bay. All the Company shops were converted, and gradually the Company homes were wired for electricity. Next, the line was extended along the front street to light up the stores and hotels, but it was not until after the war that power was available to the homes south of McLeod Road.

Cumberland had its own light company in 1902. After it was built, the Puntledge plant was the sole supplier of electricity in the district. Cumberland, Courtenay and Royston each had their own distribution plant and bought bulk power from the CC(D)L. The power plant was under the District Supervisor at Union Bay, with all the mechanical work done at the shops.

Union Bay was the only town supplied directly by the CC(D)L. In the beginning, for the first 30 kilowatt hours (a maximum for most households), electricity cost 10¢ per KWH. By 1922 it was 13¢ per KWH, with a 10% discount if paid by the end of the month. What a labour saving device for the housewives who, until then, had to daily clean the chimneys in the lamps and lanterns, then fill them with coal oil! They could now also entertain the thought of buying a toaster, washing machine, or iron.

1914 JULY ➻ Electrical Appliances from Cumberland Electric Light Co.

Electric Iron	$3.25
Electric Toaster	3.25
Electric Hair Dryer	3.00
5 Watt Tungsten Lamp	.40
10 & 15 Watt Tungsten Lamp	.45
25 & 40 Watt Tungsten Lamp	.50 [5]

In the press, in November 1919, the Boy Scouts were demanding street lights at Union Bay. A month later the Company announced that the Bay would have lights. Every third power pole was equipped with a 100 watt bulb, and the citizens were thrilled with the improvement.

The power plant that had been installed in 1913 was 25 cycle. Although 60 cycle was more popular, there was no set cycle in B.C., so the CC(D)L chose the system that offered the best deal. All the hydraulic turbines and generators were manufactured in Switzerland. Visitors, used to 60 cycle, complained that the lights flickered, but it went unnoticed by the locals. Heating elements, such as hot plates and toasters, could be used on either cycle, but appliances with motors, such as fridges, vacuums, clocks and turntables could not. The 25 cycle versions were more expensive.

By 1947 the district light companies were acquired by the B.C. Power Commission, which built the John Hart Dam at Elk Falls. All of the district, except Union Bay, was converted to 60 cycle by the summer of 1951. From homeowners in the communities which had changed to 60 cycle, people at the Bay got good deals on fridges and motors. In 1952 a B.C. Power line from Royston to Mud Bay brought electricity to 125 homes in the Fanny Bay area for the first time. Sixty cycle power went right past the doors of homes in Union Bay. In 1953 the B.C. Power Commission bought the Puntledge Power Plant and reconstructed it, changing it to 60 cycle, and Union Bay was finally in the 20th century!

The electric department at Union Bay installed and serviced all of the company's electrical equipment at the mines and dock. The power line, substations and transformers were kept in running order. Motors were rewound and repaired. Heating elements were made and repaired. The meters were read.

In connection with the coming of 60 cycle, a challenging job was done by the machine shop and electric department. The pulp mill in Port

V. Hudson

The powerhouse just before completion in August 1913

Cumberland Museum

The generators inside the powerhouse produced electricity at 13,200 volts

Alberni was built, with plans to buy power from the John Hart dam. When the mill was finished, the power line was through from the dam but the generators were not completed. So an unusual installation at the Puntlege Power Station was the placing of two 60 cycle alternators on the existing shafts of the 25 cycle alternators. This created the necessary 60 cycle to run the mill.

One of the first electrical engineers at the Bay was P.F. McNally, followed over the years by Art Lee and Syd Andrews. George Dutfield came from the company's mines in Mercoal and was the engineer during the changeover in the 1950's.

George Cooper, a recent immigrant from England, was living in Merville in 1920 when he got a job as electrician at No.4 Mine. He used to walk over a trail from Merville every Sunday night to work at the mine during the week. In '26 he moved his wife and family of four to Union Bay where, for over twenty-five years, he kept the lights on and the meters read. Several apprentices, such as Tommy Adamson, Eddie Hughes, George Cooper Jr., Bill Stokes and Don Bennie, served their term under the head electrician.

"My mother was going to a masquerade ball in Cumberland in the early '20s. She was the belle of the ball because Mr. McNally, the electrician, made her flashing earrings. Imagine, in those days! They must have had a battery."

Dunc Marshall

FIRE PROTECTION

Fire fighting in the early days was the quick formation of a bucket brigade. Water from wells, creeks and the ocean were used. A hose was connected to the water tank on the wharf for fires there or around the company yard.

When the Washer was built in 1896, a pipe was laid from the lake to service the colliery works. Stand pipes, which were used as fire hydrants, were installed, and several hose reel stations were built around the yard. After the spectacular blaze which destroyed the Wilson Hotel and surrounding buildings in 1922, and the fire which burned the Baynes Sound Hotel in 1926, interest was generated by the company and local citizens to improve fire fighting capabilities. A 1928 one-ton Model A Ford truck owned by the CC(D)L was stripped down and refitted with hose bed, reel, and tank. An 110 gallon pump was designed and cast in the foundry. All work was done by volunteers at the shops. When the new truck was tested in April 1935, the pump recorded 210 gallons per minute with a twelve foot draft. This was the first power-driven pump on the North Island.

A lot next to the Willis Hotel was bought for $300 from Fraser and Horne. The old square-fronted butcher shop which stood on the lot was renovated by J. Pollock and D. Haggart to become the first fire hall.

The Union Bay Fire Department was formed in 1935, with Johnny Fulcher as the first chief. Jake Campbell and George Watt were captains. Firefighters were W. Auchinvole, F. Bradley, W. Glover, G. Horne, R. Hudson, H. Jones, W. Peters, G. Strachan, A. Searle, C. Stubbs and W. Treloar.

A. Searle

The Union Bay Fire Department was formed in 1935. Driving the truck is Art Searle with Chief John Fulcher beside him. Standing on the running board are Bunt Bradley and Jake Campbell

Fire Hall

In 1955 this '49 Ford truck was completely stripped down and rebuilt by volunteer labour at the CC(D)L shops

T. Dutfield

Dedicated firemen proudly pose, wearing their new sweaters. Standing left to right: Gerry Stewart, Gordon Murdock, Reg Hudson, Bob Treloar, Reid Roth, Jack Ward. Sitting left to right: Ken Peters (deputy chief), Jake Campbell (chief), Des Stewart, Lyle Stewart

With his wife and two daughters, Grace and Ethel, Fulcher had lived and worked as a mechanic in Union Bay for over twenty-five years. After only a year the chief died, and was carried to his last resting place on the fire truck.

Jake Campbell took over as chief, and in that position responded to a gigantic fire at the Deep Bay Fish Cannery. Eight firemen, with their pump sucking up salt water, worked valiantly to fight the flames which were fuelled by tarred nets and two scows of fish oil. The Courtenay brigade also answered the call, and although the cannery was gutted, the twenty-five other buildings on the spit were saved.

During the next few years little was done to improve the department. The Second World War stirred renewed interest in fire protection, and the fire department was issued with steel helmets, pumps, and 1000 feet of hose. The company also replaced and extended the water system.

1944 APRIL ➾ During recent months Union Bay, one of the most vulnerable areas in the district, has vastly improved its fire-fighting preparations by installation of a modern hydrant system which cost in the neighborhood of $12,000 and which provides hydrants throughout the residential and business sections. Previously, the community faced a difficult pumping problem in the event of fire, and its small but active volunteer fire department was faced with many problems. Most of these have been solved by the new installation. [7]

In July 1947 the firefighters responded to a fire at Buckley Bay. A runaway logging truck had crashed into a pick-up truck containing three men, and pushed the vehicle into the truck shop. Gas and oil exploded so that little could be done to save the men trapped inside the inferno.

Over the years, as the department waxed and waned, E.T. Searle was secretary-treasurer, and managed by donations and grants to keep the truck going. He turned over a set of records of meticulous detail to the group who reorganized the department in the spring of 1952. This came about when the Community Club realized that fire insurance for their hall would be greatly reduced if there were properly trained firemen provided with approved equipment. Jake Campbell was retained as chief and Ken Peters became deputy chief. Two years later the positions were reversed, and George Cooper and Gordon Murdock were appointed as captains.

A hose tower was built and a siren was installed. With the restructuring of the department, the firefighters under chief Peters took a more serious attitude to their job, and attended lectures and classes on fire protection and fighting. Their equipment was kept in tip-top condition, with the hydrants freshly painted, ladders waxed, and the brass on the trucks polished. The brigade looked smart in sweaters and crests they bought through Edna Peters' store.

The Union Bay Fire Prevention District became a reality with Harry Tappin as secretary. The north boundary joined Courtenay district at Lyn-Maur Auto Court, and the jurisdiction stretched south to Tsable River. This meant financial aid annually.

1955 OCTOBER ➾ Union Bay gets a new fire truck made by the residents... The basis of the

L. Stewart

The Women's Auxiliary gather around the potbellied stove in the old firehall, making plans for a money raiser. Back left to right: Gladys Shillito, Muriel Peters, Vi Hudson, Margaret Campbell, Audrey Cooper. Front: May Stewart

unit is a 1949 three-ton Ford truck chassis. This was stripped down and rebuilt. The body and equipment were designed by J. Harry Glover and, with the exception of nozzles, hoses and pumps, all equipment was manufactured at the shops by volunteer labour. [7]

While the new truck was still under construction, on May 22, 1955 the Nelson Hotel burned. All available men and equipment fought the huge fire, with the assistance of the Courtenay department.

"There was a light southeaster blowing against us to start with, but at the height of the blaze the wind shifted, and that saved the store and the town."

Chief Ken Peters

As the fire hall was too small for the new trucks, a building project was embarked upon. Again, it was back to volunteer labour and donations. Plans were drawn up by Wilf Glover for the two storey building, to be built directly behind the old hall. Logs for lumber were donated by Rosewall Logging. Harry Chapman supervised the building, and George Dutfield the electric wiring. It took several years until it was completed and the old hall torn down.

About this time the Provincial Fire Marshall's office required all hydrants to have 2 1/2 " outlets. Prior to this, each community had a size of its own. A machine shop crew came to town, took the hydrants apart and bushed them up to standard.

Over the years the firemen attended many house, car, boat, and bush fires. Looking through their minutes, it seems that every few months one of the houses at Chinatown caught fire from an overheated stove, faulty chimney, or sparks on the roof. Luckily, they were all extinguished with no loss of life.

"Seven firemen worked the fire at Maw Tawe's house, but the building was gutted. A typical fire, burnt the Chinese type construction, tin over shingles and tar paper next to the chimney. Worked the adjoining building and saved Lin Duck's house."

Union Bay Volunteer Firemen's logbook.

A ladies' auxilary was formed during the construction, and through raffles, teas and dances, assisted financially. They contributed to the purchase of equipment and completion of the recreation room upstairs. With the firemen, they also brought back the old tradition of Guy Fawkes night.

"The women bought our first rubber turnout coats. We got them from Seattle. We bought things cheap from the War Assets, and we got called down for it by the other departments. But we had no bucks. The colliery donated most of the stuff we had. We never bought much until we started buying that truck, and then we bought accredited equipment."

Chief Ken Peters

GARBAGE

For over seventy years there was no garbage collection in Union Bay. Unlike today, nothing was disposable. There was little paper and cardboard, no plastic, and metal was expected to last forever. If it did break it was repaired and used again. Even after automobiles became the main mode of transportation, models rarely changed from one year to the next so the old jalopy served a family for many years.

In a town where no one was very well off, everything was used and reused. The word "re-cycle" was unknown, but that is exactly what every householder did. Today, containers account for much of our garbage. Back then, all large quantities of food arrived in sturdy wooden boxes which could be used to store produce from the garden and orchard. They made excellent chairs or stools and, when stacked up, useful book cases. The boxes could be taken apart and the wood used for shelving or furniture. Strong solid boxes could have hinges put on the top boards, creating a chest or toy box. Cigar boxes stored keepsakes or became jewelry boxes.

Food also arrived in sacks. Potato sacks were made of burlap which could be used over and over again for storing or transporting vegetables. For travelling, the sacks could be used as duffel bags. They could be used for upholstery and covering bed springs. Opened up, the burlap made good curtains or could partition off a room.

The uses for flour sacks were legion, limited only by the housewife's imagination. After emptying the flour, all that was required was washing the sack, and sometimes bleaching it to remove the brand's logo, such as Five Roses or Purity. As is, they could cover baked goods to keep them fresh and clean, or be converted into pillow slips, bags for shopping, school or laundry. Filled with down and feathers, they made excellent pillows and cushions. A 50 lb. sack, opened up, became a yard of material 36" wide which made a perfect tea towel. The 100 lb. sacks were large and could be sewn together to make a bed sheet.

With lace or a crocheted edge, charming curtains, hankies and doilies were made. When colourful embroidery was added, pretty table cloths were created. The material was used for many articles of clothing: nightgowns, aprons, underpants, shirts.

"Our underpants had Royal Standard on one leg and Red Rose on the other. They were as white as any linen. We used to make sheets of them. I know Liz had them for her boys' beds. They'd be the big 100 lb. sacks, and when they were opened out they were big."

Annie (Muschamp) Nelson

"In summer we used to swim a lot. I went to the hotel and got all the corks from the liquor bottles and put them in a flour sack and made myself water

A. Graham

In earlier days each home had an outhouse. Overturning these was a favourite trick on Hallowe'en

wings. That's how I learned to swim. You had to make your own fun."

Nellie (McKay) King

"Lina made all us kids bathing suits out of flour sacks, a new one every year. They were easy to make because you just cut a neck out of the bottom of the sack, and a couple of arms out of the corners, and then did a little sewing for under the crotch. Big or small, boys or girls, the bags were very adaptable."

Margaret (Glover) Matthews

Clothing was never thrown out merely because styles changed or the owner became tired of the article. It was made over or made down for children until it was truly worn out. Then any part of the material that was not ragged or torn was cut and used for wash cloths, bandages, handkerchiefs, diapers, sanitary pads, quilt squares, or patches to mend other clothes.

Containers made of glass were much prized. Jars and bottles were used to keep food dry and fresh. Large ones stored staples like beans and sugar, smaller ones were used for preserves, pickles and jams. Decorative jars were kept for herbs or home-made bath salts.

Newspapers, which were few at first, were used for starting fires, wrapping things, and lining shelves and drawers. They were also used as toilet paper, as was the old catalogue, tied up with a string nailed to the outhouse wall.

"My Grandma Peters used to recycle envelopes. She'd steam them open, turn them inside out and use them again."

Ann (Vowels) Graham

Most people had a garden where the kitchen refuse could be buried for compost, if they did not have chickens to eat it. Pets could always be counted on to finish up any table scraps that happened to be left.

Most articles for the garbage could be burned in the kitchen stove. Even tin cans would burn up except for the rims. Bottles and cans could be dumped and sunk in the ocean.

The home owner was then faced with the problem of disposing of ashes. The average house, with a stove and one fireplace burning night and day during the winter, created a lot of ashes. Each day the housewife emptied them over the back fence. One could judge the housekeeper by the state of her ash pile. The good ones had no garbage in the ashes except a bottle or can which had been carefully washed out or burned. There was nothing to attract animals.

The people who lived in the company houses were lucky. Once a year the company truck drove along behind the yards, and two or three Chinese shovelled the ashes onto the truck which dumped them on the coal hills. Non-company homeowners usually did not burn as much coal so had fewer ashes. The soft wood ash was spread on the garden. Coal ashes could be used to widen the driveway, make a parking spot, or fill potholes in the highway.

Emptying the outhouse was a topic most people did not discuss, but it got full quickly, especially if one had a big family. Union Bay had no sanitation laws. In Cumberland, "Night Scavengers" worked between 11:00 a.m. and 6:00 a.m. emptying privies for $6.00 a year. At the Bay, company house residents had services provided. A crew of Chinese dug a new hole, moved over the outhouse, and filled in the old hole. Other homeowners had to do this job themselves.

MEDICAL

The rough and ready living conditions, the constant threat of disease, and the necessary use of firearms all resulted in a need for medical services. After the collieries opened, with the company's lack of concern for human safety, there were many accidents in construction, down the mines, and on the tracks.

Through necessity, people were very resourceful. Some of the women who had learned remedies and cures from their mothers were always ready to help a sick neighbour or an injured worker. One such woman was Ellen McKay. Ever willing to give a helping hand, she was there when needed to minister to the sick.

"During the influenza epidemic, Mrs. McKay calmed down a terrified logging camp crew by telling them to stay in bed and drink all the whiskey they could lay their hands on! With no doctor or nurse available, Mrs. McKay walked three miles through the snow into the camp to bring order out of chaos. Working efficiently and with the odd harsh word to grown men, she told them how to look after themselves. Mrs. McKay made mustard plasters for the loggers, and advised them to get into bed and stay there until the flu' had been sweated out."

Mary Moore

After the flood in 1912, temporary hospitals were set up at the two houses next to Chinatown. Mrs. Renwick and Mrs. Marshall, assisted by Mr. Glover, attended to the injured.

For about ten years before Mrs. Reid arrived, Herbert Glover gave first aid to accident victims. Although untrained, he equipped himself with knowledge through reading and experience.

"Dad was the only first aid man they had in Union Bay for many years. When Lina was a little girl she pulled the potato pot over. Boiling potatoes all over her face! Mom sent someone to get Dad at the office. He had her peel potatoes and they kept putting them on her face. I guess the starch did it, she didn't have a scar."

Margaret(Glover) Matthews

The closest medical help was at Nanaimo, where there was a hospital. Sick or injured people were taken there by steamer or canoe, depending on the urgency. By the late 1880's there was a resident doctor in the district, probably the first being Dr. Struthers at Comox. In June 1889 Dr. Young arrived.

1889 JUNE ➾ Dr. Young, a rising young man in his profession, left by the *Cariboo Fly* to take up the appointment of medical officer at Union Colleries. [2]

He served Cumberland and Union Wharf for three years, coming down to the port town by train or on horseback. Apparently Dr. Young was not popular with all parties, particularly the company. His work performance was reviewed in 1892, found lacking, so applications were invited for the position. Ten were received, including Dr. Young's. The workers were allowed to vote and Dr. Young won 150 votes of the 163 cast. But feelings were running high, and a month later, after a disagreement with the company, the doctor quit. Again elections were held but with just two candidates, Dr. Roderick Fraser (brother to Jack Fraser) of Victoria, and Dr. Robert Lawrence of Ontario who became the new company doctor. Dr. Young remained in Cumberland to serve his loyal patients in a private practice.

About this time, the government agreed to contribute $500 per annum to the support of a resident doctor for Comox and Courtenay. Whenever Dr. Young's name was considered, it caused strong emotions. A very unruly meeting was held to choose a doctor. The first chairman, Sam Creech, had to be deposed and Walter Harvey took over. In the end, the majority was in favour of Dr. Young so he moved his practice to Courtenay.

In November 1893 Dr. Young went down to Nanaimo to relieve a doctor. There were many cases of typhoid, and the doctor contracted it himself. Although very ill he would not give up his work until forced to go into hospital, where he died at only thirty years of age.

Dr. Lawrence arrived in December 1892 to take over the position of company doctor. In Courtenay in 1894 there were not enough patients to support the two doctors, Millard and Westwood. The population was growing in Union, so Dr. J. Westwood moved there and became assistant Colliery physician. Once a week, the doctors visited Union Wharf to hold a clinic.

There was an obvious need for a district hospital, and citizens in all areas began to raise money.

1891 JULY ➾ Grand Ball given in Comox on behalf of the proposed new hospital. It will be a long time until it is built, because attendance was poor. On squaring accounts it was found that committee members had to go down into their own "jeans" for $2.50 to make receipts balance the expenditures. [2]

This was just the beginning of fund raising. In May 1892 a Hospital Board was formed and tenders invited to erect a suitable building. In June, the Union Coal Co. donated the site and all the lumber.

The Union & Comox District Hospital was incorporated in January 1895. The $2,000 building was a two storey structure with a kitchen, a dining room, two wards, a dressing room, and an operating room downstairs. The second storey was reserved for staff. Dr. and Mrs. Westwood lived there rent free, in return for Mrs. Westwood's services as matron.

1895 ➺ The matron, Mrs. Westwood, appears to be taking a lively interest in her work. She is, we're told, a regular graduated nurse from the hospitals of the old country and well equipped for her responsible position. The nurse, Miss Shaw, who receives $10 a month, is well liked, quiet, and attentive to her duties, but no mortal can be on duty twenty-four hours a day. She has, of late, been "spelled" by Mrs. Anderton. [3b]

The matron was involved in fund raising, and one of her first schemes, which raised $70, was an excursion to Denman Island.

1895 JUNE ➺ The excursion last Thurs. evening under the direction of Mrs. Westwood and for the benefit of the hospital, was well attended, not withstanding the unpromising state of the weather at the time of starting. About sixty went from Union. The tin roof of the long car placed at the disposal of the excursionists had been snatched off by a gust of wind and not replaced, so that the rain before leaving found its way through the top of the car in some places. Some of the gentlemen thereupon left, but the ladies, more plucky, kept their places. They were not to be frightened by a little moisture. At the Wharf, more people joined the party, and boarded the *SS Isobel* carrying a gratifyingly large contingent from Comox.

At the Denman wharf, the excursionists met with a setback. They had expected rustic teams decked out with sprigs of the forest there to meet them. But there was only one solitary vehicle there at their disposal, and that was at the top of the hill. The enterprising farmer who brought his team -"God Bless him!" said the dozen who obtained a ride - is Mr. A. McMillan. Long may he wave. The rest, including quite a number of ladies, trudged on to the two mile distant hall, and reached there at last, weary, and some of them a little pouty. The concert passed off fairly well and was followed by a pleasant dance. The refreshments were very nice and were generously provided by the ladies of Denman Island who deserve much credit. The excursionists reached home about three o'clock in the morning, and the general expression gathered from many sources is that everybody had a first rate time. [3b]

Fund raising for the hospital was an ongoing challenge accepted by the citizens of Union Bay. Whist games, teas and dances were held. In 1915 the name was changed from Union and Comox Hospital to Cumberland General Hospital. The Jubilee Wing was added in 1928, and one ward was completely furnished by Union Bay. After the Community Hall was built, the club held one dance a year in aid of the hospital.

With all the Colliery employees, as well as the crews of the visiting ships, the doctor was called often to the wharf..

1906 JANUARY ➺ The third engineer of the tramp steamer *Dulwick*, then loading for Acapulco, had been celebrating on shore. T. Hudson took him to the ship and advised him to go to bed. Disregarding this advice, he proceeded to go to shore again to celebrate New Years Eve. Mr. Hudson heard a thud and gave alarm. The sailor never regained consciousness and must have hit his head, then suffocated in the water. Dr. Staples on his arrival pronounced him quite dead. [4]

The Government appointed one of the Cumberland doctors as Marine Surgeon for the port. The first was Dr. Lawrence, followed by Dr. Staples and Dr. Gillespie. Once a week the doctor came down by horse and buggy, or in Dr. Staples' case on his bicycle, to hold a clinic in the little office at the back of the customs building. It was equipped with a dispensary full of medicines and bandages to treat the waiting patients. Home visits were arranged, and if necessary, the doctor would bundle up the patient and send him to the hospital on the train.

Getting word to a doctor often posed quite a problem, but it was much easier after the telegraph was installed.

1904 AUGUST ➺ The chief engineer of a German Steamer *Ramesis*, Mr. Reinecke, was walking on the coal wharf and slipped down a coal shute to the water where he struck a boomstick. R. Cameron, the engineer of loco No.13, saw the fall and gave the alarm. He was ordered at once to go to Cumberland to get medical assistance, others rescuing the man.

Cameron started off in an excited state and, near the bunkers, collided No.13 with some coal cars on the track, slighty injuring the loco, tangling cars all over the track, and making it impossible to continue. A rig was then dispatched for Dr. Gillespie (holidaying at Royston beach), who arrived some time later to find Mr. Reinecke with two broken ribs and badly knocked about. He was sent to Victoria next day to be near the German Consul as he couldn't speak English. Suspension of Engineer Cameron and Brakeman Duncan followed the collision. [4]

Dr. Lawrence had contributed greatly to the hospital board of which he was chairman in its formative years. He was very popular within the community and especially beloved by the Chinese. Everyone was sorry to see him leave, about the turn of the century.

In 1902 Dr. Gillespie went "back east" to be married. His wife quickly became involved with the hospital's welfare, and a Women's

Cumberland Museum

Doctors McNaughton or Hicks visited Union Bay every week for over 40 years

Auxiliary was formed with Mrs. Gillespie as president. Besides raising money, the ladies made and mended the linen and gowns.

In 1895 the miners met to form an accident fund. That first meeting, with interpreters for the European miners, was concerned with gaining compensation for three types of accidents: permanent, temporal, fatal. Also discussed was the need to "lay off" work after a fatal accident. It was decided that only the shift when and where the accident happened would lay off. Of course everything was dependent on agreement by the Company. From these early beginnings, and after several years and many meetings, the medical fund grew. Each man paid $12 per year, and in return was given admission to the hospital without further charge. Some of the logging camps also had similar schemes, and this provided the hospital with needed money for daily operations. The Alexander ward was soon added, making more beds available. There was always a representative from Union Bay on the medical fund committee. George Campbell and Jock Pollock both served as officers for long terms.

Some of the transportation problems were alleviated in 1915 when the firm of Kierstead and Burton (carriage and blacksmith builders of Cumberland) customized a car for ambulance work. The car, complete with the latest appliances for first aid work, was used for general purposes in connection with the medical and accident fund. It was driven by T. Banks, the local undertaker.

In 1907 Dr. George McNaughton arrived from New Brunswick and took a position at the hospital where he remained until retirement. Two years later, Dr. Arbuckle from Vancouver General Hospital was appointed doctor for Union Bay and the Islands, but did not stay long. Dr. Hicks, a graduate of McGill, arrived in 1911, and shortly after, Dr. Gillespie moved to Vancouver.

Both Dr. McNaughton and Dr. Hicks became institutions in Union Bay. They took turns coming every Wednesday, checked in with Mrs. Reid, talked over the condition of any patients still sick, treated anyone there with a problem, and got the list of homes to visit. Dr. Hicks had a quick, businesslike manner, while Dr. McNaughton always had time for a friendly chat. People became fiercely loyal to either one or the other. If they were sick, they hoped that it was the week for their favourite doctor's visit.

The two doctors gave freely of their time and knowledge. Besides being the health officers for the district, giving first aid classes and testing the applicants, they served on just about every board that was formed, from civic to church matters. Dr. McNaughton was a religious man who did some lay preaching and also led the fight for prohibition in the district. He served on the school board, and in 1928 became the M.L.A. for Comox District, representing the Conservative party. Dr. Hicks was also involved in the church and sang in the United Church choir. A musical man who loved to sing, he was president of the Men's Musical Society.

After King Edward had an appendectomy which was dramatically reported by radio, the procedure came into vogue. It was made even more popular in the district by the fact that both doctors had appendectomies. Dr. Hicks arrived just in time to fill in for Dr. McNaughton while he was recovering. Then early in 1913 Dr. Hicks was stricken. The newspapers faithfully reported each appendectomy.

"I was sick and in the hospital when the 1st World War broke out. Dr. Hicks was just a young man and he had a car. The boom camp here had the only phone around, so they phoned the hospital and Dr. Hicks came and picked me up. He got me to the hospital but my appendix had ruptured. I had been two or three days in pain, so they operated on me in the middle of the night. Agnes McIntosh, who later married Pete Reid, was my nurse in the hospital. I was the baby and all the nurses were good to me. She used to take me in and let me sit on Pete's bed. He was in hospital with something wrong with one eye. I was in hospital for four weeks."

Annie (Muschamp) Nelson

The hospital matron, Miss Brown, resigned to volunteer as a nurse in the B.C. army hopital in France. Miss McIntosh succeeded her as matron for a few months, until she married Peter and officially became the company nurse in the port town.

1915 AUGUST ➻ The bride, matron of Cumberland Hospital, was attired in her nurse's uniform. She was attended by the groom's sister, and given away by Dr. McNaughton. The nursing staff attended in uniform, which helped to make a very pleasing scene. [4]

They lived on the top row in the last company house next to Chinatown and had one son, Jim. Nurse Reid kept her house as spotlessly clean as a hospital; the interior was painted white and always smelled of disinfectant. Inside the back door, Pete built shelves with glass doors for the dispensary. A cot, as well as a wicker stretcher, stood ready for any emergency. Mrs Reid had a phone, and she could be summoned any time of the day or night for anything from a broken bone, to red stools from eating too many beets. Unless the patient's family sent a car, or Pete was home to drive her, Agnes' only means of transportation, rain or shine, was "shank's pony". Although she was paid to treat the families of the CC(D)L employees, everyone was attended to by this kind, skillful lady.

About 1915, Saint John's Ambulance First Aid classes were given by the doctors. First aid teams were formed at each mine. First aid men at the various locations were given extra salaries. Filling this position at the Bay were Tom and Dave Campbell. Tom also gave first aid lessons. Mrs. Reid taught home nursing to many groups. The young ladies in the Sunshine Girls, Sewing Circle, CGIT, Red Cross and Girl Guides all learned how to cool a fever, stop a nose bleed and make a bed with perfect hospital corners.

Until well into the 1930's the threat of a variety of diseases was ever present, especially given Union Bay's position as a port. Until about 1910, outbreaks of typhoid were common every few years, usually killing several people in the district. Diptheria was particularly bad in the 1890's, when yellow flags, to suggest the yellowish grey membrane that grew over the throat and nose, were flown from the cottages to denote quarantine. Some parents took their children and temporarily moved to Denman Island to escape the dreaded disease. Again, in 1912, it struck with a vengeance, and an isolation hospital was set up to care for the patients, and schools were closed.

Chinese immigrants, and travellers from the Orient, were often blamed for the introduction of an epidemic. They had to pass through the quarantine station at William Head. If they had been in contact with, or near an infected person, they were fumigated and bathed. Often Victoria citizens were first to contract the disease, then it spread to Vancouver and up Island. In 1892 there were forty-four cases of smallpox in Victoria, and people were leaving for the Comox District to escape the epidemic.

1892 JULY ➾ The Health Officer on board the *SS Isobel* from Union Wharf was vaccinating any passenger not already vaccinated. [2]

The hardest hit during a smallpox epidemic were the Indians. Although the smallpox vaccine was discovered in 1796, most people were still not vaccinated until an epidemic threatened. The method was written up in the local paper to explain the procedure and encourage participation.

1892 JULY ➾ Small pox points used in vaccination are 1 1/2" long by 1/8" wide, wafer-like, tapered at one end and made from bone. The point is dipped into a solution of warm water and puss from the udder of an infected cow. It dries instantly and is then dipped in gelatin to keep the vaccine from being rubbed off. To vaccinate, an abrasion is made on the skin of the person's bare arm. The point, after being dipped in water to melt the gelatin, is drawn back and forth across the abrasion, thus forcing vaccine into the wound. A piece of court plaster is stuck over the spot and a person is vaccinated for life. [2]

J. Reid

CC(D)L nurse Agnes Reid was "on call day or night to treat emergency medical problems. She is shown here with her husband Peter and son Jim in his army uniform

Scarlet fever remained a deadly disease into the 1930's. In 1935 schools were closed in an effort to stop its spread. The next year, fourteen year old Kiyi and ten year old Emmi Masuda died at the Japanese logging camp in Fanny Bay. Other communicable diseases, such as rheumatic fever and meningitis, left children with permanent disabilities.

Tuberculosis, although a much slower disease, was also a killer which over the years took its toll. As early as 1907 the Bay citizens put on an operetta, with the proceeds going to the consumption fund to build a sanatorium near Kamloops.

In 1915 a successful campaign was launched by the government to eradicate bovine tuberculosis. A cure for human tuberculosis was not discovered for many years. Two young girls, Annie Laird and Agnes Mckay, both died of the disease. Agnes was 21 when she died at Tranquille in 1925. George Walker contracted the disease about 1932, and infected his wife and two small children. The children died first, then their mother, Ethel (Searle). George died at Tranquille in 1940.

To aid in the early detection of the disease, a drive was launched to buy a mobile X-ray unit for the province. It was heartily supported, and not a Christmas card was mailed without a TB seal stuck on. The mobile TB clinic arrived in 1945, parked in front of the school, and everyone lined up to have their "picture taken". Organized by the Pythian Sisters, it returned each year, and in 1947, 100% of the population at the Bay was tested.

Also deserving the support of the generous people of Union Bay was the Queen Alexandra

Solarium. It was built in 1927 at Mill Bay to treat crippled children. The idea for the solarium came from a letter written by Mrs. Scott of Hornby Island to the Women's Institute of B.C., requesting help for her crippled daughter, Othoa. This was close to home, so ladies' groups held teas and sold raffle tickets. Later, after the solarium was built, people sent toys at Christmas.

Gradually, with better living conditions and improved treatments, the serious diseases began to wane. The Canadian Health Services educated the public on disease and the need for personal hygiene, as well as hygiene in the home.

1913 JUNE ➾ "Keep Out the Flies" -

- Better to screen the cradle and wear a smile than scoff at precaution and wear mourning.
- Flies in the dining room usually precede nurses in the sick room.
- Screens on the window prevent crepe on the door.
- Flies as well as bad water spread typhoid.
- A fly in the milk may mean one of the family in the grave.
- It costs less to buy a screen door than to get sick and lay off a month.
- It is a short haul from the garbage can to the dining table via the fly route. [4]

The Spanish influenza was brought to North America by returning soldiers. By the middle of September 1918, cases had developed in Victoria, Vancouver and Nanaimo. For a time it seemed that the Comox district would escape. The Government, by an order-in-council, conferred upon all municipalities the power to close theatres, schools, and places used for public gatherings. This did not cover unincorporated areas like Union Bay, which worried the Medical Health Officer, Dr. E.R. Hicks. The mayor of Cumberland sent a telegram to the provincial secretary.

1918 OCTOBER 12 ➾ Apparently no Spanish influenza here. Intend closing churches, schools, theatres, and pool rooms. Feel strongly that public meeting places and dance to be held at Union Bay tomorrow night should be closed. Continuous passenger travel between here and Union Bay, and many ships there from foreign places. Feel that public meeting places in territory adjacent to Cumberland and not in city limits, should also be closed.

Mayor Harrison [5]

However, when the first flu' case in the district was discovered, Union Bay could not be blamed. The same day that the mayor's telegram was sent, a returning soldier who had been working in the shipyards in Seattle, introduced the dreaded epidemic.

1918 OCTOBER 19 ➾ A. Peacock returned from Seattle on Wednesday. It appears that he was suffering from an attack of Spanish influenza before leaving Seattle and was on the way to recovery. Local Board of Health placed him in isolation in hospital. The passenger coach in which he travelled from Union Bay, and also the persons with whom he came in contact, were fumigated. [5]

It was hardly necessary to close public meeting places, as people were afraid to go out. The owners of camps thought they could escape by keeping the loggers in the bush and hiring no new men. But it was not long before all areas of the district had people suffering from the flu'. Emergency hospitals were set up in school houses and hotels.

In the district, the Chinese were hardest hit by the flu'. By the middle of November there were eighty-three Chinese suffering in Cumberland, thirty-three at Bevan, and twenty-nine at Union Bay. A Chinese doctor, Low Mong Yee, came from Victoria and treated the men, speeding up their recovery. The flu' knew no nationality barriers. Dr. McNaughton's 1 1/2 year old daughter died from it.

"I came down with the flu' first. I think I had the distinction of being the first white person in Union Bay to get the flu'. So many people died in Cumberland. We were really ill and in bed for a couple of weeks. Mrs. Reid would come and help us; she made a little pneumonia jacket for me. It was like a little vest of cotton batting that went next to my skin under my nightie to keep my lungs warm. Mom burned it after I got better. I was ten and Bill was twelve, and he and Dad didn't get it, but Dunc, Jessie, Mom, and I did. Donald was six months old, so he was in bed with Mom but didn't appear to take it. My Dad would come home from work and he and Bill would do the cooking. Mind you, people were very good. They would bring soups and things and leave them at the door. They were afraid to come in. Bill had to be nursemaid to us all; he did everything. A little kid of twelve, with no hot water or toilet facilities. My mother always said he deserved a medal."

Nettie (Marshall) Jones

"It came very fast. I remember I was looking after everyone in our house. I never took it. But, my gawd, at that time I'd be only twelve years old. Wiping them down, emptying chamber pots and, oh gawd!... everyone was sick but my father, and he had to work. I was the nursemaid and trying to cook. Boil water was about all I could do. Most people were afraid to come into the house in case they caught it."

Bill Marshall

With most of the suffering over by Christmas, the statistics were issued in February

District population - 3,184	Flu' Cases - 1,598	Deaths - 28 (18 of the deaths were Oriental)
Union Bay	Flu' Cases - 72	Deaths - 4 (all 4 Chinese)

Patent medicines proliferated, with cures for every disease

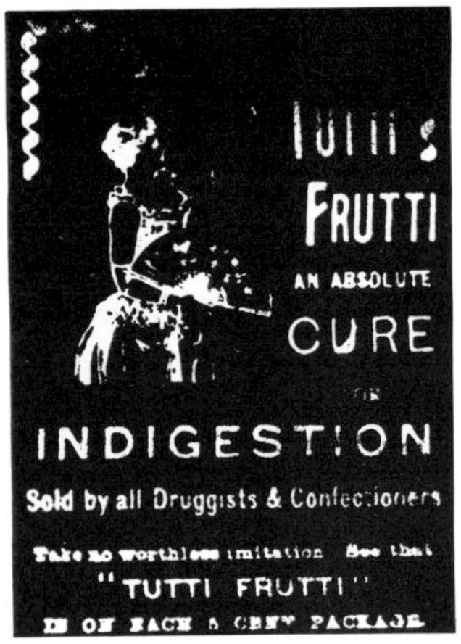

under the sun. Medicine chests held a variety of home remedies and patent medicines: Carter's Little Liver Pills, Chase's Catarrh Cure, Dodd's Kidney Pills, Eno's Fruit Salts, Kellog's Asthma Cure, Zam Buk Ointment. Most of them had their origins in herbal remedies.

A cure for diptheria was tried by many in 1891. "Provide yourself with some liquid tar and turpentine, which must be mixed on an iron plate or pan and burned near the patient, so as to make a dense smoke which he inhales. It will clear the throat of the fibrous membrane that causes death."

Drugs to kill bacteria became widely used during the Second World War. Sulfa drugs were accessible in 1939 and were particularly successful in curing pneumonia. Sulfa was added to Mrs. Reid's store of drugs, and if one of the doctors prescribed it, she would dole out the correct amount. The wonder drug, penicillin, was used to treat the wounded during the war. It was not until 1945 that it became widely used in Canada, after the War Time Prices and Trades Board took control of its distribution. The early penicillin was all given by injection, so if prescribed, the patient had to trudge up to Mrs. Reid's once or twice a day to receive the shot. Then, at last, streptomycin came into use, a drug that would kill the tuberculosis bacteria.

School Boards in the 1940's, in conjunction with the Provincial Health Nursing Service, began employing Public Health Nurses to serve the children of their district and promote preventative health. Courtenay and Comox were the leaders, and hired Miss Alice Beattie in 1941. Three years later, the other school boards joined this medical service, and another nurse, Miss Lucille Giovando, was hired. Mr. E.T. Searle was an officer on the new board.

1944 APRIL ➻ Health Nurse Scheme to cover the area not presently covered. This includes Royston, Cumberland, Fanny Bay, Union Bay, Minto, Puntledge, Bevan, Hornby and Denman Islands. For the 604 children in the area, the cost will be $1.32 per child for nurses' salary, transportation etc. So about $50 per year will be the cost to the Union Bay School Board, as a grant will come from the Provincial Board of Health. [7]

The day the health nurse visited struck fear into many a child's heart. "Is it my turn today?" "Which is worse, inoculation or vaccination?" "How far does the needle really go in?" For many children, this was their first encounter with the needle. Big boys in the eighth grade crumpled onto the floor when it was their turn to walk out to the cloak room where friendly Miss Giovando was waiting with a fresh needle filled with serum. Envied were the children whose parents conscientiously objected to immunization. In the early 1950's, polio arrived in the district, and a number of people were stricken. A serum was discovered, and in 1955 children were immunized.

Little was known about cancer, but people were reassured that it was not contagious.

1909 MAY ➻ The medical faculty of Columbia University announced that cancer is not contagious. Breathe it, handle it, or wallow in it, you simply will not get it as it is not a germ disease. You can't get cancer from eating fish, meat, vegetables, or drinking water or liquor. [4]

Scientists even went so far as to try to prove that smoking could be beneficial.

1913 ➻ Tobacco is exceedingly efficacious in the killing of microbes, state scientists. In five minutes, tobacco smoke will kill almost all microbes in the saliva and nearly completely sterilize the mouth. As proof, this experiment is offered: place several cigars in water containing millions of cholera microbes, they will all be killed in twenty-four hours. [4]

There was no connection made between smoking tobacco, and cancer. Young boys would start smoking at a very early age, often encouraged by their elders. Everyone in the district enjoyed the article about the little Comox boy.

1889 NOVEMBER ➻ The five year old son of Mr. Smith of Comox started smoking at three years of age, being introduced to it by the boarders of the house. He still smokes three cigars plus cigarettes every day, and can smoke and spit like any old timer. He'll ask a light from any man. [2]

BIRTHING & BABIES

1894 SEPTEMBER 5 ➻ At the Nelson Hotel at Union Wharf, the wife of Mr. Andrew McCartney gave birth to a daughter. [2]

The birth of the first white baby at Union Wharf was announced as far away as Nanaimo. She was named Greta. The McCartneys had moved to Union Wharf in March 1894 to operate the dining room at Howe's Hotel. Most likely, Ellen McKay was the midwife at the birth of her neice.

The sisters-in-law were the only two women at Union Wharf and must have been a great comfort to one another. It was not long before Mrs. McKay gave birth to her third child, Robert, who claimed the distinction of being the first white boy born at Union Bay. He entered the world June 29, 1895 in the family's first home, which was built on company land and stood back from the road in the woods (three houses north of the present post office).

Ellen's desire to become a nurse was fulfilled when she became the fledgling town's midwife. She drew on her own experiences at birthing, and her kind helpful nature was a comfort to all the new mothers. When she was sent for, at any time of the day or night, she'd hitch up the horses, give a few instructions to the older children and set off, often taking her youngest one with her.

"She'd come home from nursing someone and she'd say, 'You know, they haven't got a thing in the house to eat. Make up some biscuits, and when the bread is out, bring the biscuits and a loaf of bread over'. They had no tea, no sugar, no nothing! Expecting a new baby and not a bite in the house. She was the midwife; the doctor never got here because it was horse and buggy days. Mom used to stay for two weeks and look after the house and meals for them. Sometimes they'd give her $5.00 but not often. Us kids were left to run this house. Look after the cows and deliver the milk.

When Dr. Hicks came in 1911 he had his first confinement case at Union Bay and he was very nervous. Mother was there before he came, and she said, 'Doctor, you go out in the kitchen and forget all about us'. Dr. Hicks always said, 'I would have lost that baby if it wasn't for your mother'."

Nellie (McKay) King

After the turn of the century, Mrs. Booth, wife of the freight agent, lived on the company hill, and as a trained midwife from the old country, also brought several babies into the world. It was the parents' responsibility to register the child's birth. This had to be done in person in Cumberland and often posed quite a problem, with the result that some children did not get registered, or the birth dates would be incorrect.

"Often they got the dates mixed up. If Father went to Cumberland to register the baby and got a little too much of the bottle, he got the date mixed up or maybe he put down the day he was there, not the day the baby was born on."

Mary (McKay) Winterburn

Back at the turn of the century, being pregnant was no fun. For the twenty-five years she was of child bearing age, a married woman could be completely exhausted from repeated pregnancies and child rearing. Neither was it in any way glamorous. Maternity clothes did not exist. The usual garb of the "mother-to-be" was a voluminous apron worn over dresses and skirts that could no longer be buttoned. Dress-up clothes were unnecessary because she rarely went out.The roaring '20s brought in dresses that hung from the shoulder - no bust, and no waist. This developed into the "smock" which became the standard pregnancy costume, long or short, worn over skirts with an elastic waist.

Preparing a layette for the new baby was one pleasure the expectant mother could enjoy. The catalogues devoted several pages to infant wear, including two pages of fancy bonnets. When a woman realized she was pregnant, she, her mother and friends started knitting sweaters, bonnets, booties, soakers, vests and leggings. Yards of flannelette were bought to be sewn into diapers, binders, nighties, jackets and barrowcoats. If money was available, a long dress trimmed with lace and ribbons would be bought. This was very special and used for the baby's christening. The first baby christened in Union Bay church was Mary Reid.

Every morning the newborn had a bath in the dishpan on the kitchen table near the heat of the wood stove. Rubbing alcohol was put on the umbilical cord to dry it and keep it clean. Corn starch or talcum powder was then sprinkled on. Next, a binder was

M. Kine

J. Geidt

Left: The first white male born in Union Bay, Bob McKay, with his wife Bess (Muschamp) and family. Left to right: Mary, Bud, Robbie, George and Ann. Right: Little Jeremy Morrison models a flannelette barrow coat - a sleeveless wrap around vest with long skirt to keep baby warm

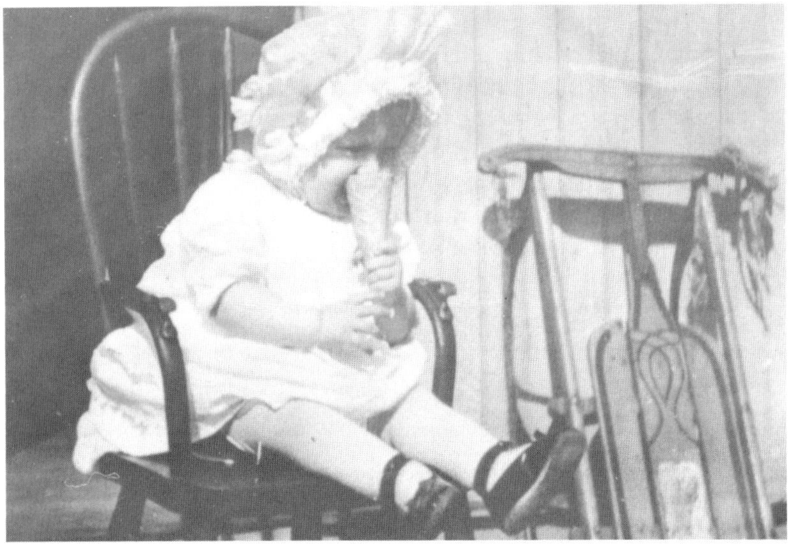

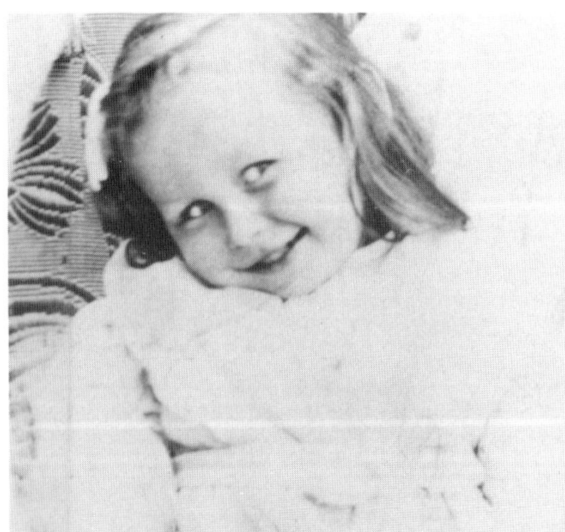

wound snugly around the tummy to keep the belly button from protruding. The diapers, made in a square and folded into a triangle, were pinned on then covered with soakers knit of wool. Rubber pants with buttons were available but mothers at the Bay preferred soakers, so it was always a little hazardous to hold a baby on your lap. Tiny vests knit of wool went next to the skin, covered most often by a barrowcoat, an ingenious item.

"All the babies wore barrowcoats. They were like a slip without shoulder straps and open down the back. The bodice part crossed over and tied like the old undershirts. The long skirt was gathered onto the bodice. It was worn over an undershirt and under the nightie or dress, for warmth. We made them of white flannelette when we made the diapers and nighties.

Thelma (Auchinvole) Dutfield

For special occasions the babies were dressed in long, flowing lawn dresses trimmed with embroidery, lace and ribbons. A knit wool sweater with matching booties always topped the outfit. When the infant was going out, a bonnet was added. If it was winter, woolen leggings kept tiny legs warm. The little one was then wrapped in a flannelette blanket and covered with a beautifully knit or crocheted shawl. This shawl was often passed down from generation to generation. When not in use it was carefully wrapped in tissue paper and stored in a cedar chest.

Little boys and girls were dressed alike in long nighties and dresses. It was not until they began to creep that you could distinguish the sex of the tot by its clothes, for then the boys were dressed in rompers.

In the very early days, by necessity, breast feeding was accepted by all. Then, with more birthing done at the hospital in Cumberland, and the advent of canned milk, infant formulas came into vogue. Besides being expensive it was very time consuming, as it was not until the '50s that powdered formulas could be bought. Sterilizing bottles and nipples on the wood and coal stove, then measuring the right amount of milk, water and sweetener to make the correct formula, kept the new mother busy. Pacific, Carnation and Eagle Brand competed for the baby market. In the early '20s at Union Bay there were a number of babies brought up on Eagle Brand, who became roly-poly little toddlers. In some cases it took them years to lose the fat.

Each birth was a happy occasion in the little town, and the arrival of twins was doubly so. Soon after moving to Union Bay, the Manson family's second set of twins, Flossie and Florence, were born in 1900, sisters to eight year old Robina and Ethel. They were Union Bay's version of the "Bobsey Twins". Mrs. Manson now had six children under eight to care for. Luckily her oldest daughter, a teenager, became a wonderful nanny, especially after another baby arrived two years later.

Then, in the 1920's the little blond McNally twin girls, Sheila and Frances, arrived. There was also a lady whose husband worked on the construction of the E&N. The family lived in a tent when she had twin boys.

The Dionne quintuplets arrived in May 1934 and caught the imagination of all of Canada. Multiple births were still a hot topic one month later when twin girls, Janette and Jacqueline, were born

W. Glover

The Glover twins, Janette and Jacqueline, fill the doll carriage

A. Mar

A rare event, the birth of Chinese twin boys, brought much attention to Alex and Ester Mar. Heather Auchinvole took Wayne and Wally for a ride in their wagon

to Harry and Winnie Glover. Their progress was measured against that of Annette, Emilie, Yvonne, Cecile and Marie.

"The twins had a favourite big old blanket, now you'd call it a security blanket like Little Linus'. When it got so dirty from dragging around and being pulled this way and that, Winnie would wash the blanket and hang it on the old pulley line in the kitchen to dry. The twins would stand under it and

E. Leighton

Curly tops Harold and Evelyn Leighton in the grandfather Baldwin's garden

cry. Drying clothes took a long time in those days. Finally, one day, Winnie cut it in half so they could go separate ways."

Thelma (Walker, Auchinvole) Dutfield

In the early 1940's the little curly tops, Harold and Evelyn, were born to Eva and Dick Leighton. They were followed by Alex and Ester Mar's twins boys, Wayne and Wally, born in 1954.

DEATH

1884 "Under the Turf"
1893 "To Brighter Chimes"
1899 "Committed to the Grave"
1905 "Death's Harvest"
1911 "Went out, even as the going down of the tide"
1920 "The Grim Reaper has taken another and he's passed to the Great Beyond"
1927 "Resident of long time standing passed to her Reward"
1936 "Follows husband across Great Divide"
1943 "Passes Away"

With very little medical assistance available, and the prevalence of diseases such as smallpox and tuberculosis, most people from an early age had experienced the loss of loved ones.

After death, the deceased was dressed in his best clothes and laid out in the front parlour on a table, daybed or sofa. The body was kept there for two days which gave family and friends time to come and "take the farewell view of the dead."

"Mr. Humphrey died of a heart attack. We delivered milk to the hotel and to get to the kitchen we had to go through the hall and past the parlour where he was lying. They just dressed dead people up and fixed them and they lay in the front room for two days. You had them at home, there was no where else to take them. Then they buried them at Cumberland."

Nellie (McKay) King

Before the turn of the century there were undertakers in Cumberland. Their job was not to preserve or beautify the corpse, but to provide a coffin, dig the hole and bury the body. Often they were agents for marble and granite headstones. Undertaking was usually a side line to another business. Alex Grant operated a furniture store, while J. Fletcher was a contractor and builder. In the big cities, ostentatious caskets of solid oak with ornamental silver mountings could be bought. At Union Wharf a family member or close friend would build the wooden box. When Andrew McKay died, the "Hindu" who worked around the farm built the coffin for his friend.

The cemetery at Cumberland was not cleared of timber and made ready until the end of 1895. Before that, people who died at Union Wharf could be buried in the Presbyterian cemetery in Sandwick or in Nanaimo. Usually, the body, accompanied by family and friends, was shipped out on the *SS Isobel* or *Thistle* to Nanaimo. There it was buried or put on the train for Victoria where it found a final resting spot.

Before the deceased took the last journey, the local preacher held a service in the family home. After that, the coffin was loaded onto the family buggy, a rented rig or a horse-drawn hearse provided by the undertaker. Then the procession set off for the graveyard.

"I can remember the day of Mr. McKay's funeral. It was about 1915 so I was maybe six years old. Bill McKay was a baby. We had a wooden kitchen table by the window that looked up to the old road and I stood on it. We watched the procession as it slowly went by. A horse drawn hearse with the box, followed by Mrs. McKay and all the kids in their big democrat wagon."

Nettie (Marshall) Jones

Early in the century, T.E. Banks in Cumberland started an undertaking business. Until the late 1920's, funerals were conducted at the family's home in Union Bay. Then the undertakers, Sutton and Piercy in Courtenay, and Banks built chapels in their mortuaries. Now bodies were taken out of the home to be embalmed and displayed in expensive caskets within the sanctimonious setting of the funeral home.

DIED

MONDAY, DECEMBER 14th, 1925

AGNES McKAY

Aged 21 years, 9 months and 15 days.

Beloved daughter of Mrs. Andy McKay, of Union Bay.

The funeral will be held from Banks' Undertaking Parlors, Cumberland, on

Saturday, December 19th, 1925
at 2.30 p.m.

to the Cumberland Cemetery for interment.

Rev. Mr. Walker, of Union Bay, officiating.

Friends and Acquaintances kindly accept this intimation.

D. Aitken

Black-bordered death notices like this one announcing Agnes McKay's death were mailed to family and friends

When settlers first came to Union Bay, obituaries were poetically written up. In 1893 when D.W. Gordon, M.P. for the district, died, the account read, "The slender thread which bound our pioneer to earth snapped asunder and so far as he is concerned, the great mystery of the future was solved."

Then, as now, the newspaper had an obituary column. Funeral write-ups were also very popular, starting first by describing the suffering and pain endured by the deceased, followed by the names of preacher, undertaker, pallbearers and chief mourners. It ended with a list, the longer the better, of the people who sent flowers and the type of arrangements sent. "Mr. & Mrs. F. Brown sent a wreath, the Walker family a cross, Mr. Fraser a pillow, Mr.& Mrs. Eade cut flowers ...."

To announce to out-of-town friends and family, death notices were mailed. These were made up by the local printer, the same as wedding announcements. The envelopes were edged in black, so that one knew on opening the post office box that someone had died.

"My uncle was away in the navy during the First World War, and what with war casulties and the flu' epidemic, half of his family was wiped out. It must have been terrible for him receiving these envelopes edged in black, when he was thousands of miles from home. He had a fabulous collection."

Muriel (Harwood) Peters

DENTAL

Going to the dentist is never a pleasant experience but years ago it was often a terrifying ordeal. Many children had to be dragged screaming into the office. Upon entering the door and encountering the antiseptic smell and the sound of the drill, adults would turn pale and feel faint.

In the very early days the first settlers had to travel to Nanaimo, Victoria or Vancouver when they had a toothache. The trip was long and arduous in a canoe, unless transportation could be arranged on the weekly visit of the mail boat. By the 1880's, dentists from the three cities were coming to the district, setting up shop in the local hotel and welcoming patients. One of the first was G.W. Hunt, who travelled by canoe to the different settlements.

1883 MAY ➾ Dentist Mr. G.W. Hunt will visit Comox in June. Silver, platinum or bone fillings put in for $1 to $2.50 each. Gold fillings $3 and up. Guaranteed satisfaction of all operations or no charge. [2]

By the 1890's, Doctors West and Curry were spending several weeks a year in Union. Dr. Curry of Nanaimo claimed as his specialty a new method for painless extractions without the use of ether or chloroform. Dr. West of Victoria boasted that he could "make artificial dentures as natural looking as your own."

Dentistry became more competitve as more dentists visited the area.

1898 ➾ Teeth Extracted	$ .50	Sale Price $.25
Excellent set of teeth	6.50	" 5.00
Silver Filling	.75	" .50
Gold Filling	1.00 and up	

After the turn of the century, dentists Dr. Kerr from Nanaimo and Dr. Dalby from Vancouver were stopping at Union Bay for two weeks and setting up an office in the Nelson Hotel. They all claimed painless work, using a variety of methods from electricity to gas and ether.

Oral hygiene was not stressed. A six month check-up was unheard of. The only reason for a visit to the dentist was a toothache. Often people suffered for months with a toothache, doctoring it themselves with oil of cloves to stop the pain. Stories are told of people trying to pull out the offending tooth themselves if a dentist was unavailable.

"Leong Mar was afflicted with a toothache. I think a lot of Chinese were a challenge for a dentist. He bought a bottle of Johnny Walker, went home, got a pair of pliers and started working on himself. The

next day he got a ride to Cumberland to see Dr. Gordon but Dr. Gordon had moved to Courtenay four years earlier. He had pulled it until the nerve broke so he just left it hanging there. All the years he worked with me all he ate was jelly roll. He carried a black lunch bucket and had green tea and one jelly roll dropped in the bucket, just the way he bought it from Hudson's."

Ken Peters

After the war Arthur Wilkinson, who married Gertie Hudson, set up a dentist office in Mrs. Hudson's front room and worked on the townspeople's teeth. He then went to Cumberland where he assisted Dr. Christie who, in 1919, opened an office in the old Royal Bank building at Union Bay under management of a Dr. Hill from Victoria. There were not enough patients to keep the office open full time, so Dr. Hill left and Dr. Christie continued to hold office hours once a week for several years.

In 1923 Dr. B. Gordon moved to Cumberland and started as a dentist specializing in bridge work, dentures, and a new method of freezing. The big needle filled with a dark solution was to be feared as much as the drill, so many people still had teeth filled without freezing. His first drill was powered by a kick wheel. Dr. Gordon drove his "Model T" loaded with his dentistry tools to Bloedel's camp. All the loggers sat around watching the patient suffer, and offering comments and encouragement.

"Most of the kids never saw a dentist, but my Dad was very fussy. Every summer he would take us all up to Cumberland to see old Dr. Gordon. He had the old foot pump drill. I never had freezing and still haven't till this day. It's mind over matter. I just think happy thoughts. Beth, she was a brat in the dentist chair. She'd kick, scratch and bite poor Dr. Gordon. One day when we were grown up we met him coming up the street. Beth said, 'Let's open our mouths so he'll recognize us'."

Alma Magnone

Probably because the early settlers and their children ate simple diets, high in starch but low in sugar, tooth decay was not as common as in the 1930's and '40s when sweets were more available. Brushing was not emphasized and most families could not afford visits to the dentist or transportation to Courtenay. Many children had a mouth full of rotten, black, broken and decaying teeth. Dr. Gordon joked that the sulfur from the burning coal on the coal hills accounted for the heavy coating of yellow tartar on the teeth of Union Bay residents. It was quite common to let the teeth rot, visiting the dentist only for extractions. Then, at about the age of fifteen, the teeth were all removed and dentures put in.

Finally, in the 1930's, the Canadian Dental Hygiene Council started to promote good mouth health with newspaper and magazine articles, essay contests, and lectures to parent groups. Teachers encouraged brushing in their health classes.

DISASTERS
ACCIDENTS

Cumberland Museum

The portion of the 100' high Trent River bridge that collapsed in 1898

Safety in the workplace, and in life in general, was not emphasized as it is today. The pace of everyday living was slower. People, not machines, were in control of their lives.

Accidents often arose from circumstances foreign to people today. Humour can be seen in what was a bizarre tragedy eighty years ago.

1910 JULY ➾ M. W. Reesman, sub-foreman and employee of Fraser River Co. at Union Bay meets horrible death. He either fainted or took a cramp. A very steady young man, dressed in his night clothes, bid his companions good-night and was never seen alive again. They searched the woods, but found him in the outhouse standing on his head, smothered to death. The verdict of the inquest was "death by smothering". [5]

Like the above, the next story could not happen today. Mr. P.M. Butler was well-known at the Bay, as he had been employed as chief engineer on the *SS Dunsmuir*, then as captain on the *Isobel*. In November 1892 he travelled from his home in Departure Bay on the *SS Joan* to Hornby Island, where he was met by Mr. Nixon in his sloop. Anxious to bag some ducks to send down to his family on the *Joan* the next day, Mr. Butler had his friend drop him and his dog near the mouth of Rosewall Creek. He arranged to fire a shot as a signal to be picked up. As dusk came and no signal was heard, Mr. Nixon put into shore and inquired of two Indians who said they had seen Butler earlier, creeping along the edge of the bush, gun in hand. The three started to search but had to stop because of darkness. Next morning they were horrified to find the missing man, lying crushed under a log. Mr. Butler had been following a cattle trail in the thicket when he stooped to crawl through a low bush and sprung the trap on an Indian "dead fall" bear trap. The fall of the heavy log across his chest had caused almost instantaneous death. The body was taken to Union Bay to await a steamer going south. Mr. Butler's dog refused to leave the scene, snarling at anyone's attempts to move him. It was seventeen days until, too weak to protest, he was sent back to the family aboard the *Isobel*.

Trains were also the source of many accidents. Several Chinese were killed or maimed under the wheels of the locomotives or coal cars. Duncan Murray, son of the local policeman, was working at his first job, as a brakeman, in 1927, when he was killed at the age of nineteen. He was runnning to make the switch at the "Y" when he tripped and fell in front of the locomotive.

The Trent River disaster was the most tragic of all the train accidents. At 7:10 a.m. on August 17, 1898 the new No.4 locomotive, travelling tender first, left the mine for the Wharf, pulling twenty cars of coal and one car of lumber. Alf Walker was at the controls with Hugh Grant stoking the boiler. Also working on the engine was young Alex Mellado, a brakeman. The rear brakeman, Matt Piercy, was riding the last car.

Cumberland Museum

Rescue workers beside Loco No.4. The engineer, brakeman and five hitchhikers were killed

As the passenger coach was only scheduled twice a week, passengers often hitched a ride in the engine or on the cars. This was against company policy, but the posted signs and notices in the newspaper did not deter anyone eager to quickly travel between the two towns. The rule was rarely enforced by the engineers, whose responsibility it was. In the cab on Wednesday morning were the following: Walter Work (son of James Work, superintendent at the Wharf), Miss Frances Horne (daughter of Wm. Horne, a blacksmith at Union Wharf), Miss Villa Grieve (a school teacher), and Richard Nightingale (contractor for the bridge repair). Two Japanese men, Nanka and Asana, rode one of the cars.

The train approached the Trent River bridge at about seven miles per hour. William Bell, a civil engineer, and his helper, Enoch Walker, were under the bridge over the deep, wide ravine, preparing a stone foundation for a new bridge. Suddenly they heard a crack like a gun exploding, looked up and sprang to the side just in time to escape the falling train and bridge. The 58 ton engine with 30 ton tender was two thirds of the way across when the bridge collapsed and the locomotive plunged, nose first, 100 feet to the gully below. It landed on its side across the river, with a tangle of coal and cars around it. Brakeman Piercy saw the coal cars going down in front of him and jumped clear. When the dust settled he was first to give assistance, and managed to free Miss Grieve who was badly injured. Piercy called for assistance and was helped by Enoch Walker. William Bell rescued fireman Grant and Miss Horne who were both seriously hurt. All the others on board were buried in the wreck, so tools and more help were needed to free them.

1898 AUGUST ➾ Bell ran as fast as his legs would carry him to the Wharf with his message of disaster. An attempt was made to acquaint the colliery office in Union by wire which was not in working order. An engine ran up to the bridge, and young Sid Hoover was dispatched on foot to the mine to carry the news. When within two miles of town he overtook a man on horseback, to whom he gave his message, and who sped forward, shouting as he reached Dunsmuir Avenue, "Trent River bridge is down, and all on the train are killed!" This was about 10:30 a.m. [4]

Superintendent Little had received the garbled phone message, realized that some disaster had happened, and ordered an engine and car to be made ready. With Dr. Bailey, Mayor Mounce, and the necessary men and equipment, it started down the track and met the messenger. It continued and reached the accident site, and the Union men joined the men from the Wharf in the rescue work. Meanwhile the news reached Cumberland.

Cumberland Museum

Debris of coal cars and coal at the bottom of the ravine

1898 AUGUST ➾ The whole town was at once in a blaze of excitement, and all available rigs were engaged and soon on the way to the scene of death, seven miles away. Men and boys on bicycles and on foot followed in a stream. Officer Thompson started immediately for Oyster River to notify Coroner Abrams. Word was sent to Courtenay and Comox, and Dr. Millard was on hand as quickly as possible. A number from Comox came over by sailing boat. [4]

The rescue party had the difficult job of finding and retrieving the remaining six bodies. Walter Work, one of the dead, had been to Cumberland to purchase his wedding suit. Dr. Millard, with the help of Mrs. C. Lowe who was camping at Trent River, treated Hugh Grant, who suffered a broken leg among other injuries. Dr. Bailey attended the badly cut and scalded Misses Horne and Grieve, then transported them by train to the Wharf. To get them to hospital, Mr. Grant and Miss Grieve were shipped by boat to Comox, then by wagon to Courtenay and finally to Cumberland. Frances Horne died the next day at Union Wharf.

1898 AUGUST ➾ Last week it was a sad sight when almost the entire population of Union Wharf followed the coffin of young Walter Work to the steamer. [4]

Coroner Abrams held a lengthy inquest where some survivors and several experts testified that the bridge was sound before the accident, while others felt that parts were unsafe and contained rot. In the end, the jury recommended that the government appoint a bridge inspector for the province and concluded with this remark:

"Taking the evidence as a whole, while we deplore the sudden taking off of

so many persons from their sphere of usefulness, yet we are unable to arrive at any other verdict than that the aforementioned deceased met their deaths from an accident caused by the falling of the Trent River bridge from some unknown cause or causes."

Signed C.H.Tarbell, Foreman

Accidents affecting children were always particularly tragic. Stoves and fireplaces were hazardous as the little ones played around the house.

"I opened the door of the little potbellied stove with the edge of my pinny, as I had seen Mom do many times. The pinny caught on fire and I was aflame. Mother rolled me in a floor rug and put out the flames. Then she left me with Hazel and Lucy, and taking Charlie, who was only one year old, ran down to the scales to tell Dad. Dad contacted the train crew, and they stopped and took me to the hospital. My face and hair were badly burned and I was in hospital a long time."

Hazel (Davis) Macartney

In 1909 two Cumberland families on an outing to Union Bay in their horse and buggy were victims of a serious runaway. The horses bolted near Fraser and Bishop's Hotel, capsizing the buggy. Eleven year old Robert Miller was killed instantly, and a brother suffered broken bones.

Another boy was killed in 1927 when he and two friends were playing on the locomotive turntable. For years after, children who heard the story from their parents were loathe to go near the spot, in case the same fate befell them.

1927 MARCH ➾ Nine year old Griffin McColgan and two playmates, Gordon Horne and Ben Abrams, went down to the bunkers on Tuesday and were playing on the turntable. Griffin pushed the mechanism which swings the turntable and it moved with him on it. The boy slipped and fell. Then, when the turntable swung back, he was caught between it and the main line, suffering such severe internal injuries that there was never any chance of saving his life. His two little playmates, seeing what had happened, rushed down and succeeded in extracting the boy. One of them carried him a quarter of a mile to some water, and the other proceeded to get help. The boy was taken to Cumberland Hospital where he died. [6]

The funeral was conducted by Rev. Hobbins from the family home. Friends of the dead boy - Reginald Hudson, Duncan Marshall, Sid Muir and Robert Searle - were pallbearers of the small flower-covered coffin.

The Washer was a hazardous place to work. Men's arms or clothing could easily be caught in the belts, pulling them into the Washer where they would be quickly mangled. Several arms were broken in this way. Tommy James had his arm caught and severely injured. Because of blood poisoning later, the arm had to be amputated. Three men lost their lives. A Japanese worker was killed in 1910, and another, Charles Nakamura, twelve years later. A Chinese worker met the same fate in 1929.

"The sleeve of my father's shirt caught in the fly wheel of a machine he was tending, and he was spun around continuously until it was brought to a halt, unfortunately too late to save him."

Kiyoshi Nakamura

Working on the wharf or trestles, especially in wet or icy weather, was extremely hazardous. Sailors slipped on the deck, or fell off the ladder getting onto the wharf. In 1912 a worker fell thirty feet to his death off the Trent River Trestle.

Logging was a very dangerous job. Every week the district could read of at least one accident in the woods, many of them fatal. (See section on logging) Even getting firewood could be hazardous. One day Massa and Tickie Hygashi were working behind their home to replenish the wood pile. A Chinese neighbour, Cod Fisher, who had once been a logger, watched the young boys with interest. There was a log lying overtop of and pinning down a tree that still had its roots firmly in the ground. Cod Fisher could see that this was a dangerous log to buck, because when the weight was removed from the tree it might spring up. He insisted that the boys let him help them. What he predicted did happen, the log flinging both Tickie and Cod Fisher into the air. Tickie escaped injury, but Cod Fisher came down head first and broke his neck. His body was placed in a large wicker stretcher and carried to Nurse Reid's front lawn until the undertaker arrived.

Car accidents happened often in the early

M. Shillito

Little Ernie Shillito stands on the turntable beside the chain and lock which were put on after a boy was killed

days but usually without loss of life. When autombiles became more powerful and were driven faster, the accidents were often fatal. As there was not the steady stream of cars on the Island Highway as there is today, children quite often played on or near the road. Five year old Jimmy Etter was hit and killed by a car in the spring of 1946 when he and his brothers were playing on Shillito's Hill. In the winter of 1949 children were sleigh riding at Buckley Bay, and Sharon Piket was killed when her sleigh hit a car as she crossed the highway.

Mah Hong died at seventy-three when he was crossing the highway at Washer Creek. He had been collecting coal at dusk, and had two buckets on a stick over his shoulders when he was hit by the car.

In 1940 the jury's verdict was speed and negligence when Andrew "Dutch" McCartney, driving on the highway south of Union Bay, hit a truck "head on". After parties and dances, young people piled into fast cars and crashes occurred. In 1946, Bud McKay was killed when his 1931 Model A roadster went off the Back Road and trapped him under it. In 1958 Douglas Campbell, nineteen years old, was killed when the car in which he and his friends were riding did not make the corner just past Laird's Crossing and hit a pole.

HUNTING & GUN ACCIDENTS

In the early days almost every man hunted for sport and to feed his family. Over the years, the combination of carelessness and primitive guns, especially the hammer fired type, resulted in many unnecessary accidents.

A logger at Doane's Camp in 1908 was accidentally killed by the discharge of a rifle in the hands of his friend. Then in 1911, Thomas Hudson's brother, Samuel, was hunting on Denman with Sandy Chapman when Sandy's gun accidentally discharged, killing Sam. Just a year later, Forrest Ray accidentally shot George Muschamp with a twelve gauge shotgun as the two teenage boys were walking on the boom in front of Muschamp's house. He died about a week later from a wound in his hip.

Tragedy struck again in January 1923 when nineteen year old Wes Peters was hunting on Protection Island with his uncle, Nelson Cook. Because snow was starting to fall, the pair decided to head for home about 3:00 p.m.

1923 FEBRUARY ➾ A few brant had passed over at the moment they were about to embark. Peters went into the boat first, leaning his loaded, single barrel, hammer shotgun against the bow of the boat. Cook followed Peters, who by this time was sitting in the boat with his back turned to the shore. As Cook brought along his decoys and other hunting paraphernalia, he picked the gun up by the muzzle, and it went off. He received the full charge in his right armpit.

Peters, whose back was turned, wheeled around to enquire who had fired the shot and was amazed to hear Cook say: "Oh my gawd, I'm shot!" Wes assisted his uncle into the boat where he collasped. He made his uncle as comfortable as possible, then dragged the boat 100 yards to the water, putting out for Union Bay as hard as he could row. He found the boat leaking so badly that he had to return and dump out everything possible, in order to keep it up in the water. He again started for the Bay, making an added effort to reach there as soon as possible. Thinking to keep his uncle warm, he covered him with his own coat. A few minutes previous to this Cook had mumbled something, and there is little doubt that he died shortly afterwards, although Peters did not realize this. After an hour and a half of steady rowing, he landed at the Fraser and Bishop's wharf, and made for the home of his aunt, Mrs. A. McLeod, and told her to get a doctor at once, his uncle having been shot and fainted in the boat. [5]

Mr.Cook left a wife and five children.

The next shooting incident happened in 1937 when Alvin Stasek went hunting by himself and was found dead from a bullet wound in his throat.

In 1948 a hunting accident happened which almost mirrored the Cook tragedy, except that it did not result in a death. Donald Campbell and Donald Kennedy skipped school one November day to go duck hunting on Langley Lake. Using an old boat that was always on the lake, the two boys loaded their rabbit-ear shotguns and took off across the lake to a peat island. As Don Campbell was pulling his gun out of the boat by the muzzle, the hammer caught on the side of the boat and discharged the shot into his hand and arm.

"I had been hunting and was just about ready to come down when I heard this hooting and hollering and these two wild-eyed kids came out of the woods. Don was staggering. The gun had gone off so close to his arm that it burned everything. The wadding and everything was still hanging out. That really saved his bacon because it wasn't bleeding."

Ken Peters

Ken loaded them into his truck and transported them to Constable Ennals house. The policeman rushed the injured boy to the hospital where his arm had to be amputated below the elbow.

The next very sad shooting accident happened at the home of Mr. and Mrs. Paul Bohn in 1958. Their son, Roy, fired what he thought was an empty gun just as his little sister, Maureen, ran around the corner of the house and she was instantly killed by the blast.

DROWNINGS

For a town with all its industry situated on the ocean, drownings were inevitable.

The first took the life of Walter E. Blackett, who held the contract to build the bridges and trestles on the railway line from Jack Hart Point to the Union Mines in 1888. The weather was so poor on June 15 that the crew stayed in bed. However, the steamer *Dunsmuir* was to deliver supplies for the new wharf early that morning, so Mr. Blackett with his timekeeper, Mr. R. Gibson, set off in a dory to an old five ton barge which was anchored out. They transferred to the larger boat and, towing the dory, sailed out to meet the *Dunsmiur* on its way south from Comox. From the steamer they took on board about four tons of iron and supplies for the camp. The *Dunsmuir* continued on her way down the Sound, and the boat, with a jib set, proceeded toward the landing. About a mile from shore they realized that they could not land on the beach in such a high surf, so turned and headed for Comox, at which time the dory swamped. Finding the rudder not strong enough to keep the boat on course, Blackett attempted to steer with an oar, but the barge fell into a trough and sank. Both men grabbed an oar and struck out for shore, loaded down with rain gear and gum boots. Gibson was rescued by the teamster who had come down to the beach to haul up the goods, but thirty-four year old Blackett disappeared in the surf.

A few years later three young sailors off the steamer *San Benito*, along with Mr. Boyle from Union Wharf, rowed to Comox in a flat-bottomed skiff.

1891 AUGUST ➸ After staying on the Spit for some time, they started off again for Union Wharf. The sail was hoisted, and Boyle and Byrne took oars and began pulling. When the others relieved the men at the oars, there was a little playful scuffling indulged in whilst the men were passing each other in the boat, causing Byrne to fall against the side of the boat. One of the others caught at him to prevent him going overboard, and their united weights caused the craft to list so much that the sail jibed, and over they went. [2]

Three of the four clung to the boat and were rescued by men from Comox; the fourth drowned.

Boat travel between Union Wharf, Comox, and the Islands kept people in touch with one another. In November 1897 two brothers, Richard and William Anderson, set off in a four-oar rowboat for their home in Comox. They were never seen again but the boat was found, full of water.

Although all the children spent many hours playing on and around the sea and creek, only one child was ever drowned. Soon after the turn of the century, four year old Kazuo, the oldest child of Mr. and Mrs. T. Nakamura, was playing near his home in a shallow pool in Washer Creek when he fell and hit his head on a rock and drowned.

Every few years a sailor (often intoxicated), a Chinese trimmer, or a wharf worker would fall off the wharf. In 1927 a Chinese worker was drowned when he fell from the gangplank, just a board 30' long and 2' wide. The captain of the ship was charged under regulations governing public harbours "for failing to provide a gangway equipped with proper side rails" and "for failing to provide a light at the gangway". The case was dismissed because the defence lawyer pointed out that Union Bay had never been proclaimed a harbour as defined in the shipping act.

Some simply drowned after hitting the water, but more often than not they hit a piling on the way down and were killed by it. Anderson was an unlucky name to have, as Lars Anderson was drowned in 1906, and Victor Anderson's body washed ashore in 1912. Then, one of the Bay's favourite characters, Adolf Anderson, the town clown, drowned in 1928 when his walking stick caught in a hole on the wharf and he fell overboard. The next year another town favourite, the well known Chinese, "Goo Goo" fell from his rowboat and drowned.

Two drownings occurred in 1908. In May the twenty-two year old son of the owner of Doane's Logging Company was bringing freight from Denman Island in a small rowboat. It capsized and Ralph drowned, but the Japanese with him managed to swim to shore. Later, in the fall, captain Seward of the barge *Oregon* rowed over to Henry Bay to have dinner with the captain of Mr. Dunsmuir's yacht, the *Dolaura*. After much food and drink the captain bid his fellow seaman goodnight and rowed off in the direction of the coal port. Later that night another captain, whose boat was loading coal, heard someone calling but could see nothing. The body was never found.

Most of the men hunted. With hunting season in the fall, several hunters were drowned while pursuing duck, brant or geese in rough weather. In December 1912 O.H. Strand, foreman of Anderson Logging, was hunting on the north end of Denman with George Roe. They were on shore when Mr. Strand rowed out in a punt to the launch which was anchored out. The little boat capsized, throwing Strand into the icy waters where he kept afloat for a half hour before he drowned. Roe, a strong swimmer, attempted to rescue his partner but the water was too rough. It was twenty-four hours before Mr. Roe was rescued off the Island.

A very similar incident took place in 1951 when Herb Muschamp, Wes Peters and his son Fred were hunting on Tree Island. Wes and Fred rowed out to retrieve three geese. As Wes leaned over to pick up the birds, a wave slapped the boat, throwing both men into the icy water. Herb became alarmed when he lost sight of his friends, so quickly made his way to Protection Island where Jack Beban was hunting. The search was delayed while Mr. Beban filled his outboard with gas. The two men then set out and located the father and son clinging to their overturned boat. About one and a half hours had elapsed, and although the men were suffering from extreme exposure, they both survived.

Wives watched the water constantly when their husbands were across the sound hunting, fearful that their spouses would attempt the crossing in the rough water. The men spent many a night on the islands in the old clam diggers' shacks or huddled around a huge bonfire that could be seen from home.

During the hunting season the body of Mr. Green was found in Tsable River after a three day search. He had fallen into the river and drowned. All the local logging camps shut down and assisted in the search. A group led by Tom McKay found the body.

Also treated as a drowning was Jack McKenzie's death in the 1940's. Jack, brother to Jim McKenzie, usually came to Union Bay when the woods shut down.

"One morning Alma Christie came knocking at our door in a nervous state. There was a body washed up on the beach. So I went down, it was Jack McKenzie. Well, he often went for a walk down the wharf at night. He smoked a lot and coughed a lot. I guess he started coughing, and choked and fell into the water. Skinny Banks, the undertaker, said he didn't drown as there was no water in his lungs... said he looked like he'd choked."

Wilf Bowden

SUICIDE

Life for many early settlers along British Columbia's isolated coast must have been very lonely, thousands of miles from family and friends. The Orientals must have felt this deeply, with no women for companionship while facing a foreign culture. Several of them, particularly when they became sick or old, chose to end their lives. A few drowned themselves. One poor fellow, sick with a pain in his side, simply walked into the sea. The powerful steam locomotives provided another way of ending it all.

1895 ➾ The engine was proceeding from the Wharf to Union Mines when a "Celestial", who stood on the trestle, jumped off right in front of the engine. The engine passed over his right arm. He died later. It is said to be his second attempt at suicide. [2]

Hanging was another method employed. One Chinese fellow was found in the toilet of a second-class coach on the E&N, suspended from a hanger by his necktie. Another man, Wong Bing, first Boss Chinaman at Union Bay, killed himself. That morning he prepared breakfast as usual for his gang, but when they left for work he stayed back, ostensibly to feed his chickens. Instead, he hanged himself from one of the rafters of the chicken house. Because he had been in ill health and depressed for some time, an inquest was considered unnecessary by Coroner Abrams.

1904 ➾ A silk scarf was tied to the roof and looped around his neck. He had stood on a box to fasten it up, then had kicked this away and had died by strangulation, there being no drop to break his neck. He was dressed in his best clothes, new boots etc. and had evidently outfitted himself for his final journey. [4]

Washer Creek also claimed some lives. One lady from Bevan, in a demented condition, threw herself into the stream. In 1952, seventy-seven year old Mah Him, blind and sick, waded into the creek. Harry Glover found his body, nearly covered with coal dust.

The white man, when he chose to take his own life, usually did so in a more violent way by using a gun.

1914 FEBRUARY ➾ Elroy Cairnes, a well-known young man of Union Bay, committed suicide by shooting himself in front of Dave Walker's home, one mile up the hill. It was beyond doubt a case of love and jealousy and a premeditated act, which a letter found on the body showed. An inquest was held and suicide while insane the verdict. [4]

Nick Knutson lived alone up McLeod Road. In 1956, old and sick, he went out to his woodshed and shot himself.

Luckily not all suicide attempts succeeded. Mrs. Byrd, a bricklayer's wife, "while suffering a protracted nervous ailment" jumped off the Government wharf. When she hit the cold water she started yelling for help. From his home on Station Road, Dick Ray heard her calls and rushed to the beach. He found a boat, rowed out, and rescued her.

LIQUOR

From the beginning, the Union Coal Company declared Union to be a dry town. Alcohol was available at the hotels in Comox and could be brought up on the boat from Nanaimo. However, to get to Union, everyone had to take the train from Union Wharf, so the Company simply forbade the transport of any intoxicants.

1889 AUGUST ➾ Mr. Frank Little, the sterling superintendent, says the "order" prohibiting the carrying of liquor into Union Mines is being strictly enforced. A passenger with a bottle of whiskey in his possession cannot get a passage on the train unless the whiskey is left behind. [2]

In the early 1890's a license was granted to the lone hotel in Union, allowing liquor to be sold in the bar, but this was the only legal outlet. A Victoria company repeatedly applied for a license but was repeatedly refused.

1895 JUNE ➺ H.A. Simpson had to be present at the Union Licensing Board at Union at 1:00 p.m. Saturday, so travelled up on the *SS Esperanza.* He left Nanaimo on Friday evening and arrived at Union Wharf in good time. At the last minute, the Union Colliery Co. refused to let him travel to Union by train in spite of the heat and lack of training, so he walked. It took him two hours and he arrived at 1:00 p.m. in time to hear the magistrate postpone the hearing until Wednesday. Then on Wednesday it was adjourned. [2]

When the Nelson Hotel was built by George Howe in 1893, it opened with a bar room, and from that day on did a roaring business. It was patronized by local workers and sailors off the many boats that called.

The Indians that lived on the beach at the mouth of Hart Creek were supplied illegally with liquor. Constable Anderson from Comox often came down to arrest whites, blacks and halfbreeds for supplying the Indians. Following a drunken brawl on Denman Island in 1895, a Comox Indian was killed. In this connection, George Howe was charged with selling liquor to an Indian. Eventually the case was dropped because the dead man was the one who bought the liquor. Therefore, it could not be proved that Mr. Howe sold it to him.

In the early 1890's, as miners brought their wives to the district, a group formed a temperance league and organized lodges of Good Templars. They brought in fiery speakers who ranted and roared about the evils of intoxicants. Because of groups like these all over British Columbia, liquor laws remained very strict. These ideals were supported by most women. Some of the settlers had even left the old country because of lax liquor laws.

"My Dad owned two grocery stores in Scotland. At that time they started selling liquor in the stores. My Dad was very much against liquor, a real teetotaler, and he lost a lot of customers. So because of that we came out to Canada."

Ethel (Campbell) Glover

In other households a more relaxed attitude had been brought from the homeland. It was very common for workers, after ten or twelve hours of hard labour, to send one of the children down to the bar with a 3 lb. lard pail for 10¢ of beer to drink with supper. The temperance people were sure many of the boys took a sip on the way home, leading to their eventual addiction.

"Every night after work, Mr. Fulcher took his lunch bucket and went across to the hotel and had it filled with beer for supper. We called that "rushing the growler."

Nellie King

With the strict law governing where and when liquor could be sold, there were many violations, and the temperance people watched for bootleggers. In 1910 a new set of laws was passed, notably that of "blacklisting" patrons who habitually became drunk and disorderly. Also the right and responsibility was given to the bartender to refuse to sell to a patron who had passed over the line of sobriety. Beer parlours, as they were becoming known, had to close for the dinner hour and from 11:00 p.m. Saturday until 5:30 p.m. on Monday. Illicit business was prevented by the law that stated that bar room blinds be left up so as to permit a clear view of the interior during prohibited hours.

The town became neatly divided into those who favoured prohibition and those who did not. Dr. MacNaughton, the popular doctor in Cumberland, led the fight for prohibition in the district. The Temperance League advertised that prohibition would mean:

- Bread to hungry Children.
- Happiness to sad and overworked women.
- The help of the community for men who are struggling with a fearful appetite.

Finally, the prohibition issue was included as a referendum with the provincal election. It passed in Union Bay, as well as the rest of B.C., and in October 1917 "John Barleycorn" made his exit. This greatly affected the hotels, and many had to close their doors, as the bar was the profit maker.

1917 NOVEMBER ➺ Mr. Alf Horne's Auction Sale attracted many buyers of goods, from far and wide. This sale marked the end of one of the Island's oldest hostelries, the Wilson House, as like many more houses of the same kind since the water brigade assumed control of affairs, it had to close its doors. [6]

Blind pigs (bootleggers) became more popular. Before, they had been a source of after-hour sales, but now were one of the few ways to get liquor. Stories abound about ways booze was obtained.

"Bill Kelly was a bootlegger, as tough as nails. The police caught him once and took him to court. 'Har, Har, Har,' he said to the judge, 'I don't care if you put me in jail, you'll have to feed me'. Jack Reid ran a butcher shop across the street. If he wanted a drink, he'd blow up a paper bag and pretend he was delivering something and go across to Kelly's, have a couple of drinks, take the wind out of the bag, put it in his pocket and go back to the shop. He thought no one knew what was going on but us kids used to watch him all the time. Later, Dale and Reid went into partnership and had a dry goods store. They were bootleggers too and kept the liquor in shoe boxes. If anyone wanted a bottle they took the shoe box off the shelf and sold it to them. Lots of people bought shoes."

Hector Hooper

Bill Gaul, an American sailing ship man, came home to Seattle one day and found a man in bed with his wife. He flew into a rage and threw the fellow over the verandah. Thinking that he had killed him, Bill shipped out on the next boat. When he got to Union Bay he jumped ship, changed his name to Kelly, and spent the rest of his life at the port. For many years he worked as a watchman on the wharf, checking for deserters.

Mr. Kelly built himself a little shack on the beach, next to Bowden's Ice Cream Parlour. In the early years he kept his home clean, and "holy stoned" (a sailor's tradition) his floor every day.

"I used to milk cows, so would pass Kelly's about six o'clock in the morning. There he would be. He would take everything out of his house that was moveable. Then he'd get two buckets of sea water and a great big stable type broom. He'd sprinkle sand and gravel on the floor, then the water, and swish it all outside. When he was finished he'd sit under the big maple tree and chew tobacco... Stag Chewing Tobacco, rather juicy stuff. When he would spit, the earth would just about shake - tremendous spats!"

Bob Pollock

Bill was a big fat man who was often a little tipsy. The kids all knew him and would chant - "Old man Kelly with a cast iron belly".

"We never teased Chinamen much but we used to tease poor old Kelly. I remember we used to sell him sacks of bark and we'd put a big block in the bottom and he'd pay us two bits. We'd pack water from the well on the spring hill for him. Then we'd go in there at night and put frogs in the buckets and they'd be croaking. His sailor friends would visit and bring him American cigarettes. He never smoked, but if he ran out of chewing tobacco he'd pop three cigarettes into his mouth and chew them. Well, we used to go and visit him and he always sat in front of a little shelf where he kept his cigarettes. This night we were talking to him and I stuck my hand up there to snitch a few cigarettes. There was a rat trap up in there. Whap! 'Hey, you young buggers,' he yelled. The trap wasn't set for us, he had traps all over.

George Cooper

As he got older he became less fastidious, and he and his home became dirtier and dirtier.

"As a little girl I often delivered milk to Mr. Kelly. He took half a pint a day and never put his bottle out, so I would have to go into his house. He always left the dirty bottle on the far end of the table, so I would take a big breath of fresh air, hold my nose and dash in. The wash tub was always on the big black stove, with overalls and socks soaking in dirty water. One day I went in and he was eating his lunch, and there were four or five cats up on the table eating from his plate too. But he was a kind old man and often gave me beer bottles to sell, or candy."

Ann (Vowels) Graham

Always a heavy drinker, the problem got worse as he got older. He'd sit at the Willis Hotel and get too drunk to walk, so some of his friends would load him onto a wheelbarrow and take him home. Finally he got sick, and the decision was made to take him to the hospital. Some of the firemen decided to clean him up first. They peeled off five or six layers of underwear before they got down to skin and were able to hose him off. It was joked that having a bath after so many years was too much for his system, as he died soon after.

"Bill Carter was another bootlegger, for after-hour drinks in the '30s. I remember Bill Marshall and I used to go and see old "Cawtter" about midnight. He'd be making hot rums in a night shirt and night cap. He was quite a picture, another tough old sailor. He would sell you a bottle or mix you a drink."

Wilf Bowden

Other bootleggers over the years were Harvey Leithhead, who was the night clerk and bartender at the Nelson Hotel, George Neill, who operated a garage, and Mah Fat, a Chinese who operated a store in Chinatown. Mah Fat sold whiskey with labels that read "Bottled in Glasgow, England".

"It was a ritual. Old Dave Haggart would come up the street, a-walkin', and Billy Bowden would come out of his shop, and the two headed up to Chinatown and into Mah Fat's store and had a couple of beers. One night old Bill staggered up the road to his home on Washer Creek Hill. When he saw three bridges over the creek he took the outside one and, by gawd, ended up in the water."

Bill Marshall

1932 OCTOBER ➾ When the Provincial Police descended on Mah Fat at Union Bay they found enough fire water to start a liquor store. He had 800 bottles of N'gor Ni and Mi Kwe Lu, Chinese drinks which taste as funny as they sound, lots of beer and a few drams of rum, and a bottle of Scotch. It took two passenger cars loaded with hooch to carry the spoils to the provincial jail at Courtenay. [6]

In the late 1920's the underage fellows felt safer patronizing the out-of-town bootleggers. A favourite was Joe Damonte who had an establishment at the foot of Boulder Hill. He sold a case of beer for $3.00.

Private stills were also set up and alcohol produced, some of which was sold.

"I remember Albert Savoy telling me that when the family first came to Denman they were very poor. His dad had a still and made whiskey, which they brought over and sold to the Chinamen in Union Bay. One time they landed at the dock and a Blue Funnel boat was expected. There were police everywhere looking for opium. The Savoys were pretty nervous until they started for home."

Ingles Dalziel

FLOODS

Washer Creek was a placid stream most of the year, but in the winter and spring it often became swollen and flooded its banks, threatening the Chinese and Japanese homes along the bank.

"A year or two after the turn of the century, a storm accompanied by torrential rain filled Washer Creek. What was once a gentle stream became a monstrous flood, swollen and dangerous. It overflowed its banks, and our father's home was swept into the river with my parents and oldest brother inside. Father lashed Mother and Kazuo to a stair. They rode out the storm and were saved."

Kiyoshi Nakamura

H. Davis

Floodwater from Washer Creek covers the Colliery yard and ball field

A little past 5:00 p.m. on Saturday, February 10, 1912 the Canadian Collieries Company dam on Langley Lake collapsed. A solid wall of swirling water about 10' high rushed down to the sea. Sweeping everything along in its path, it tore great gashes and gullies in the earth.

The dam was situated two miles back in the mountains at an elevation of about 500'. The reservoir contained more than a million gallons of water. The dam was constructed of wood, and after an unusually heavy rainfall the water started to flush over the top, which then washed out the underpinnings.

It started with a roar in the distance that became progressively louder. As people realised what was happening, they dashed for higher ground. It swept through Chinatown and Japtown, destroying most of the shacks and carrying them out to sea, with several of the inhabitants clinging to roof tops. The only casualty was a Japanese man.

E. Renwick

Debris left after the flood of 1912

The company's loss was estimated between $50,000 and $90,000, while the property loss to individuals was between $15,000 and $30,000.

The event became important news, and in less than a week, pictures of the "big catastrophe" were being shown at the Orpheum Theatre in Vancouver.

Everyone living at Union Bay that day has memories of where they were when the dam burst.

"Lester Drew and I were up at the lake that day. We had traps set up there and the water was so high we couldn't get out to them, so we left. On the way down to the Bay we heard a roar. When we arrived people told us the dam had burst."

Jim Mckay

"All I remember was the noise. We could hear sort of a rumbling all the way down here on the farm. No one seemed to know what it was."

Annie (Muschamp) Nelson

"We lived up Russell Hill, and everyone came running up the hill shouting, 'The dam has burst, the dam has burst.' Trees and Chinese houses were floating by, with the men in the top windows waving hankies, and chickens sitting on trees. Different fellows had ropes around their waists and would wade out and pull someone in. After that, we had a Japanese lady and her children staying with us. Everyone took someone in."

Harry Glover

Cumberland Museum

Chinatown buildings left standing can be seen in the centre. Roofs of washed-out buildings can be seen in the foreground

M. Haas

The FooFoo gang start the immense task of rebuilding the railroad

"We lived right next to Chinatown. I was about 7 years old and was outside playing when Billy Haggart, who lived on the top row, came yelling down the hill to warn the Chinese. Our place was just jammed full of Chinamen. Mom took them in. Some had cuts and bruises and she bandaged them up. I think Renwicks, who lived next door, took in lots too. When Chinese New Year came I never saw so much silk material and stuff like that from the Chinese. They were so thankful for what she'd done."

Bill Marshall

"Mrs. Lockner was living right in front of the Washer near Washer Creek. She ran out of the house with Johnny and Christine under each arm and got to safety on the trestle. It swept Chinatown clean and undermined a lot of the tracks and overturned steel cars in the coal yard."

Wilf Glover

"My Dad had a close call. He was in the telegraph office next to the wharf. When he heard the roar and excited shouts of men, he rushed out and ran up the hill. Next day they found what was left of the office stranded on Denman Island. Our boat house next to the boarding house was smashed to pieces."

Doug Brown

"The only thing that saved me from being in that flood was a handkerchief. I was heading to Courtenay with a team to do some ploughing, but I had a handkerchief I had borrowed from Harvey Leithead, bartender at the Nelson Hotel. He was eating so I stood out and waited for him. A few minutes later there were big logs all over the bay. I was around there until two o'clock in the morning, helping out. We got a Chinaman out of an alder tree, right in front of "Putt Putt" Jones' house. He caught the tree as it went by and hung on."

Bob McKay

"Ern, my future husband, had quite an experience. He had floated his launch up with the tide onto the bank and was working on the bottom of it. He heard a rushing sound, so he jumped into the boat and it carried him all the way down past Denman."

Violet (Glover) Rutherford

"My Dad was butchering down at Partridge's store. We lived on the top hill and I dashed down to warn him. I said, 'The thing has burst, the thing has burst'. I was afraid to say "dam" and swear."

Hazel (Davis)Macartney

"Partridge's house and store were in the old boarding house. When the flood came Mrs. Partridge was home with the kids and she ran with them to the Wilson Hotel. The old building was completely undermined and turned around on the foundations. What a mess! The house was knee deep in mud when they returned. They moved to the hotel."

Sarah (Walker) Kirkwood

"When the dam broke we came all the way up to see the damage the flood made. People came from everywhere. I remember a big stump on the middle of the ball field, and logs and wood everywhere. Everything was covered in silt."

Joe Walker

"The Chinese were digging in the silt for their mattresses where they had hid their money. That's what happened to the Jap, he went back for his money and got caught."

Nellie (McKay) King

L. Magnone

Sightseers in front of the Lockner home which was near the Washer

Afterwards, it took a long time to clean up and rebuild. Train tracks had to be repaired, bridges rebuilt, and roads cleared and levelled. The Chinese found plenty of lumber washed up everywhere to rebuild their shacks. Lockners moved to Cumberland. The Co-op store moved to the Wilson Hotel annex and the telegraph office was temporarily housed in the customs office. A new and improved dam was built.

EARTHQUAKES

Luckily, earthquakes were few and far between. The first one recorded, after Union Bay was established, was in November 1895 and was reported to have been of a sizeable force. It occurred at 4:00 p.m., and that night at 8:00 p.m. another phenomenon was witnessed, a moonlit rainbow. Seventeen years later the earth shook again.

1912 JULY The most violent earthquake ever felt occurred in the district at 10:00 p.m. The earth rocked for forty seconds. Later, less violent quakes occurred throughout the night. Louis Anderson, foreman at Doane Creek Mine, was killed as he was crushed by falling rock from the roof of the mine. [4]

Cumberland Museum

In this view of the Company houses it can be seen that all of them lost their three chimneys during the quake

Several small quakes were felt in the 1920's and '30s, but it was not until 1946 that another sizeable tremor occurred. Centered 200 miles out in the Pacific, the earthquake struck on a quiet Sunday morning in June as the sleepy inhabitants were still in bed or making breakfast.

"We lived on the back row of the Company Hill, and in the back yard my Dad and Uncle Ted Glover were working on the nearly completed 36' fish boat they were building. My twin sister, Jacqueline, and I were caring for Pollock's chickens while they were away. Maxine Stokes had stayed over, and the three of us, dressed for Sunday School, went along behind the houses to the chicken pen to let out and feed the chickens. We were busily scattering the wheat to the hungry chickens when we heard a roar in the south. It became louder and louder and the earth began to heave. Chickens squawked and flew around. I yelled 'earthquake!' and dashed for the narrow gateway. With Jacquie and Maxine pulling at my dress, all three of us tried to get through at one time. Once through, we started running home, the ground coming up to meet our every step. Without realizing it, we were running north and keeping up with the earthquake. As we passed the three houses, we saw each of their three chimneys topple, sending bricks in all directions. Then we reached our yard and watched as Mom ran out of the house, barely missed by a shower of bricks.

Dad was working outside the boat and thought Ted, who was inside, had started the motor. Ted, in the meantime, was trying valiantly to climb down the ladder. It was a miracle how the huge hull, sitting braced on narrow planks, weathered its first storm completely intact.

None of us had experienced an earthquake before and we stood around crying, wondering what would happen next. Soon we were off in different directions to see how family and friends had fared. It took some nerve, and support from Mom, to shut the chicken gate. But there was no need to worry as the chickens had all retreated into their house in the gloom that followed the quake."

Janette (Glover) Geidt

The quake struck the whole district, causing widespread damage, especially to brick buildings and chimneys. The schools were all badly hit and, as there was just a week of classes left, were closed for the summer holidays. It was felt that, had it happened on a weekday, there would have been many casualties caused by breaking glass and falling brick. A man in a small dingy off the Deep Bay spit was the only fatality in the district. A section of the spit 250' by 100' slid into the sea, creating a 15' wave. This upset the boat in which Daniel Fidler was riding and he drowned.

1946 JUNE ➺ As far as can be learned, only two casualties resulted at Union Bay. Mrs. H. Geary was struck on the arm by a falling brick and was injured quite badly. Mrs. W. Thompson, in hurrying down the steps, fell and suffered injuries to her ribs. Most of the chimneys came down and Mrs. Medrich had her fireplace fall out too. At Fraser and Horne's store many goods came off the shelves and there was considerable breakage, and the big chimney came down. It was noticeable that some of the chimneys that did not fall were turned around sideways. [6]

A few small tremors followed, just enough to keep everyone's nerves on edge. It was weeks until the chimneys were repaired, so families built barbecues of the bricks and did their cooking outdoors.

R. Ryan

A crack in the ground in the Colliery yards caused by the 1946 earthquake

CRIME

ROBBERIES

Situated on the Island Highway, within a stones throw of the ocean, the town's stores and hotels were easy targets for robbers, highwaymen and pirates.

1894 DECEMBER ➺ The Gulf is alive with saltwater highwaymen like the one that threw Constable Anderson of Comox in the water. The settler living miles from the nearest supplies often returns to find all his provisions gone. The law does little to stop them. [2]

More often than not the thieves escaped in their own boat or stole one.

1896 MAY ➺ A double-dyed robber was captured after an exciting chase. He - the robber - opened his brief but wild career of villainy by breaking into Mr. Eccles' house at Qualicum, where he stole five sacks of flour, a boat, and some other effects. Thence he proceeded to Fanny Bay and called on Mr. Cowie with a tale of woe. Mr. Cowie gave him some food and shortly after went off to the woods to work. In his absence the thief entered the house, rifled the drawers, and secured a valuable gold watch, but happily for the owner, overlooked the sum of $80 in one of the pockets of Cowie's "go-to-meeting" trousers. Our hero travelled north and called on Mr. Grieves, stole another boat, and rowed to Denman. Constable Hutchinson had, in the meantime, followed him up and finally captured the crook in the woods, where he was in possession of a loaded double-barrelled shotgun. [2]

Some even got away on the mail boat or steamers. This was particularly easy before the telegraph was installed to Nanaimo.

1896 DECEMBER ➺ A brave Japanese worker stole $500 from the Union Coal Co.and stowed away on the *Monmouthshire* heading for the Orient. The police received word too late, as the steamer had sailed. [2]

Often the crooks would work one town and move on to the next just ahead of the law. When they were caught, punishment was severe.

1910 OCTOBER ➺ Thomas Hudson, Special Police, caught two Slavs who had been robbing seven hotels and stores on the Island. He caught them in Nanoose Bay where they were asleep in a hotel. He went bravely in and adorned them with the iron jewelery while one of them was asleep. Both men had loaded revolvers and daggers under their pillows. In their possession was a number of tools for breaking and entering. They had robbed a jewelery store in Ladysmith, and the Wilson Hotel in Union Bay, as well as taking clothes from Fraser and Bishops. They each got five years. [5]

Over the years the big store was broken into at least twelve times. The thieves stole hundreds of dollars, but most often they took provisions. Two prairie boys who were caught wearing sweaters from the store also had a cache hidden under the platform at the E&N station. Two fishermen working on their boat at the dock broke in one night and made off with $300 worth of goods which they hid on Hornby Island. Another night, two men boldly loaded a truck at the back of the store, and when questioned by a neighbour, told the man they were authorized to do so and advised him to go back to bed, which he did.

A bad year for robberies was 1913, with the thieves becoming more daring and their escapades making the headlines across Canada and the United States. The most well-known episode was that of the Flying Dutchman. A "Wanted" poster was circulated by the Washington authorities in 1912.

Wanted: Henry Wagner, alias Henry Ferguson, John McDonald and Nels Jorgenson for murder of postmaster, and store and launch burglaries. "Water Pirate" Henry Ferguson alias "Jack the Flying Dutchman". Age - 39, height - 5' 10", hair - dark, eyes - steel grey, complexion - medium, weight - 180 lb.

1912 ⊷ The "Water Pirate" wears a black cap when in the boat and light coloured canvas hat when on shore. He is bowlegged and a little stooped. Generally he is armed with a 44 - calibre Colt revolver which he carries in his right hip pocket, and a 17" double-barrelled shotgun. He has a 16' long, square, copper painted boat with deck forward and aft. When last seen it had no cabin but Wagner is a skilled carpenter and known to change the structure and colour of the boat. It is driven by a powerful twin engine or small sail.

Wagner is probably accompanied by a man, Wm. Julian, described as follows: height - 5'4", hair - dark, eyes - brown, complexion - dark, age - 26 years. Both of these men are desperate characters and well-informed on the B.C. waters, where it is said they are headed. [4]

Several months before the robbery, Mrs. Bishop was working in the kitchen of the hotel when she thought she heard a noise, and went down the hall to investigate. Wagner, who was busy trying to open the safe, heard her coming and ducked into a bedroom and hid in the wardrobe. After she left he escaped.

"Mrs. Bishop's brother was up staying and he had an old pair of comfortable pants. One day he went to put them on and they weren't there. He accused her of burning them, but they were later found on Lasqueti Island.

Nellie (McKay) King

The Provincial Police were determined to catch these marauding pirates. Chief Constable David Stevenson, who was in charge of the north end of the Island, kept a file on the robberies. Gradually a pattern emerged. The crooks struck one of the Gulf Islands, then a couple of logging communities, then a store in a larger community. Fraser and Bishop's had been robbed twice. In most cases, a boat motor was said to have been heard around the time of the thefts. Because of the robberies, and the labour unrest, Union Bay had a

Canadian West

Henry Wagner, the infamous "Flying Dutchman", killed a policeman during the course of a robbery at Fraser & Bishop's store. He was hanged for his crime on August 28, 1913

full time policeman, Constable James F. McKenzie, and two young officers. Harry Westaway, a Prince Edward Islander, and Gordon Ross, a big Scotchman, worked undercover, and the general public were not supposed to know of their vocation.

"Big Mac", as the resident policeman was known, assigned the rookies to night patrol and provided them with keys to the store and adjoining post office.

On a dark rainy night in the water of Baynes Sound, the *Spray*, a pirate ship stolen from Puget Sound, sailed quietly into Union Bay harbour. Its motor was muffled by the howling sou'easter. The husky man at the wheel cut the motor and glided the boat into calmer water in lee of the Government dock. The small dark man on the bow gently eased the anchor into the water while, unbeknownst to him, the helmsman quickly removed the spark plugs from the motor. The two pirates lowered a rowboat and silently rowed to shore.

It was just after midnight when the two young police officers, standing under a large maple tree for protection against the weather, noticed a faint light in the store. They quickly entered the post office, thinking it would give them the advantage of surprise when they went through the inner door to the store. Constable Ross, who was unarmed except for his blackjack in one hand and flashlight in the other, crept stealthily into the store, followed by Constable Westaway who had his gun ready. In the eerie silence Ross swung the beam of light around the huge store. All the counters, the cash register, bins of food and shelves of merchandise showed nothing amiss. Suddenly the light beamed in on the two burglars toward the back of the store, one in a kneeling position with a revolver in his hand, and the other leaning over the counter. Immediately Ross switched off the light, and seconds later saw a flash and heard the report of a 44 Colt revolver. The bullet just grazed Ross' shoulder but got Westaway in the chest. He sank down with a groan, saying "I am shot, have you got him?" Constable Ross never hesitated but sprung forward onto the thief and a struggle ensued for the gun.

1913 MARCH ➾ Ross caught hold of the burglar and fought for possession of the gun, ultimately secured the revolver and struck the burglar over the head with it. Then the two were on the floor together fighting for dear life and the burglar called out, evidently to his accomplice, "Shoot, Bill, and shoot to kill. Never mind me." To this there was no response, and the burglar again wrenched the 44 calibre Colt revolver from Ross and struck him over the eye. They grabbed each other again and lost the gun. Ross felt Westaway at his feet, and heard him say "I am unable to help you, I am shot through the lungs." The burglar then caught Ross by the throat, and the latter grabbed the burglar by the throat and choked him off so much that he surrendered to arrest. Ross knocked the burglar out with his club, slipped a hand cuff on his wrist and pulled and knocked the burglar to the door. [5]

Constable Westaway was lying at the front door in the darkness and in a faint whisper breathed his last words, "Good-bye Gordon, good-bye." Constable Ross broke the front door glass and called for help. His cries were heard by Constable McKenzie who was patrolling the Canadian Collieries' wharf. He hurried off the coal dock and around the bay to the store to give some assistance.

Quite a sight met his eyes when he forced open the door. Counters were overturned, shelves hung off the walls, food and merchandise spattered with blood lay everywhere. One constable lay dead near the door. The other, with blood running down his face, stood unsteadily over the burglar who, with a beaten and bruised head, lay unconscious on the floor.

It was about 1:30 a.m. when Chief Stephenson in Cumberland was notified. He rounded up the Cumberland policemen and Dr. McNaughton, then set off by automobile for the scene of the crime. Upon inspecting the prisoner's bloodied, swollen features, beady eyes and powerful frame, Stephenson realized that Constable Ross had captured "The Flying Dutchman."

The dead constable and the burglar were both taken to Cumberland. An inquest was held by Coroner Abrams, with a jury from Union Bay. Alex McLeod (foreman), John Donaldson, Frank Partridge, Richard Summers, William Haggart and Alfred Horne determined that Harry Westaway met his death by a shot from the gun marked exhibit "A". It was fired by the prisoner, Henry Wagner, who with an accomplice was discovered robbing Fraser and Bishop's store at Union Bay.

Wagner supplied the name of his accomplice as William Julien, who had also fled the United States lawmen. He had been standing beside Wagner when he fired on the police, and felt the powerful Ross attack his partner. Not a brave man, he quickly made his getaway through a back window. Bill dashed around the side of the store, across the road and onto the beach, then jumped into the rowboat and made for the launch. He tried the motor several times but nothing happened. Upon close examination he realized the spark plugs were missing. He swore a string of oaths at his partner who had double-crossed him, cut the anchor rope, climbed back into the row boat, and set off for Lasqueti. His wife lived there and he had a small launch in which he could take off up north and lay low for a year or two.

"Bob and I picked up the boat over by Caesar Scott's place and towed it home. He had his exhaust under the water so you couldn't hear him. Julien cut the rope on the launch because Wagner had taken the spark plugs, just in case Julien tried to escape without him. He had to row to Lasqueti where they lived and kept everything they stole."

Jim McKay

Word reached the police detachment in Nanaimo. Constables George Hannay and Tom Richardson, working on the theory that Julien would make for home at his earliest opportunity, had the spot under surveillance when Julien arrived. After a twenty-four hour vigil, the two constables spotted the small craft and watched from under cover while he landed and entered the cabin. Moments later, Hannay entered the cabin and took Julien by surprise, then transported him back to the Nanaimo jailhouse, just two days after the murder. He was brought on the E&N to Cumberland for a preliminary hearing, and both men were held to stand trial at the Spring Assizes. Wagner was sent to Nanaimo and Julien to Victoria.

In May the trial got under way, and the chief witness against Wagner was his partner, Julien, who turned "King's Evidence" and corroborated everything Const. Ross said. He then told of the other criminal activities where he and the Flying Dutchman had co-operated, working out of Lasqueti Island using the *Spray*.

Julien received a sentence of five years behind bars. Wagner was found guilty of murder and sentenced to hang on August 28, 1913.

As the day drew near, Wagner tried several times to commit suicide, first by slashing his wrists. However, the Dutchman had escaped justice before, so he was heavily guarded.

1913 AUGUST ➾ On Wednesday morning, Wagner plunged headlong into the iron work of his cell in an effort to dislocate his neck but succeeded only in rendering himself unconscious. Then, on Wednesday night, Wagner retired under a blanket and the guard heard a gurgling sound and turned down the blanket. He found the condemned man unconscious and almost dead from suffocation, he having twisted a blanket tightly around his neck in order to stangle himself. The unconscious man was revived by Dr. Ingham, then given opiates in order that he would sleep before the march to the gallows. Hangman Ellis decided to stay with the condemned man the rest of the night, saying he "did not intend that Wagner should cheat the gallows." [5]

In the morning, Wagner proved to be no coward when he faced the gallows and the hangman. He walked briskly up the eleven stairs, stood beneath the gallows and was fitted with the black hood and noose. The trap was sprung, thus ending the life of an old style western badman, gunfighter, highwayman, smuggler and thief.

In prison on the mainland, Julien must have heaved a sigh of relief, as he feared that Wagner might escape and seek revenge. It seems William Julien was destined to a life of crime, and when released from jail, he adopted the alias Silas Walker. Soon he was right back at it with a new partner, none other than George Hannay, the policeman who had arrested him five years earlier. The pattern was familiar. The pair rented a big gasoline launch in Nanaimo and carried out systematic raids in and out of coastal towns at night. Perhaps it was them in 1919 who stole $500 worth of jewelery from the Chinese store at Union Bay.

The thieves were finally apprehended in February 1920 after the police learned that they were selling barley at $3.00 a sack. Upon investigation, many things, from needles to anchors, as well as forty-two sacks of barley, were found on their premises in Nanaimo. The grain had been stolen from Mr. Hurford's old barn on the banks of the Dyke in Comox. Found at the old barn were two new gumboots, both for the left foot, stolen from Dale and Partridge at Union Bay.

The new partners lacked Wagner's finesse and left a trail wherever they went.

1920 FEBRUARY ➾ It is an interesting fact that the presence of the two men in various places was often confirmed by their habit of smoking and chewing. Hannay invariably smoked cigars, while Julien chewed Macdonald's plug, and their trail could be followed by cigar stubs and tobacco juice. [6]

Both men received four years in prison, but the story does not stop there. In 1935 George Hannay was again arrested, this time with William Jones as partner, while robbing a general store at Parksville. As before, a large cache was found in their headquarters, taken from stores along the Island Highway, including Union Bay. Hannay, who had started his career as a policeman in Nanaimo, from where he subsequently absconded with some money, was again sent to prison for a further seven years.

Another well-known robbery took place one Thursday in July 1913. The Cumberland bank manager, F. Bosworth, and Desmond Roe stowed a bag of money in a one-horse rig and started off for Union Bay. The wagon was approaching Trent River bridge when it was surprised by two men wearing dark clothes and black slouch hats. Both men, about 5'9" and 35 years of age, spoke with foreign accents. One of the bandits had a limp. The pointed guns were not to be argued with, so the bag of money was handed over and the highwaymen made off with $2,500.

It was first thought that the gunmen had made their escape from the spit by boat to Denman Island. However, this assumption later proved to be wrong, as they were hiding out in the woods behind Union Bay before they made their way south, following the slashed trail for the E&N railway. Moore and Pethick operated a camp at Tsable River for their workers who were grading the right of way for the railway. About midnight Saturday, during a pouring rain storm, the camp's Chinese cook was nearly frightened out of his wits when he was awakened by the robbers hacking a hole in his tent. Brandishing their guns, they demanded food. The cook flew into action, giving them all they could stuff into their famished jaws, as well as a supply to take with them. Onto the cook's bed they threw down a pile of change, amounting to over $13. Before disappearing into the rain they threatened him with the words, "Now take that, and be quiet about this, or we'll attend to your case later!" From there the desperadoes found their way to Sandy Cowie's, stole a rowboat and rowed away.

Meanwhile, the hills around Union Bay were full of policemen and posses scouring the woods for the highwaymen. It was learned that the thugs had been to the camp twice the week before, forcing the cook to supply them with food. Doors were kept locked and every stranger treated with suspicion, until news came from Bellingham that they had been spotted there, purchasing new clothes.

The Royal Bank put up a $500 reward and the Provincal Government a reward of $1,500.

Canadian detectives and West Sound officers were on the case but the criminals eluded them. The lawmen believed that the loot was hidden on Orcas Island, so they waited. Less than a week after the hold-up, one of the thieves returned to Orcas Island. A gun battle ensued but the robber escaped into the woods. The next day a purse was found containing a newspaper clipping that described the men who robbed the paywagon at Union Bay. They were never apprehended nor was the money recovered.

MURDER

The other two murders connected with Union Bay were both associated with alcohol.

Three Indian canoes left Comox on a July morning in 1896, heading for the fishing grounds on the Fraser. In the first canoe were George Mitchell, Peter Comox, Beaverskin and his wife. The second canoe contained Jimmy Mitchell with his wife Louisa, and in the third was Frank Comox with his wife Mary. The party stopped at Union Wharf where Jimmy, a half breed, went to George Howe's store and obtained three bottles of whiskey. The group proceeded to Scott's Point where two of the bottles were drunk, then on to Denman where a row broke out over the remaining liquor.

"Beaverskin's canoe landed first. Me and Jimmy went ashore and Frank asked Jimmy for the whiskey. George Mitchell had gone to the wharf at Denman sometime before. Frank tried to force Jimmy to give him the whiskey. Jimmy dropped the bottle and smashed it. Jimmy struck Frank on the nose and it bled. Frank got wild after this and picked up a stone and struck Jimmy on the head. Beaverskin tried to stop them fighting. George returned just after this happened and got Frank to drop the rock. Peter held Jimmy after he was struck and we tied a handkerchief over the cut."

from Louisa's (J. Mitchell's wife) testimony. [2]

After George had subdued Frank, they camped the night at Beaverskin's fire. The next morning the canoes set off for Qualicum, with Jimmy doing his share of the paddling. They stayed several nights with Qualicum Tom, then went on to Nanaimo. Jimmy's sore head required them to rest three days before finishing the journey to Steveston. A few days later, Jimmy died of an abcess on the brain from the fracture on his skull.

After a long court case at the Nanaimo Fall Assizes, presided over by Justice Crease, the case against Frank Comox was dismissed. A second case against George Howe on the charge of supplying intoxicants to the Indians was also dismissed because of insufficient evidence.

In August 1909 Mrs. Muschamp sent her two teenagers, Lizzie and Herb out to round up the cows. The family ranch was on Baynes Sound, and the pair set out on the beautiful summer morning to find the cows, but instead met up with a murderer.

"They met old Mike Watts all covered with blood. He told them, 'I've just killed old Anderson'. I guess it scared the kids and they ran home and told Mother, and she reported it."

Annie (Muschamp) Nelson

M. Hogberg, better known as Old Man Anderson to the people at the Bay, and Mike Watts were drinking buddies. Mike, a logger, lived in a little cabin on property at the north end of Buckley Bay, later owned by Piercys. Mr. Anderson lived in Fanny Bay, alone after his wife died. The friends visited the Palmer House on Baynes Sound, had a few drinks and bought a bottle of whiskey each. They went back to Mike's cabin and continued drinking. Then Anderson left the cabin but he was angry with Watts and returned the next day.

"I think Old Man Anderson wanted someone to kill him, he wanted to die. I saw him the night before. I met him right by the bent tree. He was tracking Mike Watts down".

Bob McKay

When Constable Thomas and Coroner Abrams were summoned, they found a horrifying sight near Mike Watt's cabin.

1909 AUGUST ➾ The body of M. Hogberg was found in a terribly mutilated condition. His head was nearly severed from the body and smashed to a pulp. Beside the body was a grindstone, one of the weapons used. An axe covered with blood and hair was found in Watt's cabin, with which the ghastly wounds in the neck were made. [4]

An inquest was held at Cumberland, and a trial by judge and jury at Nanaimo in May 1910, at which Michael Watts pleaded not guilty. Lizzie Muschamp, who was only fifteen years old, was sent down to testify, as was her twelve year old brother, Herbert, who corroborated her story. The two knew Mr. Watts as an old man who talked to himself and was often drunk.

"Mr. Watts came out from his own road onto the main road and called out to me that he wanted to speak to me. He told me there was a dead body at his door and he wanted me to go and look at it. I said I did not want to see it. Watts told me he thought it was Hogberg. I said he should tell them at the Palmer Hotel. He asked me if he was dirty and I told him his face was clean but his hands were dirty. They looked as if they were blood-smeared, with dirt sticking to the blood."

Lizzie Muschamp's testimony

"Mom told me about going down to testify at the trial. Uncle Herb went too, but he was younger and slept through most of it."

Mary (McKay) Kine

Also testifying were Mr. Day, proprietor of the Palmer Hotel; Mr Burgess, a neighbour; Pete Anderson, Hogberg's son; and Dr. Gillespie. Mike Watts was charged with second degree murder and was sent to prison for ten years. As he was seventy-two he probably died in jail.

WARS

World War I

Important world news reached Union Bay through telegrams. On August 4, 1914 Fred Brown, telegrapher, received the declaration of war over the wireless and immediately phoned to the CC(D)L office. The train engineers on the wharf were notified and the engine whistles began to wail. There was a battalion of soldiers stationed at Union Bay, guarding the shipping facilities and watching for sabotage in connection with the strike at Cumberland. The officers lived in the big company house on the south side of Russell Hill. In front, on the bank, whitewashed rocks spelled out the "72nd Seaforth Highlanders". The men lived in tents on the green in front. The new post office had just been built and the basement was used as the cookhouse. Next door, the reading room of the church was taken over and used as headquarters and officers' mess. They trained around town and used the coalhills for gun practice.

"I remember during WW I Dunsmuir gave the army some lumber, rough shiplap, and the boys built a dance floor with a railing around it. The collieries put up a couple of lights. Us kids weren't allowed there but we could see it from the post office. There was a fiddler and other instruments. My sisters, Alva and Carrie, Lina Glover and all that gang had a good time - lots of men."

Doug Brown

This regiment also had a few men stationed at the bridges in case of sabotage. They stopped and checked everyone passing that way.

"They guarded the highway bridge, and the railroad bridge too. It was dark and my Mom and I were coming home from visiting the Currans. The soldier flashed his flashlight and shouted "Halt". The horse shied, threw up his head and backed up. The back wheels went down over the bridge but the buggy hung up on its steps or we would have been in the Tsable River. The dashboard was across me, my Mom had her knees trapped. Boy, was my Mom mad! She really gave it to him for scaring the horse like that."

Annie (Muschamp) Nelson

Officers of the 72nd Seaforth Highlanders in front of the house on Russell Hill that was used as a barracks

Union Bay Library

To the young boys of the little town, army life looked pretty good. After war was declared, the fifty men of this small detachment were ready to sign up new recruits. Many men were anxious to serve in the Canadian Expeditionary Forces.

1914 AUGUST Announcement- Any CC(D)L employee wanting to volunteer for active service will have his job waiting on his return. (This is believed to be the first big company in B.C. to take this patriotic step) [5]

For about a year, boys and young men from around the district came to Union Bay to enlist.

1915 MAY Desmond Roe of Union Bay left for the front this week. Art Byrd and Ben Nicholls of Cumberland travelled to Union Bay to enlist in the C.E.F. [5]

The newspapers promoted the war with stories of the German advancements, Canadian victories, and lists of men joining up. As well, they published the words to war songs like "Tipperary," "Are We Downhearted? No!" and "Be A Soldier Be A Man". A guide to the pronunciation of French, German and Belgium towns in the war zone was published.

1914 We offer a free map 3 1/2' x 2 1/2' showing clearly every city, town, village, hamlet and river in the whole European war. Each map is in a neat folder and can be obtained from the Cumberland Islander. [5]

The Conservative Government of Sir R. Borden, not wanting to take the step to enforce conscription, published propaganda to promote volunteer recruitment. They even

Courtenay Museum

New recruits on the green in front of Simon Leiser's store enlist for duty

The famous 102nd North British Columbians were mobilized. The new recruits from Prince Rupert, Kamloops, Fernie and the Comox District trained under very primitive conditions. The terrible winter of 1915/16 at Goose Spit prepared them a little for life at the front. Commanded by Lieut.-Col. J.W. Warden, the 102nd regiment left Comox Wharf in June 1916. The men were in the trenches by August 12, where they distinguished themselves.

1916 OCTOBER ➻ Dawn broke with the rain still pouring down and the higher command decided to postpone operations until the 21st. Three companies of the 102nd accordingly returned to Albert, leaving one company to hold the line. Never did the North British Columbians better deserve their reputation for fine physique than in their fight against the mud after an exhausting night in the trenches. The mud was hip high between the line and Bapaume Road, and the men had to be literally dug out by their comrades as they sank exhausted in the liquid, glue-like stickiness.

The weather cleared, the ground became somewhat drier, and on the evening of the 20th the three companies were again brought into the front line, relieving "A" Company which went into support. At midnight the barrage opened, and no finer sight has ever been seen on the battlefield than the manner in which the 102nd, scaling the parapet as one man, followed the barrage like a wall, lying down until it again lifted and advancing as it moved onward, and all in perfect uniformity.

The moment the barrage lifted over Regina Trench, the men were over the parapet. The assault was carried out with such dash, vigour and impetuosity that the Germans were completely demoralized and immediately threw up their hands in surrender.

published the wonderful benefits a soldier could enjoy.

1915 AUGUST ➻ Information for recruits.

Length of Service	To end of war plus six months.
Payment - Private	$1.00 per day + 10¢ field allowance. Clothes and equipment. His wife will receive $20.00 separation allowance (taken out of the soldiers wage). Also the Patriotic fund will assist her.
If wounded or sick	The government will care for him.
If permanently disabled	Allowance paid.
If killed	Government will provide for his widow and children until the children can look after themselves. [4]

During a three week period in 1915, sixteen Union Bay men were recruited into different battalions. Included in the sixteen were B. Geary, H. Glover, S. Hooper, W. Fraser, W. Campbell, G. Grange and F. Davidson. A few of the boys joined the Royal Navy or fledgling Canadian Navy or the Royal Airforce. Most of them joined the army with the majority in the 47th, 102nd or Bantam battalions.

H. Glover

Some Union Bay "boys" are aboard *Princess Victoria* as it departs Victoria on the journey to "do or die" for country

The casualties incurred in the assault itself were very light, amounting to about five killed and ten wounded, but within an hour and a half, there were three counter attacks, whilst throughout that day and during the ensuing night and day a ceaseless barrage of shell fire was poured into Regina Trench, with the result that the total casualty list numbered six officers and seventy of other rank wounded. But the 102nd had captured their portion of Regina Trench and had successfully held it - a feather in the cap of a raw battalion. [6]

About the same time, the 143rd B.C. Bantams, the first corps of its kind in Canada, was formed "to turn the smaller man into a first-class fighting man". This was welcome news in Union Bay where Bill Campbell, Ted and Syd Glover, Hughie Reid, and Stewart and Wally Hooper were anxious to serve their country. After a short training stint in Vernon, they were on the front line in France. (The Hooper boys were later transferred into the 72nd Highlanders when they went overseas.)

1915 DECEMBER ➾ The Battalions which have thus far been formed have held that five feet and four inches are the requisite measurements to enable a man to serve his King and country. Many a man whose heart has burned with loyalty and who has been keen "to do his bit" has been precluded by reason of the fact that he did not reach the requisite height. The British Columbia Bantams offers a place to him. [5]

By the time the National Registration was collected and posted in 1916, all able-bodied men, boys as they became eighteen, young married men and a few older men had joined the fighting forces. Emerson Muschamp was fifty years old when he went overseas, leaving son Herb to manage the dairy farm. He was behind the lines doing clerical work, and wrote out many wills for the young fighting men. Pete Anderson, married with a grown family, joined up and saw action as a sniper with the 102nd.

War expenditures and heavy borrowing finally led to runaway inflation, so in April 1917 a War Income Tax was imposed. On an income of $5000, eighty dollars was paid in tax. Supposedly to last for the war years, it was the forerunner of income tax as we know it today. A month later conscription was adopted and found few in opposition.

1917 MAY ➾ Conscription starts for all men between eighteen and thirty-five. The slacker will be hunted out of his hole and forced to be a man. Those who crossed the line to the U.S. will be brought back or forced into the Stars and Stripes army. There will be no haven or refuge for cowards. [6]

Key jobs such as farming were exempt from the list. Because of this, Jim McKay had a short army career. He was training at Vernon in 1916 when his brother Bob, who managed the family farm, got married and acquired his own farm. Jim had to return home to run the farm for his mother.

War became very real to the people in the little port as they watched the camouflaged ships come and go.

1917 JUNE ➾ The *Ixion* sailed from here with 1400 tons and will probably be the last of the Blue Funnel Line vessels to call. The Ad-

A. Hooper

Stewart Hooper in the uniform of the 72nd Seaforth Highlanders

M. Kine

Emerson Muschamp was fifty years old when he went off to war

H. Glover

Fraser Campbell and Jack Glover. Jack was killed at Passchendaele, and Fraser's brother, Bill, died at home of injuries received overseas

miralty has commandeered all of their ships on the Orient-Vancouver trade.

1917 AUGUST ➻ The *War Dog* coaled here and is headed to the UK with grain. The grim realities of war were brought home as she is painted battleship grey with gun replacements set on her stern.

1917 AUGUST ➻ A four masted barque, the *Red Jacket*, loading 4,000 tons for Honululu, is the first interned German ship taken over by the US shipping board. [6]

During the war the post office was the centre through which all the news came.

"We had a telegraph set in a small room at the head of the stairs. During the war my father sat at the telegraph, sometimes night and day, with Mr. Butters typing the bulletins as they came. They were passed out to the people who crowded into the building and up the stairs to hear the latest news."

Edythe (Brown) Hicks to Mary Moore

Two men from the Bay lost their lives. Jack Glover was killed in the trenches, and Bill Campbell, who was badly injured, returned home and died a few months later. The Glover families, with staunchly patriotic British parents, sent six of the cousins off to war. Harry's sons: Bert, Ted, Syd, and Herbert's sons: Bert and Jack, joined the army. Cousin Albert, living on his own, joined the airforce. Bert, the eldest, left first and came home badly shell-shocked, and his brother Syd was seriously injured. Both Albert and Syd brought home war brides from Britain.

1917 NOVEMBER ➻ Pte. John Glover, son of Mr. & Mrs. Herbert Glover, was killed in action on September 28, 1917 at Passchendaele near Vimy Ridge. He went overseas last November, and in January celebrated his eighteenth birthday in a trench in France. His elder brother Herbert is in the same battalion. [6]

V. Hudson

B. White

Left: This was the first interned German ship taken over by the U.S. shipping board. The *Red Jacket* is loading coal for Honululu.
Right: The three sons of Mr. and Mrs. Harry Glover: Bert, Ted and Syd. Short of stature, Ted and Syd could not enlist until the 143rd B.C. Bantams was formed

"Somewhere in France"
June 24, 1918.

My Dear Peggy:

I'm just dropping you a couple of lines to let you know I am in the best of health and sincerely hope this finds all at home the same... Marg, I just got a set of eating utensils again as I have been eating with just a fork for the past month. What would you think of me if you could only see me at it... Don't worry, I'm still the same old kid, but with a good many changes and can eat anything from Hard Tack Pudding down to sawdust, so I'm afraid you won't have any trouble cooking for me.... This war gets on a fellow's nerves in time, and I certainly wish the whole business was finished with, but still there is one consolation and that is that it can't last forever. So far I haven't had any leave and have been over here for over a year, but still can smile and have a real good laugh once in awhile... I hear from Ethel quite often. Wait till I land on the soil of Canada again and believe me I'm going to have a good time, but I'm afraid it's going to be a long time yet... Well I must close for the time being and best of luck and heaps of love to all.

Cheerio,

From your loving brother, Herbert

Letter from the front written by Herbert Glover to his sister Margaret.

Albert Shillito was living in Cumberland and had been working since he was twelve to support his widowed mother and brother Ted. The mines were on strike so Albert lied about his age and joined the 102nd when he was only fifteen years old.

"In France, Albert was shot in the leg and the bullet lodged under his knee cap. He was a year in hospital in France, and a year in England, where the doctors wanted to amputate his leg, but he wouldn't let them. Then he came back to Canada and was a year in hospital in Victoria, where they still wanted to take his leg off. When he finally came home, one leg was shorter than the other and he limped. After he had retired and we moved to Campbell River, he got in the bath one night and he heard a ping on the bath. The shell had worked its way down and came out of his calf."

Margaret Shillito

On November 11,1918, when a telegram arrived announcing the the war's end, it was proclaimed by the joyous tooting of the locomotives. That was the signal every man, woman and child was waiting for. A huge bonfire was built beside McLeod Road above the track, and everyone turned out to celebrate. People blew trumpets, beat on pots and pans, and Mrs. Baldwin danced around, shaking her tambourine.

In the larger centres, official welcoming parties met each train with returning men. At Union Bay, whether the boys arrived by steamship or train, the whole town turned out to welcome them. It was months after war's end before many of them made it home.

1919 MAY ➾ Gordon Laird, eldest son of Marshall Laird, is home from three and one half years active service of fighting in France. He was in the thick of the fighting where Canadians made a record for themselves. Gordon is looking well in spite of a wounded leg.[5]

After the war, the Great War Veterans Association was formed in the district. Many Union Bay veterans were active in the organization and W. Fraser became vice-president. One of the bi-

M. Simpson

Union Bay post office decked out in bunting and greens to celebrate the end of World War I

P. Anderson	G. Grange
D. Cameron	H. Hillier
F. Campbell	S. Hooper
W. G. Campbell	W. Hooper
J. Davis	A. Hutchinson
F. P. Davidson	G. Laird
P. Fogg	A. McCollock
W. J. Fraser	C. McTaggert
B. Geary	E. Muschamp
A. Glover	F. Nello
E. Glover	R. Ray
H. Glover	H. Reid
H. Glover	D. Roe
J. Glover	M. Roe
S. Glover	A. Shillito

W. Naylor

In 1936 Mr. and Mrs. Herbert Glover on a pilgrimage to Vimy Ridge where their son Jack was killed

monthly meetings was held at the Bay until 1920, when the G.W.V.A. hall was built in Courtenay.

The members helped erect the cairn at Sandwick in October 1919. They were active in having the Government establish the soldiers' settlement at Merville. In August, 1919 it was rumoured that land for a similar settlement had been purchased at Buckley Bay. It was even speculated that the ex-soldiers could work on the "yet to be opened" mine at Tsable River. Nothing came of the rumour and the mine did not open until twenty-six years later. In 1926 G.W.V.A. became the Royal Canadian Legion in Courtenay.

In the summer of 1936 a pilgrimage was made to France by the soldiers that fought at Vimy Ridge, joined by the parents of the men killed there. Mr. and Mrs. Herbert Glover put flowers on their son Jack's grave, and were present at Arass when King Edward unveiled the great war memorial. From France the group went to London, and were entertained in Westminster Hall and addressed by Prime Minister Baldwin. Next, they were guests of honour at a garden party at Buckingham Palace, and met the soon-to-abdicate King.

1936 SEPTEMBER ➺ "You have all tasted of that bitter cup of war; they the dead, drained it to the dregs. If you and the world can find no other way to settle disputes but war, while we are still finding and burying bodies, then this world deserves to perish."

P.M. Baldwin

ALIENS

Very soon after war was declared, the Patriotic Society was formed. It assisted the government in promoting the war cause. Anyone was suspect who was not a whole-hearted supporter of the allied forces, or who criticized the war effort. The "aliens" of German or Austrian birth were not to be trusted. They were put to work and guarded by the military.

1915 JUNE ➺ On Thursday two Germans and five Austrians from Cumberland, and twenty-two Austrians from Bevan, and four Austrians from Courtenay were sent to be interned at Union Bay until the end of the war. [5]

Dr. Richard Thrum, a scientist and coal analyst in charge of the Washer and coke ovens, was of German birth. Most people from the Bay saw him as no threat. However, several officials from the district suspected him of being a spy. Joseph Shaw, Justice of the Peace, and John MacDonald, Provincial Police at Cumberland, both thought that Union Bay's lone German was up to no good.

He started working for the company about 1908 and took out his Naturalization papers in June 1914. Therefore he could not be treated as an alien. Constable McDonald once tried to arrest him, but the Company pointed out that he was a Canadian citizen. Before coming to Canada he had served as an officer in the German army and had brothers fighting for the Germans. This made him a prime suspect. Dr.Thrum carried on his duties and built a large boat during the war.

The boat was built on the south side of Tsable River, on Keenan's property. Dr. Thrum installed a tramway powered by water from the river, to bring lumber and equipment up to the building site. A young Japanese man worked for him. Construction of the boat was watched with great interest and speculation. What would it be used for? Where would the doctor sail to? The mystery was made more intriguing by the boat itself. About 28' long and built of Honduras mahogany, it looked like Noah's ark, as the hull extended about 8' above the water line.

A gas engine was installed and it was launched in June 1917. In less than a year the boat was sold to George Broder. Dr. Thrum disappeared; some say he was arrested as a spy. The boat gained some notoriety when Broder's friend, Mr. Purvis, disappeared while boating with Mr. Broder in Coal Harbour, Vancouver. Later, Mrs. Broder fell through a broken railing on the boat and also drowned.

Another rather eccentric German family became known at the turn of the century, when Governor-General Minto visited Cumberland as guest of Mr. Dunsmuir. The Ginsbergs had a beautiful garden in "Camp", and Mr. Dunsmuir took the Earl of Minto to see it. Mrs. Ginsberg flatly refused them admission, as her husband had threatened her with a whaling if she let anyone into the yard. Later, this same couple moved near Deep Bay and occasionally came to Union Bay to shop.

"They had a wonderful farm down there. I can remember she would walk up to the Bay and have oil cloth tied on her feet for shoes. We used to look at them - real Germans. During the war they found him out in a boat. He

had match boxes - some were British boats, the others German. He was sinking the British boats. Poor man, they took him away."

Sarah (Walker) Kirkwood

WAR EFFORT AT HOME

1915 JULY This great war has been the means of making people less selfish. This is seen in so many forms, among the richest and the poorest in the land, from the gifts of country mansions for the wounded, to the poor mite's penny for the Red Cross Society. [5]

The Comox District Patriotic War Fund was started early to assist soldiers' families. Collections were made from the Company, workers and merchants. The newspaper published the donations as well as the payments distributed to servicemen's wives. The amount depended on how many children they were raising. Mrs. Fraser from the E&N station benefitted from this and received $18.50 per month.

Just weeks after war was declared, the Women's Patriotic Society was formed to send clothes and medical supplies to the men at the front. The ladies from Union Bay got busy. The sewers on their treadle machines stitched up grey flannel shirts, putties, hospital jackets, dressing gowns, flannel undervests and cholera belts. "They do not need fine sewing, but strong sewing - good turnings allowed, and in many cases the seams stitched twice." Knitting needles flew as the women produced hot water bottle covers, grey woollen socks, rifle mitts and balaclava helmets.

The newspaper published a list of necessary articles each month. Often the complete instructions for one item were given, such as for knitting a balaclava using petticoat yarn on number seven bone needles.

1914 SEPTEMBER Ladies of the Patriotic Society met at the church and gave out material to be knitted or sewn. Young girls gathered in homes and made "housewives' kits" from the following directions.

Outside to be made of coarse linen, chintz, cretonne or duck. Size 5 1/2" x 13". Interior to be lined with flannel, and to contain two small pockets, one at end and one in centre. Also attach two loose squares for pins and needles. Sew tape on end for ties. Each should contain safety pins, sewing and darning needles, small straight scissors, shirt and bachelor buttons, black darning wool, black and white linen thread, court plaster and foot-ease powder. [5]

Whether under the Patriotic Society or the Red Cross, all the ladies did their part. Mesdames Alder, Bishop, Booth, Haggart, Reid and Miss Fraser organized and led all the knitters and sewers.

1915 AUGUST A parcel of supplies for wounded soldiers has been sent to Victoria headquarters from the Red Cross workers at Union Bay per Mrs. Haggart. The ladies of the Bay have organized to assist the Red Cross and their assignments are always of the highest quality. [5]

The groups around the district held teas, sales, masquerades, and canvassed door to door. Union Bay collected money towards providing medical and surgical equipment, an X-ray machine and motor ambulances for No.5 General Hospital, C.E.F. This was the B.C. hospital in France where Miss Brown, ex-matron of Cumberland Hospital, served.

"Linen Days" were held by the Red Cross to collect old white cotton, linen, and flannelette for bandages. Each contribution had to be boiled and ironed "with no blueing or starch". The seams had to be torn off, and even pieces 4" square were of use, so every household could contribute something. New material was also collected as well as sheets, pillowcases and towels. Union Bay sent their collections to Cumberland from where 390 lbs. were mailed one month.

The fighting men were heroes to all the young boys, who anxiously awaited their eighteenth birthday. Wilf Glover, with three brothers at the front, used to bemoan "that darn war will be over before I get old enough". The girls were busy sewing and knitting, so the boys wanted to do their part. The void was filled by the Boy Scouts. In their smart uniforms and wide brimmed hats, they marched in patriotic demonstrations. They collected money for guns, linen for the hospitals, sandbags and magazines for the soldiers training at Union Bay.

1915 The wife of an officer in the R.F.A. writes that her husband has asked her to make

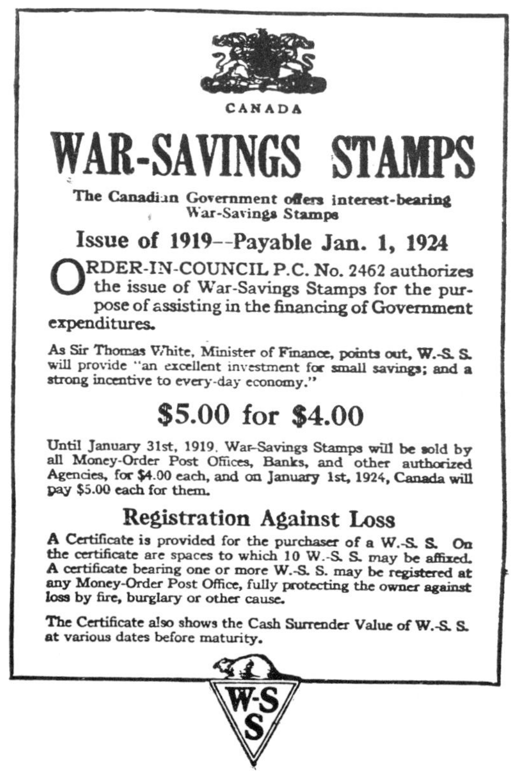

an urgent appeal on his behalf for sandbags, "because the artillery are almost more in need of sandbags than the infantry", for they have huge guns to cover as well, and the men are not dug in to the same extent that the men in the trenches are.

An infantry lieutenant writes, "We want a tremendous lot of sandbags. Our division alone has been using a million a month. If you saw a shell burst on a parapet with sandbags, and on one without, you would soon see how many lives they save."

This is how the infantry advances. Each man takes ten empty bags under his arm as he runs out. When fired at he drops and fills a bag as he lies, for cover. Then he dashes on again with his nine remaining bags to repeat the manoeuvre again and again, always leaving the filled bag to cover some man behind him. In this way the whole line advances with temporary cover, till they can dig themselves in. [5]

This appeal and description caught the Scouts' imagination across Canada and they took up the call. Homemade sandbags were collected, as well as money for sandbags at 12¢ each. Soon the War Office was knee deep in sandbags.

1915 JULY ➾ Sandbags are not needed. The British War Office is providing all the sandbags necessary and begs that no more be sent from Canada. It was a mistake to instruct the Boy Scouts to collect them. [5]

Next, word was sent home that Canadians did not have enough guns. In 1915 the CC(D)L employees started collecting funds to buy a machine gun which was to cost $1000. However, the government declared in 1916 that it could buy the necessary guns without having them donated by the people. It advised the use of money for other patriotic endeavours.

To fill that need, the government introduced the first Victory Loan campaign. Bonds bearing 5 1/2 % interest could be bought for $50, $100, $500, and $1000 at the bank and post office. Canvassers also went door to door. Citizens were expected to invest every penny they could afford, as the slogans suggested.

"Let us help to catch the Hun by buying Victory Bonds."
"Count that day lost whose low descending sun finds in your hand no Victory Bond or Gun".

Government Poster

For every year's campaign, each town was given a quota and received a flag if they reached it. Union Bay always went over the top. Even a year after the war ended, the little town went over its goal of $12,000, reaching $28,850.

Everyone was urged to keep in touch with the fighting men to keep their spirits up. Cards, letters and parcels were a little bit of home to the men on the front.

"Parcel from Home"

Oh, it isn't so much the chocolate bar
Or the package of chewing gum;
It isn't the smokes or the book of jokes
That cheers a man when he's glum.
It isn't a can of pork and beans
Though the taste is certainly grand;
Or the milk or jam, though they seem to a man
A bit of Canada canned.

No, these are not the important things
In that parcel that comes from home;
It's the love and thought that accompany it
That cheers a man quite a bit.

L-Cpl. T. McCord

Parcels had to be packed in corrugated cardboard, tin, or wooden boxes, then wrapped with canvas or linen. In February 1915 the Post Office introduced a special rate of 2¢ for letters addressed to British and Canadian troops on the continent. The address took up most of the envelope.

1915 MARCH ➾ To address mail to the front:

Rank
Name
Regimental Number
Company, Squadron, Battery or other Unit
Battallion
Brigade
1st or 2nd Canadian Contingent
British Expeditionary Force
ARMY POST OFFICE
LONDON ENGLAND [4]

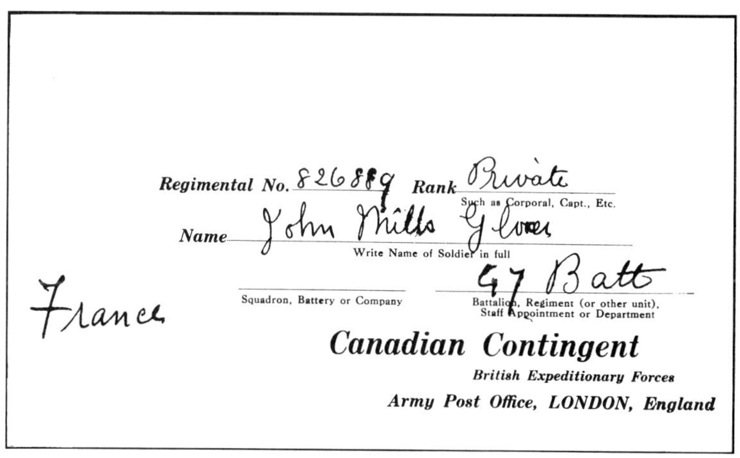
Regimental No. 826889 Rank Private
Such as Corporal, Capt., Etc.
Name John Mills Glover
Write Name of Soldier in full
France
Squadron, Battery or Company
47 Batt
Battalion, Regiment (or other unit), Staff Appointment or Department
Canadian Contingent
British Expeditionary Forces
Army Post Office, LONDON, England

WORLD WAR II

By the time of the Second World War, everyone had a radio. This meant that the people at home had access to troop movements, battles, air raids and casualties. Many homes had a map on the wall where Allied advances could be followed as Lorne Green, "the voice of doom," read the news. With a war that encompassed most of Europe, North Africa, and after 1941 the Pacific, there were many areas to report on. Over forty fighting men from Union Bay were stationed in different parts of the world, and held the interest of all the citizens.

Everyone was urged to write letters and send parcels at 12¢ a pound. Sending whole newspapers was banned in an effort to reduce the amount and weight of the mail, so articles were clipped and sent. Cigarettes could be sent to Europe duty free, in order to assure the fighting men "as many fags as they wanted." In 1941 the airgraph was introduced by the post office to send messages to the troops. Originally costing 10¢ each, they were reduced to 6¢ the next year. Letters were written on a special one page form, then reduced and photographed on microfilm. The film, containing 1,700 letters and weighing just a fraction of the original letters, was mailed to Europe. Prints were made of each letter and delivered to the troops. In 1943 an airmail service was started across the Atlantic with promise of a four day service to Britain.

A. Geary

J. Bennett

Above: George Watt, a veteran of the First World War, volunteered to serve in WWII, as did his daughter Jean

Left: One of the first local boys to enlist was Buster Geary, seen here in his uniform of the Canadian Scottish (Princess Mary's) Regiment

The first local boys to join the fighting forces were Andrew Arrol, H. (Buster) Geary and Jack McQueen. They joined "C" Company of the Canadian Scottish (Princess Mary's) Regiment which was recruiting and training at the Native Son's Hall when war was declared September 7, 1939. The boys lived at home and trained in Courtenay but it was not long before Comox Logging offered Camp 3 to the regiment, and they settled into bunk houses there.

The next recruit was Charles Davis who joined the Irish Fusiliers. From then on there was a steady stream of young men joining the army, navy, airforce and merchant marines. Albert Glover and George Watt, two veterans from the First World War, also enlisted. Both men had daughters in the forces. Thelma Glover drove truck for the WAC, and Jean Watt was a meteorologist with the RCAF. Six families had two sons involved in the war. Bob and Lizzie McKay had three sons in the service: George in the U.S. army, Robbie in the navy, and Bud in the army. The Vanyo family moved to the Bay during the war. They had three sons: Frank, James, and Alex who all saw active service with the tank corps. Frank was in the North African campaign, James was part of the D-Day invasion, and Alex took part in mop-up operations. James stayed on in Europe after the war ended, in the occupational forces. Both Frank and Alex volunteered to fight in the Pacific, but were on leave when the war with Japan ended.

The daily pay was $1.30. Each month single men received the total amount. From the married men's pay $20 was deducted and augmented with $15, for their wives. They also received $12 for each child. As well, the medical fund of the CC(D)L continued to cover the dependents of employees serving in the war, provided the monthly payments were kept up.

The feeling of war was brought close to home when troop convoys travelled Up-Island from bases at Nanaimo and Victoria. Also, the forces training at Comox and Courtenay did manoeuvers throughout the district. One group would drive down with trucks and bren gun carriers to defend Union Bay. Another group, the invaders, would arrive by landing barge under the cover of a smoke screen. Ack-ack guns fired, sirens on corvettes went woo-woo-woop, and Lysander planes flew low dropping flour bombs. Dressed in green and

J. Ibitster

The three sons of a patriotic family. Frank, James, and Alex Vanyo all saw active service with the tank corps

often in the district, or the boys travelled to Vancouver to join their favourite service.

After Pearl Harbour was attacked by the Japanese in December 1941, Hitler and Mussolini also declared war on the United States. This meant that almost all of the world was embroiled in the war. Newsreels in the movie houses showed the battles, victories, and ravages of war. They became wonderful propaganda tools to promote the war effort through victory bonds, scrap drives, and the Red Cross. Stories of prisoners of war brought home the horrors of the strife.

brown fatigues and sprouting foliage in their helmets, the soldiers hid in ditches, behind trees and under buildings as they advanced. Little boys, supplied with wooden rifles and led by Tom Jones, joined in the fight, sniping at the soldiers as they advanced toward their usual objective, the E&N track. Little girls often brought the "fighting" men drinks of water or freshly baked cookies from home. For the citizens of the port it was at once exciting and frightening.

In April 1942 a national plebiscite was held on conscription. Union Bay voted 162 for and 40 against, echoing the B.C. vote of 4 to 1. The Draft notice in 1942 included all single, divorced or widowed men between nineteen and forty, as well as married men between nineteen and twenty-five. However, most of the young boys could hardly wait until their eighteenth birthday to join Canada's fighting force, and none needed to be drafted. Recruiting officers were

1945 Mrs. John Ovans has arrived to make her home with her father-in-law, Major C.P. Ovans. Mrs. Ovans was evacuated from Hong Kong to Australia in 1940. Her husband, Lieut. J.M. Ovans RNR, has been a prisoner of war in Hong Kong since 1941, while her father is a civilian prisoner in Shanghai. [7]

In September 1942 the Shillito family received a telegram reporting that their oldest son George, able seaman in the RCN, was missing with the sinking of the *HMCS Ottawa* in the North Atlantic. With 113 men, it was the second highest loss of lives suffered by the navy to that date. Without a definite death notice, his parents went on hoping until the end of the war that somehow their son had been rescued and perhaps was a prisoner. The previous

E. Hallstrom

Courtenay Museum

Left: ***HMCS Ottawa*.** Right: Able Seaman George Shillito of ***HMCS Ottawa*** was one of the 113 men lost when the ship was torpedoed and sunk in 1942 on the North Atlantic

N. McInnes

Returning from their first mission, Ian Pollock (far right) and the rest of his crew were killed when attempting to land their Halifax bomber on a foggy day in Scotland

Christmas, George wrote to his sister Ethel.

"We had a swell spread for Christmas, with turkey and vegetables, jelly and mince pie. We were issued two bottles of beer and a tot of rum before dinner. The captain and officers came forward and visited us before dinner and boy did he ever get a good hand. He's an all round regular fellow and no fooling!"

George Shillito

Ian Pollock at age eighteen joined the RCAF. He became a bomb aimer aboard a Halifax bomber. The inexperienced crew crashed on their first mission as they were returning from a mine-laying expedition over the North Sea.

1944 NOVEMBER ➻ Mr. and Mrs. J. Pollock received word this week that their only son, Flying Officer John Robert Pollock, twenty-one, was killed in action overseas. He is being buried at Banff, Forayshire, Scotland. [7]

In 1972 Nelson McInnis, an instructor of Ian's, had his student's memory honoured when a mountain peak located in the Jervis Inlet area was named Mt. Pollock.

The town was proud of its fighting sons. Flying Officer Leroy Richardson completed an Operational Tour as navigator over Germany and received the Distinguished Flying Cross.

Citation: "This officer has completed in various capacities, numerous operations against the enemy, in the course of which he has invariably displayed the utmost fortitude, courage and devotion to duty."

Edmonton, Alta., 26 November 1949

L. Richardson

It was a proud moment for Union Bay when one of its sons received a high award for bravery. Leroy Richardson received the Distinguished Flying Cross from the Governor-General of Canada

M. Coe

Les Coe was a member of the Provost Corps that went to the Pacific Islands on mop-up operations

Following is a list of the men and women from Union Bay who served their country during the Second World War

ARMY

A. Arrol
L.W. Coe
G. Cooper
C.E. Davis
C.W. Davis
A.H. Geary
A.E. Glover
J.R. Haggart
J. Hayton
J.N. Kerpan
W.B. Macartney
A.E. McKay
G.E. McKay
S.J. McKay
G. McQueen
J. McQueen
G.H. Murdock
R. Pratt
J.M. Reid
E. Sawchuck
S. Shillito
F.C. Thomas
G.J. Watt
L.D. White
A.A. Vanyo
F.A. Vanyo
J.J. Vanyo

NAVY

W. Bateman
H. Beck
D. Carnegie
G. Chilton
J.P. Cunningham
A. Dunn
J.C. English
W.T. Farmere
J.W. Hamilton
T.G. Jones
R.A. McKay
K. Peters
H.B. Strachan
G. Shillito

MERCHANT NAVY

D.C. Haggart
D.W. Renwick

RCAF

A.L. Anderson
R. Carnegie
W.H. Hamilton
C.E. Oldale
J.R. Pollock
K.D. Renwick
D.L. Wilson
A.L. Richardson
L. Smithman
H.R. Tappin
E.G. Vaughan
Jean F. Watt (WD)
J. Williams

EXTRA!

COMOX DISTRICT FREE PRESS

With which is incorporated The Courtenay Free Press, Cumberland Islander and Cumberland News.

COURTENAY, BRITISH COLUMBIA, MONDAY, MAY 7, 1945

GERMANY SURRENDERS

Nazis Submit At 6.35 Today

Germany surrendered on Monday, May 7, 1945 at 6:35 a.mV-E Day was celebrated in the homes, schools, churches and streets.

1945 MAY ➾ Thus ends five years, eight months and six days of war which began when Hitler marched into Poland on September 1, 1939. It has been the most costly war in history. In the 2,319 days in which it raged it cost more than 40,000,000 casualties on both sides in killed, was missing and wounded. [7]

A free dance attended by 400 revellers at the Community Hall to celebrate V-E day. The Country Club donated their services and the ladies' committee provided the food.

The war finally ended on Tuesday, August 14, 1945, six years and three months after fighting began in Europe and four years after Pearl Harbour. At 4:20 p.m. the air-raid siren on top of the school announced V-J Day.

1945 AUGUST ➾ The announcement at 4:00 p.m. Tuesday by Prime Minster Clement Attlee of Great Britain that Japan had surrendered to the Allies touched off one of the most spontaneous and happy celebrations ever held in this district, surpassing even last May'sV-E Day festivities. [7]

GREEKS

In the late 1930's Japan was at war with China, and bought a great deal of scrap iron on the West Coast for its munitions factories. Ships from all over the world transported it to Japan. Many of these ships coaled at Union Bay before heading across the Pacific.

Anchored at Union Bay in the fall of 1940 was a sizeable portion of the Greek merchant navy, as well as some Yugoslavian ships. They had come for bunker coal and were loaded down with scrap for Japan. Because of the war in Europe, they were under government control. Mussolini had just invaded Greece, and the government was in such disarray that the captains did not get their sailing orders for months.

The eight or so ships were old and in disrepair. One old tub lay

D. Bennie

Greek ships anchored in the bay waiting orders to sail to Japan with scrap metal

D. Muschamp

Two Greek sailors befriended by Dover Muschamp, Mildred Hicks and May Muschamp

leaning against the dock with the ballast tanks gone. The men were half starved, and a kindly Australian captain took pity on them and gave them food. The crews were happy to stay at Union Bay as they were all frightened of crossing the Pacific in such terrible conditions. They also worried that they might get caught up in the Japanese-Chinese war.

The crews were a patriotic lot. Thirty men off one boat wired $1,000 out of their pay to the Greek government to help continue the fight with the Italians. Every time word was received that Greece had won a battle, the whistles tooted, the flags flew and the men celebrated in the beer parlours.

The boat loads of idle single men were a natural target for pimps and prostitutes.

"We were just young kids and we'd sit on the dock and watch. Some guy would haul the prostitutes all the way up from Nanaimo. He'd drive up in a big car and drop them off. The Greeks would be waiting in a whaler to row them out. The girls would be all dressed up with lots of make-up. Then they went from ship to ship and the guy would be there in the morning to pick them up. I'll tell you, they didn't look anything like they did the night before. Imagine, eight or nine ships!"

Bill Hamilton

"I was alone one day and one of the Greeks made a run through this road, through the fence and down the tracks. They had some white woman down on the boat and the husband at Cumberland heard about it and he was chasing this Greek and throwing rocks at him. I was at the window and saw it all."

Edna Peters

The sailors were allowed off their ships with special permits, and after a month became well-known in the community. Many of the officers were entertained in local homes. In December the officers decided to repay the hospitality. As the school hall was too small, Mrs. Horne gave them the use of an empty house next to the bank.

1940 DECEMBER ➻ British and Greek flags, symbols of the first democracy in the world and the great defender of the democratic way of life, were entwined last night at a Vancouver Island port when captains of some Greek ships gave graceful thanks to the people who have shown them hospitality during their long stay. [6]

The preparation took weeks, with no money spared. The captains raided the flower markets in Vancouver and Seattle for red carnations and white chrysanthemums. The house was lavishly decorated on the outside with Greek and British flags. Inside, the house was transformed with blue and white banners and greenery. Huge vases of flowers were everywhere.

1940 DECEMBER ➻ On one wall was a very animated and colorful sketch of an "evzone", one of the crack Greek mountain corps who drove the Italians back into Albania. It was painted by a wireless operater and was banked with laurel. [6]

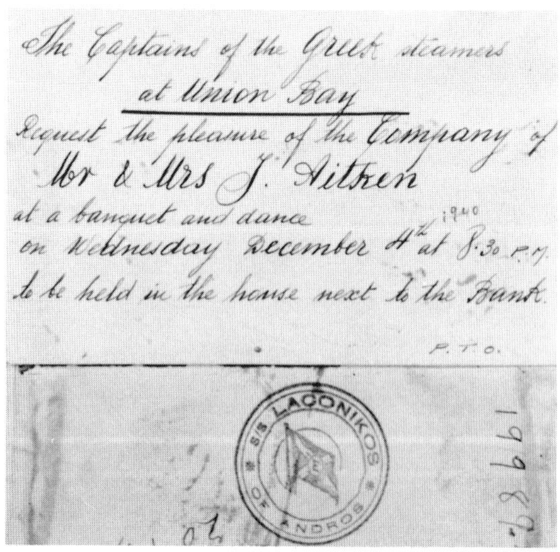

The Captains of the Greek steamers
at Union Bay
Request the pleasure of the Company of
Mr & Mrs J. Aitken
at a banquet and dance 1940
on Wednesday December 4th at 8.30 p.m.
to be held in the house next to the Bank.
P.T.O.

S/S LACONIKOS OF ANDROS

D. Aitken

An invitation to a banquet and dance hosted by the Greek ships for the community

Mrs. G.H. Dickson, Mrs. M. Horne and Miss Dorothy King received the eighty guests on behalf of the hosts. Supper was provided on a lavish scale with chicken, turkey, suckling pig and caviar on the extensive menu. Drinks were pressed into every hand and many toasts given to the success and victory of the British and Greek fighting forces. The sailors entertained the party with many songs and dances. Both nations' anthems were sung and re-sung. A local orchestra played for dancing. The party finally came to an end at four in the morning, with each lady taking home a beautiful red carnation. Several weeks later the Union Bay community reciprocated with a party for ninety people at Sunnydale Golf Course.

CIVIL DEFENCE

Early in the war, a civilian protection service called the Air Raid Precaution was formed. The police sergeant at Courtenay was in charge of the entire district. Bill Auchinvole was deputy warden for Union Bay and organized the volunteers. The men were trained in all branches of civilian protection, including first aid, fire fighting and gas decontamination. The women took nursing classes from Agnes Reid, RN.

1941 AUGUST ➾ The Comox District ARP is per capita the best in the Province. We have 827 active members, 400 of which have taken First Aid since the inception of the movement. The Government plans lectures, displays, and pictures of the Home Guard in London, to arouse people out of the attitude, "it can't happen here". [6]

On December 8, 1941 the ARP members went door to door advising and instructing the unprepared citizens about the blackout.

1941 DECEMBER ➾ *Jap Raid Expected, District Vulnerable Military Objective.* The entire Pacific Coast experienced some of the realities of war this week as Japan touched off her sudden attack on United States and Great Britain. With an air attack reported as imminent, and hostile planes reported actually approaching the Golden Gate to San Francisco, the entire coast was ordered to black out their lights. [6]

The airport at Comox and the port at Union Bay were said to be targeted by Japan. This was taken seriously. Makeshift covers were made for windows, using blankets, cardboard and tar paper. Stores were soon depleted of green window blinds, building paper, plywood, and flashlights which had to be painted so that just a slit of light showed. Car owners who had to drive at night painted their headlights, leaving a perpendicular 3" slit, 1/2" wide. Several accidents happened as cars crawled along in the dark.

The ARP men were everywhere, patrolling roads and checking even the faintest light. The second night, the chief warden toured the district at midnight.

1941 DECEMBER ➾ He was particularily pleased with the wharf at Union Bay, which is usually a blaze of flood lights. On that night there was only a glimmer of a flashlight - even the train lights had been dimmed. [7]

In less than a week the blackout was lifted, but it left the people with a real feeling of "it could happen here." Premier John Hart published a page of Blackout Orders. There were two types of blackouts:

Precautionary Blackout -
- To be used when danger is believed to exist.
- Applied to land in B.C. lying west of the Cascades.
- Announced by the ARP directly or through radio.
- All lights must be blacked out.
- Cars with appropriate lights driven less than 15 mph.

Imminent Danger Blackout -
- Used when there is a threat of immediate attack.
- Applied to all parts of the Province.
- Announced by a series of 5 blasts, repeated 3 times.
- All lights must be blacked out.
- All traffic must halt and pedestrians must walk on sidewalks only.
- The telephone to be used only for emergency.

Precautionary measures were taken at Union Bay. A huge air raid siren was installed on the school roof. Fire escapes were built on the school and teachers drilled the students on evacuation. Arrangements were made for bussed students and those living more than ten minutes from school, to bunk in at local homes. Company houses were provided with window covers made of wall board. Other people built their own which could be quickly put up and taken down, much like storm windows. By 1944 a fire hydrant system was completed, greatly increasing fire fighting capabilities. Homeowners were advised to keep sand, a shovel and a rake handy to smother incendiary bombs before a fire started.

PACIFIC COAST MILITIA RANGERS

The area from Bowser to Sayward became a division of the Pacific Coast Militia Rangers. Recruiting started in April 1942. The men who volunteered were not eligible for active service. Some were too young, some were too old and some had been rejected for medical reasons, or because they were needed in specific jobs. Captain F. Currans of Fanny Bay commanded Company No.21, with men from Bowser to Union Bay. They were a motley crew, initially equipped with only steel helmets, arm bands and their own hunting rifles. Eventually they were each issued with bone-dry jackets and pants, gas masks and 30-30 Winchester rifles. A couple of sten guns were issued to each company. In 1945 they were treated to a trip in an airplane, a first for many of them.

They trained once a week on the coal hills, with Paul Grundy and George Davis in charge. Sometimes they joined with the Cumberland company and attacked a combined force of Courtenay, Comox, and Royston. Another time, the army commandos advanced and the brave men at Union Bay defended the town with flour bombs. Following are some recollections of two young rangers, George Cooper and Bill Hamilton.

George *"Bert Geary made dummy hand grenades in the foundry and we had to learn to throw them. We practiced once a week, and I remember we used to 'take the car shop' every second Thursday. That was our objective. Good old Frankie Holmes, Jocky Pollock, and Pete Reid were inside defending it."*

Bill *On the coal hills we built a ramp covered with canvas for rifle practice. Where the ordinary fellow's toes would be on the ground, Jocky was halfway up the ramp. He was firing beside me and I couldn't concentrate on my aim because I was laughing so hard. Every time he fired he'd slide down the ramp and have to scramble back up to fire again."*

George *"They brought in army instructors to teach us. Sergeant Gardner came with a blackboard and drew up a battle - forest, guns, Japs, and everything.*
He asked, 'Now if you had twenty-eight men how would you attack this situation?'

Lou Larson hollered, 'Burn them out!'
You mean you're going to set fire to Vancouver Island?'
'Right sir, fry the bastards!'
The Sergeant tried to ignore him, 'If the bren gun is here and ...'
'Burn em out!' roared Larson.
Well, they had to kick him out. He'd been in the F.B.I. getting gassed up before practice night."

Bill *"We had just got the new sten gun and Bill Kerstead had cleaned it and done something wrong. He pushed it on to single shot and fired a couple of shots. Then he turned around and we were all standing there and the thing went onto automatic - ack ack ack. He nearly shot the whole bunch of us... and we were going to save the Island!"*

George *"John Rosengren was the powder expert and he was teaching us to make hand grenades with some dynamite that Murray Kennedy had brought. 'I'll tell you anodder ting, anyone can handle dynamite,' says John. 'You take a quarter stick of dynamite and put the cap in it and then a fuse. Then you slit the end of the fuse and put the head of a match in it. When the Japs are coming at you, you strike a match to it and throw it.' Well, we were all sitting in a circle watching, and here's this burning stick of dynamite s-s-s. Well, Tom Campbell picked it up and threw it, and it went off in the bush. Oh, we were a brave outfit!"*

"One time we took on the regular army. Gordon Horne used to bring old or broken bags of flour from the store, and we put it in little paper bags and made grenades out of it. Well, Jimmy Haggart threw one at a bren gun carrier and bonked this Sergeant or Major right on the head. The little bag of flour just turned him white. He looked like a cartoon. Boy, was that officer mad! He was livid!"

Bill *It was later said by someone of very good authority that the Rangers had quite an effect, propaganda-wise, in Japan. You know, the Japs knew we were here. They didn't know what we were like! They figured we'd be ready. They were afraid of all these carbineers crawling around the bush, that knew every tree and rock like Davey Crockett. I just wonder what would have happened if the Japs had come over the Beaufort Range."*

VICTORY LOANS

From the experience of the first war, the finance department of the federal government realized the extent to which money could be made available for war time use. The War Times Prices and Trade Board was established at the outset, to be sure that the large debts would not be incurred again. The government carried out highly successful promotional campaigns to sell both War Bonds and War

Saving Stamps. Throughout the war the CCF criticized the government for using the common man and children's money to fight the war.

The first Victory War Bonds were issued in February 1940. The second campaign was launched when two huge Hudson bombers, the first seen in the district, flew very low and dropped leaflets. Children scrambled to gather them up and read the message:

"Canada's Second War Loan Swings Into Action. Do Your Bit to Help Canada's War Effort. See Your Investment Dealer, Bank, or Stock Broker Today. BUY BONDS TO BEAT BARBARISM."

For every new bond issue a quota was given to the district, which was broken down into each town. Slogans were adopted to promote sales. A Churchill quote, ***"Give Us The Tools and We Will Finish The Job,"*** was used for the third drive in 1941. The "V for Victory" sign was taken up by everyone, and the district total of $200,000 was met in less than a month. The new twelve-sided nickel minted in 1943 had a message in morse code around the edge - ***"We Win When We Work Willingly."*** By the seventh drive, the district quota of $600,000 was met.

War Saving Stamps were sold with the same promotional gimmicks, such as ***"Stamp Out The U-Boats."*** Ninety dollars worth of stamps could buy a depth charger to sink a U-boat. Every week many children bought a 25¢ stamp with a plane, warship or tank on it, to fill a book of sixteen stamps, total cost $4.00. In five years the book could be redeemed for $5.00. Ella Davis was in charge of promoting Saving Stamps in Union Bay. She gave reports of her success: 172 stamps one month, 369 the next, and so on.

In 1944 many citizens of the Bay took a free ride on a landing barge from Royston wharf to the Comox jetty. Complete with a carnival to make money for bonds, the Navy Bond Show presented the Combined Operations School. It demonstrated what would happen on D-Day when the allied troops cracked the wall of Hitler's fortress.

1944 MAY ➾ A display of war invasion tactics was witnessed. Landing barges landed troops on the beach to storm an enemy position. Dive bombing Kittyhawk fighter planes provided overhead cover for the operation, while the objective was strongly defended by ack-ack guns, land mines, and shore batteries using live amunition. Stretcher bearers removed the casualties to beach dressing stations. Smoke generators created an effective screen to cover the troops. Roaring, diving planes, the rattle of machine guns, flashing trails of yellow and red tracer bullets, exploding shells, grenades and mines added to the realistic feeling of war. [7]

RATIONING

The food shortage came about because food had to be sent to the fighting forces and to help feed British civilians. Also, farmers were joining the army or moving to the city for better paying jobs. The National Selective Service put a stop to this in 1942. Imported foods such as sugar were often unavailable due to lack of transportation. The War Times Prices and Trade Board devised a major rationing scheme. Sugar, butter, tea, coffee and meat were rationed. It also became necessary to ration oil and gasoline because of the need in trucks, tanks, planes and ships. Gas rationing started in 1942 with sixty 5 gallon coupons issued per car per year. This was decreased to forty coupons in 1945. After Pearl Harbour, rubber also became extremely scarce.

Every member of the family received a ration book. Each new issue was distributed from the school by Mrs. Grundy and her volunteers. Covers were made to carry the ration books. They were constructed of oilcloth and bound with a blanket stitch in wool, with a different colour for each member of the family. These were a popular item at all the bazaars.

The first food rationed was sugar. As well as bulk sugar, sugar products like canned fruit, jam and candies were also rationed. Extra sugar for Christmas 1945 was welcome news as more coupons were allowed for preserves. This meant candied fruit for cakes could be purchased. Butter rationing started in December 1942 with the allowance of 8 oz. per person per week, decreasing in '45 to 6 oz.

The urgent need to ship meat to Britain made meat rationing necessary in May 1943. It started in restaurants where meat was excluded from menus on Tuesdays and Fridays. A month later, households were allowed only 1 1/3 lb. of meat per person per week. Butchers Bowden and Harwood had to attend a workshop at Nanaimo that explained the "ins-and-outs" of meat rationing.

1945 NOVEMBER ➾ Ration reminder to the public.
A list of meats not requiring ration coupons
- whole heads and tails of beef, veal, pork, lamb.

Internal Organs
- brain, liver, kidney, heart, tongue, sweetbread and tripe. [7]

Food was a weapon and "kitchen soldiers" were urged by the department of national war services to save bones and fat. Every housewife had a can into which she strained the drippings and fat, then sold to the butcher for 4¢ a pound.

"Win the war right in your own kitchen. There is enough explosive power hidden in ten pounds of fat to fire forty-nine anti-aircraft shells."

War Services Department

To help with the food shortage everyone was encouraged to plant a "Victory Garden". At the Bay most people were gardeners, but this title gave more incentive to those without a green thumb.

THE RED CROSS

W. Glover

These children rode on the Red Cross float in the 1940 May 24th parade. Back: Jack Glover, Ernie Shillito, Lorraine Watt, Bobby Treloar, Donald Campbell, Eddie Vowels. Front: Betty Jane Peters, Roni Berggren, Elsa Dickson, Margo Auchinvole

During the First World War, there was an active Red Cross Society at Union Bay which worked in conjunction with the Patriotic Society. These ladies willingly started their volunteer work once again in September 1939. Union Bay was included in the Cumberland Red Cross district along with Denman, Bevan, and No.8. Agnes Reid and Ellen McKay assisted in the formation of units at Buckley Bay and Fanny Bay, bringing them into the district as well. Agnes and Ellen were joined by Annie Campbell, Nellie King and Jessie Watt to form the executive for the first two years. The remaining years of the war were organized by a younger group of women. Mrs. Reid guided the group as vice-president. In this capacity she attended the annual general meetings at the B.C. headquarters in Vancouver, and brought home a plan for the following year's work.

1940 AUGUST ➾ As the Red Cross is the only organization to get behind the lines, it has been asked to: 1. Supply 5,000 parcels monthly for prisoners of war. 2. Find clothing for 100,000 refugees in Britain. [6]

For four years Kathleen Stubbs was president. Thelma Auchinvole was the ways and means chairlady and Winnie Glover was the work convener. The secretary-treasurer position was filled by Florence Waterfield and Ethel Glover in consecutive years.

Mrs. Auchinvole had the unenviable job of dreaming up ways to make money. Except for operating expenses, all proceeds were sent to headquarters. Any little bit helped - $12.00 made at a movie, $72.00 made at a tea, $39.00 made at a concert. Whist drives were held nearly every month at the Crib Club. Many items were donated to be raffled.

1943 OCTOBER ➾ Prizes for the Red Cross draw will be a pickled tongue donated by Mr. Bowden the butcher, and a crocheted centrepiece made by Mrs. Medrich.

1945 OCTOBER ➾ A large doll house made entirely by Mr. G. Cooper and donated to the Red Cross, was raffled and drawn at the Old Time Dance. It was won by Joan Frelone of Cumberland. [7]

Anyone with home movies was called on to show them at the Community Hall. Miss Jean McNaughton presented movies of the 24th of May which showed brightly and clearly the beautiful floats and Queen Dorothy Ward. Mrs. R. Palmer showed pictures of war scenes in Britain and local views of Their Majesties' visit to Victoria. Mr. A. Auchinvole showed scenes of coal mining and logging, as well as comic films which added to the fun.

Concerts were another money-maker. The same local talent performed time after time. Occasionally, a special guest highlighted the show.

1942 AUGUST ➾ The Union Bay unit of the Red Cross made $39.00 at a concert held in the Community Hall. Mr. Wm. Carr of Vancouver, well-known on radio and formerly of Union Bay, rendered several numbers in his fine voice. He also gave an impersonation of a well-known radio announcer. [7]

Chain teas, telephone teas, shamrock teas and many more were given in the ladies' homes. They were always accompanied by a large selection of home baking and often a bazaar table of homemade articles. Ration book holders were a hot item. Every summer a huge garden party was held in the beautiful surroundings of the manager's home. It started in the afternoon and went on until dark, with many things to spend money on. There was a fish pond, ice cream and lemonade for the children. For the adults there were games of chance, guessing games, bingo and tea cup readings. A food stall featured a bean supper, with berries and cream for dessert.

1940 JUNE ➾ The garden party for the Red Cross was held in Mrs. Geo. Dickson's beautiful garden. There were many stalls, draws, and competitions. The young girls served at the tea tables and later for dinner. There was a good selection of local entertainment as well as songs by Mrs. Chester (Miss Jean Patterson) of the Metropolitan Opera Co., in the afternoon and evening. [6]

During WW I most of the Red Cross' efforts were directed toward making clothes and supplies for the soldiers. Because England itself suffered so badly in WW II, most of the articles made and collected were for civilians and the service hospitals.

As work convener, Mrs. Glover received all the materials, yardage, wool, and one pattern per item. Her committee cut and divided everything, duplicating the patterns by hand. A room was needed to accommodate all the stock so the CC(D)L carpenters renovated the room at the back of the fire hall. Cupboards were built along the walls and large tables made for cutting patterns and fabric. Every weekday from 2:00 p.m. to 4:00 p.m. the work room was open. Wool for baby bonnets, cotton for handkerchiefs and flannel for men's shirts were distributed to home sewers and knitters.

Each province was issued with a quota to make a proportionate supply of civilian clothing. Every month the finished articles were sent off to headquarters, and Mrs. Little included the number in her news column. In January 1943 the women must have worked overtime as a total of 103 articles were made.

1941 OCTOBER ➾ This month's work done by the Union Bay Red Cross Unit totalled sixty-four. The following is a list of the items.

5 red dresses size 6	6 boys pyjamas
1 hospital shirt	4 ladies sweaters
19 pr. grey bed socks	1 pr. service socks
1 lg. quilt	1 child's quilt
1 baby layette	15 children's toques

The Red Cross has been asked for more new woolen blankets or quilts for bombed-out victims in Britain as the supply is depleted. Two dollars will buy a single blanket. [7]

"Blanket Drives" were held to make money to buy blankets, so desperately needed after each German raid over Britain. Quilts were also made by groups of women.

1941 OCTOBER ➾ Two quilts were on display at the sale of home cooking held at the Red & White store. The two quilts for bombed-out people in Britain were supervised by Thelma Auchinvole and Mrs. Medrich. [7]

The Red Cross ladies all belonged to other groups which took up special projects to help the war effort. The Sewing Club made quilts at their weekly meetings. The Church sent Christmas parcels to all of the Bay boys overseas, and the Literary Club made baby layettes.

1941 SEPTEMBER ➾ A letter from Edinburgh was received by the Union Bay Literary Society. The parcel of a baby's layette and things for mother has been given to a mother of eight children (the eldest fourteen). The baby was only four days old when its soldier father was killed. A photo was enclosed of the baby wearing the coat and bonnet which the ladies recognized as having knit. The letter said, "We wish to thank all the ladies of Canada for the many beautiful things you have sent us, and hope you will be pleased to hear how your efforts have been appreciated." [6]

In 1940 the Red Cross entered a float in the May 24th parade. Wes Peters' truck was decorated as a Red Cross Hospital. Children in the primary grades were dressed as doctors, nurses and patients. The float won second prize and $20 was added to the fund.

SALVAGE

Canadians were urged to save everything. Even Christmas cards were collected and sent to WW I veterans who remade them and sent them to Britain where there was a shortage. Mrs. McKay and her committee bagged and tied the used clothing, boots and shoes deposited in the box at the store.

1941 JUNE ➾ The "Bundles for Britain" caravan paid another visit to the district, and returned down Island well-loaded with supplies for bombed out victims of Britain. Four cartons and one bundle was loaded from Union Bay. The Red Cross workers on the truck said they wanted warm clothing for next winter. The caravan will return in three weeks. Only clean, mended clothes with six months wear still left are wanted. [7]

Nothing was wasted; everything was saved or recycled. The purpose was twofold. The government and private companies purchased scrap for use in war industries, and the money paid to the Red Cross went to further their humanitarian aims.

They held massive salvage drives with collection depots in each area of the district. The Vancouver Red Cross branch sent scows which were docked on the Courtenay River and filled with scrap. All metal was collected, especially aluminum, used in the construction of aircraft. Old batteries, rubber tires and glass bottles were recycled. Rags were collected for industry, and old woolens to be made into blankets. Used leather coats and jackets were made into stomach protectors for mine sweeper crews. Old tags were used for wrapping delicately milled parts for aircraft and ships. It was an offence to cut or destroy cloth bags. The jute, cotton or twill bags had to be returned clean to the seller. Papers and magazines were sent to a Victoria roofing company. People were encouraged to save rope, twine and string to tie up the scrap. Boxes were saved to pack bottles.

1941 OCTOBER ➾ Local Salvage Brings $1500. After the salvage barge arrived in Vancouver, this month's salvage efforts of the whole Comox District have been reported prominently in the Eastern Press as an outstanding community effort. [7]

JUNIOR RED CROSS

The Junior Red Cross was organized in most B.C. schools, and Union Bay was no exception. Besides giving the children a chance to do their bit and help the less fortunate, it taught them how meetings were conducted. Each room had a club which elected a president, secretary and treasurer. At the meetings it was decided which projects would be undertaken. Candy sales were popular. It was easy to make and easier to sell. The boys and girls collected scrap and helped with the blanket fund. Everyone learned to knit. Small squares were made, then sewed together to make colourful quilts. The McKay boys had help from their mother Bessie, who owned a knitting machine and could always be counted on for enough squares to finish a quilt.

1949 JUNE ➾ All on their own, the Primary Class held a concert at the station freight shed with proceeds going to the Blanket Fund.

1949 DECEMBER ➾ A group of young girls raised funds at a concert at Tom Campbell's home. They will use the $5.75 to buy material for layettes they plan to make for war refugees in England. [7]

Every spring and fall a concert was given, sometimes accompanied with a bazaar. One fall $130 was made.

1945 DECEMBER ➾ Union Bay children staged a fine concert for the Jr. Red Cross. This was also accompanied by a bazaar of items made entirely by the children themselves: book covers, ornaments, flower pot holders, pictures, papier-mache bowls and vases. [7]

Some of the classes sponsored country homes in Britain where children from bombed-out cities were sent. One class wrote letters and sent parcels to a farm in Kent, England.

Not through the Red Cross, but organized by the Kinsmen, the children sold and collected Shell-Out tickets at Hallowe'en. Every dime collected sent a quart of milk overseas to British children.

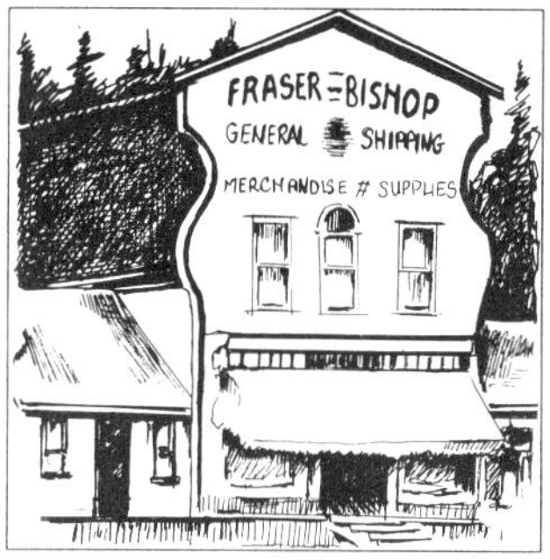

COMMERCE

GENERAL STORES

Probably the first trader at the Bay was Jack Hart, who owned a store at Comox where the Hudson Bay Post was built. He loaded a canoe with goods, including alcohol, and paddled to the "point" to trade with the Indians living there. The land, now known as the coal hills, was named Jack Hart Point.

In 1893 George Howe built the Nelson Hotel. The 18' by 22' room designated for billiards was first used as a general store for several years, until the little store was built in front of the hotel on the beach.

The first manager of Howe's store was the genial William Brown, who opened the store and remained until 1896, when he left for Vancouver. Emerson Muschamp, from McPhee & Moore's store in Courtenay, took over for five years.

Jack Fraser arrived in the district about 1891, and soon after started working for Mr. Howe. In 1898 the Yukon Gold Rush beckoned, and Jack left to seek his fortune. About 1899 George Howe's nephew, William Harwood, emigrated from England to work as a clerk. William's brother, George, came in 1907 to work on his uncle's farm on Hornby.

Three years after he left, Mr. Fraser returned, and Mr. Howe was happy to have him back in his employ. Possibly Jack used money he made in the Yukon to buy into the firm and become a partner. By 1906 the business was listed as Howe and Fraser.

M. Peters

George Howe's first store was built on the beach in front of the Nelson Hotel

Jack Fraser took over the responsiblity of managing the store and he became a very popular leader in the community. Beneath his gruff exterior was a warmth and understanding for everyone he met.

"Mr. Fraser used to say to us kids, 'Your mother should have drowned you when you were born'."

Margaret (Harwood) Bowden

"They had a root house near the store. One day Jack Roe and I sneaked in there and stole an apple. Gertie caught me; she was on our verandah looking down, so she marched me right over to Jack Fraser. He said 'What are we going to do with him? I know, you bake a nice big apple pie with that apple and don't give him any'."

Wilf Glover

The little store had everything from soup to nuts. Both Mr. Howe and Mr. Fraser built up the ship chandlery business and had a respected reputation on the waterfront in B.C. Because they regularly supplied the ships which coaled at the colliery wharf, their stock was very large for such a small town. Adolf Anderson rowed the huge flat-bottom skiff that brought supplies in from the mail boat and landed at a platform made of big boulders on the beach in front of the store. Goods purchased by the freighters were delivered the same way. The occasional side of beef slipped into the saltchuck when attempts were made to transfer the food between two boats riding the big swells in a stormy sea.

Because of the constant flow of ships from far-off places, citizens of the Bay enjoyed lemons, limes, oranges and bananas from time to time. Bananas arrived in crates padded with straw. Still on the stalks, they were hung from hooks and customers cut off bunches with a curved banana knife. The Australian ships brought exotic fruits such as pineapples, coconuts and pomegranates.

"I can remember trading detective magazines for coconuts with the crews on the ships."

Gordon Murdock

All the customers of the store carried an account, charging everything until they paid their bill at the end of the month. In the very early days of the store, all the housewives had little black books in which the store clerk listed the cost of items bought.

"When Mother went to the store she had a little black book and they wrote down what you got:

Overalls - 50¢, Soup Bone - 10¢, Slate - 15¢, Baking Powder - 50¢. Everyone was honest, they totalled it up at the end of the month and you paid your bill."

Mary (McKay) Winterburn

Month's end, when accounts were settled, was made special by Mr. Fraser's gift of a bag of goodies to each customer.

"When we paid our bill Mr. Fraser gave us a "gin-up". That's what we called it, a big bag of fruit and candy."

Ethel (Campbell) Glover

If the bill could not be paid, the month's total was "brought over" to the next month and added on. Mr. Fraser was a very benevolent man, and many a family was kept going through his generosity.When the mines or logging camps shut down, in the days before welfare or unemployment insurance, the bread winner had nowhere to turn and the family was at the mercy of the local store owner. In Union Bay people were lucky!

"It was the time of the Depression, and a family came up from Fanny Bay with a car full of kids, and wanted to charge something up. Of course, lots of these people, whenever they had money, would go up and get it cheaper at the Overwaitea in Courtenay. This time they were short and the fellow said, 'You wouldn't want to see these kids starve to death, would you?' Jack Fraser slowly walked all around the car and he came back and he says, 'Well, I don't see one of them that looks like me'. I think they got the credit anyway.

"One time he showed me two cigar boxes full of bad cheques. He helped a lot of people."

Bill Marshall

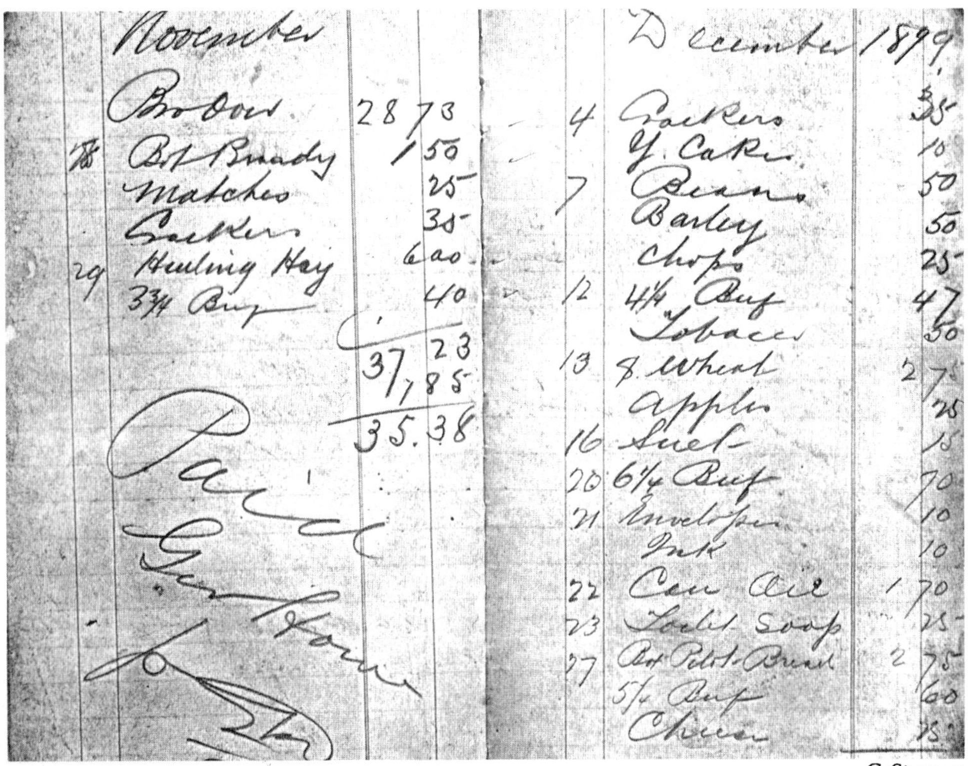

C. Stevens

A page from Ellen McKay's little black book

About 1905 Howe and Fraser built a new store, across McLeod Road from their hotel. The firm of Neil & McLeod built the 40' x 120' structure. It was a grand building with two stories and a tall facade front.

"When they took the store down there were no splices, 24' of this and 48' of that. The ceiling joists were 3" x 12" x 40'. No knots, everything was first class."

Ken Peters

In 1907 Mr. Howe retired to his farm on Hornby Island and sold his interest in the firm to Mr. Charles Bishop of Victoria. Jack Fraser was now the senior partner in the firm of Fraser and Bishop. Mr. Bishop, a natty dresser, was described by some as a "cranky rich gentleman". His wife, whose family it was rumoured owned half of Victoria, was well liked in the community. They had two children, a boy and a girl. Shortly after they arrived, the firm built two pre-fab "Aladdin Homes" just north of the store. They were handsome houses, with coloured glass framing the windows. The Bishop family settled into one, Mr. and Mrs. Kettle in the other.

On the south end of the new store, a room jutted out which was the town's first post office, with real mail boxes and its own entrance. Later, in 1913, the present post office was built and the old one became the store's office. A safe was installed, as well as bars on the windows. Several men and women were employed as accountants during the early years: Miss Gilligan, J. O'Rourke, F. Nicol, C.E. Armbrister and Miss Arrow. In 1924 Laura Little, whose husband had died in 1913, moved to Union Bay from Cumberland where she had worked as a bookkeeper for Simon Leiser. Every week, Mrs. Little would take her order book and walk round the village, taking orders from the housewives. The next day her son-in-law, George Harwood, or Alf Horne delivered the groceries in the delivery truck.

G. Francklyn

The large Fraser and Bishop store built about 1905

There were three long aisles between counters neatly arranged with merchandise. To the left of the entrance was the office, in front of which stood the serving counter with the cash register and scales. On the right wall was the door to the butcher shop, far at the back was a door to upstairs.

Situated on the Island Highway, adjacent to the wharf and with easy access to the back from the E&N tracks, the store was a favourite target for robbers. Over the years there were many break-ins, the most famous being the Flying Dutchman episode. However, none of the thieves ever got into the safe; instead they took goods, food and clothes.

All the meats, vegetables and dairy products were supplied by the beautiful farm which was tended by Hungo, the Chinese gardener. In the summer there was a bountiful crop to choose from, but in winter the only vegetables available were those that could be stored in the large root house: potatoes, beets, turnips and carrots.

"That dreadful vegetable rack just inside Fraser and Horne's store. In summer it would be full of produce, but by March, since nothing was imported, there'd be a couple of saddened turnips, miserable carrots, and soft potatoes. When the first tomatoes came from Hornby, we hadn't seen any for months, so it was pretty exciting. But the vegetable rack looked so sad in winter I used to wonder why they didn't take it away."

Margaret (Harwood) Bowden

Jack Fraser at far right with the Charlie Bishop family and friends

M. Peters

A. Watson M. Peters

Left: Gordon Horne beside the store's delivery truck. Right: Laura Little, bookkeeper, standing beside the cash register at Fraser and Horne's store

P. Dougherty

The Horne family Alf, Madeline and Pauline on the top step. Gordon with Duke and Dorothy McColgan. Donald, Margaret and Gladys McColgan stand on either side

In June 1917 Charles Bishop sold his interests to Alfred Horne, and the firm became "Fraser and Horne". Mr. Bishop and family left for Nova Scotia, and later "wintered" in California. For many years the family returned to holiday at the hotel.

Alf was born in Nanaimo in 1880 to Mr. Horne of the blacksmith firm, Horne and Renwick. He came first to Cumberland, and in 1905 he moved to Union Bay where he continued working as a blacksmith until 1913. At that time he took over the Wilson Hotel, which he owned and managed until the opportunity came to buy the interests of Mr. Bishop. Mr. Horne married the beautiful widow, Madeline, who had a little boy, Gordon. A daughter, Pauline, was born to the couple.

Jack Fraser and Alf Horne worked as a perfect team for eighteen years. Although Mr. Horne was of a retiring disposition, like Mr. Fraser he was very kind and charitable in all his dealings, helping many people in need. The store over the years was well-run, well-kept, and well-stocked.

Mr. Horne was a quiet man with a good sense of humour, who enjoyed the daily interaction with the public he served. He loved children and always gave them a treat, often to the chagrin of the mothers.

"Fanny and I would scrub the kids, dress them up and walk down to the store. Mr. Horne, with a twinkle in his eye, would pick the little ones up and set them on the counter and give them a chocolate eclair in their hot little hands. Pretty soon there was chocolate everywhere, on hands, faces, clothes. What a mess! It made us so mad, but what could you say? The kids and Mr. Horne were happy."

Winnie (Bowden) Glover

Some forty years after first coming to Union Bay, Mr. Fraser's health began to fail. He took a trip to his home in Bruce County, and soon after his return had a heart attack, followed by surgery at the Jubilee Hospital in Victoria. Although he recovered sufficiently to come home to his beloved Union Bay, he never worked again and died in November 1935.

Mr. Horne was left sole owner of the store, but only for a short time. One day in June 1937,

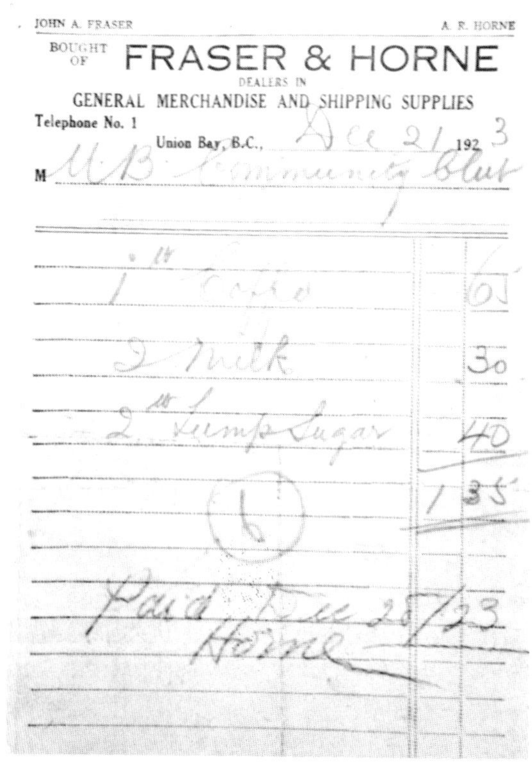

JOHN A. FRASER A. R. HORNE

BOUGHT OF FRASER & HORNE

DEALERS IN

GENERAL MERCHANDISE AND SHIPPING SUPPLIES

Telephone No. 1

Union Bay, B.C., Dec 21 1923

M U B Community Club

1 [illegible]	65
2 Milk	30
2 lb Lump Sugar	40
	1 35

Paid Dec 28/23 Horne

A familiar bill to anyone who lived in Union Bay

A. Kolzig

The new Fraser and Horne food market opened in 1948

M. Peters

Proud owners Madeline and Gordon Horne stand with Myrtle McKay behind the produce counter of the new store

A. Kolzig

Eager shoppers look over the display racks at the newly-opened store

Alf was delivering groceries on Shillito's Hill when he was seen by Nurse Reid and Mrs. Chilton to slump over the wheel. They immediately gave him first aid, but to no avail. It was a great shock to the family and community to lose such a highly esteemed man, at the young age of fifty-seven.

Mrs. Horne proved to be a very capable business woman, so she and son Gordon, with the invaluable help of Mrs. Little and George Harwood, carried on the family business. In 1948 they built a modern food market next to the old jail, so they sold the old store and stock to Sydney Ryall, who employed Edna Peters as clerk. After three years Edna bought him out, and the old building continued to serve the people of Union Bay for another ten years. Edna not only sold hardware, clothes and knick-knacks but also gave sympathy, counselling, and a cup of tea to all who needed it.

In 1954 Mrs. Horne retired from the grocery store to live near her daughter in California, and Gordon carried on the family business.

Simon Leiser, a well-known businessman from Victoria, operated what in those days was known as a "mammoth department store" at Cumberland. At Union Wharf, in 1895, he built a store at the north end of town, near the Union Coal Company. The first manager of the store was Mr. A. Lindsay, followed in a year by Brigham Brown. It was a general store, serving the many single men who lived in the boarding house.

Simon Leiser closed his store after about ten years of service. At this time the Union Bay Co-operative Society was formed and used the same building. Shares in the company were sold, 25 for $100. The members enjoyed special benefits and were supposed to share in the profits. David Haggart was very instumental in the Co-op's early success. C.M. Waggett was the first manager, followed by Frank Partridge in1909.

1912 FEBRUARY ➾ "Union Bay Co-operative Store" Mr. Frank Partridge, Mg. This house has been established three years and enjoys a splendid trade and reputation. They deal in staples and fancy groceries, dry goods, fresh and salt meats, farm products, etc. The house is under management of F. Partridge, who has officiated at a store for twenty-three years, twelve years in Cumberland and eight years in a large store in London, England. [4]

At the time of the flood in 1912 the Partridge family was living in the boarding house. It was badly undermined as was the Co-op, where some of the stock was destroyed by water. However, the share holders were not to be daunted, so they rallied round and moved to the annex attached to Humphrey's Hotel.

In the beginning the large annex was used as a dance hall until the Co-op needed it. By April 1912 they were advertising their stock-taking sale.

50 Barrels of Best "Hungarian"
Bread Flour - $7 a barrel.
75 Boxes of Winter Apples - $2 a box.

After a valiant fight to keep going, the Co-op went under in 1914. Mr. Partridge remained at the Bay and went into partnership with Fred Dale in the same building. This partnership lasted until January 1920, when Mr. Broder bought out Mr. Partridge, who moved to Cumberland and bought a clothing store.

M. Vowels

Simon Leiser's general store beside the boarding house which was across from where the Home garage stands today

The partnership of Dale and Broder lasted until the big fire in 1922 which destroyed their store, the hotel, George Smart's butcher shop, the Medical Dispensary and Hudson's house. After the fire there was a scramble to build new stores. The Wilson sisters built a 14' x 20' store on their property where the hotel had stood. George Smart built on the spot where the Medical Dispensary was. Mr. Dale took the butcher, John Reid, in as a partner and together they built a new store.

1922 MAY ➾ Dale and Reid's store will have a complete line of groceries and dry goods, and is ready for stock. The two very enterprising gentlemen gave a free dance in their new building on Friday with the local orchestra. [7]

Businesses came and went, but nobody made much money, so often fires mysteriously destroyed the shops.

"We built a butcher shop right where the hotel is and it burned down with the Wilson Hotel. Then we sold our house to Smart and it went up in smoke, then Smart moved to Courtenay."

Wilf Bowden

V. Hudson

Good friends Mrs. G. Booth and Mrs. T. Hudson

Hudson's little home was burned with the hotel, as it sat on the adjacent lot. After the fire, Tom Hudson built a lovely cottage for his family. In 1924 Mr. Hudson died, so Mrs. Hudson opened a small confectionery in a rented store nearby. In the late '20s, son Reg moved the family home close to the highway and built a store on the front. Hudson's Grocery and Confectionery store was in business for the next forty years.

Mrs. Hudson, with help from son Reg, ran the little store until 1938 when she died. In the early '40s, Reg contracted tuberculosis and was sent to Tranquille to recover, so the store was rented to William and Clara Bowden. In 1942 Mr. Bowden built a modern butcher shop onto the north end of the store. When Mr. Bowden retired in 1950, Desmond Stewart and Fred Peters ran the business for five years until Mr. Hudson's health was restored, and he and wife Vi were once again behind the counters.

I. Fudge

Reg Hudson behind the counter of his Grocery and Confectionery store

As well as the stores run by white storekeepers, there were several stores in Chinatown. Charlie Mah June operated a large general store which catered to the Chinese, selling a large variety of foods imported from China. It also carried clothes and shoes. In the 1930's the June family built a new store on the north side of Chinatown, fairly close to Washer Creek bridge. By this time daughter Vera had finished school in Victoria, and she came home to run the store. After her dad died in 1944, Vera continued running the store and supported her mother and herself. Mah Fat, who was Mr. June's accountant, also owned a store which served the Chinese population as well as many whites.

In the beginning, for the most part, the citizens of Union Bay shopped at the stores in the town, but it was a treat to shop in a larger town or city. Before the turn of the century, people with money were able to travel on the *Cariboo Fly*, the *Isobel* or the *Dunsmuir* to Nanaimo. But the workers and their families had neither the money nor the need to travel that far. Even between Union Wharf and Cumberland there was very little travel, until the merchants of the mining town decided it would be good for business.

1907 MAY ➾ The growing impact of Union Bay has caught the eye of merchants in Cumberland. With the result that a free train trip to Cumberland on Saturday evening is now the privilege of Union Bay residents. The idea emanated from City Council, the first progressive idea in many moons. Bring people to Cumberland to spend their money and all parties will benefit. [4]

Here the shoppers had many more stores from which to choose: druggist, milliner, tailor, tobacconist, etc. It wasn't until much later, when there was a good road to Courtenay and people had their own cars, that it became the trading centre of the Comox Valley.

BUTCHER

A butcher in the early days was a busy man wearing many hats to provide meat for his customers. If he did not own a farm, he had to locate and buy the animals, then transport them to his shop. Usually this was done while the animal was alive, as it was easier and cheaper to walk a cow from Curran's farm in Fanny Bay than haul it home in a buggy. Behind every butcher shop was a slaughter house, where the animals were slaughtered, bled and skinned. This was not a job for the weak-bodied or faint-of-heart.

... George Howe ...
COMOX and UNION B.C.
Dealer in All Kinds of Meats, Vegetables, etc.,
Orders Filled on Short Notice.

The hours were long. The shop was open from 9:00 a.m. to 6:00 p.m. on weekdays, and 9:00 a.m. to 9:00 p.m. on Friday and Saturday. Sunday was a day of rest, but, more often than not, on this day the butcher did the many other jobs not done during shop hours.

Over the years Union Bay had many butchers to supply meat for the local people and the many ships that took on supplies at the docks. None of them had such fitting names as Mr. Slaughter of Courtenay, Mr. Hackworth of Parksville, or Mr. Hamburger of Cumberland. The butchers at the Bay were Bowden, Griffith, Harwood, Howe, Reid, Smart and Wilcock. One could usually tell a butcher by his hands, as inevitably he had at least one finger missing.

Game was the first meat sold. Until 1913 venison, geese and ducks could be seen hanging in the butcher shops. The wild meat was shot by professional hunters like Pete Anderson, who had been a commercial hunter in Missouri. After preempting land in Fanny Bay, he made his living, for a short time, shooting deer, ducks and geese. Another commercial hunter was Gilbert Francklyn, who lived at Henry Bay and hunted on Denman and the sandspit. Both hunters sold to the butcher at Fraser and Bishop. A brace of plucked and dressed brant sold for $1.50; venison sold for 5¢ a pound. By the time the coal company started operations in the Comox Valley, the farmers of Courtenay, Denman and Hornby were producing cattle, sheep and hogs. It was shipped on the hoof to Nanaimo, and to Union via Union Wharf.

1885 AUGUST ➾ The steamship *Robert Dunsmuir* made a special trip to Nanaimo this week with cattle for Nanaimo butcher shops. [2]

After George Howe came to the district in the 1880's, he opened a butcher shop in Comox. To supply his meat market, George used a large, flat-bottomed barge to transport animals from his ranch on Hornby. Sheep, about ten to a load, were herded live into the barge and rowed over to Comox. This was one of George Harwood's first jobs when he arrived in Comox to work for his uncle. While not an easy task on a calm day with docile animals, one can only imagine the increased perils in a rough sea.

The animals were led up the beach to a small corral next to the butcher shop, where they were kept and slaughtered as business demanded. In 1889 George increased his slaughter buildings at Comox, which placed him in a better position to satisfy increasing demands for meat. Next, he expanded his commercial outlets to Union and hired other butchers to work for him.

It was not until 1893 that Mr. Howe bought five lots below Union Wharf and erected a store and hotel. By 1895 he had a large ship's chandlery business established, including a butcher shop. In 1897 most meat, regardless of the type or cut, sold for about 10¢ to 12¢ a pound. You could buy 4 lb. of mutton stew meat for 50¢, a 6 lb. roast of beef for 75¢, or 8 lb. of bacon for $1.04.

Mr. Howe acquired a small steam tug and hired Jackson Arthur to transport animals from the farm to market. Besides his ranch on Hornby, Mr. Howe let his cattle run loose behind Union Bay, and in the Henry Bay logging slash on Denman. If the butcher shop needed more beef, Mr. Howe and Hungo went with a rifle and chain block to track down the nearly-wild animals. After they shot an animal, it was dragged to the beach and loaded into the boat and rowed home.

"Mr. Howe was lots of fun. He used to take us kids with him on his wagon up the back. He had cattle running wild behind Union Bay. He would shoot a cow and bring it and us back in the wagon."

Florence (Manson) McKay

V. Hudson

In between the Wilson Hotel and the annex, Dale and Partridge built their meat market. Hudson's house can also be seen. All these buildings burned in 1922

Often the large deep-sea ships would buy the animals live, in order to ensure fresh meat after weeks on the high seas. The ships plying local waters bought the meat slaughtered but whole. The skiff was brought into play, transporting the meat out to the boats to be hauled up the sides onto the deck.

"One time a skipper off one of the Greek boats stuck his head in the door and said, '200 pork chops', and disappeared. George started sputtering away, 'Where in the so and so do you think a guy is going to find 200 pork chops?' Another time a ship wanted twelve live sheep. Gordon Horne and I were in on the act. It was quite a job to catch them and load them into a pick-up truck. We tied their legs and got them into the ship. They wanted to have fresh meat."

Harold Peters

"We deliver any Joint, any Cut, any Weight!" The sign in the butcher shop window proved true when, in January 1894, a big hog weighing 577 1/2 pounds was sold to a Whaleback ship at Union Wharf.

A huge strong man, George Howe, with help from the equally strong Hungo, did all the slaughtering and butchering for his shop. Behind the store stood the barn, and further back, nearer the track, was the slaughter house. Animals brought from the ranch or bought from a nearby farmer were slaughtered here. Many a young child went to investigate the loud squealing noises coming from the slaughter house. To their horror they saw a cow or pig suspended by one leg, while the butcher drove a wedge into its head with a hammer. Before lowering it down, the blood was let and the animal skinned. The job did not end there, for the skins had to be salted and stored in preparation for being sold to a tannery.

When Mr. Howe retired, neither Mr. Fraser nor Mr. Bishop were butchers so one had to be hired - first Arthur Blaney, then John Reid. A dapper Englishman, Paul Griffith, next took over the butcher shop. He wore puffy riding breeches above leather leggings which he kept highly polished. Over all was the huge white butcher's apron.

The Union Bay Co-operative also sold meat. In the evening, after George Davis finished work at the weigh station, he cut up meat for the Co-op. When it closed in 1916 Frank Partridge was the manager. He and Fred Dale opened a new butcher shop next to the Wilson Hotel and hired William Bowden from Quesnell's Butcher Shop in Nanaimo. At the age of ten Mr. Bowden had started his career in a slaughter house in County Durham. He learned early to drink and enjoy a cup of warm blood when the cow's throat was slit. Bill was rare among the butchers of the day, for at the end of his career he still had all ten fingers.

The 1920's saw a spate of butcher shops come and go around the Wilson Hotel. They were built, sold, burned down, and built again. After the Wilson

M. Coe

Bill Bowden in his butcher coat

Hotel burned down, taking the store with it, Butcher Bowden went to work for Fraser and Horne. He replaced George Smart who had been working at the big store for several years. Mr. Smart bought Bowden's house on the beach and turned it into a butcher shop.

In 1921 George Harwood, who had worked for several years on the Howe farm, returned to Union Bay to work for Mr. Fraser. George married Helen Little, a school teacher from Hornby, and they first lived in the "glass house." The couple had three daughters. Mr. Harwood worked closely with Mr. Bowden and learned the butchering business. It was here, in 1922, that he lost his fingers to the meat grinder. The electric machine sat on the counter with a big bucket under it to catch the ground round. George had a large tray of cut up meat. He filled the grinder and was pushing down the pieces of meat with his left hand when three of his fingers were caught in the gears and severed at the second joint. It was Bill Bowden's job to retrieve the fingers out of the meat grinder and discard the hamburger for that day.

Although an extremely painful accident, George's misfortunes were far from over. A car was soon commandeered to take Mr. Harwood to Comox hospital. In those days automobiles were unreliable, and in January the roads were in poor repair. The car broke down opposite the Royston school, two of the wheel spokes and rim coming right off. Mr. Edwards of Royston came to the rescue and transferred the injured man to his car. As they approached Happy Valley turn-off, Mr. Edward's car broke down. Here they waited until another motorist chanced along and willingly took the nearly unconscious Mr. Harwood to the hospital. Almost twelve hours had elapsed when the doctor finally sewed up his hand. Back home in Union Bay, infection set in and George suffered greatly with it. In time the hand healed, and he became very adept with just two fingers. For years after, customers marvelled at the neat way he tied up meat packages and broke the string with his little finger.

Mr. Harwood was very active in the church and often played Santa at the Christmas concert. To the unbelievers intent on identifying Santa, the glove with three limp fingers was a dead giveaway.

In 1929 William Bowden left Fraser and Horne, and butchered in Cumberland, Courtenay and Deep Bay. George Harwood took over and became the main butcher for the big store until he retired. Mr. Bowden moved back from Deep Bay in 1942 and built a butcher shop onto Hudson's store, which he operated until he retired in 1950. The families were united in 1937 when Mr. Bowden's only son, Wilfred, married Mr. Harwood's oldest daughter, Margaret.

Both men's butcher shops were kept scrupulously clean. The floor behind the counter was spread with fresh sawdust every day. A rake rested in the corner to keep the sawdust spread evenly. In the middle of the floor stood two butcher blocks, huge fir rounds mounted on four-legged stools. Hanging from nails in the blocks were knives of various shapes and sizes, and a long steel which the butcher used to hone his knives razor-sharp.

Several stout beams with "S" hooks hanging from them crossed the shop about 6' from the floor. Beef, mutton and pork carcasses hung from the hooks when not in the cooler. They also served as hangers for saws and cleavers needed to cut through bones.

When a customer came in and asked for a particular cut, the heavy carcass was lifted down to the butcher block and the desired piece cut off. Roasts were tied securely with cord that hung from a wire basket above the counter. The purchase was then wrapped in waxed butcher paper and tied up with more string.

With the customer attended to, the butcher took a large brush with long stiff bristles and scrubbed back and forth over the block to clean it. In time, the block became quite worn down.

In Fraser and Horne's butcher shop, an ammonia compressor-type freezer was installed which was run by a gas engine. This made tapered blocks of ice which were used in the hotel icebox and the large walk-in cooler at the butcher shop.

Inside the thickly insulated cooler were more hooks attached to beams on which hung the carcasses. Slatted shelves on the walls held white enamel trays containing the innards: heart, liver, kidney, tongue, sweet bread and tripe. These cheap and tasty cuts were popular with the customers.

Stew meat and ground round, the only cuts prepared ahead, were stored in the cooler. The butchers cured bacon, ham and corned beef, which stood in crocks on the cooler floor. Possibly a bowl of sausage skins were softening in water, ready to make sausages.

In the 1930's cured meats could be purchased from the large slaughterhouses in Vancouver, but before this each butcher made his own. They secretively guarded their recipes. Mr. Harwood was known far and wide for his sausages with just the right blend of spices. Mr. Bowden was just as renowned for his delicious corned beef.

The shop was always cold, as little heat was used. The butcher often wore longjohns under layers of shirts and sweaters neatly tucked under the huge white apron. A small stove was used to heat water and warm freezing hands, but the fuel was used sparingly so that the room did not become warm.

Butter, cheese and Fleishman's yeast were sold from the fridge in the butcher shop. Each tiny yeast cake was wrapped in foil and dated. If the date had expired, the butcher took it home and his wife used it in her baking, or the children ate it for a treat.

Butter, often arriving on boats from New Zealand, came in a block wrapped in wax paper and placed into a heavily waxed wooden box with dovetailed corners. The butcher needed a large knife and a good eye to cut the block into perfect one pound pieces. Some of the larger families bought whole boxes and cut it themselves. Later, the famous Comox Creamery butter came already cut and neatly wrapped into pounds.

Cheddar cheese came in big rounds and stood on a rotating table with a big knife that came down and cut a wedge of one or two pounds. With a practiced eye, the experienced butcher was within a tenth of an ounce when the piece was weighed on the large beam scales.

Many butchers' wives assisted them in several ways. All the extra fat was saved and taken home, where the wife melted it down in a large pan. Next, she painstakingly strained out the impurities through several thicknesses of cheesecloth. The fat was poured into two or three pound loaf tins where it hardened and then was taken back to the butcher shop to be sold as lard. As it was cheaper than butter, most housewives baked with lard, turning out flaky pastry and delicious cakes and cookies.

Jellied veal and head cheese, the original cold cuts, were also made by the butcher's wife. Pigs heads were boiled, then the meat removed and finely cut up. It was then seasoned and packed into a loaf pan where it set in its own jelly, and when turned out could be sliced.

Christmas was a very busy time for the butcher. More than one hundred turkeys hung from nails on every available spaces along the walls, over the counter and in front of the windows. Each bird had its feathers plucked off and head tucked neatly into a paper bag. When a bird sold, the innards had to be cleaned out, feet cut off and tendons pulled out. This was repeated so many times at Christmas and New Years that the butcher's hands became red and swollen.

Until the 1920's all turkeys came from Alberta on the railroad. If there were snowslides in the Rockies, the trains would be held up.

J. Anderson

Hilda Anderson at the entrance to her confectionery which was situated on the beach across from the school

As they contemplated Christmas dinner without a "big tom", people avidly followed the newspaper reports on the progress of the "turkey train".

1906 DECEMBER ➺ Gloom fell on the Comox District turkey fiends when it was learned that the shipment of turkeys got snowed up in the Rockies, and there would be no birds for Christmas. Later news that the tracks had been cleared and the train had arrived in Vancouver has come true. The announcement that the turkeys will soon be arriving at Union Wharf was greeted with joy. [4]

Later, the big birds were purchased locally from Mr. Smith and Mr. Gunter, two long-time turkey farmers in the valley.

CONFECTIONERY

The Cook family lived three doors north of the post office. Nelson was a carpenter, and he later built for his family a little house on the beach, south of the wharf. Steady work was hard to come by so his wife, Dora, baked tasty breads and buns for sale. Nelson kept cows, and from the beautiful rich cream made the town's first ice cream. By cutting big blocks of ice from a frozen lake or pond and storing them under sawdust, ice could be kept into summer. About 1909 the Pilsener Beer Co. installed an ice manufacturing machine at Cumberland, so ice was available. Mr. Cook built a little roadside stand from which the family sold ice cream and baked goods.

The first confectionery store in Union Bay, which was strategically placed across from the school was built by Hilda Anderson. The Anderson family had moved from Fanny Bay, and in 1903 Hilda became a naturalized Canadian, but she could not read or write English. This did not stop her from being a very good businesswoman with a shrewd eye for figures. The tiny lady was always immaculately dressed in a long black dress, covered with a beautifully embroidered white apron. On her petite feet were shiny, black button boots.

The confectionery was well stocked with peppermint candies, strawberry and wintergreen sticks, toffees, chocolates and chewing gum, all displayed in tall glass bottles. Pity the small child with a penny to spend, confronted with such a selection. Mrs. Anderson proudly declared in her Swedish accent that she sold "yiclets, yocolates and yewing gum". She was

J. Anderson

Mrs. Anderson and friend on the verandah of her second confectionery store built next to Hudson's house

W. Glover

Mrs. Bowden made the ice cream she sold in her ice cream parlour. Back: Louise and Wilf Bowden, Donna Hudson. Front: Jessie Marshall, Leona Turner

J. Anderson

Hilda Anderson posing (she couldn't drive) in the "Ford coupalay with babaloon tires" that she bought for son Andy

known to everyone as "Mrs. Yee Whiz", this being her favourite expression. The shop was often full of men off the ships, and she would become excited in all the confusion.

"One day a sailor handed her a $20 bill to pay for a 5¢ chocolate bar. Bill McCartney, who worked in the bank, could see her nervousness and offered to help her make change. 'Oh yee whiz!' she said, 'You couldn't even change your own pants, let alone change $20."

Elizabeth (Walker) Renwick

The coffee she made for movie nights and sold in her store is well remembered. She bought select coffee beans, roasted them in her oven, then ground them and brewed exquisite aromatic coffee. To go with the coffee, she baked cinnamon buns and coffee cakes.

"My grandma was a wonderful baker and made wonderful coffee. Swedish people always put the cube sugar in their mouth and drank the coffee through it. My grandpa let me do that. We never drank tea."

Hilda (Anderson) Cullen

As well as selling candies, sandwiches, baking, Almond's ice cream, and tobacco, Mrs. Anderson kept punch boards. The punch board was about 8"x10"x1/2" thick. It was full of little holes covered with a piece of paper which numbered each hole. In each hole was a tiny piece of paper with a number on it, which corresponded to an index of prizes.

"For five, ten or twenty-five cents depending on the board, you'd take a small wire pin and shove it in a hole. Out would come a little roll of paper with a number on it. If you matched the right number you won. Maybe a trinket, a kewpie doll or a big box of chocolates."

Jack Anderson

"Quite a few Swedish boats came in. I had long blond hair, and the sailors and officers would treat us kids at Anderson's candy store. I went home loaded with baskets of chocolates won through the punch board. They'd pay for it and ask me to punch out the number. I kept what I won."

Clara (Cave) Ridgway

Mrs. Anderson's oldest son, Ed, with wife Jean (Miller) and family of three, moved from Comox Lake and took over the house and store in the 1920's. Mrs. Anderson built herself a lovely home on Station Road. She was a very progressive lady and owned one of the first gramophones in town. It sat in a heavy wooden box, boasted a huge silver speaker and played cylinder records. Another first was her player piano.

"The first thing I remember about my Granny was when I came down to live with her. I actually hated it because I had to make my bed every morning, practice the piano for half an hour, and eat a big bowl of porridge which I detested."

Hilda (Anderson) Cullen

"Mrs. Anderson bought a 'Ford coupalay with babaloon tires' for Andy."

Bill McKay

In 1925 Mrs. Anderson took a trip back home to Sweden. When she came back to Union Bay, she sold her home on Station Road to Wes Peters who had just married Ina Walker. She enjoyed serving the public so built herself another store, with living accommodation at the back. This was situated next to the Hudson home. As well as confections she also sold "hot tamales", a Mexican dish made of corn meal and chicken, seasoned with hot red peppers, wrapped in corn husks and then steamed. They were delivered to her from the Oasis Restaurant in Nanaimo.

The headstrong little Swedish lady who had endeared herself to everyone, died in 1930. The new store was sold and became a barber shop.

When Butcher Bowden moved to town with his wife, Clara, and four children, he built a little house and ice cream parlour on the beach, opposite the Wilson Hotel. The jersey cow which provided the cream was tethered on a rope out back. Mrs. Bowden made her own ice cream. Into the large wooden stave barrel went the ice chips and rock salt, then a five gallon metal pail fit into the ice. Thick cream, sugar and vanilla were poured in and the kids took turns cranking the handle until the ice cream froze.

W. Glover

The Bowden family. Left to right: Clara Bowden holding Mildred, Winnie, Emily, Bill Bowden, Louise, Wilf

It was a quaint little parlour with white washed walls and lace curtains in the windows. Bent cane parlour chairs surrounded four tables. Cherry, pineapple, butterscotch, strawberry, and maple walnut sundaes, as well as banana splits, were served in heavy glass dishes.

Every Sunday during the summer months, Mrs. Bowden made a double batch of ice cream, put it on ice, and loaded it and the kids onto the little delivery truck. Jack Bradley drove them to Royston beach where they were greeted eagerly by the Cumberland people holidaying in their beach cottages. The children anxiously lined up to buy 5¢ cones.

Five years later, the Bowdens built a home on the hill north of Washer Creek. Mildred was born and the little shop was closed. About this time, the Wilson sisters were back in town, and Agnes and Jenny had a small confectionery for a few years.

In the 1930's Nell Hudson, whose husband Tom had died, rented some space near her home and opened a little store. Soon, son Reg moved the family home closer to the highway and made the front parlour into a general store and confectionery. It had four stools at the ice cream bar in front of the freezer which could hold four different flavours of Palm Dairy ice cream. Here one could buy a cone, or a "slider".

"The store bought the wafers and had a slider machine that cut the ice cream. It was like an ice cream scoop but square. You pushed it into the ice cream and when you let the lever go it pushed the ice cream out onto the crisp wafer. Boy, were they good!"

Mildred (Bowden) Coe

Ice cream to take home as a special treat could be purchased in pint or quart size waxed cardboard boxes. They were filled with scoops of ice cream, then the lid flaps were tucked down. A little later, the creameries made "ice cream bricks" of vanilla, strawberry and Neopolitan.

"I-lik-it" bars, chocolate-covered ice cream on a stick, were very popular. Made by Comox Creamery, the bars came wrapped in a paper cover with one letter of the title on it. The wrappers were saved until the word "I-lik-it" was spelled and turned in for a pint of ice cream.

M. Vowels

Art and Jessie Hastings' "Autograph Coffee Bar" built next to the school about 1948

Mrs. Hudson bought a milkshake machine and whipped up frothy milkshakes made with ice cream, milk, and vanilla, strawberry, butterscotch or chocolate syrup. Pop, sold only in 8 oz. bottles, was drunk from the bottle with waxed paper straws. A favourite were "floats" made with a scoop of ice cream floating in a tall glass of Hire's Root Beer, Coca Cola, or Rummings Orange pop.

In 1938 Mrs.Hudson died, and son Reg and his wife Vi operated the store. (see stores)

After operating the old confectionery for a short time, the Anderson's closed off the cafe and used that space for a boat repair shop. In the 1940's Art and Jessie Hastings bought the business. They reopened the tearoom until the building had to be moved for road construction. The old house was moved across the highway.

A. Graham

Alma Muschamp opened her coffee shop in the old butcher shop of Fraser and Horne's store. Betty Jane Peters waited tables for her cousin

V. Hudson

Vi Hudson who, with husband Reg, operated the store

They built a new garage with an adjoining cafe, the "Autograph", next to the school fence. Jessie sold light lunches and kept busy selling candies, pop and ice cream to the school kids. The cafe was later closed to provide more space for repairing cars.

When the Hornes moved into the new food store, the butcher shop on the end of the old store stood vacant. Alma Muschamp rented the space and with a few renovations - fresh paint, installation of a soda fountain and tables and chairs - opened a cafe. "Alma's" was a gathering place for the young and old from 1947 to '51. Everyone enjoyed the hearty sandwiches and delicious pies, fresh from the oven.

BAKER

In the early days women baked their own bread. White flour was mainly used, as the whole grain breads were thought of as a poor man's food. In 1917 a "49er" of flour cost $3.70. The heavy cotton sack was a bonus with many uses. Twice a week, six or seven big square loaves, made of white flour and risen with Royal yeast cakes, were baked to feed the hungry family. The standard dessert for dinner was thick slices of warm bread slathered with butter and homemade blackberry jam. Two pieces put together was usual fare in the children's and husband's lunch pails. The stores did not carry bread but sold Pilot bread, a dried biscuit much like a very thick soda cracker. A 50 lb. box of pilot bread cost $2.75.

By 1895 there were three bakeries in Cumberland. Fifteen loaves sold for a dollar. Soon a Scotchman named Halliday travelled to Union Bay by horse and wagon to peddle his bread. His bakeshop later became Auchterlonie's.

About 1912 Mrs. J. Cook's brother, John Kennard, with his family, moved to Union Bay. He built a house in the middle of town and from it he and his wife sold baked goods and meals.

"Mrs. Kennard used to make bread and sell the most wonderful light loaves of bread and sweet buns. They just puffed up."

Nellie King

M. Shillito

Annie Macartney, who married Joe Hastings, with her wedding cake made and decorated by Mac McCullock

Alex McCullock came to Union Bay around 1912. When war broke out he signed up and went back to Europe, fighting in France where he was injured. Returning home with a war pension, he bought the little house that had been the first bank. In the "old country" Mac had trained as a baker but he never had a shop at the Bay. However, he used to make beautifully decorated wedding cakes for all the brides.

By 1918 McBride's Bakery in Courtenay was bringing bread down and selling it at Mrs. Anderson's. Then, for a short time Rosie Leithead, Mrs. Anderson's daughter, sold her home-baking from her mother's store.

Later on, Auchterlonie's brought bread to Union Bay, delivering it door to door and selling it through the stores. Don the Baker, with his cheery disposition, was a very popular delivery boy. The children eagerly awaited his arrival, for often the bread would still be warm when he placed it unwrapped on the hall table. It was great fun to bite the corners off the fresh loaves before Mother got them into the bread box.

CATALOGUE SHOPPING

It was a matter of pride with many of the settlers that they shopped locally and supported the local stores, thereby keeping the money in the community and providing jobs.

"My Dad believed if you lived in a company town you supported the town and bought things at the stores. So Mom always shopped at Fraser and Bishops. During the strike and hard times Mr. Fraser kept a lot of people. So later, when people sent out to Vancouver for their groceries, Dad never would. I admired him for that."

Nettie (Marshall) Jones

1906 ➻ Try to buy goods locally as businessmen don't like people who send to Eatons. [4]

Some people did send out for groceries, while others made up an order a few times a year to buy special things that were not available at Union Bay stores. To obtain a cheaper freight rate, several families would go together to make one big order. An order might include crates of oranges, a bunch of bananas still on the stalk, rounds of cheese, 100 lb. sacks of flour or sugar, and canned goods by the case.

For the early pioneers there were catalogues put out by Timothy Eaton, Robert Simpson and Christie Grant. By the end of the nineteenth century, David Spencer of Victoria and Charles Woodward of Vancouver were also competing for the settlers' dollar by issuing two catalogues a year, Spring/Summer and Fall/Winter. Then, a couple of years before the first war, Woodwards issued a separate grocery list. These catalogues were sent out every three months to keep up with changing prices and seasonal merchandise.

The goods were shipped on the CPR or Union steamships that called once a week. Everything arrived in large wooden boxes that were unloaded off the ship onto the wharf.

"When the boat came in, everyone went down to get their goods with a wheelbarrow. If someone had ordered a crate of bananas, you'd snitch one."

Hector Hooper

Of course, the most fun were the catalogues themselves. To people who rarely if ever got to the city, it was a way of keeping abreast of the times, the changing fashions, new products

and the latest inventions. When they arrived, hours were spent poring over the contents.

Great lists were made of items that caught the fancy of each family member. Then, before the order was actually sent in, practicality caught up and all but the necessary items were struck from the list. Children hoped for a "surprise" package with each order. It cost $1.00 and contained an assortment of items: combs, ribbons, toys, etc.

Each edition sported a new cover, often just a different view of the department store. In the beginning, all the illustrations were done in line drawings. Then, after the 1900's, a few photos were used in the ladies' ready-to-wear departments. The next big change came during the First World War, when a few coloured photos were used.

Catalogues, which were thin at first and gradually became thicker, contained these departments: Clothing with boots, bonnets and long johns; Linens with blankets, towels and yard goods; Hardware with bird cages, tea strainers and screen doors; Furniture with wallpaper, linoleum and baby carriages; Stationery with fountain pens, visiting cards and bibles; Drugs and Patent Medicines with everything from Absorbine Jr. to Zam Buk ointment.

Soon a sports department was added, with

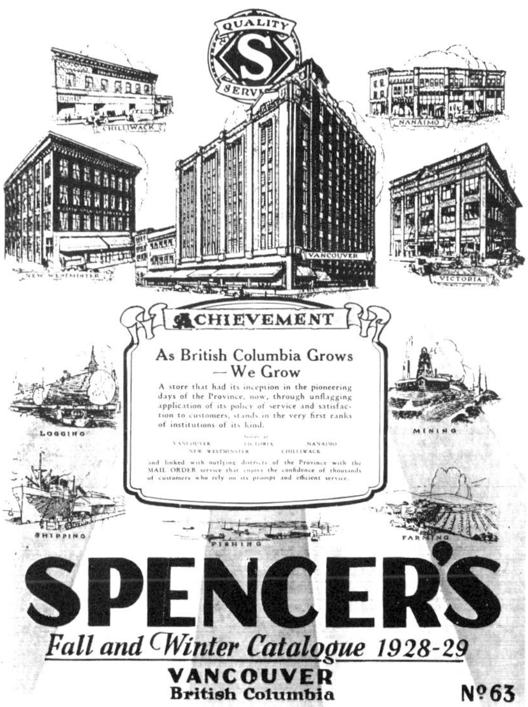

boxing gloves and playing cards, as well as a music section with all the latest hits in sheet music. Gramophones and cameras appeared in the war years, and in the 1920's radios were featured.

The British Columbia catalogues advertised special items peculiar to the needs of men working in the logging, mining and fishing industries. They also took into account the coastal weather and featured raincoats, capes, gumboots and rubbers, with a separate section for umbrellas. Every style was shown, from a girl's school umbrella for 50¢, to a black silk umbrella with a sterling handle for $9.25.

The "Personal Shopper" was popular with people wanting to give a special gift. The shopper simply sent a note stating the amount to be spent, with the age and sex of the recipient. An appropriate gift was mailed back. This service was well used at Christmas when the church ladies would send for presents for every member of the Sunday School.

Each catalogue contained an order form, and a replacement was included with every shipment. Money orders were used, as purchases had to be paid before delivery.

The approximate weight had to be estimated and money included for shipping. If too much money was sent, it was returned with the order. There was no charge for delivery to the freight dock or depot, nor any packaging costs.

Individual items less than 20 oz. were shipped by mail at 10¢ per pound. Packages up to 25 lb. went cheaper by express, and packages over 25 lb. went cheaper by freight, but were charged as a full 100. This encouraged people to fill out the 100 lb. with groceries, or combine their items with a friend's order.

Orders sent to Union Bay came by train to Vancouver, then by steamship up the coast. Later, the E&N brought freight up Island from Nanaimo. The price to Union Bay from Vancouver was 91¢ on 100 lb. By buying in large quantities and operating strictly in cash, the mail order houses were able to provide a large variety of items at very competitive prices. The careful shopper could check all the catalogues, Eatons in Winnipeg, Simpsons in Regina, and Woodwards and Spencers locally, for the best buy.

The mail order houses all promised careful, prompt delivery. Occasionally, problems did occur with the mail and freight companies which delayed orders.

"Gertie made a lot of our clothes and of course we used to send to Eatons. Gertie sent to Eatons for her wedding gown and it never came until after the wedding. But she had a very nice eyelet dress she'd made for her trousseau, so she was married in that. What a disappointment, but you couldn't put off the wedding."

Violet (Glover) Rutherford

TRAVELLING SALESMEN

The very first travelling salesman to come to Union Bay was Qualicum Tom. He lived in a log house at the mouth of the Little Qualicum River. There, he and his wife, Annie, tended an orchard which provided them with lots of apples, cherries, plums and pears. They always had something to trade or sell - if not fruit then smoked fish or a live chicken cackling in a crate. When the fish were spawning they would net large quantities of dogfish and render out the oil. The oil was sold to logging camps. It was used to grease the skids to make the logs slide as they were pulled to the beach.

Tom was a big man, well over 300 lb., with arms that reached down to his knees. Annie was a roly-poly. Whenever the couple felt the urge to "go on a toot" they loaded up the wagon and headed for Union Bay.

"You never saw any little kids when Qualicum Tom went by. We were all afraid of him and would crawl under the bed. Our parents used to say he had stolen a white boy, and he often had a blond boy with him. But I don't know why they said that because he never did anything bad and was kind to children."

Milla (Walker) McKay

Depicting Tom and Annie as evil could not have been further from the truth. They were gentle people who loved nothing better than to come to town for a visit. They stopped and talked to everyone, and Tom did like to talk, in a slow deliberate way. Annie sat patiently listening until she could bear it no longer and would lean across him and say, "Let me talk a while now, Tom." Annie particularly liked to stop at the post office to visit Mrs. Brown who could speak Chinook and made tea for her visitor.

They stopped with their produce at Fraser and Bishop's store and visited with everyone they saw. If Tom could not sell anything he always hoped to trade for some hooch.

"When they were leaving, Jack Fraser used to give me a bottle of whiskey and say, 'Put this in the back of the wagon'. So I'd go and put it in and Tom would say, 'I didn't see you put that in there'. A few yards down the road and out would come the whiskey, and they'd start celebrating."

Bob McKay

"He and Annie would be going down the road singing like sons-of-guns. One time the horse and wagon and Tom and Annie all went off the road and over the bank. Bob and I found them under their overturned wagon, happy as clams. We were delivering lumber with our team so we pulled them out."

Jim McKay

Sometimes, if the weather was poor, they stayed the night at the Muschamp farm. On the way home Tom always saved a drink for his friend, Alf Walker at Fanny Bay, who could also speak Chinook.

Occasionally the couple would get past Union Bay and make the slow trip to Cumberland or Courtenay. On one such trip the Qualicums stopped at McQuillan's livery stable to admire the latest in buggies. There, glistening and shining in all its beauty was the newest carriage, bought for and rented out to business men and young dandies. Tom couldn't resist it and rented the carriage to take Annie for a ride around town in style. Just then Cuddy Johnson, the influential owner of the Courtenay Hotel, came in and ordered the same buggy for a trip to Cumberland. Unimpressed, Bob McQuillan replied, "Sorry, first come, first served". Mr. Johnson, rather annoyed, had to settle for second best.

The door-to-door salesmen sold everything imaginable to the housewives of Union Bay. These men arrived like clockwork every month with their battered suitcases crammed full of the old tried-and-true favourites, as well as the newest inventions to save the housewife time, energy and money. Some travelled up and down the Island by car, in which they carried extra stock. Others moved from town to town on the E&N, staying at the local hotel while working the area. In the early days, they came by ship - the *Joan*, *Charmer* or *City of Nanaimo*.

The Watkins and Raleigh men arrived with a large variety of spices, flavourings, lotions and creams. And of course, who could do without the Fuller Brush man with his superior selection of brushes for every job: hair brushes, scrubbing brushes, vegetable brushes, paint brushes, nail brushes and toilet bowl brushes.

Then there were the independent fellows, who bought a suitcase, filled it with hundreds of items from a Five and Ten Cent store, and hit the road. These salesmen had a great knack for getting their foot or suitcase in the door, then mesmerizing the housewife with their fast patter.

"I remember one little skinny salesman. He coughed a lot and I'm sure had T.B. He called me Ma'am. Ma'am this and Ma'am that. Well, I felt sorry for him so I always bought something: shoe laces, thread or seam binding. One day in the '30s he came and I really didn't have much money. Out came everything and he gave me his sales pitch. When I said 'No' to everything, he quickly stuffed his goods back in the case, snarled 'Good day Ma'am', grabbed the handle and stomped out the door. When he turned down the back steps, his suitcase flew open and out tumbled all his wares. By this time he was in a rage, so I took pity on him and sent the twins out to help pick up the buttons, thread, bias tape, shoe laces, funnels, measuring cups, ribbons, toothbrushes, combs, hankies, egg timer, thumb tacks, pins, pot lid knobs, thimbles, etc. Then I decided that I really did need a new egg timer after all."

Winnie Glover

A Chinese gardener who had a beautiful farm in the Minto area peddled vegetables in the 1930's and '40s. He came door to door every week with a bountiful array of fresh vegetables, nicely displayed under a roof on the back of his pick-up truck.

Life insurance was sold door to door. The first insurance man remembered was Tommy Hudson who sold Sun Life Insurance. For years in the 1930's and '40s Fred Smith, who had been locomotive engineer for Jeremiahson

Logging, sold North American Life Insurance to his friends at the Bay. Also, the Metropolitan man knocked on the door every month to collect 50¢ which insured the life of the man-of-the-house.

BARBER

Barber Barber shave a pig,
How many hairs to make a wig?
Four and twenty that's enough,
Give the Barber a pinch of snuff.

At the end of the nineteenth century, haircuts were "two bits" and shaves were 15¢. It is debatable where the first barber shop was or the name of the barber. Some say it was in the Wilson House. A barber named Erin James had a little shop in a back room of the hotel. Others claim there was a barber who operated from a little shack on the beach, just south of Searle's house. He is remembered for his strange sleeping habits. Instead of sleeping in his shop he got his rest on planks under a big maple tree, because he had a back problem. Still others say it was Bert Miller, who lived with Tommy James. He had a little shop south of the Nelson Hotel. A friend of Bill Kelly's, he got mixed up in bootlegging and was being sought by the police. One night Tommy James spirited him away in his boat and Mr. Miller was never seen again.

Of course most families had a pair of scissors, enabling the women to cut their husbands' hair. Every three months the mother or father would set up a barber shop in the middle of the kitchen and cut all the boys hair. To reduce the number of barbering sessions, each summer the boys had their heads shaved, outdoors to save the sweeping up. For most of the boys it took till Christmas before it had grown enough for another cut.

"Come summer as soon as it was a little warm all the boys had their hair cut, right off, Yul Brynner style. I don't know if that was the standard in all families but it was in ours."

Margaret (Glover) Matthews

The most popular "tonsorial artist" in Union Bay was Jim Gunnis. He started off with a shop in the little building that had been the Royal Bank. Two beautiful barber poles with red and white spiral stripes flanked the doorway to the small shop. Business hours were from 8:30 a.m. until 9:00 p.m. every day except Wednesday afternoon and all legal holidays.

Inside was a large, black, leather barber chair, which Jim jerkily pumped up with his foot. On the back wall were two varnished wooden cupboards with glass doors, displaying shaving mugs, brushes, combs, a variety of straight razors (some with ivory handles) and a good selection of hair tonics. Off the cupboard near the chair hung the wide leather strop for sharpening the razor. It was like watching an artist preparing to create a masterpiece when Jim sharpened his favourite razor.

Most of the cutting was done with scissors, but the hand clippers were used to shape the back. They were a very efficient tool in the hands of an expert, as he squeezed the handle quickly back and forth. However, for the amateur's victim it could be a very painful business. If the clippers were taken away from the head before the teeth were completely disengaged, all the hair caught in them was pulled out. Some women, thinking they could save money and still give a professional look rather than the "bowl on the head" cut, sent to a mail-order house for a pair of clippers. One session, which often resulted in a family row, was enough to send most men back to the barber.

In the 1930's Jim the Barber moved and set up shop next to Hudson's store. Into the large front room, along with the barber chair, Jim brought in a beautiful pool table with plenty of chairs for onlookers.

"You didn't figure on a rushed job because if there was a pool game going on he'd leave you, and with scissors and comb in hand, he'd walk over to the pool table and make suggestions on a tough shot."

Bill Hamilton

Men having a shave had cause to worry as they lay back covered in a big white sheet. Jim plastered their faces with a soft badgerhair brush lathered with shaving soap from a tall mug. Then he deftly wielded the straight razor with one eye on the pool game in progress. Often he'd have to lather up two or three times to finish the shave if a close match caught his attention.

The McKay's delivered milk to the Gunnis'. Jim was alone one day in 1943 when Cassie left the milk.

"He said to me, 'If you don't see me tomorrow, have a look. I might be dead!' Sure enough, the next morning I found him dead of a heart attack."

Cassie (McKay) Stevens

Another barber who suffered the same fate was B. Collis. He was an old man in his seventies when he came to Union Bay, and only plied his trade in the little town for two years. In April 1929, Mr. Collis was sitting out front beside the barber pole when he toppled over and a customer found him dead.

After Jim the Barber died, the town was left without a barber. Joe Walker, the E&N foreman, started cutting friends' hair in his section house. Soon, more people were demanding his services. Some of Joe's loyal patrons converted a little house next to the tracks into a barber shop.

By this time haircuts were up to 50¢ and electric clippers had been introduced. Herbert Glover, who was almost bald, always asked if he would be charged the full 50¢. Joe invariably replied, "You're damned right! I'll charge two bits to cut and two bits to look where the hair should be!" However, when it was time to pay, Joe refused any money. He cut all the old-timers' hair for free. In 1951 haircuts in Courtenay went up to $1.00 and by 1959 were $1.25.

Quite often, after cutting a few heads of hair in an evening, barber and clients would go down to the Nelson House for a few beers. Joe always left the lights on so that his wife Mary would think he was still working, but this ploy did not work for long. Mary loved to listen to the radio in the evening, but the electric clippers caused static. So she knew if the radio was clear for a long stretch, that Joe had abandoned the barber shack for more comfortable surroundings.

Joe retired and the couple moved out of the section house into their new home on the Island Highway. Mary was adamant about not taking the barber chair but Joe won out. In trade for the little shack which was turned into a chicken coop, Slim Foster hauled the beloved, well-used barber chair down to the basement of the new house. It was never used again, and men had to go to Courtenay for their hair cuts.

HAIRDRESSING

Professional hairdressing came much later than barbering. Until travel to Cumberland or Courtenay became easier, the ladies cut and curled their own or friends' hair. After Violet (Glover) Rutherford came out from England, she often did several of the young beauties' hair in "Merry Widow" curls for a special party.

A house with a store front between Horne's and Campbell's was Union Bay's only beauty shop. Mrs. Wood ran it, assisted by Rachel Haggart. For a while business flourished.

It was truly a blessing to have naturally curly hair. Permanent waves were introduced in the 1920's and cost about $12. One had to get to Cumberland to have it done. Generally, perms were very fuzzy, but the pride of the possessor. Up until that time the quickest way to have curls was with a curling iron. It was easy to tell when it was being used, as the smell of singed hair from the overheated iron filled the house. The girls opened the lid of the stove and put in the metal end of the curling iron. When it was hot, it was used in the same fashion as the electric curling irons of today, but without a temperature control.

Another way to have curls was by wrapping the hair in rags. After a shampoo, mother tore up narrow strips of cloth, then labouriously wound strands of hair around them. It was left to dry, usually overnight, and produced beautiful ringlets. Thick, slightly wavy hair could look like Shirley Temple's for a couple of days, but thin, straight hair would be out by lunch time, especially if the air was damp.

Mercifully for many young girls in the 1920's, the "bobbed" hairdo came into style. Along with the flapper's short skirt, it was predicted to be the undoing of every young lass who followed fashion's dictates.

Charge of the Bobbed Brigade

Bobbed hair to the right of us
Bobbed hair to the left of us.
Bobbed hair behind us.
  Tresses asundered.

Some with a heavy crop
Some with a lighter mop
Into the barber shop,
  Walked the bobbed hundred.

Women of high degree
Women past fifty three
Determined that they shall be
  One of the numbered.

Women of every class
Mother and little lass
Flappers all join the mass
  Of the bobbed hundred.

Some with bangs
Some without
Some in curls, some in doubt
  Fear they have blundered.

Some of them look real swell
Some of them look like—well
Just as well not to tell
  On the bobbed hundred. [5]

Jobs traditionally done by men were taken over by women during the Second World War. Long hair had to be kept out of the way of machines, so it was tied up in a bandanna, Aunt Jemimah style. The snood, a net bag tied around the hair at the back, also came into vogue. The page boy or upsweep was popular for evening wear.

Home perms were welcomed in the 1940's. The plastic rods were loaned back and forth, and everyone suffered the strong waving solution in an effort to have curls. The advertisements asked, "Which twin has the Toni?" They both had.

Q. Which twin has the Toni?
A. Both

E. Hallstrom

Mrs. Ede with her daughter Nellie, grandson Gerald, and great grandson Douglas

LAUNDRY

In the very early days all the housewives did their own laundry. A few of the lucky ones had help. Mrs. Ede, who was raising a family on her own, was often hired by some of the larger families, one day a week. She was Mrs. Muschamp's sister and lived on the beach with her daughter Nellie. Later, she helped raise Nellie's four children.

The hotels hired people to do the laundry. Mammie King, the Negress, did all the laundry for the Nelson Hotel. She carried it on her head over a mile to her home at Garvin's field, where she washed and ironed all the linens. When she left in 1910, two Chinese fellows took over the job. They lived and had their large wash tubs and irons over Howe's old store on the beach. Mrs. Nakamura also had a laundry.

"Our parents were not rich, but it was not through lack of trying. To supplement his income, father worked week-ends helping mother. Behind our house he built a "dry house", and below, a "wash house". Now they were in business. Mother washed, dried and ironed, and our father delivered the clothes to their customers, on week-ends, in a two wheel cart designed and pulled much like a rickshaw. He took me with him on many occasions and I looked forward to these trips. His customers ranged south through the town to Walkers Hill, up past the CPR crossing to Glovers and Haggarts etc., and thence north to Bloedel's logging camp located on the west side of the highway, approximately two miles from our home. He covered a lot of ground during these excursions. He was affectionately called "Charlie."

Kiyoshi Nakamura

Other enterprising women also took in laundry to help out the family during hard times. After the Cave's home burned, the company gave them a house to live in on the hill. It had cold running water. Mrs. Cave took in washing, doing bedding from the logging camps. She had to heat all the water on the stove and scrub the sheets with a bar of naptha soap on a scrubbing board. Bleach was not available yet so the sheets and pillowcases were boiled in a big copper boiler on the stove. She was fortunate to have a mangle with which to wring out the water. Luckily the ceilings were high, and during the winter, sheets were hung all over the house.

"At nighttime, when everyone went to bed she'd put up lines back and forth in the kitchen, then hang the sheets on them. If we got up we'd have to weave our way through. I used to help her iron the pillow cases with a sad iron. I ironed pillow cases until I looked like them."

Clara (Cave) Ridgway

In 1909 George Booth, who was in charge of freight for CC(D)L at the Bay, became agent for the Imperial Laundry Company of Nanaimo. He collected the clothes, mainly suits and coats, then shipped them to Nanaimo on the steamer, where they were cleaned and shipped back again.

There were several Chinese laundry establishments in Cumberland, which the more affluent Bay residents patronized. The industrious Chinese excelled in the laundry business but, even in the 1920's, there was prejudice against them.

1920 APRIL ➾ WHITE WOMAN wanted to do laundry for a Cumberland Barber Shop. [5]

In the late 1920's the Comox Valley Laundry initiated a pick-up and delivery service throughout the Comox Valley, stretching as far as Campbell River and Qualicum. Monday was pick-up day at Union Bay. The company promised that all laundry would be returned the same week.

TAILORING

As well as cleaning clothes, most laundries did simple alterations. In Cumberland and Courtenay there were several tailors, both white and Chinese, who were patronized by men wanting dress suits made. Union Bay didn't have a tailor as such, just a Chinese fellow who sold ready-to-wear suits.

"The Chinese tailor had a long mirror. When you stood in front of it he held the back of the coat in, to make it look like it fit."

Jack Bradley

Mary Bennie was trained as a tailor in Cumberland by Mr. Carey. In 1905 she married William Marshall, a locomotive engineer at Union Bay. Along with raising a family of three boys and two girls, she did some tailoring, mostly alterations.

"The war started in 1914 and Union Bay became a training centre for the army. I remember the soldiers coming to the house when they were issued uniforms with trousers too long or too loose. Mom had a Singer sewing machine, and she would shorten or lengthen or take them in."

Nettie (Marshall) Jones

As well, Mrs. Marshall made all of the family's clothes. Little panties, petticoats and dresses for the girls, and underwear, shirts and pants for the boys. She made the children's clothes until they were old enough to buy their own. Then she created beautiful wedding gowns for both of her daughters.

"My mother has been known to whip up a pinafore dress before school in the morning. They'd be very plain, mind you, but a new dress nevertheless."

Nettie (Marshall) Jones

In the early days there were always costumes to be made for parties, masquerades, concerts and May Day. Mrs. Kay became famous for her creativity and volume sewing. Her husband, Andy, worked in the CC(D)L office and they had one daughter, Greta, who took part in all the concerts. Mrs. Kay would sew the costumes for a Gilbert and Sullivan operetta, or the gowns for the May Queen's entourage. She dyed and gathered hundreds of yards of cheese cloth to make dainty, ruffled dresses. She sewed rolls of braid on jackets and pants to make uniforms. Crepe paper was also used to make colourful costumes.

Winnie Bowden loved to sew, learning the skill when she was quite young at Home Economics class in Nanaimo. At thirteen she moved to Union Bay to join her family. Mrs. Marshall helped and encouraged her. When Winnie finished school she moved to Vancouver, and for one year was an apprentice to Mrs. Kincaid in an exclusive dressmaking shop which catered to the wealthy people of Vancouver. Winnie was left handed, but at school the teachers, with the help of a ruler over the knuckles, had made her write right-handed. When she arrived in Vancouver she was certain being left-handed would be a disadvantage so never told anyone, slowly struggling along. Then one day her boss had a rush order for a gown with many yards of fabric in the skirt. Together they started the hem, and in her eagerness Winnie picked up the needle with her left hand, Mrs. Kincaid going one way and she the other. They were able to sit opposite each other and work on the same garment. In this way being a "south paw" was a distinct advantage so she was encouraged to use her left hand for sewing, although she was still able to use right-handed scissors.

When her training was over she returned to Union Bay and, with her Dad's help, built a shop on property she leased next door to her parents' home. It had a store front and two small rooms - one contained a large table and treadle Singer sewing machine, the other a long mirror for fittings. Here she built up a good number of clients, charging them $5.00 to make a dress, and $10 for a lined suit or coat. Two days a month, she went over to Denman and sewed for the ladies of the Island. She created a number of beautiful wedding gowns for the young brides of the Bay. Margaret Glover's was made of cream satin, with a twelve inch lace flounce which dipped at the back. The delicate handmade lace was loaned to Margaret by the teacher's wife, Mrs. Stacey, and Winnie designed it into the dress.

W. Glover

Winnie Bowden shingling her dressmaking shop

Winnie had trained on silks, satins, lush velvets and beautiful wools bought from Saba's. At Union Bay she had little chance to use these fabrics. Money was short, and most of her work consisted of alterations and make-overs requiring little imagination or creativity. So, after a few years of tearing out old seams, "she sewed it up" and took a job in Courtenay at Laver's, where she did alterations as well as clerking.

COBBLER

Before the turn of the century, cobblers not only repaired but also made shoes and boots. Some even produced the leather by raising and slaughtering the animals, then tanning the hide.

1894 ➾ The *Joan* brought a crate of pigs from Nanaimo to the veteran shoemaker in Comox.[3a]

The catalogue was a popular place to buy footwear, but it was not always easy to get a good fit.

"I remember getting a pair of shoes once. They were so-o-o pretty - black with white soles. Unfortunately, the darn things were too tight, but I loved them so I wore them."

Margaret (Glover) Matthews

Although the catalogue featured beautiful highbutton boots of calf or kid, and smart laced oxfords in patent or satin, they were neither practical nor affordable to the settlers of Union Bay. Once the local stores were established, they carried a complete line of shoes and boots. With large families to shod, parents chose strong leather footwear with substantial soles which could be replaced when worn through.

"I have seen Dad come home from Fraser and Bishop's with a big stack of shoes. One of nearly every size."

Margaret (Glover) Matthew

Most children and adults owned only one pair of stout shoes or boots. If they were lucky, they also had gum boots for winter and a pair of canvas running shoes for summer.

"Summertime we always went barefoot, except when we went berry picking, probably in an old pair of runners with the toe out."

Doug Brown

Children's shoes had to last a long time, and were often passed down to a younger sibling. There was a ready market for the shoe repairman who could stretch the life of a pair of shoes.

William Hill was the first cobbler at Union Bay. As well as repairing shoes he also made them, but was not too particular a craftsman. In those days, when feet were smaller, his wife had big feet which looked even bigger because she wore her husbands clumsily built creations.

"Billy had promised Mrs. Hill "store-bought" shoes. So one day, with great excitement, she went into Jack Fraser's and said, 'Good morning, Jack, I want to buy a pair of shoes.'

'Oh yes, Mrs. Hill, and what size will that be?' asked Jack.

'A SMALL eight,' replied Mrs Hill."

Tom McKay

In 1920 J. Perry set up shop and became the town cobbler, followed by Ben Cave in 1922. W.T. King and C. Walker also mended shoes in the '20s.

Mr. Cave was a streetcar conductor in South Vancouver when the war broke out. He joined the army and was shell-shocked in Europe, leaving him "stone deaf" and unable to resume his profession. The government offered to retrain him, and he chose the shoe repair trade. The large CNR building was turned into a school for veterans. With the course completed in 1920, he decided to set up shop in a small town, and chose Union Bay because his relatives, the Davis family, lived there.

Opposite the Wilson Hotel was a little shack which Mr. Cave fixed up for his workshop. He had many tools, lasts of different sizes, and a big frame which was mounted with electric saw, sander, and polisher with different types of brushes. Here he could make shoes as good as new, charging $1.50 for a half sole and heel.

"Dad was a very, very good shoe repairman, and honest to the people. He always bought the best leather. He made logging boots too, right from scratch for the loggers."

Clara (Cave) Ridgway

The Cave family was beset with bad luck. Their house burned down and business was poor, as Union Bay's population could not support a full time cobbler, so Mr. Cave was forced to seek other work.

Later, in 1929, E. Collis became the barber at the Bay and also advertised as a shoe repairman. When he died suddenly, the little town was left without a cobbler.

Many fathers, through necessity, learned to repair shoes. If it could not be borrowed, all the necessary equipment could be found in the catalogue.

G295—Cobbler's Set
All complete, with three different size lasts, stand, awls, knife, hammer, and brads;
Complete set...........$ .75
Woodward's Catalogue 1912

Also for sale were soles priced from 29¢ to 59¢, depending on size and quality; heels of leather or rubber; nails and rivets; toe plates to protect the leather; caulks at 65¢ per hundred; hobnails at 36¢ a pound. The young boys loved to have hobnails in their boots, as they made a good crunching sound when they walked, and sparks when they hit rocks.

George Cooper, an electrican with the CC(D)L, gathered together the necessary tools to repair his family's shoes. He became quite proficient and started doing work for friends and neighbours, and eventually charged for the service. During the 1930's and '40s, in the evening after supper, he could be heard tap-tapping with his little hammer in the tiny workshop off the back verandah.

PHOTOGRAPHY

Before the turn of the century several photographers visited the Comox Valley, taking pictures of scenery and commercial enterprises for publications.

G. Francklyn

Gilbert Francklyn built a darkroom onto the front of his houseboat at Henry Bay and took many pictures of outstanding quality

1890 JUNE •◆ Mr. J. Becker, photographer representing "Picturesque Canada", is taking pictures in the Valley.

Photographic companies sent representatives up the Island. They could be hired to take pictures.

1889 AUGUST •◆ Mr. Uren of Mainland Photogaphic Co. will take photos of residences, groups, and scenes in the Comox Valley. [2]

Soon, flash pictures were being advertised. This required a great deal of patience on behalf of the subjects as they sat dead still with fixed poses on their faces, while the photographer exploded the flash in front of their eyes.

1893 APRIL •◆ The energetic photographer, Pierce, is in town. "Flash Light" photographs taken of your family in your own home by Elite Studios. [2]

By 1894 there was a photographic gallery established in Union by W.J. Jenkins. He advertised pictures for Christmas cards at $2.50 per dozen. After the turn of the century, several photographers - Mr. F. Watts, Mr. Powell and Mr. Hayashi - set up shop at Cumberland. They all visited Union Wharf for private sittings and to photograph the school children.

At the age of nineteen, Gilbert Francklyn packed up his camera and custom-made gun and left an affluent family in Halifax for the Pacific coast. In 1900 he built himself a houseboat on the little creek at Henry Bay. He made his living hunting for the market and developed his interest in photography. His huge camera, equipped with a Zeiss lens, had a 3' bellows. Many of the pictures he took were self-portraits, taken with a string attached to the shutter. He developed the glass negatives and made prints in a dark room built onto the end of his cabin. Many old pictures, still cherished today, of families and homes were photographed by Mr. Francklyn.

Some of his pictures, and those of the King Studio from Vancouver, were reproduced as postcards. During the First World War the soldiers sent home postcards "with their own likeness" on the front.

E. Renwick

Two Japanese sailors with their camera pose with Eva Small and Elizabeth Walker in the Nelson Hotel garden

Being a port, Union Bay was well-photographed. Even then, Japanese sailors often had a camera around their neck. A Japanese photographer took some shots of the Wilson Hotel and stores. The enlargements were returned to the Bay, but the negative had been reversed in the printing, which resulted in the lettering on the hotel sign being backwards. The photographer obviously could not read English.

In the 1920's it became increasingly popular to own a camera. Kodak's Box Brownies were the choice of most people, as they were cheap and easy to operate. A Brownie #2 sold for

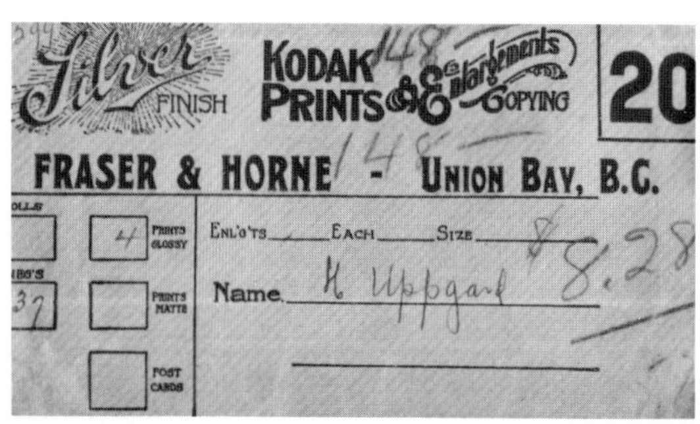

L. Kilvert

Ordered through Fraser and Horne's store, reprints from negatives cost 6¢ each

$2.75, took size 120 film, and produced pictures 2 1/4" by 3 3/4". A six exposure film cost 10¢ for development and 5¢ a print. This could be done through Fraser and Horne, but it was just as fast to send the film to Victoria or Vancouver. The best picture on the roll was attractively mounted on thick cardboard. Specials were offered, and by saving ten end flaps of the envelopes, an enlargement would be given free.

A few enterprising people bought the equipment and learned to process their own pictures. Many of Louis Magnone's home-developed photos are reprinted in this book.

The young fellow or girl who owned a Brownie was the envy of everyone. Pictures were snapped of parties, weddings, picnics, hikes and sporting events. Often the results were not that great. Heads were cut off, or the camera was moved and a blurry picture resulted. Regularly, when loading or unloading the camera, the roll became loose and some of the film exposed. Regardless of how poor, the pictures were cherished and mounted with art corners in a large, black-paged photo album.

We are certainly busy

BABIES MONTH FOR FREE SITTING IS RUNNING ALONG, JUST TWO MORE WEEKS

(Our definition of baby age—Not yet toddling about.)

Royston W.A. Garden Party next Wednesday, July 24th, at Royston.

This an excellent opportunity to learn all about Picture Making, come along and bring your cameras, C. W. S. will be delighted to assist and show you how to make BETTER photographs.

Have you tried the "COMOX FINISH" and 12 hour service If not, just send a film along, personal expert attention to every order. Kodak Films stocked.

C. W. SILLENCE, Photographer,
Royston, B. C. Phone 70M.

In the 1920's a great institution was launched in the Comox Valley when C.W. Sillence arrived from Britain, where he had trained as a photographer. From his small studio in Royston he was soon promoting the "Comox Finish" as the professional way of printing the Kodak film which he sold.

Every school child in the area remembers the little man who ducked under the black curtain to peer through the view finder of the black box mounted on a tripod. On a bright sunny day each class in turn filed outside and was arranged in rows, the boys standing on benches at the back. The smallest child was chosen to sit crosslegged on the ground at the front to hold the slate on which the name of the school and division number was chalked. The teacher took his/her place on the end. Mr. Sillence slid a glass plate into the camera, stepped to the side, smiled broadly and squeezed the rubber bulb - another school picture was recorded for posterity.

Studio portraits of weddings, babies, and families were Mr. Sillence's forte. Several generations of children were photographed sitting on the same table, playing with the same toys. Eventually the studio was moved to Courtenay, and daughter Peggy followed in her father's footsteps.

For people who could not travel to town, there were photographers who went door-to-door, taking pictures of families in their home settings.

BANKING

Originally, all money used in business transactions at Union Wharf came from the Cumberland Bank of Canada. The men were paid in cash brought down from the office at Cumberland every payday.

Then, in 1904, this report stirred interest in people with enough money to put in a bank.

1904 JUNE Two gentlemen from the Royal Bank of Canada took a trip through the Comox Valley. Ostensibly on a fishing trip, these men are secretly visiting the valley preliminary to starting a bank here. [4]

By 1905 there was a Royal Bank branch in Cumberland. The coal company used this bank, and money was brought down on payday in a wagon to Union Bay. As the town grew and business demanded, the Royal Bank decided to open a branch there. In 1909 a small building was erected on the beach opposite the jail house. This sub-branch of Cumberland opened its doors on Thursday, August 26, and was open for business every Thursday from 11:00 a.m. until 2:00 p.m.

By 1913 the bank at Union Bay was open on Friday as well as Thursday. Excitement struck the Comox Valley on July 4th when two "highwaymen" held up and robbed the paywagon in a style reminiscent of the Grey Fox. Although the bank put up a reward

Royal Bank Archives

The first bank in Union Bay built in 1909, was located on the beach across the road from the jailhouse

of $500 and the Government $1,000, the robbers were never apprehended. (See Robberies)

After the robbery, it was deemed foolish to carry the payroll every week to Union Bay, so plans were made to build a new $1200 bank, next to Fraser and Bishop's store. In the summer of 1914 the impressive building was opened. The old bank was sold and re-opened as the town's barber shop, with a red and white pole at the door. Downstairs, the new bank boasted a large vault, while a beautiful apartment was provided for the manager and his family on the top floor.

The first manager, who also doubled as teller, was R. Long, assisted by clerk Desmond Roe. Mr. Long was followed by J.S. Baird, then R. Jardin. During the war years and into the 1920's, the port was busy and growing, so the bank prospered with it. In 1919 Morton Thomas came, and managed the bank until 1931. The Thomas' were a very popular couple. Mrs. Thomas was a wonderful hostess who loved to entertain. The local women cherished invitations to her parties, just as the young folk enjoyed parties she gave for her daughter Betty.

Over the years, many of the local boys who showed an aptitude for numbers became clerks to learn the banking business. With the title of "ledger clerk", their job was bookkeeper and general "joe-boy" around the office. They worked at the Union Bay branch for a couple of years, then moved on to Courtenay and Vancouver.

After Desmond Roe came John Doney. He stayed long enough to fall in love and marry Carrie Brown, the postmaster's fourth daughter. Next was J. Matthew, and then Robert Searle, followed by his brother Ted who stayed as an assistant for three years. He left in 1922 for Vancouver, after training the next recruit for a month. Doug Brown was only fourteen when he quit school to start in the bank. After a year and a half, Doug, in turn, trained his good friend, Ray Glover, who followed him to Courtenay and then to Vancouver. Before leaving, Ray trained Lawrence McLeod, then after him came William (Happy) Macartney who was the ledger clerk through the 1930's. These young men received valuable training in the little bank at the Bay. Most of them went on to good positions in the banking and business world.

It was a community bank where there were no long line-ups at the teller's cage, and wives could sign for their husbands. Twice a month the Collieries men were paid. The office paymaster brought a list of the employees with the amount each received. The two men at the bank had to calculate and request from the main branch the exact number of dollars, quarters, dimes, nickels and pennies needed to put the right amount of cash in each pay envelope. Each man had to sign for his wages.

All of the employees except the Chinese picked up their pay at the bank. The Chinese received their pay envelopes from Mah Fat, who was Charlie Mah June's bookkeeper. Mah June submitted the men's hours to the office paymaster who, in turn, gave the total wages to the bank manager. Mah Fat collected that amount and made up his own pay envelopes.

The bank was open from 9:00 a.m. to 12 noon, and 1:00 p.m. to 3:00 p.m. Banking was carried on in a friendly manner. Mrs. Anderson, operating her confectionery, did not have anyone to relieve her so she would flag down Doug Brown on his way back to work after lunch, giving him her money and her bank book. Doug would deposit the money and return the stamped book on his way home.

Royal Bank Archives

The second bank was built in 1914 beside Fraser and Bishop's store

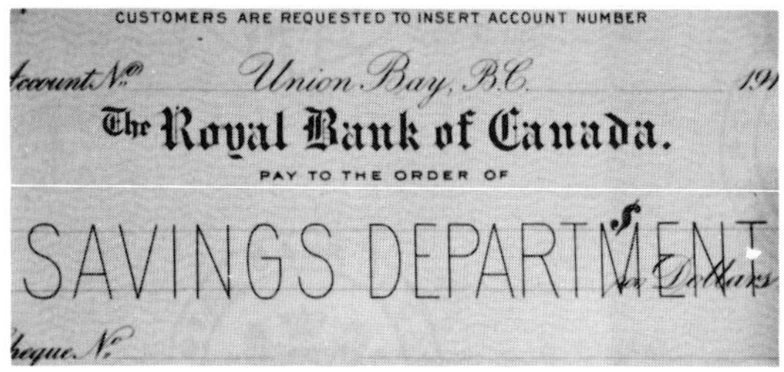

N. Eastman

The last permanent manager, R. Husband, left in 1932. Then, because no money was left at Union Bay, the vault door was taken off and put onto a vault in the basement of the Courtenay bank.

Primarily as a service to the CC(D)L, an accountant and teller came from the Courtenay branch every Friday and opened the bank. Every second week, payroll envelopes were made up for the employees. Beryl Hargood-Ash started coming down about 1943, and her fifteen years of friendly, efficient service are well remembered.

"I suppose we made up about fifty pay envelopes in my day, and I'd guess they'd average about forty to fifty dollars. Over half the recipients were Chinese, and they faithfully bought drafts and money orders in Hong Kong dollars to send to their families in China. Most of them could neither write nor read English. Some we knew by name and others by

identifying features. They were very honest and very appreciative of small favours. Vera Mar was a great help interpreting if I got into difficulties."

Beryl Hargood-Ash

The bank finally closed in 1957, and Union Bay residents had to go to Courtenay to do their banking. Some long time customers felt betrayed, so they switched from the Royal to other banks.

After the last manager left, the apartment above the bank was rented to the George Watt's, with their three girls. Mrs. Watt did the janitorial work and tended the monstrous furnace. For many years before that, Mrs. Ede was the janitor.

CREDIT UNION

The Union Bay Charter #114 of Credit Unions was incorporated in April 1944, after much organizational work by the enthusiastic members. On the first board of directors were Dave Campbell, Art Chafer, Harry Chapman, Paul Grundy, Art Hastings, Bessie McKay and Wes Peters.

Paul Grundy was the first secretary-treasurer, followed by Major Ovans, Jim Haggart and Harry Tappin. Business transactions were carried on in the secretary-treasurer's home until 1955 when Mr. Tappin took over. Then, a small building (nick-named the doll house) on E.T. Searles' property was converted into an office.

The Union Bay Credit Union has never looked back and has grown in both members and assets.

HOTELS

In the early days the main reason for building a hotel was to get a liquor license. Early in 1893 W. Sharpe, former owner of the Elk Hotel at Comox, applied for a hotel liquor license at Union Wharf. A few months later a license was granted to J.B. Holmes of Comox for a bar room at Union Wharf, on the condition that suitable premises be erected and properly furnished. Both of these men could see the potential for making money in the port, with its large population of single men, and daily visits by freighters and colliers with their thirsty crews.

At this time there were about seven hotels in the district: the Cumberland, Union, and Waverly in Cumberland; the Courtenay and Riverside in Courtenay; and the Elk and Lorne in Comox.

M. Peters

The Nelson Hotel, built in 1893, had nine guest rooms on the second floor

In June 1893 George Howe saw the potential in the growing port of Union Bay and, unlike the two men who had previously applied for liquor licenses without having a hotel, George decided to build one. He bought five lots on the townsite below Union Wharf and hired R. Sanderson of Courtenay to build his hotel. A reporter from the Weekly News visited the site just after it was completed.

1893 OCTOBER ➾ We now take a walk down the new road to Howe's. The distance is about half a mile, not far back from the beach, and through a second growth of trees which line the way and between which, on the left hand side as you go down, the Gulf waters gleam brightly. In a few minutes, we reach an opening in the midst of which stands the Nelson House. It is a noble structure 38' by 53', two stories in height, with cottage roof. Without stopping to look through it then, we yielded at the entreaty of our stomach and passed into the dining room where we enjoyed a most substantial meal. That over, we looked over the building. Taking the first storey, we came naturally to the bar room. It is 18' by 22', a corner room, connected with that is a billiard room of the same size, now being used as a store until a new building for that purpose shall be erected. The dining room is 22' by 28', like all the rooms splendidly lighted with acetylene lights. Then there is a sitting room 10' by 13', kitchen 16' by 19' with a pantry off it 6' by 16', washroom, hall etc. In the second storey are nine rooms, large, airy, and nicely furnished. Let us take a look from the front window. We are back only a little way from where the waves lap the shore. Beyond the two miles of water expanse is Denman Island, and right over it stream up like turrets the tall peaks of the Cascade Range on the Mainland. Around to the left is Texada and around still farther the eye rests on Nob Hill. It is a fine view and doubtless the place will be a popular resort: good fishing, scenery, hunting, rowing, etc. and only a mile and a fourth to Garvin's Famous Springs. [3a]

Mr. Howe, with his many business ventures, hired W.R. Brown to manage the hotel and store. In March 1894 Mr. McCartney (Mrs.

McKay's brother) came from Nanaimo to run the dining room, with his wife working as cook and hostess. Meals were 25¢ each. At the end of 1895, Mr. and Mrs. T.H. Piercy from Denman Island took charge of room and board which was $5.00 a week.

> **NELSON HOUSE**
> UNION BAY, B.C.
>
> Having taken this house, except the bar, I shall be pleased to receive the patronage of the public.
> Board per week, _ $5.
> Single meals _ 25 cents
> T.J. Piercy.

The Nelson House, with bar, store, dining room and post office, became the centre of the fledgling community. Dances, going-away parties, dinners and concerts were all held there. A New Years Eve party in 1896 was given with plenty of men and as many women as they could muster.

1896 JANUARY ➾ Dance at the Nelson House - There was a good gathering of people from the district. At 6:00 p.m. Mrs. T. Piercy served a delicious dinner of roast turkey. Dancing to the music of Roy and Grieves followed, and kept up until an early hour. Ladies present were Miss Piercy and Miss Louis of Denman, Miss McDonald of Comox, Miss Pare, Mrs. McKay, Mrs. McCartney and Mrs. Piercy, all of Union Wharf. [3b]

After the Piercys left, a Chinese cook was employed, which did not prove too popular with the regulars who lodged there. Then, in 1900, Mrs. Johnson took charge of the dining room, and many of the young men moved back and made the Nelson their home once again. About this time a third floor with six dormers was added.

Originally known as the "Saloon" or "Bar", later as the "Beer Parlour", then much later as the "Pub", the liquor outlet at a hotel was the mainstay of the establishment. Yearly, the owner had to apply for or renew his license to sell intoxicants. The Board of License Commissioners travelled up the Island and met at the little jail in Union Bay to review the requests. Strict laws had to be adhered to, especially concerning hours liquor could be sold. It even stipulated that when the bar was closed, the curtains and blinds had to be up so authorities could see that the room was truly empty. It was illegal to serve Indians and many charges resulted from this law.

Union Bay School Collection

Dormers were added to the hotel about 1900 creating six more rooms in the attic

1896 NOVEMBER ➾ Case against George Howe of Union Wharf Dimissed. George Howe was arraigned in the district court at Nanaimo on a charge of having connived at the supply of intoxicants to one Frank Comox, an Indian (the witness). After leaving Comox, witness and his companion stayed at Union Wharf, where Jimmy obtained three bottles: one rye, another of gin, and another of rum, at George Howe's saloon. Witness saw Jimmy go into the store and come out again. The store and the saloon were separated by a partition but connected by a door. The witness did not see George Howe that day. As soon as they got the liquor, the parties started out in their canoes and proceeded to drink the liquor. [2]

Howe's bar was not a big room by today's standards. As saloons of the day did not provide chairs, patrons stood at the long bar, resting one foot on the brass rail. The swinging doors welcomed the thirsty labourers, loggers, farmers, sailors and travellers to step up to the bar and order a beer, whiskey, rye, gin, scotch or sarsaparilla.

After 1905 when Jack Fraser was made a partner in the hotel and store, his sister, Miss Etta Fraser, came up from Victoria where she had been a nurse, and took over as housekeeper and hostess of the Nelson House. Patrick Doheny acted as manager for a short time.

"Miss Fraser was the official hostess at the hotel. She was a delight... an educated lady with a distinctive air and beautiful manners."

Margaret (Harwood) Bowden

Charlie Bishop bought out George Howe in 1907. The partners, Fraser and Bishop, carried out extensive renovations in 1908. At the south end the building was extended about 40'. A basement was dug and partly cemented in. Five more dormers were added. This brought the room total to thirty. The hotel had a fine spring, water tank, and flush toilets. A wide arched verandah skirted two sides of the first and second floors of the handsome building. About 1915, more rooms were built and furnished above the store to accommodate the overflow.

For the next twenty years the Nelson House was a first-class resort hotel. The grounds were landscaped, with a beautiful garden planted across the road near the beach. A tennis court was installed at the back, with lawns and gardens at the side. Jackie Witfield, a pernickety little Englishman, tended the garden with loving care under Miss Fraser's discriminating eye.

The interior was immaculate, with the decor and furnishings designed for gracious living. Many of the young girls, as they came of age, got their first job as chambermaid and waitress. They learned the art of setting a beautiful table, arranging flowers, and conversing with strangers. Mary and Nellie McKay, Matilda Walker, Elizabeth Walker and Margaret Glover are a few who benefitted from this training.

"I remember when all the rooms would be full at the hotel as well as the rooms at the annex above the store. The pilot would come and have to sleep on the couch. Miss Fraser was good, she could sure run a hotel. Everything was kept beautifully! Lovely white tablecloths and napkins... the kitchen was spotless."

Elizabeth (Walker) Renwick

The hotel catered to all types of people: officials from the coal company, salesmen waiting to catch the next train or boat, pilots who brought the freighters up the inside channel, captain's wives visiting while their husbands's ship was loading, loggers when the woods were closed because of snow or heat. Everyone received kind, friendly service from the Frasers. One year there was a lot of snow and the whole top floor was full of loggers. Most of them had no money and couldn't pay their lodging bills, but hospitality was extended and the men were able to pay when they got back to work.

A. Hardiman

In 1908 the building was extended to almost twice its size, bringing the room total to 30

T. Kovar

Jack Fraser and Jack Baird with the old gardener, Jackie Witfield, standing in the hotel garden

As well as the girls working as waitresses and chambermaids, they employed two Chinese men in the kitchen. They cooked western style under the close supervision of Miss Fraser. Wong Chee, the cook, was assisted by a fellow named Mah Young, who also did the laundry. Hungo, the gardener, had huge gardens behind the store, which supplied the kitchen with a variety of vegetables, fruits and berries. He also produced all the dairy products: milk, thick cream and freshly churned butter. Ready for the oven were chicken, beef, lamb, mutton and pork. Guests at the Nelson House truly dined in style, on long tables covered with snowy white cloths, set with flowers from the garden, silver cutlery and fine china.

Under the Fraser's care, the Nelson House attracted discriminating travellers. Their brother, Dr. Roderick Fraser of Victoria, often visited with his family, sometimes bringing with him influential people from Victoria.

"Mr. Simon Tolmie was a close friend of Jack's, and when he was Premier, often used to run up to Union Bay to escape from the worries of his office and to talk things over with his old friend."

Jack Fraser's obituary 1935, [6]

The renovated hotel had a much bigger bar room with plenty of tables to accommodate its customers. For many years Mr. Fraser employed Harvey Leithead as bartender. He was a quick man with twinkling brown eyes. The bowler hat that he wore was left over from his days as a circus barker. He attracted patrons with his non-stop patter that kept everyone roaring with laughter. At night, the bartender would double as the desk clerk and Harvey claimed there were "hot and cold running chambermaids in every room". When asked, "Any chance of getting a room

D. Muschamp

Employees of Fraser and Bishop stand in front of the hotel: bartender Harvey Leithead, butcher George Harwood, ?, gardener Jackie Witfield, owner Jack Fraser

tonight?", Harvey would jokingly reply, "Do you want a bed in it?" He claimed that the only things that grew well in his garden were "cornflakes".

"Harvey and the old characters used to sit around the lobby and play Cinch for beer. There would be Bob Byres, Andy Anderson, Nick Knutson, Cecil McQueen and Hughie McSwain. McSwain was a single man but he wouldn't eat at the hotel because of the Chinese cooks. He'd say, 'They got Fraser and they got Horne but they won't get me'."

Fred Peters

Another drawing card around the hotel for many years was the Swedish sea-dog, Adolf Anderson. In 1894 he jumped ship at Union Bay, attached himself to Jack Fraser and was his faithful retainer for thirty-four years, cleaning up around the bar and doing odd jobs. He was the town clown, known as "One-eyed Anderson"; even the press recorded his shenanigans.

J. Anderson

"Captain" Adolf Anderson, known as "One-eyed Anderson" or the "Edicated Swede", was one of several sailors that jumped ship and made Union Bay their home

1904 ➾ A man named Anderson was brought up from the wharf last Saturday suffering from an injured leg, the result of a fall from a verandah while larking with a companion. It is not yet known if the member is broken or not. [4]

1913 JANUARY ➾ New Bank Appointment - Ex-captain Adolf Anderson whose certificate was recently cancelled by the Department of Rowboats and Fisheries owing to carelessness, has after searching examination been appointed janitor of the Royal Bank. He is not likely to retain this position long owing to sudden lapses in memory. Nevertheless he is always on hand when the bank closes to draw down his hard-earned cheque. He threatened to give a banquet last week but owing to the bank manager losing the combination to the safe his cheque could not be cashed. Adolf has been stricken with a bad attack of what doctors call RYESKINDICITIS. The first symptons showed a complete disinclination to work, trembling of the hands and a zig-zag walk. This disease is likely to become quite fashionable. [4]

After Adolf broke his leg it became stiff and he was a familiar figure limping around town with his cane. He first lived at the hotel, then in a little shack by the track on McLeod Road. He claimed he was an "edicated" man and was very often intoxicated. Everyone has a story to tell about him.

"He wasn't a big man but wiry and strong. One time he carried six sacks of flour off the boat at one time. It was a bet with the deckhands, so they piled them on and he carried them off.

Nellie (McKay) King

"If a traveller paid him before he carried the suitcases up to the train or out to the dock, he would just leave the suitcases and disappear into the bar for a drink."

Doug Brown

"He could do all kinds of tricks. He could turn a glass of beer right around and not spill a drop. He'd make believe he was dead, flat on the floor, then in one motion jump straight up and scare the devil out of them. He used to amuse the skippers when they came off the big boats.

Jim McKay

"Between the store and the beach were some bushes. Anderson would be lying in there drunk and us kids would get sticks and try to roll him over. He'd say, 'Go away, its just another edicated Swede going to die'."

Hector Hooper

"The pilings used to be coated with copper sheeting as a preservative. Us kids would go down and take the copper off. We used to sell it to Adolf and he'd sell it to the junk man. Then at night he'd steal it back and sell it to him again the next morning."

Jack Anderson

B. Sherburn

Harvey Leithead, Margaret Richardson and Harry Sherburn at the ladies entrance to the beer parlour

"One-eyed Anderson used to get money from the Indians to buy them whiskey. He'd take it in a canoe and get out where it wasn't too deep then tip the canoe. He'd go tell the Indians 'Jesus, I lost your whiskey'. Then when the tide went out he'd dive down and get the bottles."

Bob McKay

"He always sang "Oh My Darling, Clementine" with a Swedish accent. They got him drunk and shanghaied him on the Charmer. He came to, down by Denman and said 'Ruby-lipsie', jumped over the rail and swam to shore."

Wilf Glover

Adolf came to his end in 1928. He was walking along the wharf with Tommy James at dusk when his cane went between the planks causing him to trip. As there were no railings on the wharf he fell over and hit his head on a brace and was killed.

Beer and hard liquor came in 90 gallon hogs-head barrels. The barrels sat under the stairs near the barroom door. You could take a bottle down and get a 26er of rye for 50¢, a drink in the bar was 25¢. Beer was 5¢ a glass and often included lunch. Draft beer could be purchased and taken home in a pail.

Bottled beer, which arrived in large barrels,was also sold.This provided a lucky boy with a job on Saturday.

"I had to go down under the hotel and stack the empty beer bottles back into big barrels, 40 dozen to a barrel. Then cover them with heavy cardboard which was held on by a hoop, which was nailed in place with a couple of shingle nails. Harvey Leithead would give me a bottle of sarsaparilla and 10¢. That was a lot of money."

Doug Brown

In the early days women did not enter the saloons, but by the 1920's a few of the more modern women joined the men. Two such ladies, Rosie Anderson and Bebe Muir, wore the latest style dresses, high heels, and hats featuring big veils which partially covered painted faces. They even smoked!

"Proper women didn't go into bars. The other women of the town looked down with askance at these ladies, possibly with some envy. Here they were socializing with their husbands and the husbands loving it."

Margaret (Harwood) Bowden

Rosie was ahead of her time, a friendly outgoing girl who led a colourful life. She married three times, once to Harvey Leithead, the bartender.

Gradually, as lifestyles relaxed in Canada, more women frequented bars, so the hotels were obliged to partition off part of the barroom for women. A separate entrance was required for "Ladies and Escorts". Single men were not permitted into the ladies' section, nor was talking between the sections allowed. In the late 1930's the Nelson House put in a "Ladies" section with its own entrance.

Mr. Bishop sold his interest in the store and hotel to Alf Horne in 1917. For another seventeen years Mr. Fraser and Mr. Horne were partners. Early in the '30s Miss Fraser moved back to Victoria, and soon after, Jack died. Alf Horne was left to manage both the hotel and store. His wife, Madeline, was a gracious, capable lady, easily filling the shoes as hostess. In two years, when Mr. Horne died, running both the store and hotel became impossible, so Madeline hired Douglas Wilson to manage the hotel. Myrtle Pratt and Emily Bowden worked as chambermaids and kitchen help.

"I worked as maid at the hotel, but by then there weren't many guests, just the pilots. I used to help Mah Young with the laundry and he taught me to count the pillows slips and towels in Chinese: Yip, gee, clom, clee, un, lo... I used to eat in the kitchen with Wong, and Gordon would sneak in and eat with us. He didn't like eating in the dining room with Mrs. Horne and Pauline because everything had to be done right - perfect manners."

Mrytle (Pratt) McKay

Mrs. Horne updated the building by having it stuccoed, then

H. Kennedy

The updated and newly stuccoed hotel reflecting the art deco of the late '30s

Cumberland Museum

The boarding house and Simon Leiser's store were undermined by the flood. The distortion to the boarding house is clearly visible

soon after sold out to J. Militich. The Militich family ran the hotel until 1942 when Pezel and Stimac took over. In the late '40s Michael Mass bought the hotel. Few people came to stay and all the rooms were in need of repair, so with no profits to put into upgrading the building, it was a losing proposition. The only part that made money was the pub. In February 1955, Mr. Mass sold out to H. Croxton of Edmonton and W. Beck of Vancouver, who started to renovate and planned to open a modern dining room. The following May, the old landmark burned to the ground in a $30,000 blaze, the third hotel at Union Bay to meet such a fate.

A large boarding house was built by the Union Coal Company in 1895, near the head of the bay, opposite Russell Hill. The large two storey building was said to have room for eighty boarders. It was built to accommodate the men constructing the large new Coal Washer.

Construction of the Washer took six months, and after that the boarding house was used to house new arrivals, until they were able to find more permanent housing. When the McKay family moved up from Nanaimo, that was their first home. In 1906 the Sikhs, initially brought in to construct the Coke ovens, were housed in the boarding house, and filled the building with the pungent smells of their curries.

In 1912 Frank Partridge was managing the Co-op store, and had his family living in the boarding house. Mr. & Mrs. Billy Hill were also living there when, in February, the Canadian Collieries power dam burst, sending flood water down the Washer Creek and onto the flats beside the wharf. The force of the water and the debris that accompanied it completely undermined the boarding house and moved it around on its foundations. When the Partridges went back in to retrieve their belongings, they were knee deep in mud. Undaunted, the family cleaned it out and continued to live there for a short time, even though the floor slanted and high tide came up to the corner of the building.

The Wilson House, built in 1899, had an inauspicious beginning. A grand opening dance was set for March 8th, but the weather was very bad so the festivities were cancelled until the next week. The weather was still poor and the newspaper reported that the dance was not well-attended due to rain. Roy and Graham provided the music, and the guests danced until 3:00 a.m. A few brave souls came from

J. Anderson

Built in 1898, the Wilson Hotel and annex was run by J. Humphrey for about 14 years

Comox and Cumberland, but not the crowd they had hoped for.

After a few years the Wilson family left Union Bay, and rented their building to Mr. and Mrs. J. Humphrey, who soon had a thriving prosperous business. The hotel was a large two storey building with about twenty rooms upstairs. Downstairs there was a spacious parlour, dining room, kitchen and saloon, with long bar, brass foot rail and spittoons. Completing the picture was a parrot said to be a hundred years old, with a large vocabulary of cuss words. Built later, and joined to the hotel by a catwalk from the second storey, was another large structure with extra guest rooms above one big hall. This was used for parties and dances, with a card room at the back.

1908 MARCH ➾ The largest dance Union Bay has ever had was given by Cpt. Ogilvie, R.N.R. There were ninety couples present at Humphrey's Hall. Mr. Humphrey is to be complimented on the tip top floor he has laid down, for it was perfection from the dancers' point of view. The hall, one of the largest in the district, was a dream of loveliness. Mrs. Humphrey simply surpassed her well-known skills in catering to the crowd. She was assisted by Miss Bessie McKay and Miss Lewis. [4]

A. Bundy

Mrs. Willis and daughter Alice on the steps of the hotel

V. Hudson

A picture taken from the Company Hill shows the back of the Wilson Hotel with the cat walk which joined the annex with large hall and rooms above, to the main building

Other young women who worked at the hotel were Lil Hill, Annie Smith, Agnes Arthur and Mrs. Matheson. Under Mrs. Humphrey, the dining room became very popular.

1908 JANUARY ➾ The Wilson Hotel at Union Bay is noted for its fresh oyster cocktail. It takes only a minute to make one. Have a luxury! [4]

Later, the hall was converted into a general store operated by Dale and Partridge. In 1910 John Humphrey died, leaving son Jack in charge until 1913, when the business was sold to Alfred Horne.

Mr. Horne had been living in Union Bay for some time, working as a blacksmith. He successfully ran the hotel until prohibition was put into law in October 1917. With the bar the mainstay of the hotel, Mr. Horne could see no future for the establishment, so he held an auction sale and sold all the furnishings. With his earnings he bought out Charlie Bishop, and became part owner of the Nelson House and store.

1917 NOVEMBER ➾ Mr. Horne's Auction Sale attracted buyers of

Union Bay Public Library

The Willis Hotel was built and operated by Mrs. I.C. Willis in 1924

goods from far and wide. This sale marked the end of one of the Island's oldest hosteleries, as, like many more houses of the same kind since the water brigade assumed control of affairs, it had to close its doors. [6]

The big building was boarded up for several years, until the Wilson sisters returned to their old home. About the same time, in 1921, prohibition was eliminated in favour of "government control". The business was sold to O.H. Fechner who had operated several hotels in Courtenay. However, it was some time before beer parlours were given the go-ahead. In the meantime, Mr. Broder, a store owner in the annex to the hotel, charged that Mr. Fechner and Lucille McCormack were selling liquor, which was later amended to selling beer. Although the police were at the Wilson Hotel when Mr. Fechner drove up with a carload of beer, he was acquitted because the prosecution failed to prove their case.

Not long after this, the hotel mysteriously burned down, taking with it the annex containing Dale and Broder's store, the medical dispensary, and Hudson's house. It even jumped across the road and burned Waddy Wilson's house. The flames were so high, with sparks jumping everywhere, that people on the Company Hill feared for their homes. It was a spectacular fire during the night of February 18, 1922, first spotted by the train crew on the wharf. The engineer, R. Ray, sounded the alarm by tooting the train whistle long and loud. His fireman, Louis Magnone, dashed down off the wharf and across the coal flats to arouse people in the hotel. He helped pull out Mr. Partridge's 1916 Model T truck that was stored in the garage. Some say as a reward he was given the pick-up, which he drove until he died.

At that time there was no fire department at the Bay, so the best that could be done was to organize a bucket brigade.

"When it burned down, I remember I went along on my bike and went in the store and helped myself to a 2 lb. box of Peggy Duff chocolates. I'll never forget that."

Doug Brown

For years, even after the firehall was built, the safe from the old hotel sat where it had been. Surrounding the safe was a thick wall of chalk, which passing children broke off to write graffiti on the back of the firehall.

It was not long before businesses were rebuilt. The Wilson sisters constructed a residence and confectionery on their property. On October 30th, 1924, Mrs. I.C. Willis opened the beautiful Willis Hotel on property north of where the Wilson Hotel stood. Local dignitaries were invited, and teenage girls were hired to wait on tables for the feast. Not long into the evening, the lights went out, and the guests truly dined in style, by candlelight. Mrs. Willis was known in the district for her excellent cuisine. She had operated the Island Rooms in Courtenay after the death of her husband in No.6 mine.

The hotel was built by Paul St. Alben on land leased from CC(D)L. For the first six months, loggers and the boom gang from Bloedel Stewart & Welch boarded at the hotel, and walked to and from work every day. When their camp was finished, the loggers moved. Mrs. Willis never planned to have a beer parlour, but business was very poor and she was urged to apply for a liquor license. She had a lawyer friend who pulled some strings to get the license, as the town already had one beer parlour. At first, just bottled beer was served.

Logs were being shipped from Fanny Bay to Japan. When a boat came in to load, fifty longshoremen came up from Chemainus and were boarded at the hotel. Oscar Stenbeck, a bricklayer nicknamed "King Oscar", lived at the hotel and helped out. The big, burly Swede with a handsome, twisted moustache took apart a partially burned house on the Company Hill. One by one, he carried the boards down the Spring Hill and built a laundry room onto the hotel. In it were showers, an auxiliary cookstove, and a little living room for Mrs. Willis and her daughter, Alice.

"Mother had a bit of money so she took me to England for three months. When we came back, the people who were running the hotel for us had stolen all the groceries from the kitchen. Mother had left gold coins in the Union Bay bank and they were gone. She suspected that one of the employees stole them. Then Dale and Reid's store burned and the hotel caught on fire. Volunteers rushed to the rescue and put it out, but they threw a lot of the furniture out the windows and it smashed. Then they decided the beer wouldn't be any good, so they smashed all the barrels and drank it. Mother was feeling so low when Waddy Wilson, the fellow who lived across the road on the beach, walked in. He had rescued all of mother's linens and taken them over to his house. He was a real friend."

Alice (Willis) Bundy

Mrs. Willis died in 1937 after a long bout with cancer, during which time Alice quit school to nurse her mother and keep the hotel going. As she was underage, she had to hire a bartender and was able to struggle on for another year on her own. Then she leased the hotel to Joe and Annie Hastings. The following year, Alice, Mrs. Willis' only child, was married to Walter Parkin. Joe and Annie graciously hosted the wedding breakfast for sixty guests.

The Hastings ran the establishment for two and a half years, but it was a losing proposition. Alice and Walter came back to manage the hotel and bought the property from the CC(D)L.

"We went back in the September when all the Greek boats were anchored out. Everytime Greece had a victory they celebrated. They were very hard to

handle, but business was good. Then fewer boats were calling... we were so young and had a baby and a big mortgage, so we sold out at a loss to the bootlegger, Joe Damonte."

Alice (Willis) Bundy

Joe Damonte ran the hotel with the help of daughter Tina, and son-in-law Toots Plump. Athough they had a few permanent boarders, the dining room closed and profits were mainly made through the liquor outlet.

"Bars being open on Sunday is nothing new to us. We used to go to the Willis Hotel when old Joe Damonte was drawing the draft beer. He'd say, 'If you don't quiet down, I'm going to cut the beer off'. Pretty soon, Joe'd bring another round and everyone would get a little louder. He'd be looking around to see if Charlie Ennals was coming."

Bill Hamilton

The next owner was Emile Rosse who ran the hotel for seven years, then Art and Daisy Hill had it for six years.

The most infamous of Union Bay hostelries was the Palmer House. It was built by Cuddy Johnson, a well-known hotel man of the district.

1908 FERUARY ➾ The Palmer House, situated about three miles below Union Bay, overlooking the gulf, was opened on Friday. The hotel has been lately built and we are informed it is a very commodious and comfortable one. Mr. and Mrs. T. Ripley of this city have been placed in charge. The surroundings are such that the new hotel should make a pleasant place for a summer holiday. [4]

James O'Da followed the Ripley's as manager, and several others followed him. The Canadian Dollar Logging Company railway met the beach just north of the hotel, with the booming ground in front of the hotel. On Saturday night, when the camps shut down, all the loggers caught the train and landed at the "Heifer Dust", with the sole purpose of getting drunk. There was no dress code and anything went: muddy caulk boots on the floor, brawls in the bar room, prostitutes in the bedrooms.

The hotel, while suffering a bad reputation, profited by relieving the loggers of their weekly pay. When prohibition became law, it spelled the end of the heyday for the "Heifer Dust", so it was abandoned. It fell into disrepair, windows were broken, and doors stolen. In 1919, at the close of his term as police constable for the city of Courtenay, Cuddy Johnson moved his family to the hotel and through hard work refurbished the old building. It was renamed the Baynes Sound Hotel, after the body of water it faced.

Guests were few so the rooms were closed, leaving only the confectionery open, selling tobacco and soft drinks. Mr. Johnson had a beautiful orchard from which he sold fruit. He also sold chickens and eggs. The police, suspicious that the hotel was again selling alcohol, made a raid in 1923 and found intoxicants for sale in the bar. Cuddy was arrested and given six months at hard labour, while his wife and children lived on at the hotel.

For the next few years the Johnson's carried on, but the days of the hotel were numbered. In the fall of 1926, a chimney fire, which was first extinguished by a bucket brigade, restarted and the building burned to the ground. It was the second hotel in Union Bay to burn. The family moved back to Courtenay, leaving only the beautiful orchard to which the locals helped themselves.

TRANSPORTATION
WATER TRAVEL

For the earliest settlers, water travel by canoe, row boat, sailing ship or steamer was the only means of transport other than "shank's pony".

"The Captain of the 'Wellington' gave my Dad a large row boat. That summer the family rowed to Hernando Island from Union Bay for the holidays."

Florence (Manson) McKay

Possibly the first ships to bring settlers and provisions north of Nanaimo were the *Beaver* and the *Otter*, steamers of the Hudson Bay. The first Courtenay settlers arrived on the *HMS Grappler* in 1862.

As the Comox District became more settled, boats began to make regular runs. Called the mail boat for years, steamers such as the *Sir James Douglas* and *Emily Harris* were the only link with the outside world.

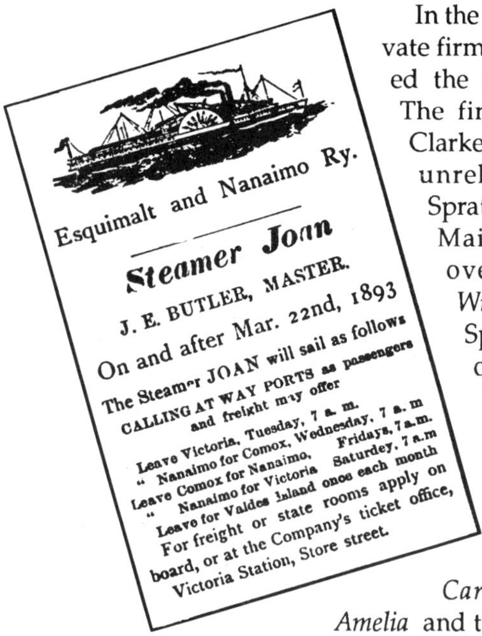

Esquimalt and Nanaimo Ry.

Steamer Joan

J. E. BUTLER, MASTER.

On and after Mar. 22nd, 1893

The Steamer JOAN will sail as follows

CALLING AT WAY PORTS as passengers and freight may offer

Leave Victoria, Tuesday, 7 a. m.
" Nanaimo for Comox, Wednesday, 7 a. m
Leave Comox for Nanaimo, Fridays, 7 a.m.
" Nanaimo for Victoria Saturday, 7 a.m
Leave for Valdes Island once each month

For freight or state rooms apply on board, or at the Company's ticket office, Victoria Station, Store street.

In the late 1870's private firms were awarded the mail contract. The first boat, W.R. Clarke's *Pilot*, was so unreliable that J. Spratt's East Coast Mail Line took over, using the *Wilson G. Hunt*. Spratt, founder of the Albion Iron Works and Victoria Machinery Depot, also used his patched up *Cariboo Fly*, the *Amelia* and the *Maude*. The latter, a sidewheeler, was commanded by a Swede, Captain Holmes, remembered for the earring he wore in one ear. These ships probably stopped at the long wharf at Quadra (Buckley Bay) to leave supplies and load coal from the fledgling mine.

The fortnightly service left Victoria for Burrard Inlet, then sailed Tuesday for Nanaimo, up the coast the next day to Comox, and back to Nanaimo on Thursday, arriving in Victoria on Saturday.

After the Union Coal Co. started and the wharf was built at Hart's Point, the mail boats and all passenger boats called at the little port, which soon replaced Comox as the major disembarking point. In the 1880's the E&N, which was owned by Dunsmuir, had boats competing for the passenger trade between Vancouver and the Island. The side wheeler, *Robert Dunsmuir*, first used as a passenger boat on this run, was given the nickname, *Dirty Bob*, because of the coal dust and livestock littering the deck. The Dunsmuir boat, which brought many of the original miners to Union Wharf, was the steam tug *Isobel*. She transported most of the machinery and building materials to the budding port.

By 1889 the *Isobel*, which could carry about 100 passengers, was making two trips per

Provincial Archives HP 39739

SS Joan

K. Drushka

The *Isobel* which brought many of the original miners and settlers to Union Wharf

J. Anderson

City of Nanaimo landing at the freight wharf

Mr. Wilson as bartender was in great request by male passengers. It will be necessary to take a complete new stock of fire water as he was pretty well cleared out.

On the return trip, in spite of half a gale in our teeth, the ship behaved well and the passengers proved themselves sailors by the gusto with which they kept time with the music. Just at gloaming the electric lights were started and added a greater brilliancy to the sailors. At 8:00 p.m. we came to port all greatly satisfied. [2]

After Captain Butler was killed in a hunting accident at Deep Bay, Captain Locke took over the *Joan*. Then, in 1896, the *City of Nanaimo* was overhauled and changed routes with the *Joan*. At a time of less than three hours to cross from Nanaimo to Vancouver, the *Joan* could better compete with the Union Steam Ship *Cutch*. So it was that many of the early settlers to Union Bay travelled to their new home across Canada to Vancouver via the CPR, across Georgia Strait to Nanaimo on the *Joan*, then up the east coast aboard the *City of Nanaimo*.

week and carrying the mail to Union Wharf. In June 1892 the mines closed temporarily, and 112 miners crowded aboard the *Isobel* and headed for the bright lights of Nanaimo. Dunsmuir could see the need for a larger boat so a new ship, named after his mother, was built at Albion Iron Works in Victoria. Captain Butler left the *Isobel* to take command of the *Joan*, which was 180' long with a 30' beam, and registered tonnage of 600 tons. Powered by 85 h.p. engines, she boasted "110 Edison electric lights", as well as sanitary and fire pumps. There was sleeping accommodation for thirty-four people in well-appointed state rooms. The cabins, saloons and dining room were also beautifully decorated. To celebrate the *Joan*'s arrival, 100 residents enjoyed an excursion from Union Wharf to Valdez Island.

1892 AUGUST The company kindly provided a train from Union to the Wharf, where the *SS Joan* sailed from at 6:30 a.m. She proceeded to Denman and then to Comox where parties joined the excursion. Breakfast was first in the commodious dining room, the start of a busy day for the well-known steward, Mr. Scott, attending to the wants of all aboard whose appetites were not diminished by the sea air. Then everyone viewed the scenery from the beautiful boat as she truly walked the waters - a thing of life. Proud owner James Dunsmuir was aboard, but the success of the excursion was due to jovial Captain Butler.

The vessel went as far north as Grant's Logging at Seymour Narrows, where the passengers went ashore and were entertained by Mr. Hugh Grant. Dancing was indulged in at intervals, the upper deck being just the thing for that purpose. Music was provided by the Roy Bros. of Union.

The *City of Nanaimo*, 159' long with a 32' beam, was originally built at False Creek in 1891 for the Mainland & Nanaimo Steam Navigation Co. Owner Wm. Rogers borrowed money from Dunsmuir to build the boat, but because trade was slow, could not make every payment. His good friend, James, foreclosed on him and acquired the boat in 1896. The E&N immediately spent $18,000 to completely overhaul the *Nanaimo*. Boilers, engine and hull were all repaired and an electric light system installed, which even provided twenty-three lights for the cattle and cargo in the hold. A derrick capable of lifting ten tons was installed on the deck. The interior saloons were richly furnished.

1896 SEPTEMBER In the dining saloon, covered with stout linoleum, handsome Spanish mahogany sideboards are provided along with walnut tables. The windows are screened with tasteful curtains of a crimson tint. The upper deck is divided into three portions: smoking saloon, general saloon, and ladies' cabin. This was furnished in exquisite taste with a beautiful Brussel's carpet and circular settee covered in dark red plush. On each side is a tier of staterooms, refurnished with basins in walnut stands (equipped with tap service), steam radiators, and electric lamps, each accommodating three persons. The interior of the whole deck is painted white, relieved by floral designs of a rose pattern. In the circle of the roof at both ends are views in and about Nanaimo. The whole appearance of the deck is light, pleasant and comfortable. Clusters of electric lights furnish the necessary light at night. [2]

The E&N was sold to the CPR in 1905 and with it went the *Joan* and *City of Nanaimo*, which continued on the same routes until 1911 when they were sold to the Terminal Navigation Co.

In 1912 all the CPR boats were painted the same colours. The black hulls and white upper decks with buff smoke stacks tipped with black were a welcome sight pulling into port. The new Princesses were especially adapted for traffic on the rugged B.C.

G. Francklyn

SS Charmer

coastline, with features borrowed from ocean, river, and coastal steamers. The ships' sides, from the main deck upwards, were built perpendicular. This feature, inherited from the riverboats, enabled the ferries to land in any condition of wind and tide at the wharf without damage. Union Bay, like most of the government wharves, had a ferry slip. Freight could be loaded through the freight doors on the ship's side and up the slip to the wharf deck. This eliminated much of the need for derricks and winches, although large unmanageable pieces of freight, like the first automobiles, were unloaded that way.

When the CPR announced that it was having a new steamer built in Scotland for the local run, everyone followed newspaper reports of her trials on the Clyde. Christened *Princess Mary*, the 210' ship with one stack could do fourteen knots and was said to be practically unsinkable due to seven watertight bulkheads. In March of 1911 she was greeted by the whole town when she arrived after a trying eighty-five day passage, to take over the east coast run in March of 1911. Everyone looked forward to a trip on this fast new ferry. Despite a petition from the east coast passengers, she was replaced a year later by the old *Charmer*, a ship that had often done relief duty on the run.

The *Charmer*, built in 1887 in San Francisco for the CN, started life as the 200' long *Premier*. Lavishly fitted for her day, she was the first ship in B.C. waters to have electricity, so she was the talk of the waterfront. After a collision with the collier *Williamette*, which killed several passengers, the *Premier* was beached near Port Angeles. She was guarded and libelled for damages by the Americans, but she was pirated back into Canadian waters by the CN and repaired. A year later, in 1894, she was renamed the *Charmer* and served on the Victoria to Vancouver run. In 1912 she replaced the new

B. Sherburn

Princess Mary

Issued July 27, 1935

POWELL RIVER - COMOX

STEAMSHIP "PRINCESS MARY"

Lv. Vancouver	11:45 p.m. Tue.	11.45 p.m. Thu.	11:45 p.m. Sat.
Ar. Powell River	6:30 a.m. Wed.	6:30 a.m. Fri.	6:30 a.m. Sun.
Lv. Powell River	8:00 a.m. Wed.	8:00 a.m. Fri.	8:00 a.m. Sun.
Ar. Hornby Island	10:00 a.m. Wed.		10:00 a.m. Sun.
Ar. Denman Island	a.m. Wed.		
Ar. Union Bay	p.m. Wed.	a.m. Fri.	a.m. Sun.
Ar. Comox	p.m. Wed.	p.m. Fri.	p.m. Sun.
Lv. Comox	2:30 p.m. Wed.	2:30 p.m. Fri.	p.m. Sun.
Ar. Powell River	p.m. Wed.	p.m. Fri.	p.m. Sun.
Lv. Powell River	11:15 p.m. Wed.	11:15 p.m. Fri.	11:15 p.m. Sun.
Ar. Vancouver	6:30 a.m. Thu.	6:30 a.m. Sat.	6:30 a.m. Mon.

Where no date shown steamship does not call.

MEAL SERVICE

Breakfasts, 35¢ to 75¢, Children 35¢ to 40¢; Table d'Hote Luncheon 50¢ and Dinner 75¢, Children 40¢; Afternoon Tea 35¢; Night Lunch, 50¢

ESQUIMALT AND NANAIMO RAILWAY

NORTHBOUND train for Nanaimo, Victoria and intermediate points leaves Union Bay at 11:35 a.m. daily except Sunday.

SOUTHBOUND train for Nanaimo, Victoria and intermediate points leaves Union Bay at 11:35 a.m. daily except Sunday

Princess on the east coast and served in this capacity, even after a collision with the *Island Princess* in 1920. Provisions were made to carry cars and she often supplemented the Nanaimo boats in auto transport during the summer. She was converted to oil in 1924 and ended up in 1932 as a floating hotel at Newcastle Island.

In the late 1920's the route was served by the *Princess Royal*. Built at Esquimalt in 1907, she was one of the few Princesses built locally. She was 228' long with one stack. At the end of her career, when she serviced the people of Union Bay, she had been converted to oil. She retired in 1932 and was sold for scrap.

In 1914 the *Princess Mary* was converted to oil and lengthened by fifty feet, adding twenty-four new staterooms and a large social hall. After 1932 she became a permanent fixture on the run to Union Bay and Comox, until the late '40s. In 1952 the stern section of the top deck was removed and taken ashore in Victoria, where it became the Princess Mary Restaurant which is still popular today. The hull became Bulk Carrier No.1 and sank the same year. *Princess Elaine*, a big ship with three stacks, carried on the service for over a year, until the maintenance was too costly and the passengers too few to continue the service.

Even after train, bus and automobile travel became the preferred way to go, steamer travel remained popular. It was the only way to get to Powell River, and it made a very relaxing trip to Vancouver. Baseball, basketball and soccer teams took the ferry to Powell River for tournaments. For a wonderful outing in the summer, the young people at the Bay took their bicycles to Comox on the boat and biked home. There was just time to sit on the deck and eat a bag lunch, or buy an ice cream cone in the dining room.

While the CPR steamships were providing Union Bay with weekly or bi-weekly passenger and freight service, the Union Steamships also called. From 1889 on, the Union Steamships, with black hulls, white upper decks and blacktipped red funnels, were a reassuring sight up many inlets where no other ferry or freight service ran. Until after WW I they were coal burners, and as most of their routes were north of Vancouver to Alaska, they naturally came to the Bay for bunker fuel. For some, it was a stop on their scheduled runs to logging claims and points north.

The pioneer of the logging camp runs was the 101' long *SS Comox*, built in Vancouver in 1891 to accommodate 200 passengers. Her hull was prefabricated in sections in Scotland and became the first steel boat built in B.C. Sharing the logging routes was the *Cassiar No.1*, also built in Vancouver, in 1901. She was also 101' long, but only licensed to carry 144 passengers. Known as the "loggers palace", she boasted a logger's saloon.

These boats travelled little-known inlets and bays, tying up at floats and booms of the hand-loggers, bringing equipment and supplies. When they stopped for bunker on the way south, the loggers poured out and into the Wilson or Nelson Hotel, some of them never making it to Vancouver. A little later, the *Cowichan* joined the logging route, and is well-remembered by the old-timers at the Bay. Nick-named *The Cow*, she inaugurated a Saturday night sailing from Vancouver to Nanaimo, then up to Union Bay on Sunday morning, arriving back in Vancouver at midnight on Sunday. It was a quick way to get to town. By 1911 the *Cowichan* was making two calls a week at Union Bay, and the hotels were

G. Francklyn

C. Stewart

Left: *SS Cowichan* landing at Denman Island. Right: Catherine Graham christens her namesake on the Denman Island ferry run. Dr. Giovando, MLA, Mr. Jones and P. Gagliardi, Minister of Highways, look on

listed on "the upcoast street-car line", which included eighteen ports with hotel accommodations. This was a popular holiday for mainland residents.

"When I was sixteen I was working for A.P. Slade's shipping department, but I could always see the boats out the door. So I went down to the boats and the fellow said, 'Sure, you can come to work right now, but you better go buy yourself a pair of pants. You can't wear those pantaloon things aboard ship.' I don't know where I got the five bucks to buy the pants, but that was my first long pants. I worked on the Union Steamships, the good ship 'Cowichan'. She made three trips a week, and one took freight and passengers to Lasqueti, Hornby, Denman, Union Bay, Comox, Blubber Bay, Vananda and Powell River. In summer she'd take holidayers to Gibson's Landing, Sechelt, and Savary Island."

Harold Peters

Remembered also is the old *Capilano*, the first British vessel to sail from B.C. to the Klondike Gold Rush in 1897. Living in a port, the people at the Bay were fortunate in that they saw history being made. Northbound ships came for bunker loaded with miners, equipment, dogs and horses. On the southward journey they were loaded with sealskins, salmon and gold. The *Coquitlam*, another familiar United Steamship, was seized by the Americans during a sealing trade dispute. Instead of being cut off from world news, as were so many small towns of that time, Union Bay knew or saw many of the key figures.

During the war, all the ships on the coast were painted battleship grey. It was the CNR's three-funnelled luxury liner *SS Prince George*, in the employ of the Canadian government, that loaded up all the Japanese of the district at Union Bay and took them from their homes to a very uncertain future.

Jack Bradley, captain of the Denman Island ferries *Moniker* and *Billy B.*

C. Stewart

Denman was a scheduled stop for most of the above boats but, with the advent of the automobile, the growing number of settlers on the Island wanted easier and faster access to the Comox Valley. Between 1923 and 1930 Alby Graham and his boat, *Diane*, with a raft attached, filled the need. On request he carried passengers, cars and freight to Buckley Bay. The landing was rough as the cars had to drive over the beach and up planks onto and off the raft.

By the late 1920's there were sixty cars on the Island and the people were demanding a better service. Meetings, petitions, and the help of Dr. McNaughton, MLA, resulted in a new service administered by the Public Works Dept. Sandy Swan was awarded the contract. With a scow lashed to it, the *MV Garry Point 11* made three scheduled trips daily, carrying three vehicles per trip.

The Baikie Bros. won the contract in 1935 and employed Jack Bradley to skipper the *MV Moniker*. Jack grew up in Union Bay. Because his father had lost his job and house in Cumberland during the strike of 1913, the family moved to a little house on the Laird property. His mother, Sara, an older sister of the Shillito brothers, had three boys and a girl. His father, Arthur, was brakeman on the coal train at the Bay for thirty-four years.

Jack started his life on the sea with Union Steamships. During the eighteen years he was captain he found himself being called to most

H. Kennedy

Tommy James' and Dave Campbell's boat, at anchor by the government wharf

H. Kennedy

Every ten years the harbour was dredged to keep it one of the best harbours on the B.C. coast

emergencies, so he prepared himself by studying first-aid. He often got instructions on how to treat patients by phone from the doctor before transporting the sick or injured person to Buckley Bay and a waiting ambulance. On January 15, 1937 during a cold stormy crossing, a three pound baby girl, Catherine Graham, was born aboard the *Moniker*.

In 1940 the Baikie Bros. bought a larger boat, the *Billy B*. By 1953 there were six scheduled trips per day. The population again outgrew the ferry and a new boat was built by the government. Seventeen years after being born crossing Baynes Sound, Catherine Graham christened her namesake.

At Union Bay Tommy James owned a gas launch which people could hire. Tommy, a short little man, lived in a shack on the beach, south of Anderson's store. When he first came to Union Bay he worked in the Washer, where his arm was caught in the machinery and badly injured. Blood poisoning set in and the arm had to be amputated. His only means of livelihood after that was by hiring out his boat. It is remembered fondly as it was the transportation to many happy occasions: a dance on Denman, a wildflower hunt on Yellow Rock, or a picnic on Tree Island. Tommy also transported loggers to and from Denman Island, and towed booms of logs.

"Old Tommy and I beachcombed; he had the boat and I did the work. He could start that boat with one hand better than I could with two. He'd get "tight" and I'd have to run the boat. One night Charlie Hendrin and him ended up high and dry on the spit."

Jim McKay

For a few years in the 1940's, a water taxi serviced a triangle from Texada Island to Powell River, Comox and Union Bay. The *Ladyslipper*, operated by Ben Nicholas, had a regular run but could be hired anytime.

WHARVES AND FREIGHT

During the construction of the railway and coal loading wharf, men, supplies and equipment were brought into Baynes Sound aboard boats like Manson's *Rustler*. The ship would come as close as possible to the beach, and large rowboats, scows or rafts were rowed out from shore and the cargo transferred. Several loads and men were lost in heavy seas during the process, and often vessels were swamped when they were beached to be unloaded.

The bay at Jack Hart Point was a natural harbour, protected from the open water of Georgia Straight by Denman Island. Unlike Royston, it was fairly deep, and was further deepened by dredging.

1902 APRIL ➾ The Government dredge *Mud Lark* is still at work deepening the water in the harbour. Vessels of the deepest draft can now load at any tide. [4]

The first dock at Union Wharf was a natural extension of the railway which was built to Union Mines in 1888. The first coal shipment left the new dock in July 1889, which is described in the chapter on the Union Colliers. The freight wharf, built beside the trestle, was 900' long and 40' wide, with a single track running down to the warehouse. Reginald Pidcock built his little ship, *Daisy*, at Courtenay and used it to carry many loads of produce from the farmers in Courtenay to Union Wharf, where it was transferred to the train and taken to Union.

In 1894 at a political rally, J.B. Holmes pointed out the need for a government wharf at Baynes Sound. However, the Union Coal Company, which carried most of the freight and passengers on their E&N boats, decided to build a more efficient dock to accommodate the new steamer, *Joan*. Tenders were called in the spring of 1895 for a freight wharf.

1895 MAY ➾ Contract for lumber for the new wharf was awarded to Urquhart Bros. Mill, who have recently installed a planer. On Tuesday they started a raft containing 60,000 board feet, which will be towed around to the point. The contract calls for 200,000 board feet. Contract for building the new wharf for the *Joan* at Baynes Sound was awarded to Geo. McLaughlin. [3b]

Built just north of the coal dock, the new wharf was much lower so that the cars did not have to go down an incline plane. The transfer slip was about 60' long and 20' wide, and could be raised or lowered to accommodate the tide. The weight of the slip, which was many tons, was counter-balanced by cast iron weights, which made it easy to raise and lower by hand-operated winches. The main structure was filled solid with rock and dross for about one-third of its length. The planks and rails were taken off the old freight section of the coal wharf and used on the new one. J. Carthew's gang of carpenters, with A. Beaton as foreman, built the new 35' x 90' freight shed.

All the supplies for the mines, shipping docks, and citizens came through this new wharf. An early form of container shipping was even practised with railroad cars loaded in Vancouver or Victoria.

1900 ➾ A carload of cattle, one of mules and one of flour has been taken to Cumberland without breaking bulk. This is a very great convenience and saving of time and expense to the merchants of Cumberland to have their merchandise thus handled without the delay and loss attendant on each time goods are handled. [4]

The main advantage of the new wharf was that it was built apart from the coal dock. The railway from the freight wharf extended about a quarter of a mile before connecting with the main line, thus leaving the coal yard track free for loading coal.

Much earlier, George Howe had built a little wharf or landing platform in front of his store.

"You remember the rock pile at Sandy Beach? That is where they brought the scows with the stuff for the store. There were all cross timbers with the rocks to hold it. The top had boards on it. The freight was put on scows and brought ashore, then wheeled up to the store. The old 'City of Nanaimo' would come in there at a real high tide and let people off."

Joe Walker

In 1909 the first Government wharf was built at the bottom of McLeod Road. The 600' wooden structure stood on piles driven in by a huge pile driver. A small float reached by a gangplank was built for the use of fishing boats and pleasure craft. Built at the end was a large freight shed. This was used only for local freight, as the CPR ships still called at the Company dock, where freight and passengers for Cumberland were transferred onto the train. Union Steamships used the new wharf exclusively.

D. Walker

M. Vowels

Left: The freight shed and dock with transfer slip built for freight steamers in 1895. Right: Swimmers at Sandy Beach beside the old landing platform in front of Howe's store. The government wharf is in the background

1909 SEPTEMBER ➾ The *SS Cowichan* sailed from the new Government Wharf on Sunday last, much to the disappointment of a few who had their baggage at the Company dock. However, transportation was done on short notice. [4]

Every boat day, come rain, shine or howling southeaster, Fraser and Bishop's gardener and handyman, Hungo, was waiting on the Government wharf to catch the rope and make the boat fast. He loaded up his wagon with mail and goods for the well-stocked store.

It was fun on a hot day to meet the boat at the new wharf and buy an ice cream cone. Some of the captains even allowed the boys and girls to take the short trip to the Company wharf.

About every ten years the harbour was dredged and the wharf would be repaired. In 1928 a new deck was put on but not enough money was provided for a railing. In December of that year Adolf Anderson tripped and was killed when he fell off the wharf onto a piling. A railing was soon added. The whole wharf was completely rebuilt with a smaller freight shed in 1939. A 115' breakwater was added on the south side to protect the float. By the late 1950's, ferries were not calling at the wharf, so when a new wharf was necessary the old one was taken down and was replaced by a narrow 5' wide wharf. The float with gang plank was renewed but the freight shed was not replaced.

Union Bay School Collection

The government wharf built opposite the Nelson Hotel in 1909

G. Francklyn

A 40' high lighthouse was erected in 1890 on Yellow Rock, later known as Chrome Island

LIGHTHOUSE

The ship which was to carry the first load of coal from Union Wharf, in July 1889, visited the port four months earlier with a few hundred tons of supplies. The largest ship to coal at Nanaimo, the *San Mateo*, with her experienced and knowledgeable skipper, Capt. Colville, came to Union Wharf to test the nearly completed facilities. He also gave a report on the navigation problems for large ships going north of Nanaimo and into Baynes Sound.

1889 MARCH ➾ The most important aid, in Captain Colville's opinion, is the erection of a lighthouse at a fair elevation, off Maple Spit, opposite Yellow Rock. A light situated on this spit would be a leading light from the Gulf, and on passing, it would be a stern light to within a very short distance of the loading wharves. On the other hand, if the light was stationed on Yellow Rock, it would only be a leading light from the Gulf and the minute the vessel entered the sound the light would be of no avail. [2]

Captain Colville further recommended a fog station be erected on the spit, and that until the construction of the lighthouse, trips by large steamships in and out of Baynes Sound be made during daylight. This report was to add considerable weight to the Comox Member of Parliament D. W. Gordon's plea to obtain the necessary aids for navigation to serve the new port. Although the captain's opinion was endorsed by all the leading pilots in British Columbian waters, the Government chose Yellow Rock, later known as Chrome Island, as the site. In January 1890, J.A. Brittancourt of Nanaimo was awarded the contract to erect a 40' high wooden structure. Attached to it was a small house, a boat house, and an oil house. In October the Superintendent of Carpenters and Mr. Gordon inspected the buildings and found them not up to specifications. Improvements were made, and two months later, on December 13 at 5:00 a.m., the light was lit, tested, and pronounced excellent by Captain Gaudin aboard the Government steamer *Sir James Douglas*. The light was small, just 35 millimetres, powered by oil and set in a round case of polished chrome reflectors. The case floated in a basin of mercury and was made to revolve by a system of weights suspended on cables. At dusk the keeper lit the light and wound the cable to the top of the tower, then the weights dropped slowly to the bottom. The keeper had to repeat this every four hours through the night, and during days of fog or snow. Added to this chore was operating the hand-held blast foghorn, until it was replaced in 1903 by a newly invented compressed air foghorn.

Walter H. Piercy was hired as the first light-tender when the light became functional on January 1, 1891. His family lived with him on the rock and were still there when Mr. Piercy died of consumption at Courtenay in 1893. Mrs. Piercy, with her four children, carried on the work for a time.

William McDonagh took charge in 1898. Unfortunately, in December 1900, the light at Yellow Rock did not warn the determined Capt. Yorke of the steamer *Alpha*. In 1898 the 700 ton *Alpha* was brought from the Atlantic to ferry miners and supplies to the Klondike goldrush. She made several successful runs, returning with fortunes in gold. But her age and the Arctic ice had taken their toll. No one wanted her so she was to be sold in the Orient, the last service of many ships. Only a few days out of Victoria, she returned with engine and firerooms flooded. After repairs she was ready to sail again, but a number of the crew refused to sail and deserted. The engineer charged that the ship was unseaworthy, and overloaded with 630 tons of salted salmon plus coal. He was arrested and jailed for ten days. In the meantime replacements were found, and the *Alpha* set sail to replenish her coal supply at Union Bay before heading to Japan. Aboard was the owner, Samuel Barber, and his brother, but no pilot.

Denman Island Museum

The *Alpha* was wrecked on Yellow Rock in 1900. The owner, captain and five seamen were lost

H. Kennedy

The government steamer *Stewart* takes on coal to be delivered to lighthouses up and down the coast

1900 DECEMBER ➾ The Wreck of the *Alpha* at Yellow Rock Light, 6:45 p.m. Saturday. Headed for the Collieries' wharves on Baynes Sound, the *Alpha* was steaming up the Gulf through the rain and snow at a normal speed, when twice the Japanese watch shouted down that there was a steady light dead ahead. The stubborn Yorke refused to alter his course and the ship struck the rock. The force of the impact drove her fast on the reef. It was low water, and the crew and passengers clung to the rigging that wasn't swept away. A hero emerged. Sailor Hanson, on the forecastle head, secured a line and watched for his opportunity. When a receding wave left the rock below him dry, he dropped down and made a fifty yard run for shore. The next wave caught him and hurled him into a crevice from which he crawled and made the line fast to a rock pinnacle. The first mate held and followed the rope, taking a second line ashore. He then coaxed most of the crew, two passengers, and two stowaways to trust themselves to the rope. Five seamen, Capt. Yorke, and Mr. Barber could not be persuaded to leave and scaled the rigging. Mr. Wilkinson, 1st mate, ended his pleading and swung off the ropes. The men on shore heard the crashing of timber at 1:00 a.m., which heralded the end of the *Alpha* on the reef. [4]

William McDonagh, the lighthouse keeper, provided temporary shelter and first aid for the twenty-six freezing men. On Sunday afternoon the Ford brothers from Hornby ferried the men to Union Wharf, where they were put up in homes and hotels. The storm which had raged for three days brought down the wires to Cumberland and scattered trees over the tracks, so that word did not reach the mining town or Victoria until Monday.

The locals on Denman salvaged bits of furniture and timbers, and collected the dog salmon which made excellent fertilizer. Three bodies were found by T. Nelson, and coffins were made by R. Swan. The bodies of Samuel Barber and the engineer were sent to Vancouver, but the third, a stowaway, was buried on the Island.

After the disaster, shipping companies and the coal company petitioned the Government for a new light. They argued that the fixed white light could be mistaken for a farm house. Finally, in 1922, a new revolving-type light was installed which flashed every six seconds.

Over the years, the Yellow Rock light has been faithfully attended by a number of keepers. During the First World War James F. Street tended the light, and his daughter Olive was born there. Soon after, the family moved to Union Bay where Mr. Street worked as a mechanic in charge of locomotive repairs. Son Frank did his apprenticeship in the machine shops. He married Gladys Piercy and Olive married Bill Burgess. Both couples, with their families, lived for many years at the Bay.

ROADS

Long before there was any industry in Union Bay, the few farmers living in the Comox district wanted a road to join them with their markets in Nanaimo, and Victoria. In the early 1860's a wagon road had been opened from Victoria to Nanaimo and had then been allowed to grow over. It was re-opened and graded in 1884, so that horse and buggy could travel between the two cities. At this time the north end went to Wellington, with a trail continuing to French Creek. Here it forked, with one branch going to Alberni and the other to Comox. For a shorter route to Alberni one could take the Comox trail to Big Qualicum, go inland, and hire a canoe to cross Horne Lake.

Possibly because the west coast water route was long and dangerous, the Government decided to build a colonization road between Nanoose Bay and Alberni. By the late 1880's, although Alberni had only 200 settlers to Comox's 2,000, it had a passable road over which the Alberni Stage Line carried passengers and mail.

The people of the Comox Valley demanded a road by writing editorials, sending off petitions and holding meetings. After the mines opened, the town of Union grew rapidly and provided a ready market for the valley farmers. However, with no road between the two settlements, produce had to be taken to Comox. There it was put on a steamer which transported it to Union Wharf, where it was then loaded onto the train for Union. Even getting to the wharf at Comox

N. King

James Street, lighthouse keeper, and his family: Mrs. Street, Frank, Olive and Phyllis

was a struggle, as the Courtenay and Puntledge bridges often washed out, and the Long Bridge along the dyke (built in 1876) was always in need of repair.

A large public meeting was held in 1889 which Premier Robson attended and was forcefully told of the necessity for a road. He promised the road, and finally, at the end of 1891, wagons could drive the five miles between Courtenay and Union. The road was narrow with not much clearing on the right of way. In January 1894 twenty-three trees fell across it in one night. This was so common an occurrence that all travellers carried saws and axes.

The little town of Union Wharf was growing. With the installation of the Washer in 1895, and the promise of coke ovens, the farmers saw another market. They argued that a road to the port would give them access not only to the regular steamer to Nanaimo but to other ships as well. They urged that the 3 1/2 mile road south of Courtenay be connected to the road that turned off at French Creek.

Finally, in 1895, the government started the project. It allotted $8,000, which was equally divided between Nanaimo and Comox so that the road could be started from both ends. Gradually, the road crews in the district started work with hired teams of oxen and horses. The best time to build roads was summer, but it was hard to man crews and harder still to get teams and wagons because they were busy on the farms. There were always complaints of the money being poorly spent or not spent at all.

The road was divided into sections of 5 or 6 miles, and let out to contractors.

Contract: To construct a portion of the Nanaimo Trunk Road.
Bayne Sound to Roys. 6th day of Sept.1895
Agreement between S. Creech of Comox and Hugh Stewart, Chief Commissioner of Lands and Works.

The road from Baynes Sound to Roys, commencing at the 12 and 1/2 mile post near Howe's Habit to the 18 and 1/4 milepost at Roys, a distance of 5 and 3/4 miles.

Will pay $3,335 on completion.

WARNING.

All persons driving over the wharf or bridges in Comox district faster than a walk, will be prosecuted according to law.

S. Creech,
Gov. Agent

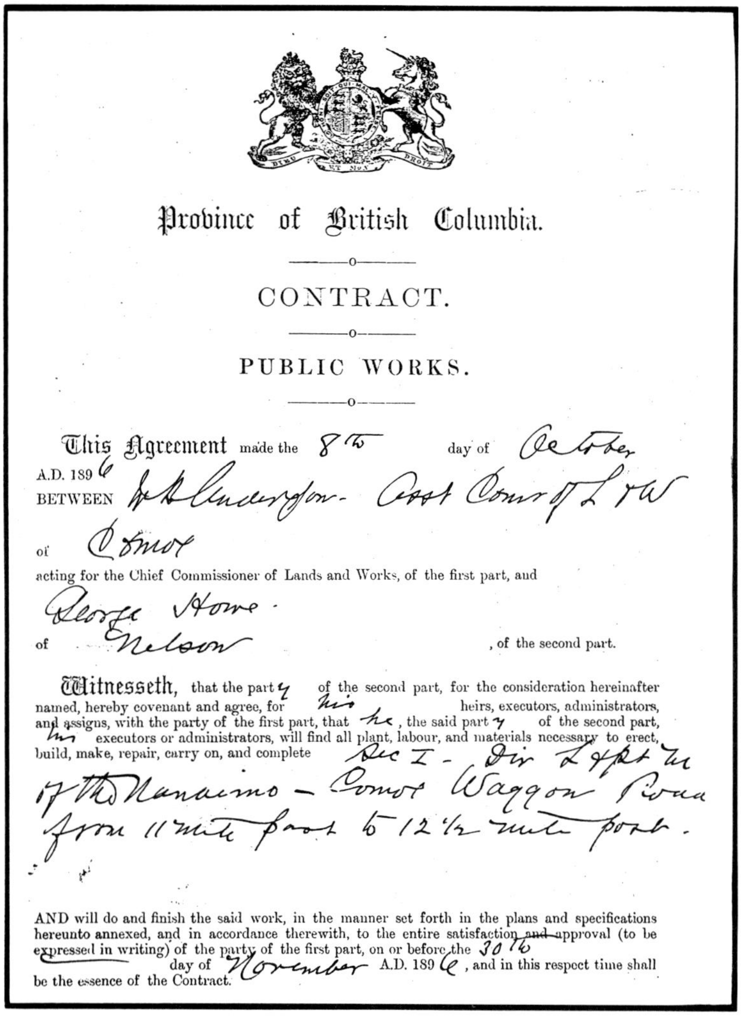

Province of British Columbia.

CONTRACT.

PUBLIC WORKS.

This Agreement made the 8th day of October A.D. 1896 BETWEEN W. A. Anderson - Asst Comr of L & W of Comox acting for the Chief Commissioner of Lands and Works, of the first part, and George Howe. of Nelson, of the second part.

Witnesseth, that the party of the second part, for the consideration hereinafter named, hereby covenant and agree, for his heirs, executors, administrators, and assigns, with the party of the first part, that he, the said party of the second part, his executors or administrators, will find all plant, labour, and materials necessary to erect, build, make, repair, carry on, and complete Sec I - Div 2 & part of the Nanaimo - Comox Waggon Road from 11 mile post to 12 1/2 mile post.

AND will do and finish the said work, in the manner set forth in the plans and specifications hereunto annexed, and in accordance therewith, to the entire satisfaction ~~and approval~~ (to be expressed in writing) of the party of the first part, on or before the 30th day of November A.D. 1896, and in this respect time shall be the essence of the Contract.

Following the line of the old Comox-Victoria trail:

- All bush and trees must be felled to a width of 12'.
- All stumps must be burned or dug out.
- Roots from other trees must be cut off.
- All stones and rocks to be removed in such a manner that no impediment shall be offered man or beast.
- All inequalities of surface to be cut down or filled up. No fillings of rotten wood accepted, hard material only to be used.
- All soft and mirey places to be corduroyed with substantial corduroy of a clear width of 8'.

Agreement with Sam Creech.

The amount paid was partly based on the figure of $2.00 for "grubbing out" a tree. On this section there were 490 trees to be taken off the road allowance. In 1896 the section to the south of Union Bay to Fanny Bay was constructed with T. Lee as contractor. He subcontracted 1 1/2 miles to Geo. Howe.

Finally, in 1899 the wagon road was declared finished. Although called a road, it left much to be desired. Some of the streams, still not bridged, had to be forded. At Big Qualicum, Qualicum Tom ran a roadhouse for travellers. He also hired out his large flat-bottomed boat to cross the river. The wagon or carriage would be put into the boat and the horses let loose to swim. In spring, when the river was high, horses, wagon and driver would often end up downstream and have to find their way through the bush back to the road. In winter, wagons got stuck in the mud. Trees blew across the road, especially between Union Bay and Qualicum, where a "Qualicum" (a westerly wind) could whip through, twisting trees this way and that.

When the automobile arrived, the roads were still very rough and narrow. There were stumps close to the edge, which several novice drivers managed to hit.

Roads were always a hot political topic. The candidates always promised more and better roads. In an effort to have smoother roads in the district, Mike Manson, MLA, tried to get a steamroller. However, he was refused on the grounds that the culverts and bridges were too weak.

Each area had a local road foreman who was responsible for keeping the road in good condition. Alex McLeod, who operated a livery stable, was the first in Union Bay. With his team and wagon he filled in potholes with gravel from the beach north of Union Bay. 1st Road, 2nd Road, 3rd Road, and 4th Road went from the highway down to the beach, where gravel was loaded onto the wagon by hand. It was spread by removing one or two floor boards, and levelled by his team pulling huge scrapers. Sometimes he hired men to clean out culverts,

G. Murdock

Ladies out for a walk on the early wagon road through Union

to slash brush along the roadway, and to repair bridges. There were three bridges between Union Bay and the railway crossing: one at Washer Creek, another 500' beyond at the bottom of the hill in front of "Japtown", and a third to span the creek near the crossing.

From Washer Creek, the road swung south to the head of the Bay and followed the shoreline, with Simon Leiser's store and the boarding house between the road and the beach. After the flood of 1912, the road was relocated closer to the company houses and past the Wilson Hotel, then followed the shoreline through the village.

Between the hotel and Russell's Hill was a very swampy area, so a sidewalk, just two 4" x 12" boards wide and 4' high in places, was constructed about 1910. The occasional hotel patron, wending his way home, ended up in the swamp. A few years later, a 4' wide boardwalk stretched from Fraser & Horne's store to Chinatown. Most of the way it followed the fences, which served as a railing.

In the 1920's Emerson Muschamp was awarded the job of road boss. Alfred Walker succeeded Alexander Cowie as foreman for Fanny Bay. All were farmers and had their own teams to help with the road work.

The Company Hill and the two access roads to it, Russell and Marshall (later called Reid), were maintained by the company, as well as the original road up to Langley Lake which left

L. Kilvert

Three little girls on the section of the board walk that was over the swamp near the Wilson Hotel

V. Hudson

The board walk stretched from Chinatown to the Nelson Hotel

E. Hallstrom

Ethel Shillito on Washer Creek bridge

G. Robertson

Marjorie Peters and Margaret Glover in front of the sign at the Government Wharf showing 60 miles to Nanaimo

the highway between the Church and post office. About 1913, when land was surveyed and lots sold, the lake road was re-routed and came straight down to the government wharf. Originally surveyed as Stanford Road, it became known as Walker's Hill because the Walker family lived at the top. Later, it received the name, McLeod Road, because Alex McLeod farmed up the hill. Station Road was constructed to connect the wharf with the E&N station in 1914.

A big improvement came in 1926, when the road beds were prepared and coated with a hard tarvia.

Contract: July 16, 1926.
Bituminous Carpet coat on portion of the Island Highway and Cumberland Road in the vicinity of Courtenay, Union Bay and Cumberland.
General Construction Co. Ltd.
per John Boyd.
- Tarvia to come by E&N tank cars to Courtenay
- Road sprayed to be 16' wide

Cost total $10,810.00

L. Bohn

Some of Campbell and Bennett's equipment used to widen and straighten the highway in 1947

M. Vowels

Many buildings had to be moved to allow the highway to be straightened. The "glass house" was relocated to the other side of the new roadway

In 1947, the Government awarded the contract to Campbell and Bennett to widen and straighten the highway from north of Buckley Bay through Union Bay. For over a year, the citizens of the Bay breathed thick dust and watched in amazement and horror as large earthmoving machines changed the nature of the town. Gone was the meandering road along the beach. As many of the homes and out buildings had been built close to the road, they had to be moved for the new highway. Hasting's store and garage were moved across the road and put between the school and jail. The old bank (Mac McCullock's house) was moved to Station Road. The "glass house" was moved across the road and south nearer the entrance to town.

Contract: June 13, 1947.
To be completed Aug. 10, 1947

Union Bay moving buildings.
Contractor: Mr.E. Warburton

- Mr. McCullock Moving House	$ 310.00
- Garages - Mrs. McKenzie, Mrs. Horne, Mr. James	356.00
- Garage & Fence Mr. Sherburn, D. Bell, E. Anderson, F. Stasek, I. Medrich, Ellen McKay	1252.00
- Rebuild Fence J.McQueen, D. Bell, Grace Haggart, F. Stevens	428.00
- Move house & shed & 2 stumps - G.Webster	431.00
- W. Glover - New steps, fence, foundation & rockpit	246.00
- W.Bowden - Move fence, rockpit & hedge	191.00
- Construction of Septic tank for Nelson Hotel	1045.00
	$ 4259.00

"The road used to go along to our driveway and then curved down to the beach past Sherburn's verandah and down by Mrs. Little's. The new road was supposed to go through our living room. Wilf was at work when the men came to the door. I said, 'You can't do that,' so they suggested moving the house back, but there was a road allowance. Then I started thinking, 'Oh, maybe we'll get a new house.' But no, they just took the frontage off - 12' and left us sitting way up high."

Ethel (Campbell) Glover

M. Peters

Alex and Belle McLeod visit with George Harwood and a guest from the hotel

democrat wagon, and buggies in which to haul supplies or transport people. His teams were also hired around the district to plow fields or bring in the harvest. During the building of the E&N he hauled lumber and supplies to where the crews were working, sometimes as far down as Qualicum. His oldest son, Bob, did most of the driving.

"Coming home I would fall asleep way at the back. I'd have a long reach on because I had hauled lumber, but the horses went themselves. I had two horses and one of them was really smart. Lots of times people would rent and ride him to Cumberland. They'd just tie up the reins, let the horse go, and he'd come home himself. He'd get a hold of the gate and shake it. Sometimes it would be eleven or twelve at night and I'd wake up and let him in."

Bob McKay

LIVERY STABLES

George Howe of the store probably had the first livery stable at Union Bay. He had a team and wagons to rent out, which Hungo drove in the early years. It was used mainly to get supplies from the wharf to the store, and to deliver groceries. Later, Alex McLeod, then Syd Glover, drove for Mr. Howe. Tommy Hudson had a livery stable too, but mainly transported people to and from Cumberland on boat day.

Andrew McKay owned a livery stable and freight business. He had four or five horses, a

After a few years of working for Mr. Howe, Alex McLeod saw the need for a freight service. He had married Belle Cook, and their home, behind which he built a two storey barn, was just south of the Nelson Hotel. Mr. McLeod also had a farm about one mile inland on the road to the lake, where he grew hay for his horses. At harvest time he loaded up the dray with hay, as well as a few local children, and hauled it down the hill to the barn. The road was eventually named after him.

Soon he had the contract for hauling all the company coal to private homes and businesses. Several logging companies burned coal in their steam locomotives, and it was a steady job keeping them supplied with coal. It was many years before the hydraulic dump but the wagon was constructed in such a way that the coal did not have to be shovelled. The wagon floor was made of 2" x 6" boards set in. First, one set of side boards would be removed, then the floor boards, one at a time, allowing the coal to fall through to a bunker. The coal was "mine run" (large and small pieces just as it

M. Vowels

M. Vowels

Left: A fun activity during harvest was a hayride to the barn. Alex McLeod's passengers are (standing): Harold and Wes Peters, (sitting): Lawrence McLeod, Myrtle Peters holding Mame, Ed Peters. Right: Alex McLeod formed a freight service and had a contract to haul all the collieries coal to homes and businesses

M. Vowels

The Sidney Peters family. Adults: Fred Vowels, Gertrude Dowling, Wes Peters, Edna Peters, Myrtle Peters, Ina Peters, Mame Vowels, Ed Peters, Harold Peters. Children: Betty Jane Peters, Eddie Vowels, Marjorie Peters, Ann Vowels

K. Peters

Wes Peters came to Union Bay from Vancouver to drive Uncle Alex McLeod's hard-tired Federal truck which delivered coal around the district

came out of the mine). At some of the camps it was not that easy.

"They'd put it in sacks and pack it on their backs. That's what crippled my Dad. A 150 lb. sack dropped on his back from the wagon. Mostly they dumped or shovelled the coal, but up at Bloedel's they had to carry it up onto the deck because they couldn't get close enough."

Fred Peters

The McLeod's only had one child, Lawrence. He was more interested in figures than freight. Mrs. McLeod's oldest sister, Myrtle Cook, married Sydney Peters and the couple had four sons and a daughter. Two of the Peters boys worked for Mr. McLeod. When he was only sixteen Wes came from Vancouver and drove the new Federal truck to deliver coal around the district. He even went as far as Campbell River. A trip with two tons of coal, and return, took six hours. Sometimes a young boy would accompany him, collecting beer bottles along the roadside. The boys could easily outrun the truck.

"A little later Uncle Alex got a Federal truck, with hard rubber tires, no doors on it. So when Wes was a boy he came over and drove the truck."

Mame (Peters) Vowels

"After Uncle Alex had a stroke I came over to help out Wes. We had two teams of horses and a Federal truck. There was coal to deliver down to Dollar camp and up to Bloedel camp, besides all the homes. There were three stores to deliver freight to, and freight, food and lots of boom chains for the logging companies."

"There used to be a 3' wide, wooden sidewalk along the front street, and I think there must have been a ditch under it. I delivered coal to the bank one time. You had to back in along the side of the building. Well, coming out, the front wheels went over the plank sidewalk but the hind wheels came to it, and went plunk! It had rubber tires and no traction. So I came home and got the team of horses, and went down there and hooked onto the front end, then lifted up the old windshield and put the reins through to the steering wheel. I got in and grabbed the reins and stepped on the gas, and the horses got us out of there."

Harold Peters

When Mr. McLeod's health failed in 1927, Wes took over the freight business at Union Bay. Coal was hauled to the rest of the district by other men: Creech, Haas, Hornby, Cochran, Hunden, Maxwell and Davis. The delivery charge for a truck load of coal was 50¢. By the time Wes' son, Fred, took over in the 1950's, it was up to $1.00. The coal man worked hard for his money.

"Everyone had a coal shed - some were downhill, some were uphill, and you shovelled it into a little hole about 24" x 24". The ones on the Company Hill were level and you just backed up your truck and shovelled it in - pretty easy! But when you went to

Courtenay - gawd, there'd be a little window down low on a house."

Fred Peters

As well as delivering coal, Wes cut wood for sale. He was also the moving man, just sweeping the coal dust out of his truck, loading on the furniture, and then covering the contents with a big tarp if the weather was poor.

In the early days, with all the horses in town, a blacksmith was necessary. In Union in 1895, Lindsay Ray and G. Murdock formed a business of horseshoeing and blacksmithing. To have your horse shod cost $2.50. Four years later Mr. Ray moved his family to Union Wharf, where he operated a blacksmith shop before becoming a locomotive engineer.

It seems there was always lots of work for the smithies, not only in horseshoeing but also in buggy repair. Runaways were a common occurrence.

1906 ➺ Trip to Union Wharf - A number of men and ladies from Cumberland hired a buggy and horses to take them to a little social dance that the Wharf is famous for. Nearing Roy's, the horses shied, the buggy struck a log and overturned, throwing everyone into the mud. The horses tore loose but the shafts stuck in the mud. The people, spattered with mud, walked the nine miles to the Wharf. It was only three miles back to town, but then the attraction did not exist there. [4]

V. Hudson

The first in Union Bay to own a car was Tom Hudson, seen here at the wheel of his 1908 Rambler

Even before the auto arrived to frighten horses, other things caused runaways: wild animals, dogs, bees, firecrackers and bikes.

1910 JULY ➺ Mrs. Partridge was travelling in her buggy to the beach when her horse was scared by a passing bicycle. It shied, throwing the lady out, where she was picked up unconscious but with no serious injury. [4]

1911 APRIL ➺ Alex Adamson and Adolf Anderson were driving out, when the horse took fright from some sheep and broke loose from the rig. Both escaped injury. Adolf says, "She bane a gude one". [5]

AUTOMOBILES

1905 AUGUST ➺ The first horseless carriages to travel the Comox roads were driven from the Union Wharf last week where they landed with a group of holiday makers, all CPR officials, from the steamer *Joan*. Capt. Troupe piloted a 12 h.p. White Sewing Machine steam car and Mr. Kerr a larger gasoline Rambler.

The party went to Courtenay and from there to the Comox Valley and then to Cumberland on Thursday morning. A delay was occasioned at Courtenay by Capt. Troupe's car requiring new ball bearings, and one further on, a mile up the road, by Mr. Kerr's car having to exchange a leaky tire. From there, after repairing, the five miles to Cumberland was made in twenty minutes. Arriving, the party

N. Eastman

Louis Magnone, the last of several owners of this Model T truck, sits in the rebuilt cab. Union Bay Fire Department is now custodian of this antique

J. Reid

D. Muschamp

D. Bennie

W. McMurtrie

G. Murdock

D. Aitken

J. Anderson

A. Hardiman

W. Glover

partook of lunch and visited friends before departing for Nanaimo, on which trip the bad state of the road necessitated such slow going that it was 2:00 a.m. Friday before the journey was completed. Much excitement was created at various points on the itinerary by the violent expressions of disapproval on the part of our country-bred horses, who no doubt scented an enemy. [4]

The first auto most old timers at the Bay remember was Tommy Hudson's.

"I remember the first car I ever saw was Tommy Hudson's Rambler, a beautiful fire truck red. It would be about 1907 I guess, because the teacher let us out of school to see it go by."

Nellie (McKay) King

Tommy bought his auto in the summer of 1908, and supplemented his livery business by immediately hiring it out as a jitney. There were other cars in the district, terrorizing man and beast. Mr. Colson, Superintendent of the coal company, drove one as did Brigham Brown of the Co-op store. His was a little Model T truck with a right hand drive. Frank Partridge acquired it when he took over the Co-op. He later sold the truck to John Reid who, in turn, sold it to Louis Magnone. It is still in Union Bay today.

Many of the early cars had no steering wheel, just a "joy stick". One such runabout was owned jointly by Fred Ray, Jimmy Haggart and Jim McNeil. Jack Fraser had a beautiful Cadillac touring car (convertible) in which he and his sister toured with the district automobile club. Alexander Cowie made regular trips up from Fanny Bay in his Rolls Royce, with Mrs. Cowie sitting beside him sporting a beautiful Panama hat trimmed with leghorn feathers, tied securely down with a scarf.

Facing Page - Top Left: **Jim Reid and his car.** ***Centre:*** **Syd McKay, Des Stewart, Dover Muschamp.** ***Right:*** **David Haggart on his motorbike.** ***2nd Row Left:*** **Harry Glover's Chev. Harry and Eugene Glover with daughter Violet and husband Ernie McMurtrie and children: Warren, Dolly and Harry.** ***Right:*** **The Renwick family set for a Sunday drive. Grace, Mrs. Renwick, Dorothy, Mr. Renwick.** ***3rd Row Left:*** **Tom McKay's new 1928 car. In rumble seat - Roy Cairnes, Dot King, Blanche Mugford. Sitting - Nellie McKay, Mrs. McKay, Ellen Magnone, Cassie and Annie McKay.** ***Right:*** **Rosie Anderson at the wheel.** ***Bottom Left:*** **All the girls love a car. Elizabeth Miles, Mildren Bowden, Doris and Edna McKay, Annie Schulson.** ***Right:*** **Wilf Bowden's convertible**

N. Eastman

Louis Magnone's first car was steered by a joy stick

V. Hudson

Tommy Hudson shows off one of the beautiful cars he sold

Tommy Hudson, an entrepreneur, became one of the first auto agents in the district. He sold Chevrolet, Dodge, Chalmer, Hudson, Essex and Cadillac cars as well as Republic trucks and trailers of one to five tons.

"My Mom had made up her mind to buy a car and Tommy heard about it, so he came down to the house. Of course my Mom was a big woman, and Tommy said, 'You'll sure look funny sitting in a Ford, a big woman like you needs a Chev'. Well, that got her back up and she thought, 'I'll buy a Ford car whether you like it or not'. And she did."

Annie (Muschamp) Nelson

It was often the woman of the house that bought the car, usually for the oldest son. The teenagers learned to drive quickly, but many men, nervous of all the power, never mastered it. Mrs. Anderson bought a car for her son, Andy, in 1917. It was an Essex which soon gained the nick-name "Ass Ache" because it was always breaking down.

Mrs. Marshall, with coaxing from son Bill, bought a car for family use.

"Mother was the business woman... she bought a Chev about 1925. Bill drove, but not my Dad. However, one day he decided to take the wheel

when they were turning off the highway into the driveway. The "engineer" went straight into the fence. He never touched it after that - he said the engine stayed on the tracks and was easier to drive."

Nettie (Marshall) Jones

Annie Nelson learned to drive early, and delivered milk to the logging camp in Deep Bay. Winnie Bowden moved up to the Bay to join her family when she was thirteen years old, and Jack Bradley, who was delivery boy for Mr. Bowden, taught her to drive. She was soon driving her class to high school in Cumberland.

C. Benson

Automobiles line up at the first gas pumps installed at Fraser and Bishop

The Davis family owned a Ford, but neither father nor mother drove. Corfield Motors put on a Ford Day in 1922. Mrs. Davis, accompanied by ten members of her family, proudly rode round the agricultural grounds with oldest son Clifford at the wheel, to win the prize for "the largest family in a Ford". Son George did not have his mother's passion for Fords but owned instead, first a Star, next a Mitchell, then a Brisco.

Besides Tom Hudson, other agents were selling cars in Union Bay. All the young men wanted to own an auto. A relation of the Wilson's had an agency at the Hotel for Starr, Durant, and Brisco cars. In 1909 they had a raffle with a Brisco as the prize, which was won by Sam Davis of Cumberland.

Mr. C. Emde ran a jitney service in Cumberland as well as being agent for the Russell cars. Then he moved to Courtenay where he had the Ford agency from 1913 to 1921.

Model "T" Runabout -	$600.00
Model "T" Touring car -	$650.00
Model "T" Town car -	$900.00

Driving the old cars was not too hard, but starting them was both difficult and hazardous. The crank handle, which released when the engine started, fit onto pins on the crank shaft and had to be spun around to start the car. If the motor backfired the crank shaft would reverse, which could easily break an arm. When storage batteries with generators were in use, starting motors with a button were installed to start the motor, but the choke usually had to be carefully regulated. The Model "T" Ford had three pedals: brake, reverse, and two speeds forward, with the gas lever on the steering wheel.

"The Grenfells lived on the top hill. Every time their father suggested a Sunday drive in his Model "T", the kids all started to cry. After driving through the back wall of his garage several times, Mr. Grenfell installed hinged doors. Part of the problem was that on the Model "T" the third pedal controlled the gears, and neutral was hard to find.

Harry Glover

"To start my McLaughlin I used to pour hot water on the manifold, and crank it to death."

Wilf Bowden

GASOLINE AND GARAGES

As there were no gasoline stations, the early owners of cars had to order drums of gasoline from Vancouver and keep spare cans in the car. Fraser and Bishop became the first gasoline retailers when they installed two Imperial pumps at the south end of their store.The gas was contained in a drum under the verandah, and to sell gas, the full length of the rack and pinion gear had to be wound down to fill 1 gal. of gas into the car's gas tank. Then it had to be wound up and back down for a second gallon.

By 1918 gas was selling for 37¢ a gallon, with the price fluctuating much as it does today. In the 1930's it was down to 32¢. In 1942, during the war, gas rationing was initiated. Each year, a car owner bought a ration book for $1.00 at the police station. A book of 60 to 70 five gallon coupons (depending on the make of the car) was issued per year. It was further decreased in 1945 to 40 coupons, with no allowance for the type of car. Ration books were carefully guarded, for if stolen or lost, they could not be replaced.

George Neil built the first garage for repairing cars and selling Imperial gasoline in 1919. Located south of the Nelson Hotel, it was built out over the beach and supported on stilts, which made a perfect pit to repair the underside of cars. The garage burned down, but was rebuilt and taken over by A.W. Kirkwood & Sons in '26. It was later sold to "Bo" Hudson.

J. Hastings

Lavina and Harry Wynne with owners Jessie (holding Donald) and Art Hastings standing in front of the hand operated Shell gas pump

G. Murdoch

Gordon and Lil Murdock operated the Home Garage into the '60s. This early view shows both a hand operated and an electric gas pump

L. Bohn

L. Bohn

Paul Bohn with his mobile welder

In the late 1920's, Ed and Jean Anderson took over Mrs. Anderson's confectionery on the beach and installed Shell Gas pumps.

"Dad sold gas and oil. On the old pumps you had to take the lever and pump up the gas and fill the glass on top of the pump. It was marked in gallons from the top down. As you filled the car the gas went down. If you wanted 20 gallons it had to be pumped up twice."

Jack Anderson

Andersons had the Shell Station for about 10 years, until they sold out to Art & Jessie Hastings in the late 1930's. When the new road was put through in 1947, the old shop was moved across the road where the Hastings continued to live, eventually building a new garage which still serves the community today.

Meanwhile, a Home Garage was built at the north end of the Bay by Geoff Kirk of Courtenay. Ernie Chandler leased the shop from him. Here Mr. Chandler built a little jalopy (dune buggie) which was the envy of all the young boys. Harold (Pop) Ward took over the garage about 1938 for four years. It was subsequently operated for a few years each by Harry Watson, Frank Charbonneau, and Cecil Stubbs in partner with Dave Campbell. Cecil died of a heart attack while working at the garage. Then Gordon Murdock owned and operated the business from 1956 into the '60s.

Paul Bohn operated the only independent machine shop in the area. About 1942 Mr. and Mrs. T. Oldale bought the Davis house and property at the crossing. Granddaughter Lil Bohn and children lived in a little house on the property. Paul was in the airforce and living in a remote area. To accomplish his dream of owning a machine shop he made extra money by trapping animals. When he came out of the service, Paul had saved enough money to buy a lathe and Lil enough for the down payment on a welder. They cleared land and built a shop. This serviced the logging camps as well as the big machines during highway construction. The work outgrew the building so a new shop was built in the '50s. It featured a travelling crane and heated floor, a first in the area.

Paul Bohn and his sons hand-made the cement bricks which Paul used to build this modern machine shop. It featured a heated floor and travelling crane

"Every night after supper while the girls and I did the dishes, Paul and the boys made sixteen bricks. They mixed the cement and poured it into templates. The next night the bricks would be set enough to take out of the moulds and they'd start again. Those little b———s really worked their a—s off. They made all but the last hundred for the construction of the new shop."

Lil Bohn

G. Francklyn

Cars travelled on the left side of the highway when this group took a Sunday outing in a Flanders 20

LICENSES & RULES OF THE ROAD

When cars first appeared on the scene, there were no laws or rules regarding travel on the roads nor any license requirements. This changed in the 1920's when a driver's license, supposedly good for a lifetime, could be bought for a $1.00 by anyone over fifteen.

"I still have the original driver's license that I got in 1927. It was supposed to be good for a lifetime, but when they came out with the new ones they called all the old ones in, and somehow I kept mine. I asked a lawyer friend if I could use it. He said, 'By law it is still good, but it will cost you $1000 to prove it, and only a $1.00 a year for a new one.'"

Henry Davis

Motorists in the district drove on the left until 1921, when a new law was brought in to make all vehicles keep to the right to conform with the rest of Canada. Huge signs were erected throughout the district to remind auto drivers and teamsters that as of January 1, 1921, everyone would drive on the right.

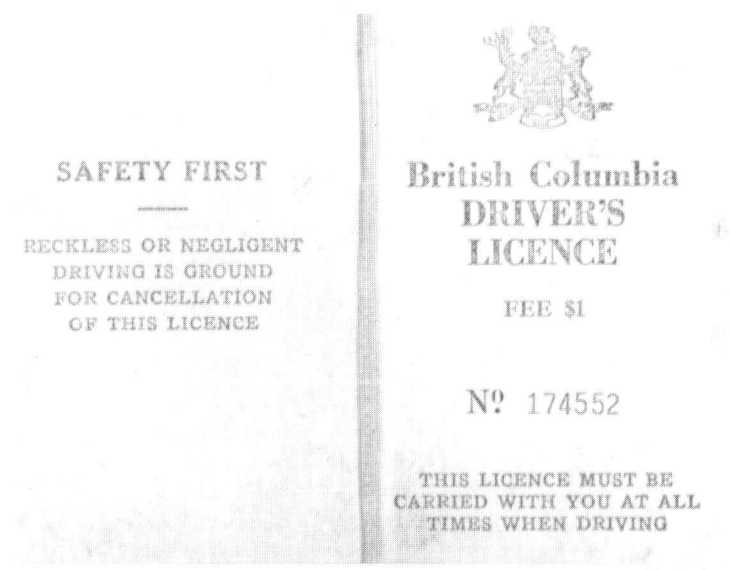

SAFETY FIRST

RECKLESS OR NEGLIGENT DRIVING IS GROUND FOR CANCELLATION OF THIS LICENCE

British Columbia
DRIVER'S
LICENCE

FEE $1

No. 174552

THIS LICENCE MUST BE CARRIED WITH YOU AT ALL TIMES WHEN DRIVING

D. Aitken

In the spring of 1939 every driver had to pass a driver's examination. After studying the little blue book, drivers filed into the McPhee Block at Courtenay to take the test given by two travelling provincial policemen.

1939 MAY •◆ First you pay your dollar and get a receipt. Then you are handed a list of twenty-five questions, against which you put a cross. You must get twenty right to pass. Then you pass on to the chair where you are tested for eyesight, very much as in the optometrist's office, and you wang on the brakes when the red light comes on. [6]

Many of the new owners of these fast machines drove at breakneck speed, sending clouds of dust up after they passed. By 1908 there were many people opposed to the new invention. Ban-the-Auto groups formed, and letters to the editor flew from this group to car owners. Taxpayers wrote, wanting at least two days a week free for horses only. In opposition to the critics, Cuddy Johnson formed an auto club.

1908 •◆ Cuddy would be better off to have money in his pocket and the auto a dream. There is not one man in the Comox District whose income warrants him in keeping even one of these horse scarers. They are the vehicle of the rich. Ye Gods! How many out of hundreds would voluntarily travel surrounded by so much rattle, dust, and stench? These people have the pig's motto: "A short life and a merry one." In every paper some luckless crowd has been smashed to pieces. Not that auto people are much use to the world, but no one asks them to fly out in that fashion. [4]

1908 ➾ These are jealous thoughts of people who want to hoard their money. We live in the 20th century, do you want to hold back progress? Is there any history of just letting the steam engine run on certain days? The auto is here to stay until more power is invented for the enjoyment of man. Cuddy Johnson [4]

The Automobile Club of B.C. promoted safety amongst its members, and petitioned the Government for more laws. In 1923 they called for a uniformity in hand signals. Road signs were erected by the club on Vancouver Island in 1925. A crew travelled up the Island, and the sign painter painted the appropriate sign while the others set in the post.

Stories of poor drivers abound, usually told about men who learned to drive later in life. Apparently Mr. Dale and Mr. Partridge competed for the title of "Barney Oldfield of Union Bay". Thelma Auchinvole and other mothers living on the main street called their children in as soon as the whistle blew at noon and 4:00 p.m., to be sure they were not on the road when the likes of Mr. Searle and Mr. Kay chugged past. Mr. Pollock, who could scarcely see over the steering wheel, found it difficult to change gears, so he drove around town in low. One day as Mr. Searle was parking next to the CC(D)L office, he bowled over the time clock.

"Yes, Dad drove, or drove at it. He owned a little Ford pick-up, no roof, just a windshield. He was working in Cumberland and I was going to High School up there. We bached together and came home on the week-ends. I only let him drive once. I got out to open the gate at home, but he went too far by to swing into the driveway. So he backed up. First thing I know he's nearly over to the Scale house - still backing up, over logs and fern patches. A big fir tree stopped him or he would have been on the beach... Then he started coming, never looked either way, up the bank and across the highway and somehow missed the gate post. I started running like mad, and got way around the house to get out of the way. He came steaming around the house just about taking the corner off and stopped against the garage door. I never rode with him again. How he got up and down those alleys in Cumberland delivering meat, I don't know. Ran over a few dogs I think."

Wilfie Bowden

"Then there would be the death defying trip to Lodge, with E.T. Searle at the helm. How they ever lived through that! Mother used to sit and wring her hands until they got home. One night he took the turn at the crossing too fast, got the railway sign between the headlights and headed for it. Down went the sign, and the large-sized Packard kept going and somehow they got her back on the road again. Nothing disastrous, but it knocked the fuel pipe loose at the fuel tank and when he parked the car in the garage all the gas ran out. Next day, dead battery, empty gas tank, and E.T. walked to work."

Ken & Muriel Peters

K. Keenan

The original Tsable River bridge and highway cut throught the Keenan farm

"I guess Hughie Reid's car wouldn't idle, and if it stopped he'd have to crank it. Us kids would always watch for him coming to the post office. He would slow it right down, jump out, run in and get his mail, then dash out and catch up with the car as it was chugging past the church. Just like a Charlie Chaplin movie."

Mildred (Hicks) Simpson

ROAD TRAVEL

Automobile travelling was always an adventure, with driver and passenger prepared for anything. All trips out of the district were dutifully reported in the local newspapers.

1907 ➾ Louis McQuade of Union Bay made a fast trip from Cumberland to Nanaimo in 7 hrs.5 min. A total of 63 miles. [4]

1908 ➾ Messers. Clinton, W. Haggart, McFarlane and Kelsey took advantage of weather and hired Mr. T. Hudson's most comfortable auto. It proved thoroughly reliable for a spin to Campbell River and back, as a respite from various arduous duties. They made the run up in 3 hr. 30 min. and back in 3 hrs. 25 min., somewhat of a record for a safe pace. [4]

1912 ➾ The roads from Cumberland to Victoria are in good condition for autoing. Mr. and Mrs. P.P. Harrison and children left Union Bay at 9:00 a.m. and reached Victoria by 6:00 p.m. [4]

A trip to Nanaimo took some preparation. There were no gasoline stations between the two towns so tins of gas had to be carried. Also, it was smart to have at least two "spares" strapped on, plus the important jack, as flats were a common occurrence.

"I can remember one night we started off for Bowser. There was Punch, Annie, and a car load of us. I don't know how many flat tires we had, but

there wasn't much time to dance before we had to turn around and come home."

Annie (Muschamp) Nelson

Unless it was the middle of summer, extra clothing, scarves, muffs, gloves and blankets were a must. With holes in the wooden floor boards for the pedals, and no heaters, even the cars with side curtains let the weather in.

During the winter it was joked that you needed a crosscut saw, an axe and a couple of Swedes with you if you wanted to get through the maze of wind-felled trees. Sometimes the roads were closed for days.

"When I worked in the Courtenay bank, I used to leave home at 7:00 a.m. and it took me an hour with those gravel roads and the ruts. The cars had no windshield wipers so I looked out the side window. I hit a bear once at Millard's Creek, $100 worth of damage."

Doug Brown

Heading south, the first thing the driver encountered was the "leap-the-dips" just north of Buckley Bay. This was a good test of everyone's tummy, as there was usually one person who got car sick. He or she always got priority and sat in the front seat. Hence a bucket was included in the supplies, which could also be used to get water out of a creek when the radiator boiled dry.

The next ordeal was the "Sand Hills" near Deep Bay. Here cars regularly got stuck as the narrow tires dug themselves into the deep loose sand, so a shovel was of help.

Halfway was Qualicum. Most travellers stopped at Qualicum Tom's Roadhouse. The passengers could get out for a stretch, and have a picnic while the overheated car cooled down.

The road was far from straight. It meandered around large trees and sometimes ran on the beach, so a tide book was valuable. It was also useful if you were planning a trip to the Islands.

1920 SEPTEMBER ➻ George Harwood owns the only car on Hornby Island and can go right round the Island roads in ten minutes. Once off the Island it is not so easy to get back on. It is only at high tide that a car can be run from the deck of the *Charmer* without breaking a spring. Mr. Harwood has his car in Courtenay for repairs. [6]

When travelling within the district there was the excitement of leaving your stomach on "Boulder Hill" or getting up "Siwash Hill" in one go and without seeing the ghost.

"Dad always insisted we dress up and go for a drive on Sundays. Dad was sitting in the front smoking his pipe and Winnie was driving up Siwash Hill. I just happened to look over the back and could see the tube coming out. I said, 'The tube's coming out.' Dad yelled back, 'Be quiet and keep your bloody mouth shut!' We got to the top and couldn't find the tube. It had flown off into the woods!"

Wilf Bowden

"Dad had a little bug, like a racing model. We were coming down Boulder Hill one time and I slipped through the floor boards right out onto the road. It was all rock, but I survived."

Jack Anderson

STAGES & JITNEYS

The district had a number of stage companies, and as soon as the roads were put through, there were regular trips made between Comox, Courtenay, Cumberland, Union Bay, and eventually Nanaimo. The first stages were run from livery stables. They were big carriages which would carry over two dozen people.

1912 ➻ The stage going back to Cumberland after meeting the mail boat tried to pass an auto south of Royston. The road was not wide enough and the stage upset throwing all twenty-seven people out. [4]

It was not always a natural progression from running a livery and stage business with horses, to a jitney service with automobiles. Some of the faithful horsemen never did change over, but such was not the case with Tommy Hudson. He was the first to have an auto, and he immediately rented it out, driving it himself after a short lesson.

1908 ➻ Mr. Hudson with passengers P.P. Harrison, Wes York, W. Hudson and Len Piket made his first trip to Nanaimo and back in his new auto. The trip was made at railroad speed without any enforced stoppage or delay on account of auto or driver. Mr. Hudson was exceptionally clever in learning to run his auto, having only a few days practice previous to the aforesaid trip. [4]

About ten years later George Neil purchased a Studebaker and ran a jitney service from his garage. In the 1920's Sandy Chapman, who had married one of Marshall Laird's daughters, and Nick Knutson, a bachelor, both had "Autos for Hire".

"Nick had a Chev "Baby Grand" with "semi-eleptic springs". He used to take the boisterous loggers up to Cumberland for some night life."

Ken Peters

Later, in the 1930's, William Carter ran a taxi company with a seven passenger jitney.

"Marge and Murray Kennedy came from Powell River on the 'Princess Mary' for their honeymoon. They hired Bill Carter to tour them around the district. It was a big Studebaker touring car."

Wilf Bowden

Next, Ray's Taxi, advertising twenty-four hour service, was stationed at the Willis Hotel. It was first owned by Ray Mosher, then operated by Ed Thompson in 1947.

For many years, after taking over the stage business, buses were still called stages. Probably the first horseless stage to operate between Union Bay and Nanaimo was started by J. Moscrop in about 1913. He drove a 30 h.p. Stanley Steamer which seated twelve passengers. Monday, Wednesday, and Friday the stage went north from Nanaimo to Cumberland, making the return trips on Tuesday, Thursday, and Saturday.

In the 1920's F. Sangster of Nanaimo operated a nine passenger stage service with his twelve cylinder Cadillac. A spectacular accident happened south of Union Bay in 1923 when the Cadillac ran into the end of a flat car attached to a logging train. The automobile turned over, trapping the occupants inside. Several strong loggers combined their strength to right the car. A broken arm was the most serious injury.

Sangster was followed by Gordon's Stage Co. who charged 5¢ a mile. By the late 1920's the Island Stage Co., the first to have a service from Victoria to Campbell River, had bought up all the smaller lines. Then in 1930 the CPR bought them out. With buses that connected with the ferries at Nanaimo, bus travel came into its own.

The bus drivers were cheerful fellows who knew everyone along the way, as well as their destinations. Don Stewart and Ray Fontana are remembered.

"Mah Him used to blink and stutter when he talked. He'd get on the bus and say 'Him-him likee one tickee Chimanusee-come-back.' Don knew he wanted a return ticket to Chemainus."

Bill Hamilton

Nanaimo-Courtenay Stage

Operated by Union Stage Co., Ltd.

T. D. COLDICUTT, Managing Director

Stages leave Courtenay for Nanaimo—8 a.m. and 10 a.m.

Stages leave Nanaimo for Courtenay—1 p.m. and 8 p.m.

Stages leave Nanaimo for Alberni—1:30 p.m. and 8 p.m.

Stages leave Nanaimo for Victoria—8:15 a.m. and 1:15 p.m.

Stage from Nanaimo at 1 p.m. connects with Campbell River Stage leaving Courtenay at 4:45 p.m. daily, also makes connections for Nanaimo with Campbell River Stage arriving at Courtenay from Campbell River at 10 a.m. daily.

PHONE FOR RESERVATION

Courtenay Tel: 105 Nanaimo Tel: 619 Alberni Tel: 11

M. Shillito

An early stage, driven by Tiny Collins, ready for a trip to Nanaimo

BIKES

The "safety bicycle" was first produced in England in the 1880's. By the turn of the century it had become popular in Canada. As a sport, cycling was popular in Nanaimo and Wellington where they had racing ovals which attracted riders from the Pacific coast. By 1911 bicycle salesmen travelled up-Island to sell their newest models at about $35.00: Standard, Humber, Massey Harris, Singer and Branford Racers. CCM became very popular in the '30s and sold at about $40.

The first bikes bought by several families had laminated wooden wheels with steel spokes. They tended to warp in the wet weather and took time to change a tire. The tire was a continuous loop of rubber tubing with a slot into which was threaded the straight inner tube, which was sealed at both ends. The opening was laced up like a soccer ball, then the tire was partially inflated and glued in place on the wheel.

A family would be lucky to have one bike to be shared by everyone for recreation and transportation. The roads were gravel, often with deep ruts, so it made for a rough ride and many flat tires. One morning the three Glover cousins, Albert, Syd, and Bert, set off on their bikes at 7:00 a.m. for Campbell River. Albert ran into the sand pit opposite Chinatown and wrecked a wheel, but the other two continued on and were back home by nightfall.

"The road was gravel and I used to bike up to work at Union Bay. I was sixteen years old, just a kid, and the side of the road was bushy and I was scared of bears and cougars. It was dark as hell when I left home at Fanny Bay and had to go all that way."

Joe Walker

For delivering papers in such a spread-out community, bikes were a must for paperboys. Most bikes, though, were used for fun and sport.

Over the years Marshall Laird was a familiar figure on his bike. Possibly he got his start on the oval at Wellington where he had lived. He and his wife had fifteen children, some of whom were grown when the family moved to Union Bay. From his home near

T. Rennison

Marshall Laird at 81 years biked to Nanaimo and was featured in Ripley's "Believe It or Not"

the colliery railway crossing he rode to the post office every day. Riding to Courtenay was but a short jaunt, and when he was in his seventies, he biked to Nanaimo in six and a half hours riding time. He attributed his excellent health to the bicycle. He never owned a car. When he was 81 he was featured in Ripley's "Believe It Or Not", a cartoon syndicated in North American newspapers.

1939 NOVEMBER

⊶ Marshall Laird, 81, who is known for his cycling, rode to Nanaimo. He hoped to do it in one day but rain forced him to stay overnight in Lantzville. He continued to the Coal City bright and early next morning, and took the train home. [7]

While growing up, most girls did not have the opportunity to learn to ride. So in the 1940's, when their children had bikes, a group of mothers decided to learn. For several months Thelma Auchinvole, Annie Campbell, Winnie Glover, Greta Kay and Isobel Stokes frightened anyone walking on the sidewalk. The telephone poles took a beating, and the kids' bikes were never the same.

TRAINS & PASSENGER SERVICE

The Wellington Colliery Railway Company

The first train to transport people in Union Wharf came about through necessity. When workers and their families arrived on the steamers they had to be transported from the port to Union mines. Soon after it was completed, the Union Coal company's railroad train met the steamer *Isobel* weekly at Union Wharf. There was always a great deal of freight and many passengers to transport to Cumberland. The railroad was a separate company affiliated with the Wellington Colliery Railroad Company.

To start with, there was one flat deck car which everybody piled onto. They held on for dear life and set off with coal dust and cinders streaming into their eyes. Then another flat deck was added, and they were improved with the addition of sides and a tin roof.

In the car shop, strictly utilitarian coaches were designed and built to transport miners from their homes to the pit head. They resembled boxcars with windows and were painted the familiar boxcar red. In the center of each car, beside a coal bin, sat a huge pot-bellied stove which was a welcome sight to the dirty, wet miners coming off shift.

Finally, a secondhand Pullman car was purchased and spruced up.

T. Rennison

Mr. and Mrs. Marshall Laird with part of their large family. Standing: Isabella Chapman, Mrs. Laird. Front: 2 cousins, Sanford Chapman, Bob Laird, a cousin, Gordon Laird, Marshall Laird, Sarah Laird

1896 AUGUST ⊶ The passenger coach is receiving a coat of paint. The trimming and design is being done by J.B. McLean. When finished it will rival any CPR coach in outward appearance. [3a]

By the turn of the century, there was a passenger train running between the two communities three or four times a week. In 1907 the Cumberland council asked the company to run a train Saturday night. This became very popular, much in favour with the Cumberland merchants and Union Bay residents alike. Several more passenger coaches were added to the rolling stock, as often the passengers numbered over 150, all eager for a night on the town. Some went to shop, some to hear the band play, some to visit friends, and everyone took in the movie before heading home.

One Sunday morning, in March 1912, the engine and lone coach jumped the track three miles from Cumberland and rolled down an embankment. The engineer was injured and the passengers badly shaken up. Although none of the paying passengers was ever seriously injured, several times people who had hitched a ride were hurt or killed. There were people riding in the cab when the Trent River bridge went down. Before that, an Indian woman, Comox Mary Ann, hitching a ride from Union Bay, was killed when she jumped off before the train reached Cumberland. She caught her dress on a bolt and was dragged onto the track and under the wheels of the following cars. Notices were posted in the papers prohibiting this practice and warning of the consequence, which was dismissal if the person was an employee.

As the E&N was nearing completion, the Wellington Colliery Railway Company also increased their service. It was now possible to go from Union Bay to Cumberland via Bevan, Puntledge, Lake Trail, and Royston, and return the same day. As well, the Comox Logging line tied into the W.C.R.C. line at Royston, allowing people to get from Headquarters and Courtenay to Union Bay.

1913 MAY The first train from Headquarters via Courtenay and Royston is expected to reach Cumberland for the May 24th celebrations. A special train from Union Bay will also bring visitors to May Day. [5]

After the E&N's inaugural trip in 1914, freight and passengers from Cumberland transferred for the trip south, at Royston. There were now about ten coaches, and in 1915 electric lights were installed in them.

The service continued more or less the same until the 1930's when, because of the automobile, people patronized the train less and less. In 1931 the passenger train was discontinued, and the mail was taken by truck from Cumberland to

E. Renwick

Loco No.20 pulling a passenger coach on the Wellington Colliery Railway

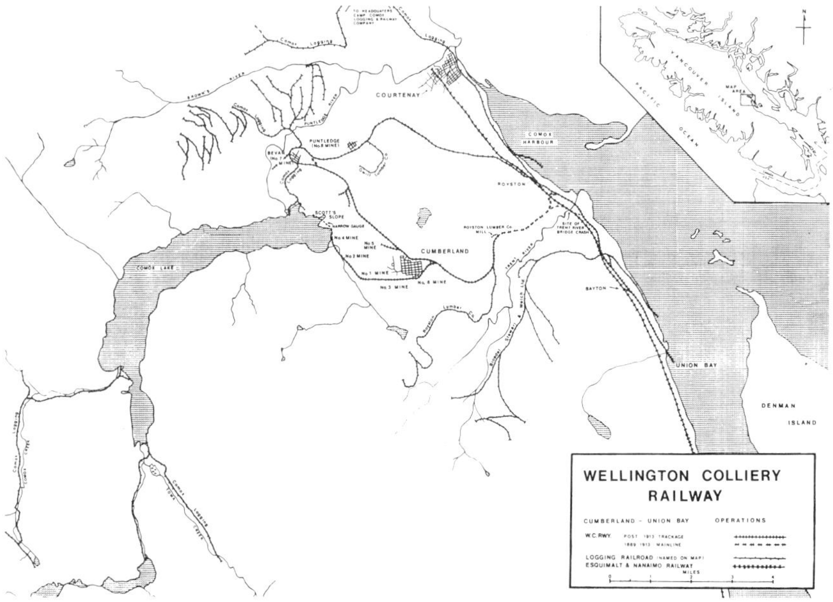

Wellington Colliery Railway Company

TIME TABLE No. 1.
EFFECTIVE OCTOBER 1st, 1914.

READ UP							STATIONS	READ DOWN						
Sat.	Fri.	Thur.	Wed.	Tue.	Mon.	Sun.	------	Sun.	Mon.	Tues.	Wed.	Thurs.	Fri.	Sat.
4.35 p.m.	7.35 p.m.	4.35 p.m.	7.35 p.m.	4.35 p.m. 9.35 a.m.	4.35 p.m.	9.35 a.m.	Cumberland	7.00 a.m. 1.00 p.m.	A.M. 10:30	7:00 a.m. 2:00 p.m.	A.M. 10:30	A.M. 7:00	A.M. 10:30	A.M. 7:00
4.10 p.m.	7.10 p.m.	4.10 p.m.	7.10 p.m.	4.10 p.m. 9.10 a.m.	4.10 p.m.	9.10 a.m.	Bevan	7.25 a.m. 1.25 p.m.	10:55	7:25 a.m. 2:25 p.m.	10:55	7:25	10:55	7:25
4.05 p.m.	7.05 p.m.	4.05 p.m.	7.05 p.m.	4.05 p.m. 9.05 a.m.	4.05 p.m.	9.05 a.m.	Puntledge	7.30 a.m. 1.30 p.m.	11:00	7:30 a.m. 2:30 p.m.	11:00	7:30	11:00	7:30
4.00 p.m.	7.00 p.m.	4.00 p.m.	7.00 p.m.	4.00 p.m. 9.00 a.m.	4.00 p.m.	9.00 a.m.	(f) Lake Trail Road	7.35 a.m. 1.35 p.m.	11:05	7:35 a.m. 2:35 p.m.	11:05	7:35	11:05	7:35
3.55 p.m.	6.55 p.m.	3.55 p.m.	6.55 p.m.	3.55 p.m. 8.55 a.m.	3.55 p.m.	8.55 a.m.	(f) Courtenay Road	7.40 a.m. 1.40 p.m.	11:10	7:40 a.m. 2:40 p.m.	11:10	7:40	11:10	7:40
3.50 p.m.	6.50 p.m.	3.50 p.m.	6.50 p.m.	3.50 p.m. 8.50 a.m.	3.50 p.m.	8.50 a.m.	(f) Minto Road	7.45 a.m. 1.45 p.m.	11:15	7:45 a.m. 2:45 p.m.	11:15	7:45	11:15	7:45
3.45 p.m.	6.45 p.m.	3.45 p.m.	6.45 p.m.	3.45 p.m. 8.45 a.m.	3.45 p.m.	8.45 a.m.	Royston	7:50 a.m. 1:50 p.m.	11:20	7:50 a.m. 2:50 p.m.	11:20	7:50	11:20	7:50
3.30 p.m.	6.30 p.m.	3.30 p.m.	6.30 p.m.	3.30 p.m. 8.30 a.m.	3.30 p.m.	8.30 a.m.	Union Bay	8:00 a.m. 2:00 p.m.	11:35	8:00 a.m. 3,00 p.m.	11:35	8:00	11:35	8:00

An extra train will leave Cumberland for Bevan on Tuesdays, Thursdays and Saturdays at 9:30 p.m.
Stations marked (f) are flag stops only.

Wellington Colliery Railway Company.

Royston to connect with the E&N. The coaches were retired to a siding at Union Bay, but dusted off every May 24th when the whole community boarded the ancient carriages for a nostalgic ride to Cumberland.

Esquimalt & Nanaimo Railway

In 1883, long before Union Bay was chosen as the port for shipping coal, the Settlement Bill was passed awarding Dunsmuir and Associates the contract to build the Esquimalt to Nanaimo railroad. The settlers of the Comox Valley objected strongly to the monopoly this company was given on the coal and mineral rights, but could do little about it. The railroad was built and the last spike driven by Sir John A. McDonald in August 1886. Mr. Fred Brown (later to be postmaster at Union Bay) came from Yale to be the first station master at Russell Station in Victoria.

After the mines were opened in Union, the growing community began to agitate for the extension of the E&N from Wellington (where it was extended to in 1887) to Courtenay. By June 1894 a survey party was as far as Englishman's River.

In 1905 the CPR purchased the E&N. Several years passed until work started, first at the south end between Wellington and McBrides Junction (near Parksville). Here it divided, one line going west to Alberni, the other north. In the summer of 1911, tenders were called to clear the right of way between McBride and Union Bay. Westholme Lumber Co. of Victoria won the contract. The company of Sabine and Stevens cleared the ten miles to Courtenay. Hundreds of men were employed, and camps were established along the way.

D. Bennie

The train stops to pick up passengers at the E&N station

M. Shillito

Newlyweds Russell and Edythe Hicks wait for the train to take them on their honeymoon

Many of the farms to the south lay in the railroad's path so they were divided, with the railroad going through the middle. Some of the farmers felt that they were not properly compensated so protested in their own way.

"Old man Larson had just a little piece of land that was going to be taken off him. So when the brush cutters came through he went out to his outhouse and put "IT" all over the damn bushes. It stopped them alright but just for a little while."

Joe Walker

"They were clearing the family farm at Fanny Bay when the railroad went through. The workers on the CPR would blast a stump and send everything over on the ranch. So my folks would load up a stump with all the rocks and branches and blow it all back. It was kind of a war - they were both clearing and didn't want extra junk on the property. Just to break the monotony more than anything."

Jack Anderson

"We were temporarily living on Station Road when they were blasting. A big root landed on the end of the pantry and broke all the fruit jars and canning Mother had stored there. We were paid for it I think."

Sarah (Walker) Kirkwood

Because Union Bay was the only port north of Nanaimo, all of the equipment, supplies, horses, mules and men for the north end of the railroad arrived at the Wharf. It was a very busy time, and the businessmen at the Bay prospered.

"They used all Hindus and horses. The little freighters used to come in with hundreds of tons of oats and hay for the horses. They rented space in people's barns to stack it in. My father's barn was just full. Lots of the people with barns made rackets of it, they stole so much. I can remember old man

McKay with his horse and wagon passing us on our way to school, with loads and loads of groceries for the camps south of Fanny Bay. Sometimes a crate of peaches or something would fall off and us kids would stash it in the bushes. When we were going home we'd stop in, find the cache and have a can of peaches."

Joe Walker

Different contractors were hired to build short sections and bridges. Canadian Bridge Co. built the bridge at Tsable River. Dominion Steel & Bridge Co. built the bridge at Trent River. Brown contracted for the Washer Creek section. Laying track after the land was cleared was fairly straightforward, but where it crossed a gully cut by a river or creek, it presented a much more difficult problem. A good deal of the gap had to be filled in to shorten the bridge span. Mules were used to carry the gravel and dirt in wagons from the "cut" behind the Company Hill where a steamshovel dug it out.

The first bridges laid were made of wood from trees cut from the surrounding forest. They were delimbed, shaped, and dragged into place by mules. After 1925 these were replaced by steel spans.

J. Walker

Joe Walker started working for the E&N at Mud Bay and became roadmaster for the north end of the Island

Hundreds of Sikhs (called Hindus at that time) were hired as labourers. They drove the teams and wagons that carried the dirt for the fill, and were the "Ghandi dancers" that laid the ties and carried the steel rails into place. The Sikhs lived in a big tent town at Union Bay, next to the right-of-way behind the church and school. Cooks prepared chapatis and curries on outdoor fires.

"They were putting the fill in. They used mules, and the men looking after them were so kind to us. They would give us fruit from the kitchen. So that's where we would head every day after school. A free handout."

Sarah (Walker) Kirkwood

By March 1914 the steel had been laid to three miles north of the Bay, and was progressing towards Courtenay. In May the platform and station were built, with an office and a freight shed with a capacity for 500 tons. From the beginning until the late 1920's, Mary Fraser was the Station Master and Freight Agent. She sold tickets from the little booth before the train arrived.

Station Road, which wound its way from the highway at the Nelson Hotel up around an impossible "S" turn to the station, was finished and lit with electric lights. With the station and "Y" (for turning trains) at Courtenay built, and the rails inspected by the end of July, the railroad was ready for the first train. On August 6th, 1914, two days after the Great War began, a locomotive decked out in bunting and flags chugged into the Union Bay station. In the cab was Michael Manson, MLA, taking a turn at the throttle. The loaded train was given a grand welcome by the delighted crowd.

For the next five years the train service was only three days a week. The train came north Tuesday, Thursday and Saturday, arriving in the late afternoon, and returned to Nanaimo on Monday, Wednesday and Friday in the mornings. Passengers wanting to go on to Victoria by train, or Vancouver by boat, had to stay over in Nanaimo.

Finally, by 1920, a daily service was inaugurated during the summer months. One train left Victoria at 9:00 a.m. while another one left Courtenay at 10:30 a.m. They connected with the Vancouver boat three days a week.

All passengers travelling to and from Denman and Hornby Islands had to come to the station at Union Bay, until a station was constructed at Fanny Bay in 1917. In 1929 Buckley Bay was made a flag stop to let off or take on passengers. This was a further convenience for the Island citizens.

The railway could not function without men to keep it running and in repair. The first section foreman was John Wilkinson, a big, bewhiskered man. For years he kept the tracks cleared, cowcatchers repaired and culverts clean. Pumping up and down his section on a velocipede, he found any potential dangers and kept tabs on his crew of men.

Joe Walker, who grew up on his father's farm at Fanny Bay, got the railroading bug early.

"Another time after the steel was laid, my mother warned me not to go

near the train. I had a red sweater, and one day when she was picking berries on Mike Watt's slashing, this work train went through with a boy in a red sweater on it. So, she nailed me. I had a red bottom when she got through with me."

Joe Walker

Joe started working for the CPR at Mud Bay, and was then sent to Alberni. He was soon in charge of a crew of sixty Chinese workers who built the Great Central Lake section. He came back to Union Bay in 1932 as section boss, where he stayed until he retired in 1965. With his wife Mary, the daughter of the section foreman at Parksville, he lived in the big section house, which was about three feet off the track, south of McLeod Road. They got so used to the freights almost coming through their bedroom at night, that Joe had to put a penny on the track so he would know in the morning if the train had gone by. In 1956 Joe became roadmaster for the north end of the Island.

A smaller section house north of McLeod Road housed the workers, who were often men transferred from the prairies. Beside it was a garage for the speeder.

Joe used a gas speeder for his daily inspection of the track. In 1923 the E&N had a big Lincoln car converted with railroad wheels. The Railroad officials took the "999 Wagon", as it was called, on periodical tours to check the line from Victoria to Courtenay. It looked very sleek and travelled fast. Many of the children who used to walk the tracks thought it was operated by railway pirates and robbers. If they heard it coming they dove straight off the track into the bushes, stinging nettles, blackberries, or whatever. Anything was better than being caught by the men in speeding car #999.

The rolling stock remained about the same over the years, with no modernization until 1955, when the Budd Car was put into service. Although capable of a high speed, the Dayliner travelled at about 45 m.p.h. because of the curves and road bed. A passenger could travel any day of the week from Victoria to Courtenay for $9 return.

D. Muschamp

David Muschamp and a twig basket made and sold by hoboes travelling the E&N rails

S. Kirkwood

Two young section hands, Bill Glover and Bill Walker, resting on the speeder beside the station

In the 1920's and '30s the E&N trains and tracks made a good transportation system for hoboes travelling up and down the island. Farms and houses run by generous women were marked in code by the tramps. There they could count on a handout or meal, sometimes in exchange for an odd job such as splitting wood. Some of the more creative men made baskets of wooden twigs and offered them for sale.

The railway attracted children's interests. It was a good place to play, jumping across the ties or balancing on the rails. It was fun to walk over the high trestle and look down. Mothers living near the track always checked on their small children at train time.

"Once, when my sister Junie was four years old she, with Sharon and Adele Campbell, were playing on the tracks and cow catchers at the McLeod Road crossing. They were talking about how big the train was, and decided that if they stood on the very end of the ties the train wouldn't hit them. When the train came down, there the three of them stood. I

D. Bennie

A float plane at the government dock

guess the engineer saw them when he turned the corner and started blowing the whistle. It hooted and hooted but the kids stayed on the ends of the ties. The train managed to stop, and had attracted everyone, including the three mothers who could see from their porches what was up. Hazel arrived with her broom and booted Adele across the cow catchers to home. Mom had her rolling pin and chased Junie up the hill with it. Annie, who never hit a child, arrived with her wooden spoon and Sharon caught a few spanks on her way up the hill.

Julie (Vanyo) Isbister

AIRPLANES

Anticipation mounted in the district on Monday, October 27, 1919 after word came by telephone that the first airplane was due to arrive. The Pathfinder II, owned by the Aerial League of Canada, was flown from its headquarters in Victoria to towns and cities on the island and mainland, to demonstrate the possibilities of commercial flying.

Lieut. N. Brown piloted the plane which left Victoria at 11:30 a.m., flying in rain until the weather cleared over Nanaimo. At Fanny Bay the pilot had to land on Keenan's flats to take on fuel. Soon the people of Union Bay heard a strange sound and looked up to see their first airplane.

1919 NOVEMBER ➻ Great excitement was caused by the passing of the Pathfinder through Union Bay. Some of the Chinamen who had never seen an aeroplane before, dropped their tools and rushed out shouting, "All same big boat, go like H—." The machine landed in Urquhart's field in Courtenay and took up passengers. T. Hudson was one of them. [5]

A white cross of cardboard boxes and a fire had been set out on Urquhart's field to guide the pilot and he made a good landing at 2:45 p.m. A large crowd had gathered to see their first airplane, and fifty-five lucky passengers had a ride.

The following May, on Empire Day, the folks had another chance to see a plane. The bi-plane, that was to be stationed at Courtenay for commercial use, flew up-island promoting the Vancouver Island Aerial Service by dropping literature on each little village it flew over. What excitement for the children of Union Bay as they dashed around picking up the fluttering pamphlets! The advantages of air travel were endless, so the pamphlet said. The main objective was to get the public favourably impressed with the airplane so that many of the excellent Canadian pilots returning from the Great War could continue their vocation in peacetime.

For many years, until the Comox airport was built, airplanes continued to be a novelty. Occasionally seaplanes attracted attention when they dropped off passengers at the government dock.

SCHOOLS

M. Vowels

In 1898 the first school was held in the company house two doors north of Russell Hill

The British Columbia government required a minimum of fifteen pupils before a school could be established. John Cook came to Union Wharf in 1896 to work on the coke ovens, leaving his family of three grown sons and five young daughters with his wife in Port Angeles. He built a house next to the Wilson Hotel and sent for them. The family with their horse *Jack* arrived on the steamer in 1898, thereby making enough children to warrant a school. Even so, they had to cheat a bit to win government approval.

"I was not old enough to go to school, but they had to have one more before they could get a teacher. So I went and slept half the day."

Mary (McKay) Winterburn

Miss E. Dalby took charge of the children, aged five to sixteen. The Company had provided one of the houses to be used as a school. This little bungalow still stands beside the highway, second house north of Russell Hill.

The next school year, a young man with an M.A. became the teacher. Mr. McKinnon was obviously an organizer, taking advantage of any dignitaries passing through.

1899 JULY ➾ The Wharf School was honoured with a number of visitors at the closing exercise. Lt. Gov. McInnis, Post Office Inspector Fletcher, Mayor of Victoria Rev. Marough and other people from Victoria and Nanaimo.

Roll of Honour		
	General Progress	C. Hooper
	Punctuality	Cleda Drew
	Deportment	R. Humphrey
	Mrs. Hooper prize for Best Speller	Archie Lane
	Lt. Gov. prize for 2nd Best Speller	C. J. Hooper
	T.Brown prize for Gentlemanly Conduct	Archie Lane
	T.Brown prize for Ladylike Conduct	Bessie McKay
	McKinnon's prize for Excellent Progress	Margaret Ray

At the conclusion, His Honour addressed the children in a few well-chosen words, dwelling particularly on the evils of the cramming system of education, and the necessity of obedience to supervisors. [4]

After such a glorious end to the school year, the parents were struck with the need to build a proper school house. The main driving force was Secretary of the Trustees, Michael Manson, who advertised for tenders to construct a frame schoolhouse. James Carthew of Cumberland won the $600 contract for the new structure.

BRITISH COLUMBIA

PUBLIC SCHOOLS

PROVINCE OF BRITISH COLUMBIA

Roll of Honor.

This Certifies that

Miss Myrtle Maud Cook

has been a pupil of

Union Bay

Public School during the past Year, and that she holds First Rank in

Proficiency

Edith M. Dalby

Union Bay

June 23rd 1898

M. Vowels

H. Glover

School children about 1908. Front: B. Campbell, B. Cutler, C. Davis, G. Davis, W. Stewart, F. Campbell, D. Renwick, G. Russell, T. Glover, G. Roe. Second row: G. Berry, M. Uchida, N. Cutler, F. Ray, N. McKay, G. Hudson, H. Wornick, N. Blackstead, C. Brown, M. Glover, R. Donaldson, L. Glover, J. McKay, J. Glover, W. Glover. Third row: M. Ray, E. Campbell, P. Renwick, C. Donaldson, O. Luck, F. Ray, S. Glover, J. Russell, L. Drew. Fourth row: H. Glover, F. Ray, S. Hooper, D. Haggart, H. Muschamp, teacher Miss Buick

Built in sixteen days, on land donated by the Union Coal Company at the south end of their property, it was finished by October 15, 1899.

Painted with the same red oxide (car-shop red) as the Company houses, the new school became known as the Little Red School House. The enrollment was now up to thirty-one pupils, so Miss M.E. Nicholas was hired to assist Mr. McKinnon. The school was one big room, with the primary children sitting two to a bench facing the blackboard on one wall, and the older ones facing the other end. The pot-bellied stove sat in the middle.

"There would be two boys appointed as janitors, they got 10¢ a day or $2.00 per month. There was a coal shed at the back. You swept the floors, took out the ashes, cleaned the boards and dusted. Then you brought in fresh kindling, wood and coal in a big coal scuttle. The outhouse was in a separate little building. Girls on one side, boys on the other. You had to put lime down that."

Wilf Glover

Over the years the Little Red School House underwent changes, and about 1909 a second room was added to the back. Mrs. Haggart and her group of workers had a bazaar, and with the proceeds painted the school house inside and out.

Even with smaller classes in two rooms it was not always easy to find teachers. So some years one teacher taught both classes from a position in the doorway between the two rooms. In 1915, with an enrollment of sixty-five, the town had outgrown the L.R.S.H. and the decision was made to build a new school. After serving the children faithfully for sixteen years, the little building was put on skids and moved back to make room for the new one.

D. Bullen

Gertrude McKay 1920-21. The interior of the Little Red School House after the partition was taken out and the stage built. Left to right: Row 1 - T. Chapman, B. Magnone, M. Turnbull, M. Navey, G. Hallstrom. Row 2 - T. Neil, _McNally, B. McKay, M. Dunn, G. Fulcher, H. Humphrey, V. Wong. Row 3 - J. Marshall, D. Ray, A. Ray, S. Muir, M. Turnbull, H. Anderson, M. Hallstrom, N. Bird. Row 4 - A. Cook, J. Abrams, H. Higashi, A. Searle. Row 5 - R. Cairnes, ?, C. Turnbull, ?, K. Nakamura, A. Schulson

S. Kirkwood

Students in front of the Little Red School House 1912 Front row: S. Nakamura, J. Roe, B. Brown, H. Glover, T. Hudson, B. Glover, F. Street, E. Brown, F. Cook, I. Walker, I. Campbell, D. Renwick, E. Fulcher, F. McKay, C. Donaldson, D. Partridge, M. Glover, C. Cooke, B. Walker. Second row: S. Walker, R. Donaldson, N. McKay, B. Arthurs, F. Ray, P. Partridge, G. Renwick. Third row: F. Ray, D. Renwick, J. Glover, G. Russell. Back row: Mr. Matheson, Miss Oliver, E. Haggart, G. Fulcher, C. Brown, G. Hudson, J. McKay, F. Campbell, W. Hooper

A. Watson

The Union Bay School in the late '20s with the L.R.S.H. still at the back

L.R.S.H. for four more years. This room looked exactly the same as the other two, with a row of tall windows that could be covered by green roller blinds. These touchy blinds were temperamental, whirring up like a skyrocket and sometimes knocking themselves off their hooks. The wooden floors were coated in black oil, making them indestructible to hob-nails and caulks.

"I remember when "Abner" was in school. He used to wear caulk boots and chew the floor all up. The steps on the boys side were all dished. Jack McQueen was nicknamed "Lil Abner" because of the big boots and the cartoon."

Bill Hamilton

For about ten more years it housed the primary class, and then the high school pupils for a few years. About 1923 it was remodelled, with a removable stage built in three sections, which was stored behind the school. The old school became the community hall where concerts, dances and sports were held until it was torn down in the late '30s.

The contract to build the new two-room school was won by G. McWilliams of Victoria for a sum of $6,300. Built with a full basement above ground, a wide stairway led up to the two rooms which each had a cloakroom, three walls of chalk board, and eight drop cord lights. A large, cold-air duct coal furnace sat in the basement, along with wash-rooms: boys on the south side and girls on the north. The toilets cost $35 each, two for the children 14" high and one for the teacher 16" high.

"We had some fun watching them build the big school. Then the day we all marched in - it was quite a day to remember. The old school just had out-houses, then it was indoors in the new school. We were putting our hands up every five min-utes. Although we had flush toilets in the post office, most kids didn't, so that was really something."

Doug Brown

A third room was added at the back in the spring of 1922, although the first two primary grades stayed in the

The next change came during the war, when stringent fire regulations came in. Fire escapes were built from each room, which served as a quick way in and out at recess. In the summer of 1944 fluorescent lights were installed. Two more classrooms, an office and a staffroom were added in 1953, with an activity room and kitchen under them. The old floors were covered with battleship linoleum. In 1957 the activity room was used as temporary quarters for two Fanny Bay classes after their school burned down.

The CC(D)L donated 1 1/2 acres to provide additional playground space at the back of the school in 1949. When the changeover for the land title was made, some strange facts came to light.

K. Carter

1922 Classroom H.V. Hildrige. From right: First row - R. McNally, M. McNally, L. Bradley, ?, K. Formby, C. Bradley, E. Bell. Second row: D. Marshall, L. Nicoll, S. Nakamura, E. Magnone, E. Humphrey, ?, H. Nakamura, ?, Third row: ?, B. Campbell, C. McKay, B. Bradley, ?, ?, ?. Fourth row:I. Broder, G. Walker, R. Ray, E. Nicol, ?, ?.

1949 MAY ➾ The Union Bay School ground may belong to royalty. On July 3, 1893 Robert Dunsmuir vested this land in the person of Her Majesty Queen Victoria for "educational purposes" and the title has remained unchanged. Property vested in a royal personnage is not the same as "crown land", and presumably power to dispose of the title now rests with the present king. [7]

In the early 1950's a P.T.A. was formed under the able leadership of Annie Campbell, Rhoda Foster and Gladys Grundy. The group enjoyed informative talks given by various educators. Myrtle Adamson, Margaret Bowden, Mildred Coe, Isobel Hood, Alice McDonald, Emily and Muriel Peters, and Audrey Sawchuck were some of the loyal workers who were invaluable to the teachers in helping with sports days and special events.

SCHOOL BOARD

The School Board became a leading force in the community, with its members very dedicated and interested in the children's education. Working as volunteers they performed their duties to the best of their abilities, feeling proud when one of the teachers hired gave a good performance, and taking the blame if classes got out of hand. From the beginning, with M. Manson heading the group, the names of G. Roe, T. Hudson, H. Glover, E.T. Searle, E. Baldwin, D. Haggart Jr., L. Magnone and G. Davis spanned the years. Herbert Glover joined the board in 1905 when eight of his children attended school, and he served until 1946 when five of his grandchildren were students there.

"About once a month you could smell cigar smoke in the school and we knew that Grandad was there on an inspection tour."

Winanne (Glover) Naylor

In the years prior to 1946, before amalgamation of all the schools into District #71, about six of the small boards formed an association, with Mr.Glover serving as president for several years.

By 1905 each Board was given $480 a year per teacher, and did everything from hiring them to deciding on the colour of the school.

"The first year I taught in Alberni. We didn't like the principal, but the Board wouldn't do anything so we all decided to quit, thinking they wouldn't let us all go, but fire Hildrige. Well, they fooled us, and I was out of a job. In those days the School Board interviewed you, and Mr. Glover came down and interviewed me at Ladysmith, to size me up. After that we became fast friends. In about three years, do you know who became principal? You guessed it - Hildrige."

Annie (Baillie) Campbell

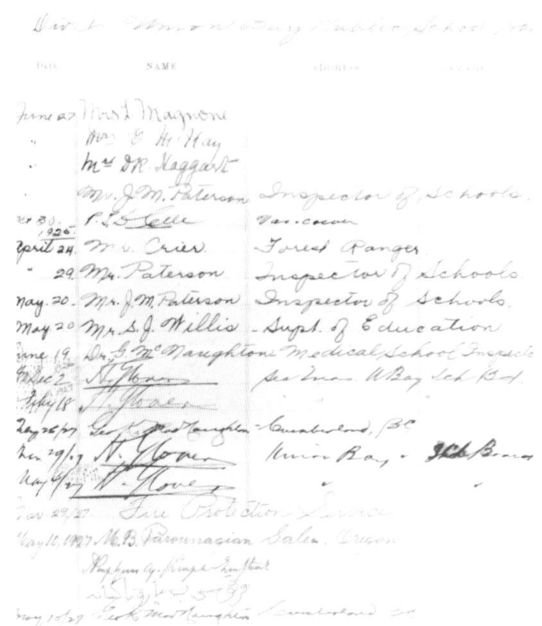

Union Bay School

A page from the school's visitor book 1924

"Mr. Haggart was an inspector on the School Board. I can remember he came one day and wrote "Fuchsia" on the board and asked who could pronounce it. No one knew the word, I don't suppose we'd ever even seen one. Ever since, though, you don't stick me on spelling fuchsia."

Sara (Walker) Kirkwood

"One day, when I was principal, a carpenter was working in the basement, banging away and very noisy. So I marched up to Mr. Glover's house and told him. He supported me and told the man he had to work after 3 o'clock."

Grace (Davis) Boudreau

After the teacher was hired, the next job for the school board was to find accommodation for him or her. Most of the teachers were single women, and room and board was sought in private homes, although a few stayed at the Nelson Hotel. Through the years Mrs. Fulcher, Mrs. Kay, Mrs. Searle, Fanny Auchinvole, Emily McKinnel and Ruby Treloar boarded teachers in their homes.

Besides the frequent visits from the School Board, the teachers lived in dread of the Inspector, who originally had the whole Island to cover. It struck fear into the hearts of the best of teachers when a student dashed in with the news that a strange man had arrived on the steamer and was making his way to the school. What to do first- tidy the room or yourself, update your plan book, put something on the board or just pray that the children would behave. He always asked the worst speller to spell, quizzed the poorest mathematician on the tables, and listened as a bumbler struggled through the adventures of Jerry and Jane.

They made reports on the teachers and schools, including recommendations and suggestions to improve education.

1912 APRIL ➾ D. L. McLaurin, Inspector of Schools, was in town on a tour of inspection and has recommended that the

B. Pollock

Teachers were hard to keep, since women had to quit after they married, as was the case when Annie Baillie married Tom Campbell

M. Simpson

School kids lined the church boardwalk when a favourite teacher was married

school provide drinking cups for the children. The cups will be chained to the taps. [5]

Undoubtedly the best remembered was E.H. Gower, who took over the north end of the Island in 1929 and monitored the schools until 1944. He was a big bald-headed man with a hawk nose, who intimidated both teachers and children.

"It was like the Chinese water torture. Mr. Gower lived north of Courtenay, and the kids would report that he'd driven past going to Alberni or Qualicum. Then we'd hear that he'd had a primary teacher in Parksville crying, and a few days later that the Fanny Bay teacher was in tears. We never knew when it would be our turn."

Donald McDonald

To augment the allotments received to run the school, the community took on special projects which bought the extras. Sports equipment, library books, and even paint were paid for by teas, sales and dances.

1927 DECEMBER ➾ A very enjoyable concert followed by a dance was held at the old schoolhouse on the 23rd. The music for the dance was supplied by Miss Fulcher, B. McLellan and G. Walker. The considerable proceeds will be used to buy books for the school library. [5]

The school janitors down through the years played a part in the life of the school. One of the early janitors was T.W. King, who had been a shoe repairman but changed professions in 1927 and was janitor for ten years. David Walker, in his later years, became janitor and fumigated the school with the pungent odour of his pipe. Some say he grew his own tobacco. After her husband died in the 1940's, Mrs. C. Formby took on the job. It was heavy work for a woman as the huge coal stoker had to be filled every day. Bill McDonald took over the job in 1955 and kept the school shining clean until 1960.

TEACHERS

"An eagle flying through the air
Caught Miss De Beau by the hair.
When he found she was a fool,
He dropped her into Union Bay School."

Poem by Jim McKay

Unfortunately, many of the early records were not kept, but over the years Union Bay School has seen many teachers come and go. Originally, the School Board was given $20 per student per year. In 1905 it was changed to $480 per teacher. Out of this had to come all the school expenses, including the teacher's salary. By the '20s, while in other districts some were only paid $60, teachers at the Bay were making $96, with the principal receiving $120, in an obvious attempt to hire and keep good instructors. It was not until after amalgamation that the principal made over $200 a month.

"Union Bay was classified as a Superior School, so teachers got a bit more money. As principal I made $1260 a year when the minimum for the province was $780. But the big thing about coming to Union Bay was the

Union Bay School Collection

C.H. Tudway 1950. Front: D. Hastings, C. Ennals, D. Cullen, J. Moore, W. Hayton, B. Shillito, L. Smith, A. Frew, T. Smith, L. Lundy. Middle: L. Stewart, M. McLellan, G. Phelan, S. Adamson, P. Glover, J. Seuriel, A. Treloar, J. Cullen, J. McKay, C. Bowden, Y. Woods, N. McDonald. Back: J. Tarnowski, G. McLellan, D. Tweedie, A. Vowels, S. Davis, Mr. Tudway, P. Glover, B. Bell, J. R?, M. Klein, R. Lundy, R. Wood

Studio One

Kay Dick 1950. Front: J. Stokes, B. Webster, C. Webster, R. Bohn, D. Muschamp, M. Grundy, D. Wynne, P. McKay, R. McKay, B. Watson. Middle: ?, M. McDonald, M. Smith, ?, P. Flint, ? Charbeneau, C. Webster, B. Flint, A. Stewart, J. Vanyo, A. Campbell. Back: G. Hudson, O. McDonald, D. Chapman, G. Hatch, H. Herbin, ?, J. Foster, R. Chapman, ?, Bill Bohn, ? Charbeneau, D. McKay

TEACHERS

Enrollment		Teacher	Salary/Month
1897-98		Miss E. Dalby	$40.00
1898-99		McKinnon	
1899-1900		McKinnon	
		Miss M. Nicholas	
1900-01		Miss Cathgart	
1901-		Miss Cathgart / Miss Carter	
1902-January		Miss O. Dingwall	
1902-03		Miss O. Dingwall	
1903-04		Miss O. Dingwall	
1904-05		Miss O. Dingwall	
1905-06		Miss Clark	
1906-07		Miss F. McKay	
1907-08		N. Hill	
1908-09	59	Miss M. Buick	$60.00
1909-10		Miss E. Milligan	
		Miss B. Frew	
1910-11	26	Miss E. Milligan	75.00
	39	Miss B. Frew	
1911-12		Miss DeBeau	
1912-13		A. Matheson	
		Miss Oliver	
1913-14	22	Paul Murray	88.00
	35	Miss M.M. Smith	68.00
1914-15	30	Paul Murray	88.00
	36	Miss M.M. Smith	68.00
1915-16		Paul Murray	
		Miss M. M. Smith	
1916-17	24	Miss R. Milligan	88.00
	41	Miss E.C. Russell	68.00
1917-18	29	Miss M.B. Henderson	85.00
	41	Miss E.C. Russell	70.00
1918-19	35	Miss M.B. Henderson	108.00
	51	Miss E.C. Russell	90.00
1919-20	42	Miss E. Russell	120.00
	51	Miss G. Davis	102.00
1920-21	40	D.J. Anderson	120.00
	39	Miss G. Davis	108.00
	38	Miss G.L. McKay	106.00
1921-22	41	R. Struthers	120.00
	38	Miss G. Davis	108.00
	32	Miss A. Baillie	96.00
1922-23	42	Mr. H.V. Hildrige	126.00
	43	Miss R. Harrison	108.00
	36	Miss A. Baillie	96.00
1923-24		Miss G. Davis	
		Miss A. Baillie	
		Miss J. Redding	
1924-25	29	William Stacey	126.00
	28	Miss G. Davis	108.00
	35	Miss A. Baillie	96.00
	28	Miss J. Redding	96.00
1925-26	18	William Stacey	132.00
	32	Miss F. Jones	110.00
	23	Miss H. Harrison	96.00
	22	Miss J. Redding	96.00
1926-27	22	W. Stacey	132.00
	31	Miss F. Jones	110.00
	24	Miss M. McIntyre	96.00
1927-28	20	W.Stacey	126.00
	28	Miss F. Jones	108.00
	23	Miss M. McIntyre	96.00
1928-29	19	W. Stacey	126.00
	20	Miss F. Jones	108.00
	31	Miss M. McIntyre	96.00
1929-30	8	W. Stacey	136.00
	24	Miss F. Jones	118.00
	31	Miss M. McIntyre	106.00
1930-31	14	W. Stacey	136.00
	22	Miss F. Jones	118.00
	32	Miss M. McIntyre	106.00
1931-32	23	C.E. Ritchie	115.00
	32	Miss M. McIntyre	98.50
1932-33	34	C.E. Ritchie	115.00
	34	Miss M. McIntyre	106.00
1933-34	27	C.E. Ritchie	136.00
	35	Miss M. McIntyre	106.00
1934-35	28	T. Crowley B.A.	136.00
	34	Miss M. McIntyre	106.00
1935-36-	24	T. Crowley	136.00
	36	Miss I. Jones	106.00
1936-37	30	D.G. McDonald	136.00

	32	Miss I. Jones	106.00
1937-38	38	D. McDonald	136.00
	37	Miss I. Jones	106.00
1938-39	36	D. McDonald	136.00
	40	Miss I. Jones	106.00
1939-40	29	D. McDonald	136.00
	26	Miss A. DeCoeur	96.00
	24	Miss I. Jones	106.00
1940-41	37	D. McDonald	136.00
	24	Miss A. DeCoeur	96.00
	23	Miss I. Jones	106.00
1941-42	22	C. Cull	135.00
	29	Miss A. DeCoeur	96.00
	22	Miss E. Watchhorn	106.00
1942-43	31	R. Kelly	135.00
	38	Miss M. Mercer	96.00
1943-44	30	D. Cameron	145.50
	33	Miss M. Mercer	105.50
1944-45	27	Mrs. M. Reynolds	145.50
	23	Mrs. A. Jordan	123.50
	28	Mrs. R. Fraser	115.50
1945-46		Mrs. M. Reynolds	150.00
	79	Miss V. Campbell	120.00
		Mrs. M. Douglas	135.00
1946-47		Mrs. M. Reynolds	205.00
	91	Mrs. V. Smith	125.00
		Miss Y. Cowan	120.00
1947-48		Mrs. M. Reynolds	240.00
		Miss E. Loewen	140.00
		Mrs. K. Dick	160.00
1948-49	94	C. Tudway	
		Mrs. A. Bryans	
		Mrs. K. Dick	
1949-50	98	C.Tudway	
		Miss B. Pottinger	
		Mrs. K. Dick	
1950-51	111	C. Tudway	
		Mrs. D. McKerrall	
		Miss T. Dennis	
		Mrs. K. Dick	
1951-52	116	C. Tudway	
		Mrs. D. McKerral	
		Miss T. Dennis	
		Mrs. K. Dick	
1952-53	116	C. Tudway	
		Mrs. A. Campbell	
		Mrs. K. Dick	
		Miss T. Dennis	
1953-54	124	C. Tudway	
		Mrs. D. McKerrall	
		Mrs. J. Montgomery	
1954-55	130	C. Tudway	
		Mrs. D. McKerrall	
		Mrs. B. Parker	
1955-56	132	D. Isenor	
		Mrs. D McKerral	
		Mrs. B. Parker	
1956-57	145	D. Isenor	
		A. Wedel / Mrs. A. Campbell	
		Mrs. J. Dutfield	
		Mrs. D. McKerrall	
1957-58	138	L. Beduz	

E. Peters

Jessie Dutfield 1960. Front: T. Piket, P. Bullen, V. Lansel, D. Bradley, N. Coe, K. Webster, K. Payne, W. Richardson, J. Lennox, E. Gould. Middle: J. Anderson, M. Stewart, S. Seba, C. Morrison, A. Horne, P. Gould, N. Corrigal. Back: B. Lund, R. Lovell, R. Sexton, G. Piket, S. Arsenault, G. Sawchuck, B. Peters, B. Grills, R. Chapman, E. Lovell

M. Coe

Annie Campbell 1960. Front: G. Handlen, C. Lund, ?, L. Anderson, D. Street, D. Scavarda, B. Walker, N. Robertson, T. Adamson, G. Murdock. Middle: M. Gould, G. Cooper, D. Richardson, S Pratt, S. McDonald, M. Richardson, L. Davies, D. Gray, A. Sawchuck, L. Lovell. Back: B. Millar, K. Cottini, G. Handlen, B. Payne, W. Coe, K. Etherington, L. Sexton, B. Dalziel, J. Webster, G. McKay, D. Anderson

	D. Geidt
	Mrs. A. Campbell
	Mrs. J. Dutfield
	Mrs. E. Dane
1958-59	L. Beduz
	H. Janzen
	Mrs. A. Campbell
	Mrs. J. Dutfield
	Mrs. E. Dane
1959-60	L. Beduz
	E. Doehnel
	Mrs. A. Campbell
	Mrs. J. Dutfield
	Mrs. E. Dane
1960-61	N. McInnis
	T.F. Williams
	Mrs. A. Campbell
	Mrs. J. Dutfield
	Mrs. E. Dane

B. Campbell

Margaret McIntyre 1931. Front: I. Pollock. G. Murdock, B. Silver, M. Bowden, L. Arrol, I. Magnone, P. Horne, A. Muschamp, D. Chapman, P. Cooper, M. Muschamp, I. Muschamp, M. Jones, I. Davis, M. Harwood, J. Watt, E. McKay, S. Shillito. Back: R. Thompson, R. Tappin, B. Sherburn, G. Shillito, J. Silver, S. McKay, J. McQueen, G. McQueen, B. McKay, A. Davis, T. Mah, T. Higashi, J. Haggart, R. McKay, ?, A. Arrol

hand-driven Gestetner machine. We could buy one work book and take it off for the whole class, and it sure beat the old jelly pad."

Donald McDonald

One problem in keeping teachers was the fact that when a lady teacher married, she could no longer teach. With many eligible bachelors in the district, such as the Campbell brothers, lots of the girls left the profession. A few years after the war ended, Tom Campbell followed his parents and three brothers and two sisters to the Bay. He stepped off the E&N dressed in the height of British fashion: a short overcoat, bowler hat and walking stick. He captured Annie Baillie's heart and thus ended a four year teaching career. Margaret McIntyre, after teaching for nine and one-half years, married Tom's brother, Jake, the local football star. Later, both women became reliable substitutes. In 1956 when Annie's children had grown and the law had changed, she came back and taught her former student's children and grandchildren, for another twelve years.

D. Bell

F. Jones 1927. Front: R. Cairns, C. Turnbull, G. Horne, W. Bowden, D. Marshall, J. Kirkwood. Second row: J. Abrams , J. Anderson, E. Searle, J. Atchison, F. Atchison, Dot King, D. McColgan, B. Davis, B. Mah. Third row: A. Ray, S. Schulson, D. Ray, M. Hobbins, D. McMurtrie, A. Magnone, E. Formby, B. Abrams, D. Muir. Top: J. Abrams, I. Atchison, M. Mah, M. Turnbull, A. McCartney

The same fate took the first two homegrown teachers, Florence and Irene Jones, who each taught six years. Florence married Syd Waterfield, and Irene captured the heart of the principal at the time, Donald MacDonald. It was a romance not lost on the pupils.

Being a port town, geography and history lessons could be made very real, something of which the more enterprising teachers took advantage. The visitors book is full of foreign names and places.

1900 ➾ The school children, under the care of Miss Nicholas, were treated to a very pleasant afternoon's enjoyment on board the ship *Hawaiian Isles*. Refreshments were served by Captain and Mrs. Rice. [4]

1901 SEPTEMBER While the *U.S.S. Albatross* was coaling at Union Bay last week, four of her officers, Dr. Bullen, C.R. Miller, A.J. Hepburn and F. Chamberlain visited the school. They each addressed the pupils, telling many thrilling tales of their travels to the delighted children. [4]

School started early in the fall - for many years in the last week of August - and went right to the end of June. With such a long school year, anything that presented itself as a possible holiday was seized upon, especially by the older boys.

"If we wanted a holiday we used to take a wet sack and stuff it down the chimney. The smoke would fill the school and we'd get a holiday."

Hector Hooper

"One spring we wanted a holiday. So Tom McKay (he was a bugger anyway) went downstairs and piddled all over the furnace and the smell came up over the whole school."

Katherine (Formby) Carter

"April 1st, we'd all turn up at school and line up. When the teacher went in to put the bell away, us boys would beat it. We'd go up the lake road, through the woods and down to Chinatown. One year the teacher decided to strap everyone. I was the smallest and they all got the strap. When I held out my hand, she said, 'Go to your seat! You're too little.' Boy, was I mad! I wanted to take my medicine like the big boys."

Wilf Glover

Any teacher with a physical handicap was taken advantage of by the students.

W. Naylor

Irene Jones 1938. Front: J. Ward, B. Hayward, J. McKay, B. Auchinvole, J. Renwick, D. Campbell, D. McKay, B. Treloar. Second row: E. Frew, W. Glover, G. Harwood, A. McKay, H. Treloar, R. Shillito, M. Peters, R. Treloar, V. Frew, L. Watt, F. Higashi. Third row: F. Peters, E. Davis, D. Murdock, A. Lowe, G. Wortendyke, S. McKay, B. Lowe. Back: B. Geary, J. Nelson, E. Shillito

J. Anderson

R. Struthers 1921. Front: F. Bradley, L. McLeod, H. Hooper, D. Brown, C. Bradley, T. Bradley, W. Fraser, ?. Second row: ?, G. Walker, T. Formby, ?, ?, C. Fraser, ?, T. Hudson, R. Ray, R. Glover, W. Cook. Third row: L. Nicols, C. Cave, L. Bowden, G. Kay, I. Broder, E. Humphrey, E. Davis, E. Humphrey, K. Muir, L. Brown, D. Good. Top row: K. Good, P. Street, N. Marshall, W. Bowden, E. Baldwin, K. Haggart, A. McKay, F. Cook

"Miss Russell, a tiny thing who walked like a chicken, was always taking fainting spells. We'd run and get the principal. Of course, we thought afterwards that it was because he was so good looking."

Kathleen (Haggart) Stubbs

"Miss Russell was supposed to have a weak heart. She'd do a fainting spell and one of us boys would run and get a cup of swamp water and revive her. When she came to and saw the cup of slimy water she'd faint again."

Tom McKay

Mr. Hill, who had a hook arm which he used to pull the children

B. Sherburn

Donald McDonald 1938. Front: S. Higashi, S. Shillito, T. Anderson, D. Muschamp, G. Frew, K. Keenan, G. Cooper, D. Renwick. Second row: D. McKay, M. Hicks, I. Nelson, V. Campbell, M. Glover, D. Ward, J. Auchinvole, D. Murdock, E. Shillito, M. McKay. Third row: E. Lowe, J. Geary, M. Muschamp, M. Alexander, I. Magnone, I. Davis, P. Cooper, L. Arrol. Fourth row: D. Fontana, B. Hamilton, B. Sherburn, R. McKay, B. McKay, J. Haggart, K. Peters, G. Murdock

around by their sweaters, did not last long.

"One day a drunk sailor came roaring into the school ground and asked us kids if we wanted a holiday. Well, you can guess what we said. The sailor beat the teacher up and shoved him out a window. One of the kids ran home and got Jimmy McNeil who had one arm too, and he came and hauled off and hit the sailor. That was good for a holiday. The teacher never came back."

Jim McKay

Another rather aggressive teacher was Mr. Struthers, who was fresh out of the British army and ran the school like a general. Needless to say the boys met him head-on. Mr. Anderson was very athletic and boasted of being the broad jump champion of the Maritimes. He would jump over a row of desks to reprimand a student, and was a deadly shot with a piece of chalk.

To start with there were no grades. Instead, first, second, third, and fourth primer were used. A pupil was expected to stay two years in each primer, at which time a silent reading test was given before he advanced. Pity the child with a learning disability, with no special help. Only aging would make him smarter, and finally, old enough to quit.

"Poor Walter, he was a big guy in grade three. He was in a wee little desk, his knees up around his chin. Mr. Anderson snapped on him about sitting up straight. Walter swore at him. Anderson grabbed him by the shoulder and Walter swung around and knocked him right down. He was expelled from school."

Bobby Pollock

"Kids were held back and held back and stayed in a grade until they knew the work. So you'd have these great big kids in grade five. It was all because of the entrance exams... when they finished grade eight they were supposed to know enough to pass."

Irene Jones

The hinged wooden seat and back for one pupil was attached to the desk top and shelf of the pupil behind. This unit, mounted on iron legs, was screwed to the floor. Later on they were mounted on wooden runners, making it easier for teachers to arrange students. Each desk top bore the names of previous occupants, painstaking-ly scratched into the wood while the teacher was not looking.

"The year of the Coronation, Col. Villiers was coming for a visit, so we decided the school needed sprucing up. I gave each kid a piece of glass and they scraped the old finish, initials and all, off their desks and smoothed the wood with sandpaper. I remember that Robbie McKay objected because his father's name was on his desk. Then they varnished them with a mahogany stain. The desks really looked good.

Donald McDonald

On the right hand side of the desk was a hole to hold a small glass ink well. One of the students had the job of filling the ink wells. With the large ink bottle in his arms, he started a syphon going by sucking on the straw, then went from desk to desk filling the wells. It was fun to have dropped a bit of dry ice into a dry well and see it boil over when the ink was added. Each pupil had a red wooden pen fitted with a straight nib, which scratched and scraped across the page as he labouriously tried to write using McLean's method.

Pupils in the very early days had few materials to work with; readers were about the only books they used. Teachers put lessons on the board which were answered on slates. The exercise had to be marked right away so the slate could be cleaned for the next lesson. Exercise books were a luxury until the late 1920's.

"Our slates were about 8"x 12" and we were supposed to have a rag to rub them off. We had an Irish teacher who used to say, "Sput on yer slate an ruub it wi' yer sleeve".

Wilf Glover

Planning lessons must have been a night-

J. Gordon

Marye Reynolds 1946. Front: Wogsey, Mrs. R., M. Auchinvole, S. Treloar, J. Bradley, J. & J. Glover, C. McCarthy, M. Stokes, J. Vanyo, B. Peters. Second row: J. Hayton, T. Smith, D. Kennedy, G. Jones, A. Juvas, B. Chapman, E. Vowels, T. McKay, H. Woods. Third row: M. Campbell, G. Stewart, E. Shillito, E. Shillito, J. Bennie, J. Glover, J. McKay

T. Dennison

Tess Dennison, 1950. Back row: B. Ray, M. Campbell, ?, L. Horne, R. Knox, D. Ward, D. Campbell, C. Tarnowski, student teacher. Middle row: A. Flint, C. Webster, H. Shillito, P. Adamson, J. Cullen, B. Vanyo, J. Chafer, J. Ward, S. Campbell, M. Stephens, S. Katovic, R. Katovic. Front: L. Webster, J. Ennals, A. Aitken, J. Aitken, J. Chapman, D. Wynne, B. McKay, J. McKay

mare, with the almost impossible task of keeping a large class of four grades all busy. With no copy machines, little seatwork could be given until the jelly pad was introduced.

"Remember the jelly pads. I used to mix up a solution of gelatin and glycerine and pour it into a cookie sheet to set. We used hectograph ink, and wrote or typed a lesson on paper. Then the paper was placed onto the jelly which absorbed the ink. Thirty or forty copies could be made, one at a time, by pressing a sheet of paper onto the jelly pad. Gradually the lines became thicker and the copies purple.

Irene Jones

There were few guide or refer-ence books, and no student records were kept from year to year.

"I got $720 a year as principal and had fifty-two kids in one room. There were no records of work, so you started out new to find their level, and all the time the pupils testing you. You taught the three R's, that's about all. Then I started playing ball with them after school and they liked me. If you play with kids you've got them."

Grace (Davis) Boudreau

Grace was unique in 1920 when she first taught at Union Bay and was principal for one year. There were very few women in administration at that time. It remained that way for years, and even in 1944 when Mrs. Marye Reynolds held the position, she was one of only a handful of lady principals in the province.

Mrs. Reynolds is also remembered for her dog that accompanied her to school each day. "Wogsy", probably a sheltie cross, trotted up and down the aisles behind her master. The poor thing was the brunt of many jokes, and received a few stabs with the boys' straight pens.

Two other principals were dog lovers - Daniel Anderson fancied brindle bulldogs, while Mr. Stacey bred springer spaniels.

"Mr. Anderson had a bulldog named Tanya from Brittany. It had four pups, and he kept one and called it "Tulip", an ugly little devil."

Bobby Pollock

"I remember Mr. Stacey. He was a wonderful teacher. He had two beautiful dogs that he always brought to school. They were curly-haired hunting dogs."

Hilda Cullen

Mr. Stacey is remembered by all, particularly the boys, as he spent many hours coaching them in different sports. He stayed for seven years, and was followed by Cecil Ritchie who produced several good track and field teams. He later returned as Superintendent of the Courtenay School District.

HIGH SCHOOL

Before the 1930's very few students went to high school. Entrance Exams were given at the end of Grade 8 for those who wanted to go on. The senior teacher spent a good deal of time tutoring these pupils, as their job was on the line if they failed. The teachers were careful to allow only the serious students, usually three or four a year, to take the exams. More than one teacher was let go when everyone failed. It didn't matter, as one teacher said, if you had a bunch of "rotten" kids that year.

"For several years Buck Stacey's grade eights never passed the exam. So in 1928 he was given an ultimatum. Either we passed or he was out. So all year he had us come to school on Saturday morning. It was kind of fun because he unbended a bit. Nine out of twelve passed...the highest average for years.

Art Searle

The schedule, a daunting three days of exams, was the same throughout B.C.

1910 ➾ Entrance exams for admission to High Schools of this province-

June 18, Tuesday	9:00-10:30	English History
	10:45-12:00	Nature Lessons
	1:00- 3:00	English Literature
	3:00- 4:30	Reading
June 19, Wednesday	9:00-11:00	Arithmetic
	11:00-12:00	Dictation & Spelling
	1:00- 3:00	Grammar & Composition
June 20, Thurday	9:00-11:30	Drawing
	1:00- 2:30	Geography
	2:30- 5:00	Canadian History [4]

The contestants anxiously awaited their results. The local newspaper printed the names of the successful students, with their mark out of 1,000. Passing mark was 500. The two triumphant candidates in 1910 were William Campbell and Jack Russell.

E. Hallstrom

William Stacey 1926. Front: E. Magnone, C. McKay, O. Kirkwood, M. Little, K. Good, K. Haggart, M. Mugford. Second row: J. Johnson, C. Fraser, D. Muir, B. Hallstrom, B. Mugford. Back row: D. Marshall, B. Searle

Very few of the students went on to matriculate from high school, the first being the Russell boys and Phyllis Partridge. U.B.C. held matriculation exams at Cumberland. In 1913 Jack Russell, at only thirteen years of age, passed and went off to university. He was a genius in mathematics, with a photographic memory, and became a scientist for the Kodak Company after graduating. His brother, George, and Phyllis Partridge also went to U.B.C., both becoming teachers. The next university student from the Bay was Mary Little. She attended U.B.C. in the 1930's and also became a teacher.

As more students passed high school entrance exams, the parents and school board had to provide access to a school. Very early, some of the candidates, like Percy Renwick, were sent to relatives in Nanaimo or Victoria. Others, like Gertrude Hudson and Ted Glover boarded with families in Cumberland during the week and walked home on Friday after school. The Cumberland School Board charged the parents $2.00 per month, or $3.00 for two students in one family, until 1917 when the government paid the tuition for "out of district students".

In 1923 a high school was started in the Little Red School House. About a dozen students were taught by Rev. Walker, but because he was not qualified, diplomas could not be issued.

"Rev. Walker took over after grade eight. We took it and fooled away our time and had a lot of fun. There was Kathleen Haggart, Irene Jones, the Good girls, Eva Baldwin, Winnie Bowden, Ray Glover and me. Also the kids rowed over from Denman every day: Harper and Jack Baikie, Norman Chalmers, Clarence Graham and Tom Piercy."

Nettie (Marshall) Jones

The boys from Denman rowed over every day, rain or shine, and several times were reprimanded by the inspector for arriving late for school.

"One very foggy day, Harper Baikie set his compass on the seat beside him and rowed northwest for a specific length of time, then southwest. He landed on the beach between the government wharf and coal wharf, which was right in front of the school.

Dunc Marshall

This high school lasted only a few years, then

N. Watson

One of the first real school buses in B.C. was this Dodge which began operation in Union Bay about 1936. Eileen Watt, Peggy Cook, Muriel Jones, Betty Watt, Margaret Harwood, Annie Schulson, David Haggart, George McKay

J. Hilton

The school bus owned by 'Pop' Ward was driven by Don Carnegie

the pupils went back to boarding in Cumberland. About 1928 Irene Jones got her first teaching job in Courtenay. She lived at home and travelled to and fro in her Chev, transporting her brother Herb, Happy McCartney, Mary Reid and Art Searle to high school. The next year Wes Peters was hired to transport the nine students to Courtenay in his Model A truck. The Government picked up half the tab.

"We wrote the exam and went to Courtenay in grade nine. Wes put a back on his truck and took us. There was Bill McKay, Jessie Waterfield, Bill McCartney, Jean Abrams, Gladys Cooper and me. Then we picked up Vi Feeley at Royston."

Hilda (Anderson) Cullen

"Wes had a canvas top that he raised and lowered with a block and tackle in his garage. A load of wood, a load of coal and then a load of kids. We sat on two benches along the sides."

Art Searle

This scheme faded into nothing by the early 1930's. So in 1933 the parents again had to solve the transportation problem.

"Dad and Mr. Haggart got together and had a meeting of the minds and decided to hire Cecil Stubbs to take the five of us. Two boys in the front, Donald Marshall and Gordon Horne, and three girls in the back, Gracie Haggart, Emily Bowden and me. It was a touring car, about a 1913 Essex. The vacuum pump would break and we'd be late for school. We liked that.

Margaret (Harwood) Bowden

Next, Ernie Chandler was the school bus man, driving a Hupmobile. The roads were usually in dreadful condition, so the pupils had lots of experiences getting to school. One day a wheel fell off and went sailing into Trent River.

When the parents thought the teaching standards were low in one school, they changed schools. This group had started in Courtenay, then switched to Cumberland, and back to Courtenay in 1936. A new motor vehicle law made it mandatory for the driver of a school bus to have a special license, so Mr. Chandler bought a converted Dodge bus and Union Bay students had their first real school bus in '36. The bus driver was owner and operator of the Home Garage. Mrs. Chandler manned the gas pumps when he was driving bus. The business was sold to Harold "Pop" Ward about 1939, and he took the students to Cumberland High. When the twenty pupils from Union Bay and Fanny Bay switched to Courtenay again in '41, it swelled the high school's enrollment enough so that a fifth teacher was hired, and Senior Matric offered. Mr. Ward sold out to Harry Watson in 1942 who, with Robert Ash, formed the Watson & Ash Transportation Co., the firm that still carries Union Bay students to Courtenay.

For years the children to the north and south of Union Bay had to make the long trek to school.

"It was a long way to walk to school, but if we got up early we could catch a ride down on the speeder with Mr. Davis when he went to work. That was kind of fun."

Thelma (Chapman) Rennison

"We finally got picked up by a school bus in about 1935. Don Carnegie was the bus driver. Before that we all used to walk together, the McKenzie, Muschamp, Nelson and McKay kids, about two miles to school.

Mary (McKay) Kine

Union Bay Library

In 1954 the library moved into the former customs office. Members of the V.I.U.L. Board look on as Ethel Glover and Mary Moore check out books on opening day

LIBRARY

Many of the early settlers were avid readers. Some of them, with only a rudimentary education, became very knowledgeable through reading. Memberships were taken out with book clubs, and the eagerly awaited publications arrived through the mail. Series books such as the Forsythe Saga were popular, with each new edition read and re-read. Books were loaned among neighbours and friends, but there were never enough to fill the winter evenings. So in 1932 Nellie King established a Government circulating library in her home. Boxes of books were sent from Victoria on the E&N and Nellie displayed them in her front room. For 25¢, membership tickets were purchased for a season of book borrowing.

Then in 1936 the Vancouver Island Union Library acquired a new library van. With about 16,000 books to catalogue, they set about encouraging communities from Cobble Hill to Campbell River to join. The Union Bay School Board took up the challenge, and decided to raise the necessary funds by a direct tax of $1.50 yearly for ratepayers, with non-ratepayers contributing on a voluntary basis. The vacant room at the school was prepared and offered free of charge.

On Saturday, September 19, 1936 Miss Jean Stewart of the V.I.U.L. officially opened the library. Stocked with a fresh set of books every four weeks, the library was open Tuesday and Thursday evenings for the public, and Wednesday afternoon for the school children. It was run by volunteers Jack Pollock and E.T. Searle. Mr. Searle represented Minto, Royston, Fanny Bay and Union Bay on the Island Library Board. Teachers and students organized whist drives for the purchase of reference books. By 1938 there were ninety-five card holders. Gladys Grundy and Grace Haggart helped with the circulation of over 700 books.

Library Week in October 1950 was observed by the opening of new quarters. The small room at the front of the church was redecorated with bookshelves for 500 books. Every Friday it was open from 2:00 to 4:00 p.m. for children, with Mary Moore encouraging the young readers. In the evening she was assisted by Rita Treloar.

In only four years the books were moved again, into the old customs office attached to the post office. The library was then open twice a week. For years Mary Moore was head librarian, with Ethel Glover as assistant. They were helped out by Peggy Woods and Eunice Thompson. Mrs. Moore started a "story hour" with songs, games and stories once a week to introduce pre-school children to reading.

CHURCH

A. Sawchuck

The Union Bay United Church was built in 1906 at a cost of $2,551

A. Sawchuck

The first sermon inside the church was given by Rev. Ross who thanked Michael Manson for leading the money raising

A Prayer for Our Church

O God, make the door of this house wide enough to receive all who need human love and Thy saving grace, and narrow enough to shut out all wordly thoughts and pride and hate. May it become indeed a sanctuary to men, women and children and may they find therein the Savior who is able to save to the utmost all who come unto God by Him. Thus may this House of Prayer become a gateway to the Eternal Kingdom through Jesus Christ, our Lord. Amen.

Rev. Welsh

The church and the preacher served as a vital link between isolated settlers and the tiny communities of the Comox District. In 1888, the same year that the Union Coal Company started their operations, the Methodist Church appointed Rev. W.W. Baer to the mission of Jack Hart Point, Denman Island, and Union. By 1889 the long-time residents of Denman had built a church. Rev. S. Forsythe followed Baer. About the same time Rev. T. Crosby aboard the *Glad Tidings* started spreading the gospel along the B.C. coast.

1892 NOVEMBER ➾ Rev. Robson of the new Methodist Church in Union came up on the Missionary steamer *Glad Tidings*. The ship had a mishap and is lying at Union Wharf. [2]

The few single men at Union Wharf had their religion dished out by ministers of any faith who travelled from Comox, Union or Nanaimo. Services were held in the dining room of the big boarding house, which had been home to most of the new settlers as they arrived. These men of God travelled from cabin to cabin on horseback, and at Union Wharf commandeered a boat and rowed to Denman, or were met by a Denman Islander.

For about five years a big-hearted Scotsman, Rev. Alex Fraser, visited each community on his white horse, broadcasting the Presbyterian message. He was followed in 1893 by Alex Tait.

1895 NOVEMBER ➾ Rev. Tait gives service in the boarding house with forty present. A good turn out of our mixed population. Whites in the front seats, Chinese and Indians (males and females with their papooses) in the back seats. [3b]

The Catholics were served by Father Durand who came up on the steamer once a month from Nanaimo, until becoming the first permanent priest at Comox in 1889. The Anglicans were represented by Rev. Willemar, then Rev. Nixon.

With the arrival of the first families, the McKays and McCartneys in 1894, the settlement took on a more permanent feeling. By 1895, with about a half dozen families, the church held its first Christmas party in the boarding house.

Church services continued, and as more families arrived - the Rushmores, Gibsons, Hoopers, Drews and Cooks - a Sunday School was started by Mrs. Cook in her home. In 1900 the Little Red School House was built and became the focus of community life, with both Church and Sunday School held there. The Mansons arrived, and Mr. Manson was instrumental in building the church.

As wharfinger he was in a position to ask for help and money from the coal company, which donated the swampy land next to the school property. They also provided the lumber from their mill, which Andrew McKay hauled to the site with his horse and wagon. Mr. Manson petitioned the captains as their boats coaled at the wharf, and so collected a bit more to add to the public subscription, which augmented grants from churches in B.C. and Winnipeg. The building and furnishings cost $2,551, and when the doors were opened on Sunday, December 2, 1906 the grand sum of $1,992 had been collected.

That day the wind howled off the ocean, beating the rain into the worshippers' faces, as they carefully made their way on the planks laid over the swamp to the church door. Rev. J. Ross welcomed everyone and invited the congregation to pull their chairs into a circle around the glowing pot-bellied stove. Mr. Harry Glover struck up a hymn of praise, and Rev. Ross launched into his sermon standing at the table cum pulpit. Possibly Mr. Manson himself passed the collection plate, which reaped $33 from the proud and thankful parishioners. On Monday evening the celebration continued with a concert in which many new settlers took part.

D. Bennie

Rev. and Mrs. Alder with Grace and Anna

1906 DECEMBER 3 ➻ The musical programme commenced at 8:00 p.m. and was listened to by a large appreciative audience, the hall being filled and every piece electing hearty applause.

Instrumental Selection - Miss Haggart
Quartette - *"Alone in the Moonlight"*
Mesdames Marshall & Renwick
Messrs H. Glover & J. Haggart
Recitation - Miss Margaret Ray
Violin Solo - T. Glover
Song - Miss Violet Glover
Quartette - Mesdames Etom, Renwick, Marshall & Simpson
Messrs T. & B. Glover, Rev. Ross & J. Haggart
Duet - Miss Glover & Mrs. Marshall
Male Quartette - T. Simpson, J. Haggart, T.& B. Glover

Rev. Ross, chairman, said he was pleased to witness the help and generosity of the public and thanked Michael Manson who he highly commended on the interest he had taken in this matter. It was almost entirely due to his efforts that the finances were raised to erect the building. [4]

The concert raised $88, leaving a balance of $438 due on the building fund. Very soon after, Rev. W. Kidd, a Presbyterian minister stationed on Denman since 1901, took over the church and was the first preacher to live at Union Bay, residing in the small room at the back of the church. In a few years the reading room and tower at the front of the church were added.

On June 13, 1909 Rev. Kidd performed the first wedding, uniting Bessie McKay and Louis Magnone.

"Rev. Kidd said he'd give the first ones married in the new church a pair of blankets, but he never gave them. No money I guess."

Nellie (McKay) King

With a strong enthusiastic congregation of young families and an active Ladies Aid, it was not long before money was raised for a manse and church hall. Rev. Kidd left in 1915 and the Rev. J.C. Alder arrived to take over. His family of three girls - Emily, Grace, and Mabel - was probably the first to live in the manse, which had been built the year before. A musical family, the girls played the organ for Sunday School and sang in the choir. Rev. and Mrs. Alder were founding members of the Union Bay Glee Club. In 1918 Rev. Alder performed the wedding of his daughter Grace to David Haggart. They brought up their family of three in Union Bay.

Rev. & Mrs. Alder left after the end of the war, but Emily, who was a clerk at Fraser and Bishop's, stayed on. Rev. J.S. Gibson was rector for one year before being replaced in Oct 1919 by J.A. Rowland, who is remembered for the big-bowled pipe that he smoked. After three years Rev. A. Walker took charge of the con-

N. King

Rev. and Mrs. Hobbins at Al and Frances Stasek's wedding

gregation, in May 1923. He also doubled as a school teacher, instructing the high school class for several years. It was during Rev. Walker's tenure that union of the church was consummated, creating the United Church of Canada in July 1925.

About the beginning of 1926 Rev. J.H. Hobbins arrived with his musical family. He saw that there was lots of music in the church, with his daughters Muriel, Joan and Dora taking an active roll. As a member of the Comox Valley Men's Musical Association, his beautiful bass voice was in demand. He sang in district musicals, once singing the part of Captain of the Pinafore.

Too soon for the music lovers, Mr. Hobbins left and was replaced in 1930 by a nautical preacher. Rev. M.F. Eby and family arrived from Port Simpson in their sail boat, the *Acadia*. As Hornby and Denman were also in his charge, being a sailor was an asset as it meant no more rowing to Denman. He provided transportation for the picnics to the Islands and outings for the boy's club.

1932 JULY ➾ Rev. M.F. Eby, accompanied by some young boys, left in his launch for a four day cruise to Texada and Lasqueti Island. G. Horne, D. Marshall, J. Abrams, and B. & N. Davis were the lucky sailors. [6]

In June 1934 Mr. Eby left, due to poor health. Soon after, he died and was buried on Quadra Island. Rev. A.O. Patterson followed and it was during his term that Rev. Ralph Connor, who had assisted materially in founding the original church, presented new hymnals to the worshippers. At this time the Church was at a low ebb and a meeting was held to consider its future.

1935 JUNE ➾ The Union Bay Church is partly supported by the mission. It was suggested that if every resident attended one service a month, there would be no need to close the church. The meeting definitely decided not to close it. [6]

Often in the lean times, just a few families kept the church doors open with funds for the preacher's salary. After two years Rev. Patterson left to be replaced by Frank Chilton. He truly put spirit back into the church and was especially enthusiastic about the young people. With three sons of his own, Bob, Ralph and Gordon, he was particularly interested in the boys of the community. The Bible Study group lead services, sang in church, enjoyed picnics and played sports.

"Rev. Chilton was about the only one who did anything for young people. He taught us how to play roller hockey with hockey sticks in the little red school house. Then he installed gym equipment in the church hall. He was just the kind of fellow who never saw anything wrong in anybody. We tried to wreck the building, but it looked O.K. to him. He really put up with something gosh terrible."

Ken Peters

In January 1938 cushioned pews were installed in the Church which seated 150. Every seat was filled at Christmas, Easter and Thanksgiving as people came to enjoy Rev. Chilton's sermons.

The year 1940 saw many changes: Rev Chilton left, Mrs. Haggart hung up her umbrella, and Mr. Glover put away his hymn books. For over thirty-five years the two faithful workers had watched ministers come and go, the church wax and wane and wax again.

Rev. Leslie and family came next. When they were away at a church conference on May 15, 1941 the manse burned to the ground. Because the fire started at 2:00 a.m., flames had already engulfed the house before the fire was discovered. Assisted by a heavy rain, the Union Bay Fire Department fought the fire and were able to save the church and post office.

M. Peters

Three dedicated church workers. Edna Peters played the organ, Helen Harwood taught Sunday School, and George Harwood sang and sat on the church board for many years

Miss Leslie, the minister's daughter, taught school at Courtenay High. She came down after the fire and sifted through the ashes where her bedroom had been and found some of her jewelry. This inspired some of the young girls and they went sifting through the ashes, being careful not to be seen.

"Marg, Verna, Mildred and I dug out this money, but we knew we couldn't spend it because it was all black and they'd know at the store where it was from. So we went up in the post office and scrubbed them all off. Poor Verna was so scared... she was sure we would get caught. After that we always imagined that Miss Leslie had it in for us kids from the Bay."

Gertrude (Harwood) Robertson

1941 JUNE ⊸ A surprise shower was given for Rev. & Mrs. Leslie who lost everything in the manse fire. Rev. & Mrs. Henderson attended along with thirty parishioners. During the evening songs were rendered by Mrs. D. Campbell and Mrs. A. Ray. [7]

Soon after, the Leslies left and were replaced by Rev. A.L. Anderson, who came down from Cumberland to conduct morning service. Immediately, the congregation and various groups started raising money to rebuild. The proceeds from teas, concerts, sales and lantern shows all added up, until just fifteen months after the fire a new manse built by Edward Baldwin was opened.

1942 AUGUST ⊸ The community gathered on the lawn of the new manse at Union Bay when the building was formally opened by Mrs. E. McKay, one of the oldest local members, who presented the key to Rev. A.L. Anderson. Mr. E. Baldwin, president of the Church Board, spoke on the joint effort of the congregation and thanked the ladies for their untiring work. Mrs. L. Magnone, on behalf of the Ladies Aid, presented a picture to be hung in the manse. [7]

Rev. Anderson, who had married a year earlier, lived in the new manse for only a year. When he left to join the airforce and become a Flight Lieutenant, Rev. and Mrs. W.R. Welsh arrived. Although not a young man, Rev. Welsh was energetic and athletic. He had a gymnastic club which used the ropes and rings which Rev. Chilton had installed in the back room.

Mrs. Welsh had a Mission Band for younger children. Although disappointed at first, as most of the kids expected to be playing in a music band, they soon came to enjoy stories of other lands remembered from Mrs. Welsh's missionary days.

"Mrs. Welsh had been a missionary, maybe in China. She made us green tea to drink. Ugh! We didn't like it much."

Shirley (Treloar) Lenner

Rev. Peter Kelly was the most distinguished minister that graced the Church at the Bay. He came after sixteen years of marine missionary work up and down the British Columbia coast aboard the *Thomas Crosby*. A chief of the Haida Indians, while at Union Bay he received the title Doctor of Divinity, and first wore his new vestments to marry Margaret Glover and Mario Marocchi in 1949.

F. Peters

The Shantyman Mission boat *Messenger II* was captained by Harold Peters

W. Glover

Dr. Peter Kelly, a chief of the Haida Indians, and his wife served the Union Bay church

The proud handsome man with a kind gentle manner was respected by all. He and Mrs. Kelly used to blend their voices in beautiful duets. Because of a dwindling population, the United Church became a three point charge in 1950. The Kellys moved to Cumberland, but he was also responsible for Union Bay and Denman until 1952. He later became a Canadian senator. The ministers that followed all lived in Cumberland, so the manse was rented out to young families.

Rev. P. Connal served from 1952 until 1956. Next came Rev. W. Seiber who ministered for two years. He was followed by Murray Henderson who, with his friendly enthusiasm,

B. White

Harry and Eugene Glover. He was church organist for 35 years

CHOIRS

When the church services were held in the Little Red School House, someone donated a small organ and Mrs. Dave Renwick played the hymns for Sunday service. When the church was built, Mrs. Renwick, the first organist, happily turned the organ duties over to Harry Glover. For several years Herbert Glover had been writing to his brother, telling about the virtues of Vancouver Island. So in 1906 he left his post as organist and choir master of the United Methodist Church in Sheffield, and with his family of four sons and two daughters, immigrated to Canada. Harry got a job in the foundry, and the family rented the "glass house" from Mammy King.

"Dad left England with his grey flannel swallow tail coat and a tall black silk hat. As we travelled across the prairie he kept looking out of the window, and then one day he opened it up and threw out the beautiful hat.'He said 'I shan't be needing this in Canada'.

Dad was known as a master organist in the old country. We had a 400 pipe organ in our parlour. When we first arrived, church was held in the school house. He could just bring the tone out of that little organ. He chose good music, the masters."

Violet (Glover) Rutherford

This little man with twinkling eyes, bushy moustache, and sporting a flower in his lapel, always arrived half an hour early for church to warm up the organ. His tiny wife, Eugene, sat with an appreciative ear as he played beautiful organ voluntaries until the congregation arrived. Harry took on the job of training the choir, and worked with the Glee Club. His volunteer work did not end there. Many Sundays he rowed the minister to Denman, hiked with him up to the Church and played for the Islanders. Later, to make it easier he acquired a motor launch and a Chevrolet car. Nearly eighty, after serving the church for thirty-five years, he retired in 1940 and was presented with a pen and pencil set by Rev. Chilton.

When Cumberland purchased a new organ Union Bay acquired the old one. This organ was restored in 1959 by the Harwood family, in honour of their mother and father's work in the church. It now sits in the Presbyterian Church on Mission Hill in Courtenay.

After Mr. Glover retired, Mrs. Grace Haggart, who had for years played for the Sunday School, took over. Later, Hazel Campbell and Mary Moore took turns. With their musical talents Mary and Hazel made a winning pair. One played the organ while the other led the choir. Hazel, a trained singer, added to the enjoyment of the congregation with her beautiful solos. For the next twenty-five years there were adult, girls, and mixed choirs, all well-trained and appreciated not only in Union Bay but around the district. Then the Campbell family moved to Campbell River, and Mrs. Moore got help from Audrey Sawchuck, another favourite soloist. Together they had a very dedicated group of young people.

brought many of the younger people back into the church.

In 1941 Harold Peters started work with the Shantyman Mission. As captain of the *Messenger II* he took the gospel to those who couldn't be reached by land. He sometimes took sick persons from primitive areas to city hospitals, and helped to rescue lost souls at sea. He often assisted in the services when he visited home port. His wife, Edna, graciously entertained many of the missionaries passing through Union Bay.

"There has never been a trail too hard, or a sea too rough for the "Skipper" in his outreach for men and women who were unreached by the church"

Percy Wills

M. Aitken

Mary Moore plays the organ and sings with daughter Marjorie

"The first time I went to church at Union Bay, Hazel Campbell was sitting in front of me and heard me singing. She told Rev. Welsh that I could sing. So the next day he biked down to Buckley Bay and asked me to sing in church.

Audrey Sawchuck

Also serving as organist over the years were Mrs. Booth, Ethel Fulcher, Kathleen Haggart, Eva Baldwin, Mrs. Edna Peters and Mrs. Margaret Woods.

For a small town there were a number of good voices, which enhanced the church services considerably. In the early days there were Mrs. Mary Marshall, James Haggart, Violet Glover and her brothers, Ted and Bert. Then came Edith Campbell, Mrs. Jean Anderson, Eva Baldwin, Mrs. Madeline Horne, Albert Glover, E.T. Searle, Mrs. Hazel Campbell, and a little later, Mrs. Audrey Sawchuck. Spanning all this time was a pillar of the church, George Harwood, with his lovely tenor voice.

"Dad Harwood sang. We suffered especially if he sang the Holy City - those high notes. We'd sit in the church and hope he'd make it through. Some were very good - some were awful. But he loved singing and the church."

Margaret (Harwood) Bowden

M. Aitken

Ruth Robertson, Audrey Sawchuck and daughter Afona wait for the ferry to Denman Island where the choir often sang

M. Peters

Faithful members of the church choir. Front: A. Campbell, A. Sawchuck, M. Moore, A. Pendlebury. Back: L. Eccleson. T. Searle, R. Robertson, M. McBride, G. Harwood, T. Pratt

SUNDAY SCHOOL

The first Sunday School was started by Mrs. Cook in her home. She played the hymns on her black walnut organ that she brought by railroad from Cleveland to a homestead in Port Angeles, and then by boat to Union Bay. Later, Sunday School was held in the Little Red School House, and Mrs. Cook had help with her growing number from George Russell and Michael Manson.

About the time the church was built, the two Haggart families, those of William and David, moved to town. Arriving at the same time was David's brother, James Haggart. David had been to Canada, then returned to Scotland and married his sweetheart, Agnes. Together they set out for Canada. By the time they arrived in Union Bay they had one son, David, and three daughters, Rachel, Nellie and Elsie. Kathleen was born at the Bay. Agnes had trained as a kindergarten teacher in Edinburgh. Her love of children was deep, so with her own five to swell the ranks of the Sunday School, it was only natural that she become the superintendent.

"Mom taught Sunday School for forty years. I remember Gordon Horne saying he wouldn't miss Sunday School for the world. She always told a lovely interesting story."

Kathleen (Haggart) Stubbs

"Old Ma Haggart in her long black skirt and black umbrella ran the Sunday School for years. God bless her! Such a kind old lady."

Doug Brown

In all kinds of weather she trudged along the main street with her Bible, hymn book, and just in case, her umbrella. In 1922 an appreciative Church Board presented Mrs. Haggart with an umbrella.

"Mother was a real community-minded person, always

doing things for everyone. She used to say, 'Cast your bread upon the water'. Then one of my sisters (all with a good sense of humour) would quip back 'and you'll get soggy toast'.

Rachel (Haggart) Bennie

Over the years Mrs. Haggart was assisted by her daughter Kathleen, and daughter-in-law Grace, as well as minister's wives, Mrs. Helen Harwood, and Eva Baldwin. The Grand Old Lady of the Sunday School died at seventy-two, just five months after retiring.

"For over thirty years, rain or fine, storm or sunshine, sick or well, this faithful servant of Jesus Christ was in her place. What patience, zest and love she must have had all these years, but she counted her task a pleasure, for she loved the work and was building for eternity. She was moulding young lives for the future, and her great work has not been in vain and will not be soon forgotten. Her influence will long be felt by those who have sat under her faithful teaching, and long after she has departed this present life. Her name will be spoken in reverence and love."

Speech on Mrs. Haggart's retirement
by Rev. F. Chilton, Feb. 1940

D. Bennie

Mrs. Hobbins, the minister's wife, and Agnes Haggart with her ever-present umbrella share a joke

Mrs. Eva Leighton and Grace Haggart carried on. Soon Mrs. Mary Moore and Mrs. Vi Stewart also became involved, and began their long association with the church.

In the 1940's Constable Ennals of the B.C. Police was posted to Union Bay and became superintendent of the Sunday School. He attracted some of the older boys back to church, and his wife Betty's class inspired the teen-age girls.

"I remember Mr. Ennals favourite verse. One I am sure he lived by... Corinthians X111, verse 13 which ends, 'And now abideth faith, hope, charity, these three; but the greatest of these is charity'."

Janette (Glover) Geidt

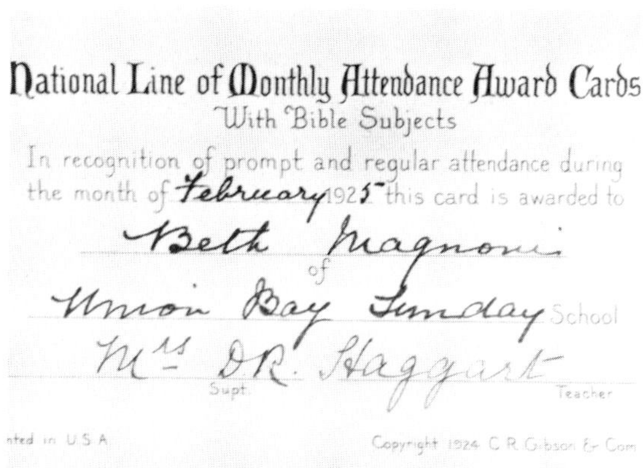

National Line of Monthly Attendance Award Cards
With Bible Subjects
In recognition of prompt and regular attendance during the month of February 1925 this card is awarded to
Beth Magnoni
of
Union Bay Sunday School
Mrs D.R. Haggart
Supt. Teacher
nted in U.S.A. Copyright 1924 C.R. Gibson & Com

N. Eastman

Mrs. Vi Stewart assisted the Ennals' and became superintendent when they left. She in turn was helped by the three Glover girls and Maxine Stokes, who taught the little ones. In the 1950's Mr. and Mrs. Harold Flint also became involved as teachers. Soon Mr. & Mrs. Woods, who had moved down from Cumberland, stepped forth and took the reins. Peggy played the organ and Bill was superintendent. The gregarious Mrs. Stewart faithfully taught her class through the years.

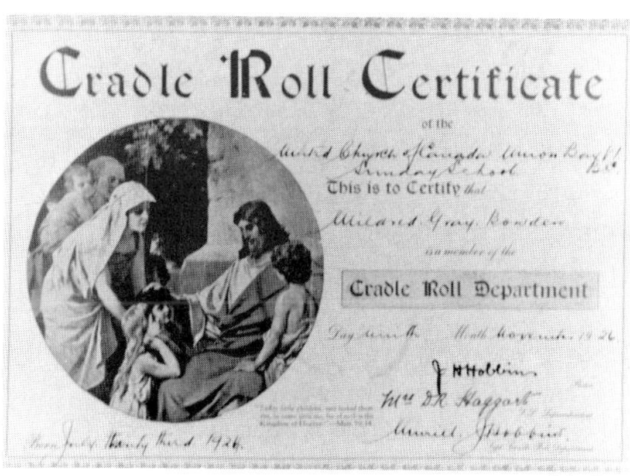

Cradle Roll Certificate
of the
United Church of Canada Union Bay
Sunday School B.C.
This is to Certify that
Mildred Gray Bowden
is a member of the
Cradle Roll Department
Mrs D.R. Haggart

M. Coe

The first Christmas concert was organized by Mrs. Cook, and featured acrostics, recitations and dialogues-

"Just Before Christmas"	Fred Ray
"Don'ts"	Bobbie Curran
"The Lecture"	Ella Cook
"Grandmamma"	Margaret Ray
"The Boy"	Bobbie Humphrey
"The Frog in My Throat"	Mary McKay
"The Old Woman"	Marnie Cook
"The Cobbler"	Bill Cook
"Taking Up the Collection"	Bessie Ray

Christmas concerts became a tradition. The story of the nativity was acted out by little boys in dressing gowns with tea towel

A. Hooper

A Vacation Bible School class. Back: G. Hendmorse, J. McKay, R. Chafer, J. Chapman, P. Glover, N. Chalmers, ___. Front: A. Stewart, D. Chapman, J. Chafer, D. McKay

D. Bennie

A Sunday School Picnic at Holmes Field

A. Sawchuck

headdresses, and little girls in white sheets with cardboard wings and tinsel halos. The tiny ones singing "Away in a Manger" always stole the show.

Every summer during the 1940's and '50s, two personable young people from the Missionary Vacation Bible School set up at the church and gave kids two weeks of learning and fun. They memorized Bible verses until they could recite them in their sleep, sang songs, played games and did handicrafts.

Summer was also time for the Sunday School picnic. In the early 1890's all the churches of the district joined forces for an annual picnic, sometimes at Denman but more often at the Wharf.

1895 JULY ➾ The district's Sunday Schools grand picnic was held at Union Wharf grounds on July 1. Children and adults enjoyed boating, games, swings and refreshments. The 300 to 400 present sat down at long tables, with about 70 at each sitting. People travelled from Denman and Comox on the *Joan*, and from Union free on the train, thanks to the management. [3b]

Later, the Bay Sunday School had it's own picnic on Tree Island if a boat was available, but usually it was held at Holmes' Field. The beautiful grassy space was perfect for races and treasure hunts, with Baynes Sound waiting to cool off the sweaty participants. Every year tired, sunburned, dusty kids and their parents trudged the mile home and declared it the best picnic ever, thanks to Mrs. Haggart and her helpers. In later years picnics were held at Kye Bay and Qualicum.

LADIES AID

With the building of the new church, the ladies of the congregation formed the Ladies Aid with Mrs. E. McKay as the first president. Another founding member was Mrs. A. Haggart, who for years welcomed each new family into the community.

Through the years these dedicated ladies worked tirelessly to keep the building and furnishings in good repair, through bean sup-

1960 Sunday School Picnic at Kye Bay. Standing: Mr. and Mrs. H. Flint. Sitting Back: G. Sawchuck, G. Emerton, B. Flint, J. Sexton. Sitting Front: A. Sawchuck, V. Lansell, P. Flint, F. Lansell, J. Lansell

C. Stewart

A Ladies Aid St. Patrick's Day tea. V. Stewart, N. King, K. Strachan, E. Peters

S. Lenner

The Ladies of the Missionary Society. Back: J. Watt, V. Stewart, M. Pollock, I. Treloar, L. Little, P. Wood. Front: E. Thompson, E. Tappin

N. King

Rev. Murray Henderson congratulates Ellen McKay for sixty years of service to the church

pers, teas and sales. Each lady brought her special talent to the group: Phemie Wynn her bedding plants, Ellen McKay her baked beans, Margaret Pollock her Scotch pancakes, Bess Magnone her mincemeat, Jessie Mackenzie her prize buttertarts, Nellie King her garden produce.

1909 APRIL ➻ Ladies of the Church present sale of work. There was a good selection of artistic and colourful articles on many stalls. Delicious ice cream and cake was served. Selections from Mrs. Haggart's gramophone greatly added to the pleasure of the evening. A handsome sum was raised which will clear the debt off the church. [4]

In 1944 the enterprising ladies produced "The Friendly Cookbook". Recipes were gathered from the congregation and friends around the district. All the local businesses put in advertisements. The sixty page book was a big success and many dog-eared copies are still in use today.

After more than sixty years Mrs. Ellen McKay was still working with the group. At the suggestion of Rev. Henderson the group adopted the name, "Ellen McKay Circle". As the group got older and members died, a few younger ladies, such as Emily Peters, joined to help keep up the tradition of supporting the church.

MISSIONARY SOCIETY

Amalgamated with the Ladies Aid in 1962 was the Helen Harwood Missionary Society. Founders of the group in the early '40s were Mrs. Welsh, Mrs. Moore and Mrs. Harwood (who died shortly after). The group met monthly, when they studied some distant part of the world, learning that country's customs, geography and history. Supplies were made and sent to Mission Hospitals in Canada and overseas, wherever needed. Missionaries on vacation spoke to the group, bringing first hand reports of their work. The first World Day of Prayer was organized by the Missionary Society.

CHURCH GROUPS

D. Aitken

Peeling potatoes at C.G.I.T. camp. F. Jones, E. Fulcher, W. Bowden, L. Brown, A. McKay

Generally speaking, the women and girls were more religious than the men and boys. In many families the wives went faithfully to church as well as serving in some other capacity, while many husbands never set foot inside the church except for a wedding.

"My dad never went to church but he saw that us kids never missed Sunday School".

Doug Brown

Those men who did attend found themselves on the Church board, and some sang in the choir. No groups were formed, probably because there were never enough men at any one time.

The young boys didn't fare much better. Mothers tried valiantly to keep them in Sunday School until they were nine or ten. In the early 1920's the Trail Rangers Club was formed and led by the minister for the next fifteen years.

W. Glover

A hike to Langley Lake. I. Crawford, L. Bowden, C. Cave, A. Baillie, E. Campbell, N. Marshall, E. Campbell, L. Brown, D. Good, K. Good

1922 NOVEMBER ➾ One of the most successful events in the social history of Union Bay took place in the old school house, given by the Trail Rangers. The boy's club has already made its good influence felt in the appearance and demeanor of the boys. [6]

1939 MARCH ➾ The young boys group and Rev. Chilton hiked out to Robt. McKay's farm and enjoyed a hot dog roast over a bonfire. [6]

In the early 1920's Mrs. Pollock and Mrs. Haggart led a club for young boys and girls. Named the Maple Leaf Club, these busy little beavers held lantern shows and sales of work. At one such sale $216 was made for church repairs. By the '30s a girls' group emerged.

1931 NOVEMBER ➾ Sunbeam Club under able leadership of Mrs. A. Horne had a Hallowe'en party. The officers of the group are President Gladys Cooper, Secretary Betty Thomas and Treasurer Grace Haggart. [7]

It is the Canadian Girls in Training that is best remembered. It was started in the fall of 1923 by Mrs. A. Haggart and Mrs. H. Harwood. The two young school teachers, Annie Baillie and Jean Redding, led the enthusiastic group of about sixteen girls, under Mrs. Haggart's watchful eye. The girls wore the official uniform of white middies with navy ties, bloomers and knee socks.

One of the first undertakings was a mother-daughter banquet to rival the Ranger's father-son dinner.

1922 DECEMBER ➾ Miss Kathleen Haggart ably filled the chair as chairman for the evening. Toasts to the King, Our Mothers, the Sunday School and C.G.I.T. were respectively proposed by Minnie Mugford, Mary Little, Margaret Johnson and Winnie Bowden. [6]

The leaders, Annie and Jean, who were only a few years older than the girls, organized many fun-filled activities. They went on hikes to the lake and Tsable River, had picnics on Tree Island, did handiwork, put on concerts and sang in church.

"We struck trouble. I wanted to give the girls a little

A. Pratt

Merry Hearts. I. Nelson, V. Campbell, D. Ward, M. Hicks, E. Bateman, D. McKay

A. Pratt

More Merry Hearts. H. Treloar, I. Robertson, R. Treloar, M. Glover, M. Militich, G. Harwood, A. McKay, M. Peters

more social life so we planned a party. The girls would ask the local boys with the understanding that it was well supervised - straight home afterwards and NO hanky-panky. There was lots of opposition. The minister, old Walker, was dead set against it, but his wife was for it and so was Mrs. Pollock. She really supported us and we had a wonderful party - no rumours afterwards. We went camping down at Parksville and lived in tents and slept on boughs. Really roughed it. I made the rule that everyone had to swim before breakfast, and we did."

Annie (Baillie) Campbell

Many of the men remember the C.G.I.T. girls.

"The boys used to wait at the Church after C.G.I.T. to walk the girls home."

Jack Bradley

"Ross Ray, Jack Bradley and I were fishing on the outside of the bar. We knew the C.G.I.T. girls were having a picnic on the spit. We landed behind a clump of trees and heard this clattering and gabbing like a bunch of geese on the tide flats. So we sneaked thru' the bush, and on our way, here were all their clothes and the girls were swimming, all respectable-like, in bathing suits. 'Doggone!' I said, 'lets play "chew raw beef" on their clothes'. So I got a-hold of the teacher's corsets and laced them around a maple tree. Ross got Annie's and did the same. We tied knots in all their clothes and pulled them tight. To this day I don't think they know who did it."

Bobby Pollock

These young ladies, according to Annie Campbell, were a wonderful group that stayed together even after they were married. Later, in the 1930's a new bunch of girls was led by Florrie Jones, also a teacher and one of the original group.

A generation later, in 1941, C.G.I.T. was formed again, with several of the original girls' daughters as members: Verna Campbell, Gertrude Harwood, Winanne Glover and Isobel Nelson. Mrs. Harwood again helped establish the group, with Hazel Campbell and Mary Moore as leaders. They were named the Merry Hearts, derived from Mrs. Moore's maiden name, Mary Hart. She kept these girls busy with many special projects. In the '50s the girls went their separate ways but still get together for reunions.

"We sang in church on all the special days: Christmas, Easter, Mother's Day. We put on concerts. One year we did a Stephen Foster night and sang negro spirituals. Mr. Harwood and Albert Glover sang too, and Mrs. Grundy was the narrator."

Winanne Glover

"Explorers", for younger girls, flourished under the organization of Peggy Wood in the late 1950's.

M. Aitken

Explorers Group. Standing : ?, ?, J. Vanyo, A. Stewart. Sitting: H. Auchinvole, P. Flint, L. Dutfield, B. Flint. Kneeling: ?, M. Moore, D. Parkinson, C. Coe

CLUBS

THE UNION BAY COMMUNITY CLUB

T. Dutfield

Original Community Club Members. Front from right: J. Stevens, A. Reid, R. Treloar, E. Tappin, Ina Peters. Second row: A. Glover, D. Davis, K. Haggart, A. Campbell, E. Renwick, F. Stasek. Third row: W. Peters, C. Stevens, H. Tappin, P. Renwick, P. Reid, T. Campbell. Back: T. Searle, C. Stubbs, G. Davis, W. Treloar, S. Waterfield

The Union Bay Community Club started out in February 1921 as the Union Bay Social Club. The executive remained the same throughout the four years of operation: Alexander Auchinvole, president; Seymour Abrams, vice-president; Ted Searle, secretary-treasurer. The honourary president was Thomas Graham, Supt. of the CC(D)L, who had promised to help with the building of a hall.

The Social Club soon absorbed the Athletic Club and its assets, and continued to support the town's teams. Twice a week the club held dances for the young people. Concerts, movies, whist drives and smoking parties were also put on for entertainment and to raise money. Mrs. Anderson donated her services, making the coffee and looking after the refreshments at all the functions. Picnics and sports days were arranged by the club. They also organized and provided funding for the first May Queen.

By having benefit dances and subscription collections, the club helped many families and people who fell on bad times. A collection of money and clothes was taken for the victims of the Merville fire. The club arranged and paid for Nelson Cook's funeral at a cost of $105, then gave his widow and children $100, and also helped her apply for the widow's pension.

All the events took place in the Little Red School House, for which the School Board collected $4.00 rent. Because there were no chairs in the hall, they had to be borrowed and returned for each event from the church. Volunteers, under Mr. Pollock's supervision, carried the chairs across the school yard to the little hall. This was done at the discretion of the presiding minister, one of whom refused to loan the chairs for card parties. Finally, in the fall of 1923, eighty chairs were bought from the Restmore Manufacturing Co. for $125. When the club folded in 1924, the chairs were sold to the School Board.

Then, after ten years of being inactive, the executive members met to disperse the funds. In June 1935 the $547 was divided: $325 was given to the Fire Brigade, $111 each to the United Church and School Board.

M. Simpson

Three hundred people attended the Inauagural Banquet when the Union Bay Community Hall opened in 1942

In the early 1940's an Old Time Dance Club formed, which soon became the Community Club, with Peter Reid, president; Bill Treloar, vice-president; Percy Renwick, secretary-treasurer; Jenny Stevens, ladies' convener. Now that the Little Red School House was gone, the sole purpose of the club was to build a hall. With $75 in assets and "a great deal of optimism", the club approached Mr. R.H. Plommer, general manager of the CC(D)L, for financial assistance. He suggested that they first raise some funds to test their optimism. The committee of hard workers set out to do just that.

Money-raising events followed one after another: a silver tea held by Mrs. Moore, a tulip tea held by Mrs. Searle, fifty-eight ladies at a costume party held by Mrs. Renwick. Telephone whist drives were held at homes that boasted telephones. A baked bean supper was held on the lawn of the Nelson Hotel. A huge garden party was given at G. H. Dickson's home. Theme dances were held at Fanny Bay and the Native Sons' Hall. A bubble dance featured a prize bubble, and a star dance a prize star. Ed and Jack Anderson built a beautiful cedar strip rowboat which they donated to the committee for a raffle. It was won by Duncan Bennie of Ladysmith.

In a short time the Committee had amassed $2,000, so they went back to Mr. Plommer who, on behalf of the CC(D)L, gave them a triangle of land opposite the Home Garage. The company also provided the club with a long-term, interest-free loan of $5,000. W.A. Owen, the company architect and construction engineer, was hired to draw up the plans and oversee the construction of the hall, which was carried out by Abe Orr of Courtenay.

The 70' x 45' floor was of edge grain fir, strapped underneath to give sufficient resiliency for dancing. The 16' high walls were finished in 8" and 10" beaded cedar shiplap which was varnished to highlight the beautiful grain. Ladies' and gentlemen's cloakrooms with plumbing were on either side of the ticket office at the entrance. The 21' x 47' adjoining dining room could comfortably seat one hundred people to eat the food prepared in the well-equipped kitchen.

At a gala affair on Friday, May 15, 1942 three hundred very proud people attended a banquet to mark the official opening of the Union Bay Community Hall. The highlight of the evening was the speech of President Peter Reid in which he turned the hall over to the people.

"Here is the Hall! It is yours, for your pleasure or business. Make the most of it as a centre of effort for the advantage and improvement of the community. Use it freely."

E.T. Searle accepted the hall on behalf of the citizens of Union Bay, naming and thanking the committee members.

"This fine hall is a monument to public spirit. I accept it on behalf of the people of Union Bay with the utmost pleasure."

The hall was declared officially open by Bill Auchinvole, Mechanical Superintendent of the CC(D)L.

"To the saying 'everything comes to those who wait' I think we could well add in this case, 'and work'. For it has been a great deal of work. Now I have great pleasure in declaring it officially open, and I ask you to rise and drink a toast to its success."

The banquet was a full course meal prepared by the ladies and served by teenage girls wearing dainty caps and aprons in patriotic colours. Entertainment followed, featuring the talents of the community, at which time the Women's Committee sang their theme song "The Spirit of Union Bay". Jimmy Walker's orchestra, with soloist Adele McMillan, made a big hit when it played for the dance which started with a grand march led by the bagpipes.

The hall was indeed enjoyed and used. It could be rented for any occasion for $7.50 by Union Bayites and for $15 by outsiders. The Committee set out to rid themselves of the mortgage by setting an ambitious schedule of a modern dance every Saturday night, featuring the very popular Country Club Orchestra. Once a month an old-time dance was scheduled, with either Mrs. King's or Johnny Lockner's Orchestra playing. For years Bill Treloar organized the dances, always seeing to it that there were enough workers to sell tickets, act as bouncers, and keep the floor in good shape.

It was war time, with soldiers stationed at Courtenay and sailors and airmen at Comox. Admission was 75¢ for men, and 50¢ for women and servicemen. The Bay dances became known far and wide, not only for the beautiful hall and fine orchestra, but also for the hearty ham or egg sandwiches and excellent coffee served by the friendly ladies of the committee. This was a feat in itself as many of the items were rationed, so ways were devised to stretch the food.

Union Bay Community Club

Mr. and Mrs. P. Renwick

are cordially invited to attend an

Inaugural Banquet

to be held in the New Hall at Union Bay
on the evening of May Fifteenth, 1942
at 7 p.m.
This banquet is preliminary to
the general public meeting
which will take place on May 23rd.

Dress: Informal
R.S.V.P.

E. Renwick

There was always a huge turnout for the Community Club banquets. c. 1947

To Double a Pound of Butter.

Dissolve one tablespoon of gelatin in one half cup of lukewarm top milk. Add the pound of soft butter and beat until smooth, adding half a teaspoon of salt and a little yellow colouring. Perfect for sandwiches.

Ella Davis

"Ella and I would go every Friday night and make two pounds into four. We had two old spatulas and they joked that we'd worn them down by scraping out the bottom during the war years. You couldn't buy a new one because they were made of rubber."

Elizabeth Renwick

At the end of the war, when all the service men and women came home, they each got a year's free admission to the dances. The mortgage was burned seven years after the hall was built.

The floor was marked with three badminton courts and a basketball court. As well, gymnastic rings, ropes, bars and horses were installed for the use of the gym club. An Athletic Club was formed in 1949 with teams in various sports.

MERCHANT NAVY CLUB

The Merchant Navy Club was started by the Women's Committee of the Community Club during the war, when many merchant marine and navy boats called at Union Bay. The women, some with sons fighting in far-off lands, talked to the crews of these boats and realized how lonely they were. Elizabeth Renwick, whose husband was the customs man, often entertained the sailors in her home so was a natural to lead the group.

"This Geordie had a terrible throat and Dr. McNaughton wanted him in the hospital, but we decided to look after him here. So we did, and while he was lying here his people in Newcastle were entertaining my Donald. He had taken a parcel for them. Donald said they must have put all their coupons out to give him something to eat. Small world!"

Elizabeth Renwick

The idea of the Merchant Navy Club was presented to the Native Sons in Courtenay, who in 1943 dedicated the proceeds of their July 1st celebration. A fund of $2,750 was created. Within the next two years eighty seagoing merchant ships had been entertained at an average cost per ship of $28.90. In October 1945 a clubroom was built in the basement of the hall and

D. Bennie

The kitchen crew make sandwiches - K. Strachan, D. King, P. Stasek, Elsie Veal

T. Dutfield

Washing up. E. Hicks, K. Mosher, M. Lockner, J. McKenzie, E. Woods and helper D. McBride

G. Murdock

The Community Hall being moved to its present site by Ed. Sawchuck in 1962

comfortably furnished for the use of the crew of any ship calling at Union Bay. Under the auspices of the Navy League of Canada, the room was opened by Commander N. Jackson of Victoria who eulogized the work of the local people in making it possible.

For every ship that arrived, the same women who put on the weekly dances held a party for the crew. The sailors looked on these ladies as their "fairy godmothers" in this part of the world. There were always lots of sandwiches, baked treats and coffee served with a friendly smile. An American ship was so grateful that they left the ladies twelve pounds of coffee, an uheard of amount during rationing.

"A British boat came in on Christmas Eve from New Westminster. Somebody there had said, 'We sure feel sorry for you bunch going to Union Bay , there's nothing there but a wharf.' Percy felt sorry for them so I had fourteen for dinner next day. Cecil and Kathleen came along and we had a singsong, and some of them played with Jack's new toys half the night. One of the boys told me, 'It's just like being at home'."

Elizabeth Renwick

Magazines were collected from the community, and Clement's Drug Store sent down their unsold ones for the sailors to read. Some sort of entertainment was provided, perhaps a home slide show. Anyone with a little talent was called upon. Many times Kathleen and Cecil Stubbs played the piano and accordion with Bill Thompson on the banjo, for dancing. Mrs. Reid and Lily Ray sang, Margot Auchinvole danced the highland fling, and Jim Reid recited poetry. Often the men entered into the fun.

"Some of them were very talented, and Kathleen and I would coax them to sing or whatever. One fellow was an organist from a big church in England. Once a Maori off an Australian boat sang 'Now is the Hour', first in Maori then in English. It brought tears to our eyes. A very young

D. Bennie

The devoted Ladies' Committee who welcomed men from the merchant navy. Front: K. Stubbs, M. Winterburn, R. Bennie. Back: J.McKenzie, M. Lockner, M. Geary, L. McKay, L. Shillito, E. Renwick, H. Slaughter

E. Renwick

Elizabeth, Jack and Percy Renwick entertain visiting sailors

With Apologies to Rudy Kipling and "On the Road to Mandelay"

By rocky Tipple Island
Through the "straights" and across
the sound
The wind sings in the rigging
But We know where we are bound.
The Seamen's hearts are happy
Their songs are blythe and gay.
And the work seems much lighter
For We're bound for Union Bay.

On the road to Union Bay
Where the whole ship's Company play
Just across the bar from Comox
With the green Denman across the Bay.

That dirty old black coal dock
By that sleepy little town
Is not a thing of beauty
Or a port of wide renown
But it offers relaxation
And a chance to make Whoo-pee
And a chance to meet the Ladies
And forget the blooming sea.

On the road to Union Bay
With Our pockets full of pay
If We're wise we'll take it easy
And remember the "Rainy Day".
But We're young and gay and carefree
So We sing this little lay
We're the Crew of the good Ship "Stewart"
On the road to Union Bay.

P.D.M.

boy was a good step dancer and had his tap shoes with him. I remember one fellow got up to sing and he could no more sing than fly. He sang 'Jealousy' and they clapped him and he sang again. When we would think he was finished he'd sing again. Couldn't get rid of him, but he did his part anyway."

Elizabeth Renwick

Both the officers and men were very grateful. They never expected such kindness so far from home in a coal shipping port.

1945 JULY There are several merchant ships in at the Bay. The Ladies Club had to divide the entertainment into two nights with fifty men being served strawberries and cream each night. Music was provided by Dave Haggart and Jules Herbin. [7]

Each social was different, but the men were always made to feel special. A warm glow spread over hosts and guests alike as each gathering ended with everyone joining to sing "We'll Meet Again".

CARDS

As in most tiny communities with little entertainment provided, card playing became an important social activity. Some of the settlers arrived with very strict morals, and associated cards with gambling. They considered cards the "devil's playthings", but for the most part no large sums of money changed hands. Card games were fun-filled evenings with friends and family. Groups got together to play bridge, whist or crib. Soon clubs formed out of these informal gatherings.

The Union Bay Crib Club had its beginnings when old friends John Fulcher, Aaron Dunn, Peter Reid and E.T. Searle frequently met to play crib. When Mr. Fulcher suggested the possibility of forming a Crib Club, the others readily agreed and canvassed prospective members. The founding meeting was held in the fall of 1924 in an old railroad coach standing in the CC(D)L yard. Over a dozen men elected John Fulcher, president; Albert Jones, vice-president; Andy Kay, secretary; Percy Renwick, treasurer. A year later Percy became the long-standing secretary. Membership was $1.00 per year with a monthly fee of 25¢. They were all set to start the first game of the UBCC when they realized they were short one man.

"It all got started one night when I was practicing baseball in the field. Old man Fulcher came along and said, 'Tom, do you know how to play crib?' 'Oh!' I said 'I play at it.' 'Well, come on over, we're short one man.' We played in a caboose over on the trestle. Gee! I was young and won every game that night and haven't done it since. I'm the only founding member still alive."

Tom McKay

History was made in the caboose in March 1923 when Spence Walker and Peter Reid were playing a game of singles. To the amazement of all Pete turned up a perfect "29" hand.

From the caboose the club moved to the dining room at the Nelson Hotel. In 1924 a Company house on the back row became vacant and the CC(D)L generously offered it rent-free to the Club, to make whatever changes might be desired. Several inside walls were knocked down to make one large room. It was furnished with handmade, square card tables and cheap wooden chairs. All the windows were boarded up and the house was never painted, so it gave the impression of an abandoned house.

Aaron Dunn and Bert Geary were appointed caterers and kept the club supplied with beer which, according to the club's historian E.T. Searle, was always used with great moderation.

"I think it was early in October that we moved into our new quarters, and what a celebration we made of it. Songs, speeches, and a hubbub of talk. Plenty of beer, but Johnny Fulcher put his foot down when one chap brought in a bottle of whiskey. That bottle went home unopened. There wasn't much play that night- too much conviviality, and we kept it up late. Early I should say. Leaving a few men still at it, it was 2:00 a.m. when I got home. And what a "wiggin" I got from the wife next day."

E.T. Searle

Cumberland Museum

An old railway coach was used as the first home for the Crib Club

Soon there was a membership of over thirty men. The Club challenged a Cumberland club, which resulted in the formation of the District League.

A women's group of bridge players was formed in the late 1920's. Greta Abrams and Mary Marshall, both known better for their infectious laugh than their bridge prowess, led the group. The "Nighthawks" was composed of about twelve ladies who enjoyed weekly card games held in the member's homes for over two decades.

Pythian Sisters' Drill Team. Front: J.McKenzie, M. Rutledge, ? Cottini, E. Chafer, M. McKay, E. McLellan, M. Spence, M. Cowden. Back: E. Peters, R. Foster, E. Woods, A. Cooper, A. Nelson, H. Slaughter, M. Kine, J. Waterman, E. Hicks, K. Strachan, M. McKay

Whist was always popular and a favourite way of raising money for charity. There was always a new twist to keep the players interested: progressive whist, court whist, telephone whist, earthquake whist and military whist. The latter, popular during the war, was scored using flags of different nations. First held in homes or the old school house, all whist games were played in the Community Hall after it was built.

PYTHIAN SISTERS

Union Temple No.12, Order of Pythian Sisters, received its charter in April 1946 at a ceremony held in the Crib Club building. Spearheading the group of fifty ladies that formed the first Temple was Hannah Slaughter who had been a Sister in Nanaimo. The first Most Excellent Chief was Jennie Waterman. In four years the lodge boasted eighty active members.

A drill team was formed, first under Staff Captain Emily McKinnell, and then Myrtle McKay. Many hours were spent in the Community Hall practicing intricate formations, with Kathleen Strachan or Milla McKay beating out the tempo on the piano. The team travelled to many competitions in B.C. and Washington, usually bringing home top honours.

Working for charitable causes has been an important part of the club's activities over the years. One of the first was to organize and assist in the Mobile Chest X-ray programme to stamp out TB. An ongoing project was the Cerebral Palsy Fund for which they raised money with walkathons, teas and cabarets. The annual Christmas Bazaar with its many stalls of home baking, crafts, white elephants and raffles was always well attended.

In later years the lodge made money by catering to banquets, weddings, and reunions. The efficent crew, first under Jennie Stevens and later Emily Peters, prepared delicious food which was cheerfully served by the ladies of the lodge.

The sisters always took time out for fun and camaraderie. Skits, original songs and poems were part of all their parties.

Past Most Excellent Chiefs

1946 - Jennie Waterman
1947 - Kathleen Stephens
1948 - Muriel Chapman
1949 - Myrtle McKay
1950 - Jessica Boskill
1951 - Isabell Hood
1952 - Kathleen Dick
1953 - Jane Anderson
1954 - Georgina Surgenor
1955 - " "
1956 - Mildred Cowden
1957 - Audrey Cooper
1958 - Ethel McLellan
1959 - Margaret Rutledge
1960 - Ann Pratt

G. Robertson

The Ladies' Literary Society in George Cooper's garden. Front: M. Pollock, A. Campbell holding Sharon, N. Parnham, H. Harwood, C. Searle, M. Little, M. Cooper, M. Abrams. Back: I. Peters, J. Watt, E. Tappin, L. Little, W. Glover

LADIES' LITERARY SOCIETY

The Ladies' Literary Club of Union Bay was formed in the 1920's. This group of book lovers met monthly for about twenty years to learn about, discuss, or debate chosen topics.

Meetings were held at the homes of members and always started with "O' Canada" and ended with "God Save the Queen". In the formative years the group was led by Catherine Bowran, Ann Glover, Helen Harwood, Laura Little, Agnes Reid and Gertrude Thomas. Later, the reins were taken up by Ethel and Winnie Glover, and Eva Leighton.

After refreshments at the close of each meeting, the topic for the next month was decided on, such as vacation spots, Shakespeare, or art. A country was often chosen, with seven or eight ladies researching and preparing papers on everything from history to dress. To keep up with current events, debates were sometimes the format for the evening. In one memorable debate Margaret Pollock and Mrs. J.A. MacDonald took the affirmative, while Jessie Watt and Madeline Horne opposed the question, "Should the Dionne quintuplets be wards of the government?"

The ladies' feminist leanings were reflected in topics like "famous women", "lives of queens", "female authors" and "Nellie McClung". The women drew on their own experiences with topics such as "food" and "gardening". Anne Glover recounted her six months pilgrimage through the U.S., Britain, France and Belgium.

Poetry or musical nights were given, with a chance for the talented members to perform.

1931 FEBRUARY ⊷ The subject for the evening was "music, composers and their compositions". The following program was rendered and thoroughly enjoyed. Outlines of the lives of composers were followed by selected compositions:

Mrs. Little, "Beethoven"
Mrs. Thomas, "Sonata Pathetique"
Mrs. Watt, "Schumann"
Miss Searle, "Melodie"
Mrs. Stacey, "Schubert"
Mrs. Horne, "Slumber Song"
Miss Steven, "Mendelssohn"
Mrs. D.N. Haggart, "Consolation" [7]

Humour was not forgotten as Catherine Bowran and Margaret Pollock starred with topics like "The Wife That Keeps the Bawbees" and "On Being Chinicked".

The Ladies' Sewing Circle with props for their skit. Front: E. Glover, L. Glover, W. Glover, G. Kay. Back: F. Stasek, M. Walker, A. Aitken, M. Campbell, E. Chafer, I. Peters, E. Hicks, A. Campbell, K. Strachan

D. Aitken

SEWING CIRCLE

In the early 1930's the Sewing Circle evolved from the group of young women who had previously been together in CGIT. They met once a week, ostensibly to knit or crochet. As well they held showers for newlywed members, talked about child raising, exchanged recipes, laughed a lot and caught up on the town gossip.

Most of them were talented knitters, sewers or crocheters who turned out beautiful handcrafted articles. Annie Campbell, not gifted with her hands, took a lot of ribbing as she worked year after year on the same pair of socks. During the war years the ladies pooled their talents and made quilts which were given to the Red Cross, either to be raffled or sent overseas.

The meetings were held at members' homes, with the biggest easy chair always left for the next mother-to-be. By sitting in it a lady announced to everyone that she was pregnant. At the wind-up party each spring, skits were put on for the enjoyment of all.

LACE CLUB

The Denman Island Lace Club was formed in the early 1920's. Soon after, E. Baldwin, N. Hudson, I. McLoughlin, B. McKay, A. Nelson and G. Swan from Union Bay joined the Denman group.

The old craft was brought back when the Union Bay Lace Club was formed in 1951. It was later named the Rose Robertson Lace Club, after Rose who had been a charter member of the Denman Island Club. She taught the new group. They first learned to make their pillows. A round plywood base was stuffed tightly with kaypok and covered with broadcloth. Aina Hooper still has the pillow on which she fancyworked the signatures of the charter members.

Bobbins of wood, ivory and bone were ordered from England. The ladies collected beads and wired them onto the ends of the bobbins for weight. Patterns were carefully copied onto linen paper then pinned onto the pillow. Linen or cotton thread was then braided around the pins to make beautiful pillow lace.

D. Bennie

The Boy Scouts' camp at Horne Lake

W. Glover

Making Pillow Lace with beaded bobbins

ORANGEMEN

Over the years several clubs were formed which dissolved after only a short time. In March 1915 an Orange Lodge was inaugurated with twenty members. An Orangeman was a Protestant patriot who loved religion and country, and was prepared to lay down his life for them. In the early days of WW I there was a great feeling of patriotism among the British settlers at Union Bay. Parades and celebrations were attended every Coronation Day, June 16, at either Cumberland or Nanaimo. After the war the group petered out.

CANADIAN CLUB

The Canadian Club, which had a chapter at Union Bay for a few years in the 1920's, was headed by Messrs. Abrams, Harwood and Searle. Members were privileged to hear speakers from many parts of the world. In the '30s the three separate Canadian Clubs of the District joined to form one club.

BOY SCOUTS

Becoming popular during the First World War was the Boy Scout movement. The boys not quite old enough for the army joined the Scouts. They assisted greatly in collecting materials for the war effort, and folded soon after. Nearly thirty years later, in 1947, a new Boy Scout troop received its charter from District Commissioner Bert Chandler. The troop was sponsored by the Knights of Pythias and enthusiastically led by Scout Master Jim Haggart and Assistant Scout Master Charlie Ennals. The boys enjoyed camping at Horne Lake, and hikes and picnics as well as parties

D. Bennie

In boat: J. Bennie, D. Bennie, D. Campbell, H. Kennedy, M. Campbell, T. McKay

with the Girl Guides. After Jim and Charlie left Union Bay the group soon ended.

About the same time a Cub group was formed. Fred Peters became the leader after attending a training camp at Camp Byng on the Sunshine Coast.

GIRL GUIDES

In 1944 an Explorer group was formed with Annie Campbell, Winnie Glover and Ina Peters as leaders. Because of the girls' interests the group changed in November 1945 to become Girl Guides. With organizational help from District Commissioner Ringrose, the twelve or so girls were led by Emily McKinnell. Divided into two patrols, Bluebirds and Wrens, the girls worked hard and obtained many badges. A year later Edna Peters became the beloved captain, and was later assisted by Winanne Glover and Mary McDonald.

Each spring the girls went on hikes. One memorable cookout was with Mrs. D. Munday, a well-known B.C. mountaineer. Also, the girls were honoured to meet Lady Baden-Powell at a huge rally in Nanaimo. They had practiced for weeks, and in three minutes could put up a tent using wooden poles lashed together with ropes. Every summer a two week camp was held at Henry Bay. Later, the troop joined the district Guide camp at Hornby or Campbell River, and had a fun and educational time under Kay Williams of Cumberland and Betty Stewart of Comox.

In 1947 a Brownie Troop was formed with Hilda Cullen as Brown Owl and Mildred Coe as Tawny Owl. One memorable event was a trip taken to Nanaimo in 1951 to see Princess Elizabeth and Prince Philip.

UNION BAY RIFLE RANGE

In the 1950's a rifle range club was started for the teenage boys. Paul Grundy was instrumental in organizing the club and purchasing equipment. Volunteers built a bulkhead to shoot into, in the crawlspace of the community hall. The boys were taught maintenance, care and safety of guns. The P.T.A. bought six small bore 22's for the group. Early instructors were Jack Anderson, Les Coe, Murray Kennedy and Frank Scavarda. Wilf Emdy, the local RCMP officer, became leader, with Don Bennie assisting him. Constable Emdy took the minute book and shooting record with him to organize, when he went home for Christmas in 1955. The plane on which he was riding crashed near Chilliwack and he was killed.

E. Peters

Girl Guide Troop c. 1947. Front: J. Bradley, M. Jones. Back: L. Watt, B. Peters, J. Vanyo, S. Treloar, Captain Edna Peters, J. Glover, G. Jones, M. Stokes, M. Auchinvole, J. Glover, A. Juvas, B. Chapman

W. Naylor

Cooking chops over a camp fire: M. Stokes, B. Chapman, A. Juvas, J. Vanyo, G. Jones, J. Glover

CELEBRATIONS

I. Fudge

Curly lilies in the woods

ANNUAL CELEBRATIONS

The settlers in Union Bay were almost all of British ancestry, and celebrated their special holidays with the same customs as in the old country. Robbie Burns' birthday was marked with a party in Scottish homes, or a hall was hired where, for one evening, everyone wished they were from the land of the "Tartan". The pipes heralded Ian Pollock into the room, bearing the haggis which Jim Reid most solemnly toasted. Burns' poems and songs were enjoyed, then Joan, Margo or Heather Auchinvole danced the Highland Fling.

Sweet Valentine cards, often done in beautiful needlework, were only sent to that very special person. Then later, lacy boxes of red and white were made in each school room to hold the many cards, handmade the night before.

In preparation for St. Patrick's Day the butchers cured crocks of corned beef which was served with cabbage (Jigg's style). Shrove Tuesday was marked with the serving of stacks of pancakes for lunch or dinner.

An aroma of hot cross buns filled the house on Good Friday, while children coloured eggs by writing on them with lard, carefully wrapping them in onion skins, then boiling them in coffee. Easter Sunday the whole family went to church, Mother sporting a new bonnet or at least new ribbons on the old one. After church, older brothers and sisters hid the eggs in the yard and it was great fun seeing who would find the prize egg. A hike up Washer Creek and the flume, where bunches of curly lilies and trilliums were picked, rounded out the day.

D. Aitken

Bouquets of trilliums for Mother's Day. Edith Humphrey, Beth Magnone, Edith Campbell, Kathleen Good

Although Mother's Day was established in the U.S. in 1912, it was several years before it was celebrated in Western Canada. Gradually, preachers adopted the theme of honouring Mother in their sermons on the second Sunday in May. Flowers were pinned on worshippers' lapels as they entered church, white for those whose mother was dead and red if she was living. The Sunday School or CGIT girls were called upon to sing hymns. The first gifts were bunches of wild flowers collected by the children, who rose early to gather them before breakfast.

Not to be confused with Empire Day, May Day has long been a Socialist holiday. This celebration for the workers and their unions was much preferred over the government-declared Labour Day in September. At Cumberland, the United Mine Workers of America observed the day by bringing in important Union officials and Socialists who gave fiery speeches to the gathered workers. Concessions were set up for free food, ice cream and pop which were enthusiastically consumed by the kids. At Union Bay the Collieries shut down, and although the schools were not closed, there was only a handful of kids left. Those whose parents did not work for the CC(D)L or whose parents were in management positions, insisted that their children attend school.

On the 24th of May,
It's the Queen's Birthday.
If they don't give us a holiday,
We'll all run away!

T. Dutfield

Cumberland Museum

D. and I. McDonald

D. and I. McDonald

Top left: John Rosengren rides his horse down Dunsmuir Avenue. Top right: The Union Bay fire engine leading the 24th of May parade. Bottom left:Themes of war and peace, such as this Union Bay Red Cross float, dominated the 1940 parade. Bottom right: These black-faced minstrels are ready to march in the parade or perform on stage

Queen Victoria's birthday was celebrated in Western Canada from the middle of the 19th century, and became a national holiday when she died. Called Empire Day until the 1950's, Victoria Day now celebrates the reigning monarch's birthday. Most of the fledgling communities held their own festivities. In 1891 Cumberland held possibly its first celebration, with sports and a dance at Comox Lake. For a few years in the '90s, excursions left Union Wharf aboard the *City of Nanaimo*, bound for celebrations in Nanaimo or Vancouver. Comox sometimes held a picnic with sports in the early days. In the 1920's Courtenay had its own celebration with May Queen and all, but Cumberland won the day and the festivities have continued there for nearly 100 years.

The Company always provided a train for the Bay people to travel to Cumberland. As years went by the train trip became one of the highlights of the day. This was the only time when the old coaches were dusted off and used. With a full head of steam the engine whistled at 7:30 a.m. to beckon everyone to the railroad yards. Children and adults piled aboard, dressed in their best bib and tucker, only to arrive at the fair ground with soot smudges on their faces and cinders in their hair.

The day started off with a parade led by the fire departments. Children in costume, several bands, the queen's coach, and many colourful floats delighted the onlookers lined up and down Dunsmuir Avenue. Everyone wondered what "get-up" Sid Williams would appear in that year.

Choosing a May Queen to reign over the day was inaugurated

M. Shillito

Maypole dancers c. 1942. C. Carlyle, E. Frew, F. Higashi, P. Duncan, R. Berggren, E. Shillito, E. ?, M. Campbell

W. Glover

Margaret Johnson, the first May Queen from Union Bay 1921

in Cumberland in 1919. It was decided to share the honour with Union Bay and Bevan in 1921, so about every four years their turn came around. The first lucky girl was Margaret Johnson, with maids of honour Edith Humphrey and Kathleen Good, and pages Willie McKay and Howard Humphrey. The boys' suits were designed and made by Mrs. Hooper, and were passed down for many years to the new little pages. Charlie Fraser with his beautiful curly hair was the queen's herald. To enable all the girls at school to participate in the event, the six older girls became attendants and the younger ones, Maypole dancers.

1921 MAY ➾ The coach was elaborately decorated with the royal colours of purple and gold, and reflected great credit on those who undertook the work. The royal coachman in his quaint English livery was very imposing. But the most attractive and interesting person in the whole parade was Queen Margaret, who looked particularly charming in a gown of white silk and a cloak of white velvet trimmed with a large white fur. She wore a picture hat of white lace and georgette. Her Maids of Honor were very prettily dressed in pale yellow silk, with picture hats, and looked extemely sweet. The page boys were adorned in purple velvet trimmed with gold braid. [5]

"Mrs. Apps taught us how to move gracefully and how to curtsey. I remember that one page boy had to carry the train, another one carried the pillow. One maid of honour carried my flowers, the other carried my crown. My sister and I and some friends made my crown with cardboard, glue and pearls."

Ann (McKay) Pratt

Reminiscent of the old-time rituals on village greens in far-off England, the queen-elect was crowned by the retiring queen in the same ceremony year after year. The mayor presented the queen with a ring, then she addressed her royal subjects and bade the festivities begin. On cue the Maypole dancers, boys in white shirts and girls in frilly dresses, wound their coloured ribbons around the Maypole to the tune "Come Lassies and Lads". Everyone crossed their fingers and prayed that "this" year the Union Bay kids wouldn't get their ribbons tangled.

D. Muschamp

Answering the call "Come Lassies and Lads" in 1938 are Maypole dancers (clockwise) P. Cooper, L. Arrol, M. Peters, D. Muschamp, I. Nelson, W. Glover

E. Peter

Not every pageboy liked dressing up in lace and frills. Kenneth Brown and Alvin (Bud) McKay, Emily Bowden and Dorothy King

Members of the royal party were given money to buy their dresses and flowers. Often the mothers or a friend sewed the gowns. The capes that the girls wore were passed down year after year. For the 1937 party, Winnie Glover made capes of white velvet for her sister, Mildred Bowden, and Irene Davis. The same capes were also worn in 1941 by Georgina Barker and Mary McKay. Winnie's own daughters wore them in 1945, as did her niece, Claire Bowden, and Jean McKay in 1949.

N. King

Tom McKay stands in front of one of the early royal coaches

The pages' original costumes varied with the times and always had to be sewn. The first pages wore velvet and flounces, then during the war the little boys were in military suits. Then it was back to ruffles and plumes.

"Greg came home and said he'd been chosen as a page, but there was no way he would be in it if he had to wear a frilly blouse. So I asked him what he wanted to be and he said, 'A Mountie'. When I went to the meeting to ask if it would be O.K., they said it would be the first time. I borrowed the local Mountie's suit and a made a pattern from it and sewed the two suits."

Audrey Sawchuck

The queen and her entourage were royally treated by the citizens of Cumberland, lunching and dining in private homes, visiting the hospitals where bouquets were presented to patients, and ending with a gala ball at night.

The May Queen Committee was always responsible to provide transportation for the royal party. In the early years elaborate floats were made. After the royal visit to Canada in 1939 by King George VI and Queen Elizabeth, a wealthy English widow with homes in Victoria and Comox bought the 1939 Buick that they toured in. Mrs. Palmer generously drove the May Queen and her party in the 24th of May and 1st of July parades, for years. Accompanied by her good friend, Mrs. M. Horne from Union Bay, they were excellent models in manners and grace for the young girls. Dorothy Ward was the first Union Bay queen to ride in the truly royal coach, and Margaret Christie the last. Then it was back to making floats or using a local convertible.

Chosen by their classmates, it is interesting to see how the same names keep returning to the May Queen party. Over the forty years there were eleven McKay descendants; the second and third queens were sisters, Helen and Beth Magnone (McKay grandchildren). Seven from the Bowden family took part and three from the Muschamp clan (Gail Hood was a maid of honour in 1957 and queen three years later). Buster and Bobby Geary were both page boys. Tom Anderson's nephew followed him twenty-six years later as page.

M. Vowels

Dr. McNaughton welcomes the royal party to the hospital where the girls will present their bouquets to lucky patients. Mrs. Palmer, owner of the car, and Mrs. Horne are chaperones

W. Glover

First May Queen Party 1921. Front row: E. Broder, E. Magnone, D. Good, L. Brown, D. Shuttleworth, C. Pollock, Bill McKay (page), M. McNalley, L. Bowden, L. Nicol, E. Bell, C. Cave. Second row: E. Nicol, M. Mugford, Howard Humphrey (page), Charlie Fraser (queen's herald). Third row: A. McKay, K. Haggart, W. Bowden, N. Marshall, G. Kay, K. Muir, E. Humphrey, P. Street. Back row: Edith Humphrey (maid of honor), Margaret Johnson (queen), Kathleen Good (maid)

A. Hardiman

1927 Queen - Ellen Magnone. Maids - Muriel Hobbins and Mazie Turnbull. Pages - Buster Geary and Graham Holland

F. Peters

1934 Queen - Lydia McKenzie. Maids - Marjorie Jones and Pauline Horne. Pages - Fred Peters and Tom Anderson

E. Peters

1930 Queen - Alma Magnone. Maids - Emily Peters and Dorothy King. Pages - Kenneth Brown and Bud McKay

M. Coe

1937 Queen - Ina Muschamp. Maids - Irene Davis and Mildred Bowden. Pages - Bob Geary and Bob Gifford

M. Kine

1941 Queen - Dorothy Ward. Maids - Mary McKay and Georgina Barker. Pages - John Hayton and Ted McKay

J. Gordon

1945 Queen - Ann McKay. Maids - Janette and Jacqueline Glover. Pages - Leslie Smith and Rudy Katovic

M. Vowels

1949 Queen - Ann Vowels. Maids - Jean McKay and Claire Bowden. Pages - David Chapman and Bruce Watson. Flower girl - Heather Auchinvole

B. Campbell

1953 Queen - Margaret Christie. Maids - Sharon Campbell and June Vanyo. Pages - Kenneth Hatch and Bruce Campbell. Flower girl - Terry Adamson plus Marjorie Moore and Margaret Foster

M. Kine

1957 Queen - Marilyn Davies. Maids - Gail Hood and Karen Bohn. Pages - Greg Sawchuck and Barry McQueen. Flower girl - Rhonda Pratt

I. Hood

1960 Queen - Gail Hood. Maids - Joanne Lansell and Sheila Bowden. Pages - Ricky Anderson and Lennie Murdock. Flower girl - Laura Scavarda

J. Geidt

The royal party rode in a truly royal coach during the years that Mrs. Palmer donated the use of her 1939 Buick first used by George VI and Elizabeth during their Canadian tour

M. Vowels

The royal float 1934

The Campbell cousins, Sharon and Bruce, were together in the 1953 royal party. After the first flower girl, Heather Auchinvole, the little girls were chosen from daughters of previous queens or maids, and this practice continues today, with no trouble in finding a little girl just the right age.

Dominion Day became a very important holiday to the new settlers, who gathered to celebrate Canada's birthday. In the early 1890's both Comox and Union held picnics or sports days. Probably the day was first celebrated at Union Wharf in 1892 when the joint Sunday Schools held their picnic. The Cumberland Brass Band, sporting new uniforms in 1896, accompanied the revellers down on the train and entertained the crowd at the annual picnic. Through the first nine years of the twentieth century the picnics continued with increased emphasis on sports, clay pigeon shoots, bike and foot races.

Then, in 1910 a Dominion Day Committee of company officials and citizens was formed, and July 1st became a big sports day with a picnic for everyone from the four coal towns. Subscriptions were collected from the workers to finance the day.

1910 JULY ➾ The free train left Cumberland at 10:00 a.m. with five box cars, three flat cars and the passenger coach crowded to the utmost capacity with excursionists. The passengers with their baskets were all eager to enjoy a picnic by the sea. Many sports were organized with the highlight being the baseball tournament.

Financial statement for Dominion Day Celebrations

Amount subscribed	$281.75
Expenditure	$270.75
Balance	$ 11.00
Receipts from Dance	$ 33.00
Balance on hand	$ 44.00

Certified and found correct
by Finance Committee D.F. Renwick
G.C. Campbell
Jas. McNeil

Added to the day's fun in 1911 were aquatic sports held at the Government Wharf. That year three trains arrived with twelve car loads of picnickers from Puntledge, Bevan and Cumberland. As well as the foot races there were tug-of-wars, log sawing and nail driving contests. Fun things like "old tub" water races, sack races and three legged-races were highlights. There were events for everyone: children, ladies, men, Chinese and Japanese with substantial prizes for the winners.

Sometime in the 1920's Courtenay took over July 1st celebrations, so the Company Picnic as it was known was held later in July.

Almost from the beginning the workers at Union Bay celebrated Labour Day, usually with a picnic. It signalled the end of summer.

1902 SEPTEMBER ➾ The train took an excursion to Union Bay where families spent Labour Day on the shore. Many carried baskets and picnicked out under the trees; others patronized the hotels. Some drove down the road toward Tsable River and thus spent the day. [4]

Like Mother's Day, Thanksgiving originated in the States and was copied by Canada. It was even celebrated in November until about 1912, when the government issued a proclamation fixing the date in October to correspond with our Canadian harvest. Before the turn of the century, the day was often celebrated with sports, football games and rifle matches. Merchants advertised Thanksgiving gifts, a commercial enterprise that did not catch on. Although an 1896 Weekly News Thanksgiving dinner menu featured turkey, cranberry sauce, lobster tail and pumpkin pie, the early settlers at the Bay were lucky just to have the pie.

The church was the focal point of this celebration. All the farmers and gardeners brought their prize produce to decorate the church. Tall stalks of corn, giant pumpkins and squash, huge potatoes, carrots and beets, piles of polished plums, pears and apples, and bottles of shimmering jams and jellies all graced the pulpit, chancel and window sills, giving the appearance of a fall fair. The scene surely inspired everyone to sing the hymn "Bringing in the Sheaves".

Sometimes the food was donated to the hospital or the poor, but in later years a sale and tea the next day netted the church a tidy sum.

Hallowe'en was a celebration for children. Pumpkins were grown and carved into jack-o-lanterns. Parents had parties for family and friends where they played games like bobbing for apples and pulling toffee. Someone would tell a ghost story by the light of the fireplace, while strange noises made on an outside window with a pin, thread and rosin frightened the listeners. Homemade candies and cookies were enjoyed.

The older boys bought firecrackers from Chinatown. They cost 2¢ for a package of tiny ones and 5¢ for large. Sometimes they would light a whole package at once, but it would be over in one long sputtering bang. So they carefully unwound them one by one, then using the string that bound them together as a punk, lit them and terrorized the town.

A little later when the homes were not so scattered, children began to dress up and wander from house to house knocking on doors. The home owner would be entertained with a song, poem or dance before guessing who was behind the mask and rewarding the performer with a treat.

The older kids played pranks. They would race through Chinatown and ring the big dinner gong, disturbing the quiet calm. Once, Jake Campbell rolled a basket bomb into the gambling house, which exploded with such force that lantern glasses were broken.

Bands of boys would roam through the town soaping windows, taking gates off fences and hiding them in the bush, or hoisting the odd one up a flagpole.

"We used to steal the horse cart from Horne's barn, take it all apart and put it on top of the freight shed. Poor Hungo had to get it down."

Jack Anderson

Possibly the worst or best prank, depending on your point of view, was the fun of turning over outhouses. Scarcely a toilet was missed as the boys moved along the Company Hill. Sometimes the man of the house would try to defend his throne, but this usually made the boys more determined.

"We had two crews. A bunch of us would go to the front of the house and make a hell of a lot of noise, then a few guys would sneak around back and tip over the outhouse. Once Lil' Abner's gang pushed the toilet over with Jocky Pollock in it. He was trying to weight it down. Jenny Stevens lived on a hill, and when she came up the path to go to the toilet, the outhouse came rolling down the hill and chased her back to the porch. Bradley's moved their outhouse ahead a few feet, then when the kids came to push it over, down in the hole they went. Next day the carpenters and Chinamen came around and put the outhouses up."

George Cooper

"There was an excellent group of young people at Union Bay, and I had a good working relationship with them. One Hallowe'en there was a large group of boys up to the usual trick or treating, and I did what I knew they wanted. I kept appearing around the area and they did what they naturally did... ran. We kept this up until about 10:00 p.m. When I stopped, I got them all in the car and we went to Royston for hot dogs. Home again in Union Bay and at a slight hint, they disappeared into the dark and home to bed. After school next day, I talked to one of the Kennedy boys and suggested it might be a good idea for all concerned to clean up and return the articles removed. Shortly, it was all back in order and everyone happy.

Cont. Charlie Ennals

During the Second World War fire crackers were outlawed. At this time the Kinsmen intoduced Hallowe'en Shell-out tickets to support their fund to send milk to British children. Sheets of 100 tickets were sold to homeowners for $1.00 and were in turn given to the children instead of the customary candies or fruit.

1944 OCTOBER ➻ This year Shell-Out tickets realized $85.35. At a Hallowe'en party Shirley Davis won the contest for both selling and collecting the most tickets. [7]

The term "trick or treat" was not widely used until the 1940's. Later, parents concerned that the fun was being lost from Hallowe'en organized parties at the Community Hall with lots of games, prizes and a grand march.

Originally a more important celebration than Hallowe'en, and a truly English tradition was the bonfire on Guy Fawkes night,

November 5. This commemorated the discovered plot to blow up the British parliament buildings and King James I in 1605 by Guy Fawkes and other Roman Catholic supporters. On Coal Beach the Chinese workers, using old railway ties and piles, built a huge hollow square about 10' x 10', to represent the parliament buildings in London. It was set aglow, then an effigy of Guy Fawkes was draped across and burned.

The children brought the biggest potato they could find to roast, and ate them burned black on the outside and not quite cooked in the middle. This fueled their energy as they roared around the beach playing hide-and-seek in the glow and shadows of the giant bonfire. Parents sat on logs, moving back further and further as the heat intensified.

In the 1930's and '40s the "big boys" took a half day off school to build the fire, using wood from the Colliery and beach.

"When we were building the Guy Fawkes fire we used to sneak over to the coal cars and pull the waste out of the journal boxes with a stick. We used it to start the fire. Then the bearings would go dry, but boy, the fire sure went."

Bill Hamilton

The teachers always attended and led everyone in a sing-song. When Donald MacDonald was principal, it was always the highlight of the evening to sing "Old MacDonald's Farm".

In 1942, due to "war conditions in the Pacific and the possibility of a black-out", the fires were banned. For a few years the custom was abandoned, then in the '60s the firemen rekindled the idea by building the bonfire and serving hot dogs and pop to youngsters who probably had no idea who Guy Fawkes was.

Christmas, in the past, was the biggest celebration of the year. It seemed that the weather was always cold and the ground covered with snow. Everyone remembers sleighriding down Russell's Hill all the way to the wharf trestle, or down McLeod's Hill and negotiating onto the Government wharf. With cold wet mittens and pants, the boys and girls scampered home to a toasty kitchen, full of the aromas of shortbread and gingerbread. If they were lucky they could sample the goodies before they were stored away in old cracker tins. Poring over the catalogue, the children dreamed of an "Eaton's beauty" or a shiny red wagon.

The first few settlers celebrated their Christmas together in the boarding house.

"It was 1895 in the old boarding house near the beach. That was the first Christmas tree I ever saw. Mrs. Drew dressed up as Mrs. Santa Claus and gave us all gifts."

Bessie (McKay) Magnone (as told to Mary Moore)

Nine years later, in 1904 Mrs. Cook taught Sunday School and had a big Christmas tree decorated with cookies for the children. The best part of the wonderful party was the gingerbread man that each child took home.

By 1906 the new church had been built, and Christmas parties were held there. A delegation of ladies travelled to Cumberland on the train and purchased presents from a fund of $80 which had been collected.

1906 DECEMBER •• Attendance was so large at the Christmas Tree Entertainment that standing room only could be had. The large tree was prettily draped and ornamented. Its branches were fairly loaded down with presents for children, and even a few getting into their second childhood were remembered. The house was fairly brought down when one of our leading bachelors, who has scarcely a hair on his head, was handed a wig. [4]

Family presents were often homemade from Mother or Father's workshop: a sturdy red sleigh, mittens, doll clothes, and cloth doll. Not wrapped, some gifts were stuffed, along with nuts and a "Jap" orange into the sock that had been hung before bed. Japanese oranges were imported before the turn of the century. In 1921 a box was $1.10, but by 1936 they were down to 59¢ a box. The box was wooden with many uses.

Fraser and Bishop had a good selection of gifts to choose from, but a trip to Cumberland was a must, even just to window shop and dream. Special presents were ordered from the catalogue. For many years the Sunday School sent the ages of all its students to Woodward's or Eaton's, and the personal shopper selected appropriate gifts and mailed them back. In later years, when the younger people had money to spend, they loved to do their shopping on Christmas Eve at Fraser and Horne's, as the shelves contained many interesting items, something just right for each member of the family. When Auntie Edna Peters took over, she gave ideas and suggestions in her good-humoured way.

But more important than the presents were the family get-togethers, with lots of delicious food. Mrs. McKay with her daughters and daughters-in-law prepared dinner for about forty-five in the large farm house. Two turkeys were stuffed and cooked in the oven of the huge coal and wood stove. Mountainous quantities of home-grown vegetables were boiled. Cranberry sauce made from berries picked in the summer at Fanny Bay was opened along with pickles and relishes. Dessert was plum pudding with hard and lemon sauce, or rich dark Christmas cake topped with almond paste. Two long tables were set in the dining room for the adults, with the youngsters sitting at the kitchen table.

The Glover families, although smaller, also got together. Each end of the long dining room table held a big "Tom" which Harry and

Herbert, wielding Sheffield knives, carved, reserving the parson's nose for themselves.

"The only time we ever had turkey was Christmas, and again at New Years. It was the most expensive meat at that time, I think about 85¢ a pound. It would be bought with its feathers on and innards in. I think it was at least dead."

Margaret (Glover) Matthews

Any festivity at the Glovers called for music. Every Christmas morning Harry sat down at the organ, pulled out all the stops, and woke the family with a rousing chorus of "Christians Awake, Salute the Happy Morn". Meanwhile Herbert was in his home playing the same piece on the piano. Carols were always enjoyed at night.

Since children grew up and often married within the community or district, both sets of parents expected the young family home for Christmas dinner.

"For years we walked up to Grandma and Grandad Bowdens and had a huge turkey meal for lunch, then walked along the tracks for another turkey dinner at Grandma and Grandad Glovers. I think they all came to our house for New Years dinner, more turkey. Guess it's good we didn't have a car and had to walk."

Jacqueline (Glover) Gordon

The New Year was celebrated by groups of friends "first-footing" on New Years Eve. This custom originated in northern England. For good luck, tradition demanded that the first to enter the house in the New Year be a dark person. This "first foot" was to carry a lump of coal in one hand and a bottle of whiskey in the other. The revellers walked and sang through the town, knocking at all the doors. They were welcomed in with a plate of Christmas goodies and a round of drinks. Needless to say, as the night wore on and more homes were visited, the "first-footers" began to stagger and their voices to slur. More than one could not face the delicious turkey dinner served the next day.

After the Community Hall was built, New Years Eve dances were held with balloons and noisemakers at midnight. Tickets were sold out early, as people from all over the district wanted to be part of the fun.

ROYAL CELEBRATIONS

The first regal visitors to pass through the Bay were both Governors-General of Canada. As guests of Mr. Dunsmuir, the Earle of Minto visited before the turn of the century, and Earle Grey arrived aboard the *Quadra* in 1906. He took time to shake a few hands before boarding the train for Cumberland where he paid a short visit. Both men are remembered for the sports they promoted: the Minto Cup of lacrosse and the Grey Cup of football. In the early '20s Governor-General Baron Byng and Lady Byng visited the Comox Valley. They travelled up the Island on the E&N then the coaches were transferred to the Wellington Colliery Railroad for the trip to Cumberland.

1937 CORONATION

In May 1937 over four thousand people, sporting souvenir buttons, attended celebrations at Lewis Park in Courtenay in honour of George VI's coronation.

Starting from Cumberland with between five and six hundred children, the Collieries train picked up kiddies from Comox Lake, Bevan and Minto, then met a train from Union Bay, Denman and Hornby schools. All train crews were on duty, provided by the Canadian Collieries by courtesy of Colonel Villiers. The arrival in Courtenay of the eleven coaches was an outstanding event. It was the longest passenger train that had ever pulled into Courtenay. The front of the locomotive was decorated with the motto "Long Live The King".

The children were each given a flag and 20¢ in refreshment tickets, then joined with the Courtenay children to form a huge parade through town to Lewis Park, where sports were held. Lunch was served in the Agricultural Hall to the out-of-town children, by a committee of men from Cumberland. A large parade was held in the afternoon, including Courtenay's May Queen, Margaret Urquhart, attended by maids of honours from around the district. Mildred Bowden

J. Lockner

Decked out with flags, No.20 is set to pull the train of coaches taking Lord and Lady Baron Byng to Cumberland

represented Union Bay. The day ended with a huge fireworks display.

This was the first coronation that was broadcast shore to shore by the CBC. The Union Bay School Board, as did all the district boards, bought each school child a commemorative mug with pictures of the new King and Queen on the side.

1937 MAY ➻ Lt. Col. C.W. and Lady Kathleen Villiers visited the school and presented children with souvenir coronation mugs. Little Winanne Glover presented Lady Kathleen with a basket of flowers. [7]

M. Coe

D. Geidt

Left: 1937 Coronation spoon presented to Mildred Bowden for being one of the attendants to the district May Queen Maudie Urquhart. Right: Commemorative mugs were bought by the Union Bay School Board and presented to each child by Colonel and Lady Villiers

1939 ROYAL TOUR

Everyone, through the newspapers and radio had followed the royal travellers across Canada. The many stories of the handsome shy king with his beautiful queen, changed the minds of many who at first expressed no interest in the visit. Businesses and schools were closed Monday and Tuesday, making a four day holiday. Many parties travelled by car, train and boat to either Vancouver or Victoria. All came home in praise of the beautiful weather, their excellent vantage point, and the royal couple. Some were positive that King George had waved directly at them or Queen Elizabeth had singled them out with her smile.

After much debate the joint School Boards decided to send the children to Victoria for the chance of a lifetime. On Tuesday, May 30, 1939 the little town was like Hamelin after the Pied Piper had lured all the children away. At 7:15 a.m. the E&N, loaded with 300 Upper Island school children, stopped at Union Bay station where the local kids, who had each paid $1.75, scrambled aboard. Accompanied by School Board chairman Herbert Glover and teachers Donald MacDonald and Mrs. F. Waterfield, they were on their way to see their king and queen.

"Yes, it was a lot of organizing to coordinate everything. The E&N had to bring out all their coaches, and there were some really old ones with straw seats. Everyone in the school went except Jack Hamilton. He said to me, 'Will we have to write a story about it when we come home?' I said, 'Well, probably.' That was enough for him, he refused to go."

Donald McDonald

At Parksville the train was joined by one from the west coast, and the "double header", with over 800 young people, sped on its way, arriving as planned after the parade was over. The children marched to Beacon Hill Park where they waited in a designated area to view the Royal Navy receiving its colours from the king. What with the sailors who lined the route, adults who pushed in front, and the speed at which the royal limo passed, it was the lucky child who got a glimpse of their majesties.

The children marched back to the E&N station and left about five o'clock. Just past Nanaimo one of the engines broke down, causing an hour delay. The tired travellers arrived home at 11:00 p.m. to find the platform crowded with parents waiting to take them home.

The School Board and many parents were annoyed with the manner in which the group was treated. An editorial summed it up.

1939 MAY ➻ The children were dogtrotted through the back steets of Victoria only to wait for two hours. Sailors and other Victoria citizens insinuated themselves between the children and the roadway so they could not see. The little ones clutching their flags felt so unwanted that they did not raise a cheer when the royal couple went by. The Upper Island has been discriminated against again by Victoria. It would have been better to stay at home and listen on the radio. [6]

1951 ROYAL TOUR

The tour of Princess Elizabeth and Prince Phillip proved to be a much better experience for the local children. A special train was again employed, this time to take 800 district children to Nanaimo. They saw both the parade and royal couple, returning much pleased with the train ride and the day's events.

WEDDINGS

A wedding was always cause for a big celebration. It was a time when the children threw rice or confetti on the happy couple, and the young bachelors tied old shoes and tin cans under the groom's wagon or car for a rousing send-off.

Union Bay School Collection

In 1909 Bess and Louis Magnone were the first couple wed in Union Bay Church

M. Ellingsen

Mary McKay on her wedding day, dressed in a tailored suit and crowned with flower-bedecked chapeau

Even after the church was built, many of the weddings were held in the bride's home or garden, in the manse, or in a hotel. Probably one of the first weddings performed at Union Bay was in 1901, when a few friends witnessed Myrtle Cook's marriage to Sydney Peters at the bride's home. The happy couple left on the *City* for Puget Sound and Vancouver. Honeymoons were saved-up for, and most couples went somewhere by boat. Louis and Bess Magnone, the first couple married in the new church, honeymooned in Seattle and while there attended the Alaska-Yukon exposition. After the E&N came through it was popular to leave by train. All the wedding guests accompanied the couple to the train station, and threw rice as the newlyweds stood on the observation deck of the last car as it chugged out of sight.

Everyone anxiously awaited the newlyweds' return to hold a "charivari". The young friends of the couple gathered after dark and made a big ruckus in front of their home. Rice, old boots and tin cans were thrown at the door. The kids beat on pots and pans until the couple appeared on the porch and threw pennies, nickels and dimes. The girls and boys scrambled around in the moonlight picking them up. The last charivari remembered at the Bay was held on the Company Hill at the end of the Second World War, when Reid Roth married Phyllis Cooper.

Popular fashions can be traced through the styles and colours

M. Shillito

Following the wedding of Hamako Nakamura to Fred Kato an Oriental wedding breadfast was served. Groom, bride, Miss Smui, S. Nakamura

M. Simpson

Throwing confetti as a newly-wed couple leave on the E&N

N. Jones

The family gather for a morning wedding in Marshall's garden. Mr. and Mrs. S. Jones, Duncan, Jessie, E. Turner, Harold and Nettie Jones, Rev. J. Hewitt (Cumberland United), Mr. Marshall, W. Glover, Mrs. Marshall, A. Thatcher, Donald

used in the many pretty weddings over the years.

1908 ➻ Mrs. Bessie (Ray) McNeil's appearing-out-dress was of Panama cloth, with hat and gloves to match.

1910 ➻ Nellie Eade wore a white cashmere gown with satin ribbons, and a large picture hat. Her cousin Lizzie Muschamp, as bridesmaid, was in a white princess style dress.

1918 ➻ After the wedding breakfast Mr. and Mrs. David Haggart left for their honeymoon in Vancouver. A very pretty effect was made by the Sunday School children who lined the platform, with boughs of dogwood forming an archway under which the bridal party walked on their way to the train.

1928 ➻ Hamako Nakamura looked charming in a gown of white crepe-de-chine and lace. Her long veil was wreathed with orange blossoms.

1929 ➻ Kathleen Clifford married Andy Anderson in a beautiful Liberty blue flat crepe silk dress with hat to match. She carried a bouquet of cream chrysanthemums.

1933 ➻ Nettie Marshall looked sweet in a powder blue rough crepe dress with a shot of grey lace. She carried a shower bouquet of pink roses. Bridesmaid Jessie was in a pink pin net dress with hat to match.

1934 ➻ When Tom McKay married Milla Walker, she looked stunning in a smart blue tweed swagger suit with blue hat. She was attended by sister Clara in a rose silk swagger suit.

In the very early days, a list of wedding presents and who they were from always appeared in the newspaper. Favourite gifts were silverware, salt cellars, bonbon baskets, table linens and rugs. Each bride down through the years has been honoured with a community shower. The gifts were always presented in a novel way. Kathleen Muir "caught" her gifts in "Cupid's Pond". Others had their gifts presented in decorated parasols, baskets, and wagons. Margaret Glover was marrying a pilot, so clues to the gifts' hiding places flew in on a tiny airplane.

Go in the kitchen,
Look under the sink.
You'll find something
That'll tickle you pink.

C. Benson

W. Glover

Harriet Hooper wore a gorgeous gown for her wedding to Albert Benson in 1910. Right: When Margaret Glover married Walter Matthews, Winnie Glover made the wedding dress which featured a deep edging of lace loaned to the bride by Mrs. Stacey

D. Bennie

Duncan and Rachel Bennie stand with the ship, pulled by little sailors Pauline Horne and Dora Hobbins, that carried shower presents

CULTURE

ARTS & CRAFTS

Artistic ability and talent were channeled into practical projects, either to wear or for the house. Women produced beautifully knit baby wear, argyle socks and sweaters. Warm Indian sweaters were made at Deep Bay by Mrs. Edwards. Some women enjoyed crocheting doilies and tablecloths while others preferred fancy work and smocking.

"Mother knit all four of her daughters' beautiful suits. She taught us all to knit, crochet and embroider. That is what we did every evening as teenagers."

Kathleen(Haggart) Strachan

DRAWING & PAINTING

Georgina (Jean Abrams) Lytton, the daughter of Greta and Seymour Abrams, grew up in Union Bay. Very early, her artistic ability was evident and she became interested in native art and culture. This influence no doubt came from her upbringing, as Adam Grant Horne, her great grandfather, was Hudson Bay Factor at Comox. His daughter, Mrs. F. Brown at the Post Office, spoke Chinook and told her grandaughter many Indian stories. A typical struggling artist, Jean often traded her originals for canvas and paint. Several of her water colours now reside in the National Art Gallery in Ottawa.

D. Geidt

A painting by Charles Pickles of the *Pamir* sailing off Cape Flattery with a load of Union Bay coal

Also preferring the medium of water colours, Charles Pickles portrayed his love of the sea. In the late 1940's Mr. and Mrs. Pickles followed their daughter, Marge Kennedy, and family to Union Bay. This very talented artist had started his working life as a British sailor on the clipper ships which carried cargo around the world. He raised his family on Cortez Island where he first started painting on pieces of cedar. He painted many English country scenes and pubs but he is best remembered for his sailing ships. With a knowledgeable eye, he knew where every rope went and what it did when he painted in the rigging of his ships. Many homes of friends and relations proudly exhibit off the large collection he left.

CARVING

David Haggart served eight years in Scotland learning his trade as a cabinet maker. He came to Union Bay in 1906 and was the company's head carpenter. As well as building, Mr. Haggart loved to carve.

"He used to sit in his chair in his little room every night and carve away. David, my brother, became a carpenter too but never took any interest in the carving part."

Elsie (Haggart) Veale

Mr. Butchart, when he was building his famous gardens, hired Mr. Haggart as head carpenter, so the family moved to Todd Inlet. The master builder crafted the forms for many cement posts and beams. The resulting arbours, some of which are still standing, had the appearance of tree branches with bark and knots.

They returned to Union Bay after the project was complete, where David built his family a fine home on McLeod Road next to the E&N tracks. He continued to whittle and carve, turning out some very unique oak furniture. Intricately embellished china cabinets were his specialty and he built one for each of his daughters as well as his neighbour, Herbert Glover.

About 1912, as boss of the car shop, Peter Reid used his carpentry talent and the available tools to create a carousel. All ten horses were smoothly carved, brightly painted and embellished. The gear drive, built in the machine shop, was run off a stationary engine. For over twenty years the merry-go-round was the feature attraction at all the picnics and sports days. In later years the the once proud stallions lay worn, fading and dusty in a corner of the car shop.

D. Geidt

D. Geidt

Left: One of the five beautifully hand carved oak china cabinets made by David Haggart. Right: Duck, brant and goose decoys carved by Wilf and Harry Glover

Wilf and Harry Glover also had access to the car shop machines, making nearly one hundred geese, brant and duck decoys, as well as silhouettes, which were used on their many hunting trips.

"We had a couple of patterns and had the run of the car shop. The lathes shaped the necks. We'd band saw out the heads and shape the bodies by knocking the corners off and they'd be round. Then we'd saw the bottoms off and hollow them out by clamping them down and drilling holes all over, then smoothing it out with a chisel. Next we'd white lead them together again and they'd float heavy side down."

Wilfred & Harry Glover

One of the Sikhs who worked on the E&N remained and worked on the McKay farm, clearing land. He spent his recreation hours carving and whittling with an axe and knife. The family remembers his beautiful work.

"The old "Hindu" carved fans, birds, and a real beautiful crib for Bill, who was the baby. He made dozens of brant decoys for us too. He had a little bit of an axe and cut them out as smooth as could be. I still have them."

Jim McKay

CONCERTS & TRAVELLING SHOWS

Too small to attract the large acts like the Chautauqua Co., Union Bay, being a port, was a stop for several travelling shows that toured the coast in the 1920's and '30s.

"What I loved and really looked forward to was when the little launch would come in with the travelling company. A variety show, music, singing, tap dancing, bears, monkeys and everything. They'd tie the bear to the maple tree across from the Home Garage during the day. Then on the stage at the Little Red School House they'd have the odd kid get up and ride on the bear."

Wilf Bowden

After depositing their passengers at Victoria or Vancouver, the liners called at the Bay for bunker. The crew often staged a concert or dance for the port people whom they had come to know. The Australian Blue Funnel

Travelling shows often featured a dancing bear

J. Anderson

Line's crew put on a good show with the whole town turning out.

Most of the entertainment was local, provided by church, school or community. Parties, concerts and smokers were popular, where performers and audience both had fun.

1910 DECEMBER ➾ A Smoker was held at Humphrey's Hall with a good program of songs, recitations, instrumental music and comic stunts. A boxing contest with young Dinkydoodle and Kid Dingheiser in barrels was a roaring go. Also the rooster fight was a howler, but the cracker eating contest beat them all. Plenty of smoke, good sandwiches and coffee enjoyed. [5]

CANADIAN-AUSTRALIAN

ROYAL MAIL LINE

CONCERT

TO BE HELD IN HUMPHRIE'S HALL, UNION BAY

THE ZEALANDIA CONCERT PARTY

NOVEMBER 21st, 1910. AT 8:30, P.M.

BY KIND PERMISSION OF Capt. J.D.S. Phillips

Overture	Union Bay Orchestra
Song	"Down in the Depths" - C. Iveson
Song, Comic	" I Love a Lassie" - H. McKenna
Geography up-to-date	J. McDuff
Song	"Take a Pair of Sparkling Eyes" - T. Miles
Comic	" Any old thing will do" - T. Hollingum
Song	"The Deathless Army" - A. Glover
Recitation	"Asleep at the Switch" - W. Kettle
Flute Solo	"Selected" - C. Kellar
Song	"Any Little Girl" - Miss Greta Brown
Duet	Selected - Messrs. Miles & McDougal
Song	Selected - A. Stephens

INTERVAL

Piano Solo	Syd Hunt
Song	"Sea, Sea, Sea" - A. Stephens
Comic Song	H. McKenna
Cornet Solo	Selected - E. Clark
Stump Speech	T. Hudson
Song	Selected - Miss Ray
P. C. Monkey	J. McDuff
Song	Selected - J. McDougall
Song	"Song of Araby" - T. Miles
Song	Selected - C. Curtain
Song	"The Lighthouse Bell" - C. Iverson
Duet	"Excelsior" - Messrs. Iveson & McDougal

GOD SAVE THE KING

J.W. Tucker, Printer, R.M.S. Zealandia

Possibly the first musical instrument at the Bay was Mrs. Cook's organ. She and her family arrived in 1898 to join husband John.

"Grandmother Cook and her brother saved their money and bought a black walnut organ. It was beautiful. She brought it across the states from Cleveland to Puget Sound, then up here."

Mamie (Peters) Vowels

Mason Rich pianos could be bought in 1894 for $360, with $40 down and $10 per month. Sheet music sold for 50¢ and could be obtained, along with phonograph records, needles and violin strings, from the Weekly News at Cumberland. George Howe bought a piano for his hotel in 1899, and people gathered there for singsongs and dances. Mrs. Anderson had her phonograph which everyone enjoyed, and in 1920 she bought a Ceilian piano.

As early as 1900, a Mrs. Davis was playing for concerts and giving piano lessons. Then Mrs. Booth took over and taught the budding musicians whose parents were lucky enough to own a piano. Many pianos were Gerard Heintzman's, as an agent travelled from Nanaimo selling them. Whether because they needed money or the children had lost interest, in 1910 Hoopers raffled off their piano for $1.00 a ticket.

When Mrs.Booth moved to Victoria, Herbert Glover took over her pupils. Then Mrs. Finch came from Cumberland and taught several students, one of whom was Ethel Fulcher who became a teacher herself and taught many of the young people in the 1920's and '30s. One of her pupils was Eva Baldwin who later gave lessons. Katherine Formby also took lessons from the above two ladies, and with her husband, Walter Carter, formed a dance orchestra. Later they made their living operating a music store and giving lessons. In the '40s Doris McDonald and J.L. Reynolds of Courtenay taught at the Bay.

Over the years there were several talented musicians and thespians who gave direction and inspiration to less gifted but enthusiastic amateurs. Bert and Ted Glover, who were trained in the old country, were the nucleus of many groups when they arrived in 1905. Then, after Bert returned from Hollywood with more training, wigs and a make-up kit, theatrical productions were very exciting. Mr. Kettle became involved and they formed a perico troupe. Dressed in frills and pompons which Mrs. Kettle made, they put on variety shows and short versions of Gilbert and Sullivan operettas.

In the 1920's Cyril Armbrister became the accountant for Fraser and Bishop. Famous for his monologues, he became a hit at all the concerts, teamed up with Ethel Fulcher on the piano. He also directed plays and concerts.

"Cyril Armbrister, a handsome man, was from a well-to-do French family of mixed blood. He loved drama and recited Robert Service. We put on plays... Jean Potter, Harry Auchinvole, Wilf Glover and others. I remember "Mrs. Flynn's Lodgers". Later Cyril went into movies and pioneered television in New York."

Grace (Davis) Boudreau

K. Carter

Costumed children pose in front of Mrs. Auchinvole's house at one of her "fancy dress balls"

D. Bennie

Greta Kay in her beautiful costume sang a song to 'Papa'!

William Carr, who worked at the shops, had a trained voice and added class to the local concerts for many years until he moved to Vancouver. Then his fans tuned in every week to hear his fine baritone voice on the CBC show "From Leister Square to Old Broadway".

There was no lack of male voices, even starting with the young. Master Jack Bradley was a budding young comedian who regularly "brought down the house" with songs like "Everybody Works but Father". Another funny man was Charlie Formby who lived with his wife, one son and two daughters on the Company Hill. He sang Cockney songs like his namesake "George" and elicited "storms of applause".

"My dad was from Liverpool, and at Union Bay he ran the conveyor on the wharf. He'd get to know the men on the English boats and bring them home. We had some great times! Dad could only play about five chords but he'd thump away and sing all the old costermonger songs."

Kay (Formby) Carter

George Harwood's fine tenor voice was always appreciated at church or in concert. He, as well as W. Baldwin, A. Glover, T. Grieg, R. Husband and Rev J.H. Hobbins, were part of the famous Comox Valley Men's Musical society that won many awards over the years. Little Dickie Ward won the hearts of all that heard him sing. He was always included on programs during the war years with songs like "Praise the Lord & Pass the Ammunition".

Not to be outdone were the women who sang at church, teas and concerts. Early singers were Mary Marshall, often accompanied by Mrs. Renwick, and Violet Glover, accompanied by her sister Gertie. Madeline Horne and Jean Anderson also sang at many functions. Later there were Hazel Campbell, Lily Ray and Dorothy Ward. Audrey Sawchuck, a war bride from Wales, brought smiles with "Pass the Plate of Happiness Around". Accompanying all of the ladies were Mary Moore, Hazel Campbell or Kathleen Strachan.

The school or Sunday school always put on a Christmas concert for which the community turned out en masse. Many of the teachers spent hours writing and rehearsing plays and songs, as well as making costumes.

One of the earliest concerts was in 1910 when Mrs. Booth trained thirty-five young people, each representing a Mother Goose character in costume and song.

Mrs. Auchinvole organized several "fancy dress balls" in the 1920's. The children came dressed in costumes, prepared to sing, dance or recite.

1920 MARCH ➾ Mrs. Auchinvole's fancy dress ball was a huge success, $100 proceeds were handed over to the Cumberland Hospital for linen. Judges Mr. T. Graham and Miss Graham of Cumberland and Mrs. J. Burns from Bevan judged the many national costumes, princes, princesses, butterflies and kewpies. The program was delightful with marches, songs, recitations. There were prizes for the best waltz and one step, which were done by the little people with great grace. [6]

"I remember at one of Mrs. Auchinvole's fancy dress balls Greta Kay dressed in a frilly dress and old fashioned bonnet singing in her innocent voice, 'What would you take for me, Papa, if someone wanted to buy? And offered you nice shiny dollars and piled them as high as the sky?' It brought the house down."

Kay (Formby) Carter

Over the years Mrs. Haggart put on many concerts, always making sure that everyone was included and having fun. A very patriotic lady, each of her concerts ended with a girl as Britannia, draped in the Union Jack at centre stage while the entire cast grouped around her to sing "The Maple Leaf Forever".

In 1927 Mrs. Haggart, with the help of other mothers, directed a play entitled "Hall Of Fame". There was a cast of about twenty girls who each depicted a famous woman of history hoping to enter the "Hall". It was so popular that they took the show to Courtenay and Denman.

"I was Rita Cleaver, and Sara Kirkwood was Joan of Arc, but she got sick and couldn't go to Denman, so I wore her costume. I could hardly walk, and when I came out the audience went into fits of laughter."

Kathleen (Haggart) Strachan

The same group of girls did a Hawaiian show, doing the Hula dance in beautiful grass skirts made from rice sacks given to them by the Chinese.

Mary Moore, another creative lady, helped with Sunday school shows and trained the CGIT girls in some very effective revues. One well-remembered concert was a Stephen Foster night.

Donald McDonald and Irene Jones coached the school children in skits and songs. One year it was a minstrel show with black-faced boys in top hats, carrying canes. The next concert featured Bruce Auchinvole singing "I'd Rather Marry an Old Man", Mel Campbell warbling "My Hat it has Three Corners", Dorothy Ward and a bevy of beauties dressed in crepe paper dresses charming the audience with "Sweet Little Alice Blue Gown", the Glover twins fighting in "I Don't Want to Play in Your Yard".

In the 1940's, when district drama and music festivals were initiated, Union Bay was always well represented. In the process, the children received lots of musical training as well as the fun of performing.

From this, the kids amused themselves by putting on well-rehearsed concerts for their families and friends. Every summer the dogwood trees on the Company Hill were turned into a theatre. If the houses had been

E. Leighton

Women in the play "Hall of Fame": Joan of Arc, Queen Elizabeth I, Florence Nightingale... The show was so good it went "on the road" to Courtenay and Denman Island

W. Glover

Hula-hula dancers dressed in grass skirts made from Chinese rice sacks. G. Kay, K. Haggart, L. Brown, W. Glover, N. Marshall, D. Good, K. Muir

D. and I. McDonald

"Sweet Little Alice Blue Gown": W. Franklyn, J. Hamilton, D. Ward, W. Glover, M. Glover, H. Treloar, E. Frew, G. Harwood, J. Auchinvole, R. Treloar

Top: Mock weddings were part of every concert. Left: "What Would You do With a Drunken Sailor?" Right: "The Old Grey Mare"

wallpapered that year, the trees were made festive with the ends of the rolls woven in and out of the branches. The "Tangle Up House" was a great place to put on a show which always featured a mock wedding.

1940 JUNE ➾ Much credit is due to a group of school children who staged a concert all on their own in the freight shed on Saturday afternoon. A collection of pennies, nickels and dimes realized $3.37 that was donated to the Jr. Red Cross blanket fund. Those taking part were R.& R. Berggren, G. Harwood, M. Glover, F.& M. & B. Peters, V.& D. Campbell, L. Watt, I. Nelson, D. Muschamp and B. Jones. [6]

Miss Searle, a little lady who lived in a tiny house next to her brother Ted, was trained in elocution and taught many children the art of using their voices. She put on recitals and often gave comic recitations herself. Later, the school principal, Mrs. Reynolds, entered her classes in many festivals, reciting such works as "The Highwayman".

Dancing lessons were another luxury in a small town, and at different times teachers came and held classes. In the late 1920's Gwen Noel taught about twenty little girls. Then, in the '30s Kay Moore gave lessons, followed by Babe McKenzie. The Auchinvole girls - Joan, Margo and Heather - took up highland dancing and won many awards.

DANCES

The "terpsichorean art" flourished in Union Bay from the early days, when the young people "tripped the light fantastic" until the "wee small hours" of the morning. As soon as the community had enough women to make a few couples, dances were "got up". Some young men and women travelled to dances in other settlements. In January 1894 a party left Union on the coal train at 10:00 a.m., were fed and joined by others at the Wharf, then rowed to Denman "while downy white feathers of winter fell". After arriving at Denman wharf they proceeded on foot to the hall at Mt. Pleasant. Instead of collapsing, the hardy settlers truly did dance until the wee small hours.

The merrymakers travelled on the *Joan*, *City of Nanaimo*, or hired Tommy James' boat. Sometimes private yachts were used.

1910 JUNE ➾ Two launch parties in the command of Captains Strand and McMurtrie journeyed to Denman on Wednesday evening to attend the strawberry festival and dance. The affair proved a decided success, all enjoying themselves, returning home in the wee small hours, tired but happy. Music was by Percy Smith, violin and Mrs. McLaughlin, piano. [5]

F. Auchinvole

Highland dancer Joan Auchinvole displays her many medals

At the Wharf in the early days, dances were held in the dining room of the big boarding house. The Nelson Hotel acquired a piano and Mr. Howe gave dances. The Wilson Hotel celebrated its opening with a dance. The music was furnished by Roy and Graham.

Before the upstairs of the new Fraser and Bishop store was partitioned into hotel rooms, it made a wonderful large dance hall which was used for a few years. Then Humphries added an annex to their hotel, creating a perfect dance hall.

When the army was stationed at Union Bay during WW I, they built a large wooden platform for dancing behind the Post Office. Dancing to an army band under the stars, several romances were started between local girls and soldiers.

The Roy Brothers of Royston, playing the fiddle, piano and cornet, formed the nucleus for many orchestras in the district. They were joined at different times by Duncan McAllister, Tommy Reed and Tom Graham. Mr. Walker and Mrs. McLaughlin from Fanny Bay often provided the music.

The first truly local dance band was formed by two of the Glover boys. Classically trained in England, and up on the latest tunes when they arrived in 1906, Bert played piano and flute while Ted played the violin. Joining them were E. Allen and Ed Clarke on cornet.

Liners, after leaving their passengers off at Victoria or Vancouver, came to the Bay for bunker coal. Many of them carried a first class orchestra to entertain the passengers as they steamed across the Pacific. Often the musicians would give a dance for the community, sometimes on board but usually in the local hall.

1908 APRIL ➻ The largest dance Union Bay has ever had was given by Capt. Ogilvie, R.N.R., with ninety couples present. The hall was a dream of loveliness, being decorated with evergreens and the large flags of all nations. Besides these, there were nautical arrangements that were a striking novelty to anyone who had only attended landlubber dances. First there was the Forecastle bell hung to beams, with the line carried through the ivy to the leader of the orchestra, who at the start of each number would give the necessary rings. Large signs designated the Starboard, Port, Cabin, and Quarterdeck, which was the card room. The Captain soon put the vessel under way with an opening speech given in a rattling good style. [4]

1919 SEPTEMBER ➻ The *Empress of Japan* came in to coal and a dance was arranged. The Captain loaned the ship's band which consisted of Philippinos with stringed instruments. Many young people came down from Courtenay and Cumberland. [6]

Travelling to dances in the early motor cars gave the young a real sense of adventure, as they set out under warm blankets with several spare tires strapped on. In the 1920's Bowser held dances in their little school house. Often the "Bay crowd", after changing several flats, would arrive just in time for the home waltz. The hall at Fanny Bay was also a popular dancing spot. Sometimes they had Swartz' orchestra from Nanaimo, but usually the musicians were Mrs. McLaughlin on piano and Mr. Walker on violin, with son Joe on whistle and drums.

"I went to dances at Tweedies Hall. Charlie Tweedie fancied himself like "Rudolf Valentino" and dressed the part. He was pretty snooty with us ordinary people. I used to dance with Clara and Milla Walker."

Bobby Pollock

For about twenty years, until it burned in 1940, the Royston Pavilion was the biggest hall on the Island, sometimes bringing in Mart Kenny to play, but more often couples danced to the local groups. In the late '30s Syd Waterfield on the violin led an orchestra which played the summer months at the pavilion.

After the new school was built, the Little Red School House became the town's hall, and the dances were held there. Union Bay boasted a seven piece band led by Alex Auchinvole Sr. on trombone, sons Bill and Alex on saxophone and drums, and Ernie King on piano. Pay for the players was $1.00 an hour. Admission was $1.00 for Gents and 25¢ for Ladies, who also provided refreshments.

T. Dutfield

A ball at the Imperial Pavilion at Royston, the largest hall on the Island

M. Adamson

Jimmy Walker's Orchestra played for the opening of the Community Hall. Left to right: D. Haggart, S. Waterfield , ?, B. Walker, A. Dixon, J. Herbin, H. Dixon, A. McMillan (vocal) A. Walker, D. Davies, J. Walker

H. Hatch

The country club orchestra played all the Saturday dances at the Bay. G. Monks, J. Hoglo, B. Clifton, B. Ardley, J. Herbin,

The Country Club logo

H. Hatch

"My husband was very musical; he played piano. He got the band music and transposed it for all the instruments. They had a clarinet, two saxophones, trombone, violin and drums."

Nellie (McKay) King

Fred Cave, a very musical fellow, and friend Scutta Nakamura wanted to join the band, so they took correspondence lessons on the saxophone. They learned to make their own reeds, and practiced at Cave's house, with help from sister Clara who played piano. Fred went on to have an orchestra for many years after leaving Union Bay.

Union Bay's Kay Formby married Walter Carter from Royston. Both musicians, they formed a band with Kay on the the piano and Wally playing violin. They played through the Depression with musicians like Bob Clifton, Bill Ardley and Bill Walker. The Carter children followed their parents into music, and in the 1940's, ten year old son Alfie on the accordian joined the group, followed a few years later by Karen on drums and trumpet, while Barb sang.

Jimmy Walker had a popular orchestra in the district in the 1930's. Sid Waterfield on violin, David Haggart on string bass and trumpet, and Roy Parkins on sax played with them and were joined by Jules Herbin who had moved from Nanaimo. Hank Hatch of Powell River was living at Courtenay, playing in the Legion. He and Jules became friends and a new group evolved. In 1943 the six devoted players spent several months writing arrangements and practicing, then called themselves the "Country Club".

Initially, Jules Herbin did all the arranging, while Hank Hatch looked after the bookings and money in his little black book. The players received $7.00 each for the four hours of music they provided. Above that, $3.00 was charged to transport the whole group. New Years Eve paid more, when the men received $12.00 for the evening. Bill Ardley built and painted music stands of plywood, and wired them with music lamps made from tin cans. The players bought red sweaters with the Country Club logo on them. For special occasions they wore black suits and bow ties.

The Country Club was in its heyday after the Community Hall was built, and became the Saturday night attraction known all over the Island. The orchestra had the big band sound of the day - Glen Miller or Tommy Dorsey. Jules or Hank would hear a new piece

Dancers on a float pulled by a team of horses from the Comox Valley Riding Club. W. Glover, D. Bennie, J. Glover, J. Bennie, D. Kennedy, M. Stokes, J. Glover, M. Campbell

on the radio, then sit down and write the music out and arrange it for the other players. They followed the pattern of fast, slow, and waltz unless the crowd was getting too rambunctious, then they would play some slow dances to calm them down. It always worked.

"We'd have some big crowds. It was the days of liquor in your car. Fights would break out and often couldn't be spotted by the bouncers - George Davis and Bill Treloar. But I had a pretty good view from the stage so if I saw a fight starting I'd keep on playing, but hit high "C" bing, bing, bing. Bill would pick it up and I'd point to where the fight was. They'd have the trouble makers out the door pretty fast.

Hank Hatch

A set was three pieces and they ended it with, "That's all folks, there ain't no more." For three decades the orchestra announced the home waltz by playing down the scale and then launching into "Let's Waltz As We Say Goodnight."

"During the war, rubber was hard to get, so women's underpants had buttons instead of elastic. After the dance Bill Treloar would take a count of the panties under the chairs. The buttons would pop off while the girls were jitterbugging and they would kick them off without missing a beat."

Hank Hatch

In the late 1940's and '50s a group of young people took a revived interest in "Old Time Dancing". Taught at the Friday night dances by good dancers like John Rosengren, Jake Campbell and Rudy Toman, plus the ladies of the Community Club, these kids put the jitterbug aside in preference for the polka, barn dance and chartreuse. Wally Carter, Mrs. King, and Johnny Lockner played the old tunes. The dancers followed Johnny around the district from Lazo and Merville to Denman and Fanny Bay.

In the 1949 July 1st parade, Maxine Stokes, Winanne, Jacquie and Janette Glover, Don and Jack Bennie, Mel Campbell, and Don Kennedy agreed to dance on a float pulled by a team from the Comox Valley Riding Club. With their crinolines starched and square dances perfected, nothing could have prepared them for the terrifying ride down Fifth Street, with Hunter Babcock on his trusty steed trying to prevent a runaway wagon.

MOVIES

The first movie theatres in the district were at Cumberland. Both the Electric Theatre and the City Hall were showing "silent howlers" by 1910. One of the first projectionists was Pete Anderson who, with James Smith, bought the City Hall in 1912.

For a few years the people at the Bay were treated to a movie once a week.

1911 ➾ Well-known motion picture men of Cumberland, Clough and McNeil, will give a motion picture performance in Courtenay's Opera House every Wed. evening, at Comox every Fri. and in Humphrey's Hall at Union Bay every Sat. evening. [4]

Pete's son, Ed Anderson, was the projectionist and his mother's phonograph, set on the piano, provided music for the silent flicks.

"I remember my grandmother's old phonograph in the big square thick box. It had a huge silver speaker like a horn about 3' wide. It played cylinder records."

Jack Anderson

FOTO-NITE

Every Tuesday at the E W Ilo-Ilo and Bickle Theatres

This week's offer $125.00

READ THE STORY ON PAGE ONE AND BE THERE NEXT TUESDAY

1911 ➺ The Cowboy and Indian frontier celebration at Cheyenne, Wy. is an exhibition of a Rodeo show. The special film has been secured at great expense so the cost will be 15¢. [5]

The Ilo-Ilo opened in 1915, and every Saturday the Colliery train took shoppers and movie goers to Cumberland. Serials came into vogue, with as many as fifteen episodes.

"They'd run the train free and take everyone up there. I used to get 15¢ - 10¢ to get into the show and 5¢ to go to Henderson's for some candy. Ray Glover, Hector Hooper, and I... lots of times it didn't cost us anything if we sneaked in."

Doug Brown

In the 1920's movies were again shown at Union Bay, in the Little Red School House by men from Courtenay. Still silent, the music was provided by local piano students.

"Remember the serial "Elmo Lincoln"? In the old silent days Nettie played the piano, to one side of the screen. She'd be thundering along with the horses, then playing romantic music for the love scenes."

Dunc Marshall

The acting careers of Lionel Barrymore, Charlie Chaplin and Rudolph Valentino were followed. Tom Mix, a cowboy actor, was extremely popular. A local actor, Bert Glover, had tried his luck in Hollywood and landed the enviable job as Tom's understudy.

The Gaiety in Courtenay and the Ilo-Ilo in Cumberland introduced "100% TALKIES" to the district in December 1929, so Mrs. Anderson's gramophone was retired. During the war, "News Reels", which contained much propaganda, became the forerunners of television news. Foto-nite also became popular, and many people with a carload headed to town for a movie and chance to win money.

SPORTS

The Sportsman's Prayer

By E.T. Searle: Dedicated to the memory of the late John Fulcher

Dear Lord, in the battle that goes on through life,
I ask but a field that is fair;
A chance that is equal with all in the strife,
A courage to strive and to dare;
And if I should win, let it be by the code,
With my faith and my honour held high;
Or if I should lose, let me stand by the road
And cheer as the winners go by.

And Lord, let my shouts be ungrudging and clear,
A tribute that comes from the heart;
And let me not give them a snarl or a sneer,
Or play any snivelling part;
Let me say, "There they ride, on whom laurels bestowed,
Since they played the game better than I":
Let me stand with a smile at the edge of the road
And cheer as the winners go by.
So grant me to conquer, if conquer I can,
By proving my worth in the fray;
But teach me to lose like a regular man
And not like a craven, I pray.
Let me take off my hat to the warriors who strode
To victory splendid and high;
Yea, teach me to stand by the side of the road
And cheer as the winners go by.

BADMINTON

The old school house was used for many sports, and in the 1930's badminton flourished. There was a very active club with Wes Peters as president and Edythe Hicks as secretary. They challenged clubs from other district towns. A friendly rivalry existed between Union Bay and Denman Island which resulted in many exciting games.

1934 MARCH M. Piercy and M. Swan lost to Annie McKay and Ethel Glover 8 to 15. G. Dalziel and I. Piercy beat Gordon Horne and Norm Davis 11 to 3. L. & T. Piket beat Reg Hudson and Andy Magnone 11 to 9. [7]

D. Bennie

A Union Bay Athletic Club float in the 1953 Dominion Day Parade. Baseball players pulling float at front: J. McKay, D. Bennie, A. Kennedy, D. Campbell, D. McKay. At back: J. Renwick, B. Geary. Girls on float - front: M. Auchinvole, G. Harwood. Back: B. Peters, R. Robertson, M. Stokes.

A. Sawchuck

Right: Ted Searle, one of Union Bay's leading citizens, was secretary for many groups and also enjoyed writing poetry

Royston Imperial Badminton Club, which played at the Pavilion, brought in national contenders. Players from the district paid $1.00 for reserved seats to see stars like Jack and Dick Underhill.

After the community hall was built, some of the older players introduced the game to the young people. A new club was formed.

LAWN TENNIS

Over the years there were several lawn tennis courts in Union Bay. The first one was constructed by the Company after the turn of the century. Few could afford rackets or the time to play, so it was used mostly by the Colliery officials. The customs man, George Roe, his wife, and a couple of the Haggart girls were tennis enthusiasts. They played in competitions in Cumberland.

The Nelson Hotel had a beautiful court behind the hotel. Used mainly by hotel guests and friends of the owners, some good matches were played on its smooth grass surface.

In 1924 a newly-organized tennis club built themselves a court on a flat area near Washer Creek.

BOXING & WRESTLING

Both wrestling and boxing were popular spectator sports around the turn of the century. John Humphrey was a promoter of wrestling and held some matches at the hall attached to his hotel. Cuddy Johnson was a contender and could wrestle with the best of them. He later became a referee.

Boxing came into its own in the 1920's when Roy Cliff of Comox became Light Heavyweight Champion of B.C. Exciting matches were held at the Royston Pavilion with as many as seven preliminary fights before the big one. The top ticket price for men was $2.00, for boys 50¢. Special accommodation was provided for the ladies. Roy's cousin, "Big Bill" McKenzie, also became popular with the fans, as did Cumberland's Harold Jones, who later married Nettie Marshall.

W. Naylor

At John Rosengren's gym class Winanne Glover and Mildred Hicks do back bends

1926 JULY •• Jonesy Meets A Tartar! Harold Jones, 142 lb., from Cumberland vs. Kid Sullivan, 140 lb., from Campbell River. Jonesy is very popular with Courtenay fans and deservedly so. He was expected to win the bout, but his opponent was always ready to come back for more - a draw. [6]

A boxing team was formed at school in the '30s, when Donald McDonald was principal. The boys practiced in the spare room. The best boxer was Gordon Chilton, who gained the nickname of Champ. His father was the United Church minister and refused to let his son compete in any matches. So Bob Sherburn was sent to the tournament and, although he did not win, made a good showing.

PRO-REC

At different times, groups of women got together and held pro-rec classes in an effort to keep fit. Anyone with a little more knowledge, or more flexible body than the others, led the group. For a few years, the ladies went to classes put on by the C.R.A. in Courtenay.

"A group of us went to Courtenay for pro-rec. After the classes we always went to Kay's and bought pie a-la-mode and hot chocolate."

Annie Campbell

GYMNASTICS

The minister Rev. W. Chilton was a very athletic man. He installed rings and ropes in the back of the church and gave gym classes to the young people. After the community hall was built some very good equipment was installed there. Under John Rosengren's careful instruction, the children learned to tumble and balance. He also worked with a small group of girls. In the summer months they could be seen practicing their acrobatic routines on the lawn beside the post office. Several shows were put on, augmented once by Herb Bradley's group from Courtenay.

BASKETBALL

Basketball is not a sport usually associated with Union Bay. However, in the early days the Union Bay Athletic and Social Club had teams. Both the men's and women's team had just five players and played in a three city league. The ladies looked smart in their bloomer type uniforms.

W. Naylor

Left: Phyllis Cooper supports Myrt McCormack. Right: Union Bay girls 1911 basketball team. Edna Geary, Mary McKay, Cleda Drew, Nettie Stant, Evelyn Campbell

1911 FEBRUARY ➾ The Comox District Men's Basketball League is now formed, which consists of clubs from Courtenay, Cumberland and Union Bay. Six games will be played, three at Courtenay and three at Union Bay. [4]

The games at Courtenay were played at the Opera House. Because Cumberland had no suitable hall, their home games were played at Union Bay in Humphrey's new hall, part of the addition to the Wilson Hotel. A train brought players and fans down for each game, which was always followed by a dance.

1913 FEBRUARY ➾ The Union Bay "Violets" and a team from Cumberland played a game of basketball which the home team won 16 to 9. The line-up from Union Bay was: Frank Work (captain), Len Piket, T. Leclair, Bert Geary, and C. Donaldson. After the game, a well-attended dance was held at Alf Horne's Hall with music by Roy's Orchestra. [4]

After a few years, games were played in the Band Hall at Cumberland and the Agricultural Hall in Courtenay. By the end of the 1920's Comox had joined the league and most games were played in the new Native Son's Hall.

1920 FEBRUARY ➾ Union Bay plays Courtenay and loses 37 to 16. The Bay's Five were:

Miller - centre	Auchinvole - forward
Davidson- guard	McKay - forward
Anderson- guard [5]	

With about five teams in the league by the early 1930's, competition was intense and scores got higher. Two players from the Bay, Art Searle and Cecil Richie (school principal), were on a district team that played in Alberni, Nanaimo and New Westminster.

With the building of its new Athletic Hall in 1937, Cumberland gradually began to dominate district basketball. When the Union Bay Community Hall was built, a basketball court was included. Teams were organized, but only for short times. Some of the local teenagers who were on Cumberland or Courtenay High School teams practiced there and had fun with pick-up teams.

BASEBALL

As soon as there were enough young men to form a pick-up team, "scrub" ball was played. Possibly the first organized team was in 1908 when the Bay played in a district league including Comox, Courtenay, Cumberland and Little River.

1908 JULY ➾ The Union Bay Baseball Club just formed is going to be a winner. Mr. Geo. Booth of the freight wharf is manager. Mr. Alex McLeod of Fraser and Bishops is field captain and Mr. Fred Ray is sec. treas. "Look out Cumberland!" [4]

The team played on the "bunker grounds" behind the trestle and were covered in coal dust at the end of the game. Some of the early stars were N. Balo, F. Curran, J. Hill, and Ed Clark who always carried a rule book in his pocket to challenge the umpire. Jim McNeil, the one-armed telegrapher, filled that position and was sometimes spelled off by Alf Horne.

1909 JUNE ➾ During the game the players disputed the umpires' call and the air was a little warm from the exhaust. [4]

Cumberland Museum

A very early Union Bay baseball team. Louis Magnone (in the bowler hat) was manager

E. Renwick

The Bay Bunch c. 1914. Front: T. Hudson (bat boy), L. Drew, P. Renwick, G. Grange, B. Campbell. Back: B. Abrams, B. McKay, F. Smith, ?, N. Balo, ?, ?

H. Davis

Each team played about ten games in the season, but besides league games, Union Bay was often challenged by local logging camps, and crews off American ships in port.

For Dominion Day Sports in 1910, the committee at the port built a "big scoring board which indicates runs and strikes for the benefit of the public." Sporting new grey and red uniforms, the Union Bay team under manager J. Humphrey won the day.

1910 JULY ➾ Dominion Day Baseball Tournament.
Bay Bunch Bump Brewery Boys.
UB- 5 Cum. Pilsener- 4
Cuddy's Bunch defeated by Local Nine in a game that went
17 innings. UB-2 Courtenay-1 [4]

A few years after the flood, it was decided that Union Bay needed a proper baseball field. The company land bordered by the Colliery road, the train trestle, and the highway was chosen. A lot of digging and earth moving was required to build up the south end. The McKay boys were popular players for the home town. With the family team and plough, Bob led the work parties.

"When we cleared the ball park we just did it, we didn't get paid. We wanted to play ball, so everyone got out and worked. It was a lovely, big, flat field."
Bob McKay

During the war years many of the young men were away in the army. An all-star team for the district was picked to tour the Island. In the nine man line-up were three Union Bay men: Balo, Clark, LeClaire.

In the 1920's the local team participated in the District Intermediate Baseball League. The league included Bevan, Courtenay, Cumberland, and a Japanese team. A couple of memorable games were played. In one contest, Courtenay beat the Bay "Bushers" 18 to 1. The return match at the shipping port saw Balo pitch a sizzler.

1921 AUGUST ➾ Union Bay Got Sweet Revenge. The game was rained out after five innings and

A winning team in the early '30s with pitchers "Wild Bill" Marshall and "Smokey" Anderson. Front: W. Glover, D. Marshall, J. Aitken, C. Bradley, A. Auchinvole, J. McKay, H. Grant (bottom). Back: B. Burgess, B. Geary, A. Searle, B. Marshall, A. Anderson, W. Peters

B. McKay

The Championship team in the Twilight League. Front: J. McKay, J. Aitken, B. Macartney, D. Marshall, A. Magnone, A. Auchinvole. Back: R. James, D. Marshall, W. Glover, B. McKay, T. McKay, J. Cummins - ump.

E. Sawchuck

Ticki Higashi up to bat while the fans cheer from the grandstand

the Bay regulars counted up 14 runs. One inning doubled up, the entire team twice at bat. Wilkinson made two home runs in that one inning. 14 to 1! Why, in nine innings at the same ratio the score would have been 25 to 2. [5]

The team roster in 1922 was:

Dangerfield	P	Fraser	3rd B
J. McKay	C	T. Johnson	RF
B. Geary	1st B	D. Renwick	CF
P. Renwick	2nd B	W. Glover	LF
B. McKay	SS		

For several years Jim Kerr coached the team. Ting Bono from Cumberland travelled around the district umpiring all the big games. During this time some good "twirlers" emerged that carried the team to many victories. Names remembered are "Dixie" Geary, "Smokey" Anderson, "Sandy" Auchinvole, and "Wild Bill" Marshall.

1933 MAY ➾ Union Bay licks the Cubs. "Wild Bill" Marshall piches a 15 to 5 victory over Cumberland. The Cubs had pitcher "Spit" Quinn but he was not playing well. [6]

The Twilight League came into its own in the1930's.

1930 JULY ➾ Union Bay wins a double header over Courtenay and Happy Valley. The Bay's McKay battery soon got working and held the Valley nine down. "Fin" McKay was in the box for his first appearance and showed he could chuck some wicked balls. Jim McKay was at the receiving end and played the position like a big leaguer. [6]

Tragedy struck in 1931 when Union Bay was playing Courtenay at the Dominion Day Sports in Lewis Park. In the 8th inning two men had been put out when Alex Auchinvole came up to bat. He swatted out a long fly which Freddie Stephens in left field ran to catch. He caught the ball against his chest, with a thud heard in the grandstand. As it was the third out he ran into the infield where he fell down dead.

"Because it was third out as soon as he caught the ball, I ran from where I was coaching at first base, to shortstop which was my position for the next inning. He crossed right in front of me, just at the pitcher's mound. I heard him say "Oh Shit", and he turned sideways and went down dead as a varmint. But the ball wasn't going fast. If you'd got it right between the eyes it wouldn't have hurt."

Dunc Marshall

For one of the Colliery picnics in the 1930's, the company built a grandstand around home plate. On summer evenings down through the years, the enthusiastic fans sat and cheered for the local boys. Most of the games were played in the evening. The sun, which was low in the west, shone directly into the batter's and umpire's eyes. In the early 1940's a huge billboard was built by the company in front of the Washer and briquet plant. It served two purposes, to advertise "Famous Comox Coal", and to block out the sun as it was setting.

For over twenty-five years the Japanese living at the Royston lumber camp were keen competitors. The young boys loved the game of baseball and some became very good players.

1924 AUGUST ➾ The Japs lost a league game to Union Bay, 17 to 4. Royston Sawmill Co.'s plucky little Nipponese team played their last league fixture in a wild loose game last Saturday. The little brown men went down fighting against superior odds. [5]

Famous Japanese teams also came from Vancouver to play an all-star district team at Courtenay. The Marshall brothers - Bill, Dunc, and "Smoothie" (Donald) - were often on the roster.

OFFICIAL LINE UP OF GAME
FRIDAY, AUGUST 22, 7 P.M.
Sponsored by Union Bay Community Club
"Has Beens" vs. *"Never Was"*

Managers
"Big Bill" Treloar — "Big Bill" Chaffer

	Batt. Average
"Pike Pole" McKay	.999
"Two Cup" Geary	.42-7/8
"One on the House" Plump	.2001
"Dead Eye Dick" Renwick	1500
"Snoose" McKay	350-2/5
"Short Ton" Peters	2240
"Brake Stick" McKay	99-1/2
"S-Hell" Gas Hastings	30¢
"One Gulp" Glover	NIL
"Don't Argue" Aiken	OUT
"Pile Expert" Campbell	247-1/2

"Answer to the Maiden's Prayer" Joe Walker

Pinch Hitters
"Full House" Dunn
"Ole Man River" Sherburn

Official Umpire
"Lookie" Richardson

First Aid
"Off Side" Jones
"Choo Choo" Ray

Water Boys
"Aces Up" Searle
"Hamburger" Bowden
"Close Shave" Guiness

Ball Finders
"Short Circuit" Cooper
"Smoothie" Marshall
"Slicker" F. Treloar

Base Umpires
"Semi-Final" Kay
"Slim Pop" Hamilton
"Hot Shot Tinny" Walters

Coaches
"Next Week" Davis
"Home Brew" Plunkey

Trainers
"Raw Beef" Harwood — "Blue Back" Anderson

Notice
Park all cars at least one mile from grounds.
Fouls are meat to these boys.
Managers and trainers are not responsible for
Flies caught (if any)
Bases stolen (if any)
After the game Coffee Doughnuts and
Bingo at Crib Club
Old-timers baseball game

During the war years, players on the Bay teams were constantly changing as the boys went off to war. A year before the Japanese were banished from the B.C. coast they still had a team in the league, led by a left-handed pitcher, "Cowboy" Kimoto.

1941 JUNE ➻ The Bay beats the Nippons in a 13 inning thriller. The Union Bay squad members were:

J. Younger	P	Higashi	3rd B
L. Coe	C & P	Renwick	RF
B. McKay	1st B	McQueen	CF
Shillito	2nd B	Kennedy	LF
Magnone	SS	James	C

Umpire: Ting Bono [7]

The big burly pitcher, Ron Pratt, was a favourite who played on many all-star teams. He moved from Little River and married Ann McKay. During the late 1940's and '50s the "southpaw" led the Bay to many victories, and also pitched for a Courtenay team which won the B.C. Senior A Baseball Championship.

1950 JUNE ➻ The hurling efforts of Lefty Pratt proved to make him the master all the way. To the delight of the enthusiastic crowd, he struck out sixteen Legionnaires. [7]

By the 1940's the second generation of ball players came of age. Four young McKays - George, Robbie, Stan, and Bud - were on the 1942 squad with their Uncle Bill. The two Renwicks, Kenneth and Donald, were also on the team. After the war Fred Peters, Jack Renwick and Bob Geary played for the Bay, as well as more McKays: Sid, Dave, Joe, Ted, Bill, Jack, Roy, Pat, and Glen.

Many of the older players became coaches or umpires. Johnny Aitken became a favourite umpire and was still officiating at games in the 1960's when his three boys - Alvin, Jim, and Dennis - were playing.

In the late 1940's and '50s, Tommy Barnes became a real baseball booster, working behind the scenes. Always smoking a fat cigar, he looked the part of a manager, but in fact did all the "Joe-jobs": cutting the grass, making the bases, keeping the equipment, rounding up the boys. A few years earlier, the old grandstand had been dismantled, so Tommy decided a new one was needed. He scrounged scrap lumber and had it planed and cut to size at the company mill, then with volunteers built the grandstand near the third base line.

K. Peters

Another winning team, wearing uniforms donated by the IWA. Front: E. Shillito, S. McKay, F. Peters, L. Richardson, D. McKay, 'Toots' Plump (coach), K. Peters. Back: G. McQueen, R. McKay, L. Coe, R. Pratt, S. Shillito

D. Bennie

Cigar-chompin' Tommy Barnes was manager of all the boy's teams in the late '40s and '50s

K. Peters

A team of young players who just won their league. c. 1958. Front: K. Hatch, D. Peters, G. McKay, D. McBride, N. Stewart. Second row: K. Scavarda, K. Webster, D. Peters, W. Kennedy, T. Piket, R. Wynn. Back row: G. Webster (coach), T. Foster, L. McDonald, G. McQueen, Mr. Weir (coach)

1909 MARCH ➻ The football match on Saturday was disgraceful. Players from No.6 and No.7 teams should have left the field when ordered to by the referee. I hope the Association will stand for good clean sport, unless they do we cannot expect the support of the public. I suggest a line 12' around the field to keep the people back. Also, the swearing should be stopped. [4]

The game reached its zenith in the 1920's when Cumberland United was in the national finals for the Canadian Football Championship. The team was sponsored by the coal company, and many claim that star players were brought by the CC(D)L from "the old country" and given a job in the mines. "Dirty" Jock Campbell, whose father Bob worked in the shops, was one such player. They were a devoted lot, playing in almost any kind of weather.

FOOTBALL

Among the English and Scottish settlers of Union Bay, football was almost a religion. Many had come from the northern cities where the teams were avidly followed by devoted fans. In 1908 a District Football Association was formed with Cumberland at the centre. Cumberland had six teams, while Bevan and Union Bay each had one. There was also fierce competition from Wellington, Nanaimo and Ladysmith.

1921 JANUARY ➻ A special train took two Cumberland football teams to Union Bay to practice because of the snow here. [5]

"When I was about 12 years old, Cumberland had a championship team. A bunch of us used to walk to Cumberland on Sunday morning to watch the football match, then walk home again. Twenty miles to see a football game!"

Hector Hooper

The Union Bay Junior Team won the Graham Cup in 1921. The next year, the No.1 and No.2 Cumberland football teams in the Junior League travelled to Nanaimo for the Island Championships.

L. Renwick

Football fans watch a game at the ball field

H. Glover

An early football team. c. 1912. Front: ?, S. Glover, T. Glover, J. McFarlane, F. Campbell. Middle: ?, L. Drew, P. Renwick. Back: G. Campbell (manager), W. Hooper, A. Glover, H. Reid, ?, B. Campbell, P. Reid (coach)

A. Searle

A championship team supported by the CC(D)L. Front: A. Auchinvole, S. Nakamura, J. Campbell, D. Johnson, T. Searle. Middle: T. Johnson, E. Mazzolini, B. Marshall, T. McKay. Back: A. Kay, A. Auchinvole, H. Auchinvole, B. Brown, B. Auchinvole, H. Reid, P. Reid

Five of the No.1 players were from Union Bay: W. Auchinvole, E. Mazzolini, S. Nakamura, J. Campbell, D. Jones. On the No.2 team three were Bay boys: W. Marshall, A. Auchinvole, T. Searle.

The Cumberland Eagles Junior Football team won the O.B. Allan Cup, top trophy in B.C. The team, including Jake Campbell and "Tweet" Charlie Bradley from Union Bay, got half way across Canada before being defeated. Other outstanding players were Bill Marshall, and the Auchinvole boys: Harry, Bill, and Alex.

1924 OCTOBER ➾ Harry Auchinvole played his first game on the UBC Football Team as centre forward and scored two goals. Club officials think he is a "find". [5]

Coaches through the years were Hughie Reid, Pete Reid, Jimmy Walters and Waddy Wilson. The latter two, both bachelors, devoted many hours to training the young people in various sports. Albert Jones, originally from England, moved to Vancouver after the war and refereed all the big games there. To procure the top notch official the coal company offered Albert a job. The Jones' family of four girls and one boy lived in the big house on the north side of Russell Hill when they moved to the Bay in 1923. Mr. Jones officiated at all the big games in the district. His nick-name was derived from blowing the whistle.

"That's how "Putt-Putt" Jones came to Union Bay. I think he was hired by the Collieries because he was an excellent referee. We were lucky to have him do our games. His son, Deacon, played too."

Dunc Marshall

The Bay boys had lots of practice as they played teams from all over the world.

"We used to play against all the boats that came in. The Blue Funnel Line had all-Australian crews and, of course, many of the ships were English. Even the Indians and Malaysians could play football. They'd come ashore and start kicking the football around. Maybe we'd have to loan them a few players to make a match. I remember once we had eighteen on each side. They weren't out to win so much as to have fun."

Wilf Glover

The three Campbell families (not related) all had sons who were talented football players. George Campbell managed a team that his two son's, Bill and Fraser (Scottie), played on. Jock Campbell (Bob Campbell's son) was brought out to the district by the coal company to play. He was nicknamed "Dirty Campbell". The same nickname went to Jake Campbell a few years later when his family, with brothers Tom, Dave and Bert, moved up from Nanaimo.

By the 1930's a new roster of names appeared: L. Coe, J. Baikie, B. Bradley, Dunc and Don Marshall, S. Nakamura, F. and J. Schoening, and A. Searle.

SPORTS DAY

Originally started as a Dominion Day celebration, the company picnic eventually evolved into a big annual sports day. It was held in July at Comox Lake, Royston or Union Bay. The towns vied for the opportunity of holding the picnic. The committee favoured the Roy farm south of the wharf at Royston. Because of the lack of facilities, Union Bay was refused for several years. Then, in 1929 a delegation presented a carefully thought-out plan to the committee. Included was a map of the field with the improvements of shade trees, seating and a playground.

1929 JULY ➾ A good deal of comment had been heard about the location chosen for this year's picnic, but the most bitter opponent to Union Bay as a picnic centre had to admit after last Saturday's affair, that it was the best picnic in the history of the employees. Some doubtful committee members now say it would make a good permanent place for the picnic. [5]

Free trains brought thousands of picnickers from all the company towns. Local CC(D)L officials took an active part in the organization. The company provided about $800, and each employee contributed, the men $1.00, the boys 50¢. Over the years, Thomas Graham or Alex Auchinvole was president, with A.S. Jones, P. Reid, T. Searle, and A. Kay heading the many committees.

Local Members of Parliament and the Legislature attended, as well as company officials from Nanaimo. This was to promote harmony and co-operation between the company, workers, and community.

1922 AUGUST ➾ Thomas Graham, general superintendent of the CC(D)L, took a leading part in the sports and addressed the large audience during the noon hour. He dwelt upon the pleasant relationship that existed between employer and employee. [5]

A. Searle

Many teams were coached by Waddy Wilson and Jimmy Walters, two bachelors who devoted many hours to young people. Front: S. Nakamura, ?, A. Auchinvole, T. Johnson, ?. Middle: H. Glover, D. Johnson, B. Mugford. Back: Waddy, T. Searle, ?, B. Glover, B. Auchinvole, Jimmy

D. Marshall

A young team of footballers. c. 1924. Front: R. McNally, T. Johnson, D. Marshall, C. Bradley, F. Bradley, G. Walker, L. Cave (ball boy). Back: T. Bradley, R. Glover, T. Formby, D. Brown, L. McLeod

The company carpenters were put to work at the carshop, building grandstands sufficient to seat 2,000 spectators. Swings, teeter-totters, "shoot the shutes," and a beautiful ten horse merry-go-round were crafted by Pete Reid and his carpenters.

"Johnny Fulcher ran the diamond drill boiler. It was on two big steel wheels with a tongue for harnessing it to a team of horses. They would pull it to Holmes Field to provide lots of hot water, or take it to the Company picnics at Royston. At the picnics it ran a stationary engine which was belted to the merry-go-round. Later, the company truck was used with a

The Company Sports Day Picnic held at Royston Cumberland Museum

Plan of Sports Field at UNION BAY, where Colliery employees' picnic will be held

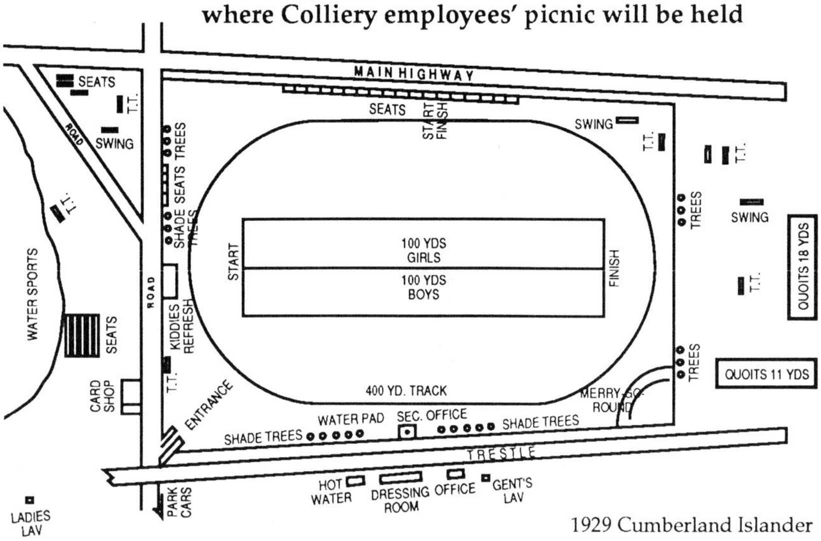

1929 Cumberland Islander

wheel taken off the truck and a belt attached to the driving wheel of the merry-go-round."

Harry Glover

Every year the Cumberland Band provided music at the picnic site. Their services were no longer needed when the electronic age took over. In 1934 the Fletcher Music Co. installed a loud speaker and broadcast all the latest tunes, as well as providing amplification for the organizers.

Great quantities of food were bought and dispensed free to the picnickers, who were supposed to be company employees or dependents. As outsiders were benefitting as well, it was decided in 1929 to issue tickets with the men's pay statements for each member of the family.

1922 JULY ➾ The Company supplied the picnickers with 1507 gallons of ice cream, 15,000 cones, 6 cases of oranges, 2,000 sacks of peanuts and 25 barrels of soft drink. [5]

Added to the goodies was a free "Giant Draw". Over 75 prizes were provided each year by local and provincial merchants who did business with the company. It was an exciting time when names were drawn for lamps, fishing rods, cameras, cushions, chocolates, etc.

Track and field events took most of the day. Footraces, relays, jumping and throwing included everyone from children to old men, with separate races for the Chinese and Japanese. Skipping, three legged, wheelbarrow and sack races were enjoyed by the children. Novelty contests such as pillow fights, cracker eating, pie eating, milk drinking and nail driving provided contestants and onlookers with lots of laughs. These events usually ended with tug-of-wars pitting Japanese against Chinese, and Bevan against Union Bay. There was a side bit of fun as the men bet on the outcome.

Dominion Day Celebration

at

UNION BAY

Wednesday, July 1st

PROGRAMME OF EVENTS

1—FOOTBALL MATCH (10 a.m.)
2—FOOTBALL MATCH (11 a.m.)

RACING (1 o'clock)

3—Girls' Race, 8 years and under, 1st prize 75c, 2nd 50c, 3rd 25c
4—Boys' Race, 8 years and under, 1st prize 75c, 2nd 50c, 3rd 25c
5—Girls' Race, 12 years and under, 1st prize $1, 2nd 75c, 3rd 50c
6—Boys' Race, 12 years and under, 1st prize $1, 2nd 75c, 3rd 50c
7—Girls' Race, 16 years and under, 1st prize $2, 2nd $1.50, 3rd 75c
8—Boys' Race, 16 years and under, 1st prize $2, 2nd $1.50, 3rd 75c
9—Young Ladies' Race, special prize given by Ramsay Bros. through Fraser and Bishop, 1st prize 5lb box of candy, 2nd prize 4lb box of candy.
10—Married Ladies Race, special prize given by W. H. Malkin and Co. through Fraser and Bishop, 1st prize 5lb Victoria Cross Tea, 2nd prize 5lb Victoria Cross Coffee.
11—Married Ladies' Race (Union Bay) special prizes given by Kelly, Douglas & Co. and F. R. Stewart through Fraser and Bishop, 1st prize One "Ajax" Ham, 2nd prize 5lb Nabob Tea, 3rd prize 5lb Nabob Coffee.
12 Old Men's Race, special prizes given by McLellan and McFeely and Turner Beaton Co., 1st prize Fishing Rod, 2nd prize Big Horn Shirt
13—Chinese Race, 1st prize $5, 2nd prize $2.50
14—Japanese Race, 1st prize $5, 2nd prize $2.50
15 100 Yards Dash (entrance fee 50c), 3 entries, 1st $7.50, 2nd $5
16—100 Yards Loggers' Race, 3 entries, 1st $7.50, 2nd $5
17 Quarter Mile (entrance fee 50c), 3 entries, 1st $7.50, 2nd $5
18 One Mile (entrance fee 50c), 3 entries, 1st $10, 2nd $7.50
19—Hurdle Race, 3 entries, 1st $7.50, 2nd $5
20—Chinese Tug of War, 8 men, prize $8
21—Putting the Shot, 1st prize $5, 2nd prize $2.50

FINAL FOOTBALL GAME, $75

22 Men's Swimming Race, 100 yards, 1st prize $7.50, 2nd prize $5
23—Boys' Swimming Race, 100 yards, 1st prize $3, 2nd $2, 3rd $1
24—Log Sawing Contest, 3 entries, 1st prize $7.50, 2nd prize $5
25 Tug of War, Union Bay v. Loggers, 8 men, prize $16

Items 22, 23, 24 and 25 will be held at Government Wharf.
Rules—Judges' decision final.

A. Hooper

Mr. and Mrs. C. Hooper dressed to enjoy the company picnic

"There was a sports day when they used to bring four or five flat cars down from Cumberland, loaded with people. They thought it was fine getting down to the Bay. There were races and swimming and climbing the greasy pole. They'd have a pole and grease it with lard and everyone would try to climb it. Then one time they had it out over the water. Then there was the greasy pig which you had to catch. You could keep him if you caught him. The Collieries helped the people organize it."

Bob McKay

R. Masters

Separate races were held for Orientals. The photo caption indicates the prejudice of the day

"In just one day I won $43. I won the slow bike race, married women's race, nail driving contest, and more. Old Hudson bet $10 when I was running and I fell on the uneven ground. He said, 'You just lost me $10 because I bet on you.' I said, 'Bet on me next race'. He did and he won $25."

Nellie (McKay) King

Competitions in quoit and boshe were carried on throughout the day. In 1929 Union Bay re-introduced water sports: swimming, diving and rowing, as well as lifesaving contests. That year, First Aid competitions were also introduced with the Sloan Challenge Shield as prize. It proved a very popular event every year, with teams of men, women, and young people from Cumberland and Bevan competing. The highlight was always the baseball game between Union Bay and Cumberland, with lots of friendly rivalry and fan support on both sides.

Union Bay School Collection

Novelty races like the sack race were fun for contestants and onlookers

TRACK & FIELD

The first Upper Island Inter-School Field Day was held at Cumberland in 1925. Three high schools - Cumberland, Courtenay, and Nanaimo - competed against one another, while the public schools were divided into two groups. Union Bay was included in the small public schools and came third to Brechin and Fanny Bay. It became an annual event, and in 1934 Union Bay hosted the Public School contest. School principal Cecil Richie led the committee. It had to raise money and prepare the program and field. Mayor Pete Maffeo came from Nanaimo to start the races. Winners were awarded silver spoons, second and third receiving ribbons. All the schools, large or small, competed against each other, and although small, the "Flying U's" did very well due to the interest and coaching of Mr. Richie.

1934 MAY ➾ Points won by each school.

Cumberland	80	Comox	25
Union Bay	48	Bevan	5
Tsolum	47	Fanny Bay	5
Courtenay	46	Royston	1
Pt. Alberni	39	Denman	1

The next two principals, T. Crowley and D. McDonald, and their staffs kept up the interest and good coaching. Through the years the "Flying U's" won many races. The big meets were cancelled during the war. Later, to allow all children to compete, standards were set for each age bracket and each child tried to make the standards for a crest. Competitions were still held for the best athletes. Some of the winning competitors were Ed Shillito, Jack Renwick, Mel Campbell and Margo Auchinvole.

During the war, Leroy Richardson, one of the best sprinters of the Comox Valley, competed in inter-service sports.

1942 OCTOBER ➾ At Varsity Stadium, Edmonton, the local boy, Leroy Richardson, won the major honours for the day, placing 1st in both the 100 and 220 yard dash and 2nd in the high jump. [7]

WATER SPORTS

Water races and sports were an important part of the Dominion Day celebrations and company picnics. With keen competition, they were held at either Union Bay or Comox Lake. The boys built a diving board onto the float and a high board onto the top of the freight shed at the Government wharf, where they practiced. Medal winners in swimming and diving were Alex and Bill Auchinvole, Harry Glover, Bill Marshall, Scutta Nakamura and Ross Ray.

"We won all the swimming races, then the diving took place. Bill Auchinvole and Harry Glover did the swan and back dive off the high board. They took 1st and 2nd. Scutta Nakamura and Alex Auchinvole did the fancy dives off the spring board and they got 1st and 2nd. I believe Union Bay won all the

D. Aitken

The 1934 winners. Front: G. Murdock, J. Reid, I. Pollock, M. Harwood, I. Magnone, I. Davis. Middle: P. Cooper, E. Shillito, A. Muschamp, M. Jones, F. McKenzie, M. Jones, P. Horne, I. Muschamp. Back: C. Richie, R. Tappin, M. Higashi, T. Higashi, G. Shillito, Y. Uchita, M. McIntyre

M. Peters

Teachers Irene Jones and Donald McDonald ready to hand out the cups. They later formed a permanent team

Union Bay School Collection

The "Flying U's" with all their trophies. c. 1937. Front: D. Ward, G. Frew, A. McKay, D. Muschamp, J. Auchinvole. Middle: I. Nelson, M. Hicks, M. Harwood, I. Magnone, P. Cooper, L. Arrol, D. Murdock, S. Higashi. Back: G. Cooper, G. Murdock, R. Chilton, G. Shillito, B. McKay, I. Pollock

swimming races that year except the underwater swim.

Tommy Formby and I had been fishing on the bar all summer, rowing a 16 ' boat across. He says to me, 'Say Bob, I've got two bits. Let's hire a boat and go in the race.' I said, 'We haven't got a chance. Look at those two miners, Ted Shillito and Sam Davis, great big fellows.' We were waiting for the gun to go when Tommy turned to me and said, 'You keep it straight and I'll do the pulling.' He was about 170 pounds and wide. So we dug in and drove a straight course. The others were zig-zagging and rammed us just as we went across the finish line but we won."

Bobby Pollock

About 1913 Billy Lempy, a young girl staying with the Strand family, swam from the Bay to Tree Island. She was accompanied by the bartender, Mickey McKay, in a rowboat. In the '20s long distance swim competitions were held from the wharf to Denman Island. Charlie Formby, who had competed in England, often won the silver cup. Later, competitions were held between Comox and Royston wharves.

1931 AUGUST ➾ The 1 1/2 mile was swum in 44 minutes by winner Harry Forse. Six men with bodies well greased and glistening entered the water. Albert Cooper from Union Bay had a good chance, but his boatman took him too far off course, allowing for tides. The mistake was realized too late to correct so he did not win. [6]

M. Simpson

Edythe Hicks getting up courage to dive and get her "beautiful" bathing costume wet

H. Glover

Bill Auchinvole executing a swan dive off the high board built onto the top of the freight shed

H. Glover

Some of the Union Bay swim team: T. Glover, B. Marshall, T. Campbell, B. Auchinvole, A. Auchinvole, H. Glover, W. Peters

The young people spent most of the summer at the beach. With the protection of Denman Island, the water was one of the warmest spots on Vancouver Island, especially at Coal Beach at the head of the Bay. It was here that Waddy Wilson, who loved sports and kids, taught many youngsters to swim. An old beached scow was fun to play on when the tide was out and dive off when the tide was in. After swimming there, kids and bathing suits alike needed a wash to clean off the coal dust.

"Remember the boats we built out of the 4" x 12" planks discarded by the Foo Foo gang when they repaired the trestle? We shaped a point in the front for the bow and because it was tippy nailed a board across and attached 4" x 4" pontoons to stabilize it. There it was, another Southsea island craft just like in the movies, and we paddled the ocean blue in the bay to our hearts content. Each day we could hardly wait for the tide to come in to float our boats. There was a fleet of them. Surely no kids anywhere in the world had more fun than us."

Kyoshi Nakamura

In the 1930's sand was barged in and dumped beside the old rock jetty. This became known as Sandy Beach, a popular swimming hole. The old warehouse made a perfect changing room. For the better swimmers at the Government wharf, the freight shed served this purpose.

M. Simpson

The Brown grandchildren enjoy the water and beach. J. Abrams, M. Hicks, B. Doney, B. Abrams, ?, L. Brown, J. Doney

G. Murdock

The water was warm and there was lots of wood to play on at Coal Beach. Left to right: G. Murdock, K. Renwick, D. Murdock, ?, M. & S. Renwick, D. Renwick. In front: D. Murdock

In 1948 Maxine Stokes, and Jacqueline and Janette Glover went to Victoria to attend the first Red Cross Swimming Instructors School held on Vancouver Island. Equipped with kickboards made in the car shop and a first aid kit supplied by Edna Peters, the girls gave free lessons at Sandy Beach and the Government wharf for five years. They read the tide book and scheduled their lessons to take advantage of the sand. The weather did not always cooperate and many lessons took place on cold, wet days. An examiner travelled from Vancouver to test the swimmers at the end of each season. Many children passed through the three levels and won Red Cross badges.

PICNICS

Union Bay was perfectly situated for recreation. There was something for everyone: a picnic lunch and swim at Sandy Beach, an end-of-school picnic at Washer Creek, a C.G.I.T. hike up to the King's Bath, a bike ride down to Tsable River, a family birthday at Barnacle Beach, a weiner roast at 4th Road, a boat trip to Tree Island.

Ask anyone about picnics and the first place mentioned is Holmes' Field. About a mile south on Baynes Sound, the beautiful grassy field was surrounded by tall trees and had room for games, races, and swimming. Sunday School picnics were always held there, with

R. Ryan

M. Vowels

M. Coe

Left: Three men line up on the diving board with local bathing beauties - J. Watt, M. Militich, M. Peters, E. & R. Shillito, D. Ward, L. & J. Veale, G. Militich. Centre: Three ladies swimming at Sandy Beach - Bell McLeod, Mary Walker, Myrtle Peters. Right: Mildred Bowden, Jack Glover and Edie Schulson at Sandy Beach. At left is the old store later used for a store house and finally a change room

B. Sherburn

Betty Thomas buried in the sand at Qualicum by her dad, M. Thomas, as Buster Sherburn looks on

M. Ellingsen

The early Union Bay families gather July 1st for a picnic on Denman Island. Families - Cook, Manson, McKay, McLeod, Richards, Street.

Mrs. Haggart organizing races and games. Everyone shared in a huge table of salads and desserts.

In the early days community picnics were organized by the church. In 1896 three Cumberland churches combined to have a gala picnic at the Wharf. The Union Cornet Band started off the day by marching to each church and marshalling the picnickers behind them to Grant's Landing. There, about 500 boarded the train, consisting of two coaches, two flat cars and one baggage car, all fitted out with seats.

1896 JULY ⊸ The afternoon was spent "a go as you please" fashion. Many enjoyed a dip in the briny deep. Three or four boats were kept busy in rowing and sailing their friends about the bay. The crowd strolled about enjoying the rest and recreation of a holiday by the seashore. The band furnished excellent selections during the day and did much to enliven the proceedings. Lemonade was the order of the day and was given out without stint, much to the satisfaction of the rising generation. The swings were well patronized. 3b

N. Jones

Everyone was well turned out for a Sunday School picnic at Holmes Field. Mrs. & Mr. B. Marshall, Mrs. A. Kay, Mrs. W. Fraser, Mrs. Hudson, Mr. & Mrs. McColgan, Mrs. Horne

F. Peters

Ladies at a Community Picnic - M. Pollock, ?, M. Geary, G. Haggart, E. Tappin, M. Horne, G. Murdock, Mrs. McIntyre

D. Bennie

Scrambling ashore and up the beach for a picnic

N. Eastman

L. Magnone takes the McKay family for a boat ride

Sometimes the excursions were held on Denman Island. With the same minister serving Union Bay, Denman and Hornby, joint picnics were often held. Several years Mr. Manson took the Bay parishioners in the *Thistle* to join the Islanders. It was the hit of the day when he scattered candies on the grass to be picked up by eager children. George Howe also took the whole town to Denman.

"George Howe had a scow and he'd take all Union Bay that wanted to go over, to Piercy's farm for a picnic once a year. Everyone took their lunch. That was a great day!"

Mary (McKay) Winterburn

Later, family and friends travelled to Tree Island for a Sunday picnic. At low tide, the men walked the beautiful sandy beaches from Denman to Seal Island, while the women collected a wonderful variety of wild flowers. Boys built forts with the driftlogs, and girls collected pails of sand cookies and pretty shells.

Louis Magnone, Harry Glover, Dick Ray and Ernie McMurtrie each had a launch that took many boat loads of picnickers to the island. However, the launch best remembered was owned by Tommy James. It could be rented for the day. Men in summer whites and ladies in large straw hats climbed aboard for a picnic on the Island.

"Several families hired Tommy James to take us over to Tree Island. When we got there Tommy was going to ferry us to shore. Old Bill Bowden, I can see him yet in a pair of ice cream pants. Well, Bill had one foot on the launch and got one foot in the row boat when she started to go. In he went and he couldn't wait to get to the surface before he started swearing at Mrs. Bowden. It had nothing to do with her at all. He gave her hell just as soon as his head came up."

Dunc Marshall

Occasionally, after leaving the picnickers at Tree Island, Tommy returned to the Bay and stopped at the beer parlour. A few times he lost track of time and the picnickers spent an anxious few hours at dusk, wondering if they would have to stay the night. For the young people it was an adventure, for the old people a scandal.

"One time Tommy James took a group of young couples over to the island and got drunk and forgot about them. It caused quite a stir in the community. I was living with Uncle Jack and Aunt Margaret, and you know how narrow-minded those people were. I remember the conversation at the dinner table. 'Imagine those young people over on that island all night and no chaperone! Oh well, Annie

G. Francklyn

F. Peters

Left: Heading to Henry Bay for a picnic. Right: Tommy James has just returned a group safely home from Hornby Island. Adults: Tommy, Mrs. and Mr. G. Harwood, M. Harwood, M. McIntyre, H. Sherburn, ?, Mrs. Sherburn. Children: B. Sherburn, M. & G. Harwood, B. Sherburn

K. Nakamura

A. Hardiman

D. Walker

Top Left: Wilf Bowden, Kyoshi Nakamura and Albert Cooper head off backpacking. Left: Resting on top of Tsable Mountain - Ross Ray, Jake Campbell, George and Bill Walker. Top right: The view of Tsable Falls was worth the hike up. Bottom left: Hikers wave from a rock island in a snow covered valley. Centre: Louis Magnone pulls the McKay girls, Mary, Frances, Nellie and Agnes up a rock cliff. Right: Skinny dipping in Tsable Lake. Dave & Jake Campbell, Harry & Wilf Glover

H. Glover

D. Aitken

H. Glover

Baillie and Tom Campbell are a bit older, they wouldn't let anything happen.'"

Bob Pollock

Young people also took hiking and camping trips on the mountains, lakes and rivers surrounding the Bay. The Beaufort Range, Rosewall Canyon, Bradley Lake and Tsable River were favourite destinations.

W. Glover

This group of young picnickers was left on Tree Island all night when Tommy James got drunk and forgot them. E. Fulcher, A. Lee, D. Renwick, A. Auchinvole, M. Glover, W. Peters, J. Campbell, H. Glover, S. Walker, A. Campbell, ?

WINTER FUN

Before the turn of the century, reports indicate that the thermometer dipped down further than it does today. During several winters Baynes Sound froze over. The mail boat could not call and wolves walked from Vancouver Island to Denman. Everyone has memories of the big snow falls, but a few feet every year was common.

1890 JANUARY ➾ At the Union Mine the snow is 5' deep and it required the united efforts of two locomotives to make the trip down to the steamer on Wednesday. They were only able to make about 30 ' at each "buck" as the snow packed hard and fast. [2]

1916 JANUARY ➾ Mines shut one week due to snow. The Chinese Theatre and several other buildings collapsed. One Comox Logging train is running between Cumberland and Union Bay for passengers. [5]

1935 JANUARY ➾ George P. Davis of Union Bay had the unusual experience of being brushed off a railway track by a snow plough and living to tell the tale. Davis was riding horseback along the CC(D)L track when he heard an engine whistle but thought it was in the yard. Snow

A. Hooper

A snow lady built by J. Chapman, K. Webster, L. Arrol, P. Glover, M. Chapman, A. Vowels, D. Chapman, J. Ennals

A. Graham

After the big snowfall in 1949 Claire Bowden and Ann Vowels shovel snow off Grandma Peter's roof

Cumberland Museum

Mr. McKay takes the family and friends for a sleigh ride

T. Dutfield

Ice skating on the frozen flooded ball field

Two excellent hills beckoned the warmly-dressed kids with their homemade or catalogue-bought sleighs. Russell Hill was steepest and fastest. It was a test for the rider to see if his sleigh could go all the way to the railway trestle. Walker's Hill at the other end of town could be as long or short as desired, depending how far the sleigh rider walked up. At the bottom there was the thrill of continuing across the highway and negotiating onto the Government wharf, without ending up on the beach. Until the 1940's, crossing the highway with a toboggan loaded with kids was safe. The few cars were kept safely in garages when it snowed.

prevented both him and the engine crew seeing each other until too late. The plough gathered the man and horse and tossed them unhurt into a snow bank. [7]

Then, as now, children loved the deep white stuff which they hoped would stay a few days before being turned to slush by a good southeaster. Snowmen were made and boys teamed up for snowball fights. The groceries were delivered by horse and sleigh.

"The McKay boys had a big sleigh and horses. We'd all pile in under the heavy blankets and keep our feet toasty warm on hot bricks. One year we went all the way to Fanny Bay and back."

Violet (Glover) Rutherford

For a few weeks every year the young people were able to ice skate on ponds and lakes. Most families had a couple of pairs of skates to be shared. If they did not quite fit, an extra pair of socks filled up the space. The novice wobbled around, skating almost on his ankles, and it was a relief to unlace the skates so a brother or sister could have a turn. The little ones wore bob skates which could be expanded each year to clamp on to shoes or boots.

During each cold spell a careful watch was kept on the ice forming on the lake. Finally the word was given that it was thick enough for skating. A group of friends would excitedly hike up Walker's Hill to Langley Lake in the cold crisp air. Donning their skates they glided over the ice, stopping on peat bogs to rest, and warming up around the bonfire on the bank.

Maple Swamp at Cumberland froze earlier than the lake, so those lucky enough to have transportation skated there. In later years good skating was found on the ponds behind Buckley Bay. Kids would catch the E&N train to Buckley Bay, then walk up the

D. Aitken

A sleigh ride in homemade sleighs. Maureen Stevens, Judy Chafer, Alvin Aitken, Ron Chafer

F. Peters

A hockey game on Langley Lake

M. Kine

D. Marshall

D. Marshall

N. King

M. Vowels

Top left: Annie McKay and a large cutthroat trout. Top centre: Two boys and a dog gone fishin', up Washer Creek. Dunc Marshall, Ray Glover and Mickey. Top right: Dunc Marshall and Bob Pollock with a steelhead caught in Washer Creek. Centre left: A good day of trout fishing. E. King, J. Golden, D. King, N. King, G. McKay, L. McKay, F. Stasek, A. McKay, A. Stasek, D. Aitcheson. Centre right: Len Peters and a catch of cod fish. Bottom left: Caught "over at the bar" these two giant spring salmon are nearly as big as the kids - Caroline Coe and Dennis Newman. Bottom right: Summer days were meant for fishing "over at the bar". Don Marshall, Kyoshi Nakamura, Art Searle, Scutta Nakamura

M. Coe

S. Nakamura

logging road to the ponds. The boys, with homemade hockey sticks, became either Maple Leafs or Canadiens. Everyone joined in. A goalie did not need skates; gumboots would do.

As early as 1921 the company flooded the football field for skating. In the 1940's and '50s the fire department flooded the baseball diamond. It was almost like being in a real rink as you sat in the grandstand and laced up your skates, then glided out over the ice like Sonja Henie.

FISHING FOR FUN AND FOOD

The ocean, lakes and streams on Vancouver Island teemed with fish, while the beaches were covered with oysters, clams and crabs. With little effort or skill, the head of the household could always have food on his table. Indeed, through the 1930's, many families lived on fish, clams and oysters.

"When times were tough we ate lots of seafood. Our belly's went up and down with the tide."

Bill McKay

One of the most precious items to accompany many of the immigrants was a Hardy fly fishing rod. These disciples of Isaac Walton would catch fish only on the fly. They treasured their little box of beautifully tied flies: Green Drake, Royal Coachman, Palmer, Brown Hackle.

1907 APRIL A party of tourists from the *Moana* took advantage of coaling at Union Wharf, and guided by Pilot Owens, tried fishing in the lake back of the Wharf. The catch numbered 30 fish with the smallest being 2' long. No bears were met, and Cpt. Owen, being well-armed, was in a position to ward off attacks. [4]

Langley Lake and Washer Creek, easily accessible to the men and boys of the Bay, abounded with cutthroat trout, steelhead and small coho. As well, Tsable River and Horne Lake were favourite spots for both fly and bait fishermen.

1910 JUNE Mr. Hudson and Mr. Ripley had a successful fishing trip to Horne Lake. They returned with 175 pounds of trout, the result of a two day fishing trip. One fish weighed 5 1/2 pounds. [5]

For recreation, a party of men would hike through the woods and mountains, fishing in all the lakes and streams. They enjoyed the trout they caught for breakfast and dinner. Later, with better transportation, fishing parties travelled to the Campbell Lakes, Buttle Lake and Elk River in pursuit of the speckled beauties.

The waters of Baynes Sound were home to a large variety of fish eager to bite a worm, spoon, fly, or flasher.

1932 OCTOBER Mr. Wm. Baikie was rowing home from Union Bay when he heard a splash. Then to his surprise a good size salmon landed in his boat. [6]

Even without a boat, fish were there for the taking. As early as 1890, herring were being scooped up in the shallow waters of the Bay. Every day there was at least one Chinese fishing off the coal or Government dock for perch, cod or crabs. When the fish were running, there would be as many as twenty men and boys on the coal wharf, fishing after work. The two corner pilings were the preferred spots as they provided more room to cast handlines. Coho from 1 1/2 pounds and up were caught, as well as many 20 pound chinooks.

1919 OCTOBER Fishing is good at the Government wharf this week, several boys having caught as many as twenty to thirty fish daily. [6]

Coho, dog salmon, chums and steelhead used to spawn in Washer Creek and its little tributaries.

"Remember when we used to go up Washer Creek with a rake after salmon. All those swamps up there in Stray Creek used to be just moving with salmon."

Tom McKay

Those lucky enough to own a boat were sure of fish every time out. Those that lived on the beach pulled their boat up under their homes. The men who lived in the company houses built boathouses into the coal banks on the spit.

"Mr. Francklyn at Henry Bay had money, but he lived over there and made boats for a hobby. Mr. Glover bought his first boat from him. It had two sets of oars and we could move right along. We were strong kids in those days. We'd row over to the bar or down to Yellow Rock to fish. He built me a beautiful boat for $25."

Doug Brown

The avid fishermen were out on the ocean whenever it was calm enough. Even on Christmas morning a few fathers rose early with the kids and caught a salmon before breakfast. Many of the big spring salmon were caught between the two wharves in the winter months. But it was nothing for men to row over to the bar for a day's fishing. Later, two horsepower Evinrude outboard motors were coaxed into life and used to get across the sound.

Fish stories were told at work, in the beer parlour, or on the street. Wherever men gathered, the latest catch was boasted of.

"Bill Carter was the envy of Dick Ray, because Bill always caught lots of salmon. He'd stand up in his double-ended boat and say, 'Come to me, me bright beauties'. Dick would say to his son Ross, 'Look at the old so-and-so'. Ross observed, 'He's catching more fish than we are.' Then Dick would snap back, 'Oh, shut up and keep rowing.'"

Bob Pollock

There were also women who liked to fish. Daughters went with their fathers, wives with their husbands, and some fished alone.

"Nellie and I went out fishing one day and we got a big salmon on, but couldn't land it. So we rowed to shore and pulled him up on the beach."

Frances (McKay) Stasek

"Mrs. Ede used to go fishing with grandaughter Nellie in a big wide canoe. I met her one day and asked her if she'd had any luck. 'I got one but the bastard got away', she replied. The little girl piped up 'Grandma had it in the boat but he jumped right out again'. On the way home I passed her again and asked, 'How ya doing, Mrs. Ede?' She lifted up a big salmon with a 3/4" rope through it's gill, tied to the boat and said. 'This bastard ain't gettin away'. Nellie was laughing.

Bob Pollock

HUNTING FOR SPORT, FOOD, AND BOUNTY

Panthers, bears and wolves were plentiful when white men first settled around Baynes Sound. Travellers usually carried a weapon for protection. Generally, a healthy animal would not attack, unless defending her young or if a person was accompanied by a small dog. Most of the bear sightings near civilization were in late summer, when berries attracted the big beasts. They were hunted for their meat.

1892 JULY •✧ Mr. R. Grant and four of his men were out prospecting timber on Mr. A. Garvin's land near Union Wharf when they heard the roar of some monstrous animal. Approaching carefully, they were joyfully surprised to find the monster, a black bear, held fast in a trap. His roars were quieted by four charges of Mr. A. McLaughlin's heavy Winchester rifle. The trap had been set by neighbours waiting for bruin's approach to bathe in Mr. Garvin's "noted mineral spring". [2]

1905 AUGUST •✧ The noon train to Union Wharf on Friday met a panther on the road just beyond Trent River. The beast ran along the track ahead of the train for a mile or more and finally turned off into the bush, just before the wagon road crossing at Laird's. T. Hudson started up the track after hearing of the incident but was not lucky enough to catch sight of the quarry. Panthers have been plentiful in the vicinity of the wharf this summer; it's not long since two whelps were killed by F. Curran. The animals, a mother and her family, were first seen by children out picking berries. [4]

N. King

"Cougar Smith" with his bag of six cougars

Cougars, which for many years were called panthers, often killed small farm animals such as sheep, calves and dogs, so were hunted vigilantly by the homesteaders. Gradually they were seen less and less near the growing town.

At the end of the First World War, two cougar hunters emerged at the north end of Vancouver Island. Robert Smith lived at Union Bay, and Cecil Smith, who was a guide for big game, came from Comox. The unrelated men were both nick-named "Cougar Smith." They bagged most of the big cats during the winter when snow drove the deer to lower levels and the cougar followed.

1922 FEBRUARY •✧ Mr. Bob Smith of Union Bay is getting famous as a slayer of cougars. He came to the Government office on Tuesday with skins of six panthers to collect the bounty. The animals he got in less than a week will net him about $300. He shot two of the destructive cats at Fanny Bay on Wednesday and secured the other four at Tsable River on Sunday. The four were together and he followed them in the snow until the last one fell to his gun. This makes thirteen since Christmas. [5]

1923 FEBRUARY •✧ With five panther skins draped round his car on his way through Courtenay to collect the bounty, Mr. Bob Smith told of his hunting. He secured the five big cats within a week around Cameron Lake. The snow was wet and excellent for tracking. His dogs are two Airedales and another little fellow of assorted pedigree. But this pup of unknown

N. King

parentage saved Mr. Smith. On the day he pursued the biggest cat he lost his way and would have had to stay in the bush for the night if the little dog had not taken up the scent and found his way out. His bag for the season is 30. [6]

Cougar Smith lived in a cabin near Sproat Lake but stayed with Mrs. McKay during the winter months. He took a shine to Nellie and she accompanied him on several hunts.

"I was only fifteen when he took me hunting. The dogs had treed a cougar and Smith called the dogs back and told me if I killed the cat with one shot I could have the gun. Well, I hit it through the eye on the first shot and he gave me the gun which I still have today."

Nellie (McKay) King

Tom McKay also hunted the big cats with the help of his cougar hounds. One year the dogs took up the scent of a wolf.

1933 MARCH ➾ Three year old fully grown male timber wolf measuring 5'10" from nose to tail was shot at Union Bay by Tom McKay and John Aitken, but not before it had thrown and killed a valuable cougar hound owned by the former. This brute is believed to be the mate of a female shot at Campbell River last year. Formerly wolves infested this area in large numbers but of later years they are rarely seen this far south. No bounty is awarded on these animals as the pelts have a commercial value. [7]

N. King

Nellie McKay proudly displays the cougar she shot through the eye with only one shot. Cougar Smith rewarded her by giving her the gun

In the 1920's the Vancouver Island marmot was proven to exist. Now, this marmot is one of six mammals on the Canadian endangered species list.

1922 AUGUST ➾ The brown-eyed cat that whistles, thought to be a hunter's fantasy, had been several times reported in the mountains around Rosewall Creek. Mr. B. Curran has shot a brace of them so now the "tall story" is believed. Known as the "whistling marmot" it has brown eyes and a short flat beaver-like tail. It climbs trees and also emits a shrill whistling noise. [6]

T. McKay

Tom McKay's cougar hound howls after the kill

A few of the settlers were commercial hunters. They peddled the meat to local butcher shops that sold venison for 5¢ a pound. When he first came to B.C., Pete Anderson supported his family by selling deer, ducks, geese and grouse to the shops in Cumberland and Union Bay. Gilbert Francklyn lived in a little cabin at Henry Bay on Denman Island where he hunted for the market. He was also a carpenter and carver, and made all of his own decoys.

1893 DECEMBER ➾ Deer hunting is the staple industry at present in activity, some of the hunters reaching six deer a week. Our "citizens of the shambles" are intending to petition the legislature to remodel the existing game laws so that wholesale slaughter will be a thing of the past. At present the ranching business is not sufficiently protected, with the result of no trade in beef. [2]

Hunting for food was necessary for many settlers. They also hunted for sport. The island was a hunter's paradise for British men who had been excluded from the aristocratic game preserves

T. McKay

John Aitken and Louis Magnone with the 5'10" timber wolf shot by Tom McKay behind Union Bay

in the old country. Deer came down to the ocean to lick the salt on the rocks and to eat sea grass. They often swam across Baynes Sound to Denman or back. A few exhausted fawns were picked up by boaters and nursed back to health. Sometimes they were kept as pets.

1886 NOVEMBER ➾ The "mighty nimrods", Mr. Emerson Muschamp, Mr. Smith and Mr. Tompkins, returned from a hunting expedition to Salmon River with the largest pair of elk horns ever seen in Comox. [2]

1932 OCTOBER ➾ Cowichan attracts many outside hunters annually for the opening of pheasant season, but it would have to be a very seasoned and devoted hunter to touch the record of Herbert Glover, Union Bay. For the last twenty-six years, Mr. Glover has visited Cowichan for the sport he desired and has not been disappointed this year, when he took home nine fine table specimens.

Cowichan Leader

As early as 1893, turkey shoots were held annually on December 24, at Howe's Hotel and later at Humphreys'. The lucky marksmen took home a bird for Christmas dinner. Trap shooting became popular in the 1920's and '30s. Al Stasek and Andy Anderson won many of the shoots. Relations, friends and city folk also came to the district to share in the abundance of game.

1931 OCTOBER ➾ Three young South Vancouver men were camped for two weeks at Langley Lake. They tramped out into the forest every day, hunting deer with no luck. One day all three of them were in the tent keeping out of the rain when they heard a shot. Upon investigation, they found a local hunter had shot a deer which was chewing on their tent ropes. [6]

Not long after the turn of the century, laws were passed regulating hunting seasons for different game, as well as the bag limit. About 1915, hunting badges (licenses) were introduced.

1917	Deer Season	Sept.15 to	Dec.15
	Duck "	Oct.15	Feb.28
	Brant & Geese	Dec.1	Mar.10
	Blue Grouse	Sept.15	Nov.14
	Pheasant	Oct.15	Oct.28

1921	**B.C. Game Bag Limit for**	Day	Season
	Deer (bucks only)	-	3
	Black Bear	-	3
	Pheasant (cocks only)	6	25
	Quail	20	150
	Ducks	20	150
	Geese	10	50
	Brant	10	50
	Grouse	12	50

With very few lawmen to enforce regulations, shooting out of season, exceeding the limit, and pitlamping were common in the area. If caught, the hunter faced possible confiscation of his gun, a fine from $10 and up, or a jail term of thirty days.

1895 OCTOBER ➾ Judge Abrams tried a Chinaman from Union Bay who was arrested with possession of five grouse out of season. He was fined $25 and the grouse were given to the hospital. [3b]

N. King

Deer shot by the McKay brothers

G. Francklyn

Gilbert Francklyn hunted for the market and sold to Fraser and Bishop's butcher shop

H. Glover

Hunting licence holder

Both rifle cartridges and shotgun shells were expensive, so many of the hunters reloaded the cardboard shells. The family hunters would get together before hunting season and take the old primer out of the used shell. New primer, the exact amount of powder, wadding, shot of a certain size and more wadding were packed into the cardboard casing, then the ends were crimped together. The main disadvantage in the early shotgun shell was the fact that the cardboard expanded if it got wet. Then the shell would not fit in the gun barrel.

Each father who hunted passed the love of the sport on to his sons. Gun safety was stressed, and dogs were trained to find and set on the birds. English Setters and Springer Spaniels were the preferred field dogs who ferreted out many coveys of blue grouse, willow grouse and pheasant. Labrador Retrievers made excellent duck hunting dogs. During hunting season, the young men brought home lots of game. They skinned and butchered the deer. Mothers, daughters and young children helped out by plucking and cleaning the birds. The family sat around in a circle with newspapers on their laps, plucking off the feathers. A gunny sack was used to save the down from the waterfowl, which would later be used to make pillows and comforters. When cleaning out the innards it was fun to cut into the gizzard and identify salal berries, grains or weeds. Great quantities of wild meat were bottled, to be enjoyed later in the year.

G. Francklyn

On the Sandspit. With decoys in the water the hunter hid behind the blind then shot when the birds came in

A few women also hunted. At the turn of the century, Mrs. Charles Hooper often hunted food for her family. She would go out alone, shoot a deer, bring it home, skin and clean it. Nellie McKay hunted with her brothers and Winnie Glover hunted with her husband. The women had their own guns, hunting coats and caulk boots.

The spit from the end of Denman to the tip of Seal Island was a popular duck and goose hunting area. Loaded with decoys and shotguns, the hunters either rowed over or had little outboard motors on their boats. Tommy James could also be hired to ferry them across Baynes Sound. They built blinds out of driftwood, stood silhouette decoys in the sand, and floated other decoys in the shallows. Then they waited for the geese, brant or ducks to join

B. McKay

Geese shot at Bradley Lake by Tom McKay, Ted Glover and Al Stasek with Cassie McKay in front

M. Coe

The hunter's cabin on Shack Island

H. Glover

A brant and goose hunting trip to Knight Inlet - T. Glover, A. Treloar, C. Ferrario, Alberto, S. Waterfield, A. Auchinvole, H. Glover

their wooden brothers. The Indian clam diggers had built little shacks on what was known as Shack Island, where parties of hunters could stay for two or three days. They also provided protection if the weather turned nasty and the hunters could not make the crossing to home. In latter years the shacks were upgraded by Jack Beban for the comfort of the hunters.

Hunting season was in fall and winter when the weather and ocean were the stormiest. Combined with firearms, this accounted for some accidents and the deaths of several Union Bay residents. (see chapter on accidents) A new regulation was introduced in 1913 which prohibited all automatic or pump repeating guns with a magazine capable of holding more than one cartridge.

In many families the men spent their holidays hunting, either close to home or in organized hunting parties. Large fishing boats were hired to take them to better geese and duck hunting grounds in the inlets along the coast. As many of the logging camps were shut for snow during duck season, the men could pursue their sport as well as put meat on the table.

After the war, parties of hunters went to the interior to hunt big game around Greenwood, where their friends, the Higashi family, had been sent during the war. Tickie drove logging truck and could advise them on the best hunting areas.

Bibliography

Books:

Abdill, George B. **This Was Railroading**. Seattle: Superior Publishing Company, 1958

Andrews, Ralph W. **This Was Logging**. Seattle: Superior Publishing Company, 1954

Audain, James. **From Coal Mine to Castle**. New York: Pageant Press, 1955

Baikie, Wallace. **Rolling With The Times**. Campbell River: Kask Graphics, 1985

Bowen, Lynne. **Boss Whistle**. Lantzville: Oolichan Books, 1982

Carroll, Leila. **Wild Roses and Rail Fences**. Comox Valley: E.W. Bickle Ltd., 1975

Collins, Robert. **A Voice From Afar**. Toronto: McGraw Hill Ryerson, 1977

Deaville, Alfred S. **Colonial Postal System and Postage Stamps.** Victoria: B.C. Banfield, 1928

Dollar, Robert. **Memoirs of Robert Dollar. Vol. 2 and 3** San Francisco: Van Gott; Knight Counichan, 1918-28

Duncan, Eric. **Fifty-Seven Years In The Comox Valley.** Courtenay: Comox District Free Press, 1934

Feely, Jean and Margery Corrigal. **A History Of "Tle-Tla-Tay".** Royston Centennial Committee

Graham, Donald. **Lights Of The Inside Passage**. Madeira Park: Harbour Publishing, 1986

Grainger, M. Allerdale. **Woodsmen Of The West**. Toronto: McClelland & Stewart, 1964

Griffiths, Bus. **Now You're Logging**. Madeira Park: Harbour Publishing, 1978

Hacking, N.R. and W.K. Lamb. **The Princess Story**. Vancouver: Mitchell Press, 1974

Hayman, John. **Robert Brown And The Vancouver Island Exploring Expedition.** Vancouver: University of British Columbia Press, 1989

Hughes, Ben. **History Of The Comox Valley, 1862 - 1946.** Nanaimo: Evergreen Press (V.I.) Ltd.

Isbister, Winnifred A. **My Ain Folk.** Comox Valley: E.W. Bickle Ltd., 1983

Isenor, D.E. et al. **For Our Children, A History Of Comox Valley Schools.** Courtenay: School District #71, 1980

Isenor, D.E. et al. **The Land Of Plenty.** Campbell River: Ptarmigan Press, 1987

Isenor, D.E., E. Stephens, D. Watson. **One Hundred Spirited Years**. Campbell River: Ptarmigan Press. 1988

Johnstone, William. **Coal Dust In My Blood.** B.C. Provincial Museum, Heritage Record No. 9, 1980

Killian, Crawford. **Go Do Some Great Thing.** Vancouver: Douglas and McIntyre, 1978

Lindsay, F.W. **The B.C. Outlaws.** Kelowna: Regatta Press, 1963

Lyons, C.P. **Milestones On Vancouver Island.** Nanaimo: Evergreen Press, 1958

Melvin. **Post Offices Of B.C.** Vernon: Melvin, 196-

Norris, John. **Strangers Entertained.** Vancouver: Evergreen Press, 1971

Ormsby, M.A. **British Columbia History.** Canada: McMillan, 1958

Paterson, Thomas W. **Ghost Towns Of Vancouver Island.** Langley: Stagecoach Publishing Co. Ltd., 1976

Paterson, Thomas W. **British Columbia Shipwrecks**. Langley: Stagecoach Publishing Co. Ltd., 1976

Paterson, Thomas W. **Outlaws Of Western Canada**. Langley: Stagecoach Publishing Co. Ltd., 1977

Rushton, Gerald A. **Whistle Up The Inlet**. Vancouver: Douglas and McIntyre, 1974

Rushton, Gerald A. **Echos Of The Whistle**. Vancouver: Douglas and McIntyre, 1980

Smith, E. and D. Gerow. **Hornby Island: The Ebb And Flow**. Campbell River: Kask Graphics, 1988

Stubbs, Dorothy. **All About Us**. Courtenay: Glacier Press, 1979

Turner, Robert D. **Vancouver Island Railroads**. San Marino: Golden West Books, 1973

Turner, Robert D. **The Pacific Princesses**. Victoria: Sono Nis Press, 1977

Watt, R.D. **The Shopping Guide Of The West**. Vancouver: J.J. Douglas Ltd., 1977

Sawchuck, Audrey et al. **Union Bay United Church 1905-1985**. Church History Committee, 1985

Wabran, John T. **British Columbia Coast Names 1592-1906**. Ottawa: Government Printing Bureau, 1909

World Book. **The World Book Encyclopedia**. Toronto: World Book - Childcraft International Inc., 1985

Unpublished

Aitken, Annie. **Annie's Scrapbook of Clippings.**

Egger, Margaret. **Margaret's Scrapbook of Clippings and Notes.**

Gallacher, Daniel T. **B.C. Coal Production to 1891.**

Johnstone, Bill. **Bill's Scrapbook of Clippings.**

Lytton, Wayne. **A Tribute to My Mom, Georgina (Abrams) Lytton.**

Moore, John. **Diary of Shipping Agent.**

Moore, John and Mary. **Guest Book of Shipping Agent.**

Peters, Emily. **Emily's Scrapbook of Clippings.**

Pickles, Charles. **The Four Masted Barque Pamir.**

Pratt, Ann. **Pythian Sisters' Album of Clippings and Notes.**

Sampson, Steve. **Union Bay Fire Department Log Book.**

Searle, E.T. **Book of Original Poems. Diary of Shipping Agent. Union Bay Glee Club Minute Book. Union Bay Social Club Minute Book.**

Periodicals

Newspapers
- Comox Argus
- Comox District Free Press
- Cumberland Islander
- Cumberland News
- Nanaimo Free Press
- Victoria Colonist
- Vancouver Province
- Weekly News. Courtenay and Cumberland

Directories of British Columbia
- Henderson's Gazetteer
- William's Official B.C. Directory
- Wrigley's B.C. Directory

Cummings, Doug. **Canadian Collieries (Dunsmuir) Ltd.** Vancouver, The Steam Chest "Hi-Baller" Railway Club, June 1960

Grant, Charles. **Old Time Logger.** Victoria Colonist: July 5, 1964

Hacking, Norman. **Trailer Snug Harbour For "Man Of Sail".** Vancouver Province: Sept 11, 1974

Hughes, Michael C. **The Coke Ovens Of Union Bay.** Industrial Archeology

Johnstone, William. **Union Bay.** Victoria Daily Colonist: July 10, 1977

Lomax, Alfred L. **The Coke Ovens Of Union Bay.** Victoria Daily Colonist: September 25, 1960

Moore, John and Mary. **Demolition Marks End Of Era.** Comox Free Press: 1960

Muralt, Darryl. **Quadra, The Town That Almost Came To Be.** Victoria Daily Colonist: March 1982

Sharcott, Margaret. **Early Mines - Baynes Sound Coal Co.** Victoria Colonist: October 17, 1971

Archival Documents

Canadian Collieries (Dunsmuir) Ltd. **Originals 1860-1925, Deeds and Survey books**

Canadian Collieries (Dunsmuir) Ltd. Graham, Thomas. **Originals 1871-1908, Contracts and indenture notes**

Department of Lands and Works of the Nelson District of Vancouver Island. Pre-emptions GR112 Certificate of Improvements GR 112

B.C. Liquor Control Board, **Applications and transfers for bar rooms, 1894-1960 (selected years)**

Attorney General, **Inquests and Trials** GR 429 1898-1913

B.C. Provincial Police. **W.W. I Alien Enemies Form A.**, Cumberland GR 57

Mackenzie, J.D. **The Coal Measures of Cumberland and Vicinity, 1922**

Minister of Mines Annual Reports. Selected years 1889 to 1960

B.C. Provincial Police Force Superintendent Originals 1910-1912

B.C. Surveys and Land Records GR 1088, Vancouver Island Rights Act 1917-25

Sound and Moving Images Division
Interviewee:
- Grant, Charles. **Logging and Milling in the Cumberland Area**
- King, Nellie. **Union Bay**
- Smith, Sydney, G. **Bloedel, Stewart and Welch**

Department of Public Works
- GR 54-File 270 Union Bay School building 1899
- GR 54-File 536 Union Bay School building 1915
- GR 71-File 27 Road building: Bituminous Carpet. Comox District, July 16, 1926
- GR 71-File 609 Renovations to old police building. Union Bay, March 15, 1926
- GR 71-File 661 Island Highway: Fanny Bay to Union Bay. Revision, August 25, 1947
- GR 71-File 690 Moving Union Bay buildings for road rerouting. August 10, 1947
- GR 87-File 19 Extension of Section I, Courtenay to Nanaimo Trail. September 30, 1874
- GR 1039-File 43 Comox District Road, Baynes Sound to Royston. September 6, 1895

Index